Horizons

Phonics and Reading

1

Teacher's Guide

Author: Polly A. Wood, M.A.

Editor: Alan L. Christopherson, M.S.

Alpha Omega Publications, Inc. • Rock Rapids, IA

804 N. 2nd Ave. E., Rock Rapids, IA 51246-1759

Printed in the United States of America

ISBN 978-0-7403-0326-5

Introduction

Introduction

Horizons Phonics and Reading Grade 1 is another addition to the exciting and innovative Horizons curriculum line. Just like the other Horizons materials, there are 160 lessons and 16 tests contained in the two student workbooks. An extensive Teacher's Guide provides plenty of tips and teaching strategies. A reduced student page is included in the Teacher's Guide, along with the instructions and information the teacher will need for the lesson.

Language development begins with listening and is followed by speaking. The listening and speaking skills that a child develops during the first years of life prepare them for learning the skills of reading and writing. The reading and writing skills they learn allow them to communicate the sounds they have heard and spoken. This program will capture the interest of young students with the interesting illustrations and colorful pages. Reading skill develops as the students master the phonics concepts. After its initial presentation, each concept appears a second time as a "review" and is reinforced a third time as a "checkup."

Teacher-directed lessons explore the phonetic sounds and guide the students as they practice the concepts. This material will help the student become a proficient reader one step at a time.

Two readers contain stories that follow each lesson. These allow the student to apply the phonics concepts they were taught in the lesson. Memorization of phonics/spelling rules assists the student in recognizing the relationship between letters and speech sounds—a skill that will enable them to decode new words. The phonics and reading program has three major components: **The Student Workbooks**, **The Readers**, and **The Teacher's Guide**.

The Student Workbooks

Horizons Phonics and Reading Grade 1, Book One contains Lessons 1–80, plus a test after every ten lessons. *Horizons Phonics and Reading Grade 1, Book Two* contains Lessons 81–160, plus a test after every ten lessons.

The Readers: A Note to Teachers and Parents

The Horizons First Grade Phonics Readers are to be used as a companion to the Horizons First Grade Student Workbooks. For each lesson in the Student Workbooks there is a corresponding story in the Readers. The story will illustrate and demonstrate the primary concept of the lesson. NOTE: Most first grade students should not be expected to read the first forty stories independently. The teacher or parent should read the stories to the student. The student can sound out some of the shorter, single-syllable words. After lesson forty, most first grade students should be able to start reading the stories independently. The student may still require some help with some of the words. The teacher or parent should make word cards for the words that the student does not know. The word cards should be reviewed with the student frequently. As the student's vocabulary increases, the student may be able to go back to the first forty stories and read them independently.

The teacher or parent should ask the student questions before and after reading the story. Help the student anticipate what is going to happen in the story after reading the title or looking at the pictures. There are comprehension questions at the end of each story. The answers to these questions should be discussed. The teacher or parent may have the student write out the answers to the questions if so desired.

At this stage, the skill level of each student will vary. It is not necessary for the student to sound out and read every word in a story. This skill will develop gradually over the course of this unit. Enjoy the learning process as it happens!

Lesson Preparation

The *Horizons Phonics and Reading Grade 1* program contains a total of 160 lessons. Typically, one lesson should be completed each day during the school year. Prepare for each day by carefully reviewing the material provided in the *Teacher's Guide*. The **Overview** is a summary of the concepts and activities that will be covered in the lesson. The **Materials and Supplies** is a list what will be needed for the lesson. Get these items assembled before starting class with the students. The **Teaching Tips** are classroom teaching procedures that give special instructions for each activity of the lesson. Take your time in going over these procedures. Thoroughly think through what you will say and do, so that you have a plan in your mind before teaching the lesson to the students. The **Answer Keys** are reduced student pages with answers. These pages allow you to have both the **Teacher Notes** and the **Student pages** in front of you as you teach the lesson.

The students are to complete the activities after you have gone over the instructions, discussed the pictures, and reviewed the words. Allow sufficient time for the students to do each activity before going on to the next. Compliment and encourage the students as they work.

Lesson length will vary from two to four pages of student activities. Doing the four-page lessons at one sitting is not necessary, nor is it recommended. Do the first two pages and take a break or work in another subject. After the break, pass out the second set of pages. Do some review, and then complete the lesson with the students. Each group of students is different, so be flexible and vary the routine.

Additional Resources in the Teacher's Guide

The following reproducible pages are available in the **Teacher Resources** section of this handbook:

- Alphabet flashcards that may be colored by the students and laminated, if desired.
- Phonics rules flashcards to be used during lesson presentation and/or to be copied for student use:

1. Long vowel sounds
2. Short vowel sounds
3. Silent **e** words
4. Hard and soft sounds of **c** and **g**
5. Consonant digraphs (beginning and ending)
6. Vowel pairs
7. Punctuation
8. Capitalization
9. Compound words
10. Plurals – words ending in **ss, ch, sh**, or **x**
11. Plurals – words ending in vowel plus **y**
12. Plurals – words ending in **f** and **fe**
13. Suffixes **-ed, -ing, -ful, -ly, -less, -ness, -s, -y**
14. Suffixes **-er** and **-est**
15. Doubling ending consonants and adding suffixes **-ed**, **-er**, **-est**, **-ing**
16. Adding suffixes to words ending in silent **e**
17. Suffixes **-y**, **-en**, **-able**
18. Consonant blends (beginning and ending)
19. Vowel digraphs
20. The sounds of **x**
21. Adding **-er** and **-est** to words ending in **y**
22. Contractions
23. R-controlled vowels
24. Vowel diphthongs
25. **Y** as a vowel
26. Synonyms, Antonyms, Homonyms
27. Words with **qu**
28. The sounds of **s**

NOTE: The flashcards are numbered for ease of location in the **Teacher Resources** section of the **Teacher's Guide**. The numbers do not necessarily match the lesson numbers.

est informative texts." NAEP also reported that such illiteracy persists in the higher grades. The report found that nearly one-third (31 percent) of eighth-graders and nearly one-third (30 percent) of twelfth-graders are also reading at a "below basic" level. The latter figures probably understate the problem, because many poor readers drop out of school before twelfth grade.

Other researchers have come to similar conclusions regarding how widespread students' reading problems really are. National longitudinal studies have measured the ability of children to recognize individual words in text. Their data suggest that more than one child in six (17.5 percent) will encounter a problem in learning to read during the crucial first three years of school. Further evidence comes from the sharp rise in the number of students who are diagnosed as learning disabled or are referred to special education because they cannot read at the proper grade level.

In contrast to popular belief, reading failure is not concentrated among particular types of schools or among specific groups of students. To the contrary, students who have difficulty reading represent a virtual cross-section of American children. They include rich and poor, male and female, rural and urban, and public and private school children in all sections of the country. According to the NAEP assessment, for example, nearly one-third (32 percent) of fourth graders whose parents graduated from college are reading at the "below basic" level.

In short, the failure of a substantial number of students to learn to read during the critical first three years of school is a national problem - one that confronts every community and every school in the country.

A Common Stumbling Block: Phonemic Awareness

Whatever the reason children fail to read by the end of the third grade, most non-readers share a common problem. They have not developed the capacity to recognize what reading experts call phonemes. Phonemes are the smallest units of speech—the basic building blocks of speaking and writing. The word "cat," for example, contains three phonemes: the /k/, /a/, and /t/ sounds. Phonemes are often identical to individual letters, but not always. The word "ox," for example, has two letters but three phonemes: the /o/, /k/, and /s/ sounds.

Researchers have demonstrated that accomplished readers are adept at recognizing phonemes and putting them together to construct words and phrases. They do this quickly, accurately, and automatically. The absence of this critical linguistic skill makes it difficult for children to decode and read single words, much less sentences, paragraphs, and whole stories. Teaching phonemic awareness and discrimination among phonemes is imperative for all students.

Solutions in the Classroom

Teaching beginners to read must be highly purposeful and strategic. Effective techniques have been developed for helping students, including those with learning disabilities, to develop phonological awareness, word recognition, and other advanced skills required for reading.

Phonological awareness activities build on and enhance children's experiences with written (e.g., print awareness) and spoken language (e.g., playing with words). A beginning reader with successful phonological awareness and knowledge of letters ostensibly learns how words are represented in print.

Intervention for learners who have difficulty with phonological awareness must be early, strategic, systematic, and carefully designed. It must be based on a curriculum that recognizes and balances the importance of both phonics instruction and the appreciation of meaning.

For children who have difficulty reading, effective reading instruction strategies should be used to build phonological awareness and alphabetic understanding. These strategies should be explicit, making phonemes prominent in children's attention and perception. For example, teachers can model specific sounds and in turn ask the children to produce the sounds. In addition, opportunities to engage in phonological awareness activities should be plentiful, frequent, and fun.

Instructional strategies should consider the characteristics that make a word easier or more difficult to read. These include: the number of phonemes in the word; phoneme position in words (initial sounds are easier); phonological properties of words (e.g., continuants, such as /m/, are easier than stop sounds, such as /t/); and phonological awareness dimensions, including blending sounds, segmenting words, and rhyming.

Many early readers will require greater teacher assistance and support. Using a research-based strategy known as scaffolding, teachers should provide students with lots of instructional support in the beginning stages of reading instruction, and gradually reduce the support as students learn more about reading skills. The ultimate goal is for students to read on their own without the help of a teacher.

A Balanced Approach

Unfortunately, it is not always easy for teachers to recognize students with reading difficulties. When they do, teachers sometimes find themselves caught between conflicting schools of thought about how to treat reading disabilities. One school of thought gives considerable attention to the teaching of phonics in the early stages of reading. Another school of thought emphasizes the whole language approach. Should teachers rely on phonics instruction, whole language instruction, or a combination of the two?

The U.S. Department of Education and the National Institute of Child Health and Human Development (NICHD) have supported the review of hundreds of studies done in recent years on reading instruction and disabilities. This body of research suggests that the relatively recent swing away from phonics instruction to a singular whole language approach is making it more difficult to lift children with learning disabilities out of the downward learning spiral and, in fact, may impede the progress of many students in learning to read with ease.

Few dispute the value of giving children opportunities to write, surrounding children with good literature, and generally creating a rich literate environment for students. But for many children this is not enough. Such children will have continued difficulty with reading unless they master the decoding skills associated with phonics instruction.

Research makes clear that children do not learn to read the way they learn to talk. Speech is a natural human capacity, and learning to talk requires little more than exposure and opportunity. In contrast, written language is an artifact, a human invention, and reading is not a skill that can be acquired through immersion alone. Beginning readers benefit from instruction that helps them understand that the words they speak and hear can be represented by written symbols — and that letters and the sounds associated with them, when combined and recombined, form words — just as they benefit from experiences that make reading fun.

California's experience with a chosen reading approach is instructive. A decade ago, the state became a leader in the movement to embrace whole language instruction. However, as a result of low reading scores, a task force was formed and has recently adopted a more balanced reading approach that includes building phonological awareness along with the reading of meaningful and engaging texts.

Research indicates that reading can be taught effectively with a balanced approach that uses the best of both teaching approaches. Such an approach incorporates phonics instruction with the rich literacy environments advocated by whole language instruction.

Reading: The Key to Success

As already discussed, reading is the gateway to learning. Facility to understand and use written language has always been a prerequisite to the efficient acquisition of knowledge, and it is becoming increasingly important in today's information society. In the past, it may have been possible for persons who were illiterate to obtain a good job, support a family, and live a comfortable life, but those days are gone. Children who do not learn to read today can expect to live on the margins of society in every way.

Lesson Plans

Lesson 1 - Beginning Consonant/Vowel Sounds

Overview:

- Print beginning consonant letters
- Print beginning vowel letters
- Complete words by writing the vowel
- Blend consonant-vowel pairs
- Blend consonant-vowel-consonant words

Materials and Supplies:

- Teacher's Guide & Student Workbook
- White board or chalkboard
- Alphabet flashcards
- Story: *Dan's Dog* (see note on p. 3 under "Readers: A Note to Teachers and Parents")

Teaching Tips:

Discuss the pictures so that the student is able to identify them correctly. Have the student practice printing the upper case and lower case alphabet on paper or on the white board.

Activity 1. Review the names of the pictures together. Have the student print the upper case and lower case consonant letters for the beginning sound of each picture.

Pictures: **bow, house, gum, pin, star**
wagon, cap, map, drum, bus
dog, leaf, jar, fire, bed
kite, lamp, nail, seven, pig

Letters: **Bb, Hh, Gg, Pp, Ss**
Ww, Cc, Mm, Dd, Bb
Dd, Ll, Jj, Ff, Bb
Kk, Ll, Nn, Ss, Pp

Activity 2. Review the names of the pictures together. Write the vowels on the board. Have the student print the upper case and lower case vowel letters for the beginning sound of each picture.

Pictures: **apple, elephant, inch, octopus, up**
ice cream, ax, umbrella, off, ant
ostrich, astronaut, olive, iguana, engine
elk, on, otter, egg, igloo

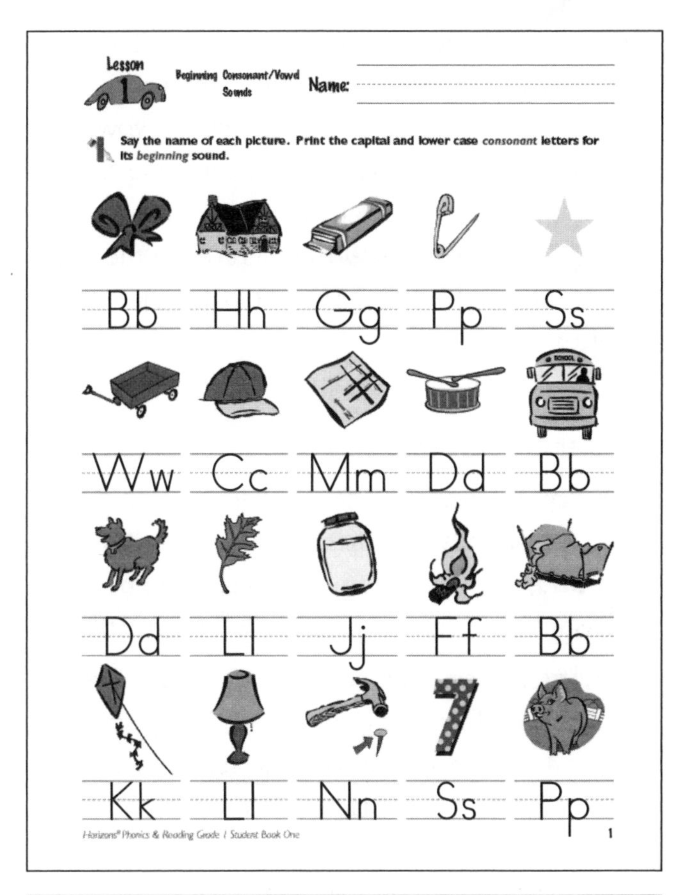
Lesson 1 Beginning Consonant/Vowel Sounds Name:

1. Say the name of each picture. Print the capital and lower case *consonant* letters for its *beginning* sound.

Bb Hh Gg Pp Ss
Ww Cc Mm Dd Bb
Dd Ll Jj Ff Bb
Kk Ll Nn Ss Pp

Horizons® Phonics & Reading Grade 1 Student Book One 1

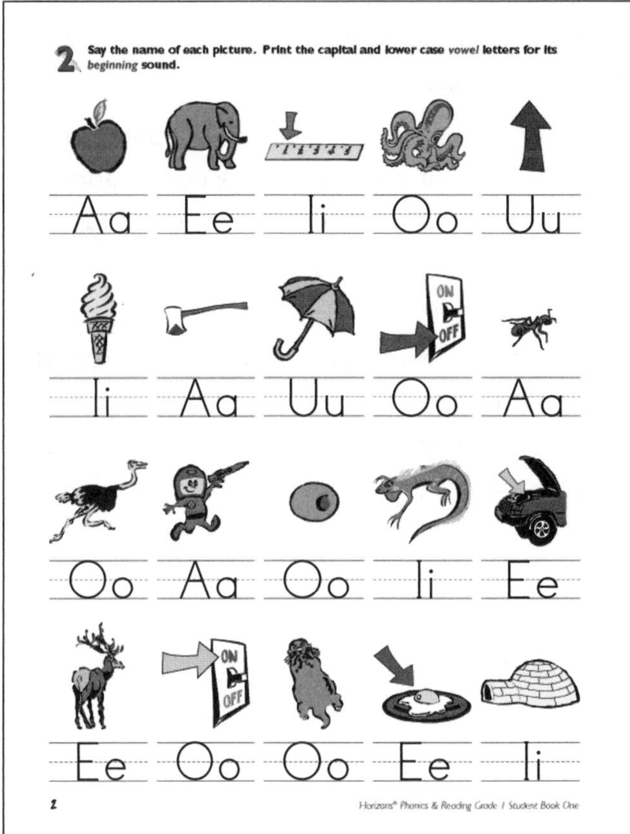
2. Say the name of each picture. Print the capital and lower case *vowel* letters for its *beginning* sound.

Aa Ee Ii Oo Uu
Ii Aa Uu Oo Aa
Oo Aa Oo Ii Ee
Ee Oo Oo Ee Ii

2 Horizons® Phonics & Reading Grade 1 Student Book One

Letters: **Aa, Ee, Ii, Oo, Uu**
Ii, Aa, Uu, Oo, Aa
Oo, Aa, Oo, Ii, Ee
Ee, Oo, Oo, Ee, Ii

Activity 3. Review vowel sounds using flash cards. Write the words **dad, fed, hit, Bob,** and **nut** on the white board, leaving out the vowel. Say each word and have a student tell you the letter for the missing vowel. Write the vowel completing the word. Review the pictures in the student book and have the student write the missing letters.

Pictures: **bed, gum, hot, bat, pig**

Letters: **e, u, o, a, i**

Activity 4. Practice each individual sound and blend the sounds together. For example: ***buh*** *plus* ***aa*** *is* ***baa***, etc. These combinations could be put on flashcards or a flip chart for future practice.

Activity 5. Using the combinations from the previous activity, blend beginning and ending sounds and read the words. Remind the students that names of people and places are proper nouns and begin with a capital letter. Review each ladder several times. It might be helpful to review these types of activities several times over the next couple of weeks.

Activity 6. Practice each individual sound and blend the sounds together. These combinations could be put on flashcards or a flip chart for future practice.

Activity 7. Using the combinations from the previous activity, blend beginning and ending sounds and read the words. Review each ladder several times. It might be helpful to review these types of activities several times over the next couple of weeks.

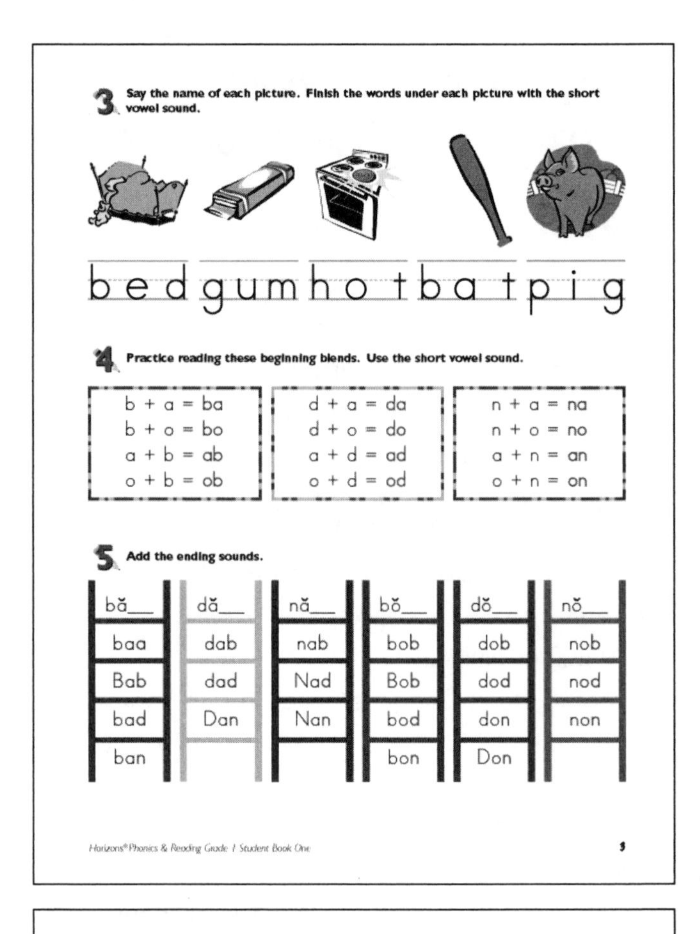

3 Say the name of each picture. Finish the words under each picture with the short vowel sound.

bed gum hot bat pig

4 Practice reading these beginning blends. Use the short vowel sound.

b + a = ba	d + a = da	n + a = na
b + o = bo	d + o = do	n + o = no
a + b = ab	a + d = ad	a + n = an
o + b = ob	o + d = od	o + n = on

5 Add the ending sounds.

bă__	dă__	nă__	bŏ__	dŏ__	nŏ__
baa	dab	nab	bob	dob	nob
Bab	dad	Nad	Bob	dod	nod
bad	Dan	Nan	bod	don	non
ban			bon	Don	

Horizons® Phonics & Reading Grade 1 Student Book One 5

6 Practice reading these ending blends. Use the short vowel sound.

a + b = ab	a + d = ad	a + n = an
o + b = ob	o + d = od	o + n = on

7 Add the beginning sounds.

__ăb	__ăd	__ăn	__ŏb	__ŏd	__ŏn
Bab	ad	an	bob	odd	on
dab	add	ban	Bob	bod	bon
nab	bad	Dan	dob	dod	don
	dad	Nan	nob	nod	Don
	Nad				non

4 Horizons® Phonics & Reading Grade 1 Student Book One

Lesson 2 - Middle Consonant Sounds

Overview:

- Print middle consonant sounds in words
- Blend consonant-vowel pairs
- Blend consonant-vowel-consonant words
- Match rhyming words

Materials and Supplies:

- Teacher's Guide and Student Workbook
- White board or chalkboard
- Alphabet flashcards
- Story: *Jim and the Soccer Ball*

Teaching Tips:

Help the student say the name of each picture, emphasizing the consonant sound in the middle of the word. Review the consonants with the student.

Activity 1. Review the names of the pictures together. Have the student print the upper case and lower case consonant letters for the middle sound of each picture. At the end of the activity, have the student tell the consonant sounds that come at the beginning, middle, and end of each word that was completed on the page.

Pictures: **kitten, apple, rabbit, hammer**
spider, seven, tiger, lemon
boxes, wagon, robot, zipper
penny, fiddle, kettle, dollar

Letters: **Tt, Pp, Bb, Mm**
Dd, Vv, Gg, Mm
Xx, Gg, Bb, Pp
Nn, Dd, Tt, Ll

Activity 2. Practice each individual sound and blend the sounds together. For example: ***fuh*** *plus* ***a*** *is* ***fa***, etc. These combinations could be put on flashcards or a flip chart for future practice.

Activity 3. Using the combinations from the previous activity, blend beginning and ending sounds and read the words. Remind the students that names of people and places are proper nouns and begin with a capital letter. Review each ladder several times. It might be helpful to review these types of activities several times over the next couple of weeks.

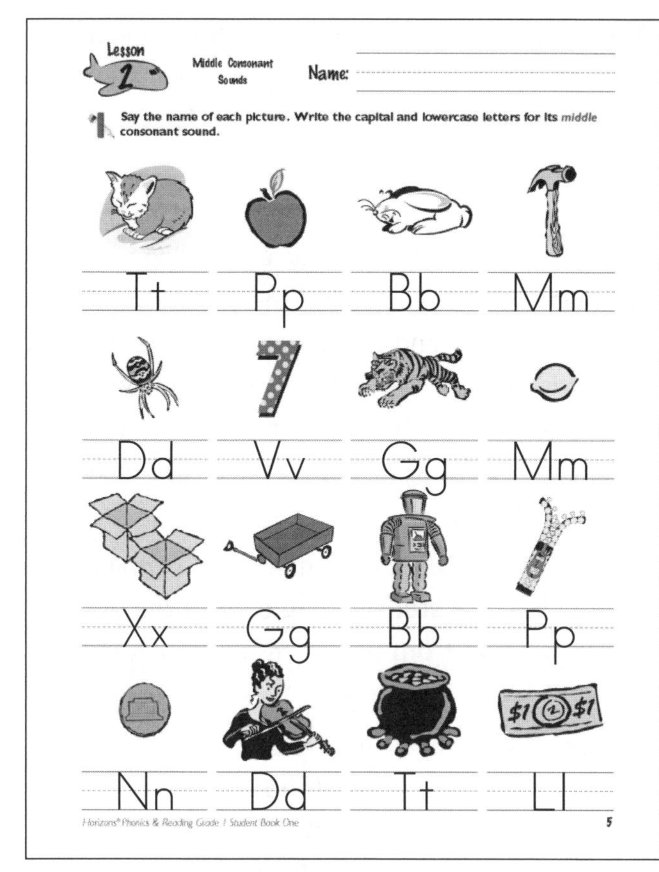
Lesson 2 Middle Consonant Sounds Name:

1. Say the name of each picture. Write the capital and lowercase letters for its *middle* consonant sound.

Tt Pp Bb Mm
Dd Vv Gg Mm
Xx Gg Bb Pp
Nn Dd Tt Ll

Horizons® Phonics & Reading Grade 1 Student Book One 5

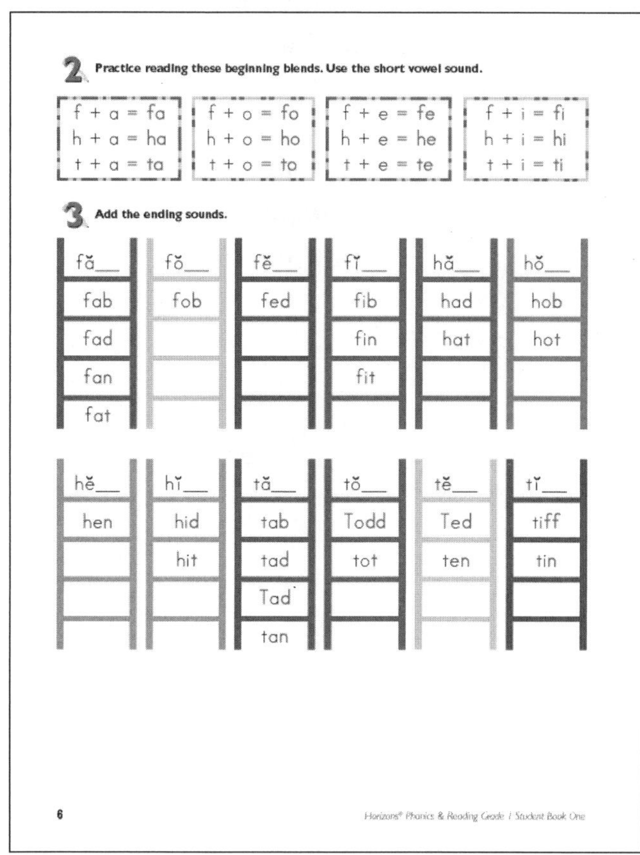
2. Practice reading these beginning blends. Use the short vowel sound.

f + a = fa	f + o = fo	f + e = fe	f + i = fi
h + a = ha	h + o = ho	h + e = he	h + i = hi
t + a = ta	t + o = to	t + e = te	t + i = ti

3. Add the ending sounds.

fă__	fŏ__	fĕ__	fĭ__	hă__	hŏ__
fab	fob	fed	fib	had	hob
fad			fin	hat	hot
fan			fit		
fat					

hĕ__	hĭ__	tă__	tŏ__	tĕ__	tĭ__
hen	hid	tab	Todd	Ted	tiff
	hit	tad	tot	ten	tin
		Tad			
		tan			

6 Horizons® Phonics & Reading Grade 1 Student Book One

Activity 4. Practice each individual sound and blend the sounds together. These combinations could be put on flashcards or a flip chart for future practice.

Activity 5. Using the combinations from the previous activity, blend beginning and ending sounds and read the words. Remind the students that names of people and places are proper nouns and begin with a capital letter. Review each ladder several times. It might be helpful to review these types of activities several times over the next couple of weeks.

Activity 6. Review the formation of rhyming words. Have the student read each of the words and draw a line from the word on the left its the rhyming word on the right.

Rhyming words: **Nan/Dan**
dab/nab
hid/lid
Ron/Don
fat/bat
Bob/rob
red/fed
bib/rib
sad/lad
bet/net

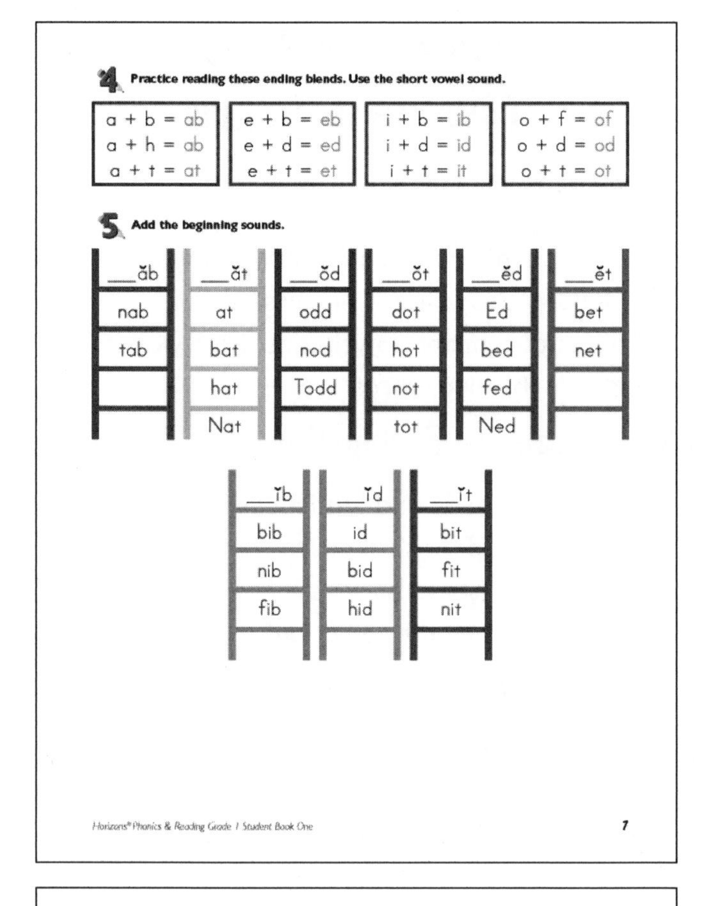

4 Practice reading these ending blends. Use the short vowel sound.

a + b = ab	e + b = eb	i + b = ib	o + f = of
a + h = ab	e + d = ed	i + d = id	o + d = od
a + t = at	e + t = et	i + t = it	o + t = ot

5 Add the beginning sounds.

___ăb	___ăt	___ŏd	___ŏt	___ĕd	___ĕt
nab	at	odd	dot	Ed	bet
tab	bat	nod	hot	bed	net
	hat	Todd	not	fed	
	Nat		tot	Ned	

___ĭb	___ĭd	___ĭt
bib	id	bit
nib	bid	fit
fib	hid	nit

Horizons® Phonics & Reading Grade 1 Student Book One 7

6 Draw a line to match the words that rhyme.

Nan	rob
dab	lid
hid	fed
Ron	rib
fat	bat
Bob	lad
red	fan
bib	net
sad	nab
bet	Don

8 Horizons® Phonics & Reading Grade 1 Student Book One

Lesson 3 - Ending Consonant Sounds

Overview:

- Print ending consonant sounds in words
- Blend consonant-vowel pairs
- Blend consonant-vowel-consonant words
- Match pictures to words

Materials and Supplies:

- Teacher's Guide and Student Workbook
- White board or chalkboard
- Alphabet flashcards
- Story: *The Cat in the Van*

Teaching Tips:

Activity 1. Review the names of the pictures together. Have the student print the lower case **consonant** letters for the ending sound of each picture.

Pictures: **coat, top, pen, star, bell**
bed, leaf, hot, box, glass
map, cat, bag, bus, cap

Letters: **t, p, n, r, l**
d, f, t, x, s
p, t, g, s, p

Activity 2. Have the student think of some words that have the ending sound of **x**, **p**, **k**, or **m**.

Activity 3. Review the names of the pictures together. Have the student print the lower case consonant or vowel letters for the beginning sound of each picture.

Pictures: **up, bus, leg, man, sun**
milk, ladder, kiss, seal, back

Letters: **u, b, l, m, s**
m, l, k, s, b

Activity 4. Review the names of the pictures together. Have the student print the lower case consonant for the middle sound of each picture.

Pictures: **robot, tiger, lemon, spider, seven**

Letters: **b, g, m, d, v**

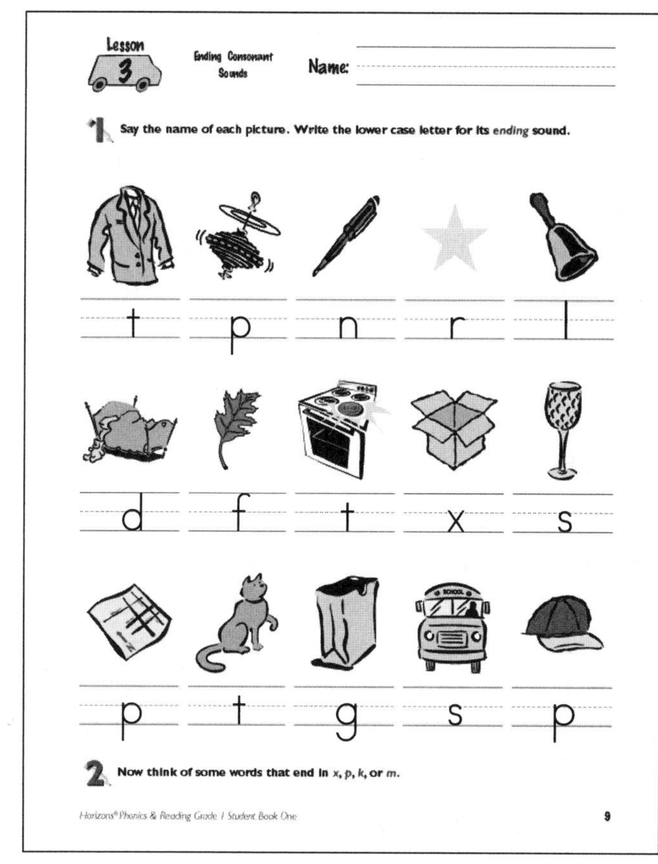
Lesson 3 Ending Consonant Sounds Name:

1 Say the name of each picture. Write the lower case letter for its *ending* sound.

t p n r l

d f t x s

p t g s p

2 Now think of some words that end in *x*, *p*, *k*, or *m*.

Horizons® Phonics & Reading Grade 1 Student Book One 9

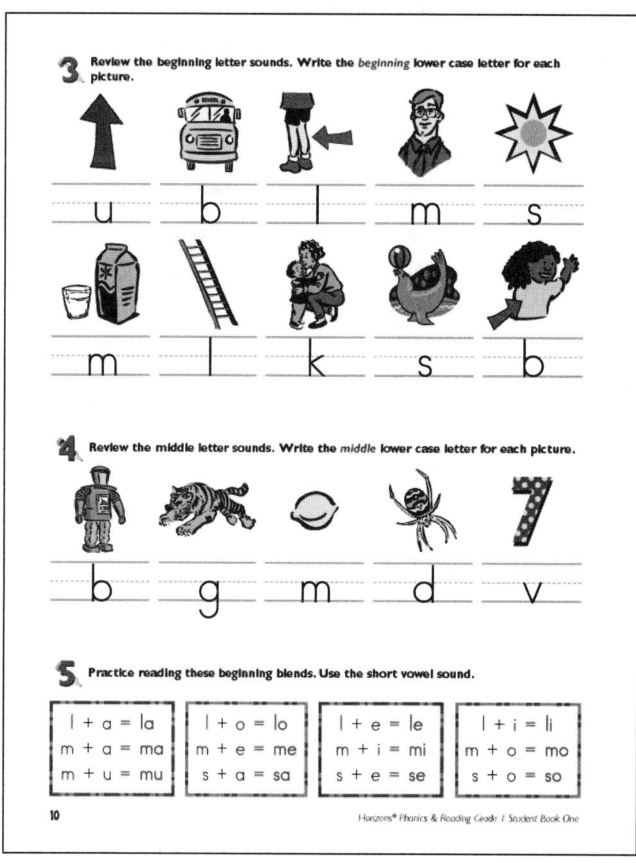
3 Review the beginning letter sounds. Write the *beginning* lower case letter for each picture.

u b l m s

m l k s b

4 Review the middle letter sounds. Write the *middle* lower case letter for each picture.

b g m d v

5 Practice reading these beginning blends. Use the short vowel sound.

l + a = la	l + o = lo	l + e = le	l + i = li
m + a = ma	m + e = me	m + i = mi	m + o = mo
m + u = mu	s + a = sa	s + e = se	s + o = so

10 Horizons® Phonics & Reading Grade 1 Student Book One

Activity 5. Practice each individual sound and blend the sounds together. For example: ***luh** plus **a** is **la***, etc. These combinations could be put on flashcards or a flip chart for future practice.

Activity 6. Using the combinations from the previous activity, blend beginning and ending sounds and read the words. Remind the students that names of people and places are proper nouns and begin with a capital letter. Review each ladder several times. It might be helpful to review these types of activities several times over the next couple of weeks.

Activity 7. Practice each individual sound and blend the sounds together. These combinations could be put on flashcards or a flip chart for future practice.

Activity 8. Using the combinations from the previous activity, blend beginning and ending sounds and read the words. Review each ladder several times. It might be helpful to review these types of activities several times over the next couple of weeks.

Activity 9. Study the pictures with the student and read the words together. Have the student draw a line from each word to the picture it matches.

Pictures:		
	fat	**bus**
	bib	**hat**
	fuss	**dad**
	bed	**mess**
	hen	**hot**

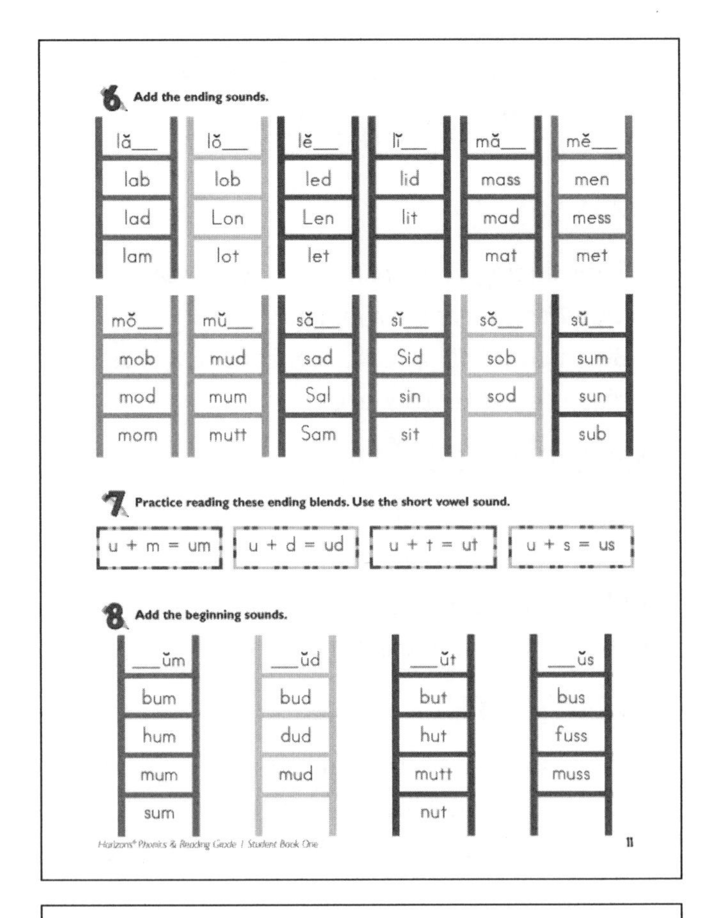

6 Add the ending sounds.

lă__	lŏ__	lĕ__	lĭ__	mă__	mĕ__
lab	lob	led	lid	mass	men
lad	Lon	Len	lit	mad	mess
lam	lot	let		mat	met

mŏ__	mŭ__	să__	sĭ__	sŏ__	sŭ__
mob	mud	sad	Sid	sob	sum
mod	mum	Sal	sin	sod	sun
mom	mutt	Sam	sit		sub

7 Practice reading these ending blends. Use the short vowel sound.

u + m = um | u + d = ud | u + t = ut | u + s = us

8 Add the beginning sounds.

__ŭm	__ŭd	__ŭt	__ŭs
bum	bud	but	bus
hum	dud	hut	fuss
mum	mud	mutt	muss
sum		nut	

Horizons® Phonics & Reading Grade 1 Student Book One 11

9 Draw a line to match the pictures to the words.

bib
bed
mess
hat
bus
dad
hen
hot
fat
fuss

12 Horizons® Phonics & Reading Grade 1 Student Book One

Lesson 4 - Short Vowel Sounds

Overview:

- Identify pictures with short vowel sounds
- Match pictures to words with short vowel sounds
- Read, sort, and write words by their short vowel sounds

Materials and Supplies:

- Teacher's Guide and Student Workbook
- White board or chalkboard
- Alphabet flashcards
- Phonics rule flashcard in **Teacher Resources**
- Story: *Nan's Hat*

Teaching Tips:

Review short vowel sounds using flashcards or the white board. Discuss the pictures in each activity so that the student is able to identify them correctly.

Activity 1. Review the names of the pictures together. Have the student draw a circle around the pictures with the short **ă** sound.

Pictures: **face, hat, cat, hand**
kite, bat, cake, ax
fan, tape, bed, castle

Activity 2. Review the names of the pictures together. Have the student draw a square around the pictures with the short **ĕ** sound.

Pictures: **bed, feed, shed, desk**
red, shell, net, wet
tent, hat, ten, bell

Activity 3. Review the names of the pictures together. Have the student draw an X through the pictures with the short **ĭ** sound.

Pictures: **lips, pig, dog, fish**
pins, six, kite, shell
mitt, boat, castle, bike

Activity 4. Review the names of the pictures together. Have the student underline the pictures with the short **ŏ** sound.

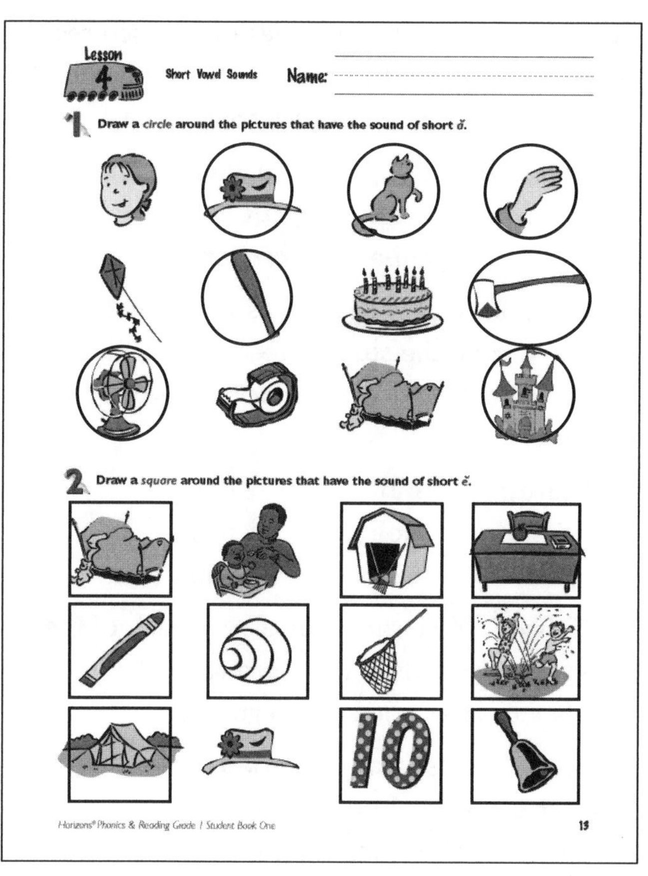
Lesson 4 Short Vowel Sounds Name:

1. Draw a circle around the pictures that have the sound of short ă.

2. Draw a square around the pictures that have the sound of short ĕ.

Horizons® Phonics & Reading Grade 1 Student Book One 13

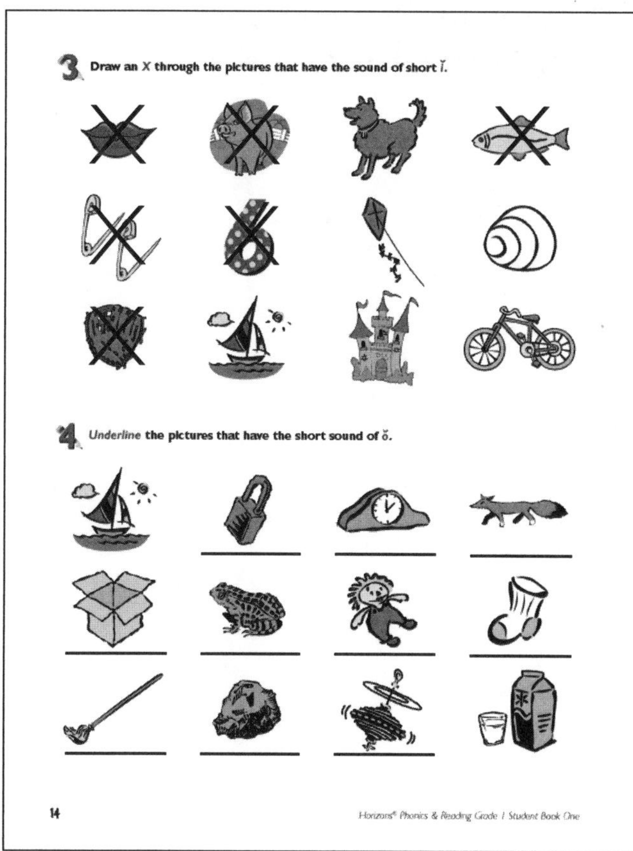
3. Draw an X through the pictures that have the sound of short ĭ.

4. Underline the pictures that have the short sound of ŏ.

14 Horizons® Phonics & Reading Grade 1 Student Book One

Pictures: **boat, lock, clock, fox**
box, frog, doll, sock
mop, rock, top, milk

Activity 5. Review the names of the pictures together. Have the student draw a circle around the pictures with the short **ŭ** sound.

Pictures: **bus, doll, mug** (or **cup**), **fruit**
sun, bugs, run, cut
rug, tuba, tub, crutch

Activity 6. Review the names of the pictures together. Have the student read each of the short vowel words and match the correct word to the picture.

Pictures:		
	bat	**pin**
	doll	**net**
	cut	**run**

Activity 7. Have the student read each of the short vowel words in the word list and sort the words into their correct categories.

Short ă words: **cat, lab, mad**
Short ĕ words: **bed, hen, met**
Short ĭ words: **bib, lid, pig**
Short ŏ words: **hot, mop, sod**
Short ŭ words: **hut, mud, sum**

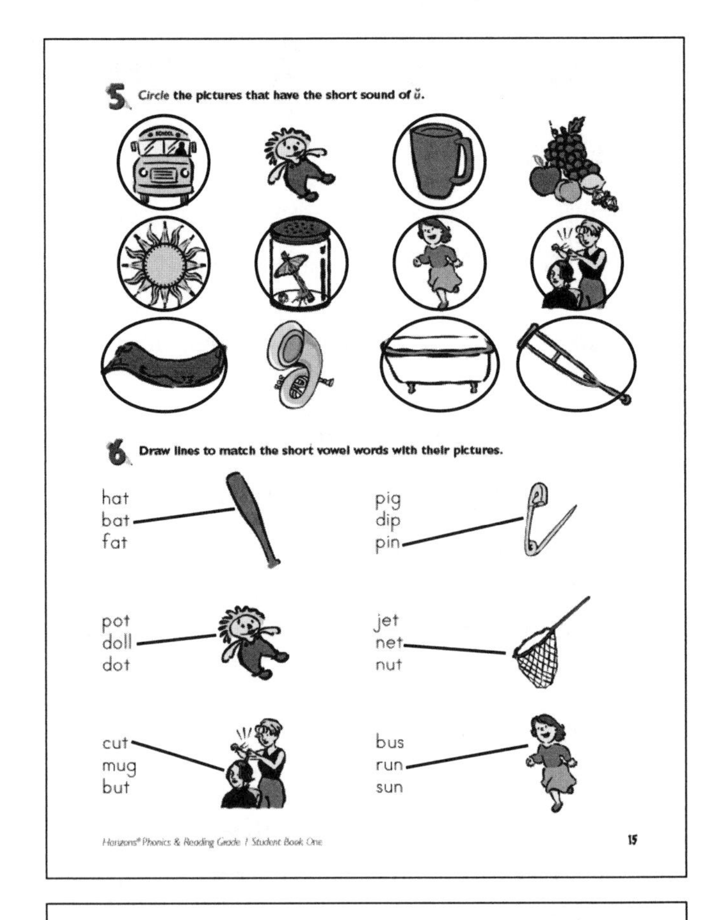
5 Circle the pictures that have the short sound of ŭ.

6 Draw lines to match the short vowel words with their pictures.

hat
bat
fat

pig
dip
pin

pot
doll
dot

jet
net
nut

cut
mug
but

bus
run
sun

Horizons® Phonics & Reading Grade 1 Student Book One 15

7 Read the list of words. Write each word under the correct short vowel sound.

Word List

bed	hen	lab	met	pig
bib	hot	lid	mop	sod
cat	hut	mad	mud	sum

Short ă: cat, lab, mad
Short ĕ: bed, hen, met
Short ĭ: bib, lid, pig
Short ŏ: hot, mop, sod
Short ŭ: hut, mud, sum

16 Horizons® Phonics & Reading Grade 1 Student Book One

Lesson 5 - Long Vowel Sounds

Overview:

- Identify pictures with long vowel sounds
- Blend consonant-vowel pairs (short vowel sound)
- Blend consonant-vowel-consonant words (short vowel sound)

Materials and Supplies:

- Teacher's Guide and Student Workbook
- White board or chalkboard
- Alphabet flashcards
- Phonics rule flashcard in **Teacher Resources**
- Story:

Teaching Tips:

If desired, use the phonics rule flashcard in the **Teacher Resources** section to review the long vowel rule: "**The long vowel says its name**." Use the alphabet flashcards to review both the short vowel and long vowel sounds.

Activity 1. Review the names of the pictures together. Have the student draw a circle around the pictures with the long **ā** sound.

Pictures: **rake, hat, train, hand**
tray, hay, cake, cane
fan, tape, plate, rain

Activity 2. Review the names of the pictures together. Have the student draw a square around the pictures with the long **ē** sound.

Pictures: **leaf, tent, sweep, team**
eagle, tree, jet, vet
meat, bee, seal, sleep

Activity 3. Review the names of the pictures together. Have the student draw an X through the pictures with the long **ī** sound.

Pictures: **kite, mice, lid, pine**
bird, chick, tiger, wrist
bike, spider, dime, white

Activity 4. Review the names of the pictures together. Have the student underline the pictures with the long **ō** sound.

Lesson 5 Long Vowel Sounds Name:

1. Draw a circle around the pictures that have the long ā sound. Long ā says its name.

2. Draw a square around the pictures that have the long ē sound. Long ē says its name.

Horizons® Phonics & Reading Grade 1 Student Book One 17

3. Draw an X through the pictures that have the long ī sound. Long ī says its name.

4. Underline the pictures that have the long ō sound. Long ō says its name.

18 Horizons® Phonics & Reading Grade 1 Student Book One

Pictures: **hoe, snow, shoe, bone**
bowl, nose, phone, rose
road, mop, rope, box

Activity 5. Review the names of the pictures together. Have the student draw a circle around the pictures with the long **ū** sound.

Pictures: **tuba, cute, mule, glue**
cupcake, suit, flute, fruit
bus, up, cube, mug (or **cup**)

Activity 6. Practice each individual sound and blend the sounds together. For example: ***puh** plus **a** is **pa***, etc. These combinations could be put on flashcards or a flip chart for future practice.

Activity 7. Using the combinations from the previous activity, blend beginning and ending sounds and read the words. Remind the students that names of people and places are proper nouns and begin with a capital letter. Review each ladder several times. It might be helpful to review these types of activities several times over the next couple of weeks.

Activity 8. Practice each individual sound and blend the sounds together. These combinations could be put on flashcards or a flip chart for future practice.

Activity 9. Using the combinations from the previous activity, blend beginning and ending sounds and read the words. Remind the students that names of people and places are proper nouns and begin with a capital letter. Review each ladder several times. It might be helpful to review these types of activities several times over the next couple of weeks.

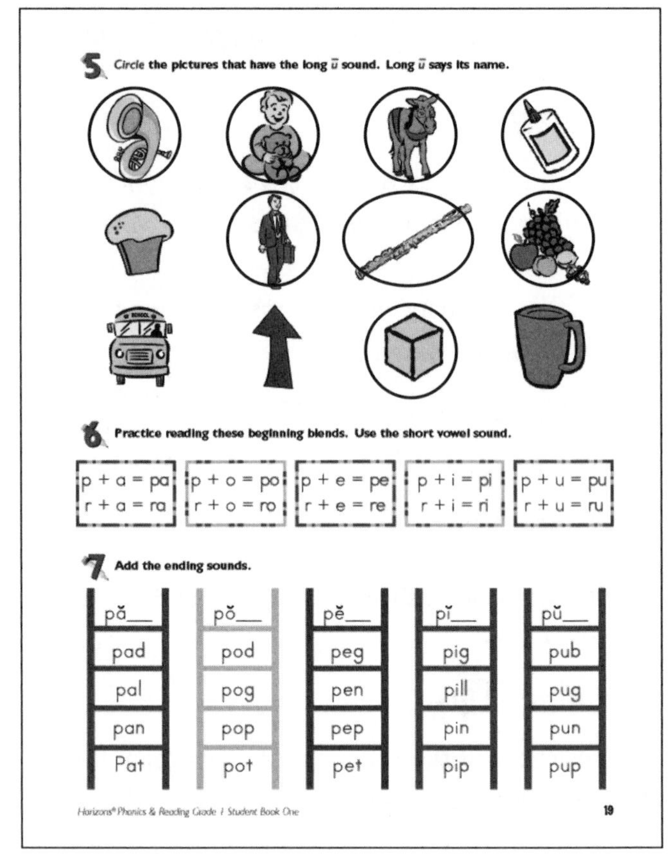

5 Circle the pictures that have the long ū sound. Long ū says its name.

6 Practice reading these beginning blends. Use the short vowel sound.

p + a = pa	p + o = po	p + e = pe	p + i = pi	p + u = pu
r + a = ra	r + o = ro	r + e = re	r + i = ri	r + u = ru

7 Add the ending sounds.

pă__	pŏ__	pĕ__	pĭ__	pŭ__
pad	pod	peg	pig	pub
pal	pog	pen	pill	pug
pan	pop	pep	pin	pun
Pat	pot	pet	pip	pup

Horizons® Phonics & Reading Grade 1 Student Book One 19

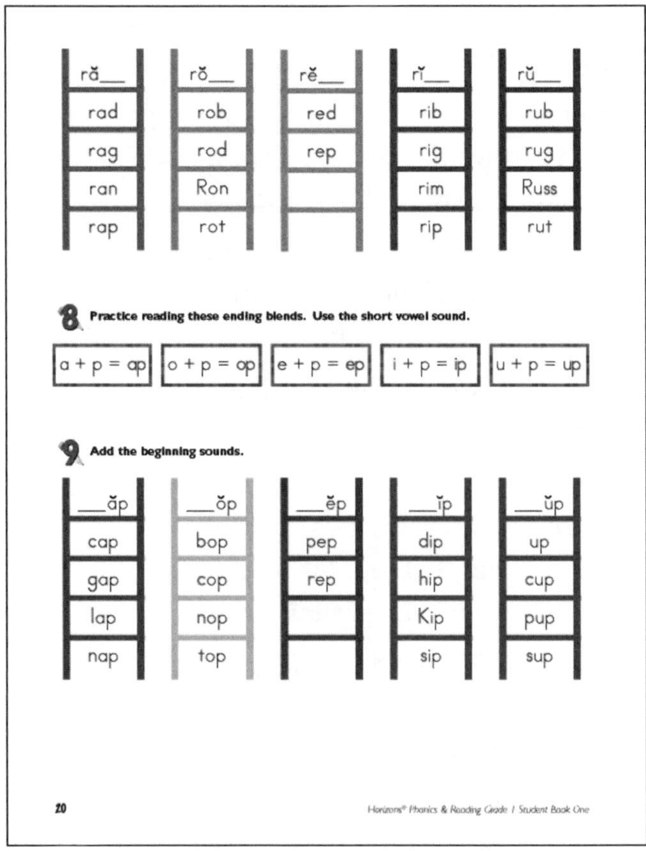

ră__	rŏ__	rĕ__	rĭ__	rŭ__
rad	rob	red	rib	rub
rag	rod	rep	rig	rug
ran	Ron		rim	Russ
rap	rot		rip	rut

8 Practice reading these ending blends. Use the short vowel sound.

a + p = ap	o + p = op	e + p = ep	i + p = ip	u + p = up

9 Add the beginning sounds.

__ăp	__ŏp	__ĕp	__ĭp	__ŭp
cap	bop	pep	dip	up
gap	cop	rep	hip	cup
lap	nop		Kip	pup
nap	top		sip	sup

20 Horizons® Phonics & Reading Grade 1 Student Book One

Lesson 6 - Silent e Rule

Overview:

- Review short vowel sounds
- Review long vowel sounds
- Introduce diacritical markings for long vowel sounds and silent **e**
- Blend consonant-vowel pairs
- Blend consonant-vowel-consonant words

Materials and Supplies:

- Teacher's Guide & Student Workbook
- White board or chalkboard
- Alphabet flashcards
- Phonics rule flashcard in **Teacher Resources**
- Story: *Nate Skates*

Teaching Tips:

Read and discuss the Silent **e** rule with the student. Demonstrate diacritical markings for silent **e** and long vowel sounds. Explain that the line drawn above a vowel to show that it has a long sound is called a **macron**. The silent **e̸** has a line drawn through it to show that it makes no sound.

Activity 1.

Have the student read each of the short vowel words. Discuss the formation and meaning of the diacritical markings for long vowels and for silent **e**. Do several examples on the board for the student to practice on paper. Instruct the student to add a silent **e** to each word in the activity and make the appropriate diacritical markings to the silent **e** and the long vowel. Have the student read the new words with their long vowel sound.

Activity 2.

Review the names of the pictures together. Have the student add the silent **e** to the word and make the appropriate diacritical markings to the silent **e** and the long vowel. Have the student read the new words with their long vowel sound.

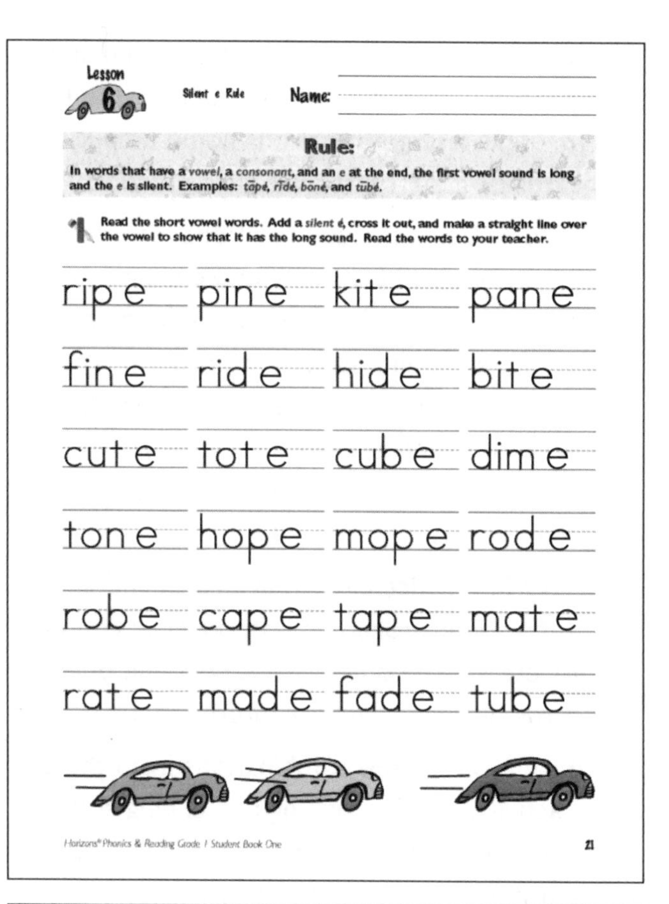

Lesson 6 Silent e Rule Name:

Rule:

In words that have a *vowel*, a *consonant*, and an *e* at the end, the first vowel sound is long and the *e* is silent. Examples: *tāpé*, *rīdé*, *bōné*, and *tūbé*.

1. Read the short vowel words. Add a *silent é*, cross it out, and make a straight line over the vowel to show that it has the long sound. Read the words to your teacher.

ripe pine kite pane
fine ride hide bite
cute tote cube dime
tone hope mope rode
robe cape tape mate
rate made fade tube

Horizons® Phonics & Reading Grade 1 Student Book One 21

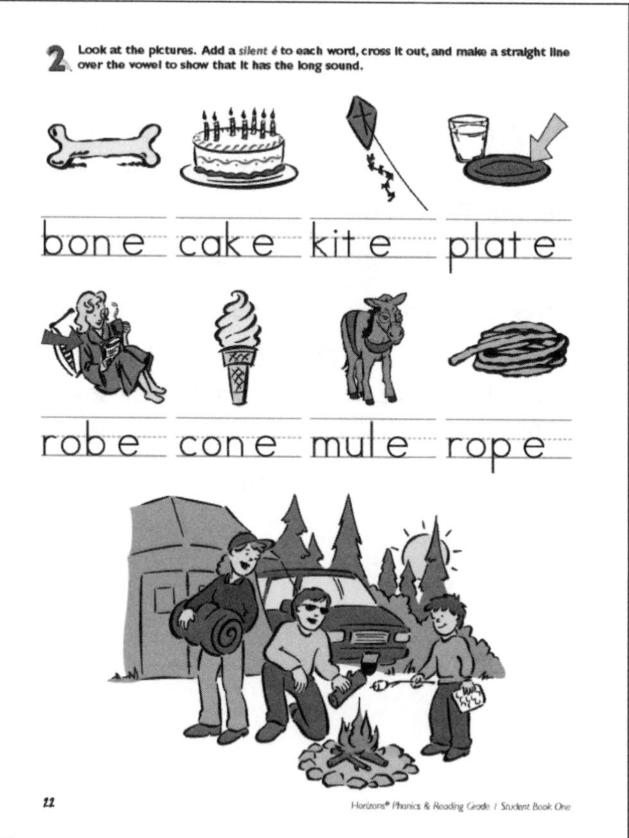

2. Look at the pictures. Add a *silent é* to each word, cross it out, and make a straight line over the vowel to show that it has the long sound.

bone cake kite plate
robe cone mule rope

22 Horizons® Phonics & Reading Grade 1 Student Book One

Pictures: **bone, cake, kite, plate**
robe, cone, mule, rope

Activity 3. Practice each individual sound and blend the sounds together. For example: ***juh** plus **a** is **ja***, etc. These combinations could be put on flashcards or a flip chart for future practice.

Activity 4. Using the combinations from the previous activity, blend beginning and ending sounds and read the words. Remind the students that names of people and places are proper nouns and begin with a capital letter. Review each ladder several times. It might be helpful to review these types of activities several times over the next couple of weeks.

Activity 5. Practice each individual sound and blend the sounds together. For example: ***vuh** plus **a** is **va***, etc. These combinations could be put on flashcards or a flip chart for future practice.

Activity 6. Using the combinations from the previous activity, blend beginning and ending sounds and read the words. Review each ladder several times. It might be helpful to review these types of activities several times over the next couple of weeks.

Activity 7. Practice each individual sound and blend the sounds together. For example: ***yuh** plus **a** is **ya***, etc. These combinations could be put on flashcards or a flip chart for future practice.

Activity 8. Using the combinations from the previous activity, blend beginning and ending sounds and read the words. Review each ladder several times. It might be helpful to review these types of activities several times over the next couple of weeks.

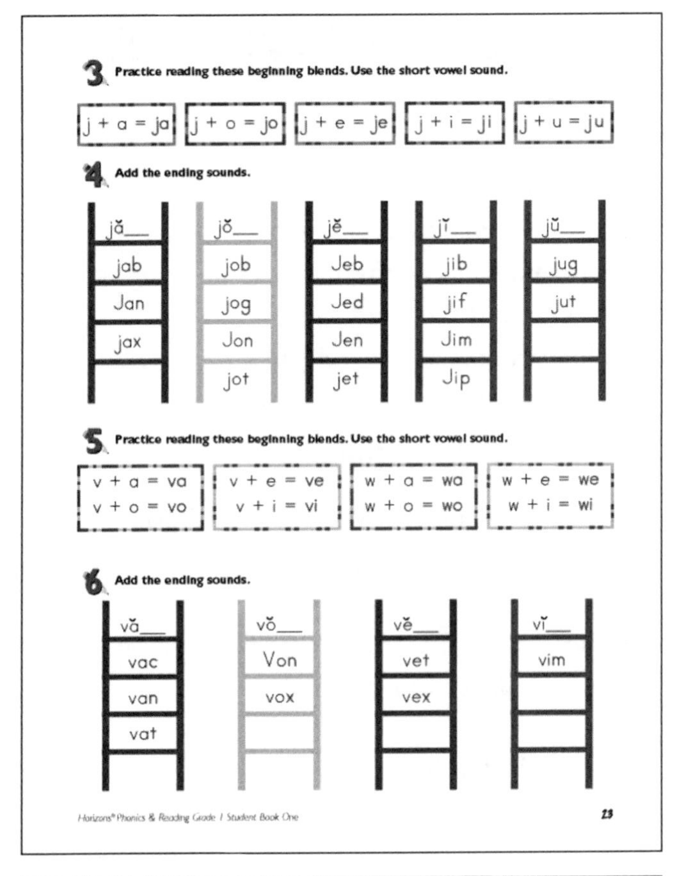

3 Practice reading these beginning blends. Use the short vowel sound.

j + a = ja | j + o = jo | j + e = je | j + i = ji | j + u = ju

4 Add the ending sounds.

jă__: jab, Jan, jax
jŏ__: job, jog, Jon, jot
jĕ__: Jeb, Jed, Jen, jet
jĭ__: jib, jif, Jim, Jip
jŭ__: jug, jut

5 Practice reading these beginning blends. Use the short vowel sound.

v + a = va, v + o = vo | v + e = ve, v + i = vi | w + a = wa, w + o = wo | w + e = we, w + i = wi

6 Add the ending sounds.

vă__: vac, van, vat
vŏ__: Von, vox
vĕ__: vet, vex
vĭ__: vim

Horizons® Phonics & Reading Grade 1 Student Book One — 23

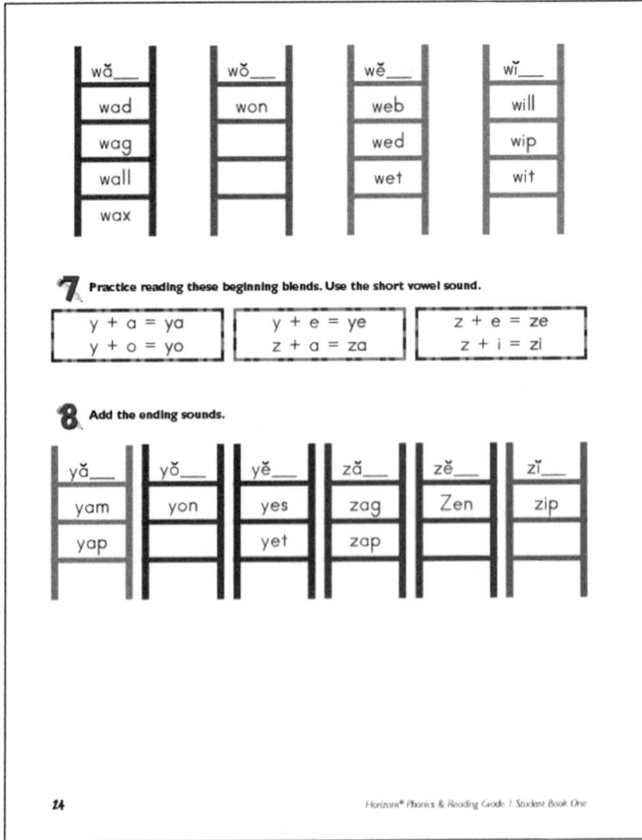

wă__: wad, wag, wall, wax
wŏ__: won
wĕ__: web, wed, wet
wĭ__: will, wip, wit

7 Practice reading these beginning blends. Use the short vowel sound.

y + a = ya, y + o = yo | y + e = ye, z + a = za | z + e = ze, z + i = zi

8 Add the ending sounds.

yă__: yam, yap
yŏ__: yon
yĕ__: yes, yet
ză__: zag, zap
zĕ__: Zen
zĭ__: zip

24 — Horizons® Phonics & Reading Grade 1 Student Book One

Lesson 7 - Hard & Soft Sounds of c & g

Overview:

- Identify soft **c** and hard **c** sounds in words
- Identify soft **g** and hard **g** sounds in words
- Complete a crossword puzzle using words with the sounds of hard and soft **c** and **g**
- Blend consonant-vowel pairs
- Blend consonant-vowel-consonant words

Materials and Supplies:

- Teacher's Guide & Student Workbook
- White board or chalkboard
- Phonics rule flashcard in **Teacher Resources**
- Story: *Cecelia Goes to the City*

Teaching Tips:

Read and discuss the hard and soft sounds of **c** and **g**. Discuss the pictures in each activity so that the student is able to identify them correctly. Discuss the crossword puzzle with the student, explaining how one word builds off another.

Activity 1. Discuss the pictures in the activity. Have the student identify each picture and determine whether the hard or soft sound of **c** is heard. Have the student underline all the pictures with the sound of hard **c** first. Go through the activity again and tell the student to circle the pictures that have the soft **c** sound.

Pictures: **corn, ceiling, cry, city**
cook, police, cake, recess
face, cat, pencils, castle
cane, slice, can, price

Activity 2. Discuss the pictures in the activity. Have the student identify each picture and determine whether the hard or soft sound of **g** is heard. Have the student underline all the pictures with the sound of soft **g** first. Go through the activity again and draw a square around the pictures that have the hard **g** sound.

Pictures: **gum, giraffe, pig, garden**
grapes, giant, gift, rug
pigeon, girl, gem, bag
grass, sugar, glass, carriage

Lesson 7 Hard & Soft Sounds of c & g Name:

Rule:
When *c* is followed by *e*, *i* or *y*, it makes the soft sound as in the word *city*. When *c* is followed by *a*, *u*, or *o*, or a *consonant*, it makes the hard sound as in the word *cat*.

1 *Underline* the pictures that have the sound of *hard c*. Draw a *circle* around the pictures that have the *soft c* sound.

Horizons® Phonics & Reading Grade 1 Student Book One 25

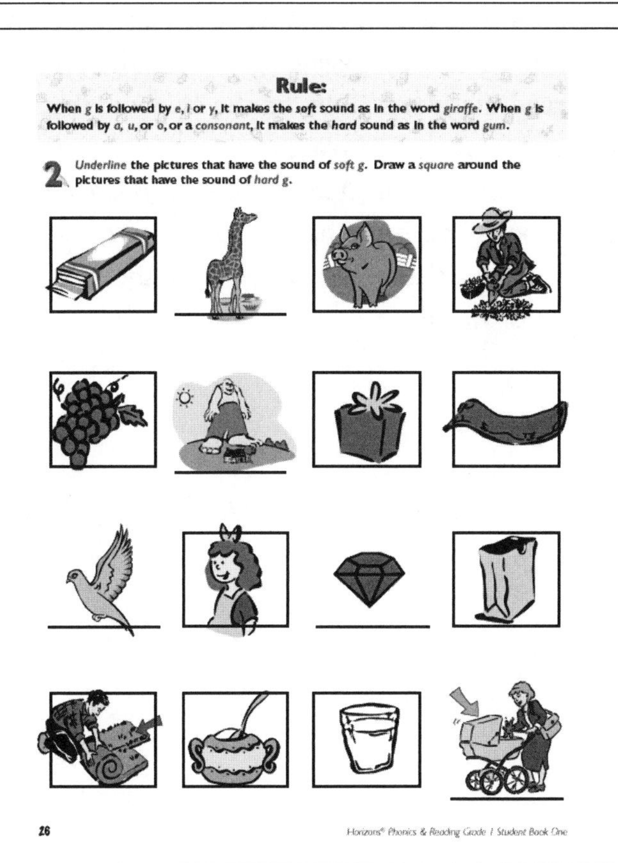
Rule:
When *g* is followed by *e*, *i* or *y*, it makes the *soft* sound as in the word *giraffe*. When *g* is followed by *a*, *u*, or *o*, or a *consonant*, it makes the *hard* sound as in the word *gum*.

2 *Underline* the pictures that have the sound of *soft g*. Draw a *square* around the pictures that have the sound of *hard g*.

26 *Horizons® Phonics & Reading Grade 1 Student Book One*

Activity 3. Have the student match the picture clues to the words in the word list before completing the puzzle. Explain that in a crossword puzzle, one word builds upon another, and the words can be written either across or down. If necessary, demonstrate some simple words on the white board or chalkboard and show how the words connect.

Across: **1. gum**
2. cane
3. slice
5. face

Down: **1. gems**
4. cake

Activity 4. Practice each individual sound and blend the short vowel and consonant sounds together. For example: ***eh*** *plus* **v** *is* **ev**, etc. These combinations could be put on flashcards or a flip chart for future practice.

Activity 5. Using the combinations from the previous activity, blend beginning and ending sounds and read the words. Remind the students that names of people and places are proper nouns and begin with a capital letter. Review each ladder several times. It might be helpful to review these types of activities several times over the next couple of weeks.

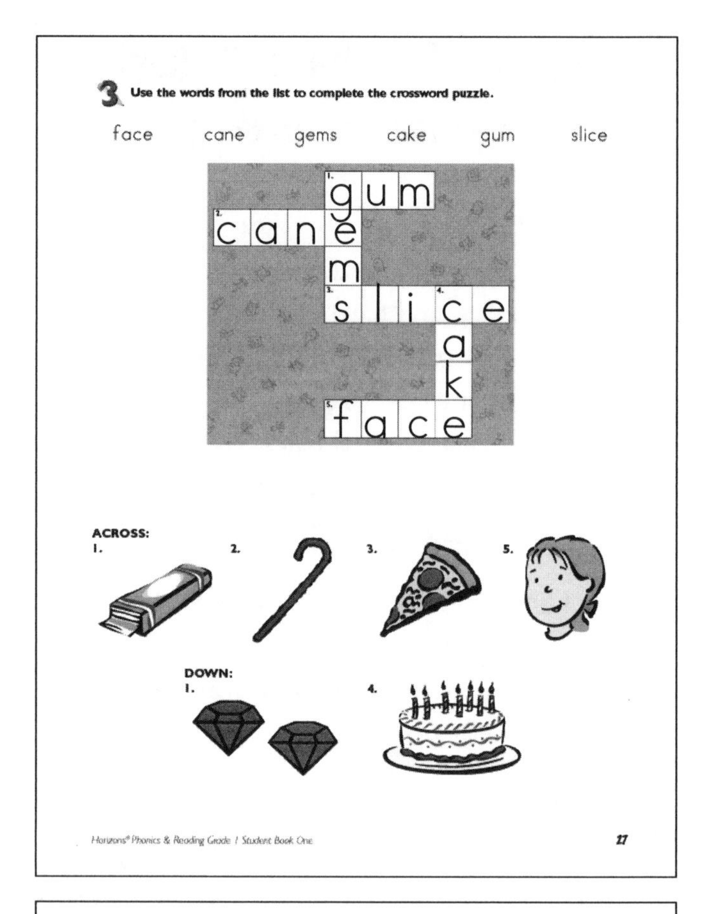

3 Use the words from the list to complete the crossword puzzle.

face cane gems cake gum slice

ACROSS: 1. gum 2. cane 3. slice 5. face

DOWN: 1. gems 4. cake

Horizons® Phonics & Reading Grade 1 Student Book One 27

4 Practice reading these ending blends. Use the short vowel sound.

e + v = ev	a + x = ax	o + x = ox
e + x = ex	i + x = ix	u + x = ux

5 Add the beginning sounds.

___ ĕv	___ ăx	___ ŏx	___ ĕx	___ ĭx	___ ŭx
Bev	ax	ox	hex	Dix	lux
	fax	box	Rex	fix	tux
	lax	fox	Tex	mix	
	Max	lox	vex	nix	
	sax	nox		pix	
	tax	pox		six	
	wax	sox			
		vox			

28 Horizons® Phonics & Reading Grade 1 Student Book One

Lesson 8 - Consonant Digraphs th, ch, wh

Overview:

- Identify beginning/ending sounds of **th** and **ch**
- Identify beginning sound of **wh**
- Identify the correct consonant digraph in a word
- Complete sentences using words with consonant digraph **ch**
- Complete words using digraphs **th**, **ch**, and **wh**

Materials and Supplies:

- Teacher's Guide & Student Workbook
- White board or chalkboard
- Phonics rule flashcard in **Teacher Resources**
- Story: *Lee's Teeth*

Teaching Tips:

Read and discuss the rule about consonant digraphs **th**, **ch**, and **wh**. Ask the student to think of other words with these digraphs.

Activity 1. Discuss the pictures in this activity so that the student is able to identify them correctly. Have the student circle the first consonant digraph if the picture illustrates a word *beginning* with that sound. The student should circle the last consonant digraph if the pictured word *ends* with that sound. Demonstrate on the chalkboard or white board if necessary.

Pictures: **thin, bath, thick, math**
pinch, chair, chick, inch

Activity 2. Discuss the pictures in this activity so that the student is able to identify them correctly. The student will write the consonant digraph **wh** under each picture.

Pictures: **wheat, wheel, whip, whistle, whale**

Activity 3. Discuss the pictures in this activity so that the student is able to identify them correctly. Have the student circle the correct consonant digraph for each word illustrated.

Pictures: **thick, whistle, chair, whip**

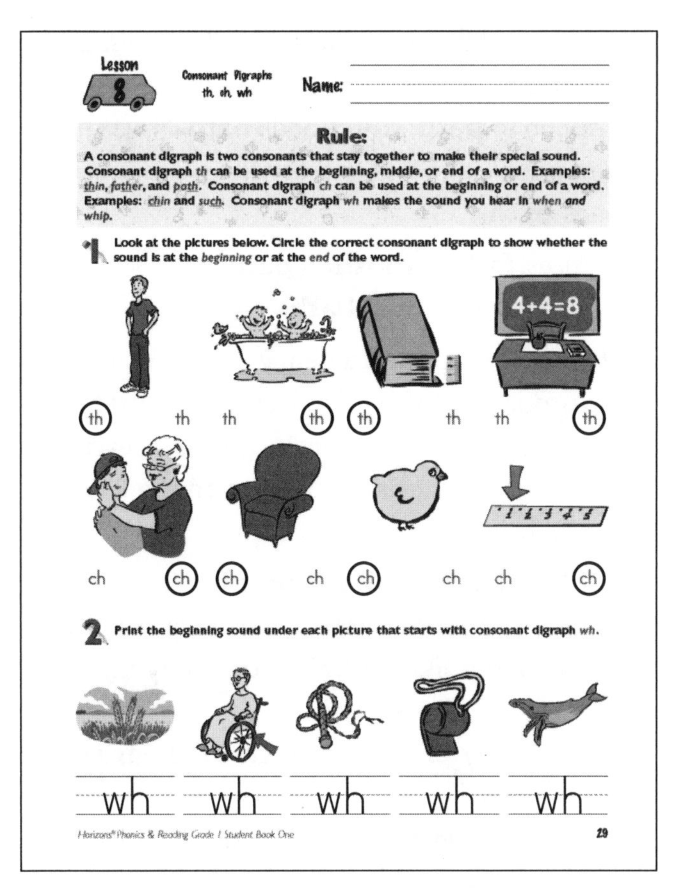
Lesson 8 Consonant Digraphs th, ch, wh Name:

Rule:
A consonant digraph is two consonants that stay together to make their special sound. Consonant digraph th can be used at the beginning, middle, or end of a word. Examples: thin, father, and path. Consonant digraph ch can be used at the beginning or end of a word. Examples: chin and such. Consonant digraph wh makes the sound you hear in when and whip.

1. Look at the pictures below. Circle the correct consonant digraph to show whether the sound is at the beginning or at the end of the word.

4+4=8

th th th th th th th th

ch ch ch ch ch ch ch ch

2. Print the beginning sound under each picture that starts with consonant digraph wh.

wh wh wh wh wh

Horizons® Phonics & Reading Grade 1 Student Book One 29

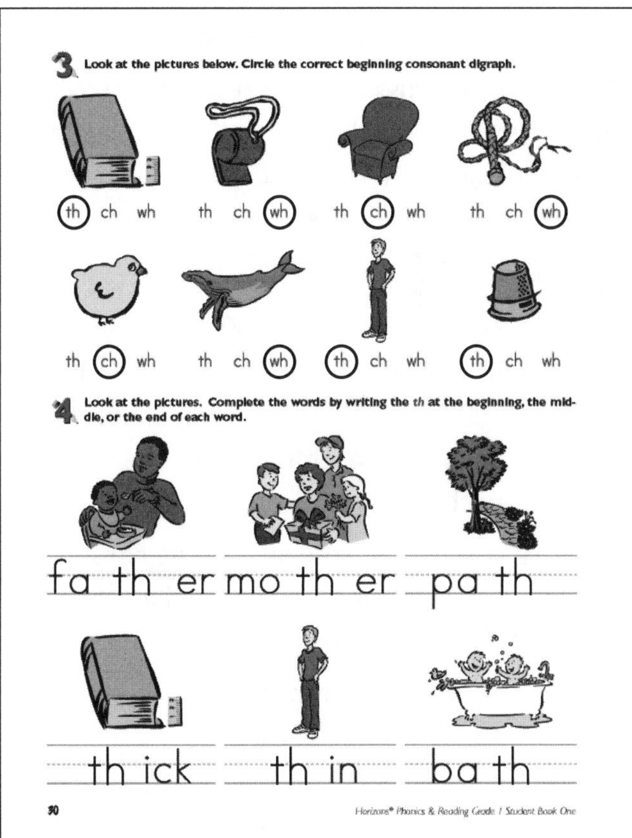
3. Look at the pictures below. Circle the correct beginning consonant digraph.

th ch wh th ch wh th ch wh th ch wh

th ch wh th ch wh th ch wh th ch wh

4. Look at the pictures. Complete the words by writing the th at the beginning, the middle, or the end of each word.

fa th er mo th er pa th

th ick th in ba th

30 Horizons® Phonics & Reading Grade 1 Student Book One

chick, whale, thin, thimble

Activity 4. Discuss the pictures in this activity so that the student is able to identify them correctly.

Discuss the different sounds that **th** makes: the *voiced* sound in **this, that,** and **them,** or the *voiceless* sound in **path, think,** and **math.** Have the student think of other words with the different sounds of **th.**

Pictures: **father, mother, path**
thick, thin, bath

Activity 5. Help the student read the words in the word list and the sentences. The student will choose which word correctly completes each sentence and will print that word on the line.

Sentences:

1. **Jill and Kim are chums.**
2. **They like each other very much.**
3. **They like to bake, and they like to play chess.**
4. **They chat with each other as they play.**
5. **Dad had to chop wood for the fireplace.**
6. **He did not want us to get a chill.**

Activity 6. Discuss the pictures in this activity so that the student is able to identify them correctly. Have the student write **ch** at the beginning or the end of each word.

Words: **pinch, lunch, chat**

Activity 7. Have the student add the consonant digraph **th** to each of the words and listen as they read the words to you.

Words: **with, moth, thin, thud**
path, math, this, that

Activity 8. Have the student add the consonant digraph **ch** to each of the words and listen as they read the words to you.

Words: **chin, chaff, chip, chap**
such, chug, rich, much

Activity 9. Have the student add the consonant digraph **wh** to each of the words and listen as they read the words to you.

Words: **whip, whiff, whim, wham**
when, whet, whip, whiz

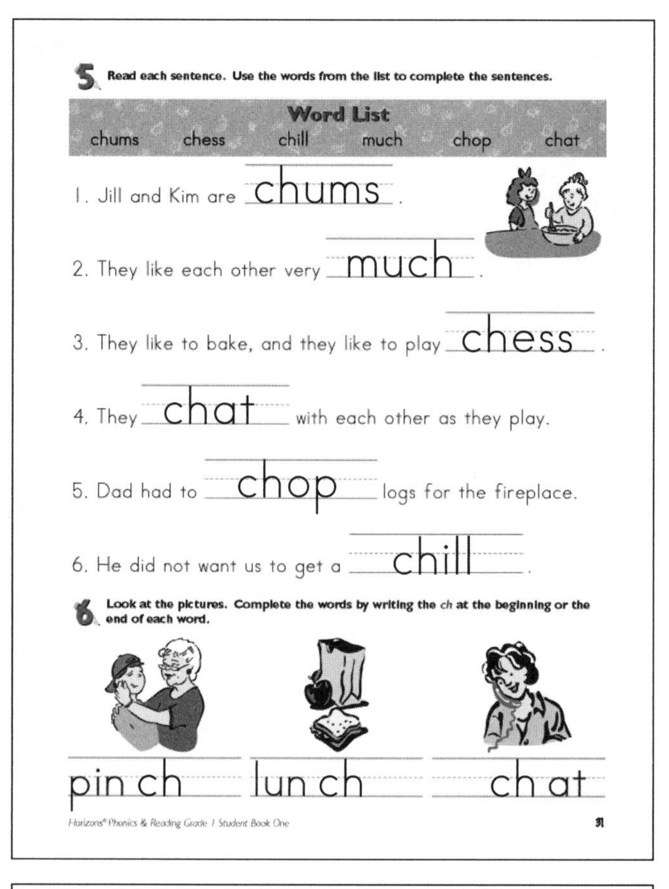

5 Read each sentence. Use the words from the list to complete the sentences.

Word List
chums chess chill much chop chat

1. Jill and Kim are chums.
2. They like each other very much.
3. They like to bake, and they like to play chess.
4. They chat with each other as they play.
5. Dad had to chop logs for the fireplace.
6. He did not want us to get a chill.

6 Look at the pictures. Complete the words by writing the *ch* at the beginning or the end of each word.

pinch lunch chat

Horizons® Phonics & Reading Grade 1 Student Book One 31

7 Add *th* to each of the words below, then read the words to your teacher.

with moth thin thud
path math this that

8 Add *ch* to each of the words below, then read the words to your teacher.

chin chaff chip chap
such chug rich much

9 Add *wh* to each of the words below, then read the words to your teacher.

whip whiff whim wham
when whet whip whiz

32 Horizons® Phonics & Reading Grade 1 Student Book One

Lesson 9 - Vowel Pairs
ai, ay, ee, ea

Overview:

- Complete words by using correct vowel pairs
- Reading and writing words with vowel pairs
- Adding long ē to short vowel words to make new words
- Picture/word match
- Sentence completion

Materials and Supplies:

- Teacher's Guide & Student Workbook
- White board or chalkboard
- Phonics rule flashcard in **Teacher Resources**
- Story: *The Peach Tree*

Teaching Tips:

Read and discuss the rule about vowel pairs. Demonstrate the correct diacritical markings for each vowel pair: āi̸, āy̸, ēe̸, ēa̸. Ask the students to think of additional words for each vowel pair. Discuss the pictures in each activity so that the student is able to identify them correctly. (**Optional**: You may have the students place diacritical markings on all the vowel-pair words they write.)

Activity 1. Discuss each picture and have the student complete each word with the correct vowel pair.

Pictures: **seal, paint, play, sweep**
bee, tree, rain, creek
teeth, read, sleep, team

Activity 2. Have the student read each of the words in the word list and write the words under the correct pictures.

Pictures: **leaf, peek, rain, seal**
seat, tray, tree, team

Activity 3. Have the student add long ē in the correct place in each word to make a new word with the long ē sound. Stress to the student that the **e** does not always go at the end of the word to make the long vowel sound.

Lesson 9 Vowel Pairs ai, ay, ee, ea Name:

Rule:
A vowel pair is two vowels that come together to make one long vowel sound. The first vowel is long, and the second vowel is silent. Examples: *ai/rain, ay/say, ee/tree,* **and** *ea/read.*

1 Say the name for each picture. Finish the words under each picture with the correct vowel pair.

s ea l p ai nt pl ay sweep

bee tree r ai n creek

teeth r ea d sl ee p t ea m

Horizons® Phonics & Reading Grade 1 Student Book One 33

2 Write the name of each picture. Use the words from the list.

Word List
team seat leaf seal tree peek tray rain

leaf peek rain seal

seat tray tree team

3 Add long ē before the vowel each word to make a new word with the long ē sound.

ten teen
sat seat
mat meat
cram cream

34 Horizons® Phonics & Reading Grade 1 Student Book One

Words: **ten** = **teen**
sat = **seat**
mat = **meat**
cram = **cream**

Activity 4. Have the student add the vowel pair **ay** to each of the words and read the completed words back to you.

Words: **play, pray, tray, hay**
stay, may, Jay, gray

Activity 5. Discuss each picture so that the student can correctly identify them. Read the words and have the student draw a line to match the words with the correct pictures.

Pictures:		
	teeth	**meat**
	eagle	**feet**
	sweep	**tree**
	seal	**team**
	bee	**sleep**

Activity 6. Help the student read the sentences and the word choices for each one. Have the student choose which word will complete each sentence correctly. The student is to underline the correct word and print it on the line.

Sentences:

1. **We like to go to the zoo.**
2. **The seals are fun to see.**
3. **I like the eagles best.**
4. **We rest under a shade tree.**
5. **We use the benches for seats.**
6. **Our feet get tired after lots of walking.**
7. **We will see the lions next.**
8. **They have big teeth.**
9. **Then we will each have a cold drink.**
10. **We will come see the animals again soon!**

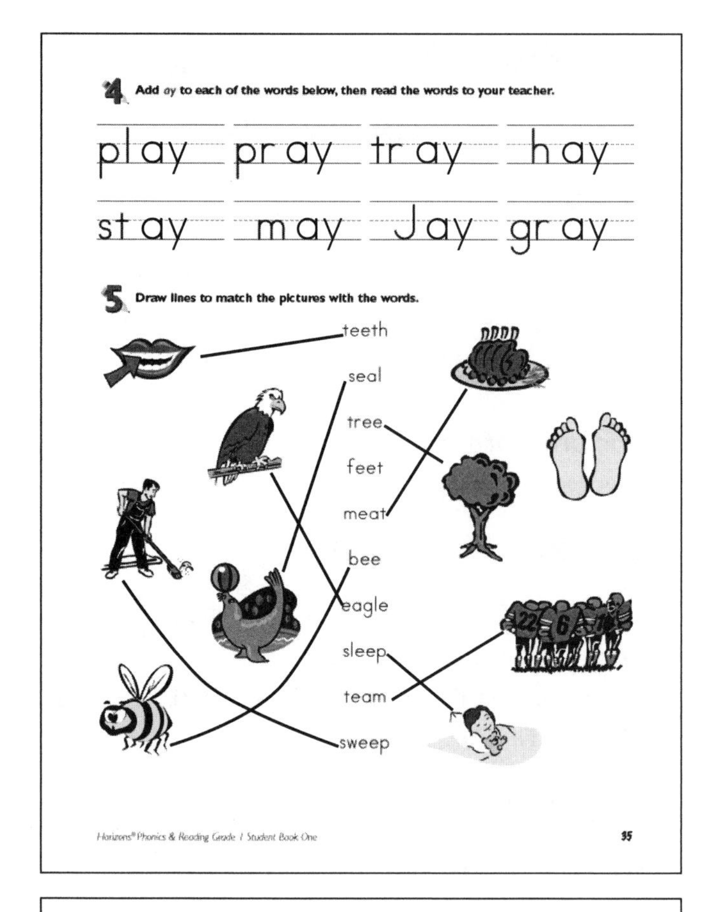

4. Add *ay* to each of the words below, then read the words to your teacher.

play pray tray hay
stay may Jay gray

5. Draw lines to match the pictures with the words.

teeth
seal
tree
feet
meat
bee
eagle
sleep
team
sweep

Horizons® Phonics & Reading Grade 1 Student Book One 95

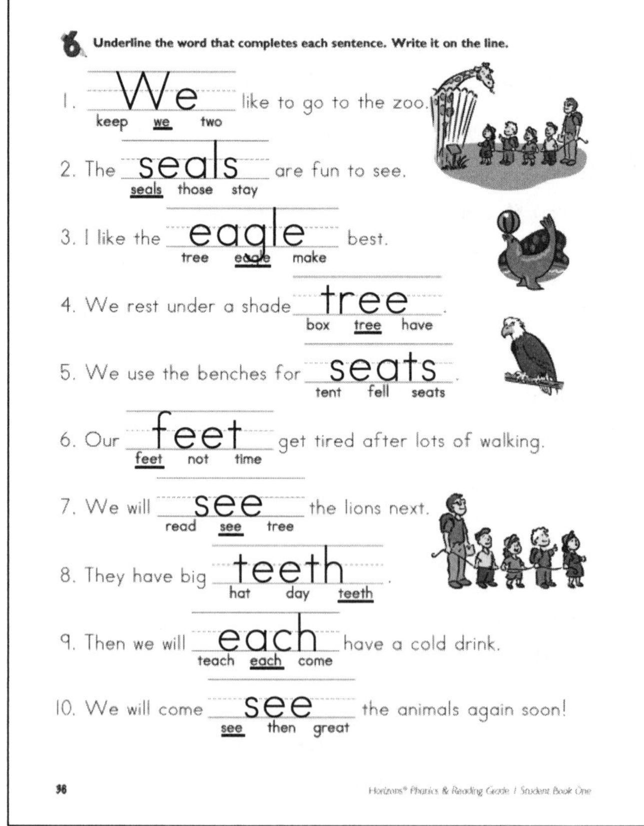

6. Underline the word that completes each sentence. Write it on the line.

1. We like to go to the zoo. (keep <u>we</u> two)
2. The seals are fun to see. (<u>seals</u> those stay)
3. I like the eagle best. (tree <u>eagle</u> make)
4. We rest under a shade tree. (box <u>tree</u> have)
5. We use the benches for seats. (tent fell <u>seats</u>)
6. Our feet get tired after lots of walking. (<u>feet</u> not time)
7. We will see the lions next. (read <u>see</u> tree)
8. They have big teeth. (hat day <u>teeth</u>)
9. Then we will each have a cold drink. (teach <u>each</u> come)
10. We will come see the animals again soon! (<u>see</u> then great)

96 Horizons® Phonics & Reading Grade 1 Student Book One

Lesson 10 - Vowel Pairs
ie, oa, oe

Overview:

- Read and place diacritical markings on words with vowel pairs **ie**, **oa**, and **oe**
- Word completion

Materials and Supplies:

- Teacher's Guide & Student Workbook
- White board or chalkboard
- Phonics rule flashcard in **Teacher Resources**
- Story: *The Old Goat*

Teaching Tips:

Read and review the rule about vowel pairs. Demonstrate the correct diacritical markings for each vowel pair: **īe̸, ōa̸, ōe̸**. Ask the students to think of additional words for each vowel pair. Discuss the pictures in each activity so that the student is able to identify them correctly.

Activity 1. Have the student read each word under the picture and make the correct diacritical markings.

Words: **hoe, coat, road, pie**
doe, toe, toad, boat
goat, soap, toast, tie

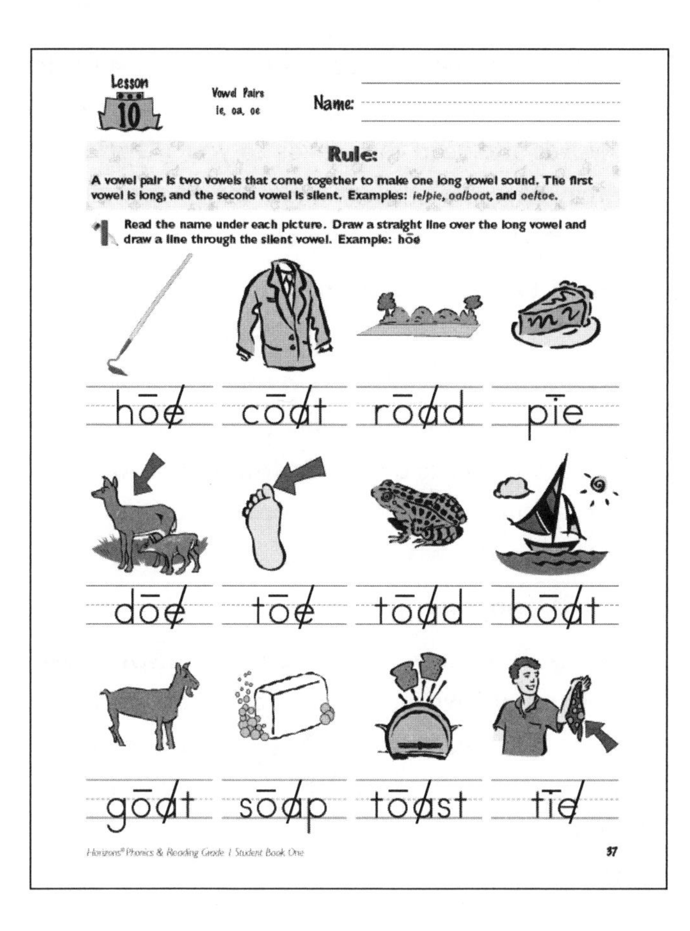

Lesson 10 | Vowel Pairs ie, oa, oe | Name:

Rule:

A vowel pair is two vowels that come together to make one long vowel sound. The first vowel is long, and the second vowel is silent. Examples: *ie/pie*, *oa/boat*, and *oe/toe*.

1 Read the name under each picture. Draw a straight line over the long vowel and draw a line through the silent vowel. Example: hōe

hōe̸ cōa̸t rōa̸d pīe̸

dōe̸ tōe̸ tōa̸d bōa̸t

gōa̸t sōa̸p tōa̸st tīe̸

Horizons® Phonics & Reading Grade 1 Student Book One 37

Activity 2. Review the sound that the vowel pair **oa** makes. Tell the student to add **oa** to each of the words and read the words to you. (**Optional**: You may have the student make the proper diacritical markings on the words.)

Words: **toad, float, Joan, road**
roast, toast, soap, goat

Activity 3. Review the sound that the vowel pair **oe** makes and have the student complete each of the words in this activity. (**Optional**: You may have the student make the proper diacritical markings on the words.)

Words: **toe, hoe, Joe, doe**

Activity 4. Review the sound that the vowel pair **ie** makes and have the student complete each of the words in this activity. (**Optional**: You may have the student make the proper diacritical markings on the words.)

Words: **lie, pie, die, tie**

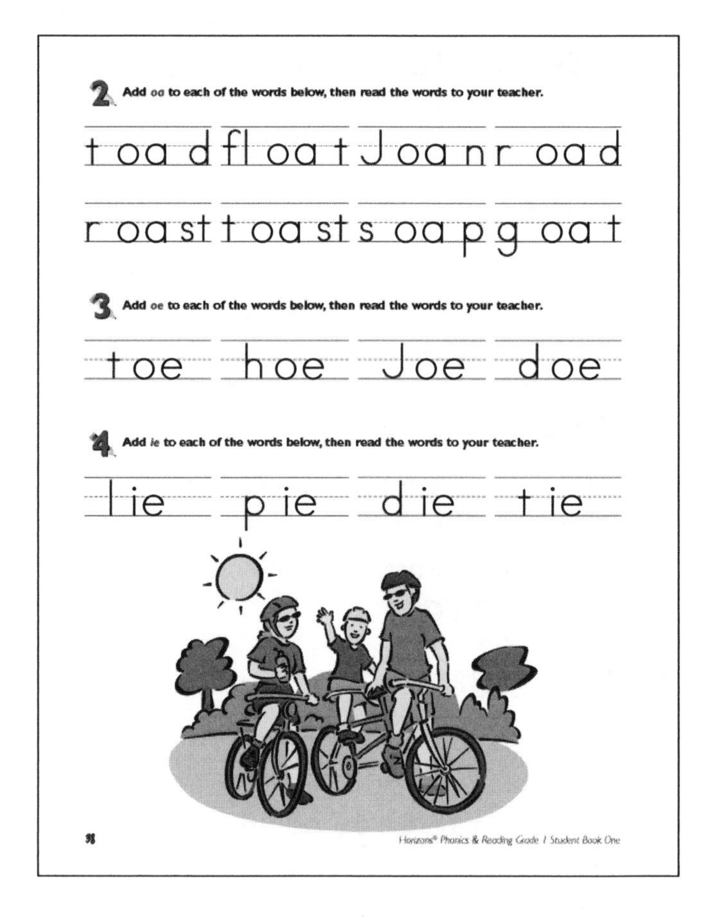

2. Add *oa* to each of the words below, then read the words to your teacher.

toad float Joan road
roast toast soap goat

3. Add *oe* to each of the words below, then read the words to your teacher.

toe hoe Joe doe

4. Add *ie* to each of the words below, then read the words to your teacher.

lie pie die tie

Horizons® Phonics & Reading Grade 1 Student Book One

Test 1

Lessons 1–10

Instructions:

Have the student name all of the pictures in the test to make sure that he/she can identify them. Review the positions of **beginning**, **middle**, and **end** in words to make sure that the student understands the concept. Review the silent **e** rule with the student. Help the student pronounce all of the words in the test. Answer any questions the student may have. This test should not be timed.

Activity 1. Read the instruction with the student. Instruct the student to write the beginning lower case consonant for each picture.

Pictures: **goat, bus, van**
top, cat, map

Letters: **g, b, v**
t, c, m

Activity 2. Read the instruction with the student. Instruct the student to write the ending lower case consonant for each picture.

Pictures: **car, bed, lamp**
dog, man, desk

Letters: **r, d, p**
g, n, k

Activity 3. Read the instruction with the student. Instruct the student to write the middle lower case consonant sound he hears for each picture.

Pictures: **table, tiger, ladder**
kitten, zipper, ruler

Letters: **t, g, d**
t, p, l

Activity 4. Read the words with the student. Instruct the student to draw a line to match the picture with the words in the list.

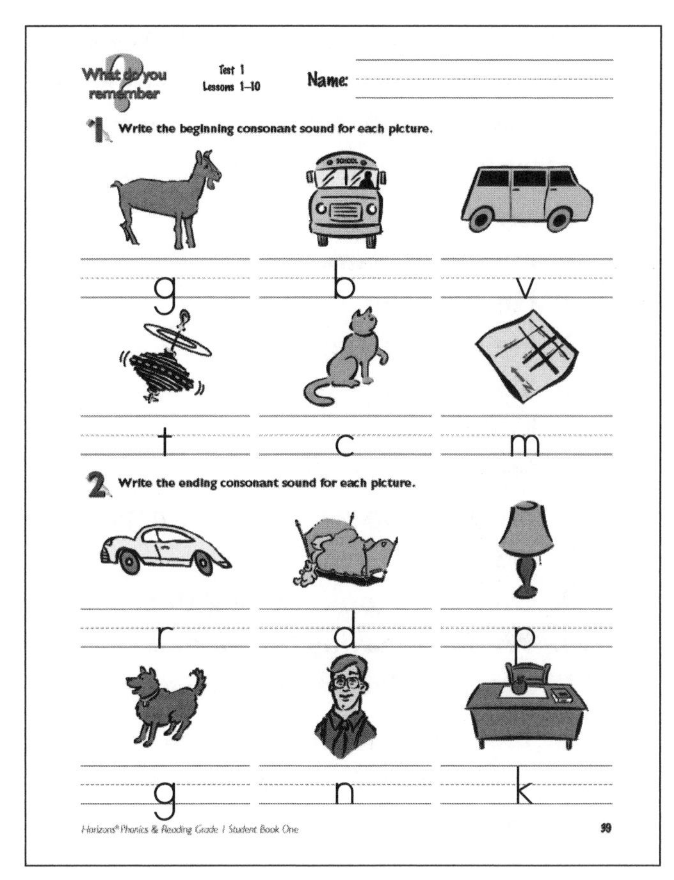
What do you remember
Test 1
Lessons 1–10
Name:

1. Write the beginning consonant sound for each picture.

g b v
t c m

2. Write the ending consonant sound for each picture.

r d p
g n k

Horizons® Phonics & Reading Grade 1 Student Book One 39

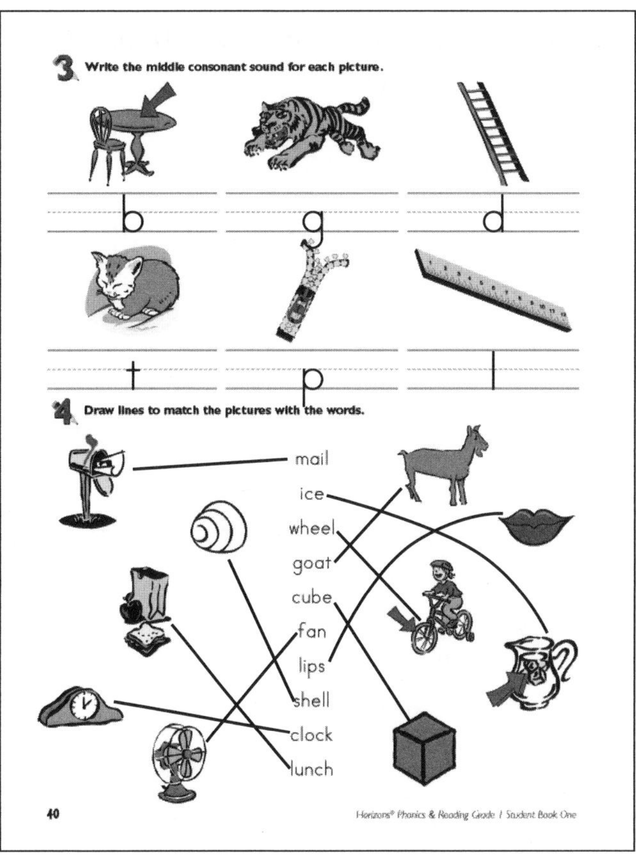
3. Write the middle consonant sound for each picture.

b g d
t p l

4. Draw lines to match the pictures with the words.

mail
ice
wheel
goat
cube
fan
lips
shell
clock
lunch

40 Horizons® Phonics & Reading Grade 1 Student Book One

Pictures:	**mail**	**goat**
	shell	**lips**
	lunch	**wheel**
	clock	**ice**
	fan	**cube**

Activity 5. Read the instructions and the word choices with the student. Make sure that the student underlines the correct word choice as well as writing it on the lines.

Sentences:

1. **My dog is Sam.**
2. **He is brown.**
3. **He likes to play.**
4. **We go to the park.**
5. **I take my mitt.**
6. **My dog and I play ball.**
7. **My dog runs as fast as he can.**
8. **He likes to get the ball.**
9. **One day I took my dog to school.**
10. **We were having "show and tell."**
11. **The kids liked to pet my dog.**

Activity 6. Read the instructions with the student and stress the importance of adding the diacritical markings to the words they write on the lines.

Words: **fine, robe, made, cute, tube, bite, dime, tape**

5 **Underline the word that completes each sentence. Write it on the line.**

1. sat / Sam / map — My dog is Sam.
2. brown / jump / man — He is brown.
3. bed / play / can — He likes to play.
4. fat / bib / park — We go to the park.
5. wind / mitt / sat — I take my mitt.
6. wig / pig / ball — My dog and I play ball.
7. tap / runs / nap — My dog runs as fast as he can.
8. bath / get / gas — He likes to get the ball.
9. jet / school / tan — One day I took my dog to school.
10. ball / pet / tell — We were having "show and tell."
11. pet / liked / ham — The kids liked to pet my dog.

Horizons® Phonics & Reading Grade 1 Student Book One 41

6 **Read the short vowel words. Add a silent e, cross it out, and make a straight line over the vowel to show that it has the long sound.**

1. Add silent e to fin: fīne
2. Add silent e to rob: rōbe
3. Add silent e to mad: māde
4. Add silent e to cut: cūte
5. Add silent e to tub: tūbe
6. Add silent e to bit: bīte
7. Add silent e to dim: dīme
8. Add silent e to tap: tāpe

42 Horizons® Phonics & Reading Grade 1 Student Book One

Lesson 11 - Capitalization & Punctuation

Overview:

- Add punctuation to sentences
- Copy sentences, adding correct punctuation
- Copy sentences, adding correct capitalization and punctuation

Materials and Supplies:

- Teacher's Guide & Student Workbook
- White board or chalkboard
- Phonics rule flashcards in **Teacher Resources**
- Story: *Jim and the Soccer Ball*

Teaching Tips:

Activity 1. Review the punctuation and capitalization rules with the student. Use the white board or chalkboard to write examples of short sentences. Discuss whether the sentences are statements, questions, or exclamations. Have the student read the sentences and add the correct punctuation on the line provided.

Sentences:

1. **My dog likes bones.**
2. **I am seven years old.**
3. **How old are you?**
4. **I love my mom and dad.**
5. **Look out for that car!**
6. **Mike likes to eat chips.**
7. **Wow! Look at that!**
8. **What is your name?**
9. **Will you be my pal?**
10. **Stop! Come back!**

Lesson 11 Capitalization & Punctuation Name:

Rules:

A sentence is a complete thought that tells *who did what*. Every sentence must start with a capital letter and end with a period (.) at the end of a statement, a question mark (?) at the end of a question, or an exclamation mark (!) to show excitement or a command.

1. **Read the sentences. Write a *period* if the sentence is a statement, a *question mark* if the sentence is a question, or an *exclamation mark* if the sentence shows excitement.**

1. My dog likes bones_.
2. I am seven years old_.
3. How old are you_?
4. I love my mom and dad_.
5. Look out for that car_!
6. Mike likes to eat chips_.
7. Wow_! Look at that_!
8. What is your name_?
9. Will you be my pal_?
10. Stop_! Come back_!

. ? ! . ? ! . ? ! . ? ! . ? !

Rule:

An abbreviation is a short form of a word. A period (.) is used after an abbreviation. Examples: *Mr.* and *Mrs.*

2. **Read the sentence and copy it on the lines below. Add the correct punctuation.**

Mr and Mrs Dix will meet with Mr Jones today

Mr. and Mrs. Dix will meet with Mr. Jones today.

Horizons® Phonics & Reading Grade 1 Student Book One 45

Activity 2. Discuss the formation of abbreviations. Use the white board or chalkboard to illustrate how **Mister** and **Mistress** become **Mr.** and **Mrs.** Have the students think of other words they have seen that are abbreviations. Examples: gallon = gal., et cetera = etc., inches = in.

Sentence:

Mr. and Mrs. Dix will meet with Mr. Jones today.

Activity 3. Help the student read the sentences. Review the rules capitalization and punctuation and have the student copy each sentence on the lines below with the correct capitalization and punctuation.

Sentences:

1. **Sam and I will go to a ball game.**
2. **Will Ed and Jim go with us?**
3. **Mr. Jones will take us to the game.**
4. **Do you want a hot dog?**
5. **Wow! He hit a home run!**
6. **We had a nice day with Mr. Jones.**

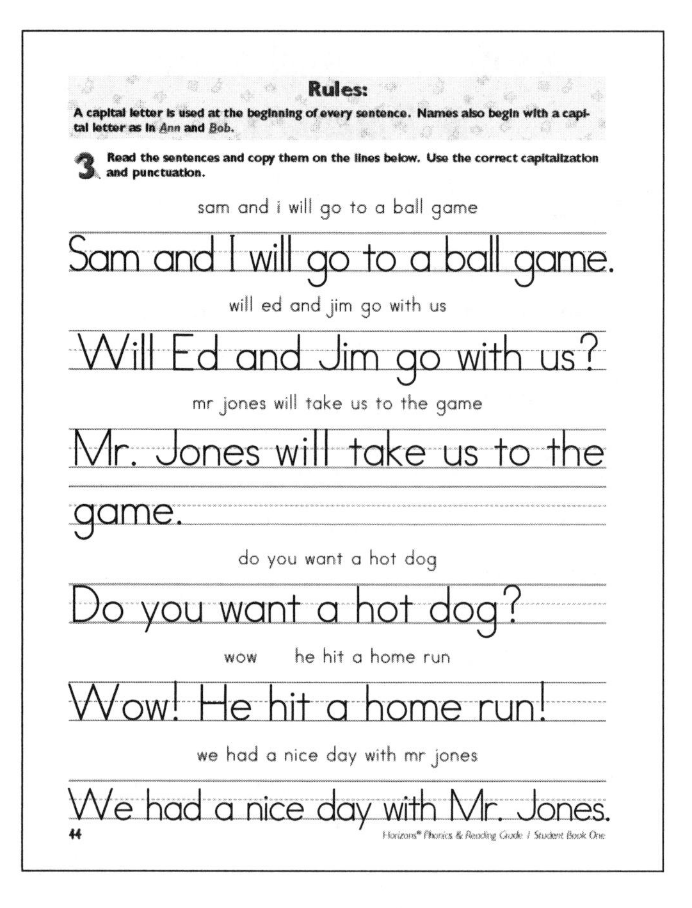

Rules:

A capital letter is used at the beginning of every sentence. Names also begin with a capital letter as in *Ann* and *Bob*.

3 **Read the sentences and copy them on the lines below. Use the correct capitalization and punctuation.**

sam and i will go to a ball game

Sam and I will go to a ball game.

will ed and jim go with us

Will Ed and Jim go with us?

mr jones will take us to the game

Mr. Jones will take us to the game.

do you want a hot dog

Do you want a hot dog?

wow he hit a home run

Wow! He hit a home run!

we had a nice day with mr jones

We had a nice day with Mr. Jones.

44 Horizons® Phonics & Reading Grade 1 Student Book One

Lesson 12 - Review: Long Vowel & Short Vowel Sounds

Overview:

- Auditory recognition of long and short vowel sounds
- Rhyming words
- Matching pictures to words
- Sentence completion

Materials and Supplies:

- Teacher's Guide & Student Workbook
- White board or chalkboard
- Alphabet flashcards
- Phonics rule flashcards in **Teacher Resources**
- Story: *Mike's Kite*

Teaching Tips:

Review phonetic sounds using alphabet flashcards. Read through all the words in the activities with the student. Discuss the pictures in each activity so that the student is able to identify them correctly. (**Optional**: You may have the student place diacritical markings on the words he writes.)

Activity 1. Read the words in the word box. Discuss the rules and ask the student to identify which words have vowel pairs, which words have silent **e**, and which words have the short vowel sound. Instruct the student to write the words under the correct categories. Ask for verbal responses for examples of short **ŭ** words.

Long **ā**:	**fail, rate**	Short **ă**:	**rat, zap**
Long **ē**:	**eat, week**	Short **ĕ**:	**mess, fed**
Long **ī**:	**dime, white**	Short **ĭ**:	**lid, wig**
Long **ō**:	**coat, toe**	Short **ŏ**:	**rob, cot**
Long **ū**:	**flute, blue**		

Activity 2. Help the student read the words in the activity. The student will draw lines to match the words that rhyme. Ask for verbal examples of additional long vowel rhyming words.

Rhyming words: **pain/gain** **eat/treat** **boat/moat** **bike/like**

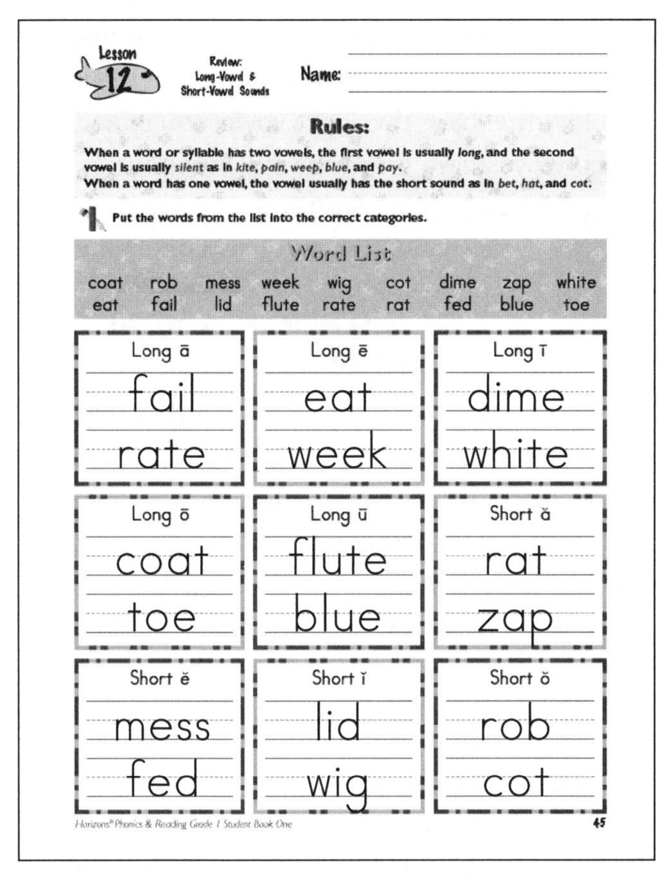
Lesson 12 Review: Long-Vowel & Short-Vowel Sounds Name:

Rules:
When a word or syllable has two vowels, the first vowel is usually *long*, and the second vowel is usually *silent* as in *kite, pain, weep, blue,* and *pay*.
When a word has one vowel, the vowel usually has the short sound as in *bet, hat,* and *cot*.

1. Put the words from the list into the correct categories.

Word List
coat rob mess week wig cot dime zap white
eat fail lid flute rate rat fed blue toe

Long ā	Long ē	Long ī
fail	eat	dime
rate	week	white

Long ō	Long ū	Short ă
coat	flute	rat
toe	blue	zap

Short ĕ	Short ĭ	Short ŏ
mess	lid	rob
fed	wig	cot

Horizons® Phonics & Reading Grade 1 Student Book One 45

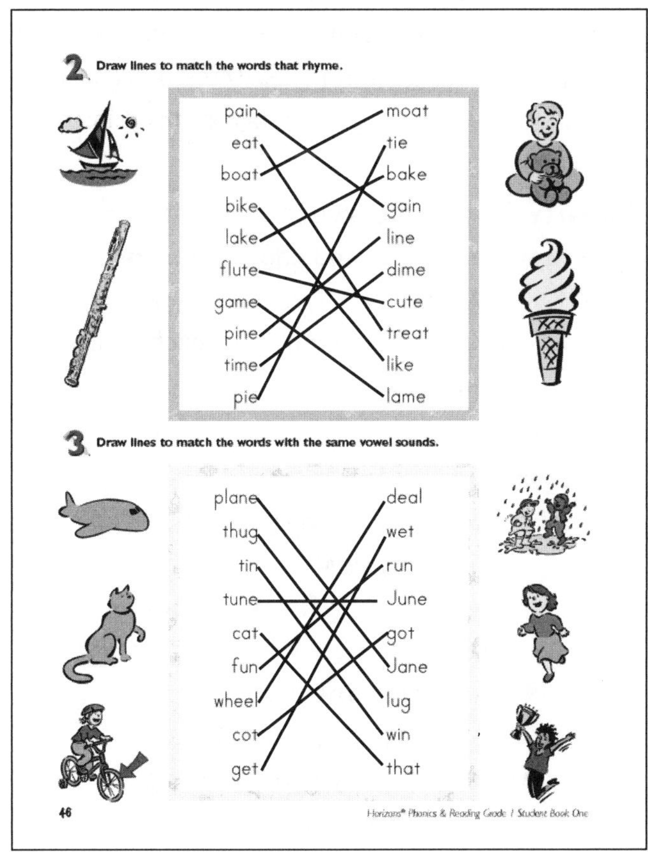
2. Draw lines to match the words that rhyme.

pain, eat, boat, bike, lake, flute, game, pine, time, pie
moat, tie, bake, gain, line, dime, cute, treat, like, lame

3. Draw lines to match the words with the same vowel sounds.

plane, thug, tin, tune, cat, fun, wheel, cot, get
deal, wet, run, June, got, Jane, lug, win, that

46 Horizons® Phonics & Reading Grade 1 Student Book One

lake/bake **flute/cute**
game/lame **pine/line**
time/dime **pie/tie**

Activity 3. Help the student read the words in

the activity. The student will draw lines to match the words that rhyme. Have the student identify which words have the short vowel sound and which words have the long vowel sound.

Rhyming words:	**plane/Jane**	**thug/lug**
	tin/win	**tune/June**
	cat/that	**fun/run**
	wheel/deal	**cot/got**
	get/wet	

Activity 4. Discuss each picture so that the student can correctly identify them. Read the words and have the student draw a line to match the words with the correct pictures.

Pictures:	**flute**	**week**
	van	**frog**
	clock	**duck**
	pine	**cat**
	cane	**lid**

Activity 5. Have the student write a sentence, using at least three of the words in the list in Activity 4. Remind the student that the sentence should begin with a capital letter and end with the appropriate punctuation mark. Remind the student to capitalize any proper names used in the sentence.

Activity 6. Help the student read the sentences and the word choices and choose the correct word for each sentence. The student will underline the word that best completes each sentence and print it on the line.

Sentences:

1. **Jim rides a bus to class.**
2. **He likes school very much.**
3. **Jim sits at a desk.**
4. **In the morning, he reads books.**
5. **In the afternoon, he works on math.**
6. **Mike is Jim's best pal.**
7. **They like to play outside.**
8. **Jim and Mike like to play tag.**
9. **At lunch, they sit together.**
10. **Jim is glad that he has such a good pal.**

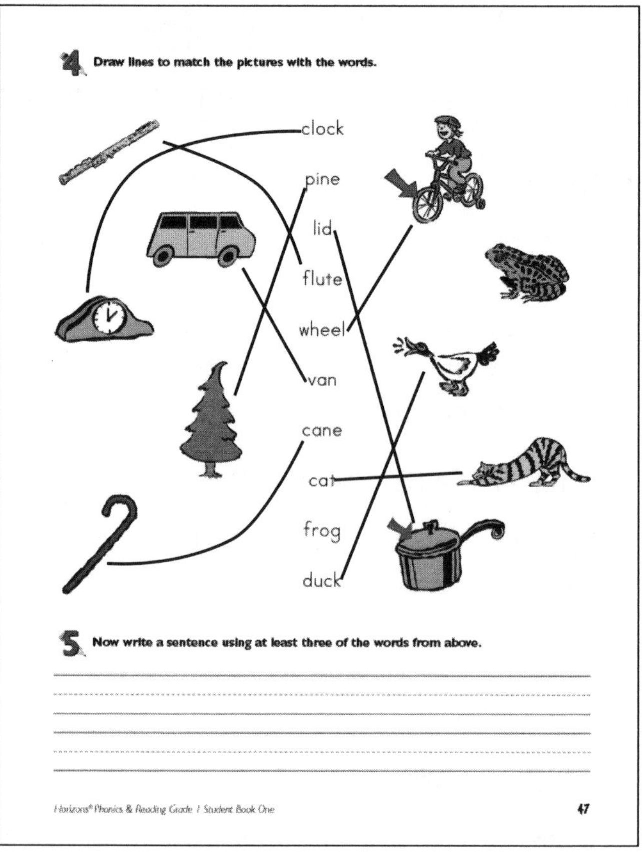
4. Draw lines to match the pictures with the words.

clock
pine
lid
flute
wheel
van
cane
cat
frog
duck

5. Now write a sentence using at least three of the words from above.

Horizons® Phonics & Reading Grade 1 Student Book One 47

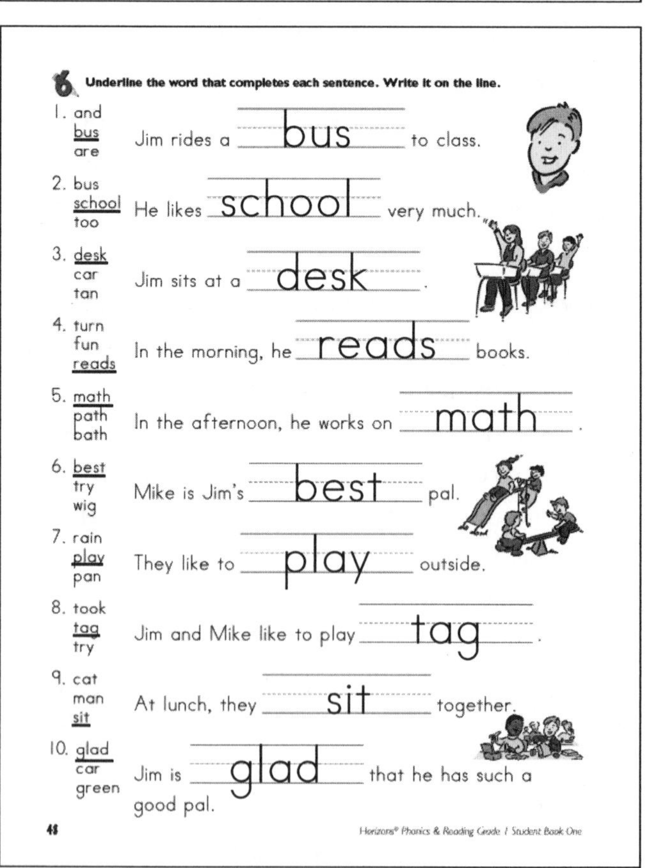
6. Underline the word that completes each sentence. Write it on the line.

1. and / bus / are — Jim rides a bus to class.
2. bus / school / too — He likes school very much.
3. desk / car / tan — Jim sits at a desk.
4. turn / fun / reads — In the morning, he reads books.
5. math / path / bath — In the afternoon, he works on math.
6. best / try / wig — Mike is Jim's best pal.
7. rain / play / pan — They like to play outside.
8. took / tag / try — Jim and Mike like to play tag.
9. cat / man / sit — At lunch, they sit together.
10. glad / car / green — Jim is glad that he has such a good pal.

48 Horizons® Phonics & Reading Grade 1 Student Book One

Lesson 13 - Compound Words

Overview:

- Write two words that make up the compound word
- Choose correct compound to word to match the clue
- Complete crossword puzzle using compound words
- Write correct compound words in sentences

Materials and Supplies:

- Teacher's Guide & Student Workbook
- White board or chalkboard
- Word cards (as necessary)
- Phonics rule flashcards in **Teacher Resources**
- Story: *The Big Backyard*

Teaching Tips:

Make word cards for the compound words presented in the lesson. Review them with the student as necessary. Help the student pronounce the words in the lesson. Explain the rule for compound words and review the examples. See if the student can think of some more examples.

Activity 1. Review the rule for compound words. Help the student read the words in the activity. Review the pictures with the student. The student will write the two words that make up each compound word.

Words:		
	dog	**house**
	back	**yard**
	sun	**light**
	scare	**crow**
	cup	**cake**
	rail	**road**
	rain	**coat**
	my	**self**
	pop	**corn**
	pea	**nut**

Activity 2. Go over the words in the list. Help the student read the sentences. The student will print the correct word to go with each clue.

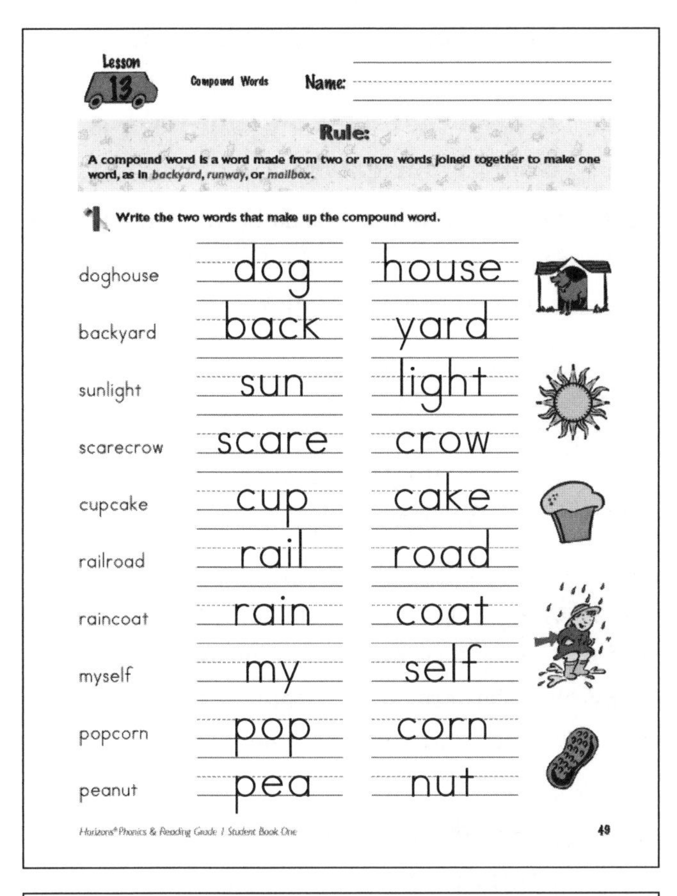
Lesson 13 Compound Words Name:

Rule:
A compound word is a word made from two or more words joined together to make one word, as in *backyard*, *runway*, or *mailbox*.

1 Write the two words that make up the compound word.

doghouse	dog	house
backyard	back	yard
sunlight	sun	light
scarecrow	scare	crow
cupcake	cup	cake
railroad	rail	road
raincoat	rain	coat
myself	my	self
popcorn	pop	corn
peanut	pea	nut

Horizons® Phonics & Reading Grade 1 Student Book One 49

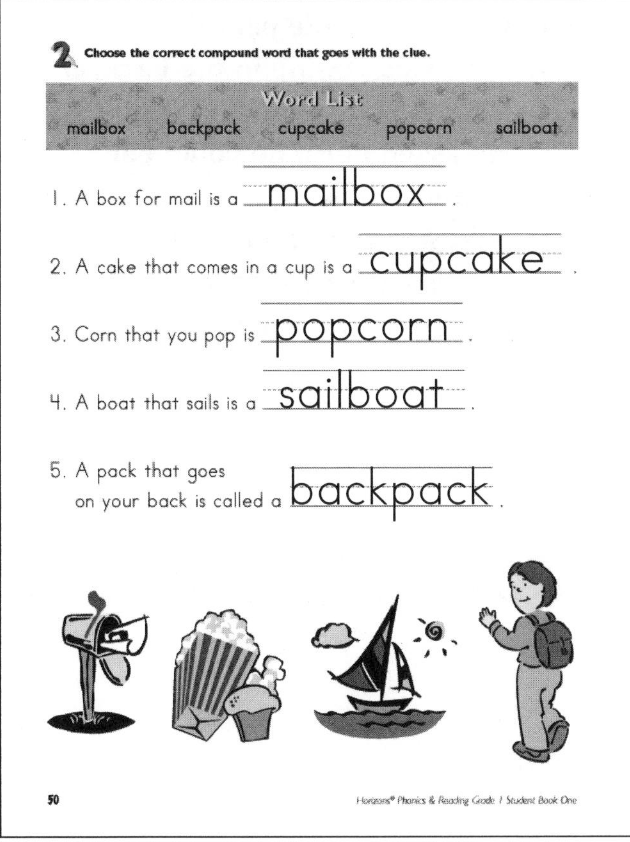
2 Choose the correct compound word that goes with the clue.

Word List
mailbox backpack cupcake popcorn sailboat

1. A box for mail is a mailbox.
2. A cake that comes in a cup is a cupcake.
3. Corn that you pop is popcorn.
4. A boat that sails is a sailboat.
5. A pack that goes on your back is called a backpack.

50 Horizons® Phonics & Reading Grade 1 Student Book One

Sentences:

1. **A box for mail is a mailbox.**
2. **A cake that comes in a cup is a cupcake.**

3. **Corn that you pop is popcorn.**
4. **A boat that sails is a sailboat.**
5. **A pack that goes on your back is called a backpack.**

Activity 3. Review the words in the list. Help the student read the crossword puzzle clues. Assist the student as necessary with the crossword puzzle.

Across: **1. sailboats**
3. scarecrow
4. doghouse

Down: **2. seaweed**
3. sandbox

Activity 4. Help the student read the sentences and the word choices. The student will underline the words that correctly complete the sentences and print the words on the lines.

Sentences:

1. **It was time for Mike to eat breakfast.**
2. **His mom made pancakes.**
3. **Mike was playing in the backyard.**
4. **His mother called him inside.**
5. **He asked her if he could eat outside.**
6. **Mike got to eat outdoors.**
7. **He also ate a cupcake.**
8. **Next time, he will have oatmeal.**

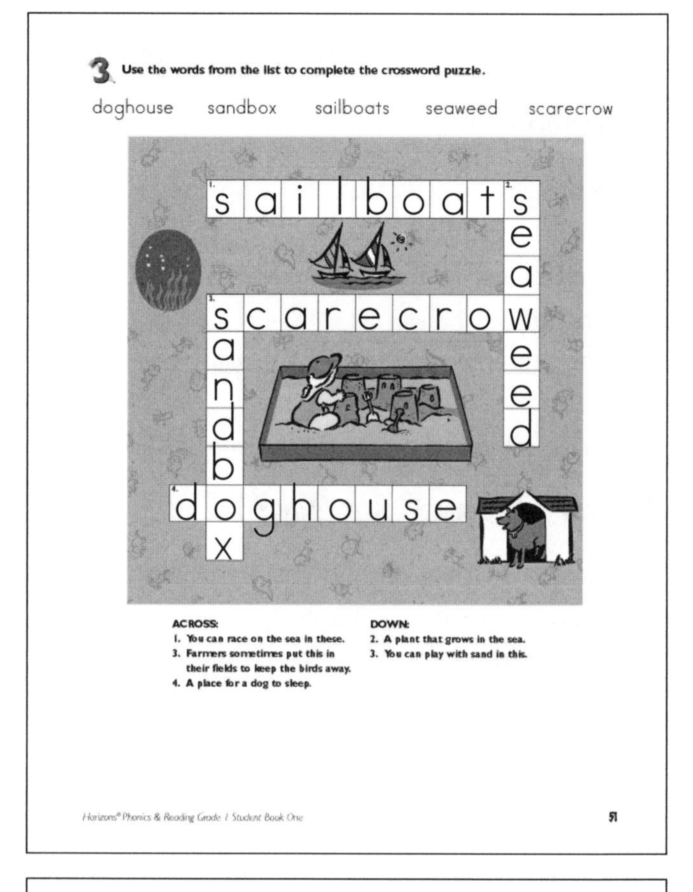

3 Use the words from the list to complete the crossword puzzle.

doghouse sandbox sailboats seaweed scarecrow

ACROSS:
1. You can race on the sea in these.
3. Farmers sometimes put this in their fields to keep the birds away.
4. A place for a dog to sleep.

DOWN:
2. A plant that grows in the sea.
3. You can play with sand in this.

Horizons® Phonics & Reading Grade 1 Student Book One 51

4 Underline the compound word that completes each sentence. Write it on the line.

1. It was time for Mike to eat breakfast. (mailbox, breakfast, cans)
2. His mom made pancakes. (trucks, pancakes, stores)
3. Mike was playing in the backyard. (uphill, grape, backyard)
4. His mother called him inside. (keep, inside, around)
5. He asked her if he could eat outside. (mine, table, outside)
6. Mike got to eat outdoors. (over, outdoors, are)
7. He also ate a cupcake. (cupcake, kite, raincoat)
8. Next time, he will have oatmeal. (may, oatmeal, mailbox)

52 Horizons® Phonics & Reading Grade 1 Student Book One

Lesson 14 - Making Words Plural

Overview:

- Circle pictures that show more than one
- Write sentences using plurals
- Write plural forms of words (**ss**, **ch**, **sh**, **x** rule)
- Write plural form of words (vowel + **y** rule)
- Write base word for plural words
- Write plural form of words (**fe** or **f** rule)

Materials and Supplies:

- Teacher's Guide & Student Workbook
- White board or chalkboard
- Word cards (as necessary)
- Phonics rule flashcard in **Teacher Resources**
- Story: *Kim and the Roses*

Teaching Tips:

Discuss all of the pictures in the lesson so that the student is able to identify them. Review all of the rules with the student. There are many rules in this lesson. You may have to go over them several times. Give many examples of each rule, using the white board or chalkboard. Have the student think of examples, also.

Activity 1. Review the rule. Instruct the student to circle all of the pictures that show more than one.

Pictures: **dogs, bed, cars, trees**
ball, tent, pencils, pins
doll, books, rose, peanuts

Activity 2. The student will write two sentences using some of the words that name the pictures from Activity 1. Remind the student about correct punctuation and capitalization.

Activity 3. Review the rule. Help the student read the words as necessary. Instruct the student to write the plural form of the word by adding **es** to the end of each word.

Words: **dresses, classes, boxes, brushes, peaches, lunches, crashes, glasses, foxes, churches**

Lesson 14 Making Words Plural Name:

Rule:
A word is *plural* if it means "more than one." Example: *trucks, cars, plates,* and *things.*

1. Circle the picture of the things that are more than one.

2. Write two sentences. Use words that name some of the pictures from above.

Horizons® Phonics & Reading Grade 1 Student Book One 53

Rule:
When a word ends in *ss, ch, sh,* or *x,* you usually add *es* at the end to make the word plural.

3. Write the plural form of each word.

dress	dresses	lunch	lunches
class	classes	crash	crashes
box	boxes	glass	glasses
brush	brushes	fox	foxes
peach	peaches	church	churches

4. Write a sentence using two of the words from above. Draw a picture to go with your sentence.

54 Horizons® Phonics & Reading Grade 1 Student Book One

Activity 4. Have the student write a sentence, using at least two of the words from Activity 3. Remind about correct punctuation and capitalization. The student may draw a picture if desired.

Activity 5. Review the rule. Help the student read the words in the activity. The student will write the plural form of each word by adding an **s** to the end of each word.

Words: **turkeys, monkeys, jays, toys, plays, donkeys, chimneys**

Activity 6. Remind the student that a base word is a word that does not have a prefix or a suffix. Help the student read the words as necessary and instruct the student to print the base word for each word on the line.

Words: **dress, church, toy, turkey, brush, fox, class**

Activity 7. Go over the rule. Help the student read the words in the activity and identify the pictures as necessary. The student will print the plural form of each word by changing the **f** or **fe** to a **v** and adding **es**.

Words: **leaves, shelves, elves, halves, lives, wives, knives, wolves, calves, scarves**

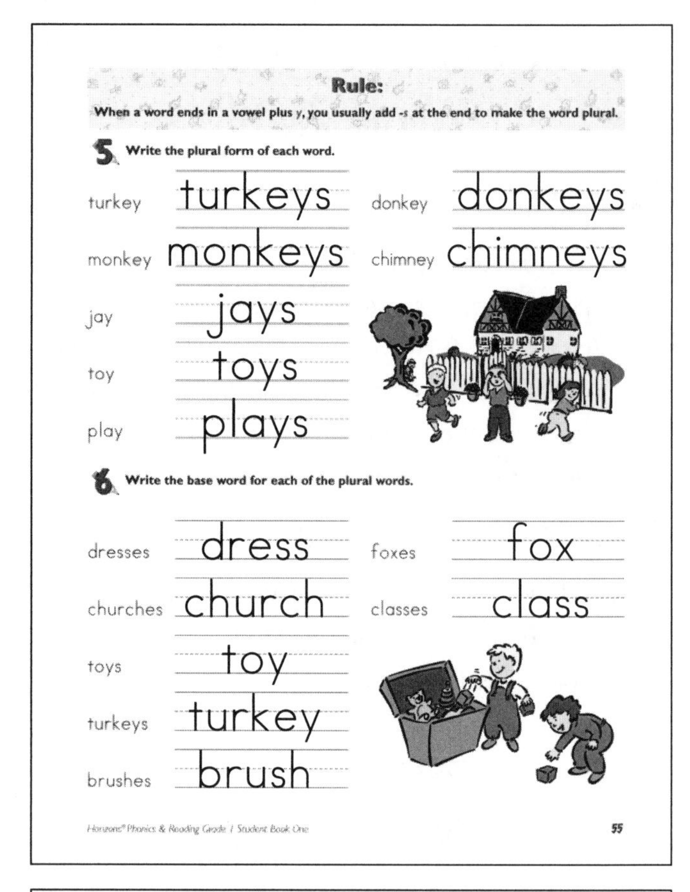

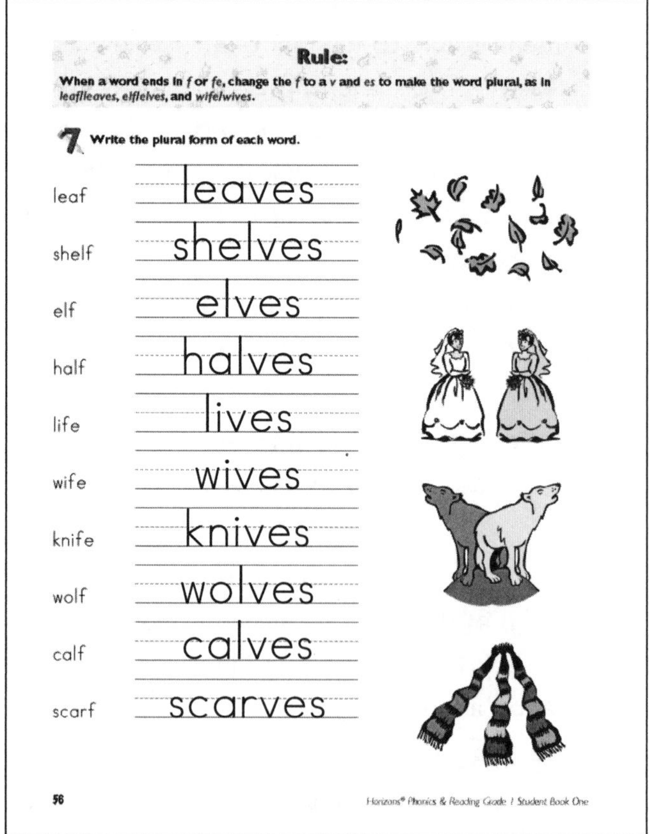

Lesson 15 - Suffixes in Short Vowel Words

Overview:

- Make new words by adding suffixes **-s, -ed,** and **-ing**
- Write base words for words with suffixes
- Complete sentences adding correct suffixes to base words
- Add suffixes **-er, -ed, -est,** and **-ing** (double consonant rule)

Materials and Supplies:

- Teacher's Guide & Student Workbook
- White board or chalkboard
- Word cards (as necessary)
- Phonics rule flashcards in **Teacher Resources**
- Story: *Bill and Jeff*

Teaching Tips:

Go over the rules in the lesson. Since there are many rules, you may want to review them several times. Refer to the **Teacher Resources** section of this teacher handbook for reproducible flash-cards with phonics rules.

Activity 1. Discuss the rule. Assist the student in reading the words in the activity as necessary. The student will print new words on the lines by adding **s, ed,** and **ing** to the ends of the words.

Words:

rains	**rained**	**raining**
lifts	**lifted**	**lifting**
cleans	**cleaned**	**cleaning**
mends	**mended**	**mending**
opens	**opened**	**opening**
peeks	**peeked**	**peeking**

Activity 2. Review the rule about base words. Have the student write the base word for each of the words shown.

Words: **rain, play, clean, open, mend**

Activity 3. Review the rule about the suffixes **-er** and **-est**. Assist the student in reading the sentences and the words under the lines. Have the student complete the sentences by adding either **er** or **est** to the word and writing it on the line.

Sentences:

1. Bill is taller than his brother, Jeff.

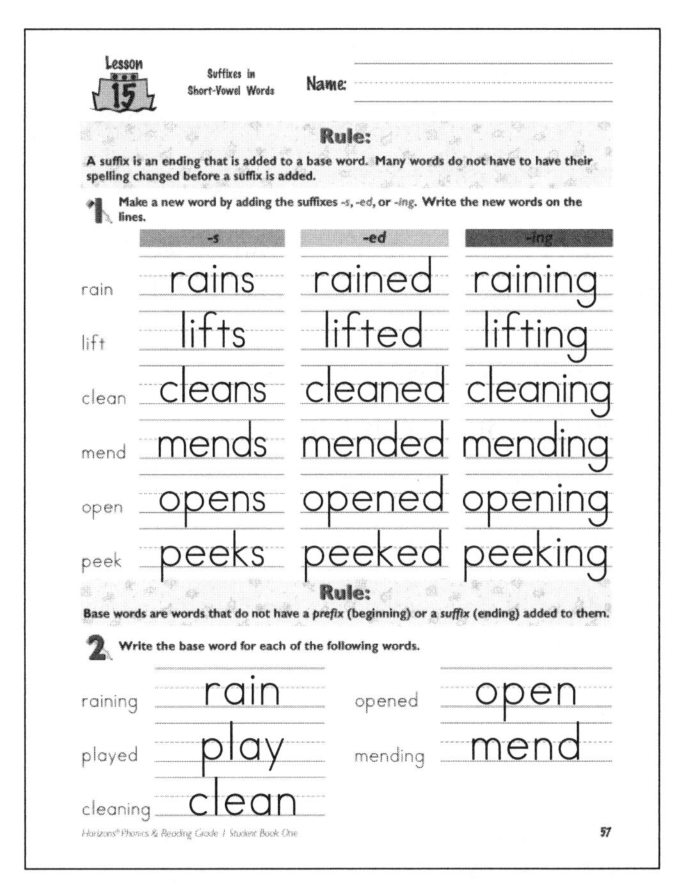
Lesson 15 Suffixes in Short-Vowel Words Name:

Rule:
A suffix is an ending that is added to a base word. Many words do not have to have their spelling changed before a suffix is added.

1. Make a new word by adding the suffixes -s, -ed, or -ing. Write the new words on the lines.

	-s	-ed	-ing
rain	rains	rained	raining
lift	lifts	lifted	lifting
clean	cleans	cleaned	cleaning
mend	mends	mended	mending
open	opens	opened	opening
peek	peeks	peeked	peeking

Rule:
Base words are words that do not have a *prefix* (beginning) or a *suffix* (ending) added to them.

2. Write the base word for each of the following words.

raining rain — opened open
played play — mending mend
cleaning clean

Horizons® Phonics & Reading Grade 1 Student Book One 57

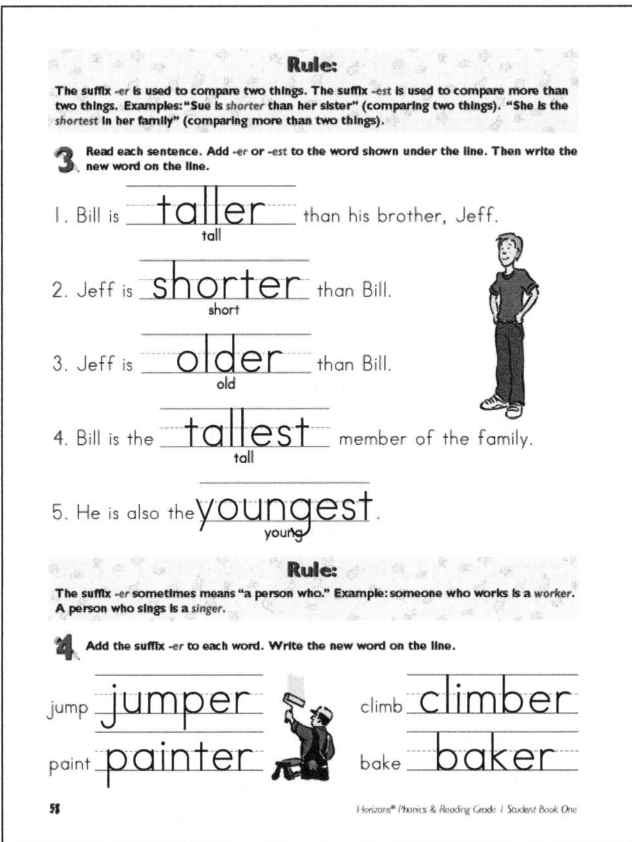
Rule:
The suffix *-er* is used to compare two things. The suffix *-est* is used to compare more than two things. Examples: "Sue is *shorter* than her sister" (comparing two things). "She is the *shortest* in her family" (comparing more than two things).

3. Read each sentence. Add *-er* or *-est* to the word shown under the line. Then write the new word on the line.

1. Bill is taller (tall) than his brother, Jeff.
2. Jeff is shorter (short) than Bill.
3. Jeff is older (old) than Bill.
4. Bill is the tallest (tall) member of the family.
5. He is also the youngest (young).

Rule:
The suffix *-er* sometimes means "a person who." Example: someone who works is a *worker*. A person who sings is a *singer*.

4. Add the suffix *-er* to each word. Write the new word on the line.

jump jumper — climb climber
paint painter — bake baker

58 Horizons® Phonics & Reading Grade 1 Student Book One

2. **Jeff is shorter than Bill.**
3. **Jeff is older than Bill.**
4. **Bill is the tallest member of the family.**
5. **He is also the youngest.**

Activity 4. Review the rule with the student, and have him add the suffix **-er** to each of the words. Have the student read the words to you. Ask for additional examples.

Words: **jumper, climber, painter, baker**

Activity 5. Go over the rule. Use the white board or chalkboard as necessary to write down examples of the rule. Have the student read the words, print new words on the lines by adding the suffix **-ed** to the words.

Words: **ripped, begged, fanned, stopped, tipped**

Activity 6. Go over the rule. Use the white board or chalkboard as necessary to write down examples of the rule. Have the student read the words, print new words on the lines by adding the suffix **-er** to the words.

Words: **hotter, flatter, batter, winner, runner**

Activity 7. Go over the rule. Use the white board or chalkboard as necessary to write down examples of the rule. Have the student read the words, print new words on the lines by adding the suffix **-est** or **-ing** to the words.

Words: **hottest, gladdest, running, flattest, winning, spinning**

Activity 8. Help the student read the sentences as necessary, add the correct suffix to the word under the line and write the new word on the line.

Sentences:

1. **Today was the hottest day of summer.**
2. **We went swimming.**
3. **Jimmy made the biggest splash.**
4. **He is the shortest one of all of us.**
5. **We had fun playing in the pond.**
6. **We laughed when a frog hopped by Jimmy's foot.**
7. **I tried skipping like the frog.**
8. **When we went home, we all napped.**

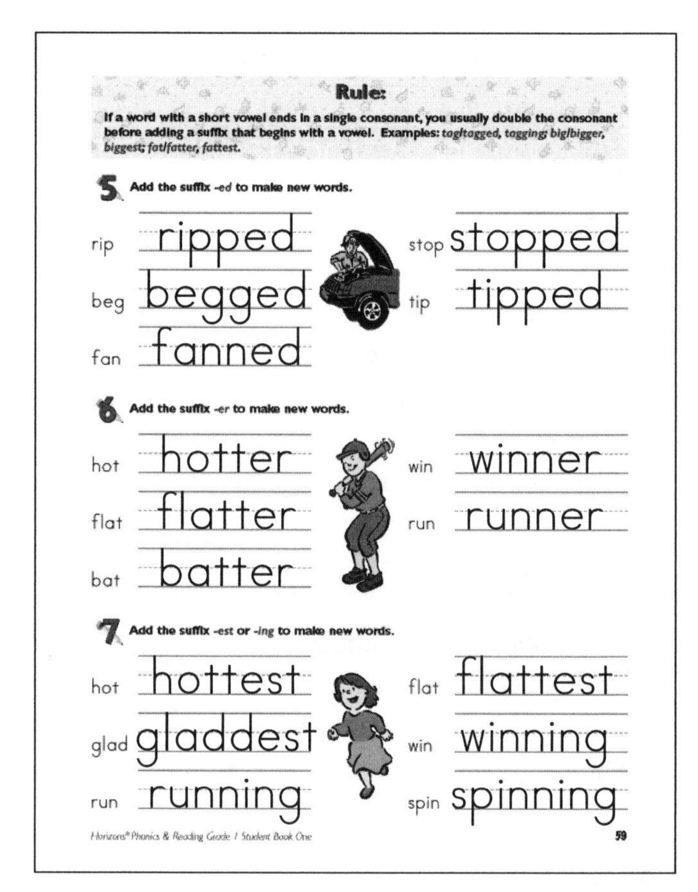

Rule:
If a word with a short vowel ends in a single consonant, you usually double the consonant before adding a suffix that begins with a vowel. Examples: *tag/tagged, tagging; big/bigger, biggest; fat/fatter, fattest.*

5. Add the suffix *-ed* to make new words.

rip ripped
beg begged
fan fanned
stop stopped
tip tipped

6. Add the suffix *-er* to make new words.

hot hotter
flat flatter
bat batter
win winner
run runner

7. Add the suffix *-est* or *-ing* to make new words.

hot hottest
glad gladdest
run running
flat flattest
win winning
spin spinning

Horizons® Phonics & Reading Grade 1 Student Book One 59

8. Read each sentence. Add the correct suffix to the word under the line. Then write the new word on the line.

1. Today was the hottest (hot) day of summer.
2. We went swimming (swim).
3. Jimmy made the biggest (big) splash.
4. He is the shortest (short) one of all of us.
5. We had fun playing (play) in the pond.
6. We laughed when a frog hopped (hop) by Jimmy's foot.
7. I tried skipping (skip) like the frog.
8. When we went home, we all napped (nap).

9. What would you do on a hot day? Write your answer below.

60 Horizons® Phonics & Reading Grade 1 Student Book One

Activity 9. Have the student write one sentence answering the question, **"What would you do on a hot day?"** Remind the student about correct capitalization and punctuation.

Lesson 16 - Suffixes in Silent e Words

Overview:

- Practice writing words adding suffixes **-es**, **-er**, and **-est**
- Identify and write base words
- Complete sentences by adding correct suffixes to base words
- Sentence writing

Materials and Supplies:

- Teacher's Guide & Student Workbook
- White board or chalkboard
- Word cards (as necessary)
- Phonics rule flashcards in **Teacher Resources**
- Story: *Baking Cookies*

Teaching Tips:

Go over the rule and the examples. Have the student think of additional examples of the rule. Make word cards for the words in the lesson as necessary.

Activity 1. Review the rule. The student will add the suffixes **-es**, **-er**, or **-est** to make new words and print the new words on the lines. Aid the student with suffix selection and spelling as needed.

Words: bake/**bakes, baker**
take/**takes, taker**
make/**makes, maker**
dive/**dives, diver**
slice/**slices, slicer**
cute/**cuter, cutest**

Lesson 16 Suffixes in Silent e Words Name:

Rule:
If a word ends in silent e, drop the e before adding a suffix that begins with a vowel.
Examples: *bake/baking, write/writer, slice/slicing.*

1. Add the suffixes -es, -er, or -est to each word. Write the new words on the lines.

bake	bakes	baker
take	takes	taker
make	makes	maker
dive	dives	diver
slice	slices	slicer
cute	cuter	cutest

2. Now write the base word for each word below.

shining	shine	writer	write
bravest	brave	bakes	bake
hoping	hope	smiles	smile
used	use	hiding	hide

Horizons® Phonics & Reading Grade 1 Student Book One 61

Activity 2. Help the student read the words as necessary. The student will write the base word for each of the words listed. Aid the student with spelling as needed.

Words: **shine, brave, hope, use, write, bake, smile, hide**

Activity 3. Help the student read the sentences and sound out unfamiliar words. Have the student add the correct suffix to the base word and write the new word on the lines.

Sentences:

1. **Jill was baking cookies.**
2. **Her pal Kim was making them with her.**
3. **They used a wooden spoon to mix things.**
4. **Mom smiled as she watched them.**
5. **She hoped the cookies would be good.**
6. **The girls were taking turns adding things.**
7. **Mom liked the way the shared the spoon.**
8. **Jill and Kim were being safe by having Mom use the stove.**

Activity 4. Have the student write a sentence or two about foods that they have helped to make. Emphasize correct punctuation and capitalization.

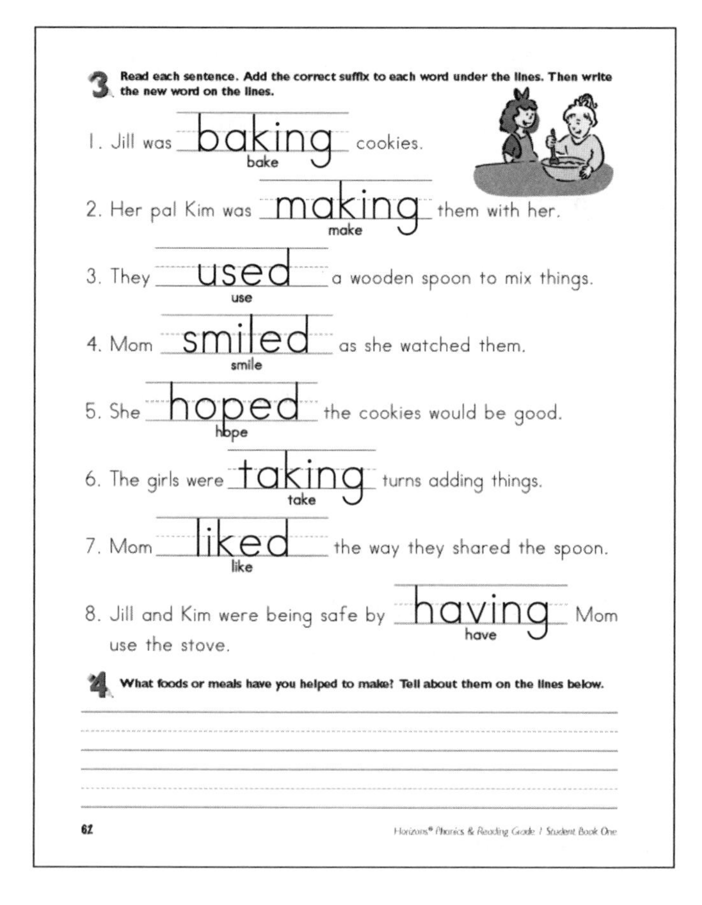

3 Read each sentence. Add the correct suffix to each word under the lines. Then write the new word on the lines.

1. Jill was baking cookies. (bake)
2. Her pal Kim was making them with her. (make)
3. They used a wooden spoon to mix things. (use)
4. Mom smiled as she watched them. (smile)
5. She hoped the cookies would be good. (hope)
6. The girls were taking turns adding things. (take)
7. Mom liked the way they shared the spoon. (like)
8. Jill and Kim were being safe by having Mom use the stove. (have)

4 What foods or meals have you helped to make? Tell about them on the lines below.

62 Horizons® Phonics & Reading Grade 1 Student Book One

Lesson 17 - Suffixes -ful, -ly, -less, -ness, Consonant Digraph sh

Overview:

- Make new words by adding correct suffixes to base words
- Complete sentences by adding correct suffixes to base words
- Identify and write base words
- Sentence writing
- Complete words by adding consonant digraph **sh**
- Identify consonant digraph **sh** as a word beginning or word ending
- Rhyming words with consonant digraph **sh**

Materials and Supplies:

- Teacher's Guide & Student Workbook
- White board or chalkboard
- Word cards (as necessary)
- Phonics rule flashcards in **Teacher Resources**
- Story: *Mark's Scooter*

Teaching Tips:

Review the rules about suffixes **-ful**, **-ly**, **-less**, and **-ness**. Review the base words also. Review the consonant digraph **sh** rule and have the student think of additional examples for both rules. Use the white board or chalkboard to illustrate examples of both rules. Make word cards for any unknown words in the lesson.

Activity 1. Go over the rule. Help the student read the words in the activity. The student will make new words by adding **-ful**, **-ly**, **-less**, or **-ness** to the base words and print the new words on the lines.

Words: hope/**hopeful, hopeless**
use/**useful, useless**
kind/**kindly, kindness**
care/**careful, careless**
glad/**gladly, gladness**

Activity 2. Help the student read the sentences

Lesson 17 Suffixes -ful, -ly, -less, -ness, Consonant Digraph sh Name:

Rule:
A suffix is an ending that is added to a base word to make a new word. Usually when the suffixes *-ful*, *-ly*, *-less*, or *-ness* are added, the spelling of the base word does not change.
Examples: *painful, sadness, hopeless, quickly.*

1 Make new words by adding *-ful*, *-ly*, *-less*, or *-ness* to the base words.

hope hopeful, hopeless
use useful, useless
kind kindly, kindness
care careful, careless
glad gladly, gladness

2 Read each sentence. Add the suffix *-ful*, *-ly*, *-less*, or *-ness* to the base word. Write the new word on the line in the sentence.

1. Mary had to be careful (care) riding her bike.
2. She wanted to ride safely (safe).
3. Her mom gladly (glad) helped her to get on her bike.
4. Mary's bike was very colorful (color).

Horizons® Phonics & Reading Grade 1 Student Book One 63

3 Write the base word for each of the words below.

neatness neat
badly bad
thankful thank
careless care
spoonful spoon
loudly loud
goodness good
sickness sick
hopeful hope

4 Write a sentence using at least two of the words from above.

64 *Horizons® Phonics & Reading Grade 1 Student Book One*

and the base words, add the correct suffix to the base word, and write the new word on the lines.

Sentences:

1. **Mary had to be careful riding her bike.**

2. **She wanted to ride safely.**
3. **Her mom gladly helped her to get on her bike.**
4. **Mary's bike was very colorful.**

Activity 3. Assist the student in reading the words as necessary, and have the student write the correct base word for each of the words with suffixes.

Words: **neat, bad, thank, care, spoon, loud, good, sick, hope**

Activity 4. Have the student write a sentence, using at least two words from Activity 3. Emphasize correct punctuation and capitalization.

Activity 5. Discuss the sound consonant digraph **sh** makes. Have the student add **sh** to the words and read the words aloud.

Words: **wish, rush, shed, shut**

Activity 6. Discuss consonant digraph **sh** as a word ending or word beginning. Identify each picture. Have the student circle the first **sh** if it is a word beginning or the second **sh** if it is a word ending. Have the student say the words aloud.

Pictures: **dish, fish, ship, shop**
cash, shell, shirt, shed

Activity 7. Have the student read each of the words in the list and draw a line to connect the words that rhyme.

Rhyming words: **shell/tell**
cash/hash
shut/hut
wish/fish
ship/rip
rush/gush

Activity 8. Instruct the student to add **sh** to each of the words and read the words aloud.

Words: **shin, sham, shun, dash**
mash, shag, shed, mush

Rule:
A consonant digraph is two consonants that stay together to make their special sound. Consonant digraph *sh* can be used at the beginning or end of a word, as in *shed* and *hash*.

5. Look at the pictures. Finish the words under each picture with the *sh* sound.

wish rush shed shut

6. Look at the pictures below. Circle the correct *sh* to show whether the *sh* sound is at the *beginning* or at the *end* of the word.

sh sh sh sh sh sh sh sh
sh sh sh sh sh sh sh sh

Horizons® Phonics & Reading Grade 1 Student Book One 65

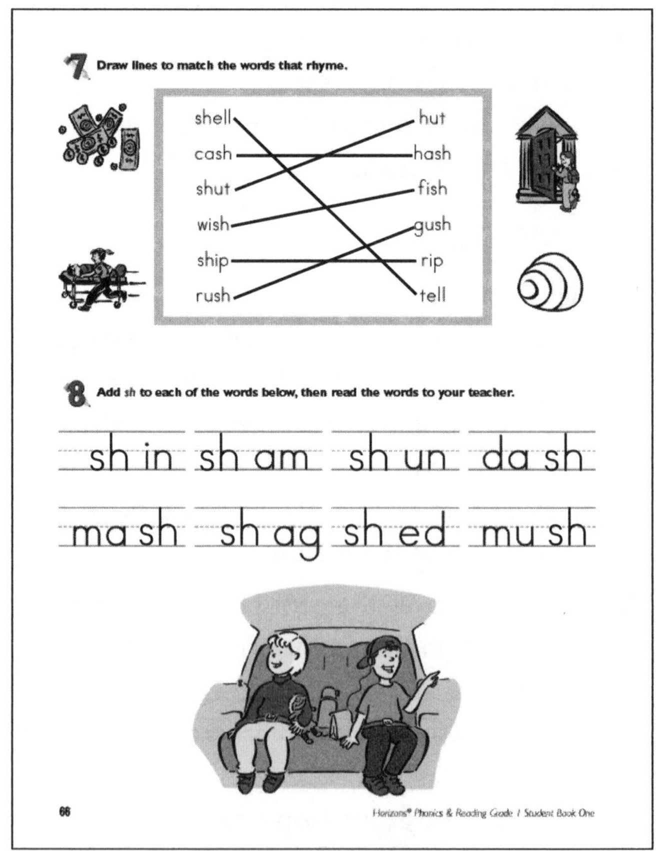
7. Draw lines to match the words that rhyme.

shell hut
cash hash
shut fish
wish gush
ship rip
rush tell

8. Add *sh* to each of the words below, then read the words to your teacher.

shin sham shun dash
mash shag shed mush

66 Horizons® Phonics & Reading Grade 1 Student Book One

Lesson 18 - Suffixes -y, -en, -able, Consonant Blends cl, cr

Overview:

- Make new words by adding the correct suffixes
- Identify base words in words with suffixes
- Complete sentences by adding suffixes to base words
- Complete words by adding consonant blends **cl** and **cr**
- Sentence completion

Materials and Supplies:

- Teacher's Guide & Student Workbook
- White board or chalkboard
- Word cards (as necessary)
- Phonics rule flashcards in **Teacher Resources**
- Story: *The Frosty Night*

Teaching Tips:

Review the rules about suffixes **-y**, **-en**, and **-able**. Review the base words, also. Discuss consonant blends **cl** and **cr**, and have the student think of additional examples for both rules. Use the white board or chalkboard to illustrate examples of both rules. Make word cards for any unknown words in the lesson.

Activity 1. Help the student read the words as needed. The student will add the suffix **-y** to each of the words and write the new words on the lines. Have the student read the words aloud.

Words: **windy, tricky, speedy, handy, dusty**

Activity 2. Help the student read the words as needed. The student will add the suffix **-en** to each of the words and write the new words on the lines. Have the student read the words aloud.

Words: **weaken, darken, sharpen, harden, loosen**

Activity 3. Help the student read the words as needed. The student will add the suffix **-able** to each of the words and write the new words on the lines. Have the student read the words aloud.

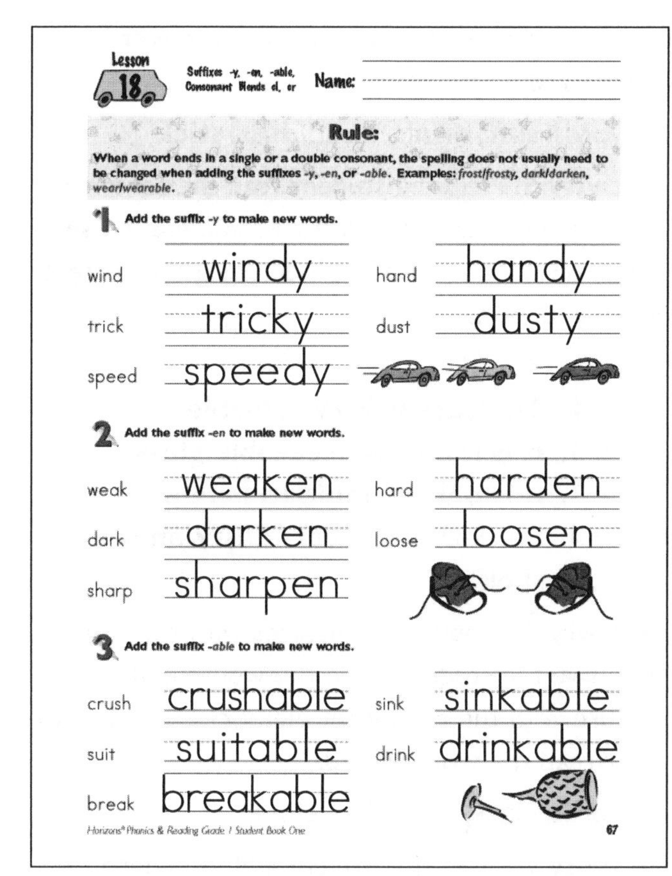
Lesson 18 Suffixes -y, -en, -able, Consonant Blends cl, cr Name:

Rule:
When a word ends in a single or a double consonant, the spelling does not usually need to be changed when adding the suffixes -y, -en, or -able. Examples: frost/frosty, dark/darken, wear/wearable.

1. Add the suffix -y to make new words.
wind windy hand handy
trick tricky dust dusty
speed speedy

2. Add the suffix -en to make new words.
weak weaken hard harden
dark darken loose loosen
sharp sharpen

3. Add the suffix -able to make new words.
crush crushable sink sinkable
suit suitable drink drinkable
break breakable

Horizons Phonics & Reading Grade 1 Student Book One 67

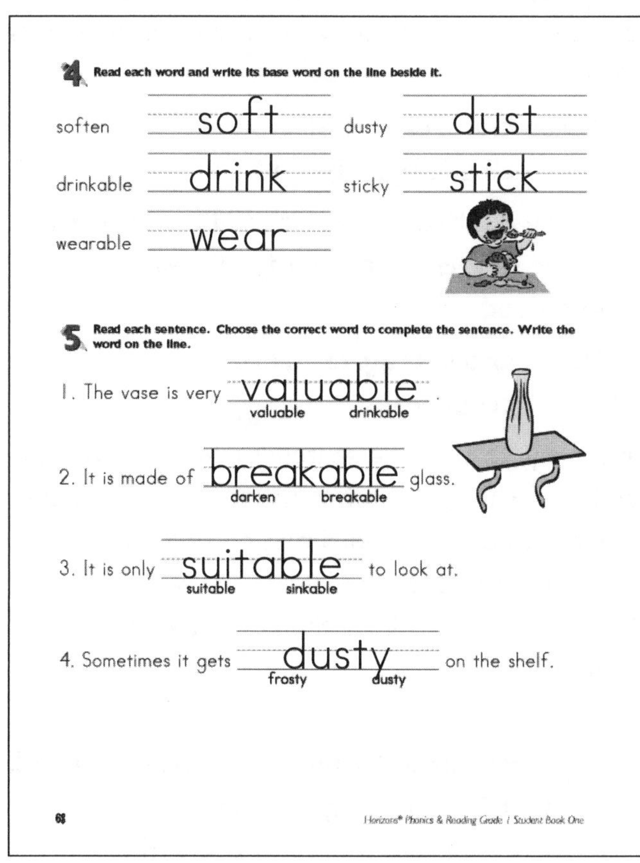
4. Read each word and write its base word on the line beside it.
soften soft dusty dust
drinkable drink sticky stick
wearable wear

5. Read each sentence. Choose the correct word to complete the sentence. Write the word on the line.
1. The vase is very valuable. (valuable drinkable)
2. It is made of breakable glass. (darken breakable)
3. It is only suitable to look at. (suitable sinkable)
4. Sometimes it gets dusty on the shelf. (frosty dusty)

68 Horizons Phonics & Reading Grade 1 Student Book One

Words: **crushable, suitable, breakable, sinkable, drinkable**

Activity 4. Help the student read the words as

needed, instruct him to write the base word for each word on the line.

Words: **soft, drink, wear, dust, stick**

Activity 5. Help the student read the sentences and write the correct word to complete the sentence on the line. NOTE: Underlining the correct word is optional.

Sentences:

1. **The vase is very valuable.**
2. **It is made of breakable glass.**
3. **It is only suitable to look at.**
4. **Sometimes it gets dusty on the shelf.**

Activity 6. Identify the pictures with the student, and have the student finish the words under each picture with the consonant blend **cl**. Have the student read the words aloud.

Words: **class, cliff, clap, clock**

Activity 7. Have the student add the consonant blend **cl** to each of the words and read the words aloud.

Words: **clam, clan, clef, clod**
clog, clop, clip, club

Activity 8. Have the student add the consonant blend **cr** to each of the words and read the words aloud.

Words: **cram, crag, crib, cross**
crop, crab

Activity 9. Read the sentences with the student, assisting with words when necessary. Instruct the student to pick the word that correctly completes the sentences and write the word on the line. NOTE: Underlining the correct word is optional.

Sentences:

1. **Be careful when you cross the road.**
2. **It is time to go to class.**
3. **Mom had a clog in the sink.**
4. **Jan looked at the clock to tell the time.**
5. **The baby sleeps in a crib.**
6. **We will hike to the top of the cliff.**

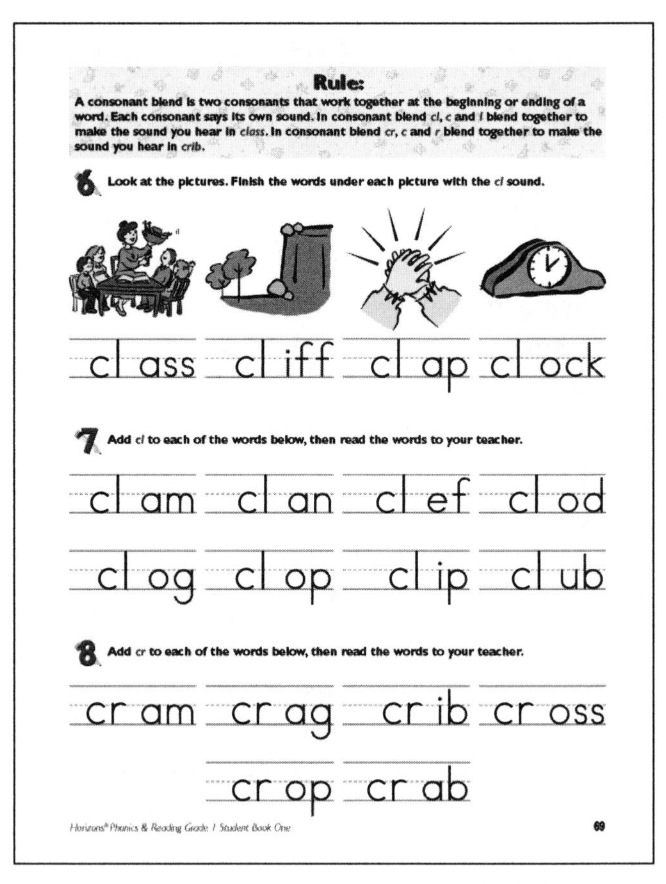

Rule:
A consonant blend is two consonants that work together at the beginning or ending of a word. Each consonant says its own sound. In consonant blend *cl*, *c* and *l* blend together to make the sound you hear in *class*. In consonant blend *cr*, *c* and *r* blend together to make the sound you hear in *crib*.

6 Look at the pictures. Finish the words under each picture with the *cl* sound.

cl ass cl iff cl ap cl ock

7 Add *cl* to each of the words below, then read the words to your teacher.

cl am cl an cl ef cl od
cl og cl op cl ip cl ub

8 Add *cr* to each of the words below, then read the words to your teacher.

cr am cr ag cr ib cr oss
cr op cr ab

Horizons® Phonics & Reading Grade 1 Student Book One 69

9 Read each sentence. Choose the correct word to complete the sentence. Then write the word on the line.

1. Be careful when you cross the road. (cross / class)
2. It is time to go to class. (clap / class)
3. Mom had a clog in the sink. (crop / clog)
4. Jan looked at the clock to tell the time. (clot / clock)
5. The baby sleeps in a crib. (club / crib)
6. We will hike to the top of the cliff. (cliff / clef)

70 Horizons® Phonics & Reading Grade 1 Student Book One

Lesson 19 - Review: Plurals & Suffixes, Consonant Blends bl, br

Overview:

- Sentence completion
- Spelling plural words correctly
- Crossword puzzle
- Choosing correct spelling of plural words
- Correct word selection for a poem
- Adding consonant blends **bl** and **br** to words

Materials and Supplies:

- Teacher's Guide & Student Workbook
- White board or chalkboard
- Word cards (as necessary)
- Phonics rule flashcards in **Teacher Resources**
- Story: *Going Shopping*

Teaching Tips:

Review all applicable rules from Lessons 11–18. Assist the student in reading the words and sentences as necessary. Use word cards if needed.

Activity 1. Help the student read the sentences and the word choices. The student will choose the correct words to complete the sentences and print the words on the lines.

Sentences:

1. **Julie's family was going to move.**
2. **They were packing their boxes.**
3. **They had been looking for a house for months.**
4. **Moving day was the coldest day of the year.**
5. **Julie stayed in the truck where it was warmer.**
6. **She knew she would soon be helping.**

Activity 2. Have the student read each of the words in the word list and print the correct spellings for each misspelled word on the lines.

Words: **foxes, churches, toys, wolves, jays**

Activity 3. Help the student read the words in the list and in the clues. Help the student complete the crossword puzzle as necessary.

Across: **2. wives**
4. smoothest
5. snowy

Down: **1. glasses**
3. leaves

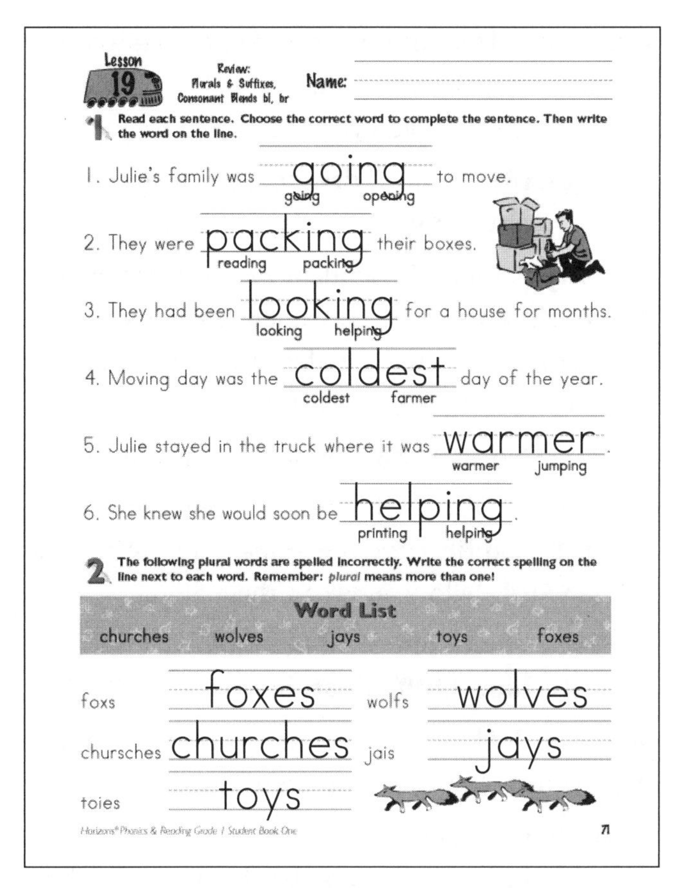

Lesson 19 Review: Plurals & Suffixes, Consonant Blends bl, br Name:

1. Read each sentence. Choose the correct word to complete the sentence. Then write the word on the line.

1. Julie's family was going to move. (going / opening)
2. They were packing their boxes. (reading / packing)
3. They had been looking for a house for months. (looking / helping)
4. Moving day was the coldest day of the year. (coldest / farmer)
5. Julie stayed in the truck where it was warmer. (warmer / jumping)
6. She knew she would soon be helping. (printing / helping)

2. The following plural words are spelled incorrectly. Write the correct spelling on the line next to each word. Remember: *plural* means more than one!

Word List: churches wolves jays toys foxes

fox**s** — foxes
wolfs — wolves
chursches — churches
jais — jays
toies — toys

Horizons® Phonics & Reading Grade 1 Student Book One 71

3. Use the words from the list to complete the crossword puzzle.

wives glasses snowy leaves smoothest

ACROSS:
2. Husbands have ___.
4. The water on the lake is the ___ when it isn't windy.
5. The day was cold and ___.

DOWN:
1. She has trouble seeing, so she needs ___.
3. In the fall, trees drop their ___.

72 Horizons® Phonics & Reading Grade 1 Student Book One

Activity 4. Help the student identify the words that are misspelled. The student will circle the words that are spelled correctly.

Words: **toys, boxes, dresses, brushes, elves, churches**

Activity 5. Help the student read the poem and the words in the list. The student will choose the words that correctly complete the poem and print them in the correct places in the poem.

Words: **flying, crawling, harder, smelly, hairy**

Activity 6. Discuss the rule for consonant blends **bl** and **br**. Have the student add **bl** to each of the words below and read them aloud.

Words: **bleed, bless, bliss, blank blot, bluff, bleat, blame**

Activity 7. Have the student add **br** to each of the words below and read them aloud.

Words: **brim, brag, brat, brush brand, brink, bribe, broke**

4 Circle the plural words that are correctly spelled.

1. toys / toies
2. boxes / boxxs
3. dresses / dresss
4. brushs / brushes
5. elfs / elves
6. churchs / churches

5 Read the poem. Choose the correct words from the list to complete the poem.

Some bugs are flying.
They have wings.
Some bugs are crawling.
They have other things.
Some bugs are harder
And covered with a shell.
Some bugs even have
A way to make them smell!
But no matter how smelly
Or hairy they are,
I like bugs and I keep them in a jar!

Word List: crawling, smelly, flying, hairy, harder

Horizons® Phonics & Reading Grade 1 Student Book One 73

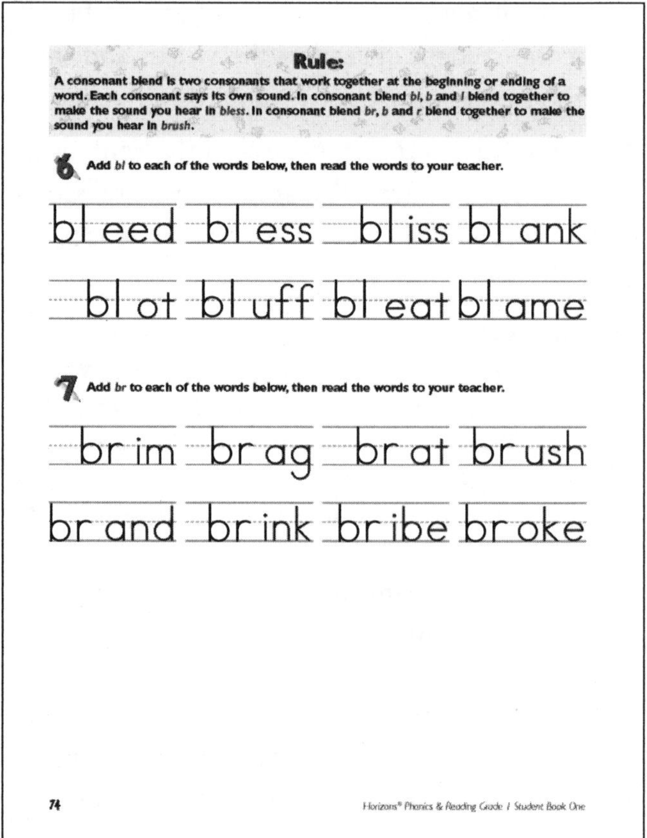

Rule:
A consonant blend is two consonants that work together at the beginning or ending of a word. Each consonant says its own sound. In consonant blend *bl*, *b* and *l* blend together to make the sound you hear in *bless*. In consonant blend *br*, *b* and *r* blend together to make the sound you hear in *brush*.

6 Add *bl* to each of the words below, then read the words to your teacher.

bl eed bl ess bl iss bl ank
bl ot bl uff bl eat bl ame

7 Add *br* to each of the words below, then read the words to your teacher.

br im br ag br at br ush
br and br ink br ibe br oke

74 Horizons® Phonics & Reading Grade 1 Student Book One

Lesson 20 - Review: Vowel Pairs, oa, ee, ie, ay, ai, ea

Overview:

- Sentence completion
- Identify words with vowel pairs in sentences
- Write correct words to answer riddles

Materials and Supplies:

- Teacher's Guide & Student Workbook
- White board or chalkboard
- Word cards (as necessary)
- Phonics rule flashcards in **Teacher Resources**
- Story: *Kay's Kitten*

Teaching Tips:

Review the rule for vowel pairs. Write the vowel pairs on the white board or chalkboard, and drill the student on the correct pronunciation of each vowel pair. Use diacritical markings if desired. Ask the student for examples of words to illustrate each of the different vowel pairs. Assist the student as necessary in reading the sentences and riddles. (**Optional**: You may have the student place diacritical markings on all the vowel pair words he writes.)

Activity 1. Help the student read the sentences and the word choices. If desired, you may instruct the student to underline the word that will correctly complete each sentence. The student will write the correct word on the line.

Sentences:

1. **Mary wanted to teach her brother to skate.**
2. **Mary tried to show him.**
3. **He did not feel like listening.**
4. **He wanted to eat pie.**
5. **They decided to try again next week.**

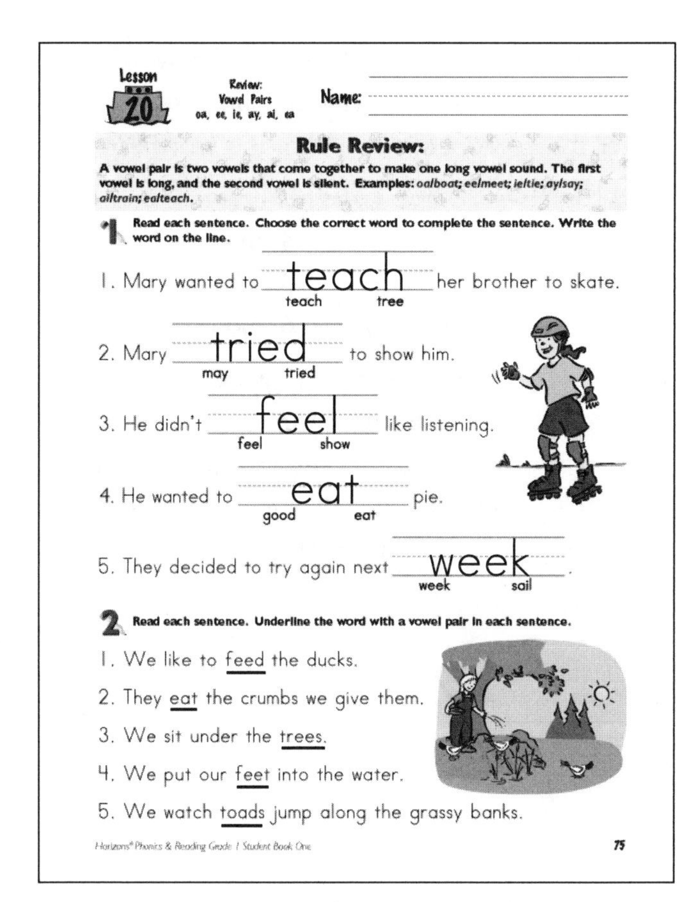

Lesson 20 Review: Vowel Pairs oa, ee, ie, ay, ai, ea Name:

Rule Review:

A vowel pair is two vowels that come together to make one long vowel sound. The first vowel is long, and the second vowel is silent. Examples: *oa/boat; ee/meet; ie/tie; ay/say; ai/train; ea/teach.*

1 Read each sentence. Choose the correct word to complete the sentence. Write the word on the line.

1. Mary wanted to teach her brother to skate. (teach / tree)
2. Mary tried to show him. (may / tried)
3. He didn't feel like listening. (feel / show)
4. He wanted to eat pie. (good / eat)
5. They decided to try again next week. (week / sail)

2 Read each sentence. Underline the word with a vowel pair in each sentence.

1. We like to feed the ducks.
2. They eat the crumbs we give them.
3. We sit under the trees.
4. We put our feet into the water.
5. We watch toads jump along the grassy banks.

Horizons® Phonics & Reading Grade 1 Student Book One 75

Activity 2. Help the student read the sentences, and have him underline the words in each sentence that contain a vowel pair.

Words: **feed, eat, trees, feet, toads**

Activity 3. Help the student read the words in the word list and in the riddles. The student will select the correct answer from the word list for each riddle.

Words:	**1. tie**	**4. play**
	2. train	**5. wheels**
	3. leaves	**6. eat**

Activity 4. Assist the student as necessary in making up a riddle. Remind the student about correct spelling, punctuation, and capitalization. Have the student share his riddle with others in the class or with a family member.

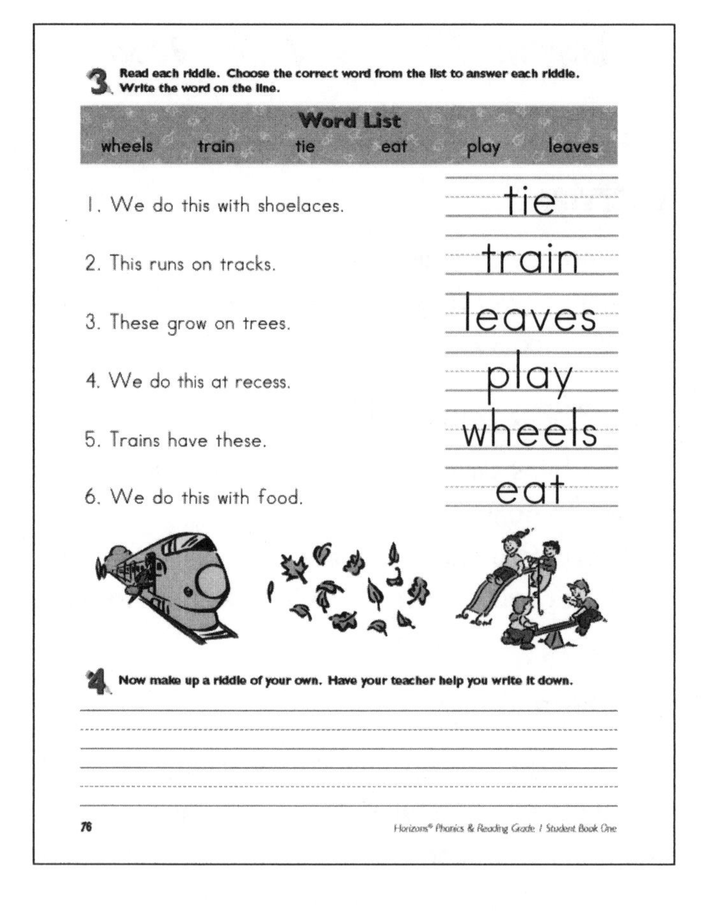

3 Read each riddle. Choose the correct word from the list to answer each riddle. Write the word on the line.

Word List

wheels train tie eat play leaves

1. We do this with shoelaces. tie
2. This runs on tracks. train
3. These grow on trees. leaves
4. We do this at recess. play
5. Trains have these. wheels
6. We do this with food. eat

4 Now make up a riddle of your own. Have your teacher help you write it down.

76 Horizons® Phonics & Reading Grade 1 Student Book One

Test 2

Lessons 11–20

Instructions:

Have the student name the pictures in the test. Review the correct way to mark short and long vowel sounds in words. Review the definition of a compound word. Practice compound words, if necessary. Review the definition of the word plural. Review the rules for suffixes that were presented in the lessons. Review the definition for base word. Review the rule for vowel pairs. The teacher should be available to answer any questions that the student may have during the test.

Activity 1. Instruct the student to **write the entire word** and place the correct diacritical markings.

Activity 2. Read the instructions and the words with the student.

Words:	**back**	**yard**
	mail	**box**
	sun	**shine**
	sail	**boat**
	cup	**cake**
	to	**day**

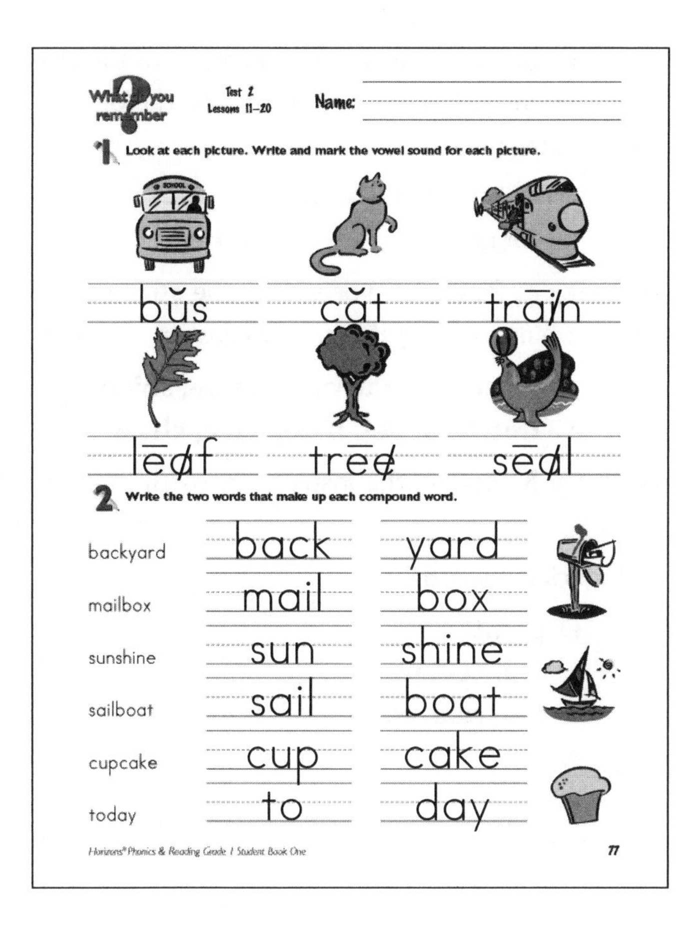

What do you remember

Test 2
Lessons 11–20

Name:

1. Look at each picture. Write and mark the vowel sound for each picture.

bŭs	căt	trāin
lēaf	trēe	sēal

2. Write the two words that make up each compound word.

backyard	back	yard
mailbox	mail	box
sunshine	sun	shine
sailboat	sail	boat
cupcake	cup	cake
today	to	day

Horizons® Phonics & Reading Grade 1 Student Book One 77

Activity 3. Read the singular words with the student, and instruct him to write the plural forms on the lines next to the words.

Words: **dresses, foxes, wolves**
brushes, classes, churches

Activity 4. Read the words with the student, and instruct him to write the base words on the lines.

Words: **jump, tall, farm, use, safe, shine**
hot, hop, pet, hide, bake, chase

Activity 5. Review the instructions with the student.

Underlined words:

1. **paint**
2. **painted, pie**
3. **pie, real, eat**
4. **play**

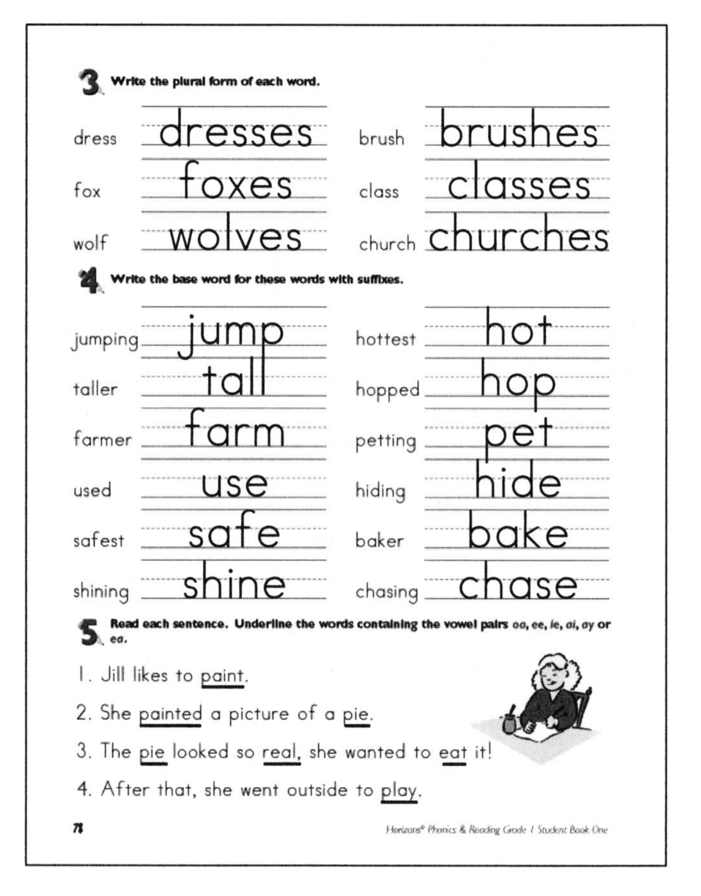

3 Write the plural form of each word.

dress	dresses	brush	brushes
fox	foxes	class	classes
wolf	wolves	church	churches

4 Write the base word for these words with suffixes.

jumping	jump	hottest	hot
taller	tall	hopped	hop
farmer	farm	petting	pet
used	use	hiding	hide
safest	safe	baker	bake
shining	shine	chasing	chase

5 Read each sentence. Underline the words containing the vowel pairs *oa, ee, ie, ai, ay* or *ea*.

1. Jill likes to paint.
2. She painted a picture of a pie.
3. The pie looked so real, she wanted to eat it!
4. After that, she went outside to play.

71 Horizons® Phonics & Reading Grade 1 Student Book One

Lesson 21 - Vowel Digraphs au, aw, ea, ei, ew, oo, Consonant Blend fl

Overview:

- Identify vowel digraphs in sentences
- Put vowel digraphs in correct categories by sound
- Read and complete sentences and a story
- Add consonant blend **fl** to words

Materials and Supplies:

- Teacher's Guide & Student Workbook
- White board or chalkboard
- Word cards (as necessary)
- Phonics rule flashcards in **Teacher Resources**
- Story: *Paul's Book*

Teaching Tips:

Review the rule about vowel digraphs. Illustrate different digraphs on the white board or chalkboard. Ask the students for examples of each. Differentiate between a vowel pair, which says the long vowel sound of the first vowel, and a vowel digraph in which two vowels make a short vowel sound or a special sound all their own. NOTE: The vowel pair **ea** may also be categorized as a vowel digraph when it has the short **ĕ** sound as in **head** or **bread**.

Activity 1. Go over the rule again. Help the student read the sentences. The student will circle the words that have the vowel digraphs **oo, ea, aw, au**, or **ei**.

Words to be circled:

1. **looked, saw, noon**
2. **read, eight, book**
3. **cool, new, sweater**
4. **stood, saw, flew, overhead**

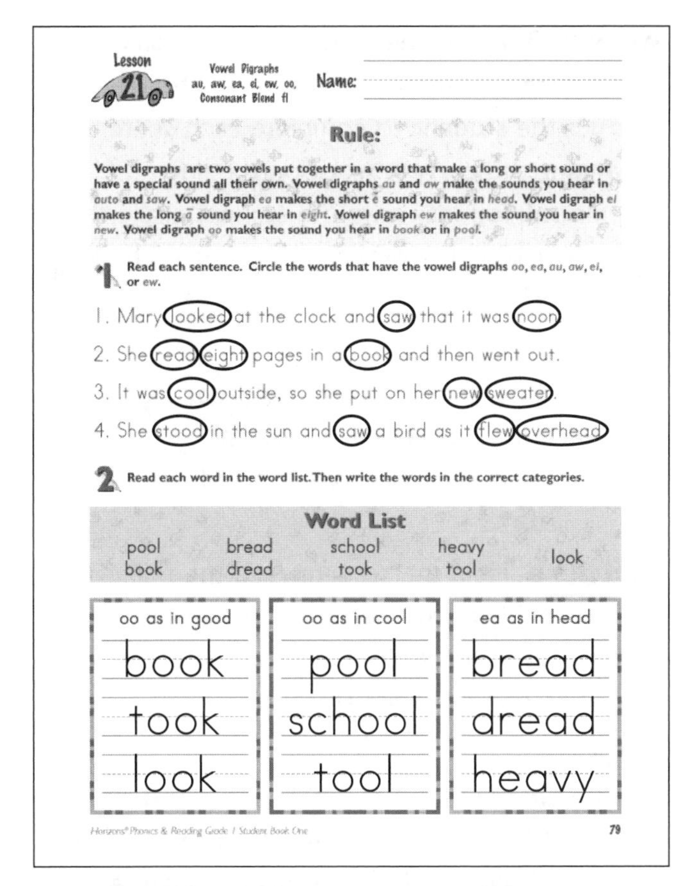

Lesson 21 Vowel Digraphs au, aw, ea, ei, ew, oo, Consonant Blend fl Name:

Rule:

Vowel digraphs are two vowels put together in a word that make a long or short sound or have a special sound all their own. Vowel digraphs *au* and *aw* make the sounds you hear in *auto* and *saw*. Vowel digraph *ea* makes the short ĕ sound you hear in *head*. Vowel digraph *ei* makes the long ā sound you hear in *eight*. Vowel digraph *ew* makes the sound you hear in *new*. Vowel digraph *oo* makes the sound you hear in *book* or in *pool*.

1 **Read each sentence. Circle the words that have the vowel digraphs *oo*, *ea*, *au*, *aw*, *ei*, or *ew*.**

1. Mary looked at the clock and saw that it was noon.
2. She read eight pages in a book and then went out.
3. It was cool outside, so she put on her new sweater.
4. She stood in the sun and saw a bird as it flew overhead.

2 **Read each word in the word list. Then write the words in the correct categories.**

Word List

pool book bread dread school took heavy tool look

oo as in good	oo as in cool	ea as in head
book	pool	bread
took	school	dread
look	tool	heavy

Horizons® Phonics & Reading Grade 1 Student Book One 79

Activity 2. Help the student read the words in the list as necessary. Make word cards for the words that are still unknown to the student. The student will write the words from the list in the correct categories.

oo as in good: **book, took, look**
oo as in cool: **pool, school, tool**
ea as in head: **bread, dread, heavy**

Activity 3. Assist the student as necessary in reading the sentences and the word choices. Instruct the student to complete each sentence by writing the correct word on the line. (**Optional**: You may have the student circle the other words with vowel digraphs: **shawl, head, Paul, food, good**)

Sentences:

1. **She threw the shawl over her head.**
2. **Did Paul chew his food?**
3. **The stew was very good on a cold day.**

Activity 4. Help the student read the unfinished story and the words in the list. Make word cards as necessary. The student will use the words from the list to complete the story.

Story:

I like to read books. They are good. When I crawl into bed at night, my mom reads to me. I yawn when the story is done because I am tired. I look forward to reading another one!

Activity 5. Review the consonant blend rule. Have the student add **fl** to each of the words and read them aloud.

Words: **flag, flew, flap, flat**
flop, flaw, flood, flip

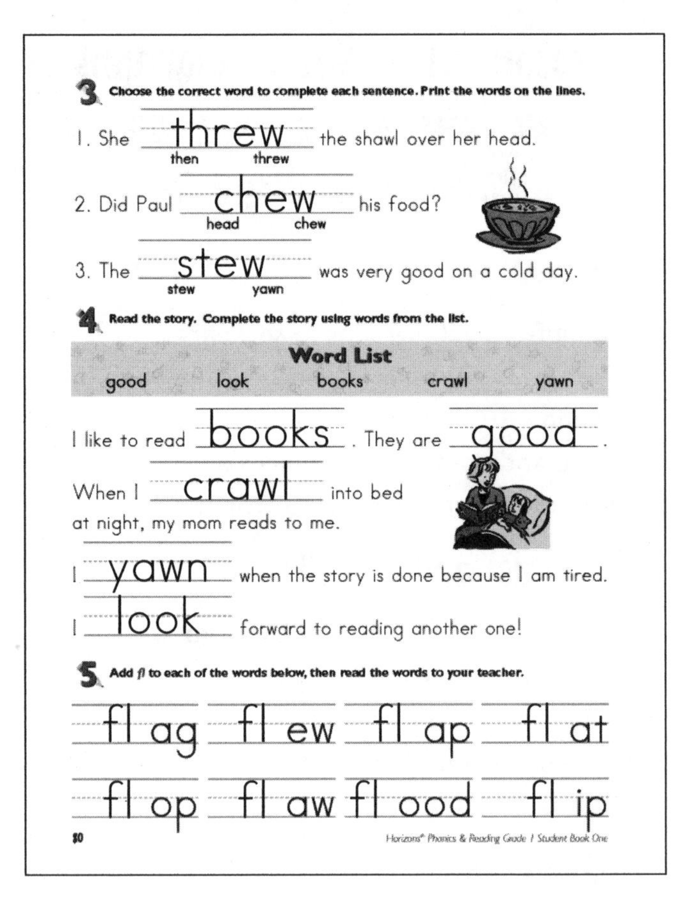

3 Choose the correct word to complete each sentence. Print the words on the lines.
1. She threw the shawl over her head.
then threw
2. Did Paul chew his food?
head chew
3. The stew was very good on a cold day.
stew yawn
4 Read the story. Complete the story using words from the list.
Word List
good look books crawl yawn
I like to read books. They are good.
When I crawl into bed at night, my mom reads to me.
I yawn when the story is done because I am tired.
I look forward to reading another one!
5 Add fl to each of the words below, then read the words to your teacher.
fl ag fl ew fl ap fl at
fl op fl aw fl ood fl ip
50
Horizons® Phonics & Reading Grade 1 Student Book One

Lesson 22 - Review: Vowel Pairs & Vowel Digraphs

Overview:

- Put words into correct categories
- Write a story using words from list
- Read story and answer questions using words from story
- Word search puzzle

Materials and Supplies:

- Teacher's Guide & Student Workbook
- White board or chalkboard
- Word cards (as necessary)
- Story:

Teaching Tips:

Review the vowel pair and vowel digraph rules. Give examples of each on the white board or chalkboard. Ask the student for examples of each. Emphasize that the vowel pair **ea** can also be a vowel digraph when it has the short sound as in **head**.

Activity 1. Help the student read the words from the list as necessary. The student will put the words into the correct categories.

Vowel Pairs:	**rain, street, tie, say, eat**
Vowel Digraphs:	**head, book, saw, caught, weigh**

Activity 2. Help the student read the words in the list as necessary. The student will write a short story, using some of the words in the list. Help the student with writing and spelling as necessary. Emphasize correct capitalization and punctuation.

Activity 3. Have the student draw a picture about the story he has written.

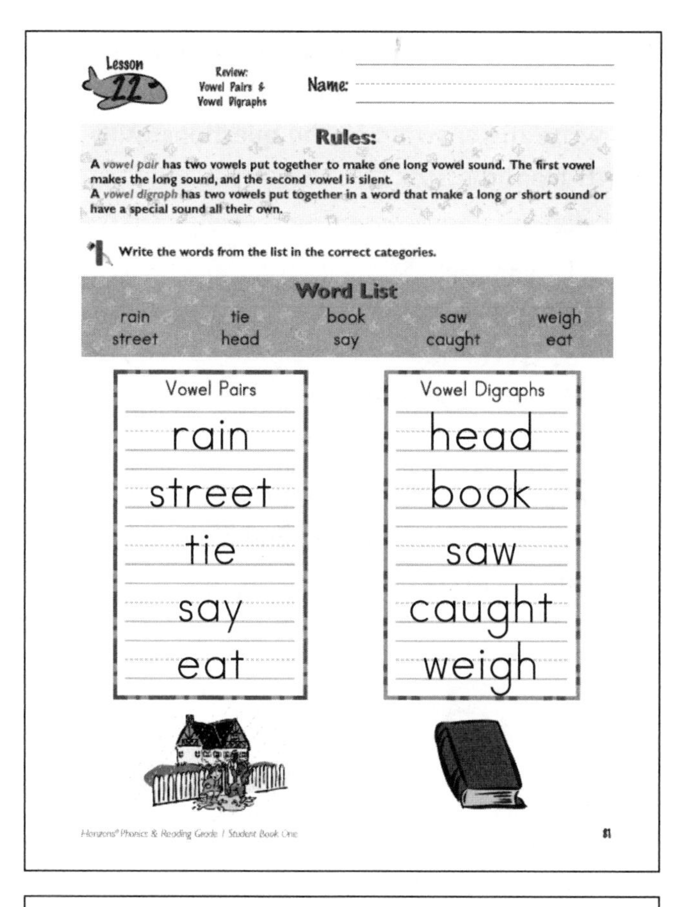

Lesson 22 Review: Vowel Pairs & Vowel Digraphs Name:

Rules:

A *vowel pair* has two vowels put together to make one long vowel sound. The first vowel makes the long sound, and the second vowel is silent.
A *vowel digraph* has two vowels put together in a word that make a long or short sound or have a special sound all their own.

1. Write the words from the list in the correct categories.

Word List				
rain	tie	book	saw	weigh
street	head	say	caught	eat

Vowel Pairs	Vowel Digraphs
rain	head
street	book
tie	saw
say	caught
eat	weigh

Horizons® Phonics & Reading Grade 1 Student Book One 51

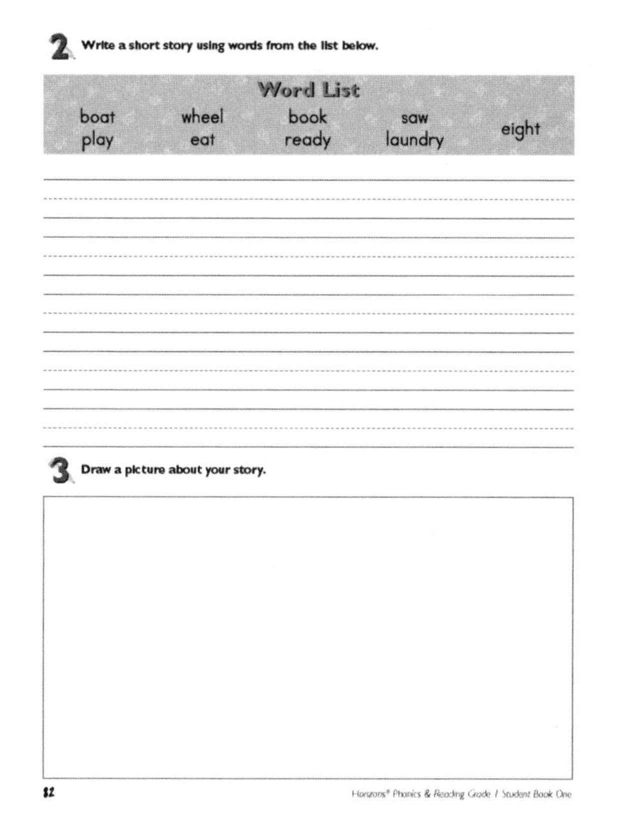

2. Write a short story using words from the list below.

Word List				
boat	wheel	book	saw	eight
play	eat	ready	laundry	

3. Draw a picture about your story.

52 Horizons® Phonics & Reading Grade 1 Student Book One

Activity 4. Assist the student as necessary in reading the story and the questions. The student will write the answers to the questions using words from the story.

Answers:

1. **soccer**
2. **Rams**
3. **Saturday**
4. **goal keeper**
5. **eight**

Activity 5. Help the student read the words in the list. The student will find and circle the words from the list in the puzzle.

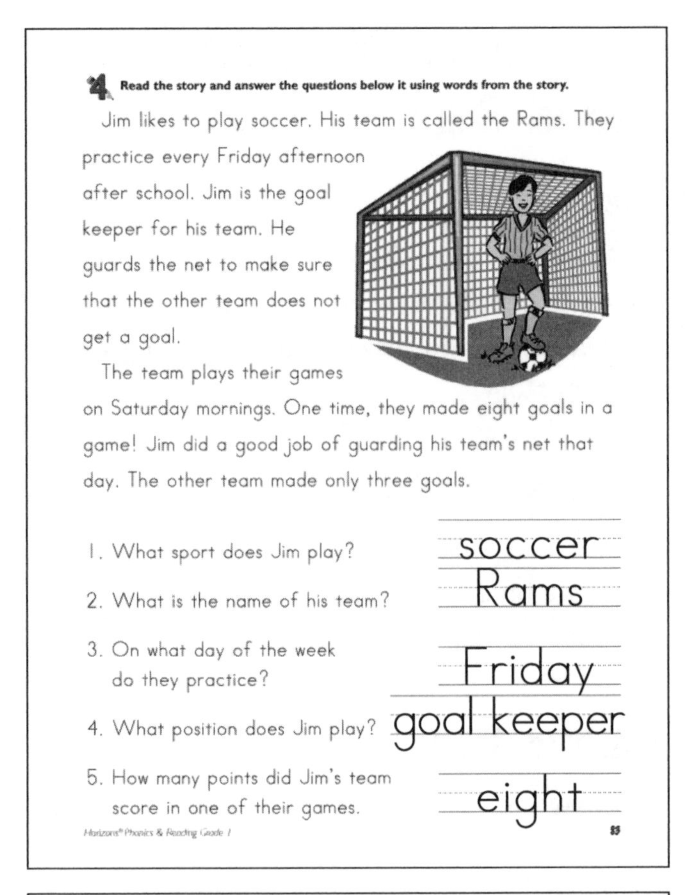

4 **Read the story and answer the questions below it using words from the story.**

Jim likes to play soccer. His team is called the Rams. They practice every Friday afternoon after school. Jim is the goal keeper for his team. He guards the net to make sure that the other team does not get a goal.

The team plays their games on Saturday mornings. One time, they made eight goals in a game! Jim did a good job of guarding his team's net that day. The other team made only three goals.

1. What sport does Jim play? soccer
2. What is the name of his team? Rams
3. On what day of the week do they practice? Friday
4. What position does Jim play? goal keeper
5. How many points did Jim's team score in one of their games. eight

Horizons® Phonics & Reading Grade 1 85

5 **Word Search – Find and circle the words in the puzzle. Look for the words that are in the list below.**

coat	toad	keep	weight
pie	claw	each	pause

r	e	p	i	e	c	k	r	s
o	n	e	f	s	k	e	e	p
w	e	i	g	h	t	a	i	r
a	o	c	a	c	s	c	r	i
s	z	p	r	l	s	h	a	t
t	o	c	o	a	t	r	u	p
e	e	m	t	w	o	s	w	a
t	a	l	c	r	a	w	k	u
r	s	e	e	r	d	o	p	s
s	a	m	t	o	t	r	i	e

84 Horizons® Phonics & Reading Grade 1 Student Book One

Lesson 23 - Consonant Digraphs bt, ph, Consonant Blends dr, gr

Overview:

- Categorize **ph** and **bt** digraphs
- Sentence completion
- Add consonant blends **gr** and **dr** to words
- Auditory recognition of beginning consonant blends **br**, **cr**, **dr**, and **gr**

Materials and Supplies:

- Teacher's Guide & Student Workbook
- White board or chalkboard
- Word cards (as necessary)
- Phonics rule flashcards in **Teacher Resources**
- Story: *The Elephant at the Zoo*

Teaching Tips:

Differentiate between a consonant digraph and a consonant blend. A consonant digraph is two vowels that combine to make their own sound (as in **phone**) or one consonant that speaks while the other is silent (as in **doubt**). Illustrate examples on the board. Review the rule for consonant blends before having the student complete Activity 3. Help students read the words and sentences in the lesson as necessary. Identify the pictures in Activity 4.

Activity 1. Help the student read the words in the list. The student will write the words in the correct categories.

Digraph **ph: telephone, elephant, digraph**
Digraph **bt: doubt, subtle**

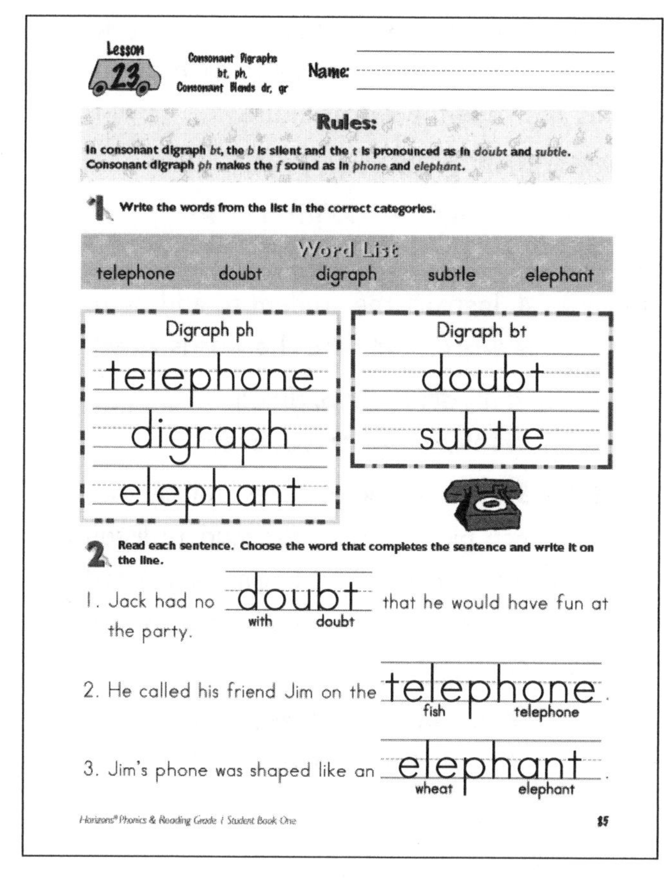
Lesson 23 Consonant Digraphs bt, ph, Consonant Blends dr, gr Name:

Rules:
In consonant digraph *bt*, the *b* is silent and the *t* is pronounced as in *doubt* and *subtle*.
Consonant digraph *ph* makes the *f* sound as in *phone* and *elephant*.

1 Write the words from the list in the correct categories.

Word List
telephone doubt digraph subtle elephant

Digraph ph	Digraph bt
telephone	doubt
digraph	subtle
elephant	

2 Read each sentence. Choose the word that completes the sentence and write it on the line.

1. Jack had no doubt that he would have fun at the party. (with / doubt)
2. He called his friend Jim on the telephone. (fish / telephone)
3. Jim's phone was shaped like an elephant. (wheat / elephant)

Horizons Phonics & Reading Grade 1 Student Book One 55

Activity 2. Help the student read the sentences and the word choices. Have the student underline the word that completes each sentence and write the word on the line.

Sentences:

1. **Jack had no doubt that he would have fun at the party.**
2. **He called his friend Jim on the telephone.**
3. **Jim's phone was shaped like an elephant.**

Activity 3. Review the consonant blend rule. Instruct the student to add **gr** to each of the words and read the words aloud.

Words: **grill, grab, grip, grub**
grain, great, grope, gripe
grim, digraph, groan, grunt

Activity 4. Instruct the student to add **dr** to each of the words and read the words aloud.

Words: **drill, drab, drip, drain**
drink, drew, drive, draw

Activity 5. Identify the pictures and say the name of each picture. Have the student listen to see which consonant blend begins each word. Have the student circle the correct consonant blend for each picture.

Pictures: **brown, crib, grave, drain**
brick, grass, drum, grill

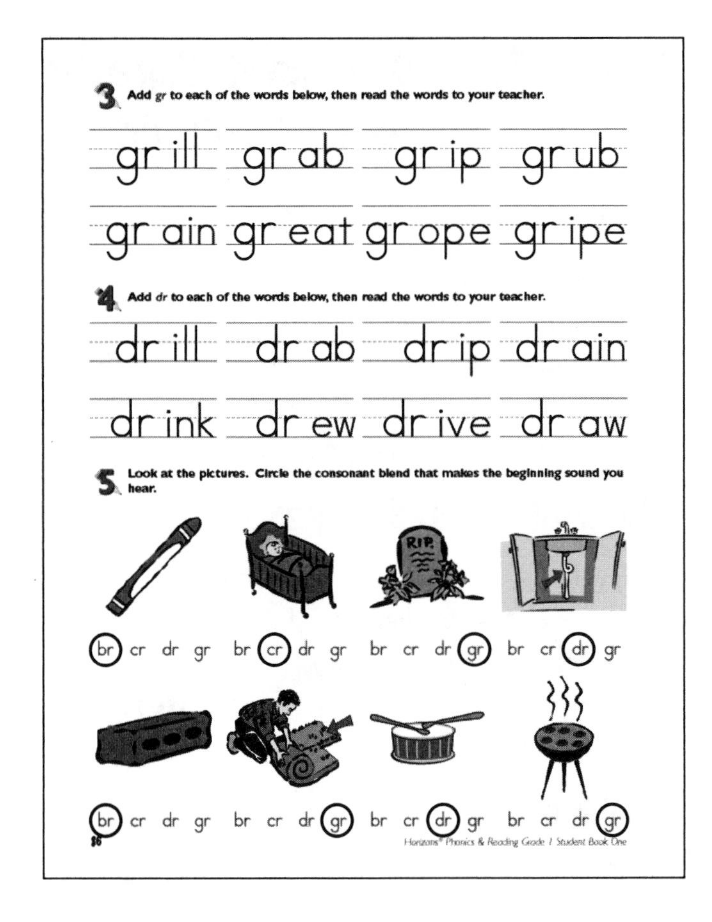

3 Add *gr* to each of the words below, then read the words to your teacher.

gr ill gr ab gr ip gr ub

gr ain gr eat gr ope gr ipe

4 Add *dr* to each of the words below, then read the words to your teacher.

dr ill dr ab dr ip dr ain

dr ink dr ew dr ive dr aw

5 Look at the pictures. Circle the consonant blend that makes the beginning sound you hear.

br cr dr gr br cr dr gr br cr dr gr br cr dr gr

br cr dr gr br cr dr gr br cr dr gr br cr dr gr

86 Horizons® Phonics & Reading Grade 1 Student Book One

Lesson 24 - Consonant Digraphs gm, mn, Consonant Blends gl, sp

Overview:

- Mark consonants in words
- Cross out silent consonants

Materials and Supplies:

- Teacher's Guide & Student Workbook
- White board or chalkboard
- Word cards (as necessary)
- Story: *The Column of Numbers*

Teaching Tips:

Help the student read the words and identify the pictures. Discuss the rule with the student.

Activity 1. Help the students read the words in this activity. Define any of the words with which the students are unfamiliar. Before completing the activity, ask the students to identify another consonant digraph that appears in the words (ph).

diaphragm: Circle **d, p, h, g, m** – cross out the **g**
column: Circle **c, l, m, n** – cross out the **n**
solemn: Circle **s, l, m, n** – cross out the **n**
phlegm: Circle **p, h, l, g, m** – cross out the **g**

Activity 2. Review the consonant blend rule. Have the student add **gl** to each of the words and read them aloud.

Words: **glad, glass, glop, glen**

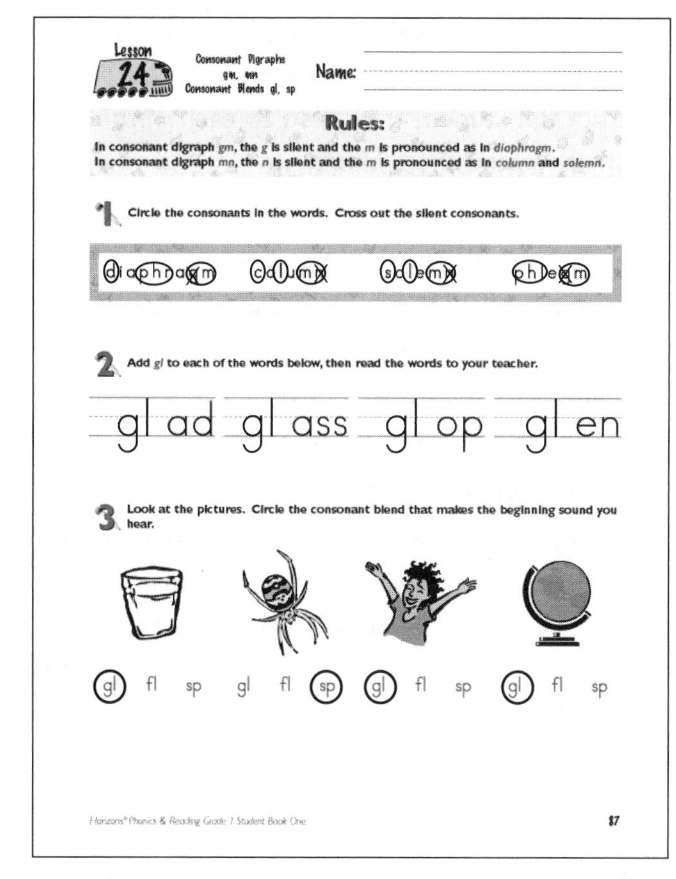

Lesson 24 Consonant Digraphs gm, mn Consonant Blends gl, sp

Name:

Rules:

In consonant digraph *gm*, the *g* is silent and the *m* is pronounced as in *diaphragm*.
In consonant digraph *mn*, the *n* is silent and the *m* is pronounced as in *column* and *solemn*.

1 Circle the consonants in the words. Cross out the silent consonants.

diaphragm column solemn phlegm

2 Add *gl* to each of the words below, then read the words to your teacher.

gl ad gl ass gl op gl en

3 Look at the pictures. Circle the consonant blend that makes the beginning sound you hear.

gl fl sp gl fl sp gl fl sp gl fl sp

Horizons Phonics & Reading Grade 1 Student Book One 17

Activity 3. Help the student identify the pictures and circle the correct beginning consonant blend they hear.

Pictures: **glass, spider, glad, globe**

Activity 4. Discuss the consonant blend rule for **sp**, and have the student think of examples. Instruct the student to add **sp** to each of the words and read them aloud.

Words: **spill, spin, spell, spot**
spend, wisp, clasp, grasp

Activity 5. Help the student identify the pictures and listen for the beginning consonant blend as you say the name of each picture. The student is to circle the beginning sound he hears.

Pictures: **spool, Spot, spade, glue**

Activity 6. Help the student identify the pictures and listen for the beginning or ending consonant blend as you say the name of each picture. The student is to circle the beginning or ending sound he hears.

Pictures: **wasp, spill, clasp, grasp**

4. Add sp to each of the words below, then read the words to your teacher.

sp ill sp in sp ell sp ot

sp end wi sp cla sp gra sp

5. Look at the pictures. Circle the consonant blend that makes the *beginning* sound you hear.

gl fl (sp) gl fl (sp) gl fl (sp) (gl) fl sp

6. Look at the pictures below. Circle the sp to show whether the sound is at the *beginning* or at the *end* of the word.

sp (sp) (sp) sp sp (sp) sp (sp)

Horizons® Phonics & Reading Grade 1 Student Book One

Lesson 25 - Review: Consonant Digraphs & Consonant Blends

Overview:

- Identify consonant digraphs in words
- Sentence completion
- Add **ch** or **tch** to words
- Auditory recognition of consonant digraphs and consonant blends

Materials and Supplies:

- Teacher's Guide & Student Workbook
- White board or chalkboard
- Word cards (as necessary)
- Story:

Teaching Tips:

On the white board or chalkboard, review the rules for consonant digraphs. Stress the difference between consonant digraphs and consonant blends. Ask for examples of each. Go over any word cards that were made for Lessons 23–24.

Activity 1. Review the meanings of the unfamiliar words. Instruct the student to circle the consonant digraphs in each word.

Digraphs:	column:	**mn**
	elephant:	**ph**
	phone:	**ph**
	doubt:	**bt**
	phlegm:	**ph, gm**
	match:	**tch**
	patch:	**tch**
	diaphragm:	**ph, gm**
	much:	**ch**

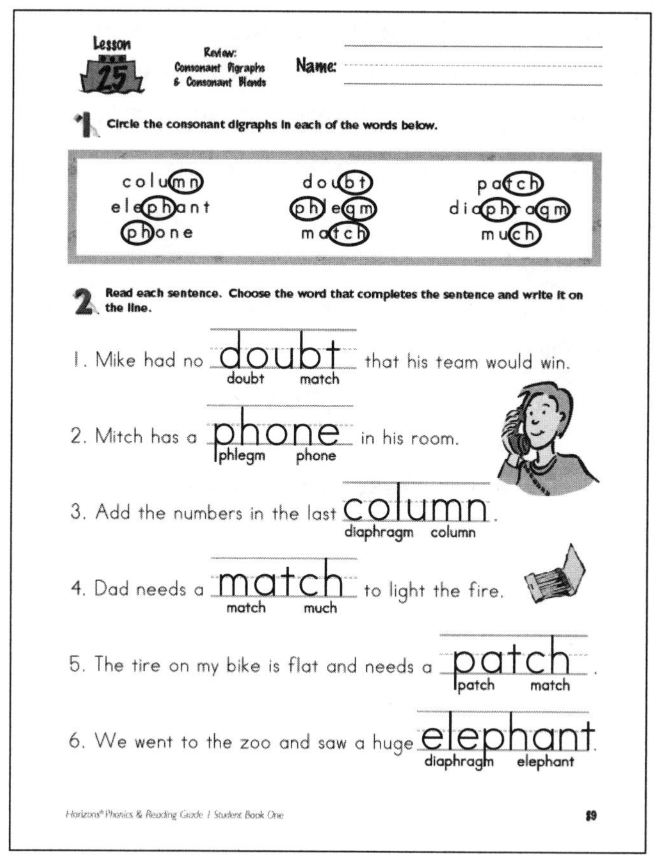
Lesson 25
Review: Consonant Digraphs & Consonant Blends
Name:

1. Circle the consonant digraphs in each of the words below.

column	doubt	patch
elephant	phlegm	diaphragm
phone	match	much

2. Read each sentence. Choose the word that completes the sentence and write it on the line.

1. Mike had no doubt that his team would win. (doubt / match)
2. Mitch has a phone in his room. (phlegm / phone)
3. Add the numbers in the last column. (diaphragm / column)
4. Dad needs a match to light the fire. (match / much)
5. The tire on my bike is flat and needs a patch. (patch / match)
6. We went to the zoo and saw a huge elephant. (diaphragm / elephant)

Horizons® Phonics & Reading Grade 1 Student Book One 59

Activity 2. Help the student read the sentences and the word choices. If desired, you may have the student to underline the word that will correctly complete each sentence. The student will write the correct word on the line.

Sentences:

1. **Mike had no doubt that his team would win.**
2. **Mitch has a phone in his room.**
3. **Add the numbers in the last column.**
4. **Dad needs a match to light the fire.**
5. **The tire on my bike is flat and needs a patch.**
6. **We went to the zoo and saw a huge elephant.**

Activity 3. Help the student identify the pictures. The student will add **ch** or **tch** to the words below the pictures and read the words aloud.

Words: **chin, catch, patch, match**

Activity 4. Help the student identify the pictures and listen for the consonant blend as you say the name of each picture. The student is to circle the consonant blend he hears.

Pictures: **clap, glasses, flowers, blue**
crown, drain, grapes, bread
flute, wasp, grass, Spot

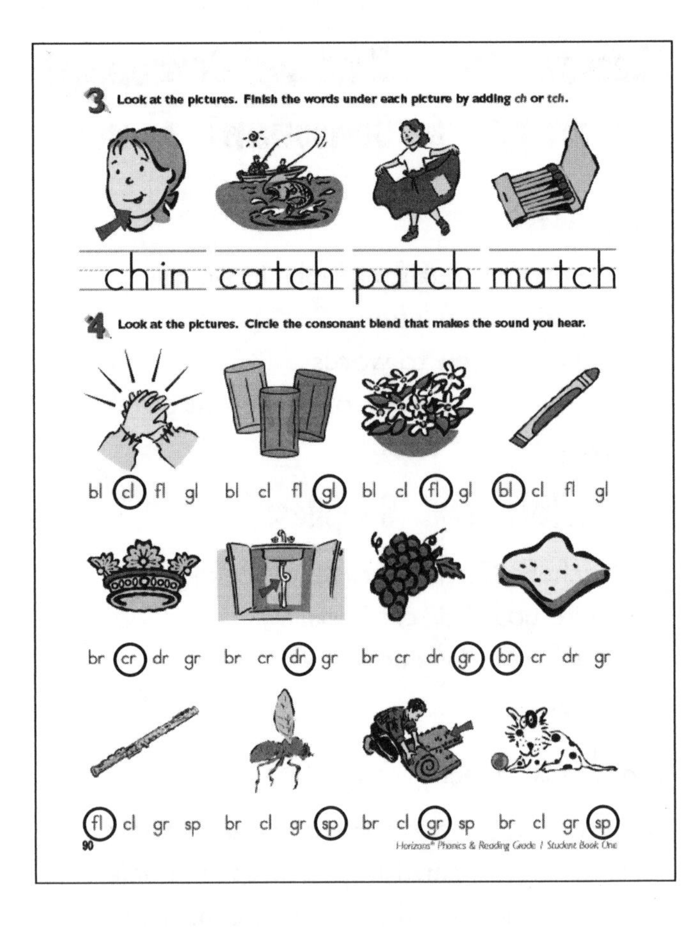

3. Look at the pictures. Finish the words under each picture by adding *ch* or *tch*.

chin catch patch match

4. Look at the pictures. Circle the consonant blend that makes the sound you hear.

bl cl fl gl   bl cl fl gl   bl cl fl gl   bl cl fl gl

br cr dr gr   br cr dr gr   br cr dr gr   br cr dr gr

fl cl gr sp   br cl gr sp   br cl gr sp   br cl gr sp

90   Horizons® Phonics & Reading Grade 1 Student Book One

Lesson 26 - Consonant Digraph ck, Ending Consonant Blends nd, nt

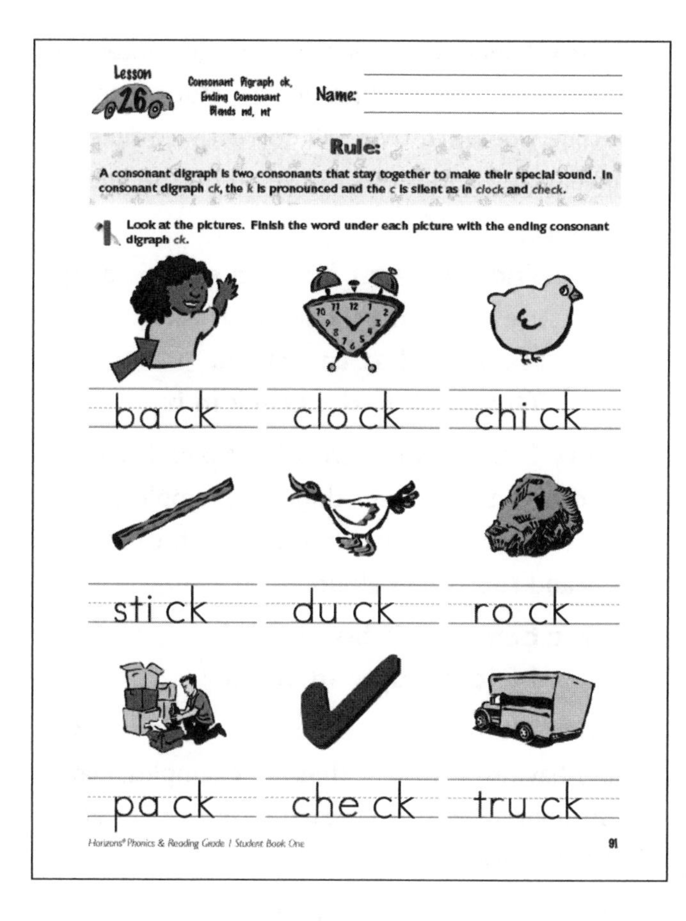
Lesson 26 Consonant Digraph ck, Ending Consonant Blends nd, nt Name:

Rule:

A consonant digraph is two consonants that stay together to make their special sound. In consonant digraph *ck*, **the** *k* **is pronounced and the** *c* **is silent as in** *clock* **and** *check*.

1 **Look at the pictures. Finish the word under each picture with the ending consonant digraph** *ck*.

back	clock	chick
stick	duck	rock
pack	check	truck

Horizons® Phonics & Reading Grade 1 Student Book One 91

Overview:

- Add consonant digraph **ck** to words
- Sentence completion
- Add ending consonant blends **nd**, **nt** to words

Materials and Supplies:

- Teacher's Guide & Student Workbook
- White board or chalkboard
- Word cards (as necessary)
- Phonics rule flashcards in **Teacher Resources**
- Story: *The Tick of the Clock*

Teaching Tips:

Review the rule for consonant digraph **ck**. Stress the difference between consonant digraphs and consonant blends. Review all the words and identify the pictures in the lesson. Make word cards as necessary.

Activity 1. Assist the student in identifying the pictures. The student will add the consonant digraph **ck** to the end of each of the words and read the words aloud.

Words: **back, clock, chick**
stick, duck, rock
pack, check, truck

Activity 2. Help the student read the sentences and the word choices. Instruct the student to underline the word that will correctly complete each sentence and write the word on the line.

Sentences:

1. **The boy went back to see his dog.**
2. **He needed to check on him.**
3. **He looked at the clock.**
4. **The clock had a crack in it.**

Activity 3. Discuss the consonant blend rule for **nd** and have the student think of examples. Instruct the student to add **nd** to each of the words and read them aloud.

Words: **bend, send, bond, fond**
hand, fund, tend, band

Activity 4. Discuss the consonant blend rule for **nt** and have the student think of examples. Have the student to add **nt** to each of the words and read them aloud.

Words: **cent, hint, pant, vent**
hunt, sent, plant, bent

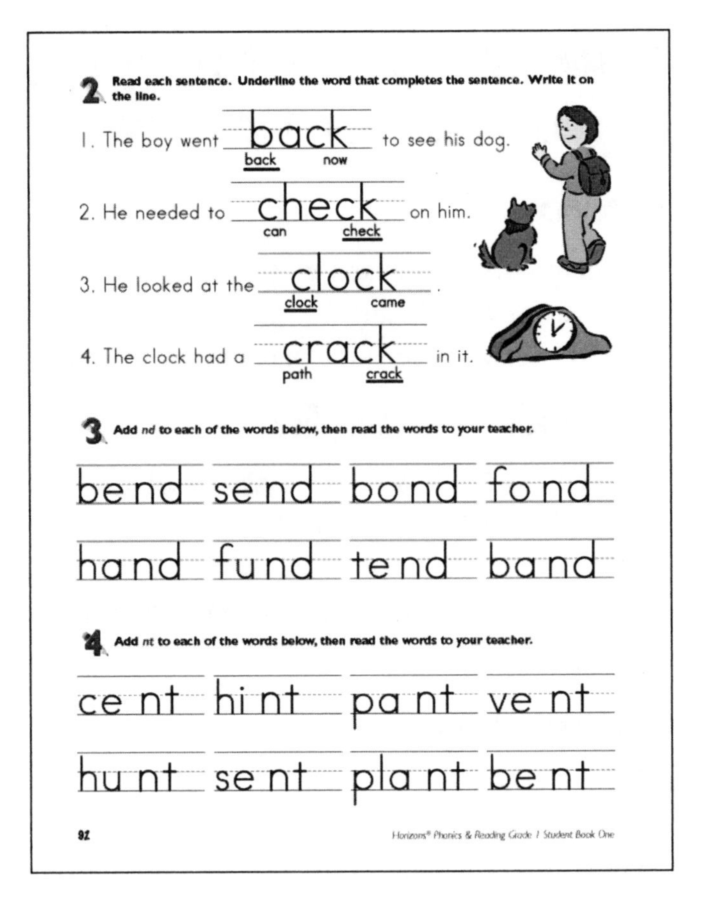

2 Read each sentence. Underline the word that completes the sentence. Write it on the line.
1. The boy went back to see his dog.
back now
2. He needed to check on him.
can check
3. He looked at the clock.
clock came
4. The clock had a crack in it.
path crack
3 Add nd to each of the words below, then read the words to your teacher.
bend send bond fond
hand fund tend band
4 Add nt to each of the words below, then read the words to your teacher.
cent hint pant vent
hunt sent plant bent
92
Horizons® Phonics & Reading Grade 1 Student Book One

Lesson 27 - Consonant Digraph gh, Consonant Blends ng, nk

Overview:

- Word/picture matching
- Sentence completion
- Auditory recognition of digraph **gh** and ending consonant blends **ng**, **nk**

Materials and Supplies:

- Teacher's Guide & Student Workbook
- White board or chalkboard
- Word cards (as necessary)
- Phonics rule flashcards in **Teacher Resources**
- Story: *The Rough Road*

Teaching Tips:

Go over the rule. Help the student think of some more examples for each part of the rule.

Activity 1. Help the student read the words and identify the pictures. The student will draw lines to match the pictures with the words.

Pictures:	**rock**	**night**
	laugh	**right**
	weigh	

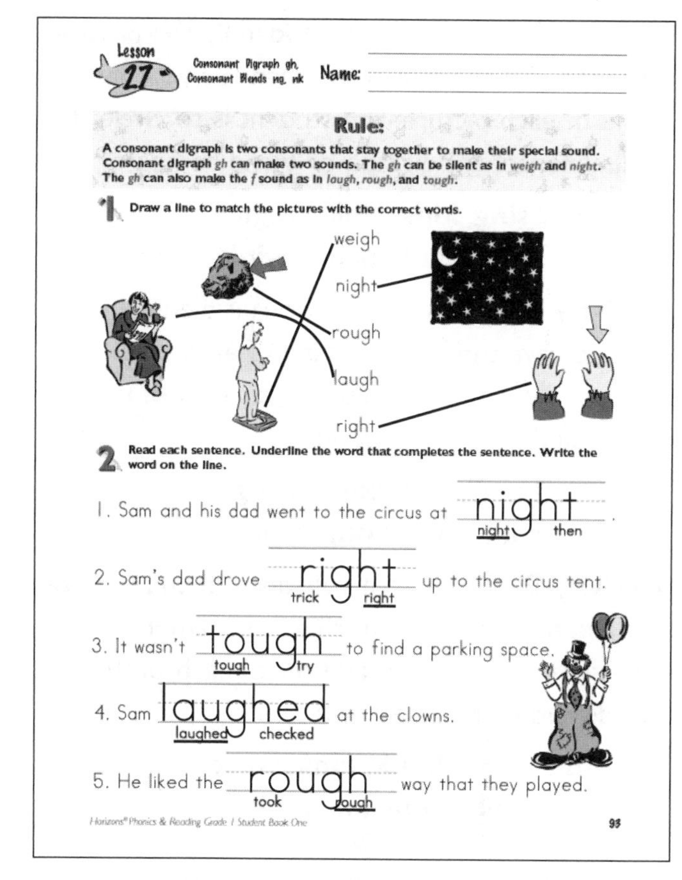

Lesson 27 Consonant Digraph gh, Consonant Blends ng, nk Name:

Rule:

A consonant digraph is two consonants that stay together to make their special sound. Consonant digraph *gh* can make two sounds. The *gh* can be silent as in *weigh* and *night*. The *gh* can also make the *f* sound as in *laugh*, *rough*, and *tough*.

1. Draw a line to match the pictures with the correct words.

weigh
night
rough
laugh
right

2. Read each sentence. Underline the word that completes the sentence. Write the word on the line.

1. Sam and his dad went to the circus at night. (night / then)
2. Sam's dad drove right up to the circus tent. (trick / right)
3. It wasn't tough to find a parking space. (tough / try)
4. Sam laughed at the clowns. (laughed / checked)
5. He liked the rough way that they played. (took / rough)

Horizons® Phonics & Reading Grade 1 Student Book One 93

Activity 2. Help the student read the sentences and the word choices. Instruct the student to underline the word that will correctly complete each sentence and write the word on the line.

Sentences:

1. **Sam and his dad went to the circus at night.**
2. **Sam's dad drove right up to the circus tent.**
3. **It wasn't tough to find a parking space.**
4. **Sam laughed at the clowns.**
5. **He liked the rough way that they played.**

Activity 3. Help the student identify the pictures and listen for the consonant blend as you say the name of each picture. The student is to circle the ending consonant digraph or blend he hears.

Pictures: **sing, king, sink, laugh**
ring, tank, drink, wink

Activity 4. Discuss the consonant blend rule for **ng**, and have the student think of examples. Instruct the student to add **ng** to each of the words and read them aloud.

Words: **lung, gang, bang, wing**
sung, zing, song, hang

Activity 5. Discuss the consonant blend rule for **nk**, and have the student think of examples. Instruct the student to add **nk** to each of the words and read them aloud.

Words: **crank, honk, tank, wink**
dunk, bank, ink, junk

3. Look at the pictures. Circle the consonant digraph or blend that makes the ending sound you hear.

gh (ng) nk gh (ng) nk gh ng (nk) (gh) ng nk

gh (ng) nk gh ng (nk) gh ng (nk) gh ng (nk)

4. Add *ng* to each of the words below, then read the words to your teacher.

lung gang bang wing
sung zing song hang

5. Add *nk* to each of the words below, then read the words to your teacher.

crank honk tank wink
dunk bank ink junk

94 Horizons® Phonics & Reading Grade 1 Student Book One

Lesson 28 - Review: Consonant Digraphs ck, gh, Consonant Blend sk

Overview:

- Crossword puzzle
- Sentence writing
- Auditory recognition of consonant digraph **sk**
- Alphabetical order
- Story completion

Materials and Supplies:

- Teacher's Guide & Student Workbook
- White board or chalkboard
- Word cards (as necessary)
- Phonics rule flashcards in **Teacher Resources**
- Story: *The Circus*

Teaching Tips:

Review the rules. Go over examples of each rule using the chalkboard or white board. Go over word cards as necessary. Discuss alphabetical order and give examples of simple words on the chalkboard or white board. Ask the student to tell you which word comes first, second, etc.

Activity 1. Review the words in the list. Help the student read the crossword puzzle clues. Assist the student as necessary with the crossword puzzle.

Across: **1. night**
2. clock
4. rough

Down: **1. neck**
3. laugh

Activity 2. Assist the student in reading the words in the word list as necessary. Instruct the student to use as many of the words in the list as possible to write three sentences. Remind the student to observe proper capitalization and punctuation.

Activity 3. Discuss the consonant blend rule for **sk**, and have the student think of additional examples. Identify the pictures, and instruct the student to add **sk** to each of the words. Have the student read the words aloud.

Words: **desk, tusk, task, mask**

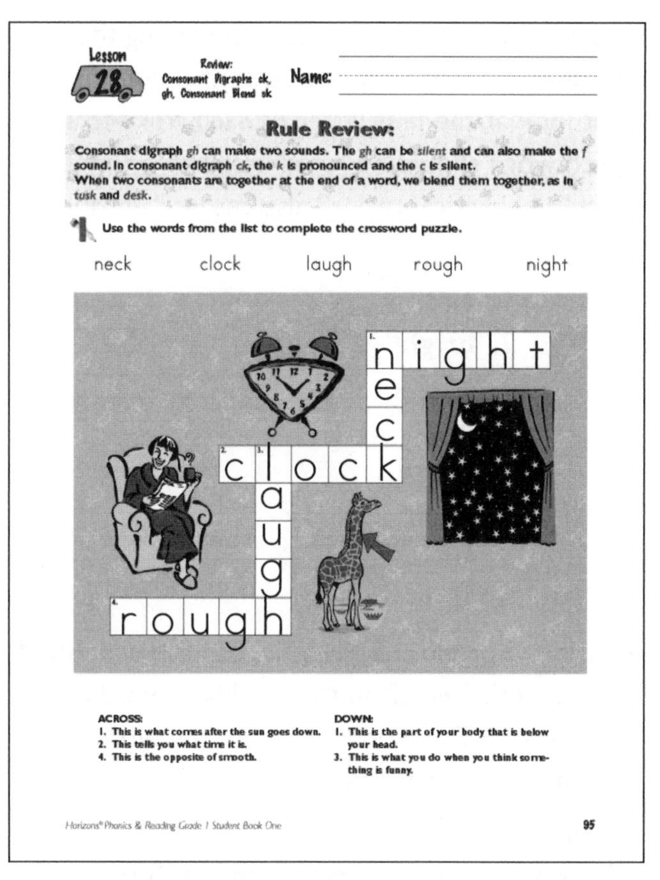

Lesson 28 Review: Consonant Digraphs ck, gh, Consonant Blend sk Name:

Rule Review:

Consonant digraph *gh* can make two sounds. The *gh* can be *silent* and can also make the *f* sound. In consonant digraph *ck*, the *k* is pronounced and the *c* is silent.
When two consonants are together at the end of a word, we blend them together, as in *tusk* and *desk*.

1. Use the words from the list to complete the crossword puzzle.

neck clock laugh rough night

ACROSS:
1. This is what comes after the sun goes down.
2. This tells you what time it is.
4. This is the opposite of smooth.

DOWN:
1. This is the part of your body that is below your head.
3. This is what you do when you think something is funny.

Horizons® Phonics & Reading Grade 1 Student Book One 95

2. Write three sentences. Use some of the words from the list.

Word List

bought check thick brought trick thought crack track

1.

2.

3.

3. Look at the pictures. Finish the words under each picture by adding the ending consonant blend *sk*.

de sk tu sk ta sk ma sk

96 Horizons® Phonics & Reading Grade 1 Student Book One

Activity 4. Assist the student in reading the words in the word list as necessary. Have the student look at the first letter of each word to see which word should be listed first. Explain that the term "alphabetical order" also means "alphabet order."

Words: **1. ask**
2. bright
3. check
4. fight
5. laugh
6. neck
7. sink
8. tusk

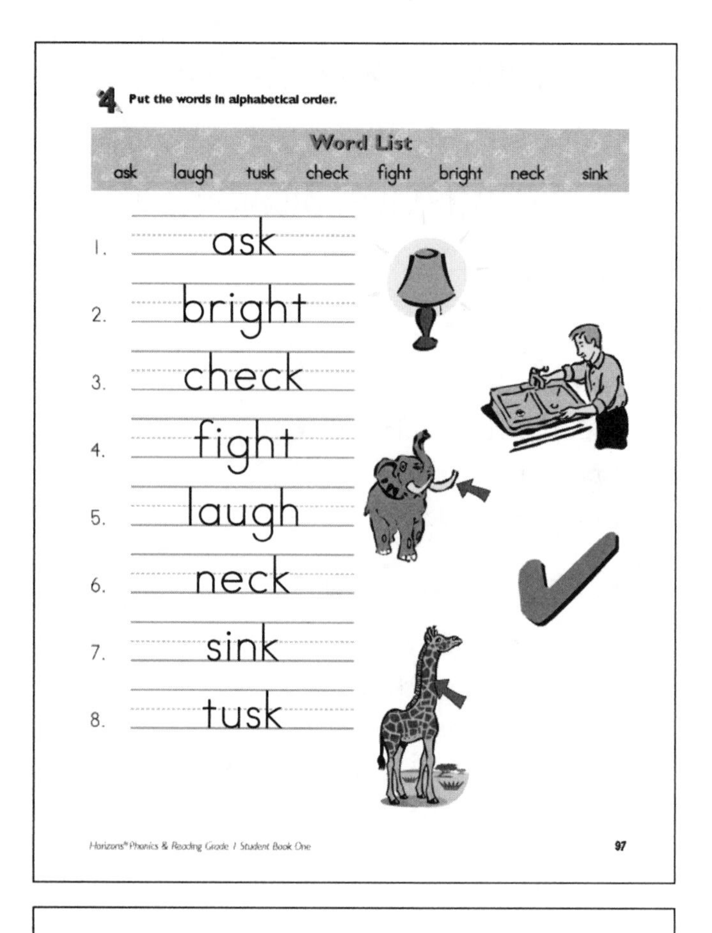

Activity 5. Help the student read the unfinished story and the words in the list. Make word cards as necessary. The student will use the words from the list to complete the story.

Story:
Dawn liked to go to the circus. She thought that the clowns were funny. They made her laugh. They always played so roughly. They tumbled around and knocked each other down. They wore colorful collars around their necks. Dawn's dad bought her some popcorn.

Lesson 29 - Review: Consonant Digraphs gn, ch, tch, Consonant Blends mp, lp

Overview:

- Match pictures to words
- Complete words by adding consonant digraphs
- Match words to clues
- Add consonant blends **mp** and **lp** to words

Materials and Supplies:

- Teacher's Guide & Student Workbook
- White board or chalkboard
- Word cards (as necessary)
- Phonics rule flashcards in **Teacher Resources**
- Story: *The Beaver*

Teaching Tips:

Assist the student as needed in reading the words and identifying the pictures in the lesson. Review the rules for consonant digraph **gn** and **ch**, and ask the student for examples. Review the consonant blend rule, and ask the student for examples of words with ending consonant blends **mp** and **lp**.

Activity 1. Help the student read the words and identify the pictures. Have the student draw lines to match the pictures to the words in the list.

Pictures:	chair	chin
	sign	**gnaw**
	chorus	**catch**

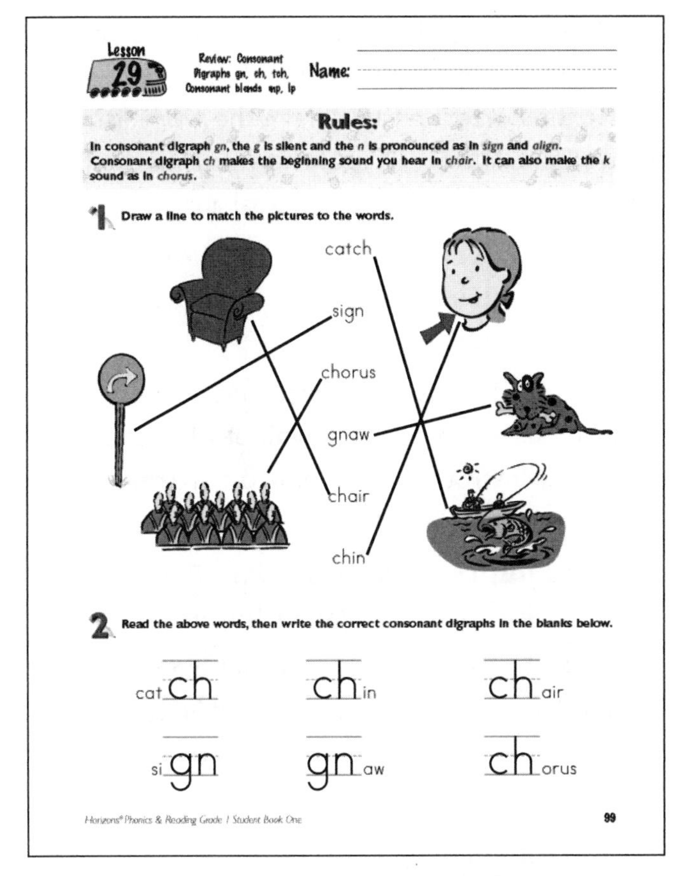

Lesson 29 Review: Consonant Digraphs gn, ch, tch, Consonant blends mp, lp Name:

Rules:

In consonant digraph *gn*, the *g* is silent and the *n* is pronounced as in *sign* and *align*. Consonant digraph *ch* makes the beginning sound you hear in *chair*. It can also make the *k* sound as in *chorus*.

1. Draw a line to match the pictures to the words.

catch
sign
chorus
gnaw
chair
chin

2. Read the above words, then write the correct consonant digraphs in the blanks below.

catch chin chair
sign gnaw chorus

Horizons® Phonics & Reading Grade 1 Student Book One 99

Activity 2. Instruct the student to look at the words in Activity 1 to complete this activity. Have the student complete the words by adding the correct consonant digraph. Have the student read the words aloud.

Words: **catch, sign, chin, gnaw, chair, chorus**

Activity 3. Help the student read the words in the word list and in the riddles. The student will select the correct answer from the word list for each riddle. NOTE: One of the words in the list is a "distractor" and is not an actual answer.

Words: **1. chin** **2. sandwich** **3. sign** **4. chorus** **5. gnaw**

Activity 4. Discuss the consonant blend rule for **mp**, and have the student think of additional examples. Instruct the student to add **mp** to each of the words and read them aloud.

Words: **lump, camp, limp, damp jump, bump, lamp, hump**

Activity 5. Discuss the consonant blend rule for **lp**, and have the student think of additional examples. Instruct the student to add **lp** to each of the words and read them aloud.

Words: **gulp, help, kelp, yelp**

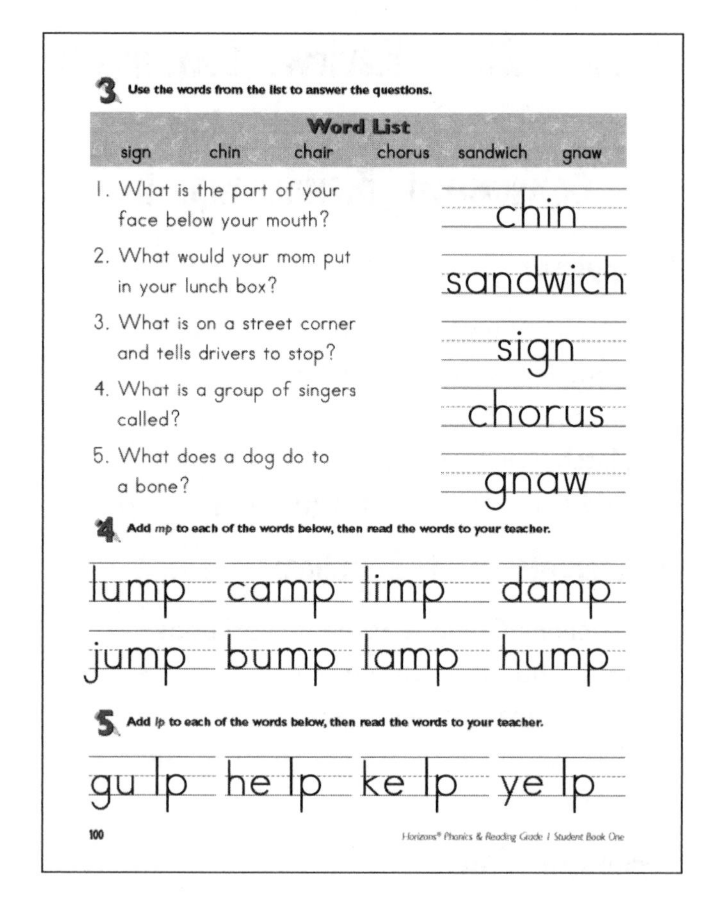

3 Use the words from the list to answer the questions.
Word List
sign chin chair chorus sandwich gnaw
1. What is the part of your face below your mouth?
chin
2. What would your mom put in your lunch box?
sandwich
3. What is on a street corner and tells drivers to stop?
sign
4. What is a group of singers called?
chorus
5. What does a dog do to a bone?
gnaw
4 Add mp to each of the words below, then read the words to your teacher.
lump camp limp damp
jump bump lamp hump
5 Add lp to each of the words below, then read the words to your teacher.
gu lp he lp ke lp ye lp
100
Horizons® Phonics & Reading Grade 1 Student Book One

Lesson 30 - Consonant Digraphs hn, kn

Overview:

- Word/picture matching
- Riddles
- Rhyming words
- Sentence writing

Materials and Supplies:

- Teacher's Guide & Student Workbook
- White board or chalkboard
- Word cards (as necessary)
- Phonics rule flashcards in **Teacher Resources**
- Story: *Sir John, the Knight*

Teaching Tips:

Review the consonant digraph rule for **hn** and **kn**. Ask for examples of other consonant digraphs that have been studied so far. Help the student identify the pictures and the words in the lesson.

Activity 1. Identify the pictures, and have the student draw lines from the pictures to the correct words.

Pictures:	knock	knife
	knee	John
	knights	knot

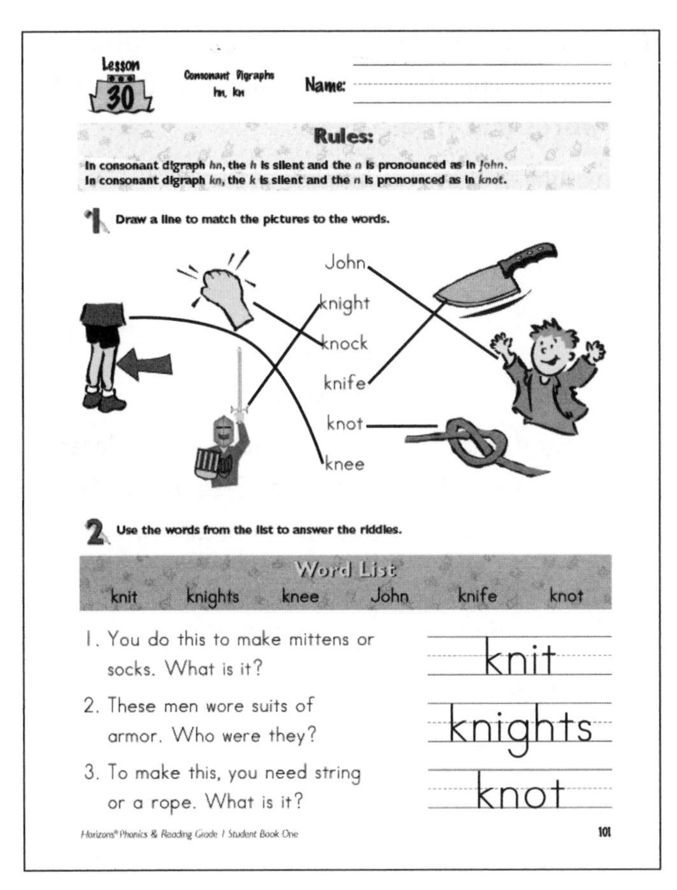

Lesson 30 — Consonant Digraphs hn, kn — Name:

Rules:
In consonant digraph *hn*, the *h* is silent and the *n* is pronounced as in *John*.
In consonant digraph *kn*, the *k* is silent and the *n* is pronounced as in *knot*.

1. Draw a line to match the pictures to the words.

2. Use the words from the list to answer the riddles.

Word List: knit knights knee John knife knot

1. You do this to make mittens or socks. What is it? knit
2. These men wore suits of armor. Who were they? knights
3. To make this, you need string or a rope. What is it? knot

Horizons® Phonics & Reading Grade 1 Student Book One 101

Activity 2. Help the student read the words in the word list and the riddles. The student will use the words from the list to answer the riddles.

Words:	**1. knit**	**4. knee**
	2. knight	**5. John**
	3. knot	**6. knife**

Activity 3. Help the student read the words in the activity. The student will draw lines to match the words that rhyme.

Rhyming words: **shot/knot**
life/knife
right/knight
free/knee
row/know
sit/knit

Activity 4. Instruct the student to use at least four of the words from Activity 3 to write three sentences. Emphasize correct punctuation and capitalization.

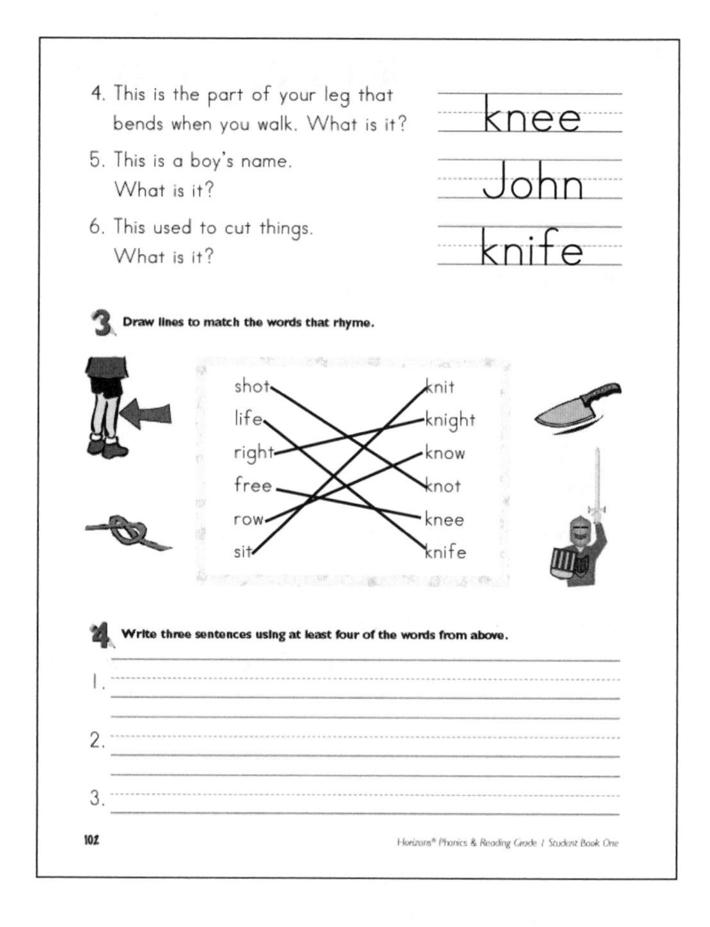

4. This is the part of your leg that bends when you walk. What is it?
knee
5. This is a boy's name. What is it?
John
6. This used to cut things. What is it?
knife
3 Draw lines to match the words that rhyme.
shot
life
right
free
row
sit
knit
knight
know
knot
knee
knife
4 Write three sentences using at least four of the words from above.
1.
2.
3.
102

Test 3

Lessons 21-30

Instructions:

Read through the test with the student. Read all of the directions to the student, checking for understanding. Review the definitions for vowel digraphs, consonant blends, and consonant digraphs. Review the way to cross out silent consonants in words. The teacher should be available to answer any questions that the student may have during the test.

Activity 1. Review the instructions with the student. Make sure they understand the difference between vowel digraphs and vowel pairs.

Circled words:

1. **played, eight**
2. **saw, shooting**
3. **Paul, bread**
4. **stood**
5. **caught, football**

Activity 2. Review the instructions, and remind the student to underline the correct word to complete the sentence as well as writing it on the line.

Sentences:

1. **Mary is talking on the phone.**
2. **She doubts that she can go outside.**
3. **She is talking to her nephew.**
4. **His name is Phil.**

What do you remember? Test 3 Lessons 21-30 Name:

1 Read each sentence. Circle the words that contain vowel digraphs oo, ea, aw, au, or ei.

1. The children played eight games at recess.
2. Jim saw the shooting star.
3. Paul likes white bread for sandwiches.
4. We stood and waited for our moms.
5. Jack caught the football and ran to the end zone.

2 Read each sentence. Underline the word that correctly completes the sentence. Write the word on the line.

1. Mary is talking on the phone. (can / phone)
2. She doubts that she can go outside. (catch / doubts)
3. She is talking to her nephew. (trick / nephew)
4. His name is Phil. (name / Phil)

3 Circle the consonants in these words, then cross out the consonants that are silent.

climb solemn diaphragm

Horizons Phonics & Reading Grade 1 Student Book One 105

Activity 3. Review the instructions with the student, and stress that all consonants are to be circled. Some will be crossed out, as well.

Activity 4. Read the words in the list with the student, and assist as needed with any words in the sentences.

Sentences:

1. **Jan had to check on her little brother.**
2. **There was a crack in the clock.**
3. **There are thirty sheep in the flock.**
4. **We went back to our house.**

Activity 5. Read the words in the list with the student.

Silent **gh**:		Digraph **gh**:	
	right		**rough**
	high		**enough**
	night		**tough**
	weigh		**laugh**

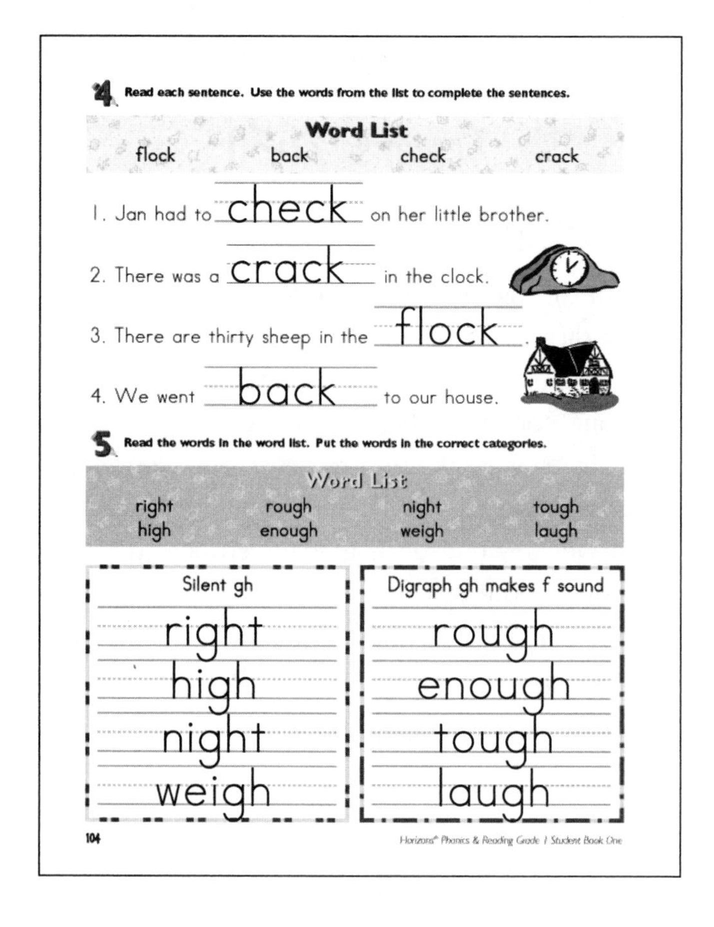

4 Read each sentence. Use the words from the list to complete the sentences.
Word List
flock back check crack
1. Jan had to check on her little brother.
2. There was a crack in the clock.
3. There are thirty sheep in the flock.
4. We went back to our house.
5 Read the words in the word list. Put the words in the correct categories.
Word List
right rough night tough
high enough weigh laugh
Silent gh
right
high
night
weigh
Digraph gh makes f sound
rough
enough
tough
laugh
104
Horizons Phonics & Reading Grade 1 Student Book One

Lesson 31 - Consonant Digraph mb

Overview:

- Word/picture match
- Sentence completion
- Story writing

Materials and Supplies:

- Teacher's Guide & Student Workbook
- White board or chalkboard
- Word cards (as necessary)
- Phonics rule flashcards in **Teacher Resources**
- Story: *The Lamb Who Liked to Climb*

Teaching Tips:

Go over the rule. Have the student name each of the pictures in the activity. Make word cards as needed.

Activity 1. Have the student identify the pictures and draw a line to match the pictures with the words.

Pictures: **comb** **bomb** **limb** **climb** **lamb**

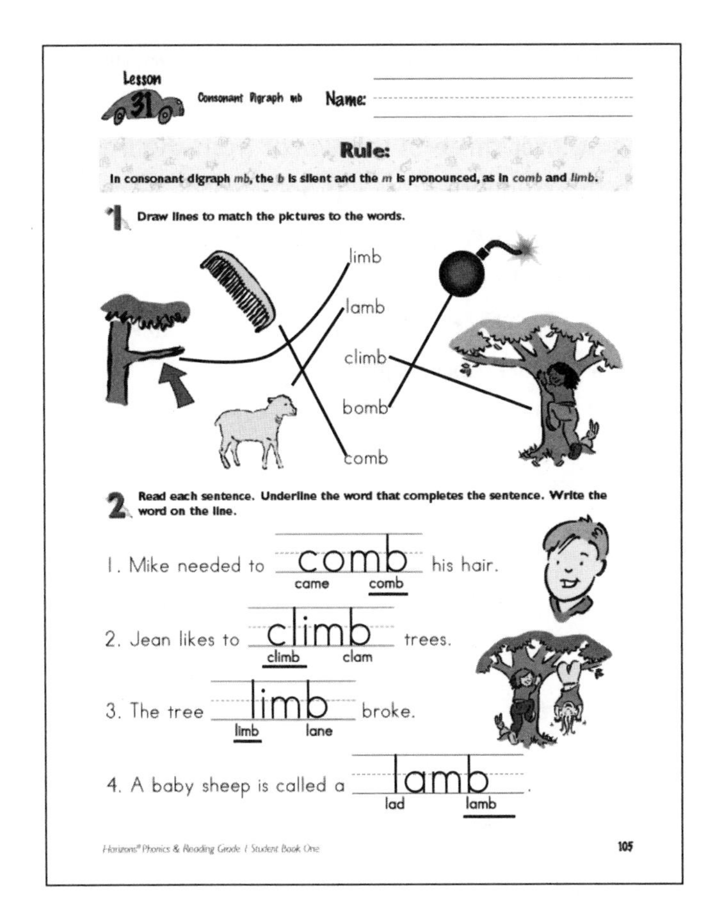

Lesson 31 Consonant Digraph mb Name:

Rule:

In consonant digraph *mb*, the *b* is silent and the *m* is pronounced, as in *comb* and *limb*.

1 Draw lines to match the pictures to the words.

limb
lamb
climb
bomb
comb

2 Read each sentence. Underline the word that completes the sentence. Write the word on the line.

1. Mike needed to comb his hair. (came / comb)
2. Jean likes to climb trees. (climb / clam)
3. The tree limb broke. (limb / lane)
4. A baby sheep is called a lamb. (lad / lamb)

Horizons Phonics & Reading Grade 1 Student Book One 105

Activity 2. Help the student read the sentences and the word choices. Instruct the student to underline the word that will correctly complete each sentence and write the word on the line.

Sentences:

1. Mike needed to comb his hair.
2. Jean likes to climb trees.
3. The tree limb broke.
4. A baby sheep is called a lamb.

Activity 3. Have the student read the words in the word list. The student will write a short story using at least three of the words from the list. Help the student with ideas and spelling as necessary. Remind the student about correct punctuation and capitalization.

Activity 4. The student may use this space to draw a picture about his story.

3 Write a short story using at least three of the words in the word list.

Word List

limb lamb climb bomb comb

4 Draw a picture to go with your story.

106 Horizons® Phonics & Reading Grade 1 Student Book One

Lesson 32 - Consonant Blends

sc, scr

Overview:

- Word/picture matching
- Sentence completion
- Adding consonant blend **scr** to words
- Crossword puzzle

Materials and Supplies:

- Teacher's Guide & Student Workbook
- White board or chalkboard
- Word cards (as necessary)
- Phonics rule flashcards in **Teacher Resources**
- Story: *The Science Class*

Teaching Tips:

Help the student identify the pictures and the words in the lesson. Use the white board or chalkboard to review the rules for consonant blends **sc** and **scr**. Have the student give examples of each.

Activity 1. Have the student identify the pictures and draw a line to match the pictures with the words.

Pictures:	**scene**	**scent**
	scrape	**scrap**
	scared	

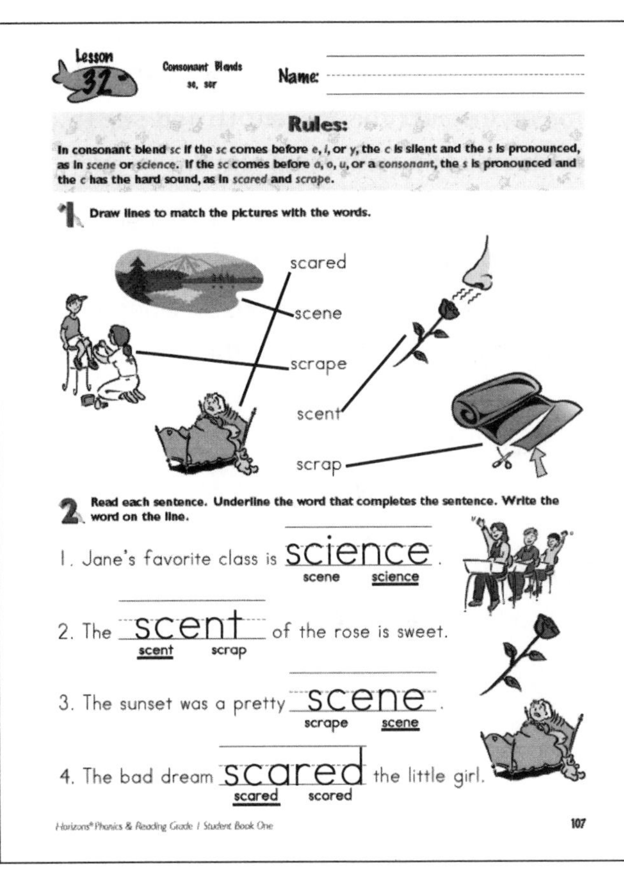

Lesson 32 Consonant Blends sc, scr Name:

Rules:

In consonant blend *sc* if the *sc* comes before *e*, *i*, or *y*, the *c* is silent and the *s* is pronounced, as in *scene* or *science*. If the *sc* comes before *a*, *o*, *u*, or a *consonant*, the *s* is pronounced and the *c* has the hard sound, as in *scared* and *scrape*.

1 Draw lines to match the pictures with the words.

scared
scene
scrape
scent
scrap

2 Read each sentence. Underline the word that completes the sentence. Write the word on the line.

1. Jane's favorite class is science. scene science
2. The scent of the rose is sweet. scent scrap
3. The sunset was a pretty scene. scrape scene
4. The bad dream scared the little girl. scared scored

Horizons® Phonics & Reading Grade 1 Student Book One 107

Activity 2. Help the student read the sentences and the word choices. Instruct the student to underline the word that will correctly complete each sentence and write the word on the line.

Sentences:

1. **Jane's favorite class is science.**
2. **The scent of the rose is sweet.**
3. **The sunset was a pretty scene.**
4. **The bad dream scared the little girl.**

Activity 3. Discuss the consonant blend rule for **scr** and have the student think of additional examples. Instruct the student to add **scr** to each of the words and read them aloud.

Words: **scrape, scrap, scratch, scram**

Activity 4. Review the words in the list. Help the student read the crossword puzzle clues. Assist the student as necessary with the crossword puzzle.

Across: **1. scene**
2. scrap
3. scent

Down: **1. scared**
2. scratch

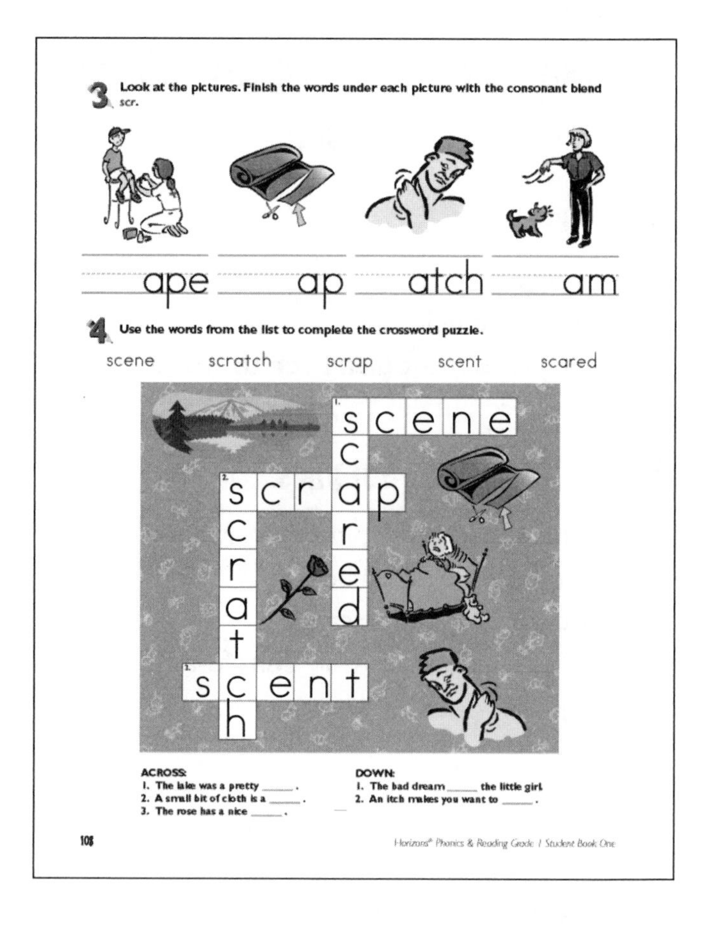

3 Look at the pictures. Finish the words under each picture with the consonant blend scr.

ape ap atch am

4 Use the words from the list to complete the crossword puzzle.

scene scratch scrap scent scared

ACROSS:
1. The lake was a pretty _____ .
2. A small bit of cloth is a _____ .
3. The rose has a nice _____ .

DOWN:
1. The bad dream _____ the little girl.
2. An itch makes you want to _____ .

108 Horizons® Phonics & Reading Grade 1 Student Book One

Lesson 33 - Review: Consonant Digraph wh, Consonant Blends pl, sl, sm

Overview:

- Picture naming
- Sentence completion
- Adding consonant blends **pl**, **sl**, and **sm** to words
- Auditory recognition of beginning consonant blends **pl**, **sl**, and **sm**

Materials and Supplies:

- Teacher's Guide & Student Workbook
- White board or chalkboard
- Word cards (as necessary)
- Phonics rule flashcards in **Teacher Resources**
- Story: *Jan's Wheel*

Teaching Tips:

Assist the student as needed in identifying the pictures and reading the words in the lesson. Review the rules for consonant digraphs and consonant blends. Ask students for examples of consonant digraph **wh** and consonant blends **pl**, **sl**, and **sm**.

Activity 1. Help the student identify each picture. Have the student write the correct name underneath each picture, using the words from the list.

Pictures: **wheat, wheel, white, whine**

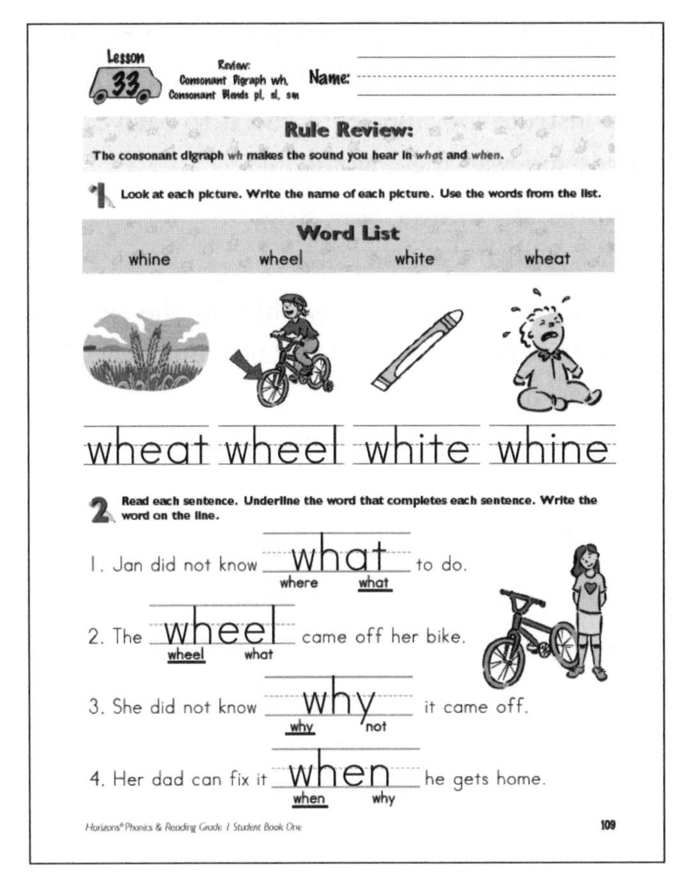

Lesson 33 Review: Consonant Digraph wh, Consonant Blends pl, sl, sm Name:

Rule Review:

The consonant digraph *wh* makes the sound you hear in *what* and *when*.

1 Look at each picture. Write the name of each picture. Use the words from the list.

Word List

whine wheel white wheat

wheat wheel white whine

2 Read each sentence. Underline the word that completes each sentence. Write the word on the line.

1. Jan did not know what to do. (where / what)
2. The wheel came off her bike. (wheel / what)
3. She did not know why it came off. (why / not)
4. Her dad can fix it when he gets home. (when / why)

Horizons® Phonics & Reading Grade 1 Student Book One 109

Activity 2. Help the student read the sentences and the word choices. Instruct the student to underline the word that will correctly complete each sentence and write the word on the line.

Sentences:

1. **Jan did not know what to do.**
2. **The wheel came off her bike.**
3. **She did not know why it came off.**
4. **Her dad can fix it when he gets home.**

Activity 3. Discuss the consonant blend rule for **sl** and have the student think of additional examples. Instruct the student to add **sl** to each of the words and read them aloud.

Words: **slam, sled, slip, slug**
slid, slot, slit, slat

Activity 4. Help the student identify the pictures, circle the beginning consonant blend he hears in each word.

Pictures: **play, sleep, smile, plate**

Activity 5. Have the student add **sl** or **sm** to each of the words and read them aloud.

Words: **smile, slip, smell, sled**

Activity 6. Have the student add **pl** to each of the words and read them aloud.

Words: **plan, plop, plug, plot**

3 Add *sl* to each of the words below, then read the words to your teacher.

sl am sl ed sl ip sl ug
sl id sl ot sl it sl at

4 Look at the pictures. Circle the consonant blend that makes the beginning sound you hear.

sl sm (pl) (sl) sm pl sl (sm) pl sl sm (pl)

5 Look at the pictures. Finish the words under each picture with the consonant blend *sl* or *sm*.

sm ile sl ip sm ell sl ed

6 Add *pl* to each of the words below, then read the words to your teacher.

pl an pl op pl ug pl ot

110 Horizons® Phonics & Reading Grade 1 Student Book One

Lesson 34 - Consonant Digraph wr

Overview:

- Word/picture match
- Sentence completion
- Story completion

Materials and Supplies:

- Teacher's Guide & Student Workbook
- White board or chalkboard
- Word cards (as necessary)
- Phonics rule flashcards in **Teacher Resources**
- Story: *The Wrong Sign*

Teaching Tips:

Assist the student as needed in identifying the pictures and reading the words in the lesson. Review the rules for consonant digraph **wr**, and ask students for examples.

Activity 1. Have the student read the words and identify the pictures and draw a line to match the pictures with the words.

Pictures:	**write**	**wreck**
	wrap	**wrench**
	wren	**wrist**

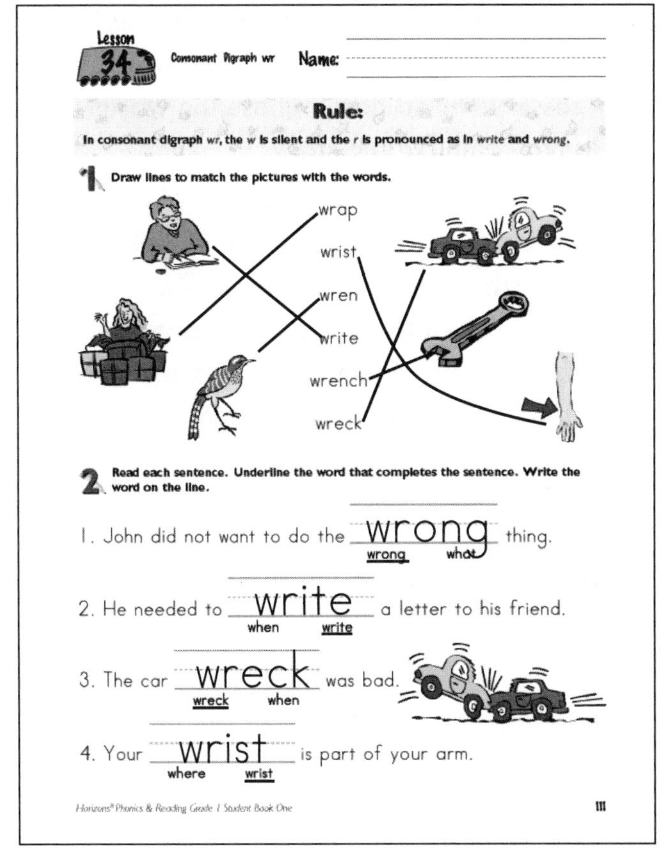
Lesson 34 Consonant Digraph wr Name:

Rule:

In consonant digraph *wr*, the *w* is silent and the *r* is pronounced as in *write* and *wrong*.

1 Draw lines to match the pictures with the words.

wrap
wrist
wren
write
wrench
wreck

2 Read each sentence. Underline the word that completes the sentence. Write the word on the line.

1. John did not want to do the wrong thing. (wrong / what)
2. He needed to write a letter to his friend. (when / write)
3. The car wreck was bad. (wreck / when)
4. Your wrist is part of your arm. (where / wrist)

Horizons® Phonics & Reading Grade 1 Student Book One 111

Activity 2. Help the student read the sentences and the word choices. Instruct the student to underline the word that will correctly complete each sentence and write the word on the line.

Sentences:

1. **John did not want to do the wrong thing.**
2. **He needed to write a letter to his friend.**
3. **The car wreck was bad.**
4. **Your wrist is part of your arm.**
5. **The wren had a nest in the tree.**
6. **Dad fixed my bike with a wrench.**

Activity 3. Help the student read the unfinished story and the words in the list. Make word cards as necessary. The student will use the words from the list to complete the story.

Story:

I will write a note to Jim. I will tell him about the wren that made a nest in the tree. I will tell him that I had a wreck with my bike. The tire on the bike was wrong. My dad fixed it with a wrench.

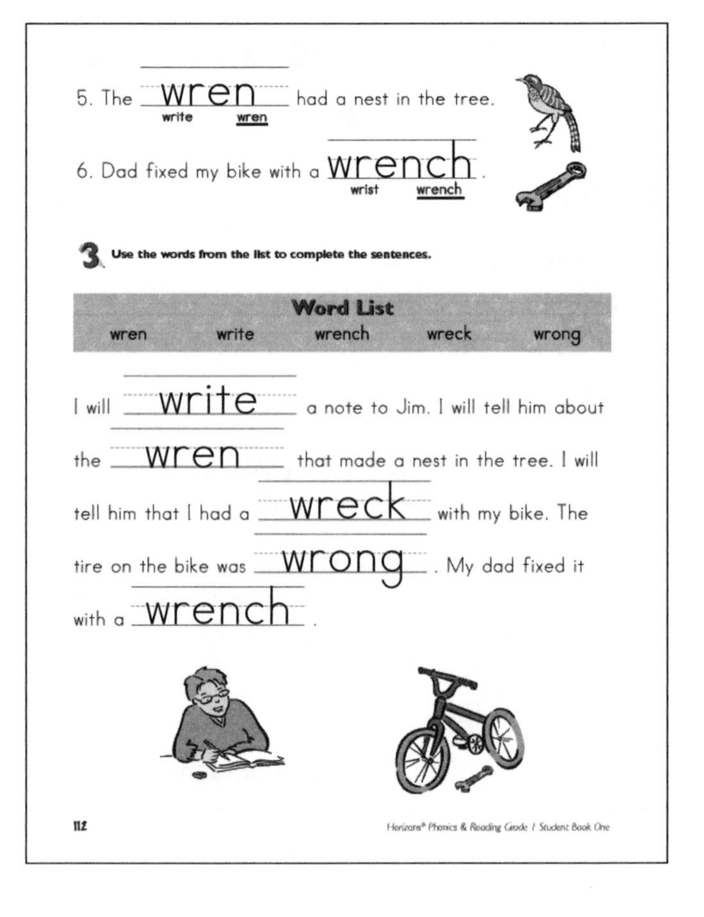

5. The wren had a nest in the tree.
write wren

6. Dad fixed my bike with a wrench.
wrist wrench

3 Use the words from the list to complete the sentences.

Word List				
wren	write	wrench	wreck	wrong

I will write a note to Jim. I will tell him about the wren that made a nest in the tree. I will tell him that I had a wreck with my bike. The tire on the bike was wrong. My dad fixed it with a wrench.

112 Horizons® Phonics & Reading Grade 1 Student Book One

Lesson 35 - Review: Consonant Digraphs gn, hn, kn, mb, wh, wr, ch

Overview:

- Auditory recognition of beginning sounds
- Sentence completion
- Story writing

Materials and Supplies:

- Teacher's Guide & Student Workbook
- White board or chalkboard
- Word cards (as necessary)
- Phonics rule flashcards in **Teacher Resources**
- Story: *The Wrong Sign*

Teaching Tips:

Review the rules from Lessons 30–34. Write examples for each rule, using the chalkboard or white board. Review word cards as necessary. Assist the student as needed in identifying the pictures and reading the words in the lesson.

Activity 1. Review each of the pictures and have the student write the correct beginning or ending consonant digraph in the space provided underneath each picture.

Pictures: **comb, sign, chair, whine**
chorus, knife, write, John

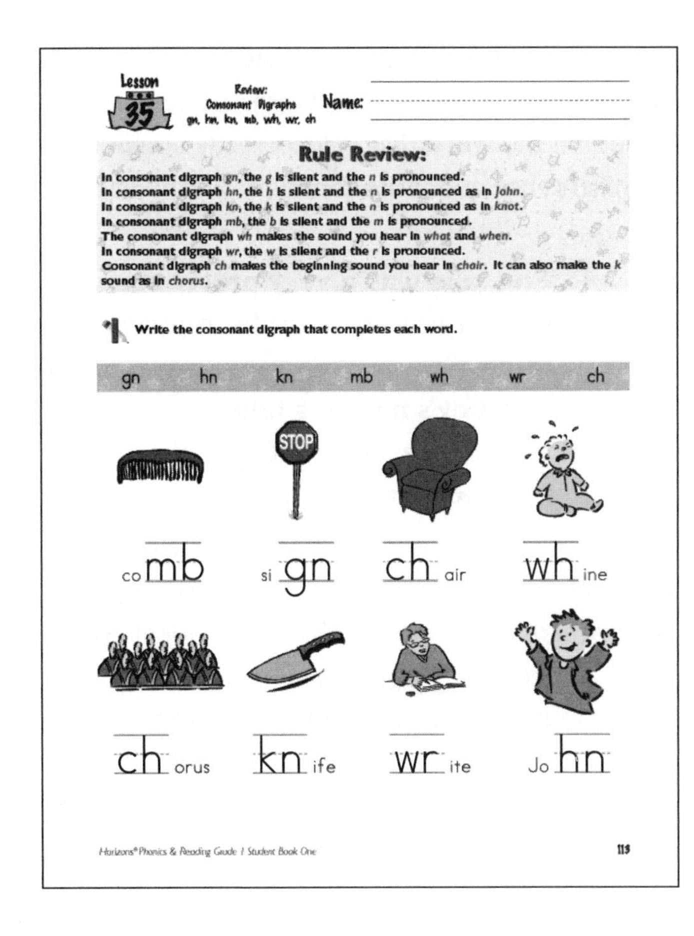

Lesson 35 Review: Consonant Digraphs gn, hn, kn, mb, wh, wr, ch Name:

Rule Review:

In consonant digraph *gn*, the *g* is silent and the *n* is pronounced.
In consonant digraph *hn*, the *h* is silent and the *n* is pronounced as in *John*.
In consonant digraph *kn*, the *k* is silent and the *n* is pronounced as in *knot*.
In consonant digraph *mb*, the *b* is silent and the *m* is pronounced.
The consonant digraph *wh* makes the sound you hear in *what* and *when*.
In consonant digraph *wr*, the *w* is silent and the *r* is pronounced.
Consonant digraph *ch* makes the beginning sound you hear in *chair*. It can also make the *k* sound as in *chorus*.

1. Write the consonant digraph that completes each word.

gn hn kn mb wh wr ch

co mb · si gn · ch air · wh ine

ch orus · kn ife · wr ite · Jo hn

Horizons® Phonics & Reading Grade 1 Student Book One 113

Activity 2. Help the student read the sentences and the word choices. Instruct the student to underline the word that will correctly complete each sentence and write the word on the line.

Sentences:

1. **The lake was a very pretty scene.**
2. **We do not want to do the wrong thing.**
3. **The boy's name is John.**
4. **The wheel came off my bike.**
5. **I like to wrap gifts.**

Activity 3. Help the student read the words from the list. The student will write a short story, using words from the list. Help the student with ideas and with spelling as needed. Remind the student about correct punctuation and capitalization.

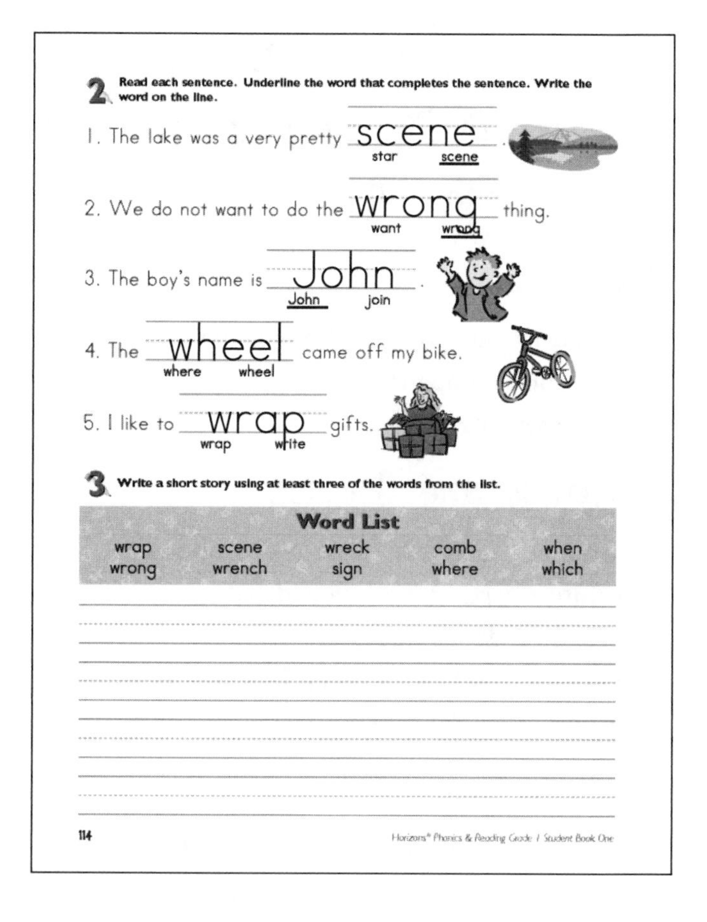

2 Read each sentence. Underline the word that completes the sentence. Write the word on the line.

1. The lake was a very pretty scene. (star / scene)
2. We do not want to do the wrong thing. (want / wrong)
3. The boy's name is John. (John / join)
4. The wheel came off my bike. (where / wheel)
5. I like to wrap gifts. (wrap / write)

3 Write a short story using at least three of the words from the list.

Word List				
wrap	scene	wreck	comb	when
wrong	wrench	sign	where	which

114 Horizons® Phonics & Reading Grade 1 Student Book One

Lesson 36 - Words with x

Overview:

- Sentence completion
- Picture naming
- Story completion
- Add the letter **x** to words

Materials and Supplies:

- Teacher's Guide & Student Workbook
- White board or chalkboard
- Word cards (as necessary)
- Phonics rule flashcards in **Teacher Resources**
- Story: *The Fox in the Box*

Teaching Tips:

Review the rules about the letter **x.** Ask if the student can think of any additional words that begin with the letter **x.** Very few words in our language begin with this letter. You may wish to have the student use a dictionary to count how many words start with **x.** Review the two sounds of the letter **x.** Assist the student as needed in identifying the pictures and reading the words in the lesson.

Activity 1. Help the student read the sentences and the word choices. Instruct the student to underline the word that will correctly complete each sentence and write the word on the line.

Sentences:

1. **Meg kept her toys in a box.**
2. **Meg's mom can fix the car.**
3. **The fox chased a rabbit.**
4. **A suffix comes at the end of a word.**
5. **He cuts wood with an ax.**

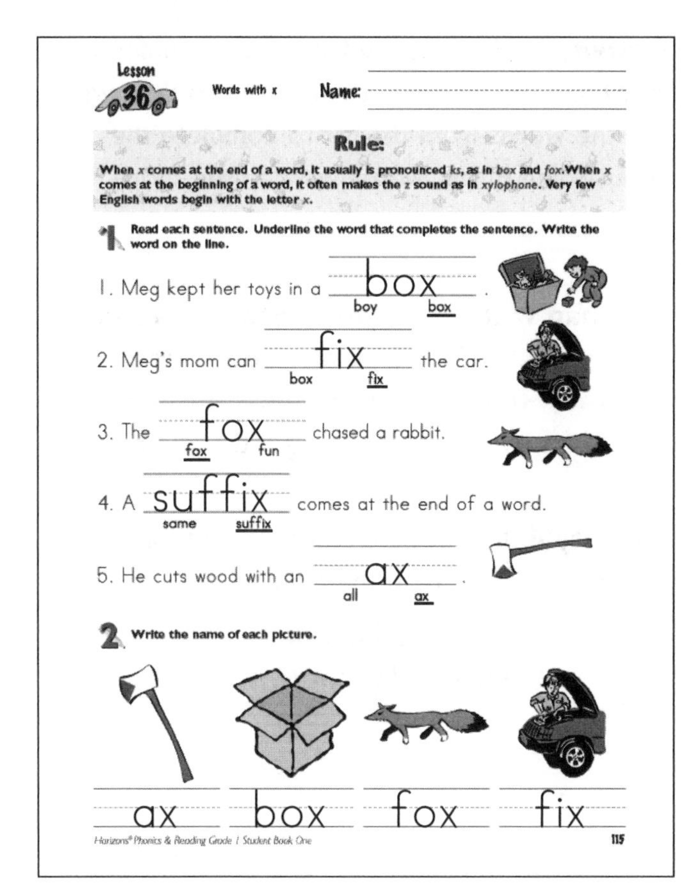

Lesson 36 Words with x Name:

Rule:

When *x* comes at the end of a word, it usually is pronounced *ks*, as in *box* and *fox*. When *x* comes at the beginning of a word, it often makes the *z* sound as in *xylophone*. Very few English words begin with the letter *x*.

1 Read each sentence. Underline the word that completes the sentence. Write the word on the line.

1. Meg kept her toys in a box. (boy / box)
2. Meg's mom can fix the car. (box / fix)
3. The fox chased a rabbit. (fox / fun)
4. A suffix comes at the end of a word. (same / suffix)
5. He cuts wood with an ax. (all / ax)

2 Write the name of each picture.

ax box fox fix

Horizons® Phonics & Reading Grade 1 Student Book One 115

Activity 2. Identify the pictures with the student, and instruct the student to write the name of the picture underneath in the space provided. The student may refer to Activity 1 if necessary.

Pictures: **ax, box, fox, fix**

Activity 3. Help the student read the unfinished story and the words in the list. The student will use the words from the list to complete the story. Some of the words will be used more than once.

Story:

A man with an ax went into the woods. He went to fix a box of wood to take home. He saw a fox run into the box to hide from a dog. The dog did not find the fox.

Activity 4. Instruct the student to add **x** to each of the words and read them aloud.

Words: **fax, boxes, fix, mix**
Max, fox, six, tax

3 Read the story. Write the words that complete the story on the lines. Use the words from the list. You will have to use some of the words two times.

Word List

ax fix box fox

A man with an ax went into the woods. He went to fix a box of wood to take home. He saw a fox run into the box to hide from a dog. The dog did not find the fox.

4 Add x to each of the words below, then read the words to your teacher.

fax boxes fix mix

Max fox six tax

116 Horizons® Phonics & Reading Grade 1 Student Book One

Lesson 37 - Beginning Consonant Blends pr, tr, fr, sn

Overview:

- Picture/word match
- Adding consonant blend **sn**, **fr** to words
- Auditory recognition of beginning consonant blends **pr**, **tr**, **fr**
- Picture naming

Materials and Supplies:

- Teacher's Guide & Student Workbook
- White board or chalkboard
- Word cards (as necessary)
- Phonics rule flashcards in **Teacher Resources**
- Story: *Fred's Lesson*

Teaching Tips:

Assist the student as needed in identifying the pictures and reading the words in the lesson. Use the white board or chalkboard to review the rules for beginning consonant blends, and ask the student for additional examples.

Activity 1. Have the student identify the pictures and draw a line to match the pictures with the words.

Pictures:	trap	track
	press	frog
	print	snack

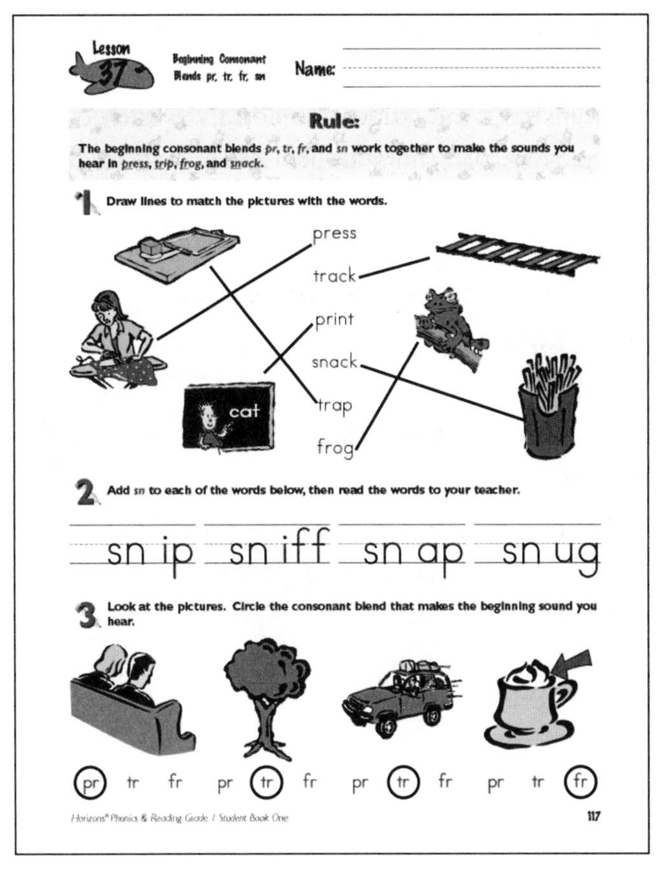

Lesson 37 Beginning Consonant Blends pr, tr, fr, sn Name:

Rule:

The beginning consonant blends *pr*, *tr*, *fr*, and *sn* work together to make the sounds you hear in *press*, *trip*, *frog*, and *snack*.

1 **Draw lines to match the pictures with the words.**

press
track
print
snack
trap
frog

2 **Add *sn* to each of the words below, then read the words to your teacher.**

sn ip sn iff sn ap sn ug

3 **Look at the pictures. Circle the consonant blend that makes the beginning sound you hear.**

pr tr fr pr tr fr pr tr fr pr tr fr

Horizons® Phonics & Reading Grade 1 Student Book One 117

Activity 2. Discuss the consonant blend rule for **sn**, and have the student think of additional examples. Instruct the student to add **sn** to each of the words and read them aloud.

Words: **snip, sniff, snap, snug**

Activity 3. Review each of the pictures, and have the student circle the correct beginning consonant blend underneath each picture.

Pictures: **pray, tree, trip, froth**

Activity 4. Discuss the consonant blend rule for **fr**, and have the student think of additional examples. Instruct the student to add **fr** to each of the words and read them aloud. Remind the student that one of the words (Frank) is a proper name and needs to be capitalized.

Words: **froth, frog, Frank, fresh**

Activity 5. Identify the pictures with the student, and instruct the student to add the correct beginning consonant blend to the word underneath the picture.

Pictures: **snack, press, track, frost**
snip, trap, frog, print

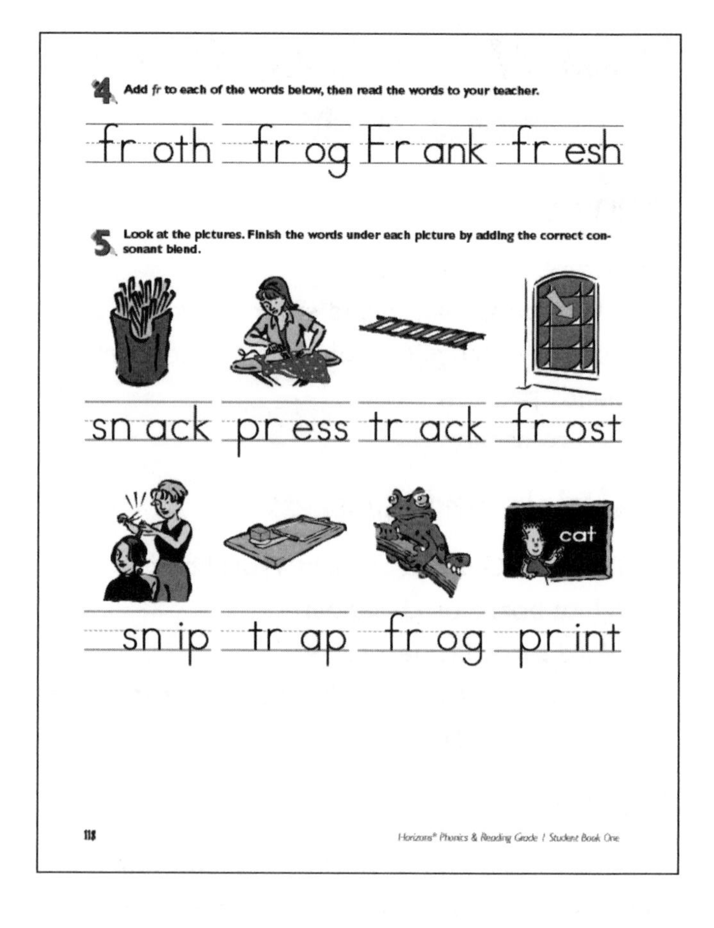
4. Add *fr* to each of the words below, then read the words to your teacher.

fr oth fr og Fr ank fr esh

5. Look at the pictures. Finish the words under each picture by adding the correct consonant blend.

sn ack pr ess tr ack fr ost

sn ip tr ap fr og pr int

Horizons® Phonics & Reading Grade 1 Student Book One

Lesson 38 - Contractions with Will & Not

Overview:

- Word/contraction match
- Print contractions to match words
- Sentence completion using contractions

Materials and Supplies:

- Teacher's Guide & Student Workbook
- White board or chalkboard
- Word cards (as necessary)
- Story: *Jim Didn't Want to Go*

Teaching Tips:

Discuss how contractions are formed. Review the rule, and use the white board or chalkboard to demonstrate the formation of a contraction.

Activity 1. Have the student read all of the words in the activity and draw lines to match the contractions with the phrases from which they are made.

Words: **we'll/we will**
they'll/they will
you'll/you will
he'll/he will
she'll/she will
I'll/I will

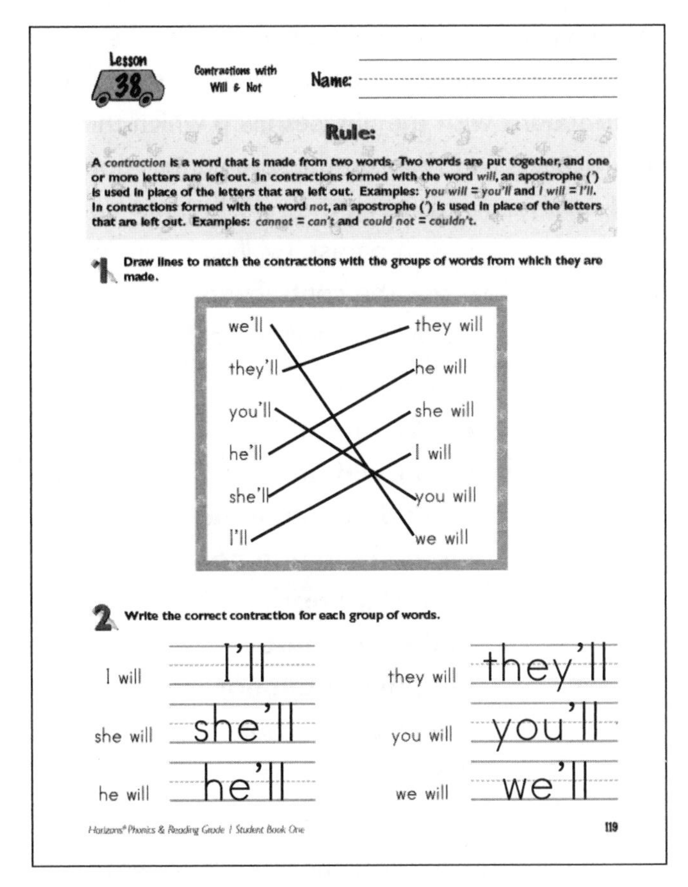

Lesson 38 — Contractions with Will & Not — Name:

Rule:

A *contraction* is a word that is made from two words. Two words are put together, and one or more letters are left out. In contractions formed with the word *will*, an apostrophe (') is used in place of the letters that are left out. Examples: *you will* = *you'll* and *I will* = *I'll*. In contractions formed with the word *not*, an apostrophe (') is used in place of the letters that are left out. Examples: *cannot* = *can't* and *could not* = *couldn't*.

1. Draw lines to match the contractions with the groups of words from which they are made.

we'll	they will
they'll	he will
you'll	she will
he'll	I will
she'll	you will
I'll	we will

2. Write the correct contraction for each group of words.

I will	I'll	they will	they'll
she will	she'll	you will	you'll
he will	he'll	we will	we'll

Horizons® Phonics & Reading Grade 1 Student Book One 119

Activity 2. Have the student read each of the phrases and write the correct contraction for each phrase.

Words: **I'll, she'll, he'll, they'll, you'll, we'll**

Activity 3. Have the student read all of the words in the activity and draw lines to match the contractions with the phrases from which they are made. NOTE: Explain that the contraction for **will not** seems to break the rule. It came from an old-fashioned English phrase (*woll not*) that we no longer use; however, the contraction that was derived from this phrase (*won't*) is still used.

Words:
- **don't/do not**
- **can't/cannot**
- **won't/will not** *(see NOTE, above)*
- **shouldn't/should not**
- **wouldn't/would not**
- **didn't/did not**
- **hadn't/had not**
- **couldn't/could not**
- **doesn't/does not**
- **wasn't/was not**

Activity 4. Help the student read the sentences and the phrases. Instruct the student to write the correct contraction of the phrase.

Sentences:

1. **Jim doesn't want to go to the party.**
2. **He is afraid that he won't know anyone.**
3. **Jim's mom says that he shouldn't worry.**
4. **He still didn't want to go.**

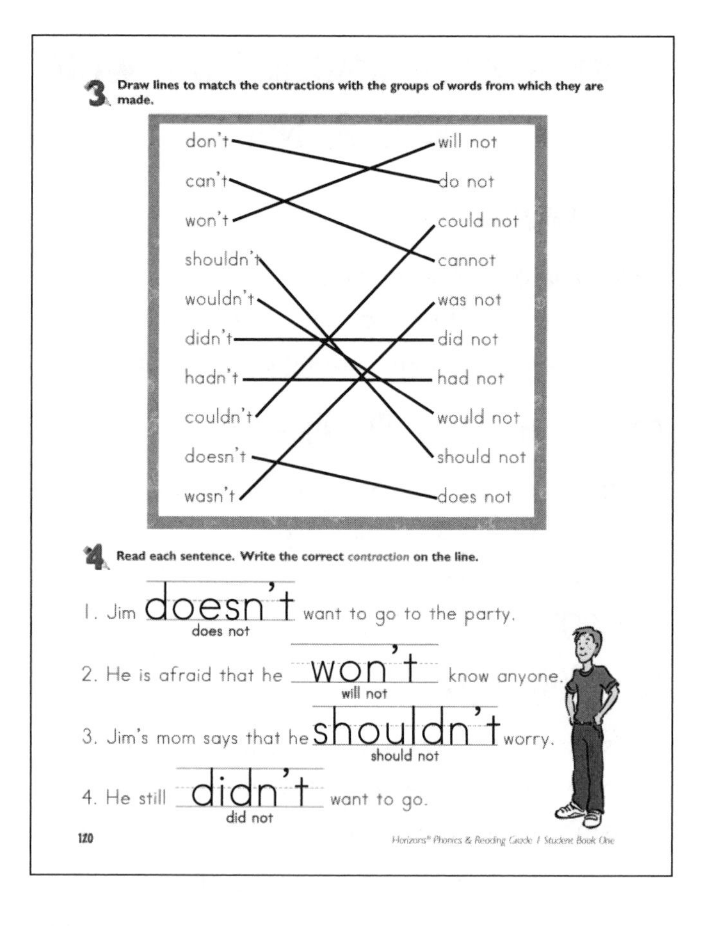

3 Draw lines to match the contractions with the groups of words from which they are made.

don't	will not
can't	do not
won't	could not
shouldn't	cannot
wouldn't	was not
didn't	did not
hadn't	had not
couldn't	would not
doesn't	should not
wasn't	does not

4 Read each sentence. Write the correct contraction on the line.

1. Jim doesn't want to go to the party. (does not)
2. He is afraid that he won't know anyone. (will not)
3. Jim's mom says that he shouldn't worry. (should not)
4. He still didn't want to go. (did not)

120 Horizons® Phonics & Reading Grade 1 Student Book One

Lesson 39 - Ending Consonant Blends lk, lt, lf, ft

Overview:

- Auditory recognition of consonant blends **lk, lt, lf, ft**
- Word completion
- Rhyming words
- Write correct words to answer riddles

Materials and Supplies:

- Teacher's Guide & Student Workbook
- White board or chalkboard
- Word cards (as necessary)
- Phonics rule flashcards in **Teacher Resources**
- Story: *The Fair*

Teaching Tips:

Review the consonant blend rule for **lk, lt, lf, ft.** Use the white board or chalkboard to illustrate. Ask the student for examples. Assist the student as needed in identifying the pictures and words in the lesson.

Activity 1. Review the pictures, and instruct the student to listen as you say the name of each picture. Have the student circle the ending consonant blend he hears.

Pictures: **wilt, milk, lift, elk**
sift, melt, shelf, malt

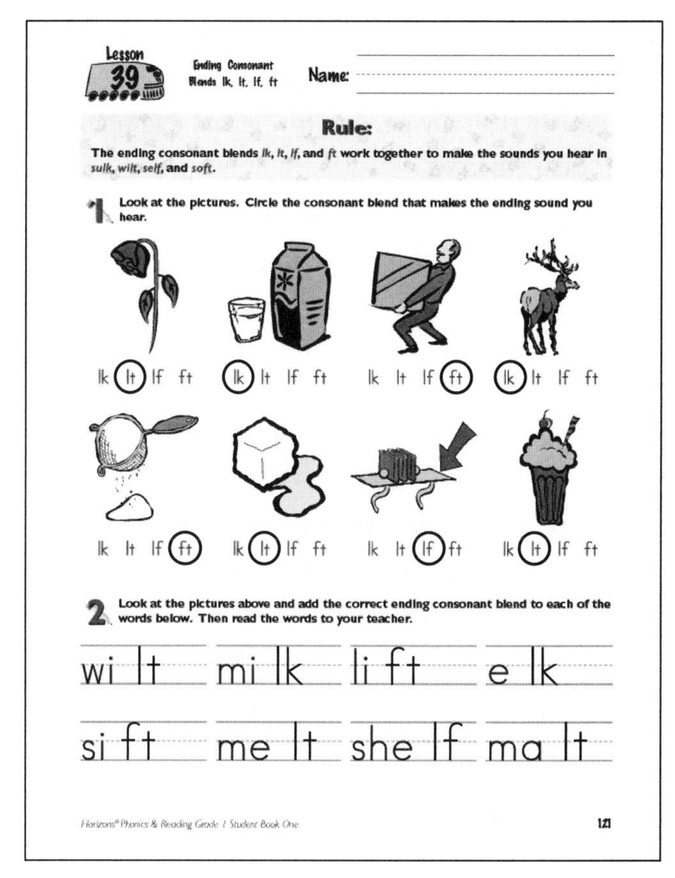

Lesson 39 Ending Consonant Blends lk, lt, lf, ft Name:

Rule:

The ending consonant blends *lk, lt, lf,* and *ft* work together to make the sounds you hear in *sulk, wilt, self,* and *soft.*

1 Look at the pictures. Circle the consonant blend that makes the ending sound you hear.

lk lt lf ft | lk lt lf ft | lk lt lf ft | lk lt lf ft

lk lt lf ft | lk lt lf ft | lk lt lf ft | lk lt lf ft

2 Look at the pictures above and add the correct ending consonant blend to each of the words below. Then read the words to your teacher.

wilt milk lift elk

sift melt shelf malt

Horizons Phonics & Reading Grade 1 Student Book One 121

Activity 2. The words in this activity correspond to the pictures in Activity 1. The student will complete the words by adding the correct ending consonant blends that he circled in Activity 1. Have the student read the words aloud.

Words: **wilt, milk, lift, elk**
sift, melt, shelf, malt

Activity 3. Help the student read the words in the activity. The student will draw lines to match the words that rhyme. Ask for verbal examples of additional rhyming words.

Rhyming words: **shelf/self**
melt/belt
bolt/molt
lift/gift
wilt/tilt
soft/loft
milk/silk

Activity 4. Have the student read the words in the list, and assist the student as necessary in reading the riddles. Instruct the student to write the correct answer to each riddle on the line.

Words: **1. melt** **2. sift** **3. silk** **4. salt** **5. elk** **6. gift**

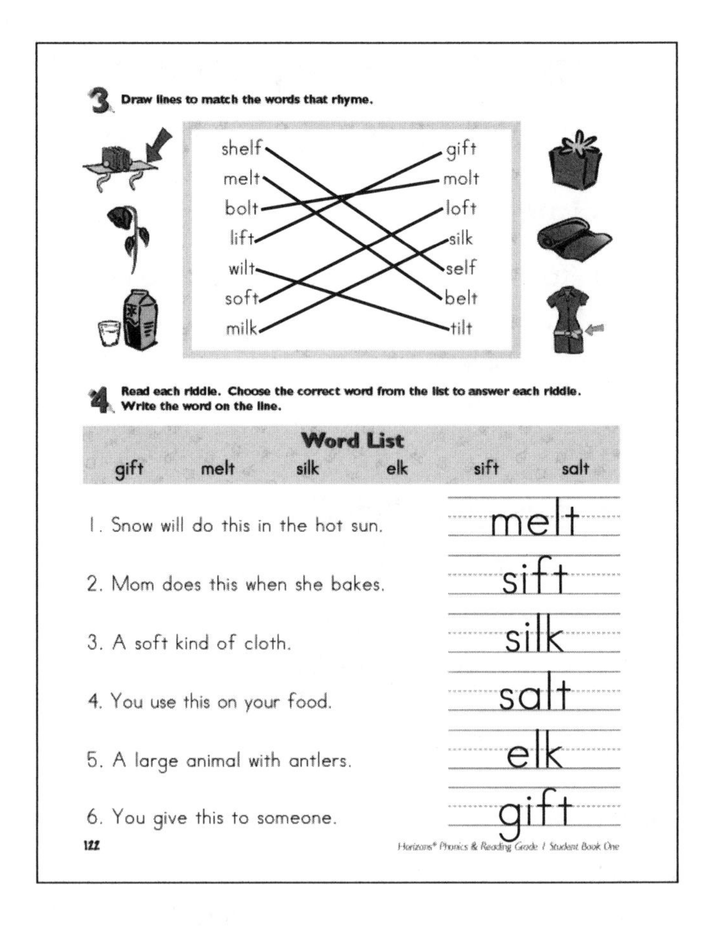

3 Draw lines to match the words that rhyme.

shelf	gift
melt	molt
bolt	loft
lift	silk
wilt	self
soft	belt
milk	tilt

4 Read each riddle. Choose the correct word from the list to answer each riddle. Write the word on the line.

Word List

gift melt silk elk sift salt

1. Snow will do this in the hot sun. melt
2. Mom does this when she bakes. sift
3. A soft kind of cloth. silk
4. You use this on your food. salt
5. A large animal with antlers. elk
6. You give this to someone. gift

122 Horizons® Phonics & Reading Grade 1 Student Book One

Lesson 40 - Review: Contractions with Will & Not

Overview:

- Choose contractions from the story
- Sentence completion
- Write two words for each contraction

Materials and Supplies:

- Teacher's Guide & Student Workbook
- White board or chalkboard
- Word cards (as necessary)
- Phonics rule flashcards in **Teacher Resources**
- Story: *Mike Won't Come In*

Teaching Tips:

Review the contractions from Lesson 38. Have the student write examples from both lessons on the chalkboard or white board. Review word cards as necessary.

Activity 1. Help the student read the story as necessary. The student will circle the contractions in the story and write the two words for each contraction on the lines.

Contractions:

1. **was not**
2. **did not**
3. **would not**
4. **we will**
5. **I will**

Lesson 40 — Review: Contractions with Will & Not — Name:

Rule Review:

A *contraction* is a word that is made from two words. Two words are put together, and one or more letters are left out. An apostrophe (') is used in place of the letters that are left out.

1. Read the story. Circle each of the contractions in the story. On the lines below the story write the *two words* for each contraction you circled.

Spot was a little dog. He was white with black spots. He wasn't a mean dog. He liked everyone.

His owner, Mark, went out to play one day. Mark took Spot with him. It was a very nice day. They played fetch with a ball. Mark didn't want to come in when his mom called him. But Mark knew that if he disobeyed his mother, he wouldn't get to play outside the next day. Mark took Spot and went inside.

Spot thought to himself, "We'll go out and play tomorrow. I'll have fun with Mark." And he did!

1. was not
2. did not
3. would not
4. we will
5. I will

Activity 2. Help the student read the sentences and the phrases underneath. Instruct the student to write the correct contraction for the phrase on the line.

Sentences:

1. **You shouldn't do mean things.**
2. **I wouldn't like that.**
3. **We won't be there.**
4. **I'll be your friend.**

Activity 3. Have the student write the two words that make up each contraction on the lines below.

Words:

1. **will not**
2. **should not**
3. **he will**
4. **could not**
5. **had not**
6. **we will**
7. **they will**
8. **I will**
9. **would not**
10. **cannot**

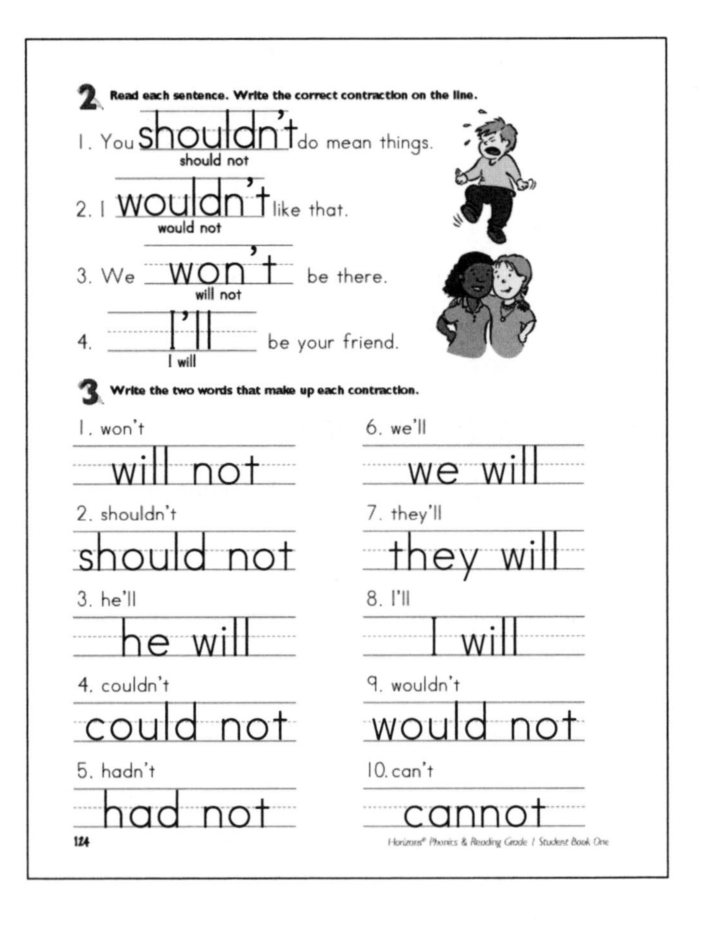

2 Read each sentence. Write the correct contraction on the line.

1. You shouldn't do mean things. (should not)
2. I wouldn't like that. (would not)
3. We won't be there. (will not)
4. I'll be your friend. (I will)

3 Write the two words that make up each contraction.

1. won't — will not
2. shouldn't — should not
3. he'll — he will
4. couldn't — could not
5. hadn't — had not
6. we'll — we will
7. they'll — they will
8. I'll — I will
9. wouldn't — would not
10. can't — cannot

124 Horizons® Phonics & Reading Grade 1 Student Book One

Test 4

Lessons 31-40

Instructions:

Review the definitions of consonant blends and consonant digraphs. Review the sounds of **x** at the beginning and the end of a word. Review the definition of a contraction. Have the student give some examples of contractions. Read through the test with the student. Identify the pictures, and help the student with any words that he/she is still unsure of. The teacher should be available to answer any questions that the student may have during the test.

Activity 1. Identify the pictures with the student, and make sure he understands the instructions.

Words:
1. **wrench**
2. **scene**
3. **whine**
4. **wheat**
5. **scared**
6. **wreck**

Activity 2. Read the words in the list and the sentences with the student.

Sentences:
1. **Jim put his toys in a box.**
2. **He saw a fox in the woods.**
3. **John likes to play the xylophone.**
4. **He chops wood with an ax.**

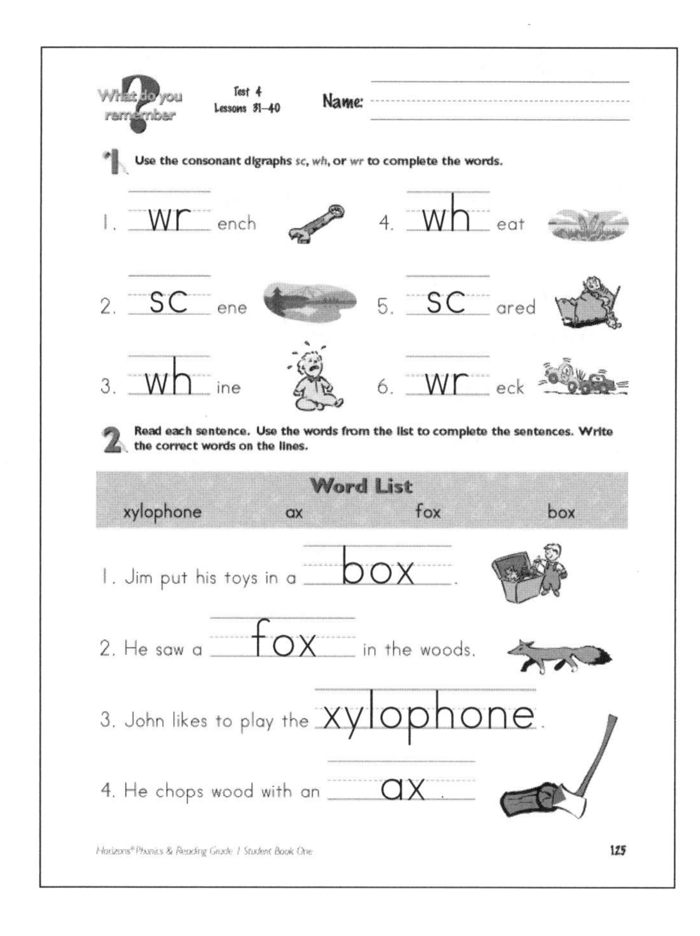

What do you remember

Test 4
Lessons 31–40

Name:

1. Use the consonant digraphs *sc*, *wh*, or *wr* to complete the words.

1. wr ench
2. sc ene
3. wh ine
4. wh eat
5. sc ared
6. wr eck

2. Read each sentence. Use the words from the list to complete the sentences. Write the correct words on the lines.

Word List			
xylophone	ax	fox	box

1. Jim put his toys in a box.
2. He saw a fox in the woods.
3. John likes to play the xylophone.
4. He chops wood with an ax.

Horizons® Phonics & Reading Grade 1 Student Book One 125

Activity 3. Review the instructions and the contractions with the student.

Words: **did not** **you will**
are not **cannot**
would not **will not**

Activity 4. Identify the pictures and review the instructions with the student.

Pictures: **comb, shelf, clock, bath**
press, scene, wrench, snip

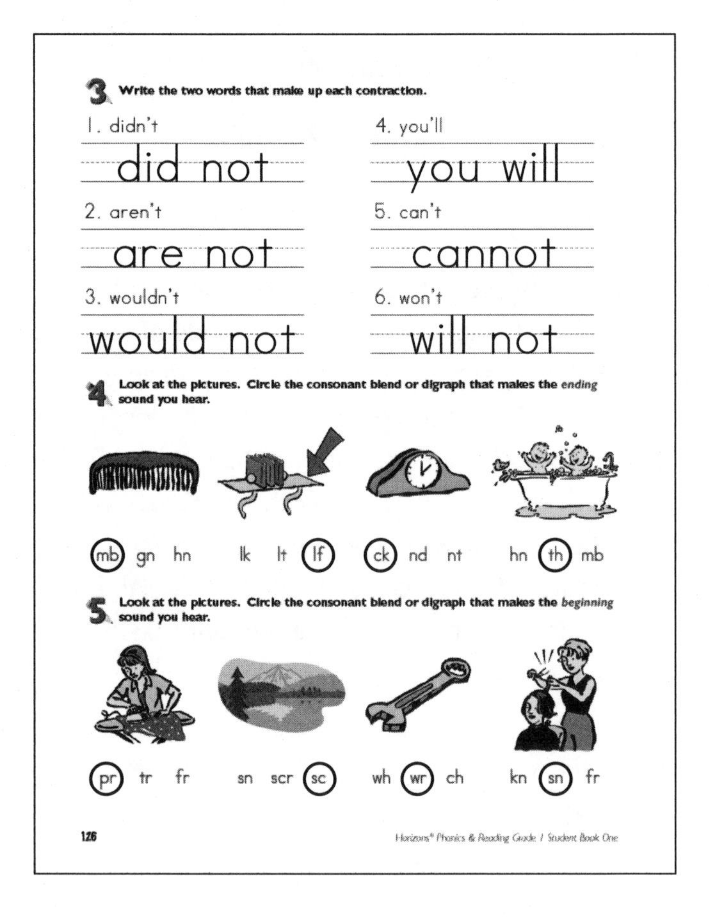

3 Write the two words that make up each contraction.

1. didn't — did not
2. aren't — are not
3. wouldn't — would not
4. you'll — you will
5. can't — cannot
6. won't — will not

4 Look at the pictures. Circle the consonant blend or digraph that makes the *ending* sound you hear.

(mb) gn hn | lk lt (lf) | (ck) nd nt | hn (th) mb

5 Look at the pictures. Circle the consonant blend or digraph that makes the *beginning* sound you hear.

(pr) tr fr | sn scr (sc) | wh (wr) ch | kn (sn) fr

126 Horizons® Phonics & Reading Grade 1 Student Book One

Lesson 41 - Contractions with Have

Overview:

- Write contractions for phrases
- Sentence completion
- Choose contractions from story

Materials and Supplies:

- Teacher's Guide & Student Workbook
- White board or chalkboard
- Word cards (as necessary)
- Phonics rule flashcards in **Teacher Resources**
- Story: *They've Gone Away*

Teaching Tips:

Assist the student as needed in reading the words and identifying the pictures in the lesson. Discuss the rule for contractions with **have**. Use the white board or chalkboard to illustrate.

Activity 1. Instruct the student to read the phrases and write the correct contraction for each set of words.

Words: **I've, we've, they've, you've**

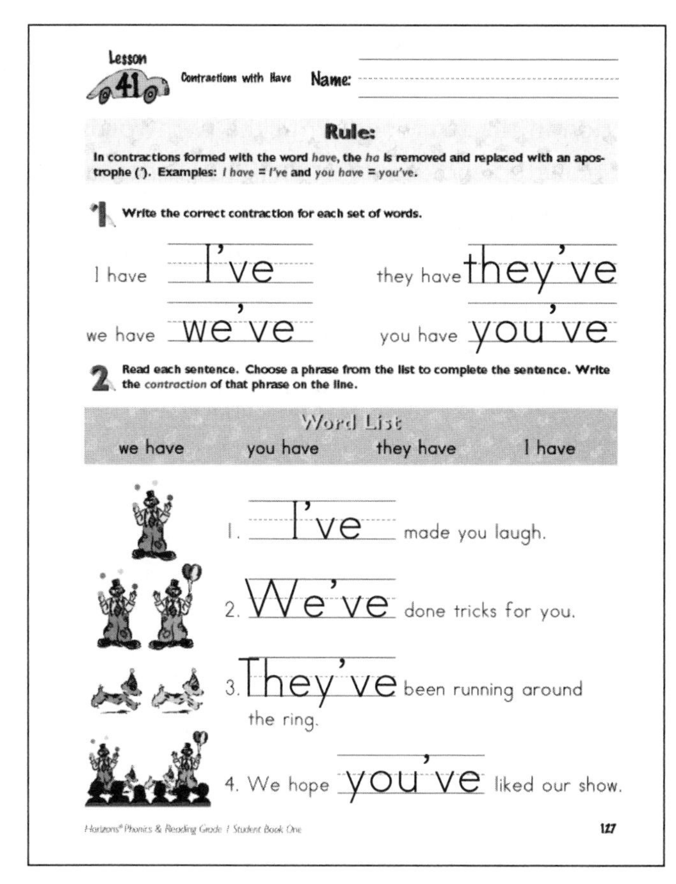

Lesson 41 Contractions with Have Name:

Rule:

In contractions formed with the word *have*, the *ha* is removed and replaced with an apostrophe ('). Examples: *I have* = *I've* and *you have* = *you've*.

1 Write the correct contraction for each set of words.

I have I've they have they've

we have we've you have you've

2 Read each sentence. Choose a phrase from the list to complete the sentence. Write the *contraction* of that phrase on the line.

Word List

we have you have they have I have

1. I've made you laugh.
2. We've done tricks for you.
3. They've been running around the ring.
4. We hope you've liked our show.

Horizons® Phonics & Reading Grade 1 Student Book One 127

Activity 2. Have the student read the phrases in the word list. NOTE: Since the pictures in this activity are clues to the correct answers, you will need to discuss the first two pictures in particular. The picture of one clown refers to the singular pronoun "I." The picture of two clowns refers to the plural pronoun "we." Instruct the student to write the contraction for the correct phrase on the line.

Sentences:

1. **I've made you laugh.**
2. **We've done tricks for you.**
3. **They've been running around the ring.**
4. **We hope you've liked our show.**

Activity 3. Assist the student as needed in reading the story. The student will underline each contraction in the story and write the two words that make up each contraction. (NOTE: capitalization of items 1, 2 and 4 is at your discretion. The emphasis is on the words that make up the contractions. You may wish to point out that since these items appear at the beginning of the sentence, they should be capitalized.)

Words:

1. **we have**
2. **they have**
3. **I have**
4. **you have**

3 **Read the story. Underline the contractions. On the lines below the story, write the** *two words* **that make up each contraction.**

We've been planning to have a party. Mom and Dad have been helping us. They've sent out the invitations. I've been planning the games. My sister said, "You've done a good job!"

1. we have
2. they have
3. I have
4. you have

123 Horizons® Phonics & Reading Grade 1 Student Book One

Lesson 42 - Contractions with Is, R-Controlled Vowels ar, or

Overview:

- Show examples of each contraction
- Change sets of words into correct contractions
- Write two words that mean the same as each contraction
- Sentence completion
- Add r-controlled vowels **ar** and **or** to words

Materials and Supplies:

- Teacher's Guide & Student Workbook
- White board or chalkboard
- Word cards (as necessary)
- Phonics rule flashcards in **Teacher Resources**
- Story: *It's a Nice Day*

Teaching Tips:

Review the rules for contractions with is and for the r-controlled vowels **ar** and **or**. Use the white board or chalkboard as necessary to demonstrate. Ask the student for additional examples of **ar** and **or** words. Assist the student as necessary in reading the words and identifying the pictures in the lesson.

Activity 1. Have the student read the phrases and write the contraction for each phrase in the space provided.

Lesson 42 Contractions with Is, R-Controlled Vowels ar, or Name:

Rule:

In contractions formed with the word *is*, the *i* is removed and replaced with an apostrophe ('). Examples: *he is* = *he's* and *she is* = *she's*.

1. Write the contraction for each set of words.

he is	she is	it is
he's	she's	it's

2. Read each sentence. Use the contractions from the list to complete each sentence.

It's She's He's

1. She's going to wear a dress to school.
2. He's going to wear his new pants.
3. It's going to be a good day at school.

Horizons® Phonics & Reading Grade 1 Student Book One 129

Activity 2. Have the student read the sentences and complete them using the correct contraction.

Sentences:

1. **She's going to wear a dress to school.**
2. **He's going to wear his new pants.**
3. **It's going to be a good day at school.**

Activity 3. Have the student read the contractions and write in the space provided the two words that make up each contraction.

Words: **she is, it is, he is**

Activity 4. Identify the pictures with the student, and have the student add the correct r-controlled vowel to the words below the pictures. Have the student read the words aloud.

Pictures: **star, short, farm, stork**

Activity 5. Instruct the student to add **ar** to each of the words and read them aloud.

Words: **cart, march, park, dart**

Activity 6. Instruct the student to add **or** to each of the words and read them aloud.

Words: **porch, born, corn, storm**

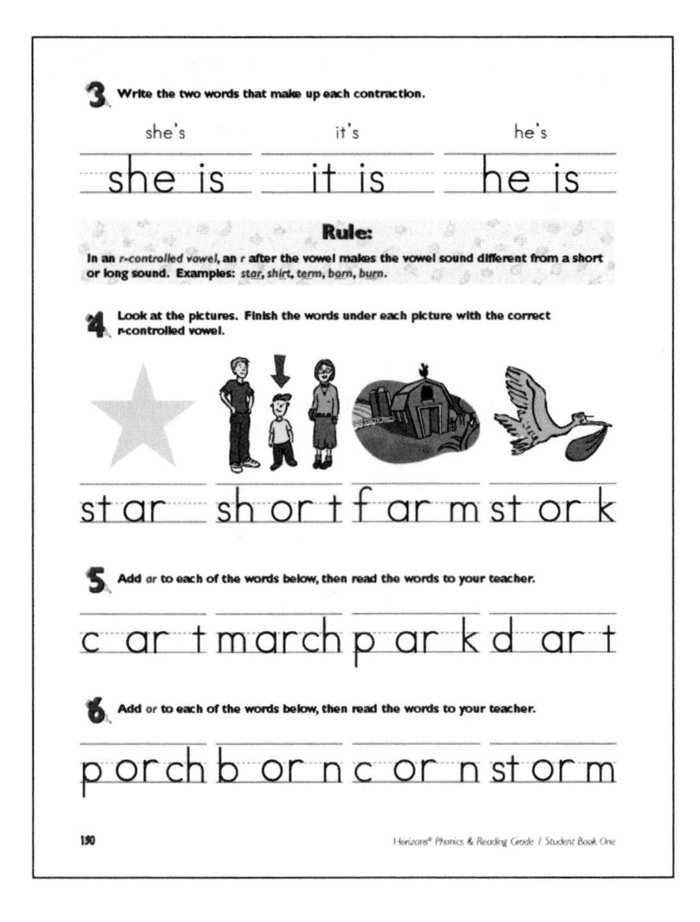

3. Write the two words that make up each contraction.

she's — she is
it's — it is
he's — he is

Rule:
In an *r-controlled vowel*, an *r* after the vowel makes the vowel sound different from a short or long sound. Examples: *star, shirt, term, born, burn.*

4. Look at the pictures. Finish the words under each picture with the correct r-controlled vowel.

star short farm stork

5. Add *ar* to each of the words below, then read the words to your teacher.

cart march park dart

6. Add *or* to each of the words below, then read the words to your teacher.

porch born corn storm

190 Horizons® Phonics & Reading Grade 1 Student Book One

Lesson 43 - Review: Contractions with Have & Is

Overview:

- Write two words that make up each contraction
- Write a story using contractions from list
- Sentence completion

Materials and Supplies:

- Teacher's Guide & Student Workbook
- White board or chalkboard
- Word cards (as necessary)
- Phonics rule flashcards in **Teacher Resources**
- Story: *She's a Good Dog*

Teaching Tips:

Review the rules on contractions from Lessons 41 and 42. If desired, use the chalkboard or white board to illustrate how contractions are made.

Activity 1. Have the student read the contractions and write the two words which make up each contraction.

Words: **you have, she is, we have**
it is, he is, I have

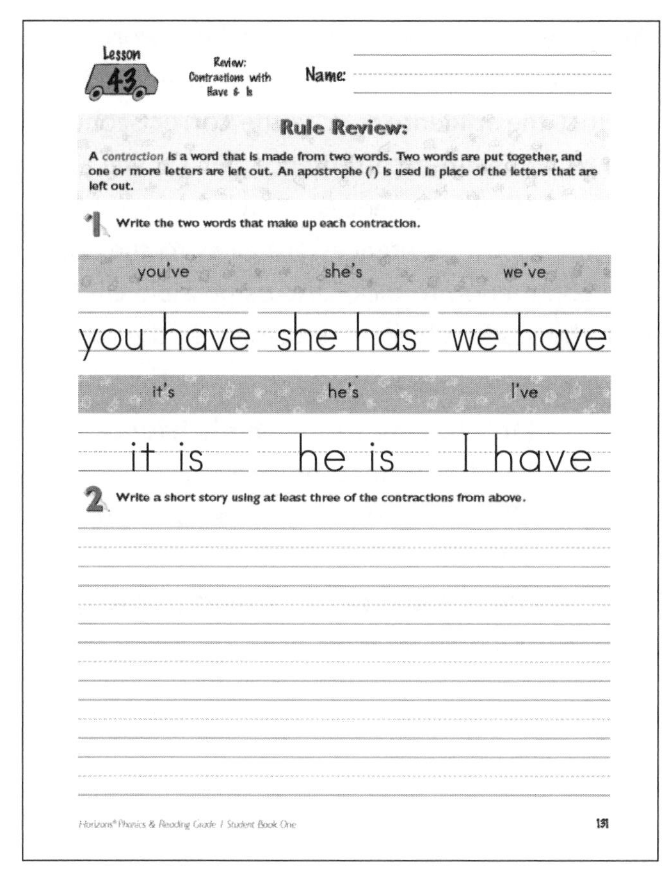

Lesson 43 Review: Contractions with Have & Is Name:

Rule Review:

A *contraction* is a word that is made from two words. Two words are put together, and one or more letters are left out. An apostrophe (') is used in place of the letters that are left out.

1. Write the two words that make up each contraction.

you've she's we've

you have she has we have

it's he's I've

it is he is I have

2. Write a short story using at least three of the contractions from above.

Horizons® Phonics & Reading Grade 1 Student Book One 131

Activity 2. The student will write a short story, using at least three of the contractions from Activity 1. Help the student with ideas and spelling as needed. Remind the student about capitalization and punctuation.

Activity 3. Have the student read the words in the list and the sentences, assisting as needed. Instruct the student to write the correct contraction to complete each sentence. NOTE: The pictures beside the sentences, as well as the other pronouns in the sentences, are clues to the correct contraction to pick. Discuss possible choices with the student before he completes the activity.

Sentences:

1. **He's having fun with his friend.**
2. **I've been here before.**
3. **We've done our homework for school.**
4. **She's walking her friend home.**
5. **It's a rainy day.**

3 Read each sentence. Use the contractions from the list to complete each sentence. Use each contraction only once.

Word List

We've It's She's He's I've

1. He's having fun with his friend.
2. I've been here before.
3. We've done our homework for school.
4. She's walking her friend home.
5. It's a rainy day.

192

Horizons Phonics & Reading Grade 1 Student Book One

Lesson 44 - Contractions with Am & Us

Overview:

- Match contractions to pictures
- Write the two words that make up each contraction
- Sentence completion

Materials and Supplies:

- Teacher's Guide & Student Workbook
- White board or chalkboard
- Word cards (as necessary)
- Phonics rule flashcards in **Teacher Resources**
- Story: *I'm Playing*

Teaching Tips:

Review the rule for contractions with **am** and **us**. Illustrate on the chalkboard or white board, if desired. Review the pictures and the words in the lesson with the student.

Activity 1. Have the student identify the pictures and draw a line to match the pictures with the sentences.

Pictures: **I'm eating.**
Let's ride.
Let's play.
I'm running.

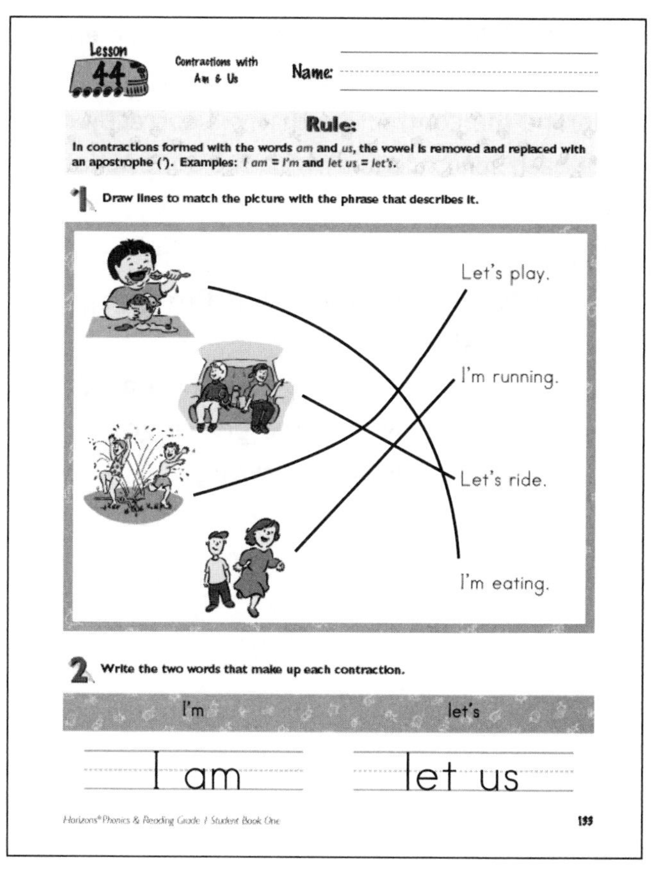

Lesson 44

Contractions with Am & Us

Name:

Rule:

In contractions formed with the words *am* and *us*, the vowel is removed and replaced with an apostrophe ('). Examples: *I am* = *I'm* and *let us* = *let's*.

1 Draw lines to match the picture with the phrase that describes it.

Let's play.
I'm running.
Let's ride.
I'm eating.

2 Write the two words that make up each contraction.

I'm — I am
let's — let us

Horizons® Phonics & Reading Grade 1 Student Book One 133

Activity 2. Have the student read the words and write the phrases that make up each contraction.

Words: **I am, let us**

Activity 3. Help the student read the sentences and the word choices. Instruct the student to underline the contraction that will correctly complete each sentence and write the contraction on the line.

Sentences:

1. **My mom knows that I'm going outside.**
2. **She said, "Let's go to the park."**
3. **I'm happy that we get to go.**
4. **Let's play on the swings.**

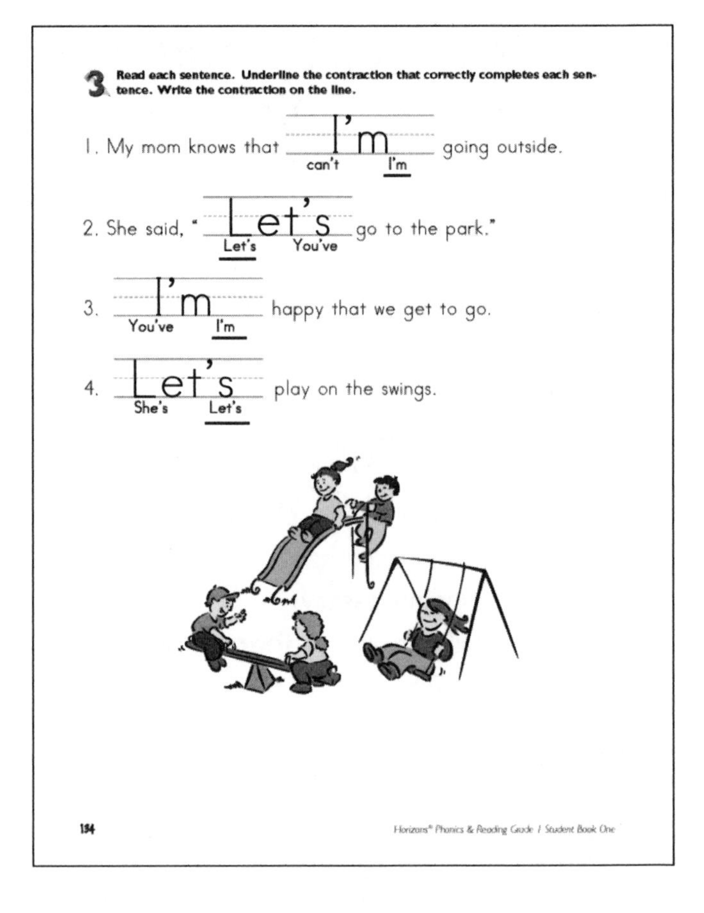

3 **Read each sentence. Underline the contraction that correctly completes each sentence. Write the contraction on the line.**

1. My mom knows that I'm going outside.
   can't <u>I'm</u>
2. She said, "Let's go to the park."
   <u>Let's</u> You've
3. I'm happy that we get to go.
   You've <u>I'm</u>
4. Let's play on the swings.
   She's <u>Let's</u>

154 Horizons® Phonics & Reading Grade 1 Student Book One

Lesson 45 - Contractions with Are, Consonant Blends spr, spl

Overview:

- Matching pictures to sentences
- Write two words that make up each contraction
- Sentence completion
- Adding consonant blends **spr**, **spl** to words

Materials and Supplies:

- Teacher's Guide & Student Workbook
- White board or chalkboard
- Word cards (as necessary)
- Phonics rule flashcards in **Teacher Resources**
- Story: *The Spring Dress*

Teaching Tips:

Review the rules regarding contractions with **are** and consonant blends **spr** and **spl**. Illustrate examples on the chalkboard or white board if desired. Ask the student for examples of words beginning with **spl** and **spr**.

Activity 1. Have the student identify the pictures and read the sentences. Tell the student to draw a line to match the pictures with the sentences.

Pictures: **You're my best friend.**
They're running.
They're climbing.
We're having a party.

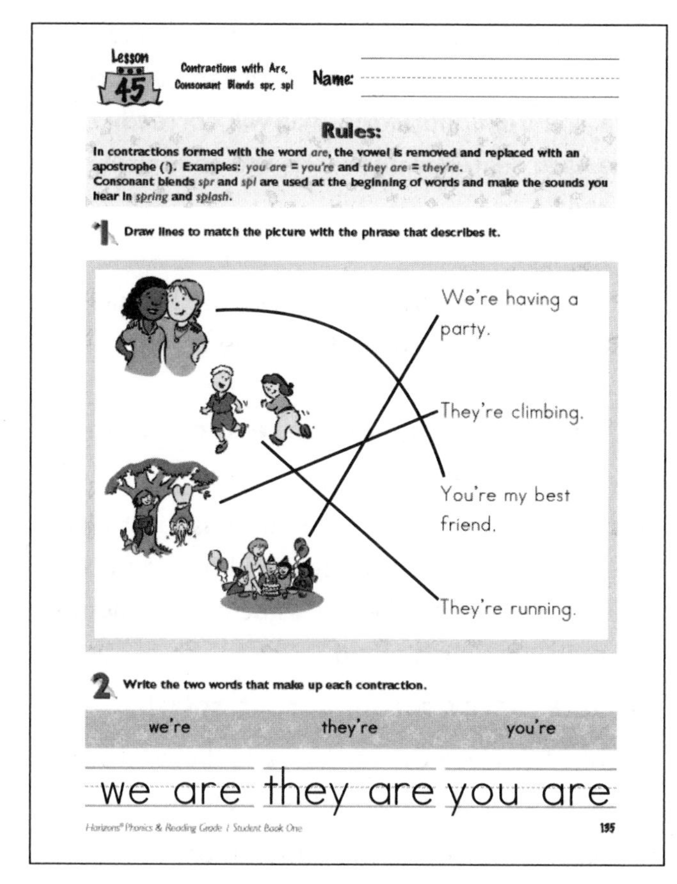

Lesson 45 Contractions with Are, Consonant Blends spr, spl Name:

Rules:

In contractions formed with the word *are*, the vowel is removed and replaced with an apostrophe ('). Examples: *you are* = *you're* and *they are* = *they're*.
Consonant blends *spr* and *spl* are used at the beginning of words and make the sounds you hear in *spring* and *splash*.

1. Draw lines to match the picture with the phrase that describes it.

2. Write the two words that make up each contraction.

we're they're you're

we are they are you are

Horizons® Phonics & Reading Grade 1 Student Book One 195

Activity 2. Have the student read the words and write the phrases that make up each contraction.

Words: **we are, they are, you are**

Activity 3. Help the student read the sentences and the word choices. Instruct the student to underline the contraction that will correctly complete each sentence and write the contraction on the line.

Sentences:

1. **We're having a picnic in the park.**
2. **They're going to come to the picnic.**
3. **You're going to have a lot of fun in the park.**

Activity 4. Review the rule for consonant blends **spl** and **spr**. Have the student add the correct consonant blend to the words below the pictures and read the words aloud.

Pictures: **spray, spring, sprout, splash**

Activity 5. Have the student add the consonant blend **spl** to the words and read the words aloud.

Pictures: **splash, split, splint, splat**

3 **Read each sentence. Underline the contraction that correctly completes each sentence. Write the contraction on the line.**

1. We're having a picnic in the park.
   Let's We're
2. They're going to come to the picnic.
   They're They'll
3. You're going to have a lot of fun in the park.
   I'll You're

4 **Look at the pictures. Finish the words under each picture with the consonant blend** ***spl*** **or** ***spr*****.**

spray spring sprout splash

5 **Add** ***spl*** **to each of the words below, then read the words to your teacher.**

splash split splint splat

196 Horizons® Phonics & Reading Grade 1 Student Book One

Lesson 46 - Review: Contractions with Am, Are, & Us, Consonant Blend st

Overview:

- Story writing using contractions from a list
- Matching pictures to sentences
- Adding beginning and ending consonant blend **st** to words
- Auditory recognition of consonant blend **st**

Materials and Supplies:

- Teacher's Guide & Student Workbook
- White board or chalkboard
- Word cards (as necessary)
- Phonics rule flashcards in **Teacher Resources**
- Story: *Steph Didn't Stay*

Teaching Tips:

Review the rules from Lessons 44 and 45 about contractions. Discuss the rule about consonant blend **st**. Emphasize that this consonant blend can go at the beginning or end of a word. Ask the student to think of words with the beginning and ending consonant blend **st**.

Activity 1. Have the student read the words in the list and write three sentences, using as many of the contractions as possible.

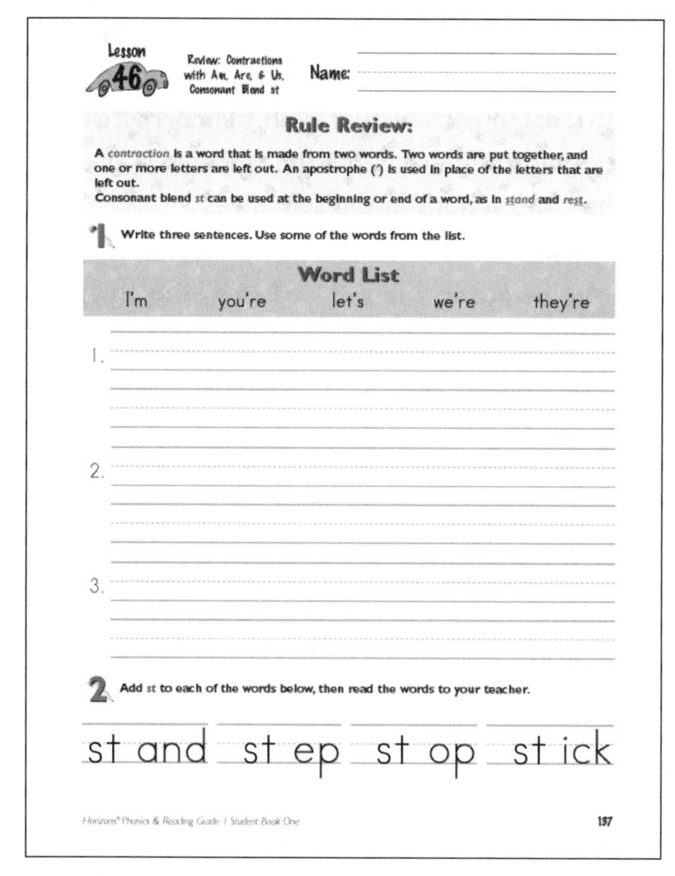

Lesson 46 Review: Contractions with Am, Are, & Us, Consonant Blend st Name:

Rule Review:

A *contraction* is a word that is made from two words. Two words are put together, and one or more letters are left out. An apostrophe (') is used in place of the letters that are left out.
Consonant blend *st* can be used at the beginning or end of a word, as in *stand* and *rest*.

1 Write three sentences. Use some of the words from the list.

Word List

I'm you're let's we're they're

1.

2.

3.

2 Add st to each of the words below, then read the words to your teacher.

st and st ep st op st ick

Horizons® Phonics & Reading Grade 1 Student Book One 137

Activity 2. Have the student add **st** to the beginning of the words and read them aloud. Ask the student for additional examples of **st** words.

Words: **stand, step, stop, stick**

Activity 3. Review the pictures and the sentences with the student. Have the student draw a line to match each picture with the correct sentence that describes it. Tell the student to circle all of the contractions in the sentences.

Pictures:

We're going for a drive.	**I'm going to hit a home run.**
Let's go to the park to play.	**You're a good dog.**
	They're playing tag.

Activity 4. Have the student add **st** to the ending of the words and read them aloud. Ask the student for additional examples of words that end in **st**.

Words: **cost, blast, best, fast**

Activity 5. Help the student to identify the pictures and circle the appropriate **st** to show whether the consonant blend appears at the beginning or the end of the word.

Pictures: **rest, stairs, nest, fist**

Lesson 47 - More Contractions with Is, Consonant Blends tw, sw

Overview:

- Write two words that make up each contraction
- Complete sentences by using contractions
- Sentence writing using contractions
- Adding consonant blend **tw, sw** to words
- Auditory recognition of consonant blends **tw, sw**

Materials and Supplies:

- Teacher's Guide & Student Workbook
- White board or chalkboard
- Word cards (as necessary)
- Story: *The Twins*

Teaching Tips:

Review the rules for contractions with **is** and for the consonant blends **tw** and **sw**. Have the student list as many examples as possible of words with **tw** and **sw** in them. Review the pictures and words in the lesson.

Activity 1. Instruct the student to read each of the contractions and write the two words that make up each contraction.

Words: **he is, they are, she is, that is, it is**

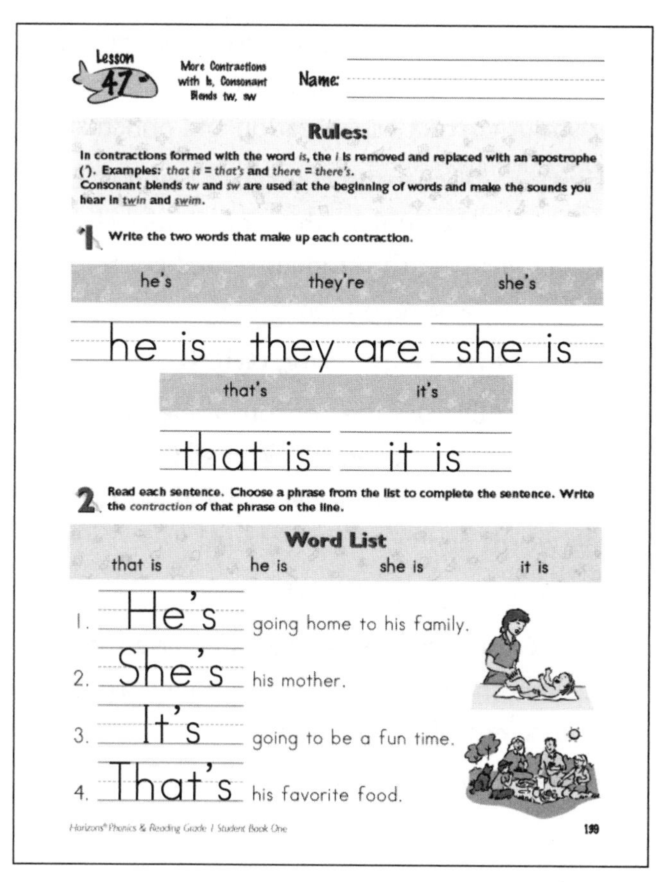

Lesson 47 More Contractions with Is, Consonant Blends tw, sw Name:

Rules:

In contractions formed with the word *is*, the *i* is removed and replaced with an apostrophe ('). Examples: *that is* = *that's* and *there* = *there's*.
Consonant blends *tw* and *sw* are used at the beginning of words and make the sounds you hear in *twin* and *swim*.

1 **Write the two words that make up each contraction.**

he's — he is
they're — they are
she's — she is
that's — that is
it's — it is

2 **Read each sentence. Choose a phrase from the list to complete the sentence. Write the *contraction* of that phrase on the line.**

Word List
that is he is she is it is

1. He's going home to his family.
2. She's his mother.
3. It's going to be a fun time.
4. That's his favorite food.

Horizons® Phonics & Reading Grade 1 Student Book One 199

Activity 2. Help the student read the words in the list and the sentences. Instruct the student to select the phrase that will correctly complete each sentence and write the contraction for that phrase on the line. Discuss possible choices with the student. Pronouns in some sentences will offer clues to the correct contraction.

Sentences:

1. **He's going home to his family.**
2. **She's his mother.**
3. **It's going to be a fun time.**
4. **That's his favorite food.**

Activity 3. Have the student write a sentence to go with each of the contractions. Remind the student about correct capitalization and punctuation.

Activity 4. Discuss the consonant blend rule for **tw**, and have the student think of additional examples. Instruct the student to add **tw** to each of the words and read them aloud.

Words: **twist, twins, twig, twitch**

Activity 5. Discuss the consonant blend rule for **sw**, and have the student think of additional examples. Instruct the student to add **sw** to each of the words and read them aloud.

Words: **swing, swell, swift, swept**

Activity 6. Discuss the pictures, and have the student circle the correct consonant blend as you say the names of the pictures.

Pictures: **twins, switch, swing, twig**

3 Write a sentence to go with each contraction.

1. that's
2. there's
3. he's

4 Add tw to each of the words below, then read the words to your teacher.

tw ist tw ins tw ig tw itch

5 Add sw to each of the words below, then read the words to your teacher.

sw ing sw ell sw ift sw ept

6 Look at the pictures. Circle the consonant blend that makes the beginning sound you hear.

sw (tw) (sw) tw (sw) tw sw (tw)

140 Horizons® Phonics & Reading Grade 1 Student Book One

Lesson 48 - Review: All Contractions

Overview:

- Sentence completion
- Match contractions with correct words
- Story completion

Materials and Supplies:

- Teacher's Guide & Student Workbook
- White board or chalkboard
- Word cards (as necessary)
- Phonics rule flashcards in **Teacher Resources**
- Story: *The Kitten Who Wouldn't Come Down*

Teaching Tips:

Go over the rules for contractions. Have the student write examples for each contraction on the chalkboard or white board. Review word cards as necessary.

Activity 1. Have the student read the sentences and the words in the list aloud. The student will use the contractions from the list to complete the sentences.

Sentences:

1. **We'll be sure that we say hello.**
2. **Don't go too far away.**
3. **I've been here for a long time.**
4. **That's all that there is.**

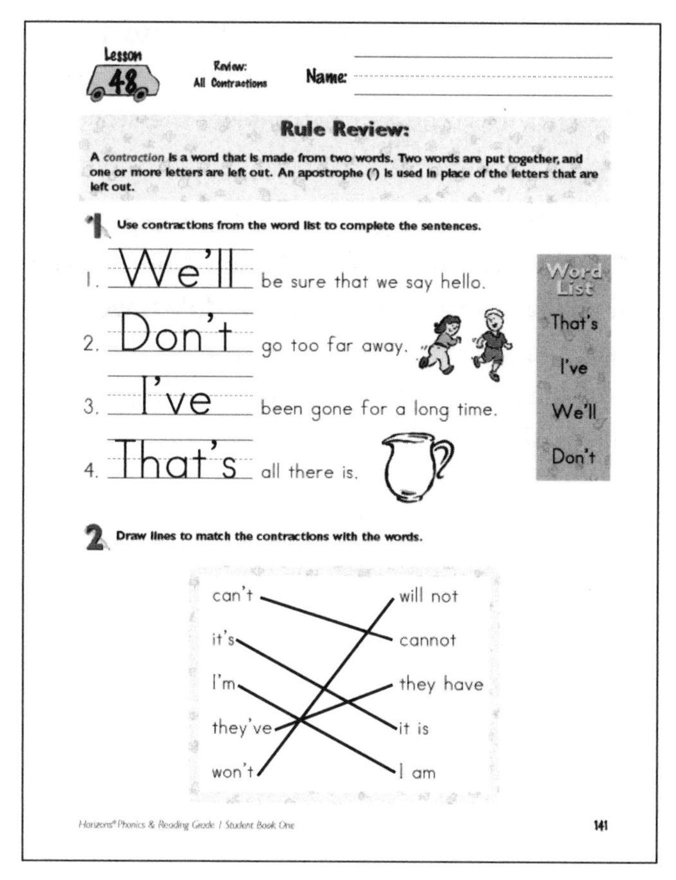

Lesson 48 Review: All Contractions

Name:

Rule Review:

A *contraction* is a word that is made from two words. Two words are put together, and one or more letters are left out. An apostrophe (') is used in place of the letters that are left out.

1 Use contractions from the word list to complete the sentences.

1. We'll be sure that we say hello.
2. Don't go too far away.
3. I've been gone for a long time.
4. That's all there is.

Word List: That's, I've, We'll, Don't

2 Draw lines to match the contractions with the words.

can't	will not
it's	cannot
I'm	they have
they've	it is
won't	I am

Horizons Phonics & Reading Grade 1 Student Book One 141

Activity 2. Have the student read the words aloud. The student will draw lines to match the contractions with the two words that make up each contraction.

Matching words:

can't/cannot
it's/it is
I'm/I am
they've/they have
won't/will not

Activity 3. Have the student read the story and the words in the list aloud. The student will use the words from the list to complete the story.

Story:

The kitten can't get down from the tree. She's sitting on a high branch. She doesn't want to climb down. They didn't have any trouble getting the kitten down. Aren't you glad the kitten has such caring friends?

3 Use contractions from the list to complete the story.
Word List
didn't can't she's doesn't aren't
The kitten can't get down from the tree.
She's sitting on a high branch.
She doesn't want to climb down. They
didn't have any trouble getting the kitten
down. Aren't you glad the kitten has such
caring friends?
142
Horizons® Phonics & Reading Grade 1 Student Book One

Lesson 49 - Review: Compound Words

Overview:

- Word/picture match
- Divide compound words into syllables
- Story completion

Materials and Supplies:

- Teacher's Guide & Student Workbook
- White board or chalkboard
- Word cards (as necessary)
- Phonics rule flashcards in **Teacher Resources**
- Story: *The Baseball Team*

Teaching Tips:

Review Lesson 13. Review as needed any word cards that were made for Lesson 13.

Activity 1. Have the student name the pictures and read the words aloud. Have the student draw a line to match the pictures with the words.

Pictures:		
	peanut	**doghouse**
	mailbox	**raincoat**
	cupcake	
	backpack	**railroad**

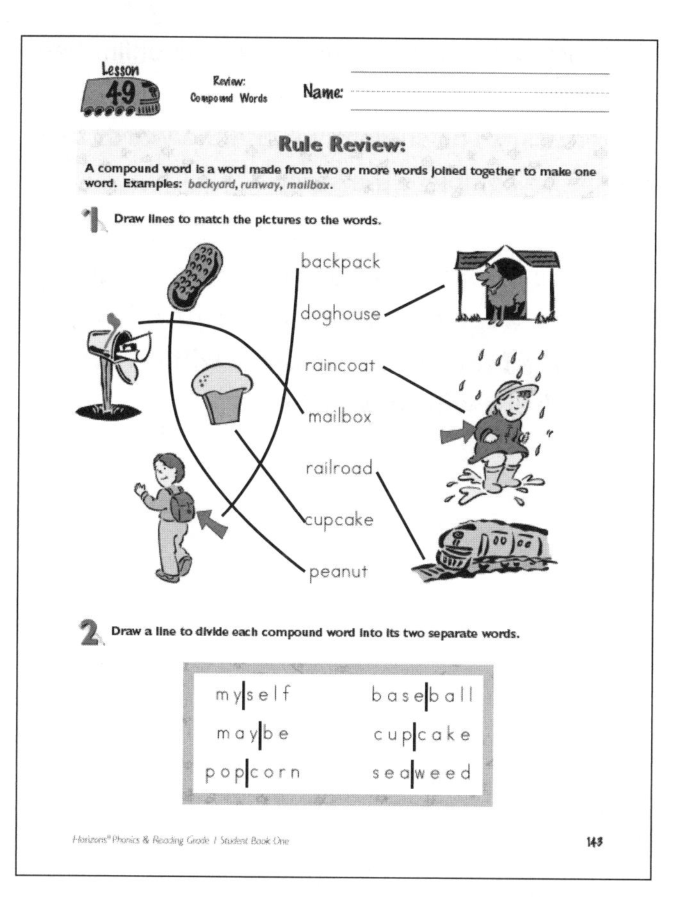

Activity 2. Have the student read the words aloud. The student will draw a line in each compound word to separate it into its two parts.

Words:		
	my / self	**base / ball**
	may / be	**cup / cake**
	pop / corn	**sea / weed**

Activity 3. Help the student read the unfinished story and the words in the list. Make word cards as necessary. The student will use the words from the list to complete the story.

Story:

I went to the mailbox to get the mail. I had to wear my raincoat because it was raining. Maybe tomorrow it will be nice and there will be sunshine.

Lesson 50 - Review: Suffix -ing

Overview:

- Write words adding suffix **-ing** to base words
- Sentence completion
- Crossword puzzle

Materials and Supplies:

- Teacher's Guide & Student Workbook
- White board or chalkboard
- Word cards (as necessary)
- Phonics rule flashcards in **Teacher Resources**
- Story: *The Buzzing Bees*

Teaching Tips:

Review Lesson 15 as necessary. If needed, go over any word cards that were made for this lesson. Review the meaning of the term "base word."

Activity 1. Have the student read the words aloud. The student will write new words by adding **ing** to the end of each base word.

Words: **running, digging, hopping**
passing, missing, buzzing

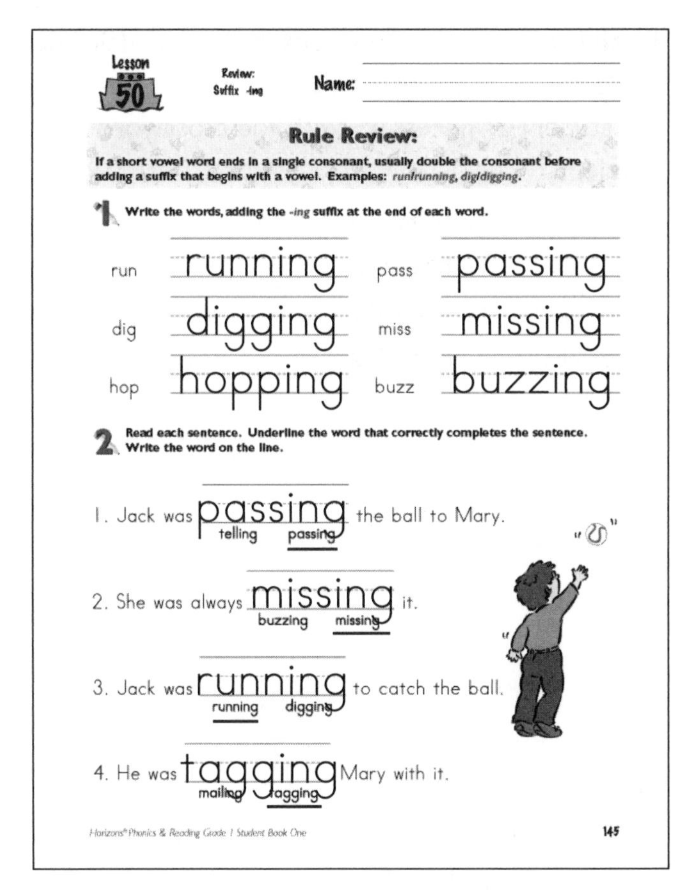

Lesson 50 Review: Suffix -ing Name:

Rule Review:

If a short vowel word ends in a single consonant, usually double the consonant before adding a suffix that begins with a vowel. Examples: *run/running, dig/digging.*

1 Write the words, adding the *-ing* suffix at the end of each word.

run running pass passing
dig digging miss missing
hop hopping buzz buzzing

2 Read each sentence. Underline the word that correctly completes the sentence. Write the word on the line.

1. Jack was passing the ball to Mary. telling passing
2. She was always missing it. buzzing missing
3. Jack was running to catch the ball. running digging
4. He was tagging Mary with it. mailing tagging

Horizons® Phonics & Reading Grade 1 Student Book One 145

Activity 2. Help the student read the sentences and the word choices. Instruct the student to underline the word that will correctly complete each sentence and write the word on the line.

Sentences:

1. **Jack was passing the ball to Mary.**
2. **She was always missing it.**
3. **Jack was running to catch the ball.**
4. **He was tagging Mary with it.**

Activity 3. Review the words in the list. Help the student read the crossword puzzle clues. Assist the student as necessary with the crossword puzzle.

Across: **1. digging**
3. tagging
4. netting

Down: **2. getting**

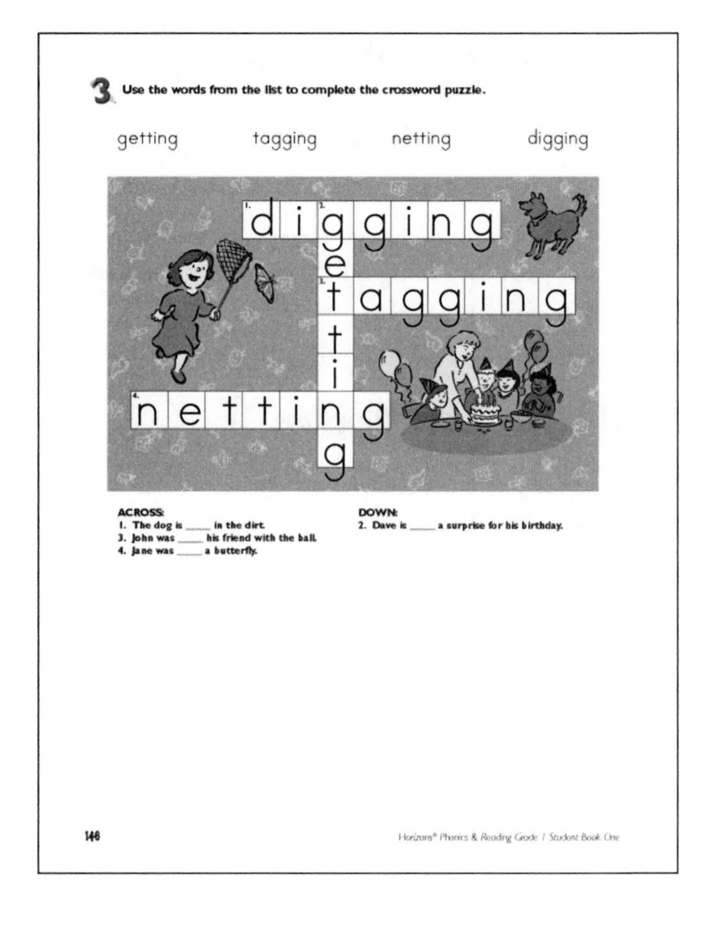
3 Use the words from the list to complete the crossword puzzle.

getting tagging netting digging

ACROSS:
1. The dog is _____ in the dirt.
3. John was _____ his friend with the ball.
4. Jane was _____ a butterfly.

DOWN:
2. Dave is _____ a surprise for his birthday.

146 Horizons® Phonics & Reading Grade 1 Student Book One

Test 5

Lessons 41-50

Instructions:

Review the definition of a contraction. Have the student give examples of contractions with **not, have, am, us**, and **are**. Review consonant blends and the suffix **-ing**. Review compound words. Read through the test with the student. Help the student with any words that he/she is still unsure of. The teacher should be available to answer any questions that the student may have during the test.

Activity 1. Review the instructions with the student.

Words:		
	did not	**I am**
	are not	**we have**
	I will	**it is**
	you will	**you are**
	I have	**we are**
	let us	**will not**

Activity 2. Make sure the student has correctly identified the pictures.

Pictures: **twins, stairs, swing, sweep**

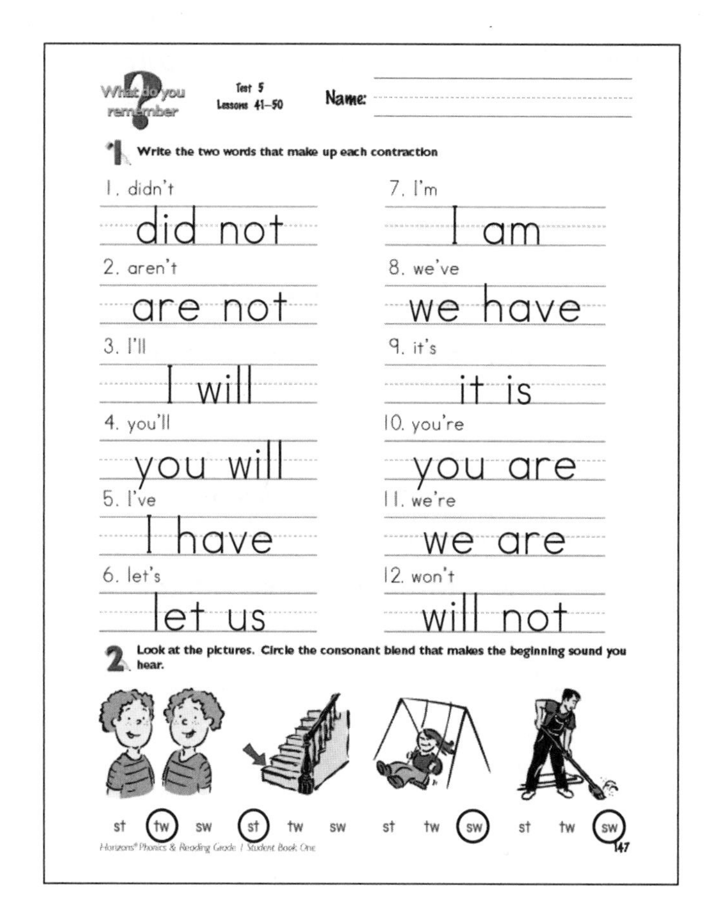

What do you remember

Test 5
Lessons 41–50

Name:

1. Write the two words that make up each contraction

1. didn't did not	7. I'm I am
2. aren't are not	8. we've we have
3. I'll I will	9. it's it is
4. you'll you will	10. you're you are
5. I've I have	11. we're we are
6. let's let us	12. won't will not

2. Look at the pictures. Circle the consonant blend that makes the beginning sound you hear.

st (tw) sw | (st) tw sw | st tw (sw) | st tw (sw)

Horizons® Phonics & Reading Grade 1 Student Book One 147

Activity 3. Make sure the student has correctly identified the pictures.

Pictures: **spring, spray, splash, sprout**

Activity 4. Make sure the student has correctly identified the pictures.

Pictures: **nest, stick, switch, twig**

Activity 5. Review the directions with the student.

Words: **running**, **passing**, **digging**, **missing**, **hopping**, **buzzing**

Activity 6. Review the directions with the student.

Words: **back / pack**
cup / cake
pea / nut
dog / house

3. Look at the pictures. Circle the consonant blend that makes the beginning sound you hear.

spl (spr) spl (spr) (spl) spr spl (spr)

4. Look at the pictures. Finish the words under each picture with correct consonant blend.

ne st st ick sw itch tw ig

5. Write the words, adding the *-ing* suffix at the end of each word.

run running pass passing
dig digging miss missing
hop hopping buzz buzzing

6. Draw a line to divide each compound word into its two separate words.

back|pack cup|cake pea|nut dog|house

148 Horizons® Phonics & Reading Grade 1 Student Book One

Lesson 51 - Review: Suffix -ed

Overview:

- Make new words by adding suffix **-ed** to base words
- Sentence completion
- Choose correct words from story

Materials and Supplies:

- Teacher's Guide & Student Workbook
- White board or chalkboard
- Word cards (as necessary)
- Phonics rule flashcards in **Teacher Resources**
- Story: *Max Painted a Picture*

Teaching Tips:

Review Lesson 15 as needed. Discuss the rule and ask the student for additional examples. Illustrate on the chalkboard or white board if desired.

Activity 1. Have the student read the words aloud. The student will write new words by adding **ed** to the end of each base word.

Words: **fixed, passed, wanted, mail**
cleaned, painted, played, helped

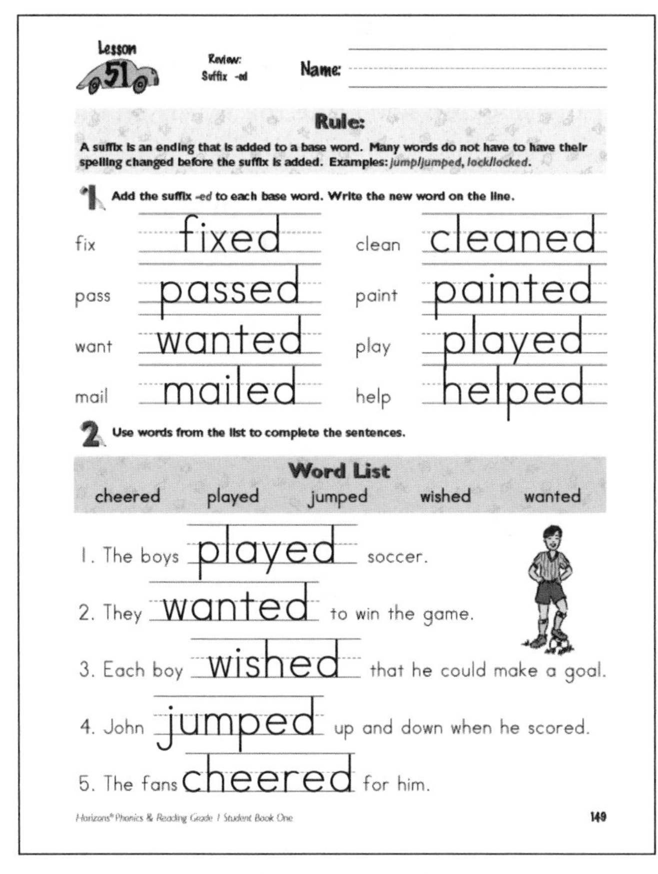

Lesson 51 Review: Suffix -ed Name:

Rule:
A suffix is an ending that is added to a base word. Many words do not have to have their spelling changed before the suffix is added. Examples: *jump/jumped, lock/locked*.

1 Add the suffix -ed to each base word. Write the new word on the line.

fix fixed clean cleaned
pass passed paint painted
want wanted play played
mail mailed help helped

2 Use words from the list to complete the sentences.

Word List
cheered played jumped wished wanted

1. The boys played soccer.
2. They wanted to win the game.
3. Each boy wished that he could make a goal.
4. John jumped up and down when he scored.
5. The fans cheered for him.

Horizons® Phonics & Reading Grade 1 Student Book One 149

Activity 2. Help the student read words in the list and the sentences. Instruct the student to select the word that will correctly complete each sentence and write the word on the line.

Sentences:

1. **The boys played soccer.**
2. **They wanted to win the game.**
3. **Each boy wished that he could make a goal.**
4. **John jumped up and down when he scored.**
5. **The fans cheered for him.**

Activity 3. Have the student read the story aloud. The student will underline all of the words with the suffix **ed** and write the words on the lines.

Words:	**1. fished**	**5. pulled**
	2. jumped	**6. helped**
	3. looked	**7. waited**
	4. hooked	

3 **Read the story. Underline all of the words containing the suffix *-ed*. Write the words on the lines.**

Dad and I fished in the lake. The fish jumped in and out of the water. Dad looked at his pole. He had hooked a fish! Dad pulled the fish out of the lake. Then Dad helped me bait my hook, and we both waited for a fish to bite.

1. fished
2. jumped
3. looked
4. hooked
5. pulled
6. helped
7. waited

150 Horizons® Phonics & Reading Grade 1 Student Book One

Lesson 52 - Review: Suffixes -s & -es, R-Controlled Vowels er, ir, ur

Overview:

- Add suffix **-s** or **-es** to base words
- Circle base words
- Sentence completion
- Add r-controlled vowels **er**, **ir**, **ur** to words

Materials and Supplies:

- Teacher's Guide & Student Workbook
- White board or chalkboard
- Word cards (as necessary)
- Phonics rule flashcards in **Teacher Resources**
- Story: *The Cat Who Jumps*

Teaching Tips:

Assist the student as needed in identifying the pictures and reading the words in the lesson. Review the rules from Lesson 42 for r-controlled vowels as needed. Discuss the rule for **er**, **ir**, and **ur** words, and ask the student for additional examples.

Activity 1. Have the student read the words aloud. Discuss the correct endings for each word with the student. The student will write new words by adding **s** or **es** to the end of each base word.

Words: **jumps, brushes, touches, plays**
churches, needs, plans, walks

Activity 2. Have the student read aloud the words in the list. The student will find the base word in each word and circle it.

Words:	**like**	**play**	**touch**	**hop**
	jump	**run**	**brush**	**walk**

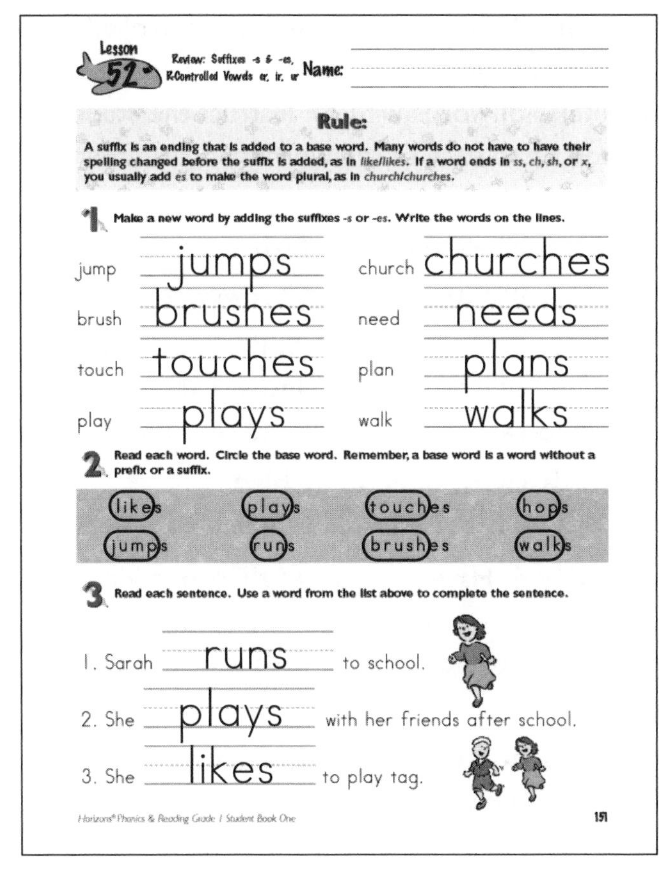

Lesson 52 Review: Suffixes -s & -es, R-Controlled Vowels er, ir, ur Name:

Rule:

A suffix is an ending that is added to a base word. Many words do not have to have their spelling changed before the suffix is added, as in *like/likes*. If a word ends in *ss*, *ch*, *sh*, or *x*, you usually add *es* to make the word plural, as in *church/churches*.

1 **Make a new word by adding the suffixes -s or -es. Write the words on the lines.**

jump jumps church churches
brush brushes need needs
touch touches plan plans
play plays walk walks

2 **Read each word. Circle the base word. Remember, a base word is a word without a prefix or a suffix.**

likes plays touches hops
jumps runs brushes walks

3 **Read each sentence. Use a word from the list above to complete the sentence.**

1. Sarah runs to school.
2. She plays with her friends after school.
3. She likes to play tag.

Horizons® Phonics & Reading Grade 1 Student Book One 151

Activity 3. Help the student read the sentences and the word choices from Activity 2. Instruct the student to select the word that will correctly complete each sentence, and write the word on the line. NOTE: There may be more than one correct answer for the sentences; however, the pictures are visual clues to a possible correct answer.

Sentences:

1. **Sarah runs to school.**
2. **She plays with her friends after school.**
3. **She likes to play tag.**

Activity 4. Discuss the rule for r-controlled vowels, and have the student think of additional examples of words with **er**. Instruct the student to add **er** to each of the words and read them aloud.

Words: **clerk, jerk, her, fern**
perch, herd, serve, swerve

Activity 5. Have the student think of additional examples of words with **ir**. Instruct the student to add **ir** to each of the words and read them aloud.

Words: **twirl, skirt, firm, bird**
whirl, birth, dirt, flirt

Activity 6. Have the student think of additional examples of words with **ur**. Instruct the student to add **ur** to each of the words and read them aloud.

Words: **burst, purse, church, lurch**
fur, purr, surf, spur

Rule:
In an *r-controlled vowel*, an *r* after the vowel makes the vowel sound different from a short or long sound. Examples: *star, shirt, term, born, burn.*

4. Add *er* to each of the words below, then read the words to your teacher.

cl er k j er k h er f er n
p erch h er d s er ve swerve

5. Add *ir* to each of the words below, then read the words to your teacher.

tw ir l sk ir t f ir m b ir d
wh ir l b ir th d ir t fl ir t

6. Add *ur* to each of the words below, then read the words to your teacher.

b ur st p ur se church l ur ch
f ur p ur r s ur f sp ur

152 Horizons® Phonics & Reading Grade 1 Student Book One

Lesson 53 - Review: Suffix -ful

Overview:

- Add suffix **-ful** to base words
- Circle base words
- Write a story, using words from list
- Sentence completion

Materials and Supplies:

- Teacher's Guide & Student Workbook
- White board or chalkboard
- Word cards (as necessary)
- Phonics rule flashcards in **Teacher Resources**
- Story: *The Helpful Friend*

Teaching Tips:

Assist the student as needed in identifying the pictures and reading the words in the lesson. Review Lesson 17, if needed, and ask the student for additional examples of words ending in suffix **-ful.**

Activity 1. Have the student read the words aloud. The student will write new words by adding **ful** to the end of each base word.

Words: **helpful, painful, hopeful, careful, joy-ful**

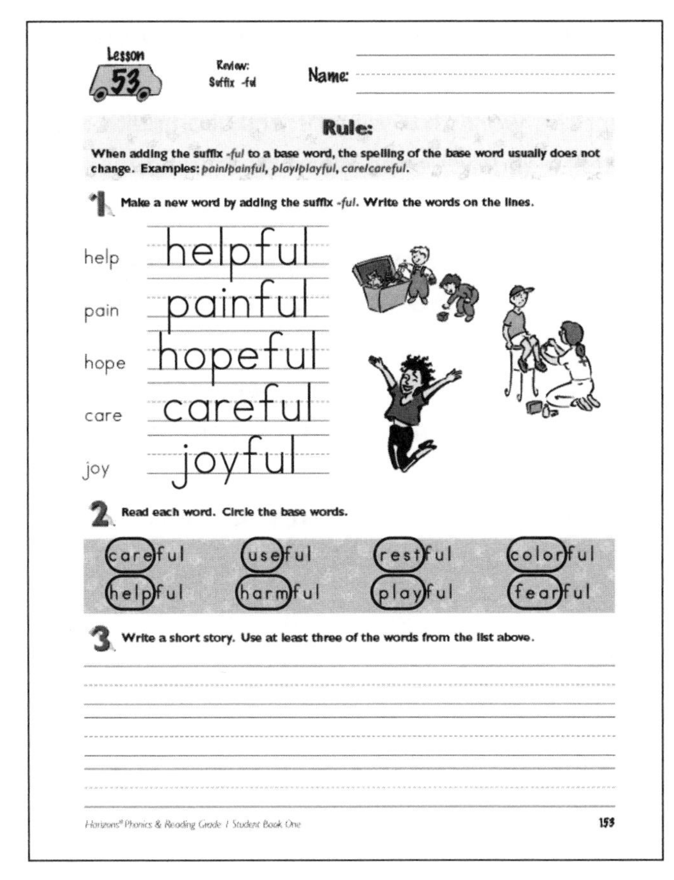

Lesson 53 Review: Suffix -ful Name:

Rule:

When adding the suffix *-ful* to a base word, the spelling of the base word usually does not change. Examples: *pain/painful, play/playful, care/careful.*

1. Make a new word by adding the suffix *-ful*. Write the words on the lines.

help helpful
pain painful
hope hopeful
care careful
joy joyful

2. Read each word. Circle the base words.

careful useful restful colorful
helpful harmful playful fearful

3. Write a short story. Use at least three of the words from the list above.

Horizons® Phonics & Reading Grade 1 Student Book One 153

Activity 2. Have the student read aloud the words in the list. The student will find the base word in each word and circle it.

Words:	**care**	**use**	**rest**	**color**
	help	**harm**	**play**	**fear**

Activity 3. The student will write a short story using words from Activity 2. Help with ideas and spelling as necessary. Remind the student about correct punctuation and capitalization.

Activity 4. Help the student read the words in the list and the sentences. Instruct the student to select the word that will correctly complete each sentence and write the word on the line.

Sentences:

1. **Jason's new puppy was very playful.**
2. **The map was helpful when we got lost.**
3. **The butterfly was very colorful.**
4. **Chad got a painful scrape on his knee.**
5. **"Be careful when you cross the street," said Mom.**

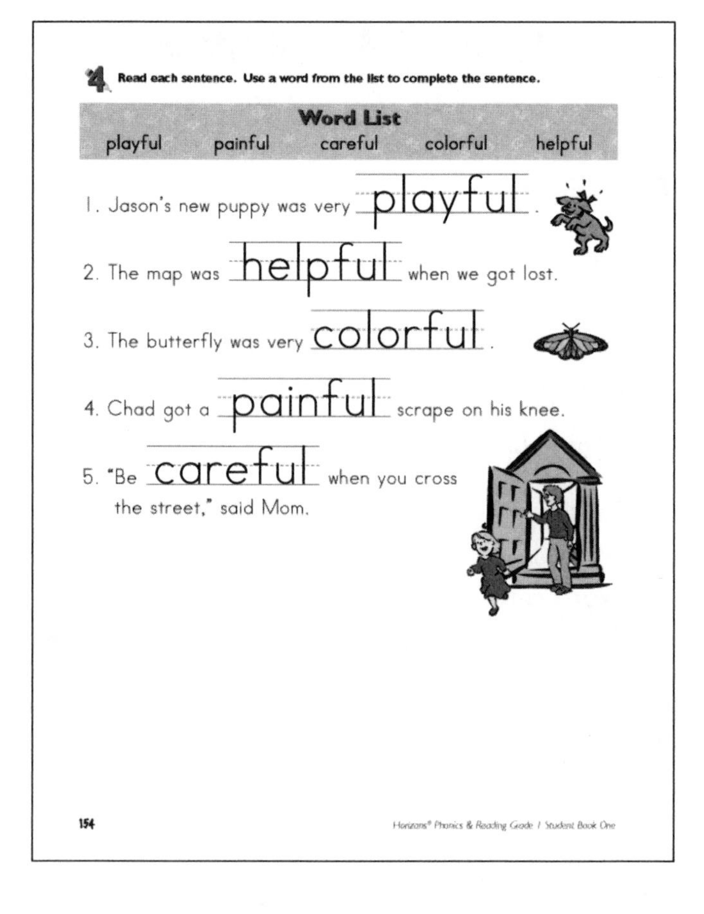

Lesson 54 - Review: Suffixes -ness & -less

Overview:

- Add suffixes **-ness** and **-less** to base words
- Match suffixes to base words
- Sentence completion

Materials and Supplies:

- Teacher's Guide & Student Workbook
- White board or chalkboard
- Word cards (as necessary)
- Phonics rule flashcards in **Teacher Resources**
- Story: *The Careless Boy*

Teaching Tips:

Review words from Lesson 17 if needed. Go over the rule and assist the student as needed in reading the words in the lesson. Introduce and explain the matching activity to the student.

Activity 1. Have the student read the words aloud. The student will write new words by adding **ness** and **less** to the end of each base word.

Words: **darkness, loudness, sharpness, softness**
helpless, careless, fearless, useless

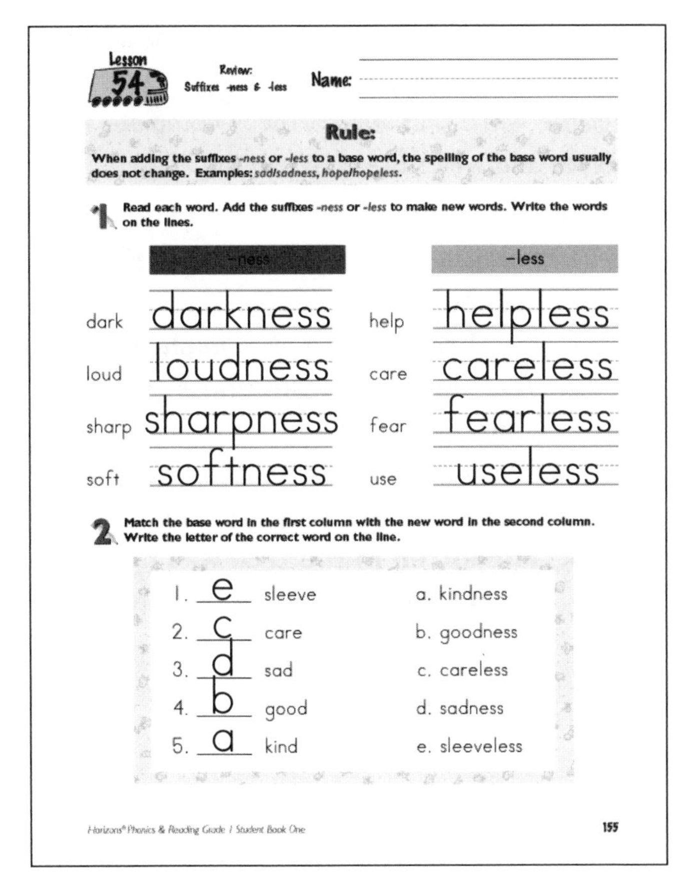

Lesson 54 Review: Suffixes -ness & -less Name:

Rule:
When adding the suffixes *-ness* or *-less* to a base word, the spelling of the base word usually does not change. Examples: *sad/sadness, hope/hopeless.*

1. Read each word. Add the suffixes *-ness* or *-less* to make new words. Write the words on the lines.

	-ness		-less
dark	darkness	help	helpless
loud	loudness	care	careless
sharp	sharpness	fear	fearless
soft	softness	use	useless

2. Match the base word in the first column with the new word in the second column. Write the letter of the correct word on the line.

1. e sleeve — a. kindness
2. c care — b. goodness
3. d sad — c. careless
4. b good — d. sadness
5. a kind — e. sleeveless

Horizons® Phonics & Reading Grade 1 Student Book One 155

Activity 2. Have the student read all of the words aloud. The student will match the base words in the first column with the new words in the second column and write the letters on the lines.

Answers:

1. **e (sleeveless)**
2. **c (careless)**
3. **d (sadness)**
4. **b (goodness)**
5. **a (kindness)**

Activity 3. Help the student read words in the list and the sentences. Instruct the student to select the word that will correctly complete each sentence and write the word on the line.

Sentences:

1. **He needed a light to see in the darkness.**
2. **The broken glass was useless.**
3. **We should show kindness to other people.**
4. **If you are careless when you ride your bike, you may get hurt.**
5. **The kitten in the tree was helpless. It could not get down by itself.**

3 Use words from the list to complete the sentences.

Word List

useless careless helpless kindness darkness

1. He needed a light to see in the darkness.
2. The broken glass was useless.
3. We should show kindness to other people.
4. If you are careless when you ride your bike, you may get hurt.
5. The kitten in the tree was helpless. It could not get down by itself.

156 Horizons® Phonics & Reading Grade 1 Student Book One

Lesson 55 - Review: Suffix -ly

Overview:

- Add suffixes to base words
- Sentence completion
- Write each word next to its definition
- Match base words with words with suffix **-ly** added

Materials and Supplies:

- Teacher's Guide & Student Workbook
- White board or chalkboard
- Word cards (as necessary)
- Phonics rule flashcards in **Teacher Resources**
- Story: *Riding Safely*

Teaching Tips:

Review the words from Lesson 17 if needed. Go over any word cards as necessary. Review the rule and have student write examples on the chalkboard or white board. Assist the student as needed in reading the words in the lesson.

Activity 1. Have the student read the words aloud. The student will write new words by adding **ly** to the end of each base word.

Words: **gladly, softly, lovely, safely, slowly**

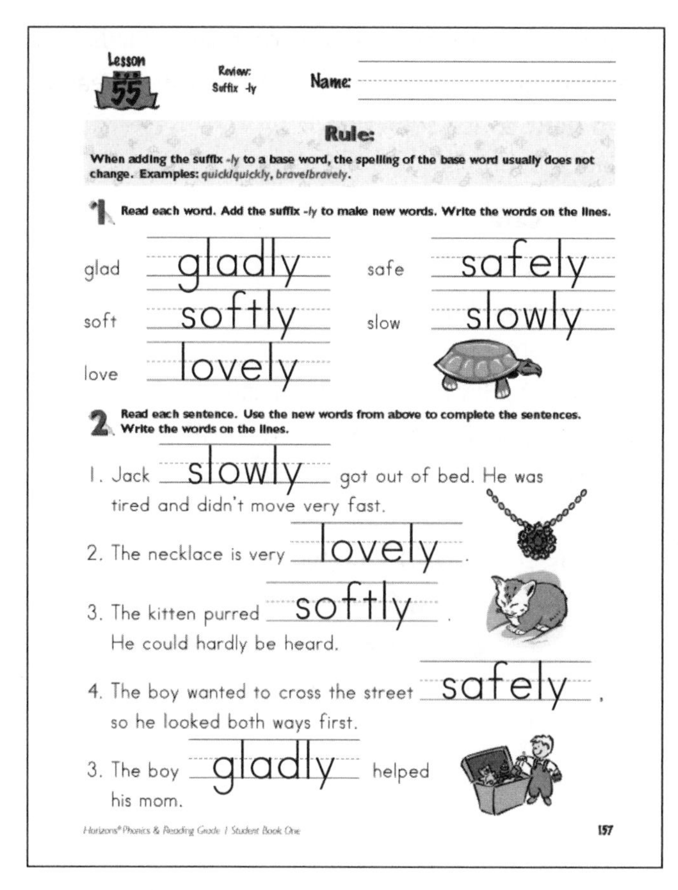

Lesson 55 Review: Suffix -ly Name:

Rule:
When adding the suffix -ly to a base word, the spelling of the base word usually does not change. Examples: *quick/quickly, brave/bravely.*

1 Read each word. Add the suffix -ly to make new words. Write the words on the lines.

glad gladly safe safely
soft softly slow slowly
love lovely

2 Read each sentence. Use the new words from above to complete the sentences. Write the words on the lines.

1. Jack slowly got out of bed. He was tired and didn't move very fast.
2. The necklace is very lovely.
3. The kitten purred softly. He could hardly be heard.
4. The boy wanted to cross the street safely, so he looked both ways first.
3. The boy gladly helped his mom.

Horizons® Phonics & Reading Grade 1 Student Book One 157

Activity 2. Help the student read the sentences. Instruct the student to select the word from Activity 1 that will correctly complete each sentence and write the word on the line.

Sentences:

1. **Jack slowly got out of bed. He was tired and didn't move very fast.**
2. **The necklace is very lovely.**
3. **The kitten purred softly. He could hardly be heard.**
4. **The boy wanted to cross the street safely, so he looked both ways first.**
5. **The boy gladly helped his mom.**

Activity 3. Have the student read the words and the definitions aloud. The student will write each word next to its definition.

Words:

1. **safely**
2. **gladly**
3. **bravely**
4. **slowly**

Activity 4. Have the student read all of the words aloud. The student will draw lines to match the base words with the words containing suffixes.

Words: **brave/bravely**
safe/safely
lone/lonely
sudden/suddenly

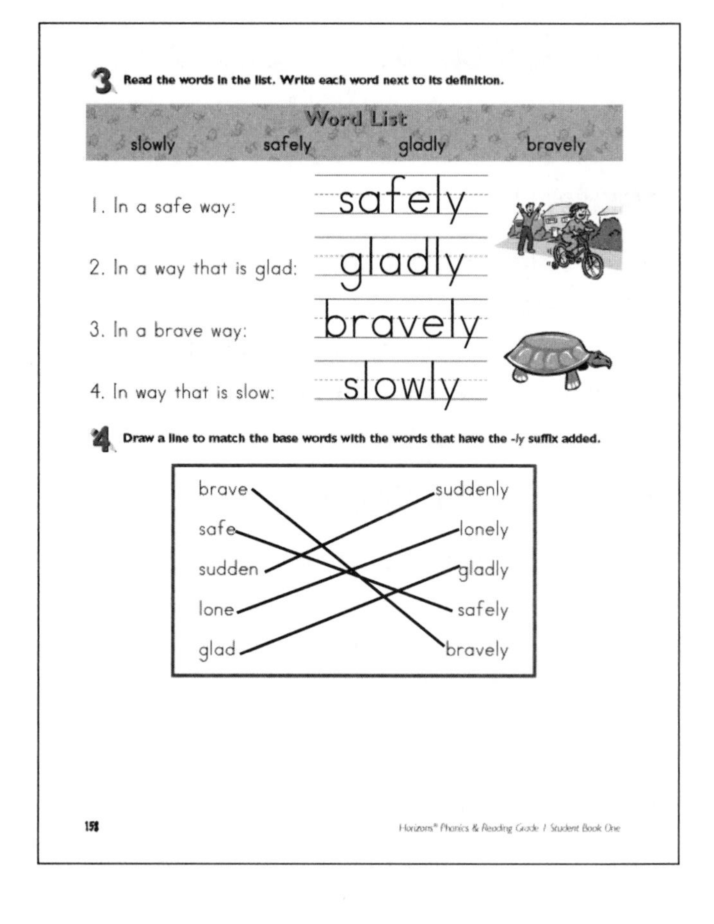
3 Read the words in the list. Write each word next to its definition.

Word List
slowly safely gladly bravely

1. In a safe way: safely
2. In a way that is glad: gladly
3. In a brave way: bravely
4. In way that is slow: slowly

4 Draw a line to match the base words with the words that have the -ly suffix added.

brave	suddenly
safe	lonely
sudden	gladly
lone	safely
glad	bravely

158 Horizons® Phonics & Reading Grade 1 Student Book One

Lesson 56 - Review: Suffixes -y, -en, -able

Overview:

- Add suffixes to base words
- Sentence completion
- Circle base words

Materials and Supplies:

- Teacher's Guide & Student Workbook
- White board or chalkboard
- Word cards (as necessary)
- Phonics rule flashcards in **Teacher Resources**
- Story: *The Wooden Box*

Teaching Tips:

Review the rule. Go over any word cards that were made for Lesson 18. Have the student write additional examples on the chalkboard or white board.

Activity 1. Have the student read the words aloud. The student will write new words by adding **y** to the end of each base word.

Words: **tricky, curly, thirsty, windy, speedy**

Activity 2. Have the student read the words aloud. The student will write new words by adding **en** to the end of each base word.

Words: **soften, sharpen, wooden, darken, frighten**

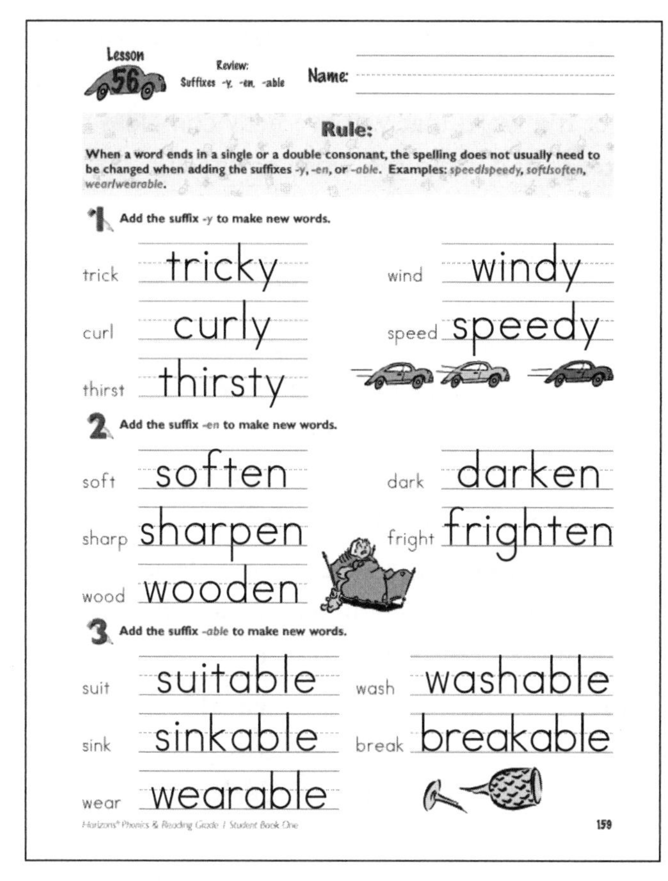

Lesson 56 Review: Suffixes -y, -en, -able Name:

Rule:

When a word ends in a single or a double consonant, the spelling does not usually need to be changed when adding the suffixes -y, -en, or -able. Examples: *speed/speedy, soft/soften, wear/wearable*.

1. **Add the suffix -y to make new words.**

trick tricky | wind windy
curl curly | speed speedy
thirst thirsty

2. **Add the suffix -en to make new words.**

soft soften | dark darken
sharp sharpen | fright frighten
wood wooden

3. **Add the suffix -able to make new words.**

suit suitable | wash washable
sink sinkable | break breakable
wear wearable

Horizons® Phonics & Reading Grade 1 Student Book One 159

Activity 3. Have the student read the words aloud. The student will write new words by adding **able** to the end of each base word.

Words: **suitable, sinkable, wearable, washable, breakable**

Activity 4. Help the student read the words in the list and the sentences. Instruct the student to select the word that will correctly complete each sentence and write the word on the line.

Sentences:

1. **His clothes were not suitable for cold weather.**
2. **The glass was very breakable.**
3. **The race car was very speedy.**
4. **The boy had curly red hair.**
5. **Dad had to sharpen the ax before he could chop wood.**

Activity 5. Have the student read aloud the words in the list. The student will find the base word in each word and circle it.

Words:				
	speed	**curl**	**wood**	**fright**
	suit	**break**	**soft**	**speed**
	sharp	**trick**	**dark**	**wash**

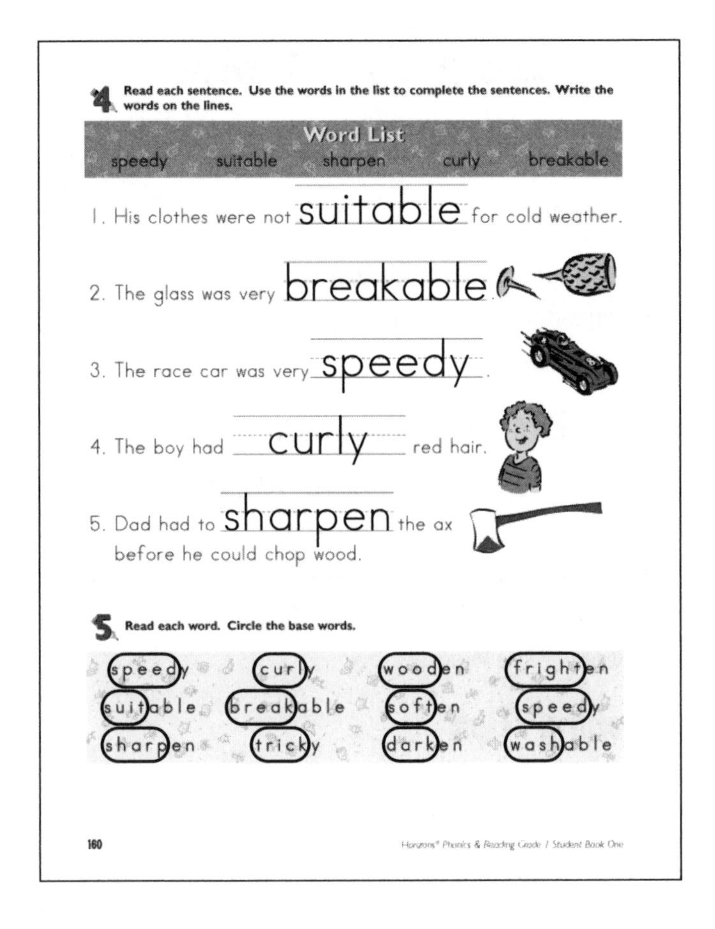

4 Read each sentence. Use the words in the list to complete the sentences. Write the words on the lines.

Word List

speedy suitable sharpen curly breakable

1. His clothes were not suitable for cold weather.
2. The glass was very breakable.
3. The race car was very speedy.
4. The boy had curly red hair.
5. Dad had to sharpen the ax before he could chop wood.

5 Read each word. Circle the base words.

speedy	curly	wooden	frighten
suitable	breakable	soften	speedy
sharpen	tricky	darken	washable

160 Horizons Phonics & Reading Grade 1 Student Book One

Lesson 57 - Review: Suffix -er

Overview:

- Add suffix **-er** to base words
- Draw pictures to show meanings of words
- Sentence completion

Materials and Supplies:

- Teacher's Guide & Student Workbook
- White board or chalkboard
- Word cards (as necessary)
- Phonics rule flashcards in **Teacher Resources**
- Story: *The Deeper Hole*

Teaching Tips:

Review the rule. Go over any word cards that were made for Lesson 15. Have the student write additional examples on the chalkboard or white board. Assist the student as needed in reading the words in the lesson.

Activity 1. Have the student read the words aloud. The student will write new words by adding **er** to the end of each base word.

Words: **faster, darker, softer, deeper, lighter, smarter**

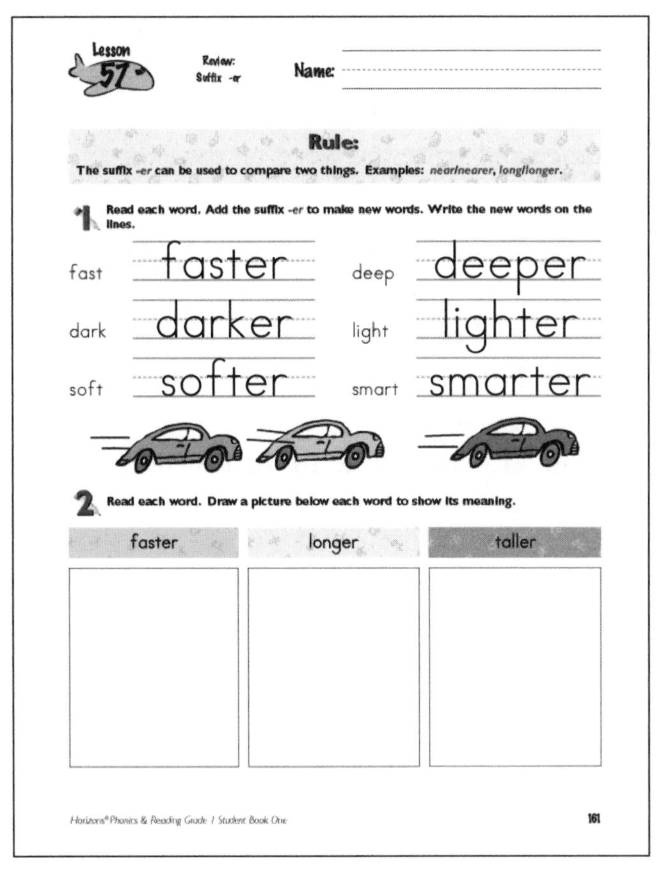
Lesson 57 Review: Suffix -er Name:

Rule:
The suffix *-er* can be used to compare two things. Examples: *near/nearer, long/longer.*

1. Read each word. Add the suffix *-er* to make new words. Write the new words on the lines.

fast faster deep deeper
dark darker light lighter
soft softer smart smarter

2. Read each word. Draw a picture below each word to show its meaning.

faster longer taller

Horizons® Phonics & Reading Grade 1 Student Book One 161

Activity 2. Have the student read each word and draw a picture to illustrate the meaning of the word. Help the student with ideas if needed. Emphasize that their picture will need at least two things, since words with the **-er** suffix compare one thing with another.

Activity 3. Help the student read the words in the list and the sentences. Instruct the student to use the word that will correctly complete each sentence and write the word on the line.

Sentences:

1. **Susan runs faster than Mary**
2. **The water is deeper at the other end of the pool.**
3. **My cat's fur was softer after I brushed it.**
4. **He is taller than his brother.**

3 Read each sentence. Use the words from the list to complete each sentence. Write the words on the lines.

Word List

deeper taller softer faster

1. Susan runs faster than Mary.
2. The water is deeper at the other end of the pool.
3. My cat's fur was softer after I brushed it.
4. He is taller than his brother.

162 Horizons® Phonics & Reading Grade 1 Student Book One

Lesson 58 - Adding Suffix -er to Words Ending in y, Review Long Vowel ā

Overview:

- Add suffix **-er** to base words
- Sentence completion
- Matching base words to words with suffix **-er** added
- Rhyming words with long **ā**
- Identify words with long **ā** sound

Materials and Supplies:

- Teacher's Guide & Student Workbook
- White board or chalkboard
- Alphabet flashcards
- Word cards (as necessary)
- Story: *The Happier Day*

Teaching Tips:

Review the rule for adding suffix **-er** to words that end in **y**. Do several examples on the white board or chalkboard. Have the student think of other examples. Review the rule for long vowel sounds: **"The long vowel says its name."**

Activity 1. Have the student read the words aloud. The student will write new words by adding **er** to the end of each base word.

Words: **busier, sunnier, funnier, happier, sillier, earlier**

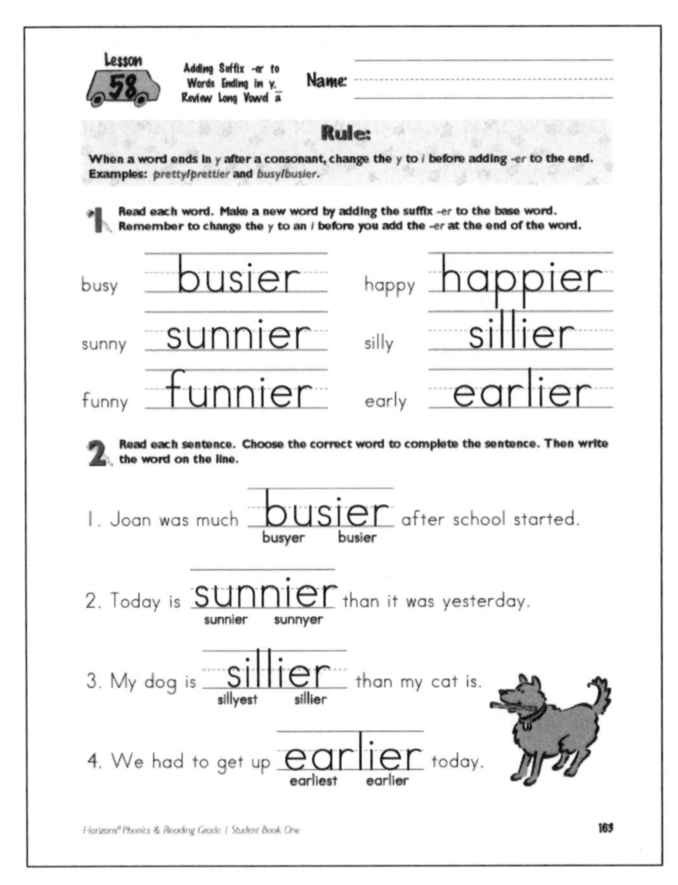

Lesson 58 — Adding Suffix -er to Words Ending in y, Review Long Vowel ā

Name:

Rule:

When a word ends in y after a consonant, change the y to i before adding -er to the end. Examples: *pretty/prettier* **and** *busy/busier.*

1 Read each word. Make a new word by adding the suffix -er to the base word. Remember to change the y to an i before you add the -er at the end of the word.

busy busier — happy happier

sunny sunnier — silly sillier

funny funnier — early earlier

2 Read each sentence. Choose the correct word to complete the sentence. Then write the word on the line.

1. Joan was much busier after school started. (busyer / busier)
2. Today is sunnier than it was yesterday. (sunnier / sunnyer)
3. My dog is sillier than my cat is. (sillyest / sillier)
4. We had to get up earlier today. (earliest / earlier)

Horizons® Phonics & Reading Grade 1 Student Book One — 163

Activity 2. Help the student read the sentences and the word choices. If desired, you may instruct the student to underline the correct spelling of the word that will complete each sentence. Have the student write the word on the line.

Sentences:

1. **Joan was much busier after school started.**
2. **Today is sunnier than it was yesterday.**
3. **My dog is sillier than my cat is.**
4. **We had to get up earlier today.**

Activity 3. Have the student read all of the words aloud. The student will draw lines to match the base words with the words containing suffixes.

Words: **happy/happier**
sunny/sunnier
windy/windier
silly/sillier
early/earlier

Activity 4. Have the student read the words aloud.

Activity 5. Have the student read all the words in the list aloud. The student will find ten long **ā** words and circle them.

Words: **ape, tape, race, pane, brave, flake, snake, sane, drape, paint**

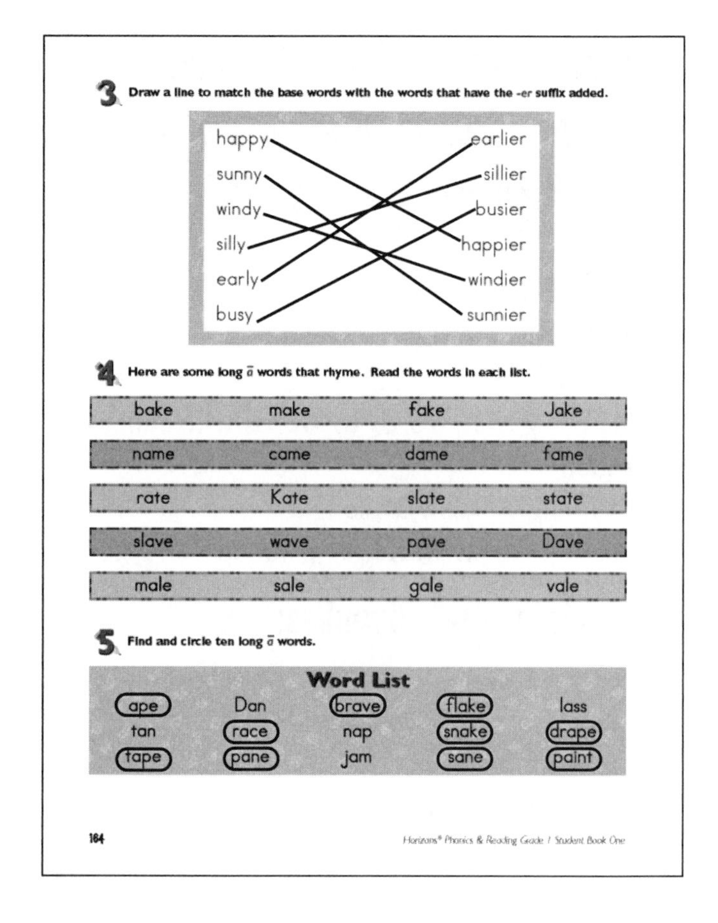

3 Draw a line to match the base words with the words that have the -er suffix added.

happy	earlier
sunny	sillier
windy	busier
silly	happier
early	windier
busy	sunnier

4 Here are some long ā words that rhyme. Read the words in each list.

bake	make	fake	Jake
name	came	dame	fame
rate	Kate	slate	state
slave	wave	pave	Dave
male	sale	gale	vale

5 Find and circle ten long ā words.

Word List

ape	Dan	brave	flake	lass
tan	race	nap	snake	drape
tape	pane	jam	sane	paint

164 Horizons® Phonics & Reading Grade 1 Student Book One

Lesson 59 - Review: Suffix -est, Long Vowels ī & ō

Overview:

- Add suffix **-est** to base words
- Draw pictures to show meanings of words
- Sentence completion
- Identify words with long ī and long ō sound

Materials and Supplies:

- Teacher's Guide & Student Workbook
- White board or chalkboard
- Alphabet flashcards
- Word cards (as necessary)
- Phonics rule flashcards in **Teacher Resources**
- Story: *The Darkest Room*

Teaching Tips:

Define and illustrate comparative words (**-er** suffix) and superlative words (**-est** suffix). Show that *comparative* means comparing one thing with another thing, and *superlative* means one thing is the best of all. Review the rule for long vowel sounds: **"The long vowel says its name."**

Activity 1. Have the student read the words aloud. The student will write new words by adding **est** to the end of each base word.

Words: **nearest, fastest, deepest, softest, darkest, longest**

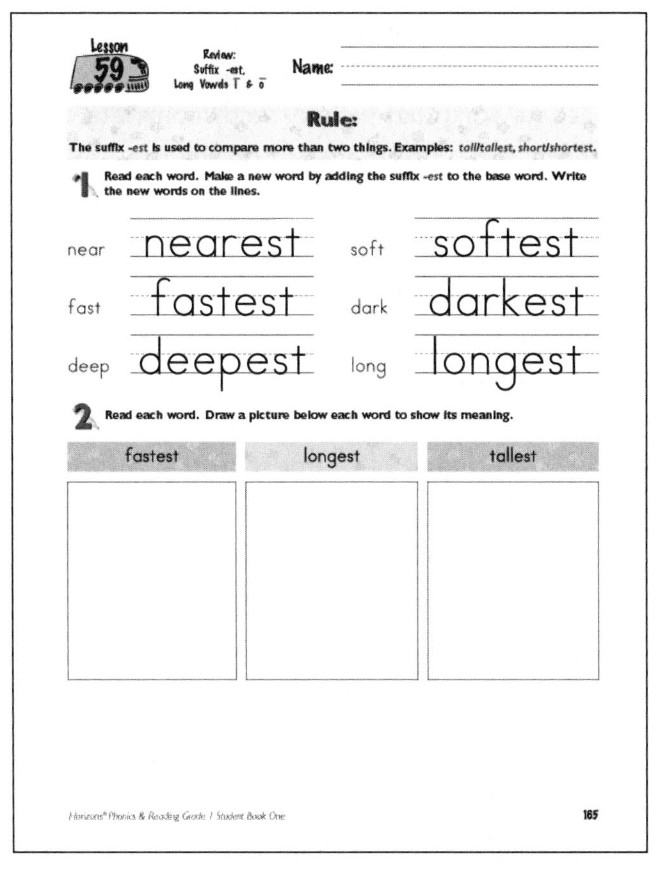

Lesson 59 Review: Suffix -est, Long Vowels ī & ō Name:

Rule:

The suffix -est is used to compare more than two things. Examples: *tall/tallest, short/shortest.*

1 **Read each word. Make a new word by adding the suffix -est to the base word. Write the new words on the lines.**

near nearest soft softest

fast fastest dark darkest

deep deepest long longest

2 **Read each word. Draw a picture below each word to show its meaning.**

fastest	longest	tallest

Horizons® Phonics & Reading Grade 1 Student Book One 165

Activity 2. Have the student read each word and draw a picture to illustrate the meaning of the word. Help the student with ideas if needed. Emphasize that each picture will need at least three things in it, since words with the **-est** suffix show that one thing is the best of all (superlative). Refer back to Lesson 57 where words with the **-er** suffix (comparative) are used.

Activity 3. Help the student read words in the list and the sentences. Instruct the student to select the word that will correctly complete each sentence, and write the word on the line.

Sentences:

1. **Her cat has the softest fur.**
2. **Nora is the fastest runner in her class.**
3. **Jim is the tallest boy on his team.**
4. **Math is my hardest class.**
5. **The lake is deepest in the middle.**

Activity 5. Have the student read all the words in the list aloud. The student will find all the long ī words and draw a square around them.

Words: **bike, site, glide, pride, pike, smile, hive, trike, slime, shine**

Activity 6. Have the student read all the words in the list aloud. The student will find all the long ō words and draw a square around them.

Words: **mope, hope, phone, smoke, scope, scroll, drove, joke, pole, molt**

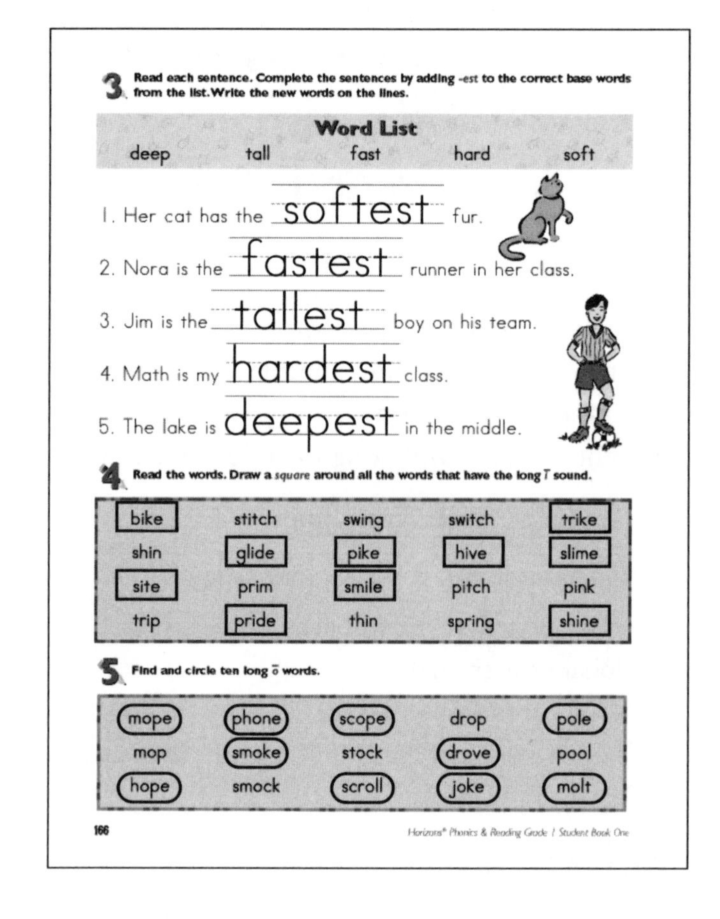

3 Read each sentence. Complete the sentences by adding -est to the correct base words from the list. Write the new words on the lines.

Word List				
deep	tall	fast	hard	soft

1. Her cat has the softest fur.
2. Nora is the fastest runner in her class.
3. Jim is the tallest boy on his team.
4. Math is my hardest class.
5. The lake is deepest in the middle.

4 Read the words. Draw a *square* around all the words that have the long ī sound.

bike	stitch	swing	switch	trike
shin	glide	pike	hive	slime
site	prim	smile	pitch	pink
trip	pride	thin	spring	shine

5 Find and circle ten long ō words.

mope	phone	scope	drop	pole
mop	smoke	stock	drove	pool
hope	smock	scroll	joke	molt

166 Horizons® Phonics & Reading Grade 1 Student Book One

Lesson 60 - Adding Suffix -est to Words Ending in y, Review R-Controlled Vowels

Overview:

- Add suffix **-est** to base words ending in **y**
- Sentence completion
- Auditory recognition of r-controlled vowel sounds
- Adding r-controlled vowels to words

Materials and Supplies:

- Teacher's Guide & Student Workbook
- White board or chalkboard
- Word cards (as necessary)
- Phonics rule flashcards in **Teacher Resources**
- Story: *The Funniest Clown*

Teaching Tips:

Review rule for adding **-est** to words ending in **y**. Use the white board or chalkboard to write examples. Ask the student for additional examples. Review the rules for r-controlled vowels and illustrate examples on the chalkboard or white board. Ask the student for additional examples. Assist the student as needed in reading the words in the lesson.

Activity 1. Have the student read the words aloud. The student will write new words by changing the **y** to an **i** and adding **est** to the end of each base word.

Words: **sillier, happier, funnier, earlier, sunnier, windier**

Lesson 60 Adding Suffix -est to Words Ending in y, Review R-Controlled Vowels Name:

Rule:

When a word ends in y after a consonant, change the y to i before adding -est to the end. Examples: *pretty/prettiest* and *lonely/loneliest*.

1 Read each word. Make new words by adding the suffix -est to the end of each word. Remember to change the y to i before you add -est.

silly silliest early earliest
happy happiest sunny sunniest
funny funniest windy windiest

2 Complete the sentences by adding -est to the base word. Remember to change the y to an i before adding -est to the end. Write the new words on the lines

1. Today is the happiest day of my life! (happy)
2. March is the windiest month of the year. (windy)
3. The white bunny has the fluffiest fur. (fluffy)
4. They are the silliest boys I have ever known! (silly)

Horizons® Phonics & Reading Grade 1 Student Book One 167

Activity 2. Help the student read the sentences and the base word. Instruct the student to add the suffix **-est** to each base word and write the word on the line to complete the sentence.

Sentences:

1. **Today is the happiest day of my life!**
2. **March is the windiest month of the year.**
3. **The white bunny has the softest fur.**
4. **They are the silliest boys I have ever known!**

Activity 3. Identify the pictures with the student. Have the student listen as you say the name of each picture. Instruct the student to circle the correct r-controlled vowel sound underneath each picture.

Pictures: **short, bird, stork, corn**
church, car, skirt, farm

Activity 4. Discuss r-controlled vowel sounds and have the student think of examples. Instruct the student to add the correct r-controlled vowel to each of the words and read them aloud.

Words: **purse, horse, cart, serve**

Rule Review:

In an *r-controlled vowel*, an *r* after the vowel makes the vowel sound different from a short or long sound. Examples: *star, shirt, term, born, burn.*

3 Choose the correct r-controlled vowel for the sound you hear in the pictures.

ar er ir or ur　ar er ir or ur　ar er ir or ur　ar er ir or ur

ar er ir or ur　ar er ir or ur　ar er ir or ur　ar er ir or ur

4 Look at the pictures. Finish the words under each picture with the correct r-controlled vowel sound.

purse　horse　cart　serve

168　*Horizons® Phonics & Reading Grade 1 Student Book One*

Test 6

Lessons 51-60

Instructions:

Review the definition of a base word. Have the student give some examples of base words when presented with words that have **-ed**, **-ful**, **-er**, **-est**, **-en**, or **-es** suffixes. Review the rule for r-controlled vowels, and ask the student for examples. Read through the test with the student. Help the student with any words that he/she is still unsure of. The teacher should be available to answer any questions that the student may have during the test.

Activity 1. Review the directions with the student.

Words:		
	jump	**help**
	show	**hope**
	fluffy	**hard**
	pretty	**soft**
	sunny	**small**
	happy	**dress**
	tall	**church**
	care	**silly**

Activity 2. Make sure the student has correctly identified the pictures.

Pictures: **short, purse, car, farm**

What do you remember? Test 6 Lessons 51–60 Name:

1 Read each of the words. Write the correct *base words* on the lines.

jumped	jump	helpless	help
showed	show	hopeful	hope
fluffiest	fluffy	harden	hard
prettier	pretty	soften	soft
sunniest	sunny	smaller	small
happier	happy	dresses	dress
tallest	tall	churches	church
careful	care	silliest	silly

2 Choose the correct r-controlled vowel for the sound you hear in the pictures.

ar er ir or ur · ar er ir or ur · ar er ir or ur · ar er ir or ur

Horizons® Phonics & Reading Grade 1 Student Book One 169

Activity 3. Make sure the student can read the sentences and the base words.

Sentences:

1. **Jack was hopeful that his team would win.**
2. **Joan is a very cheerful girl.**
3. **There are two churches on my street.**
4. **Be sure that you pet the cat softly.**
5. **This has been the sunniest day this week.**
6. **I am taller than my brother.**

Activity 4. Make sure the student has correctly identified the pictures.

Pictures: **corn, serve, burn, shirt**

3 **Read each sentence. Complete each sentence by adding the correct suffix to the base word. Write the new words on the lines.**

1. Jack was hopeful that his team would win. (hope)
2. Joan is a very cheerful girl. (cheer)
3. There are two churches on my street. (church)
4. Be sure that you pet the cat softly. (soft)
5. This has been the sunniest day this week. (sunny)
6. I am taller than my brother. (tall)

4 **Look at the pictures. Finish the words under each picture with the correct r-controlled vowel sound.**

c or n   s er ve   b ur n   sh ir t

170   Horizons® Phonics & Reading Grade 1 Student Book One

Lesson 61 - Review: Suffixes -er & -est, Long Vowel ū

Overview:

- Sentence completion
- Identify words with long **ū** sound
- Crossword puzzle
- Rhyming words with long **ū** sound

Materials and Supplies:

- Teacher's Guide & Student Workbook
- White board or chalkboard
- Alphabet flashcards
- Word cards (as necessary)
- Phonics rule flashcards in **Teacher Resources**
- Story: *Luke and Sue*

Teaching Tips:

Review the rule for suffixes **-er** and **-est.** Assist the student as needed in reading the words in the lesson. Review the rule for long vowel sounds: **"The long vowel says its name."**

Activity 1. Help the student read the sentences and the base words. Review the sentences with the student to determine whether the sentence is comparing two things or more than two things. Instruct the student to add the correct suffix to the base words and complete each sentence by writing the new word on the line.

Sentences:

1. **He is the tallest boy in his class.**
2. **She thinks that her red dress is prettier than her blue one.**
3. **My dog is the friendliest dog on my street.**
4. **We stayed at Bill's house longer today than we did yesterday.**
5. **An ant is smaller than a bird.**

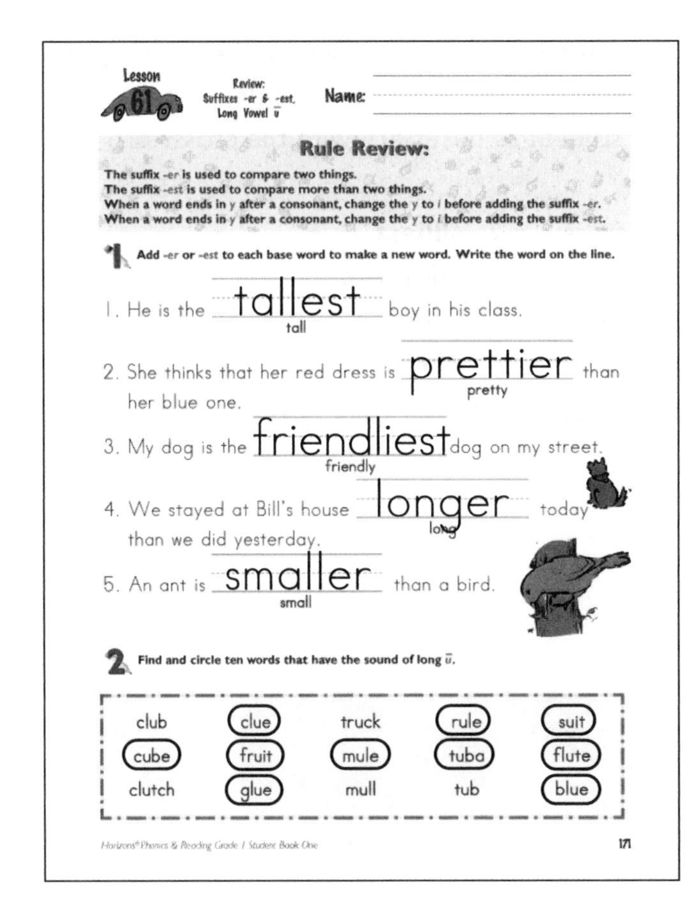

Lesson 61 Review: Suffixes -er & -est, Long Vowel ū Name:

Rule Review:
The suffix -er is used to compare two things.
The suffix -est is used to compare more than two things.
When a word ends in y after a consonant, change the y to i before adding the suffix -er.
When a word ends in y after a consonant, change the y to i before adding the suffix -est.

1. Add -er or -est to each base word to make a new word. Write the word on the line.

1. He is the tallest (tall) boy in his class.
2. She thinks that her red dress is prettier (pretty) than her blue one.
3. My dog is the friendliest (friendly) dog on my street.
4. We stayed at Bill's house longer (long) today than we did yesterday.
5. An ant is smaller (small) than a bird.

2. Find and circle ten words that have the sound of long ū.

club	clue	truck	rule	suit
cube	fruit	mule	tuba	flute
clutch	glue	mull	tub	blue

Horizons® Phonics & Reading Grade 1 Student Book One 171

Activity 2. Have the student read the words aloud. The student will circle the ten words that have the long **ū** sound.

Words: **cube, clue, fruit, glue, mule, rule, tuba, suit, flute, blue**

Activity 3. Review the words in the list. Help the student read the crossword puzzle clues. Assist the student as necessary with the crossword puzzle.

Across: **2. silliest**
4. windiest

Down: **1. sunnier**
3. earlier

Activity 4. Have the student read the words aloud.

3 Use the words from the list to complete the crossword puzzle.

earlier windiest silliest sunnier

ACROSS:
2. That clown is the ____ one I have ever seen.
4. Today is the ____ day we've had all week.

DOWN:
1. Today is ____ than yesterday.
3. We had to wake up ____ today.

4 Here are some long ū words that rhyme. Read the words in each list.

blue	glue	clue	true
cube	tube	rude	dude
due	cue	Sue	hue

172 Horizons® Phonics & Reading Grade 1 Student Book One

Lesson 62 - Adding Suffix -es to Words Ending in y, Review Long Vowel ē

Overview:

- Add suffix **-es** to base words ending in **y**
- Picture/word matching
- Identify words with long **ē** sound
- Write a story, using words from a list
- Rhyming words with long **ē** sound

Materials and Supplies:

- Teacher's Guide & Student Workbook
- White board or chalkboard
- Word cards (as necessary)
- Story: *The Purple Candies*

Teaching Tips:

Assist the student as needed in identifying the pictures and reading the words in the lesson. Review the rules for suffix **-er** added to words ending in **y** and for long vowel **ē**.

Activity 1. Have the student read the words aloud. The student will write new words by changing the **y** to an **i** and adding **es** to the end of each base word.

Words: **ponies, bunnies, cities, stories, lilies, cherries, candies, pennies**

Activity 2. Identify the pictures and discuss which pictures represent more than one. Instruct the student to circle the word that goes with each picture.

Pictures: **bunny, lilies, pennies**

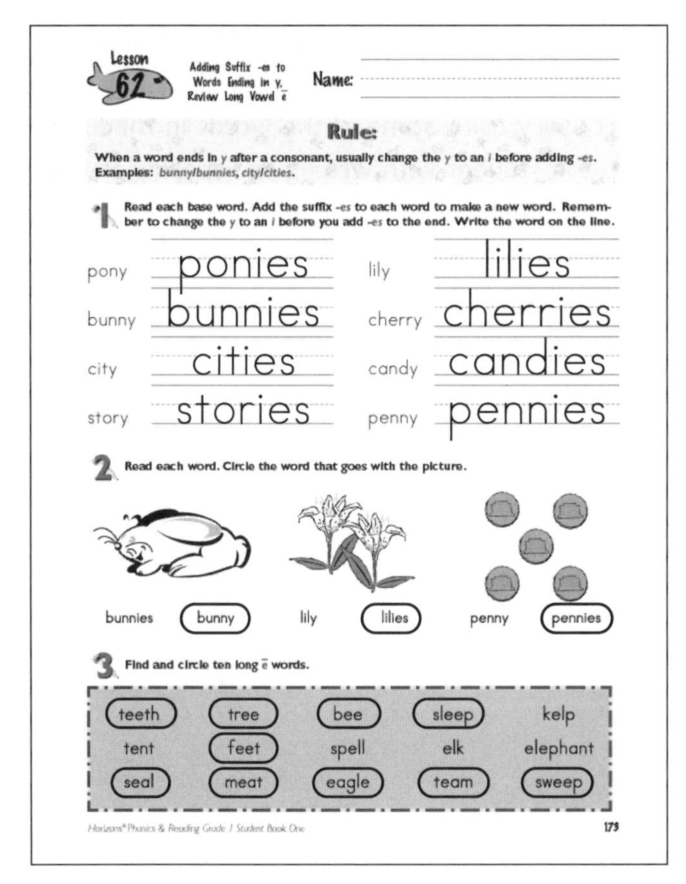

Lesson 62 Adding Suffix -es to Words Ending in y, Review Long Vowel ē

Name:

Rule:

When a word ends in y after a consonant, usually change the y to an i before adding -es. Examples: *bunny/bunnies, city/cities.*

1 Read each base word. Add the suffix -es to each word to make a new word. Remember to change the y to an i before you add -es to the end. Write the word on the line.

pony	ponies	lily	lilies
bunny	bunnies	cherry	cherries
city	cities	candy	candies
story	stories	penny	pennies

2 Read each word. Circle the word that goes with the picture.

bunnies (bunny) lily (lilies) penny (pennies)

3 Find and circle ten long ē words.

(teeth)	(tree)	(bee)	(sleep)	kelp
tent	(feet)	spell	elk	elephant
(seal)	(meat)	(eagle)	(team)	(sweep)

Horizons® Phonics & Reading Grade 1 Student Book One 173

Activity 3. Have the student read the words aloud. The student will circle the ten words that have the long **ē** sound.

Words: **teeth, seal, tree, feet, meat, bee, eagle, sleep, team, sweep**

Activity 4. Help the student read the words in the list as necessary. The student will write a short story, using some of the words in the list. Help the student with writing and spelling as necessary. Emphasize correct capitalization and punctuation.

Activity 5. Have the student read the words aloud.

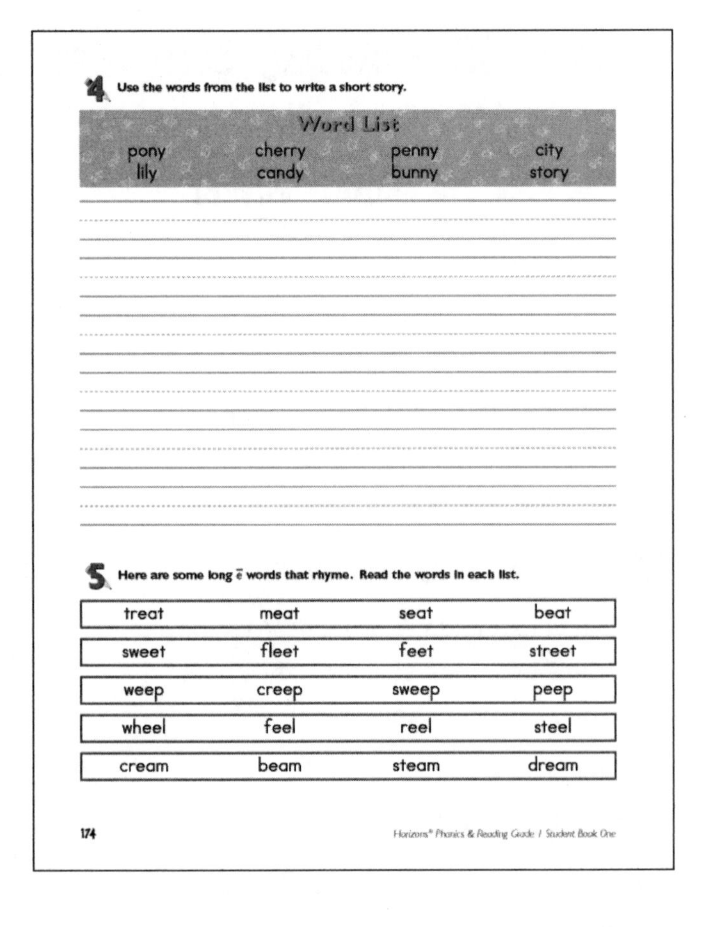
4. Use the words from the list to write a short story.

Word List

pony	cherry	penny	city
lily	candy	bunny	story

5. Here are some long ē words that rhyme. Read the words in each list.

treat	meat	seat	beat
sweet	fleet	feet	street
weep	creep	sweep	peep
wheel	feel	reel	steel
cream	beam	steam	dream

174 Horizons® Phonics & Reading Grade 1 Student Book One

Lesson 63 - Review: Suffix -es, -er, -est in Words Ending in y

Lesson 63 Review: Suffixes -es, -er, -est in Words Ending in y Name:

Rule Review:

When a word ends in y after a consonant, change the y to *i* before adding the suffix -es.
When a word ends in y after a consonant, change the y to *i* before adding the suffix -er.
When a word ends in y after a consonant, change the y to *i* before adding the suffix -est.

1 Read each sentence. Use words from the list to complete each sentence.

Word List
pennies stories parties daisies candies

1. We planted daisies in our yard.
2. I ate three candies for a snack.
3. One dollar is worth 100 pennies.
4. I went to two birthday parties in one day!
5. Mom read two stories to me before bedtime.

Horizons® Phonics & Reading Grade 1 Student Book One 175

Overview:

- Sentence completion
- Add suffixes **-es**, **-er**, and **-est** to base words
- Word search

Materials and Supplies:

- Teacher's Guide & Student Workbook
- White board or chalkboard
- Word cards (as necessary)
- Story: *The Fluffiest Bunnies*

Teaching Tips:

Assist the student as needed in reading the words in the lesson. Review the rules for suffixes **-es**, **-er**, and **-est**.

Activity 1. Help the student read the words in the list and the sentences. Instruct the student to select the word that will correctly complete each sentence, and write the word on the line.

Sentences:

1. **We planted daisies in our yard.**
2. **I ate three candies for a snack.**
3. **One dollar is worth 100 pennies.**
4. **I went to two birthday parties in one day!**
5. **Mom read two stories to me before bedtime.**

Activity 2. Have the student read the words aloud. The student will write new words by changing the **y** to **i** and adding **es, er,** or **est** to the end of each base word. Two of the words will have more than one suffix added.

Words: **ponies, babies, happier, happiest cherries, families, funnier, funniest**

Activity 3. Help the student read the words in the list. The student will find and circle the words from the list in the puzzle.

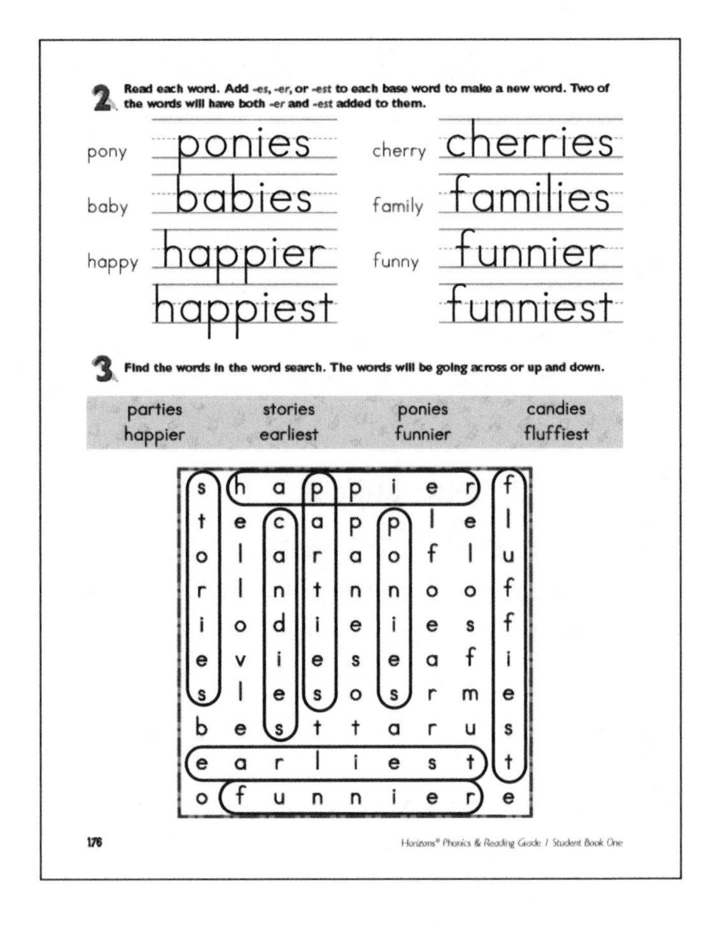

2 Read each word. Add *-es, -er,* or *-est* to each base word to make a new word. Two of the words will have both *-er* and *-est* added to them.

pony	ponies	cherry	cherries
baby	babies	family	families
happy	happier	funny	funnier
	happiest		funniest

3 Find the words in the word search. The words will be going across or up and down.

parties	stories	ponies	candies
happier	earliest	funnier	fluffiest

s	h	a	p	p	i	e	r	f
t	e	c	a	p	p	l	e	l
o	l	a	r	a	o	f	l	u
r	l	n	t	n	n	o	o	f
i	o	d	i	e	i	e	s	f
e	v	i	e	s	e	a	f	i
s	l	e	s	o	s	r	m	e
b	e	s	t	t	a	r	u	s
e	a	r	l	i	e	s	t	t
o	f	u	n	n	i	e	r	e

176 Horizons® Phonics & Reading Grade 1 Student Book One

Lesson 64 - Story Writing

Overview:

- Writing an imaginative story

Materials and Supplies:

- Teacher's Guide & Student Workbook
- White board or chalkboard
- Word cards (as necessary)
- Story: *The Lonely Prince*

Teaching Tips:

The student will be writing an imaginative story. He or she may write about any topic that is approved by the teacher. The student will write the rough draft on a piece of paper, and write the final copy on the lines provided in the workbook. The teacher or writing partner may help the student with ideas as necessary. The teacher should also help with spelling, punctuation, and capitalization. The student may use a dictionary if needed. The teacher or writing partner should help the student correct any errors in the rough draft before writing the final copy in the workbook.

Activity 1. Have the student write an imaginative story about a topic of his choice.

Lesson 64 Writing Lesson: Story Writing Name:

1. Write a story.

Your story can be about anything that you would like to write about. Before you write your story, talk to your teacher about ideas. Try to come up with three different things to write about. Then choose from your list of three.

After you have written your story, read it with your teacher or your writing partner. Have your teacher check your story. Make sure that you have spelled all the words correctly and that you have used capital letters where they are needed (names of people and places). Then you may write your final copy with no mistakes.

Write your first copy on a separate sheet of paper. Write your final copy on the lines on the back of this page.

173

Horizons® Phonics & Reading Grade 1 Student Book One

Lesson 65 - Review: Contractions

Overview:

- Sentence completion
- Matching contractions with phrases
- Identifying contractions in a story

Materials and Supplies:

- Teacher's Guide & Student Workbook
- White board or chalkboard
- Word cards (as necessary)
- Story: *The Lemonade Stand*

Teaching Tips:

Use the chalkboard or white board to review how contractions are formed. Have the student write examples of contractions on the chalkboard or white board.

Activity 1. Help the student read the sentences and the phrases. Instruct the student to make a contraction of the phrase to complete each sentence and write the contraction on the line.

Sentences:

1. **We're having a lot of fun.**
2. **They've brought games with them.**
3. **Joan isn't feeling well.**
4. **I'm making popcorn.**
5. **He's drinking lemonade.**

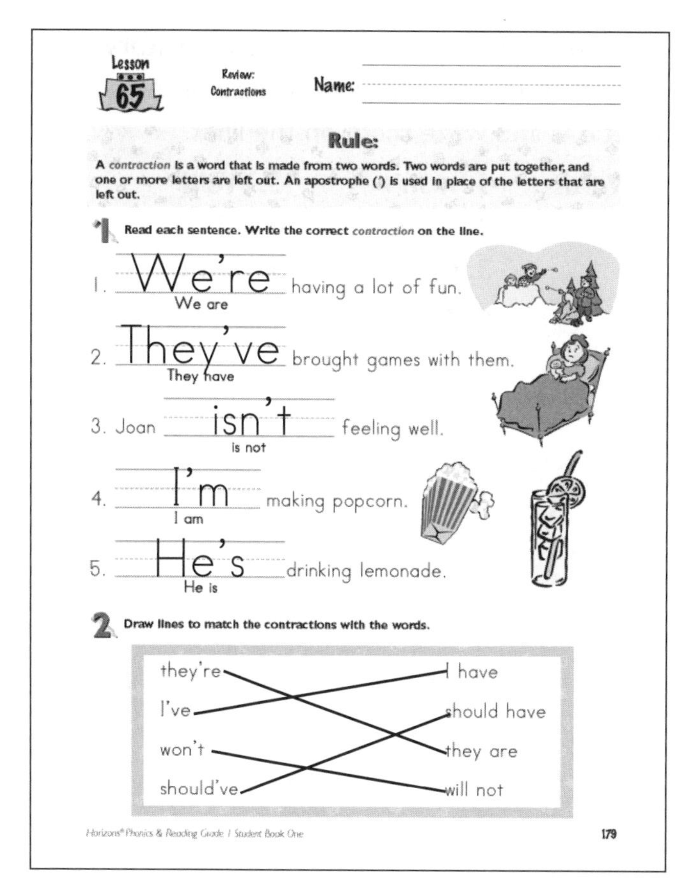

Lesson 65 Review: Contractions Name:

Rule:

A *contraction* is a word that is made from two words. Two words are put together, and one or more letters are left out. An apostrophe (') is used in place of the letters that are left out.

1 Read each sentence. Write the correct *contraction* on the line.

1. We're having a lot of fun. (We are)
2. They've brought games with them. (They have)
3. Joan isn't feeling well. (is not)
4. I'm making popcorn. (I am)
5. He's drinking lemonade. (He is)

2 Draw lines to match the contractions with the words.

they're	I have
I've	should have
won't	they are
should've	will not

Horizons® Phonics & Reading Grade 1 Student Book One 179

Activity 2. Have the student read all of the words aloud. The student will draw lines to match the contractions with the correct phrases.

Words: **they're/they are**
I've/I have
won't/will not
should've/should have

Activity 3. Have the student read the story aloud. The student will underline all of the contractions and write them on the lines.

Words:	**1. won't**	**5. We'll**
	2. she's	**6. I'll**
	3. I've	**7. don't**
	4. aren't	

3 Read the story. Underline the contractions in the story. On the lines below the story, write the *two words* that make up each contraction.

Joan says that she won't be going to the zoo with us tomorrow. She has a bad cold. Her mom says that she's too sick to go anywhere. I've had colds before, and they aren't any fun. We'll stop by her house on the way home and try to cheer her up. I'll be sure that I don't get too close to her!

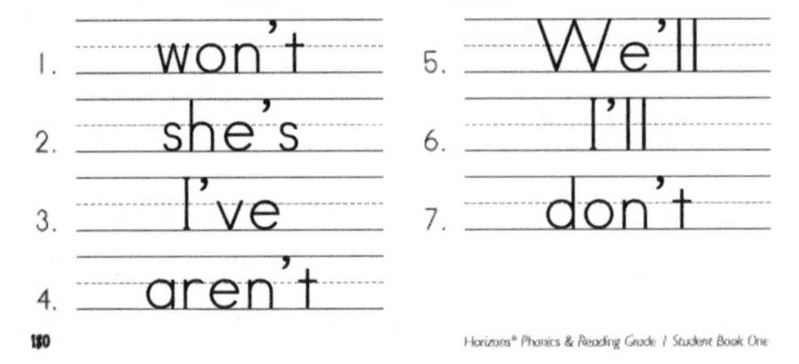

1. won't
2. she's
3. I've
4. aren't
5. We'll
6. I'll
7. don't

150 Horizons® Phonics & Reading Grade 1 Student Book One

Lesson 66 - Review: Vowel Pairs ai & ay

Overview:

- Word/picture match
- Sentence completion

Materials and Supplies:

- Teacher's Guide & Student Workbook
- White board or chalkboard
- Word cards (as necessary)
- Story: *Art Class*

Teaching Tips:

Go over the rule. Review any word cards from Lesson 20 as necessary. Have the student write examples of the rule on the chalkboard or white board. Assist the student as needed in identifying the pictures and reading the words in the lesson.

Activity 1. Have the student read the words in the list aloud. Review the pictures to make sure the student can correctly identify them. Instruct the student to write the correct words from the list underneath the pictures.

Pictures: **spray, play, train**
drain, pray, wait

Activity 2. Help the student read the words in the list and the sentences. Instruct the student to select the word(s) that will correctly complete each sentence and write the word(s) on the line(s).

Sentences:

1. **Today in art class we used clay.**
2. **I made a toy train.**
3. **After our projects dried, we painted them.**
4. **In my art class, work seems more like play.**

2 Read each sentence. Use a word from the list to complete each sentence. Write the word on the line.
Word List
clay today painted train play
1. Today in art class we used clay.
2. I made a toy train.
3. After our projects dried, we painted them.
4. In my art class, work seems more like play.
182
Horizons® Phonics & Reading Grade 1 Student Book One

Lesson 67 - Review: Vowel Pairs ee & ea

Overview:

- Word/picture match
- Sentence completion

Materials and Supplies:

- Teacher's Guide & Student Workbook
- White board or chalkboard
- Word cards (as necessary)
- Story: *The Teacher Reads a Book*

Teaching Tips:

Assist the student as needed in identifying the pictures and reading the words in the lesson. Review the rule for vowel pairs **ee** and **ea**. Have the student write examples of the rule on the chalkboard or white board. Review any word cards from Lesson 20 as necessary.

Activity 1. Identify the pictures and have the student read the word choices aloud. The student is to circle the word that goes with the picture and write the word on the line.

Pictures: **seat, wheel, teach**
read, sleeping, wheat

Lesson 67 Review: Vowel Pairs ee & ea Name:

Rule:

A vowel pair is two vowels that come together to make one long vowel sound. The first vowel is long, and the second vowel is silent. Examples: *ee/wheel* and *ea/teach*.

1. Read each word. Circle the word that goes with the picture. Write the word on the lines.

seem (seat) — seat
spell (wheel) — wheel
(teach) tree — teach
(read) sleep — read
running (sleeping) — sleeping
wheel (wheat) — wheat

Horizons® Phonics & Reading Grade 1 Student Book One 183

Activity 2. Help the student read the words in the list and the sentences. Instruct the student to select the word that will correctly complete each sentence and write the word on the line.

Sentences:

1. **He is reading a good book.**
2. **By 8:00, I'm sleeping.**
3. **My bike needs a new wheel.**
4. **My mom is teaching me to cook.**
5. **It was time to eat, so I took my seat at the table.**

2 **Read each sentence. Use a word from the list to complete each sentence. Write the word on the line.**

Word List

sleeping wheel eat teaching seat reading

1. He is reading a good book.
2. By 8:00, I'm sleeping.
3. My bike needs a new wheel.
4. My mom is teaching me to cook.
5. It was time to eat, so I took my seat at the table.

184 *Horizons® Phonics & Reading Grade 1 Student Book One*

Lesson 68 - Review: Vowel Pairs ie & oe

Overview:

- Sentence completion
- Picture/word match
- Read short story, answer questions

Materials and Supplies:

- Teacher's Guide & Student Workbook
- White board or chalkboard
- Word cards (as necessary)
- Story: *The Cherry Pie*

Teaching Tips:

Assist the student as needed in identifying the pictures and reading the words in the lesson. Review the rules for vowel pairs **ie** and **oe**. Go over any word cards from Lesson 20 as necessary. Have the student write examples of the rule on the chalkboard or white board.

Activity 1. Help the student read the sentences and the word choices. Instruct the student to circle the word that will correctly complete each sentence and write the word on the line.

Sentences:

1. **Joe was playing outside.**
2. **He saw a doe in the woods.**
3. **It stopped to lie down in the grass.**
4. **Joe stopped to tie his shoe.**

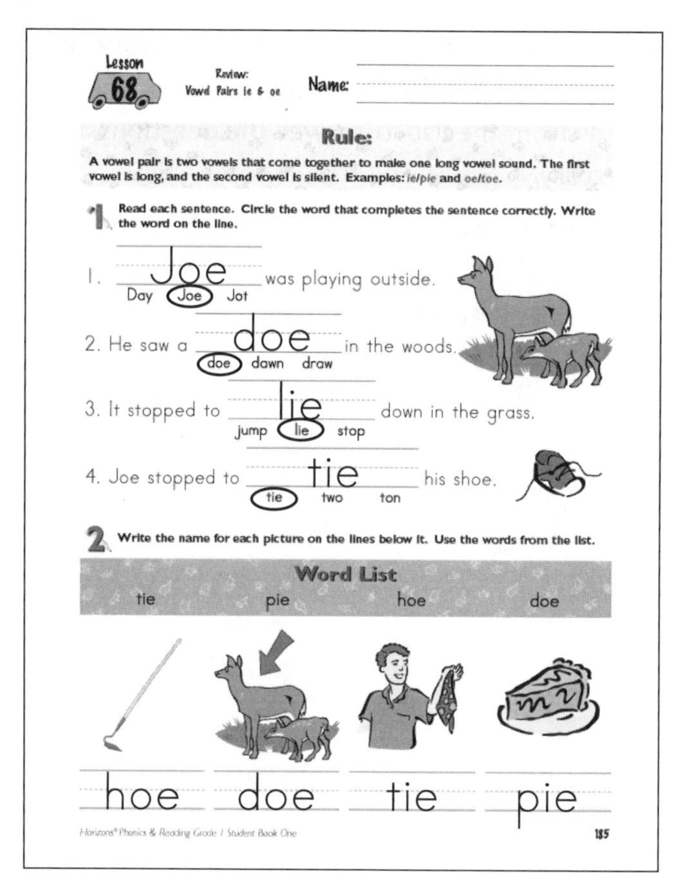

Lesson 68 Review: Vowel Pairs ie & oe Name:

Rule:
A vowel pair is two vowels that come together to make one long vowel sound. The first vowel is long, and the second vowel is silent. Examples: *ie/pie* and *oe/toe*.

1 Read each sentence. Circle the word that completes the sentence correctly. Write the word on the line.

1. Joe was playing outside. (Day, Joe, Jot)
2. He saw a doe in the woods. (doe, dawn, draw)
3. It stopped to lie down in the grass. (jump, lie, stop)
4. Joe stopped to tie his shoe. (tie, two, ton)

2 Write the name for each picture on the lines below it. Use the words from the list.

Word List
tie pie hoe doe

hoe doe tie pie

Horizons Phonics & Reading Grade 1 Student Book One 135

Activity 2. Have the student identify the pictures and write the correct word from the list under each picture.

Pictures: **hoe, doe, tie, pie**

Activity 3. Have the student read the story and the words in the list. The student will use the words from the list to answer the questions after the story.

Answers: **1. pie**
2. Joe
3. peach

3 **Read the story. Circle all the words that have the vowel pairs *ie*, *ea*, and *oe* in them. Use the words from the story to answer the questions after the story.**

Sarah and her mom made a pie. They made peach pie. Sarah liked peach pie best. Sarah's brother Joe helped as much as he could. He was only three years old.

When the pie was cool, each of them had a slice. It was very good!

Sarah said, "Let's make cherry pie next time."

Mom said, "That's a good idea, Sarah!"

1. What did Sarah and her mom make? pie
2. Who helped Sarah and her mom make the pie? Joe
3. What kind of pie did they make? peach

186 Horizons® Phonics & Reading Grade 1 Student Book One

Lesson 69 - Letter Writing

Overview:

- Writing a friendly letter

Materials and Supplies:

- Teacher's Guide & Student Workbook
- White board or chalkboard
- Word cards (as necessary)
- Story: *The Letter*

Teaching Tips:

The student will be writing a friendly letter. Go over the five parts of a letter with the student. Have the student practice writing the different parts of the letter on the chalkboard or white board. Help the student with ideas for the letter as necessary. The teacher or writing partner should help with letter structure and spelling as needed. The student will write the rough draft of the letter on paper and the final copy of the letter on the lines provided in the student workbook.

Activity 1. Write a friendly letter.

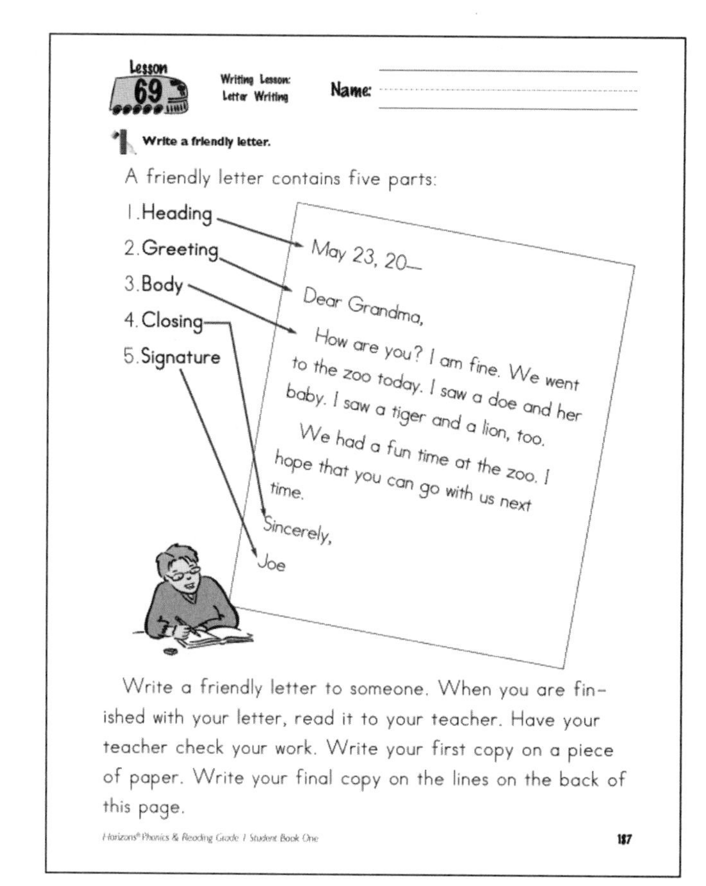

Lesson 69 Writing Lesson: Letter Writing Name:

1. Write a friendly letter.

A friendly letter contains five parts:

1. Heading
2. Greeting
3. Body
4. Closing
5. Signature

May 23, 20—

Dear Grandma,

How are you? I am fine. We went to the zoo today. I saw a doe and her baby. I saw a tiger and a lion, too.

We had a fun time at the zoo. I hope that you can go with us next time.

Sincerely,

Joe

Write a friendly letter to someone. When you are finished with your letter, read it to your teacher. Have your teacher check your work. Write your first copy on a piece of paper. Write your final copy on the lines on the back of this page.

Horizons® Phonics & Reading Grade 1 Student Book One 187

188 Horizons® Phonics & Reading Grade 1 Student Book One

Lesson 70 - Review: Vowel Digraph oo

Overview:

- Sentence completion
- Rhyming word match
- Picture/word match
- Sentence writing

Materials and Supplies:

- Teacher's Guide & Student Workbook
- White board or chalkboard
- Word cards (as necessary)
- Story: *The Cool Pool*

Teaching Tips:

Review the rule. Have the student write examples of the rule on the chalkboard or white board. Go over any word cards from Lesson 21 as necessary. Assist the student as needed in identifying the pictures and reading the words in the lesson.

Activity 1. Help the student read the sentences and the word choices. Instruct the student to underline the word that will correctly complete each sentence and write the word on the line.

Sentences:

1. **The air is very cool today.**
2. **Joe is reading a very thick book.**
3. **We will ride the bus to school.**
4. **Dad uses an ax to chop wood.**
5. **She shares a room with her sister.**

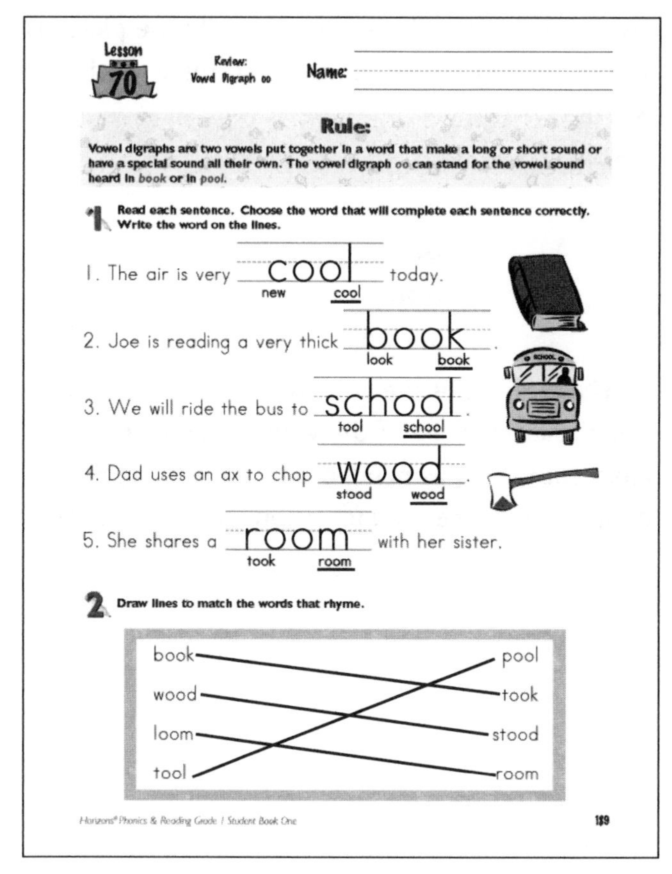
Lesson 70

Review: Vowel Digraph oo

Name:

Rule:

Vowel digraphs are two vowels put together in a word that make a long or short sound or have a special sound all their own. The vowel digraph oo can stand for the vowel sound heard in *book* or in *pool*.

1 **Read each sentence. Choose the word that will complete each sentence correctly. Write the word on the lines.**

1. The air is very cool today. (new / cool)
2. Joe is reading a very thick book. (look / book)
3. We will ride the bus to school. (tool / school)
4. Dad uses an ax to chop wood. (stood / wood)
5. She shares a room with her sister. (took / room)

2 **Draw lines to match the words that rhyme.**

book	pool
wood	took
loom	stood
tool	room

Horizons® Phonics & Reading Grade 1 Student Book One 189

Activity 2. Help the student read the words in the activity. The student will draw lines to match the words that rhyme. Ask for verbal examples of additional rhyming words.

Rhyming words: **book/took**
wood/stood
loom/room
tool/pool

Activity 3. Have the student identify the pictures and draw a line to match the pictures with the words.

Pictures: **tool**
room
book
noon
school

Activity 4. Have the student write a sentence using at least three of the words in Activity 3. Help with ideas as needed, and remind the student about correct punctuation and capitalization.

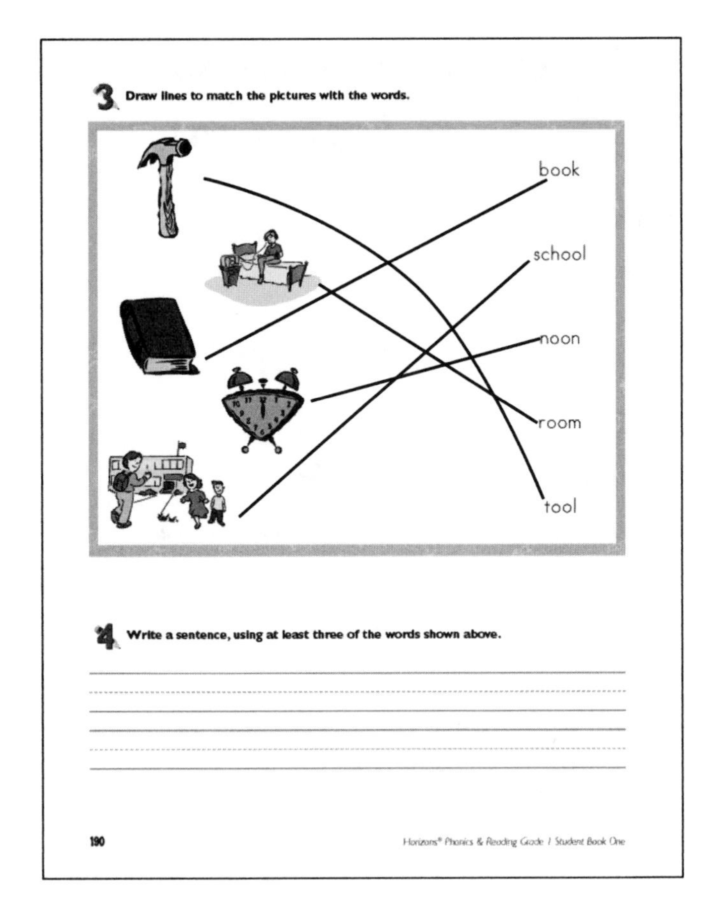
3 Draw lines to match the pictures with the words.

book
school
noon
room
tool

4 Write a sentence, using at least three of the words shown above.

190 Horizons® Phonics & Reading Grade 1 Student Book One

Test 7

Lessons 61-70

Instructions:

Review the suffixes **-est**, **-er**, and **-es** in words that end in a consonant and a **y** or when comparing two or more items. Review the definition of a contraction. Have the student give examples of contractions with **not**, **have**, **will**, **is**, **am**, and **us**. Review the rule for vowel pairs and ask the student for examples. Read through the test with the student. Help the student with any words that he/she is still unsure of. The teacher should be available to answer any questions that the student may have during the test.

Activity 1. Review the sentences and the base words with the student.

Sentences:

1. **They have the prettiest yard on our street.**
2. **He is the smallest boy in his class.**
3. **Joan's hair is curlier than Ruth's hair.**
4. **New York and Boston are two cities.**
5. **Mom read two stories to me last night.**

Activity 2. Review the instructions with the student.

Words:		
	do not	**we will**
	cannot	**he is**
	will not	**let us**
	should have	**I am**

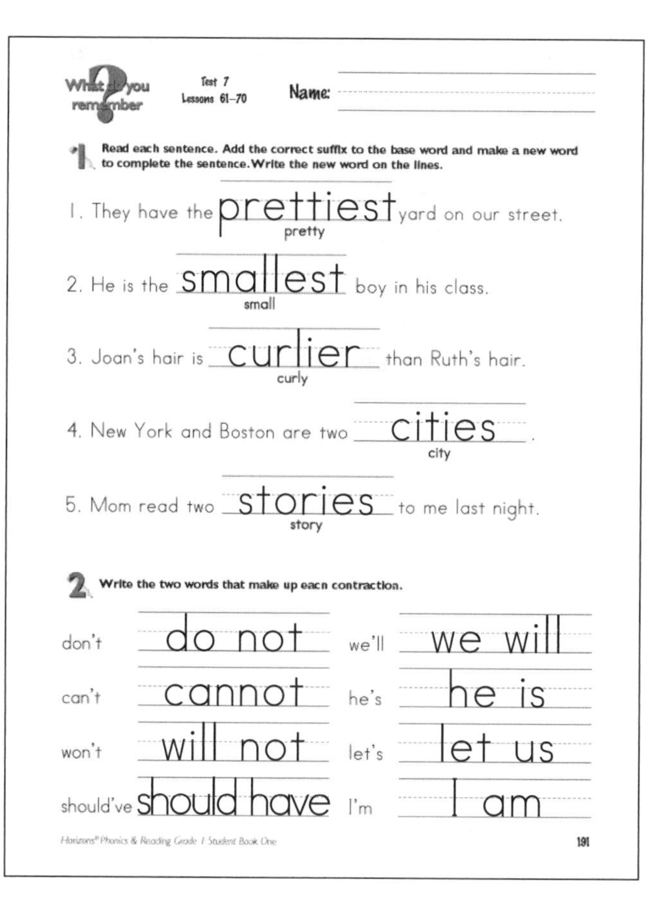

Test 7
Lessons 61–70

Name:

1. Read each sentence. Add the correct suffix to the base word and make a new word to complete the sentence. Write the new word on the lines.

1. They have the prettiest yard on our street. (pretty)
2. He is the smallest boy in his class. (small)
3. Joan's hair is curlier than Ruth's hair. (curly)
4. New York and Boston are two cities. (city)
5. Mom read two stories to me last night. (story)

2. Write the two words that make up eacn contraction.

don't	do not	we'll	we will
can't	cannot	he's	he is
won't	will not	let's	let us
should've	should have	I'm	I am

Horizons® Phonics & Reading Grade 1 Student Book One 191

Activity 3. Review the riddles and the words in the list with the student.

Words: **tie**
toe
paint
play
train
wheels

Lesson 71 - Review: Vowel Digraph ea

Overview:

- Sentence completion
- Picture/word match
- Story completion

Materials and Supplies:

- Teacher's Guide & Student Workbook
- White board or chalkboard
- Word cards (as necessary)
- Story: *The Red Sweater*

Teaching Tips:

Review the rule. Have the student write examples of the rule on the chalkboard or white board. Review any word cards from Lesson 21 as necessary. Remind the students that when **ea** has the **short sound** as in **bread**, it is a vowel digraph. When it has the **long sound** as in **read**, it is classified as a vowel pair.

Activity 1. Help the student read the sentences and the word choices. If desired, you may instruct the student to underline the word that will correctly complete each sentence. Have the student write the correct word on the line.

Sentences:

1. **The bird ate the bread on the sidewalk.**
2. **He ran ahead of me.**
3. **She is wearing a heavy coat today.**
4. **I will spread butter on my bread.**
5. **He has a hat on his head.**

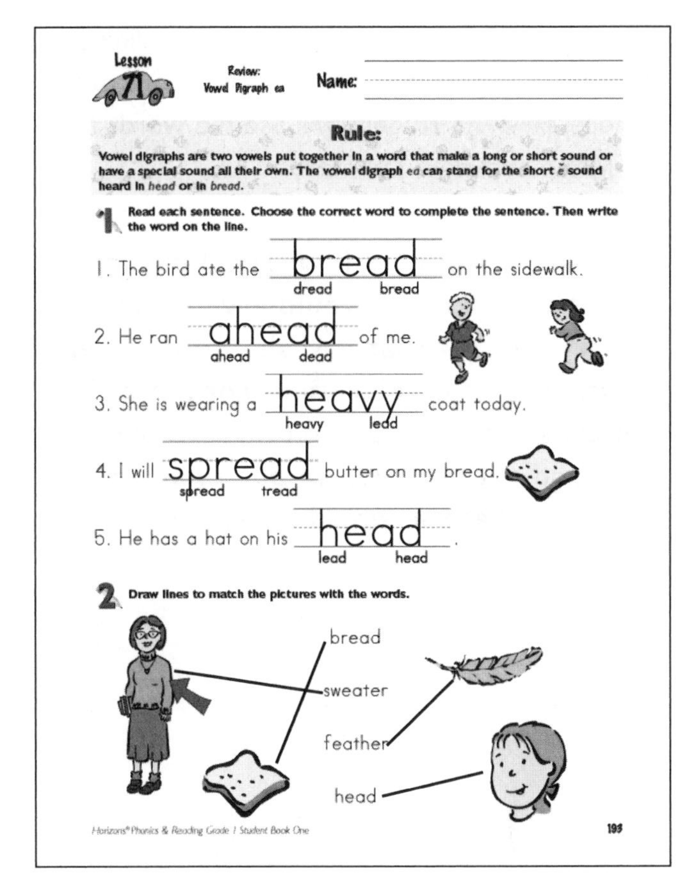

Lesson 71 Review: Vowel Digraph ea Name:

Rule:

Vowel digraphs are two vowels put together in a word that make a long or short sound or have a special sound all their own. The vowel digraph *ea* can stand for the short ĕ sound heard in *head* or in *bread*.

1 Read each sentence. Choose the correct word to complete the sentence. Then write the word on the line.

1. The bird ate the bread on the sidewalk. (dread, bread)
2. He ran ahead of me. (ahead, dead)
3. She is wearing a heavy coat today. (heavy, lead)
4. I will spread butter on my bread. (spread, tread)
5. He has a hat on his head. (lead, head)

2 Draw lines to match the pictures with the words.

bread
sweater
feather
head

Horizons® Phonics & Reading Grade 1 Student Book One 193

Activity 2. Have the student identify the pictures and draw a line to match the pictures with the words.

Pictures:	**sweater**	**feather**
	bread	**head**

Activity 3. Help the student read the unfinished story and the words in the list. Make word cards as necessary. The student will use the words from the list to complete the story.

Story:

When Jan woke up, it was cold outside. She knew that she would have to wear a heavy sweater that day. She went to get some breakfast. Her mom got her a slice of bread to make some toast. After she ate and got dressed, Jan put a hat on her head so that she would be warm.

3 **Read the story. Use the words from the list to complete the story.**

Word List

bread sweater head breakfast

When Jan woke up, it was cold outside. She knew that she would have to wear a heavy sweater that day. She went to get some breakfast. Her mom got her a slice of bread to make some toast. After she ate and got dressed, Jan put a hat on her head so that she would be warm.

194 Horizons® Phonics & Reading Grade 1 Student Book One

Lesson 72 - Review: Vowel Digraphs au & aw

Overview:

- Sentence completion
- Matching words with same vowel sounds
- Story completion

Materials and Supplies:

- Teacher's Guide & Student Workbook
- White board or chalkboard
- Word cards (as necessary)
- Story: *Paul Mows the Lawn*

Teaching Tips:

Review the rule. Have the student write examples of the rule on the chalkboard or white board. Review any word cards from Lesson 21 as necessary. Assist the student as needed in reading the words in the lesson.

Activity 1. Help the student read the words in the list and the sentences. Instruct the student to select the word that will correctly complete each sentence and write the word on the line.

Sentences:

1. **August is usually a hot month.**
2. **My brother mows the lawn.**
3. **My friend's name is Paula.**
4. **I like to drink with a straw.**
5. **When I am tired, I yawn.**
6. **The man had to haul the junk away.**

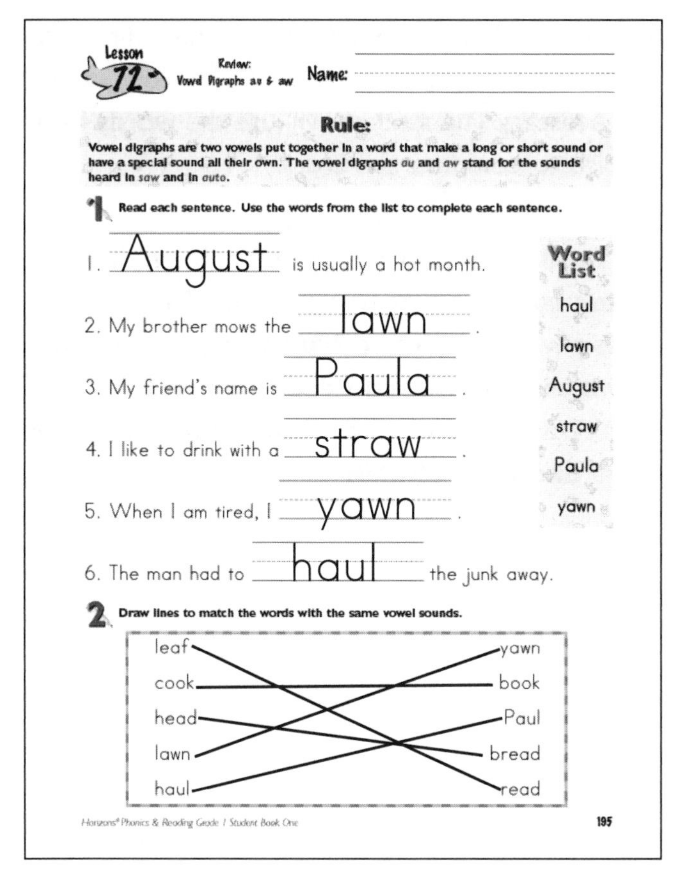
Lesson 72 Review: Vowel Digraphs au & aw Name:

Rule:

Vowel digraphs are two vowels put together in a word that make a long or short sound or have a special sound all their own. The vowel digraphs au and aw stand for the sounds heard in saw and in auto.

1 Read each sentence. Use the words from the list to complete each sentence.

Word List: haul, lawn, August, straw, Paula, yawn

1. August is usually a hot month.
2. My brother mows the lawn.
3. My friend's name is Paula.
4. I like to drink with a straw.
5. When I am tired, I yawn.
6. The man had to haul the junk away.

2 Draw lines to match the words with the same vowel sounds.

leaf, cook, head, lawn, haul — yawn, book, Paul, bread, read

Horizons® Phonics & Reading Grade 1 Student Book One 195

Activity 2. Have the student read the words aloud. The student will draw lines to match the words with the same vowel sounds.

Words: **leaf/read**
cook/book
head/bread
lawn/yawn
haul/Paul

Activity 3. Help the student read the unfinished story and the words in the list. Make word cards as necessary. The student will use the words from the list to complete the story.

Story:

Paul didn't want to mow the lawn. It was August, so it was hot outside. Paul's dad also wanted him to haul some trash. Paul wanted to be inside drawing pictures. Paul gave a big yawn and went outside to do as his dad had told him.

3 **Read the story. Use the words from the list to complete the story.**

Word List

yawn drawing lawn August haul

Paul didn't want to mow the lawn. It was August, so it was hot outside. Paul's dad also wanted him to haul some trash. Paul wanted to be inside drawing pictures. Paul gave a big yawn and went outside to do as his dad had told him.

196 Horizons® Phonics & Reading Grade 1 Student Book One

Lesson 73 - Review: Vowel Digraphs ei & ew

Overview:

- Picture/word match
- Sentence completion
- Crossword puzzle
- "Silly sentence" completion

Materials and Supplies:

- Teacher's Guide & Student Workbook
- White board or chalkboard
- Word cards (as necessary)
- Story: *The Neighbor in Number Eight*

Teaching Tips:

Review the rule. Have the student write examples of the rule on the chalkboard or white board. Review any word cards from Lesson 21 as necessary. Assist the student as needed in reading the words in the lesson.

Activity 1. Have the student identify the pictures and draw a line to match the pictures with the words.

Pictures:	flew	weight
	eight	**stew**
	sleigh	**reindeer**

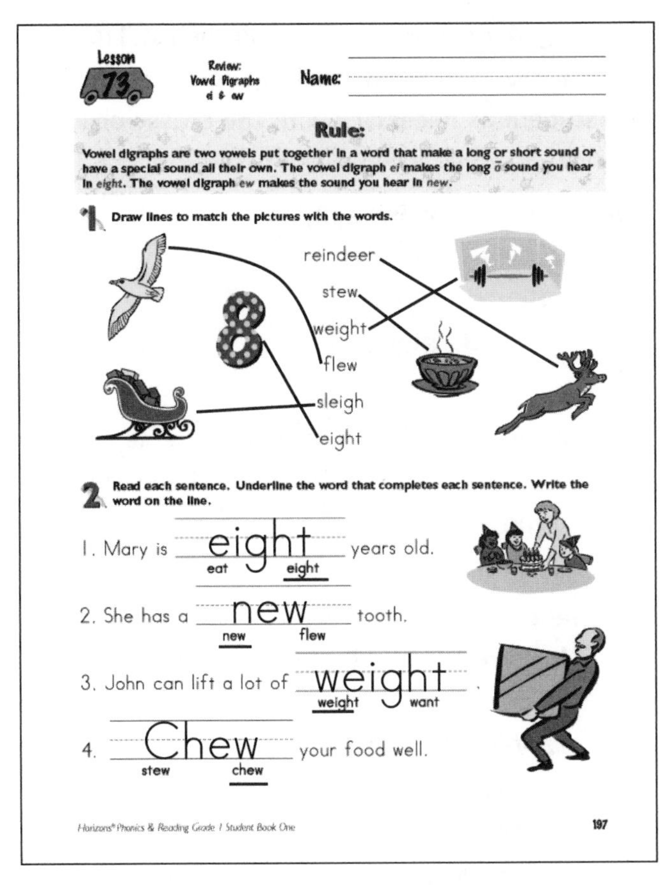

Lesson 73 Review: Vowel Digraphs ei & ew Name:

Rule:

Vowel digraphs are two vowels put together in a word that make a long or short sound or have a special sound all their own. The vowel digraph ei makes the long ā sound you hear in eight. The vowel digraph ew makes the sound you hear in new.

1. Draw lines to match the pictures with the words.

reindeer
stew
weight
flew
sleigh
eight

2. Read each sentence. Underline the word that completes each sentence. Write the word on the line.

1. Mary is eight years old. (eat / eight)
2. She has a new tooth. (new / flew)
3. John can lift a lot of weight. (weight / want)
4. Chew your food well. (stew / chew)

Horizons® Phonics & Reading Grade 1 Student Book One 197

Activity 2. Help the student read the sentences and the word choices. Instruct the student to underline the word that will correctly complete each sentence, and write the word on the line.

Sentences:

1. **Mary is eight years old.**
2. **She has a new tooth.**
3. **John can lift a lot of weight.**
4. **Chew your food well.**

Activity 3. Review the words in the list. Help the student read the crossword puzzle clues. Assist the student as necessary with the crossword puzzle.

Across: **2. reindeer**
4. weight

Down: **1. new**
3. eight
4. sleigh

Activity 4. Have the student read the sentences and the words from the list aloud. The student will use the words from the list to complete the "silly sentences."

Sentences:

1. **Wouldn't it be silly if reindeer rode in sleighs?**
2. **Wouldn't it be silly if seven came after eight?**
3. **Wouldn't it be silly if a baby could lift weights?**
4. **Wouldn't it be silly if freight trains had faces?**

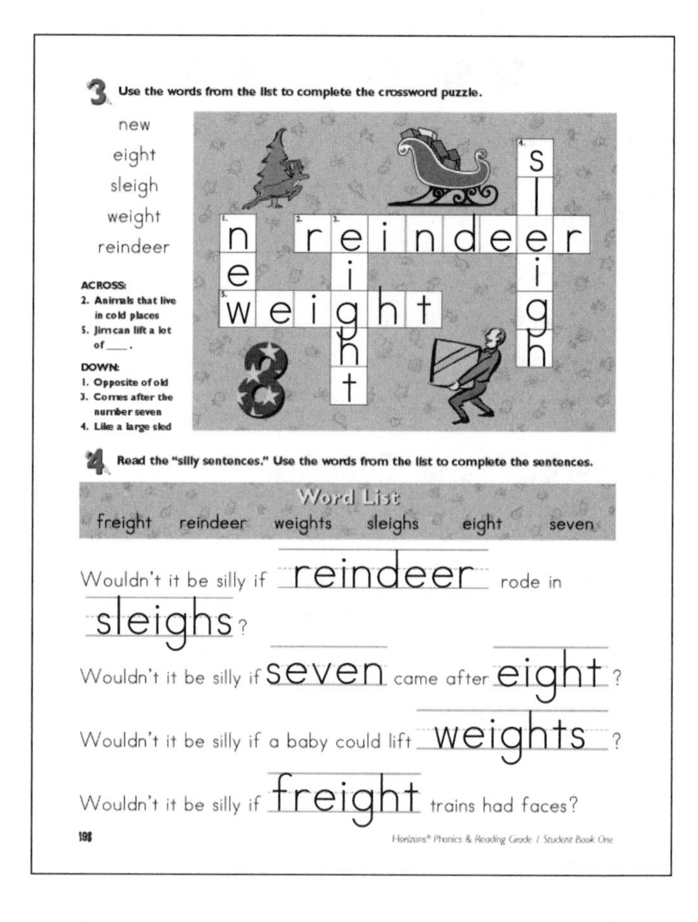

3 Use the words from the list to complete the crossword puzzle.

new
eight
sleigh
weight
reindeer

ACROSS:
2. Animals that live in cold places
5. Jim can lift a lot of ___.

DOWN:
1. Opposite of old
3. Comes after the number seven
4. Like a large sled

4 Read the "silly sentences." Use the words from the list to complete the sentences.

Word List
freight reindeer weights sleighs eight seven

Wouldn't it be silly if reindeer rode in sleighs?

Wouldn't it be silly if seven came after eight?

Wouldn't it be silly if a baby could lift weights?

Wouldn't it be silly if freight trains had faces?

198 Horizons® Phonics & Reading Grade 1 Student Book One

Lesson 74 - Vowel Diphthongs
ou & ow

Overview:

- Picture/word match
- Write correct word to answer riddles
- Story writing

Materials and Supplies:

- Teacher's Guide & Student Workbook
- White board or chalkboard
- Word cards (as necessary)
- Story: *The Brown House*

Teaching Tips:

Review the rule. Have the student write examples of the rule on the chalkboard or white board. Assist the student as needed in identifying the pictures or reading the words in the lesson.

Activity 1. Assist the student as needed to identify the pictures in the activity. Have the student draw lines to match the pictures with the words.

Pictures:		
	cloud	**owl**
	crown	**brown**
	mouse	**cow**
	down	**mouth**

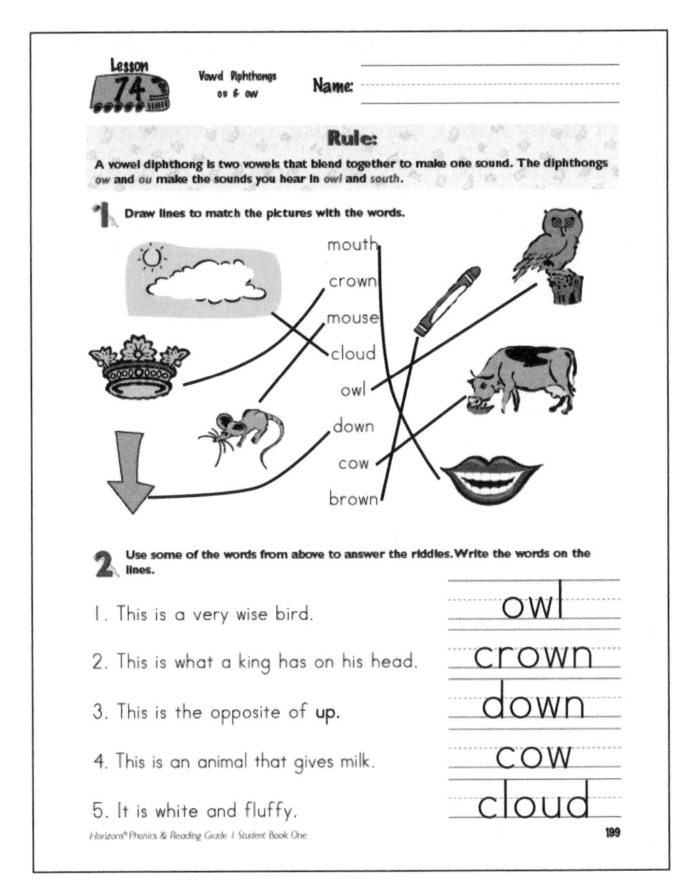

Lesson 74 Vowel Diphthongs ou & ow Name:

Rule:

A vowel diphthong is two vowels that blend together to make one sound. The diphthongs *ow* and *ou* make the sounds you hear in *owl* and *south*.

1. Draw lines to match the pictures with the words.

mouth
crown
mouse
cloud
owl
down
cow
brown

2. Use some of the words from above to answer the riddles. Write the words on the lines.

1. This is a very wise bird. owl
2. This is what a king has on his head. crown
3. This is the opposite of up. down
4. This is an animal that gives milk. cow
5. It is white and fluffy. cloud

Horizons® Phonics & Reading Grade 1 Student Book One 199

Activity 2. Help the student read the words in the word list and in the riddles. The student will select the correct answer from the word list for each riddle.

Words:		
	1. owl	**4. cow**
	2. crown	**5. cloud**
	3. down	

Activity 3. Help the student read the words in the list as necessary. The student will write a short story about the picture, using some of the words in the list. Help the student with writing and spelling as necessary. Emphasize correct capitalization and punctuation.

Lesson 75 - Sounds of ow

Overview:

- Word categorization
- Word completion
- Sentence completion
- Words with the long ō sound of **ow**

Materials and Supplies:

- Teacher's Guide & Student Workbook
- White board or chalkboard
- Word cards (as necessary)
- Story: *The Snow Fort*

Teaching Tips:

Review the rule. Have the student write examples of the rule on the chalkboard or white board of both sounds of **ow**. Assist the student as needed in identifying the pictures or reading the words in the lesson.

Activity 1. Have the student read the words in the list aloud. The student will write the words in the correct categories, according to the sound of the **ow** each word makes.

ow as in cow: **drown, brown, owl, town**
ow as in snow: **low, flow, below, show**

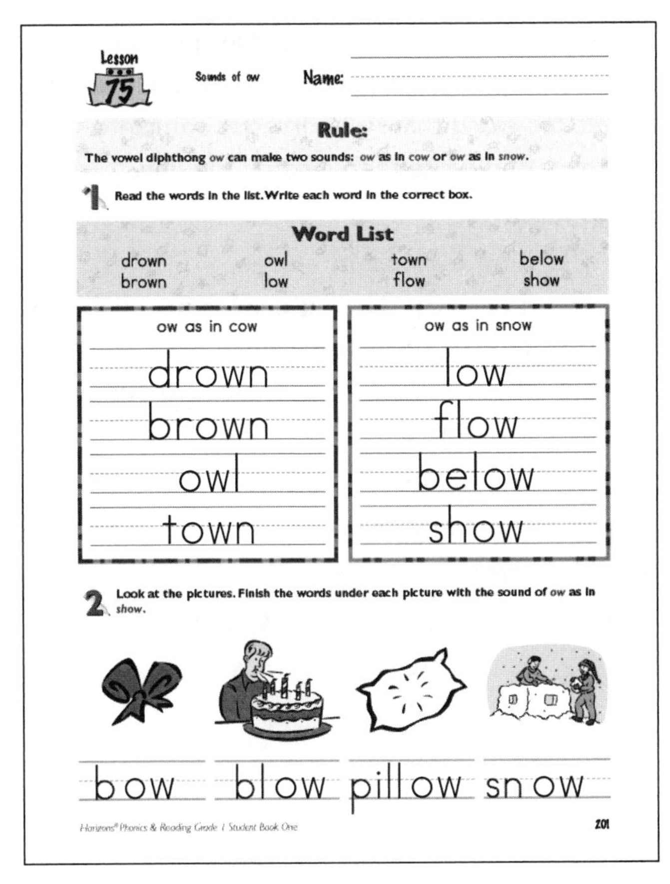

Lesson 75 Sounds of ow Name:

Rule:
The vowel diphthong *ow* can make two sounds: *ow* as in *cow* or *ow* as in *snow*.

1. Read the words in the list. Write each word in the correct box.

Word List

drown	owl	town	below
brown	low	flow	show

ow as in cow	ow as in snow
drown	low
brown	flow
owl	below
town	show

2. Look at the pictures. Finish the words under each picture with the sound of *ow* as in *show*.

bow blow pillow snow

Horizons® Phonics & Reading Grade 1 Student Book One 201

Activity 2. Have the student identify the pictures and add **ow** to each of the words below the pictures. Ask the student to read the words aloud. Ask the students for additional examples of words with the long ō sound of **ow**.

Pictures: **bow, blow, pillow, snow**

Activity 3. Help the student read the words in the list and the sentences. Instruct the student to select the word that will correctly complete each sentence and write the word on the line.

Sentences:

1. **The owl sat in a tree.**
2. **The king wore a crown on his head.**
3. **I sleep on a soft pillow.**
4. **We made a snowman in front of our house.**

Activity 4. Have the student read the words in the list aloud and write the words with the long **ō** sound of **ow** on the lines below.

Words: **1. pillow** **2. show** **3. below** **4. flow** **5. snow**

3 **Read each sentence. Use the words from the list to complete the sentences.**

Word List

crown pillow snowman owl

1. The owl sat in the tree.
2. The king wore a crown on his head.
3. I sleep on a soft pillow.
4. We made a snowman in front of our house.

4 **Read each word in the list. On the lines below, write the *ow* words that have the long ō sound.**

Word List

pillow	now	below	crown
show	clown	flow	snow

1. pillow
2. show
3. below
4. flow
5. snow

202 Horizons® Phonics & Reading Grade 1 Student Book One

Lesson 76 - Vowel Diphthongs oi & oy

Overview:

- Word/picture match
- Sentence completion
- Read short story and answer questions

Materials and Supplies:

- Teacher's Guide & Student Workbook
- White board or chalkboard
- Word cards (as necessary)
- Story: *The Coin Collection*

Teaching Tips:

Review the rule. Have the student write examples of the rule on the chalkboard or white board of **ow** and **oi** words. Assist the student as needed in identifying the pictures or reading the words in the lesson.

Activity 1. Have the student identify the pictures and draw a line to match the pictures with the words.

Pictures:	**boil**	**coin**
	toys	**boy**
		soil

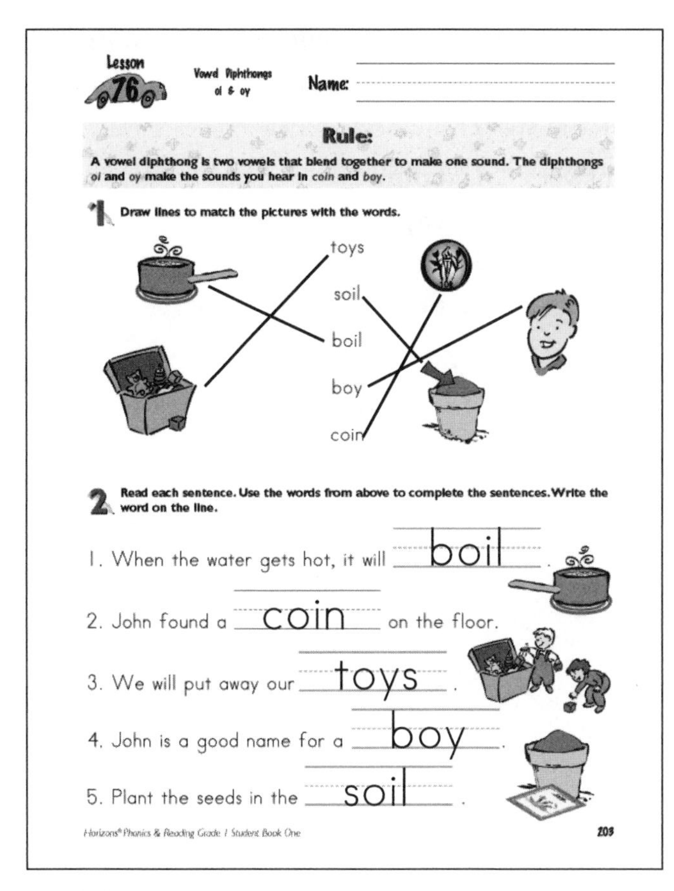
Lesson 76 Vowel Diphthongs oi & oy Name:

Rule:
A vowel diphthong is two vowels that blend together to make one sound. The diphthongs oi and oy make the sounds you hear in *coin* and *boy*.

1 Draw lines to match the pictures with the words.

toys
soil
boil
boy
coin

2 Read each sentence. Use the words from above to complete the sentences. Write the word on the line.

1. When the water gets hot, it will boil.
2. John found a coin on the floor.
3. We will put away our toys.
4. John is a good name for a boy.
5. Plant the seeds in the soil.

Horizons® Phonics & Reading Grade 1 Student Book One 203

Activity 2. Help the student read the sentences. Instruct the student to select the word from Activity 1 that will correctly complete each sentence and write the word on the line.

Sentences:

1. **When the water gets hot, it will boil.**
2. **John found a coin on the floor.**
3. **We will put away our toys.**
4. **John is a good name for a boy.**
5. **Plant the seeds in the soil.**

Activity 3. Help the student as needed in reading the story. The student will answer the questions after the story.

Answers: **1. coins**
2. toys
3. yes
4. no

3 **Read the story and answer the questions.**

Roy is a boy who likes to collect coins. He has a lot of coins from many different places.

Some of Roy's friends think that his coins are toys, but Roy lets them know that his coins are not toys at all.

1. What does Roy like to collect? coins
2. What do Roy's friends think his coins are? toys
3. Does Roy have a lot of coins? yes
4. Do all the coins come from just one place? no

204 Horizons® Phonics & Reading Grade 1 Student Book One

Lesson 77 - Review: Vowel Diphthongs ou & ow

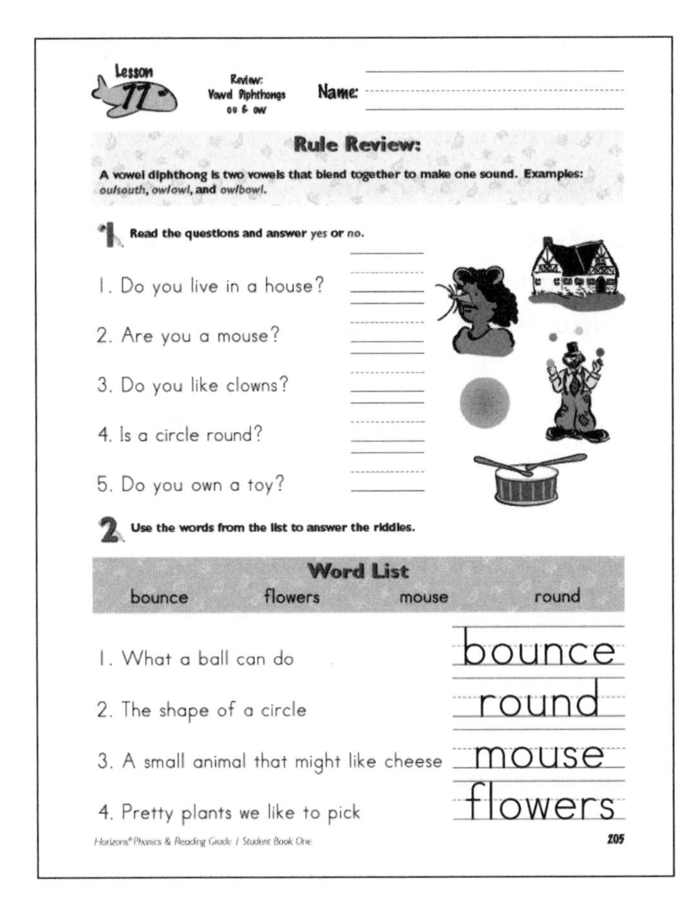
Lesson 77

Review: Vowel Diphthongs ou & ow

Name:

Rule Review:

A vowel diphthong is two vowels that blend together to make one sound. Examples: *ou/south*, *ow/owl*, **and** *ow/bowl*.

1 Read the questions and answer *yes* **or** *no*.

1. Do you live in a house?
2. Are you a mouse?
3. Do you like clowns?
4. Is a circle round?
5. Do you own a toy?

2 Use the words from the list to answer the riddles.

Word List

bounce flowers mouse round

1. What a ball can do — bounce
2. The shape of a circle — round
3. A small animal that might like cheese — mouse
4. Pretty plants we like to pick — flowers

Horizons® Phonics & Reading Grade 1 Student Book One 205

Overview:

- Yes/no questions
- Riddles
- Indicate words with long ō sound
- Word completion

Materials and Supplies:

- Teacher's Guide & Student Workbook
- White board or chalkboard
- Word cards (as necessary)
- Story: *The Mouse in the House*

Teaching Tips:

Review the rule. Have the student write examples of the rule on the chalkboard or white board. Assist the student as needed in identifying the pictures or reading the words in the lesson.

Activity 1. Have the student read the questions aloud. The student will answer the questions using **yes** or **no**. (Answers will vary.)

Activity 2. Have the student read the words in the list, and assist the student as necessary in reading the riddles. Instruct the student to write the correct answer to each riddle on the line.

Words: **1. bounce** **2. round** **3. mouse** **4. flowers**

Activity 3. Have the student read the words in the list aloud and write the words with the long **ō** sound on the lines below.

Words: **flow, show, snow**

Activity 4. Have the student identify the pictures and add **ou** or **ow** to each of the words below the pictures. Ask the student to read the words aloud.

Pictures: **snow, flower, mouse, blow**

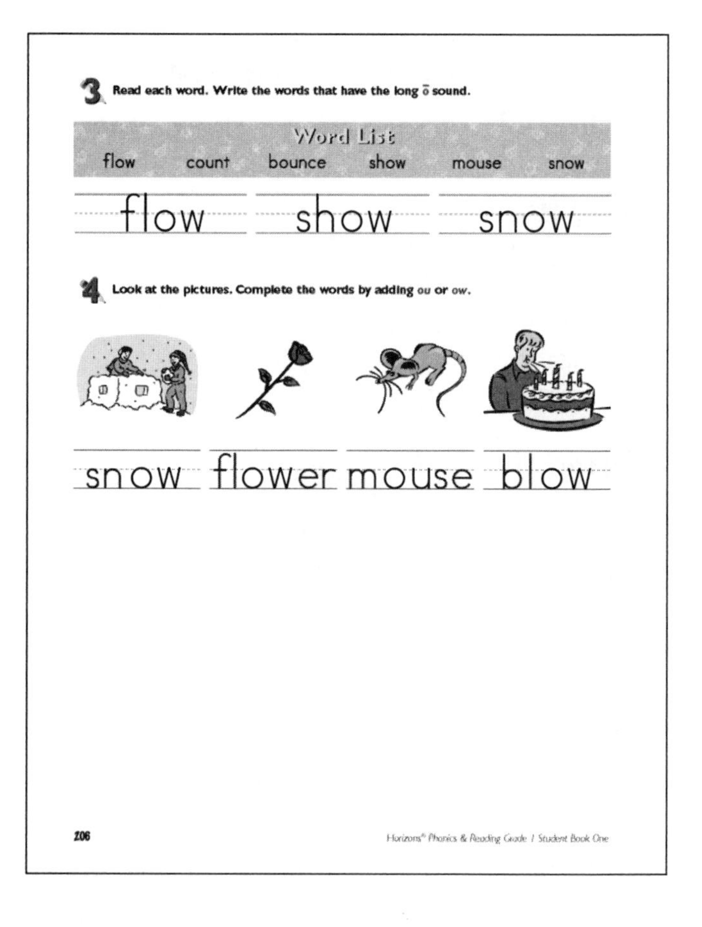

3 Read each word. Write the words that have the long ō sound.

Word List

flow count bounce show mouse snow

flow show snow

4 Look at the pictures. Complete the words by adding ou or ow.

snow flower mouse blow

106 Horizons® Phonics & Reading Grade 1 Student Book One

Lesson 78 - Review: Vowel Diphthongs oi & oy

Overview:

- Word/picture match
- Story completion
- Rhyming words

Materials and Supplies:

- Teacher's Guide & Student Workbook
- White board or chalkboard
- Word cards (as necessary)
- Story: *Seeds in the Soil*

Teaching Tips:

Review the rule. Have the student write examples of the rule on the chalkboard or white board. Assist the student as needed in identifying the pictures or reading the words in the lesson.

Activity 1. Have the student identify the pictures and draw a line to match the pictures with the words.

Pictures:		
	joy	**coin**
	toil	**toy**
		voice

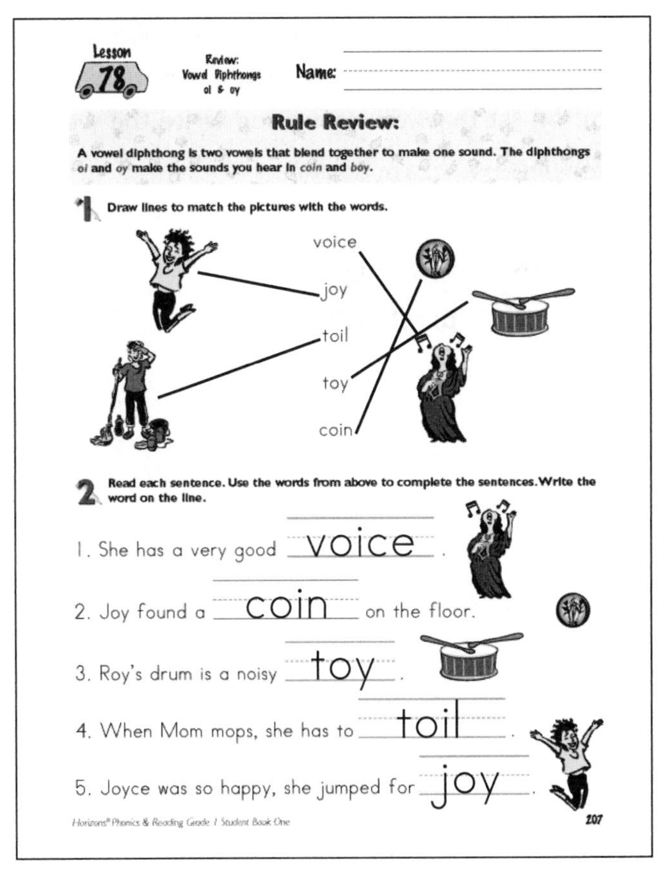

Lesson 78 Review: Vowel Diphthongs oi & oy Name:

Rule Review:

A vowel diphthong is two vowels that blend together to make one sound. The diphthongs *oi* and *oy* make the sounds you hear in *coin* and *boy*.

1 **Draw lines to match the pictures with the words.**

voice
joy
toil
toy
coin

2 **Read each sentence. Use the words from above to complete the sentences. Write the word on the line.**

1. She has a very good voice.
2. Joy found a coin on the floor.
3. Roy's drum is a noisy toy.
4. When Mom mops, she has to toil.
5. Joyce was so happy, she jumped for joy.

Horizons® Phonics & Reading Grade 1 Student Book One 107

Activity 2. Help the student read the sentences. Instruct the student to select the word from Activity 1 that will correctly complete each sentence and write the word on the line. If desired, have the student circle or underline other **oi** or **oy** words in the sentences.

Sentences:

1. **She has a very good voice.**
2. **Joy found a coin on the floor.**
3. **Roy's drum is a noisy toy.**
4. **When Mom mops, she has to toil.**
5. **Joyce was so happy, she jumped for joy.**

Activity 3. Have the student read the words in the activity aloud. The student will use the words from the list that will rhyme and write the words on the lines.

coin: **join**

toy: **boy, enjoy**

oil: **broil, soil, toil**

Lesson 79 - Review: Vowel Digraph ew

Overview:

- Crossword puzzle
- Story writing using words from a list

Materials and Supplies:

- Teacher's Guide & Student Workbook
- White board or chalkboard
- Word cards (as necessary)
- Story: *Drew's Jewelry*

Teaching Tips:

Review the rule. Have the student write examples of the rule on the chalkboard or white board. Assist the student as needed in identifying the pictures or reading the words in the lesson.

Activity 1. Have the student read the clues and the words in the list aloud. The student will use the words from the list to complete the crossword puzzle. Help the student with the puzzle as necessary.

Across: **1. knew**
3. drew
4. flew

Down: **2. new**
3. dew
4. few

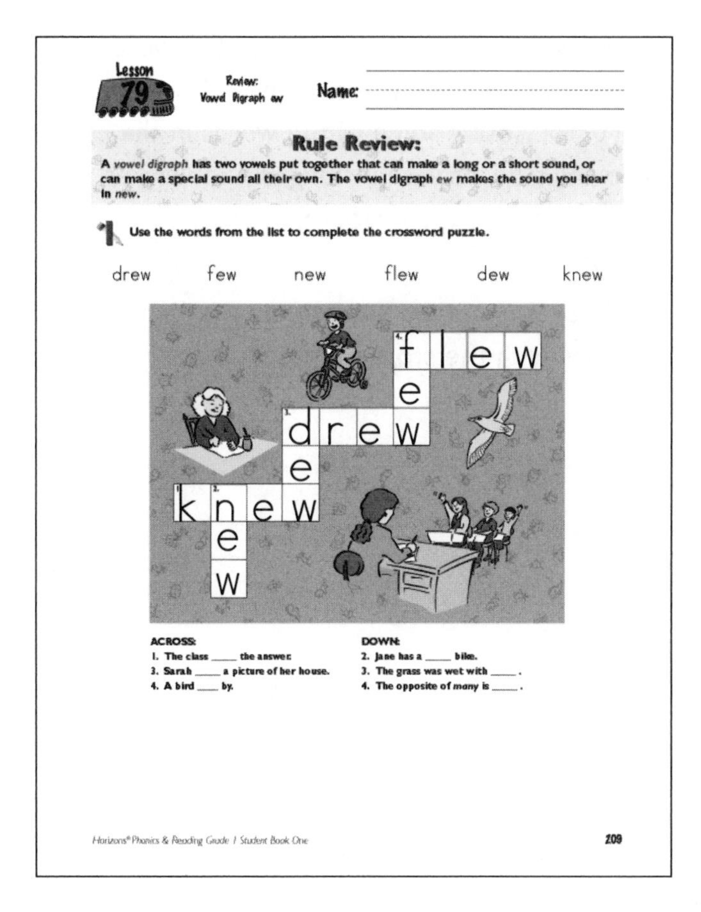
Lesson 79 Review: Vowel Digraph ew Name:

Rule Review:

A *vowel digraph* has two vowels put together that can make a long or a short sound, or can make a special sound all their own. The vowel digraph *ew* makes the sound you hear in *new*.

1. Use the words from the list to complete the crossword puzzle.

drew few new flew dew knew

ACROSS:
1. The class ____ the answer.
3. Sarah ____ a picture of her house.
4. A bird ____ by.

DOWN:
2. Jane has a ____ bike.
3. The grass was wet with ____ .
4. The opposite of *many* is ____ .

Horizons® Phonics & Reading Grade 1 Student Book One 209

Activity 2. Help the student read the words in the list as necessary. The student will write a short story using some of the words in the list. Help the student with writing and spelling as necessary. Emphasize correct capitalization and punctuation.

Activity 3. Have the student draw a picture to go along with the story he has written.

2 Write a short story, using words from the list.

Word List

drew	knew	new	crew	threw
blew	flew	grew	jewel	stew

3 Draw a picture to go with your story.

210 Horizons® Phonics & Reading Grade 1 Student Book One

Lesson 80 - Review: All Diphthongs

Overview:

- Sentence completion
- Auditory recognition of **ow, oy, ou** sounds

Materials and Supplies:

- Teacher's Guide & Student Workbook
- White board or chalkboard
- Word cards (as necessary)
- Story:

Teaching Tips:

Review the rule. Have the student write examples of the rule on the chalkboard or white board. Assist the student as needed in identifying the pictures or reading the words in the lesson.

Activity 1. Help the student read the sentences and the word choices. Instruct the student to underline the word that will correctly complete each sentence and write the word on the line.

Sentences:

1. **The pan will boil soon.**
2. **We all got in the car and went to town.**
3. **A foot of snow fell last night.**
4. **Mike is a boy in my class.**
5. **I want to join the Girl Scouts.**
6. **Jane's eyes are brown.**

Lesson 80 Review: All Diphthongs Name:

Rule Review:

A vowel diphthong is two vowels that blend together to make one sound. The diphthongs *oi* and *oy* make the sounds you hear in *coin* and *boy*. The diphthongs *ou* and *ow* make the sounds you hear in *south* and *owl*. The vowel diphthong *ow* can also make the long ō sound that you hear in *bowl* and *snow*.

1 **Read each sentence. Underline the word that completes each sentence. Write the word on the line.**

1. The pan will boil soon. (foil, boil)
2. We all got in the car and went to town. (town, south)
3. A foot of snow fell last night. (snow, go)
4. Mike is a boy in my class. (toy, boy)
5. I want to join the Girl Scouts. (toil, join)
6. Jane's eyes are brown. (brand, brown)

Horizons® Phonics & Reading Grade 1 Student Book One 211

Activity 2. Help the student identify the pictures. Have the student listen as you say the name of each picture. The student will circle the correct vowel diphthong he hears.

Pictures: **toys, snow, boy, boil**
joy, bow, crown, mouth
blow, clown, bowl, mouse

2 Look at the pictures. Circle the correct vowel diphthong.

ow oy ou   ow oy ou   ow oy ou   ow oy oi

ow oy ou   ow oy oi   ow oy ou   ow oy ou

ow oy oi   ow oy ou   ow oy ou   ow oy ou

212   Horizons Phonics & Reading 1, Workbook One

Test 8

Lessons 71-80

Instructions:

Review the rule for vowel digraphs and diphthongs. Ask the student for examples. Review the two sounds of **ea** and **ow**. Have the student name all of the pictures in the test. Read through the test with the student. Help the student with any words that he/she is still unsure of. The teacher should be available to answer any questions that the student may have during the test.

Activity 1. Make sure the student can correctly identify the pictures and read the words.

Pictures:	**eight**	**joy**
	seat	**stew**
	coin	**bread**
	snowman	**cow**

Activity 2. Instruct the student to use words from Activity 1 to complete this activity.

Sentences:

1. **We had bread and stew** [either order] **for lunch.**
2. **A cow gives us milk.**
3. **Please sit in your seat.**
4. **I am eight years old today.**
5. **When it snows, we can make a snowman.**

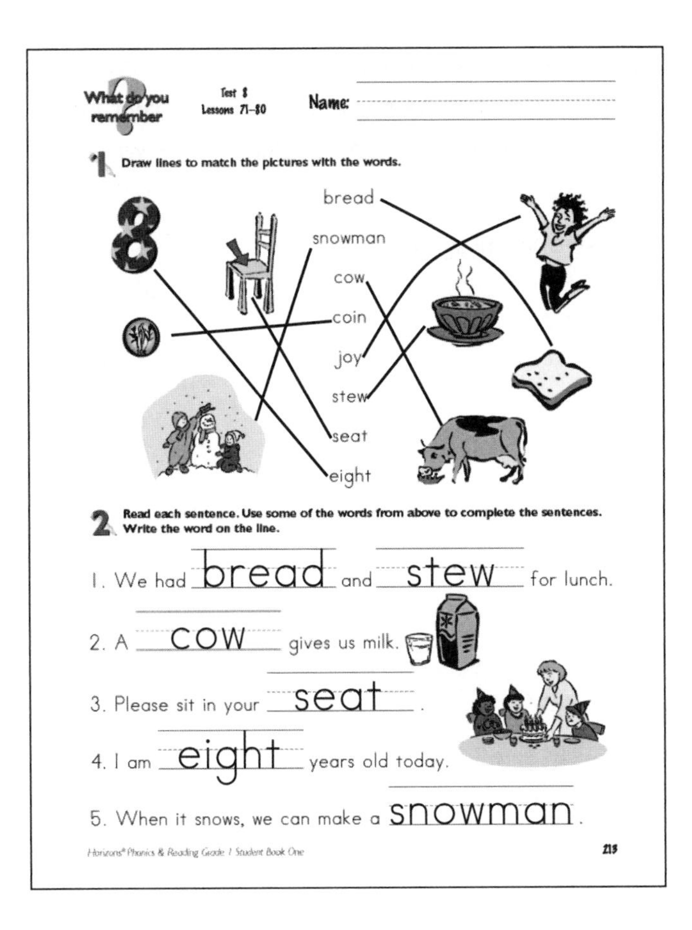

What do you remember Test 8 Lessons 71–80 Name:

1. Draw lines to match the pictures with the words.

bread
snowman
cow
coin
joy
stew
seat
eight

2. Read each sentence. Use some of the words from above to complete the sentences. Write the word on the line.

1. We had bread and stew for lunch.
2. A cow gives us milk.
3. Please sit in your seat.
4. I am eight years old today.
5. When it snows, we can make a snowman.

Horizons® Phonics & Reading Grade 1 Student Book One 215

Activity 3. Review the words in the list with the student. Remind the student to use correct punctuation, capitalization, and spelling when writing the sentences.

Answers will vary.

3 Write three sentences using words from the list.

Word List			
bread	cow	joy	seat
snowman	coin	stew	eight

1.

2.

3.

214 Horizons® Phonics & Reading Grade 1 Student Book One

Lesson 81 - Prefix re-

Overview:

- Add prefix **re-** to base words
- Match word with meanings
- Sentence completion
- Word/picture match

Materials and Supplies:

- Teacher's Guide & Student Workbook
- White board or chalkboard
- Word cards (as necessary)
- Story: *The Letter to Grandma*

Teaching Tips:

Review the rule. Have the student write examples of the rule on the chalkboard or white board. Assist the student as needed in identifying the pictures or reading the words in the lesson.

Activity 1. Have the student read the words aloud. The student will write new words by adding the prefix **re-** to the beginning of each base word.

Words: **redo, remake, reload**
reread, rewrite, retie

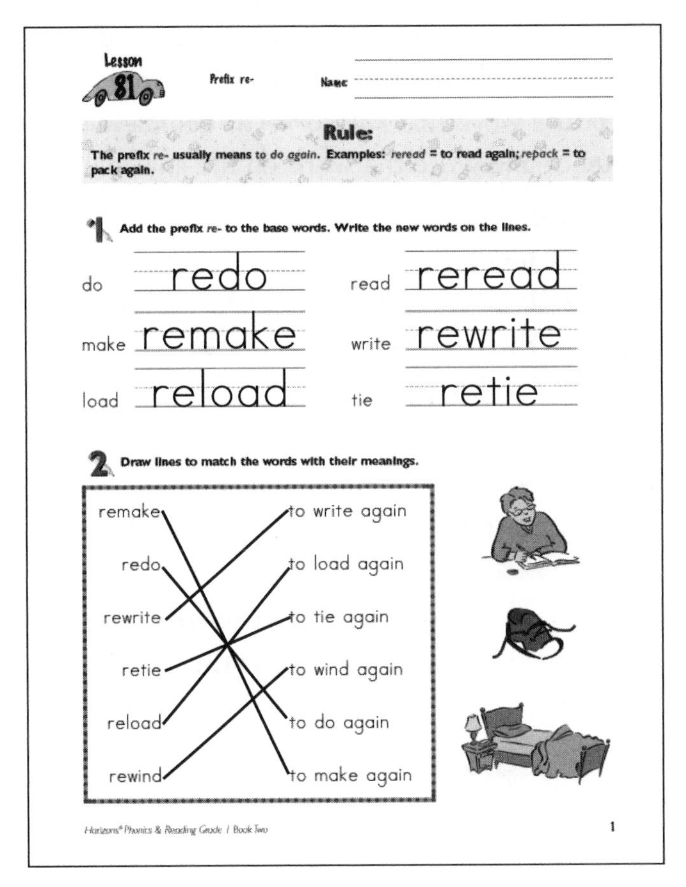
Lesson 81 Prefix re- Name:

Rule:
The prefix *re-* usually means *to do again*. Examples: *reread* = to read again; *repack* = to pack again.

1. Add the prefix re- to the base words. Write the new words on the lines.

do redo read reread
make remake write rewrite
load reload tie retie

2. Draw lines to match the words with their meanings.

remake — to write again
redo — to load again
rewrite — to tie again
retie — to wind again
reload — to do again
rewind — to make again

Horizons® Phonics & Reading Grade 1 Book Two 1

Activity 2. Have the student read the words and the meanings aloud. The student will draw lines to match the words with their meanings.

remake:	**to make again**
redo:	**to do again**
rewrite:	**to write again**
retie:	**to tie again**
reload:	**to load again**
rewind:	**to wind again**

Activity 3. Help the student read the words in the list and the sentences. Instruct the student to select the word that will correctly complete each sentence and write the word on the line.

Sentences:

1. **Jacob had to remake his bed.**
2. **Joan needed to retie her shoes.**
3. **Please rewind the clock.**
4. **I will rewrite my letter to my grandma.**

Activity 4. Have the student identify the pictures and draw a line to match the pictures with the words.

Pictures:	**rewind**	**rewrite**
	remake	**retie**

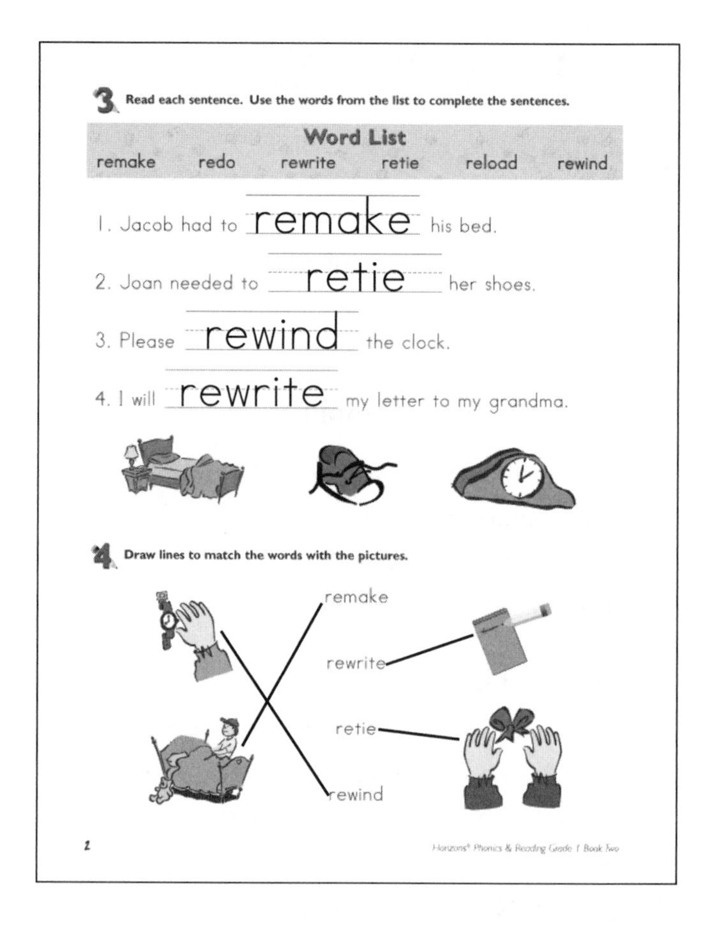

Lesson 82 - Prefix un-

Overview:

- Add prefix **un-** to base words
- Match words with meanings
- Sentence completion
- Word/picture match

Materials and Supplies:

- Teacher's Guide & Student Workbook
- White board or chalkboard
- Word cards (as necessary)
- Story: *Grocery Shopping*

Teaching Tips:

Review the rule. Have the student write examples of the rule on the chalkboard or white board. Assist the student as needed in identifying the pictures or reading the words in the lesson.

Activity 1. Have the student read the words aloud. The student will write new words by adding the prefix **un-** to the beginning of each base word.

Words: **unlock, unload, unusual, untie**
unhappy, undress, unwrap, unlikely

Activity 2. Have the student read the words and the meanings aloud. The student will draw lines to match the words with their meanings.

Words:		
	unwrap	**unlock**
	unlikely	**untie**
	undo	**unsafe**
	unpack	**unusual**
		unhappy

Activity 3. Help the student read the words in the list and the sentences. Instruct the student to select the word that will correctly complete each sentence and write the word on the line.

Sentences:

1. **Jason had to unpack the boxes.**
2. **It is unsafe to ride your bike after dark.**
3. **Jane was unhappy when she had to go inside.**

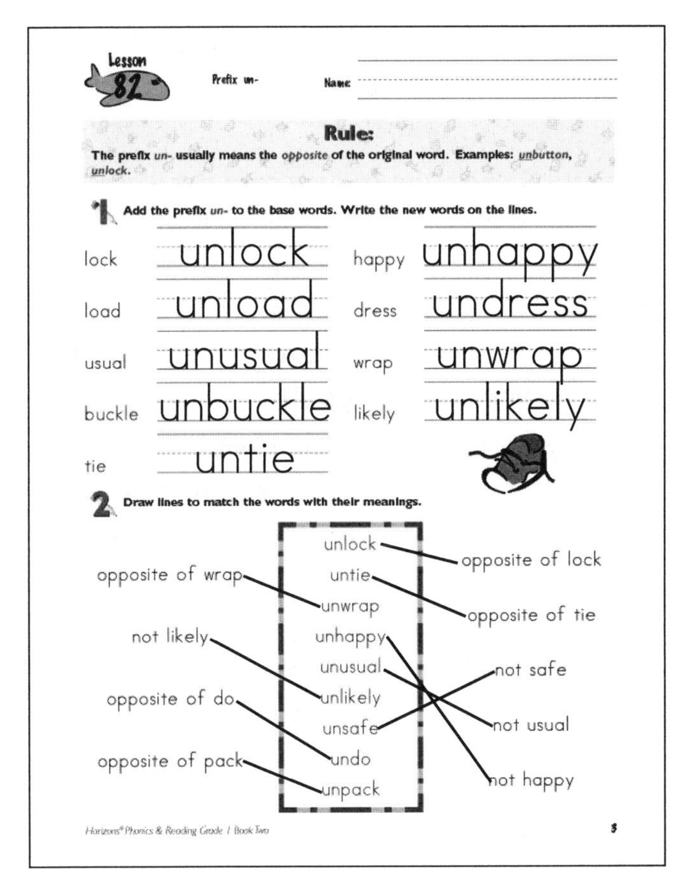
Lesson 82 Prefix un- Name:

Rule:
The prefix *un-* usually means the *opposite* of the original word. Examples: *unbutton*, *unlock*.

1. Add the prefix *un-* to the base words. Write the new words on the lines.

lock	unlock	happy	unhappy
load	unload	dress	undress
usual	unusual	wrap	unwrap
buckle	unbuckle	likely	unlikely
tie	untie		

2. Draw lines to match the words with their meanings.

opposite of wrap	unlock	opposite of lock
not likely	untie	opposite of tie
opposite of do	unwrap	not safe
opposite of pack	unhappy	not usual
	unusual	not happy
	unlikely	
	unsafe	
	undo	
	unpack	

Horizons® Phonics & Reading Grade 1 Book Two 3

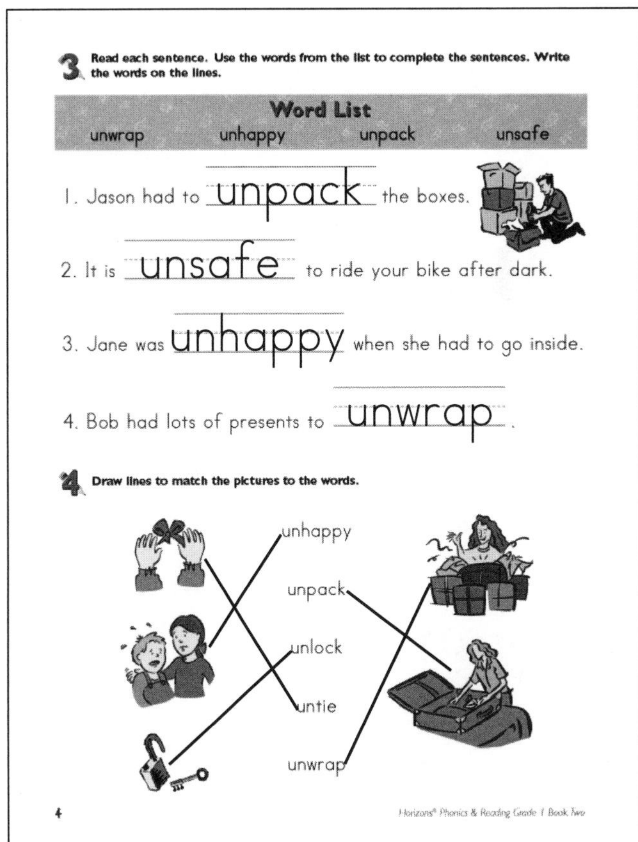
3. Read each sentence. Use the words from the list to complete the sentences. Write the words on the lines.

Word List
unwrap unhappy unpack unsafe

1. Jason had to unpack the boxes.
2. It is unsafe to ride your bike after dark.
3. Jane was unhappy when she had to go inside.
4. Bob had lots of presents to unwrap.

4. Draw lines to match the pictures to the words.

unhappy
unpack
unlock
untie
unwrap

4 Horizons® Phonics & Reading Grade 1 Book Two

4. **Bob had lots of presents to unwrap.**

Activity 4. Have the student identify the pictures and draw a line to match the pictures with the words.

Pictures: **untie** **unwrap**
unhappy **unpack**
unlock

Activity 5. Help the student read the words in the list as necessary. The student will write two sentences, using as many of the words in the list as possible. Help the student with writing and spelling as necessary. Emphasize correct capitalization and punctuation.

Activity 6. Have the student identify the pictures and read the words. Discuss the pictures as necessary. Instruct the student to add the prefix **-un** to each of the words and read the words aloud.

Words: **unwrap, unhappy, unbutton**
unsafe, untied, unload
unlock, unpack, unwind

5 Write two sentences using words from the word list.
Word List
unhappy unpack unlock untie unwrap
1.
2.
Horizons® Phonics & Reading Grade 1 Book Two
5

6 Look at the pictures. Finish the words under each picture with the prefix un-. Then read the words to your teacher.
unwrap
unhappy
unbutton
unsafe
untied
unload
unlock
unpack
unwind
6
Horizons® Phonics & Reading Grade 1 Book Two

Lesson 83 - Review: Prefixes -re & -un

Overview:

- Story completion
- Word/picture match
- Crossword puzzle
- Complete sentences by adding prefixes **re-** and **un-** to base words
- Match words with meanings

Materials and Supplies:

- Teacher's Guide & Student Workbook
- White board or chalkboard
- Word cards (as necessary)
- Story: *Charlie's Chores*

Teaching Tips:

Review the rules. Have the student write examples of the rule on the chalkboard or white board. Assist the student as needed in identifying the pictures or reading the words in the lesson.

Activity 1. Have the student read the story and the words from the list aloud. The student will use the words from the list to complete the story.

Story:

Mark has a list of things that he has to do every day. If he doesn't do things correctly, he has to redo them. When he gets up, he has to remake his bed. He sometimes rewinds his clock. He doesn't want to have to retie his shoes, so he does it right the first time. He also repacks his backpack for school. He likes to reread the same book every night before he goes to bed.

Activity 2. Have the student identify the pictures and draw a line to match the pictures with the words.

Pictures:	**rewrite**	**unload**
	repack	**reread**

Activity 3. Review the words in the list. Help the student read the crossword puzzle clues. Assist the student as necessary with the crossword puzzle.

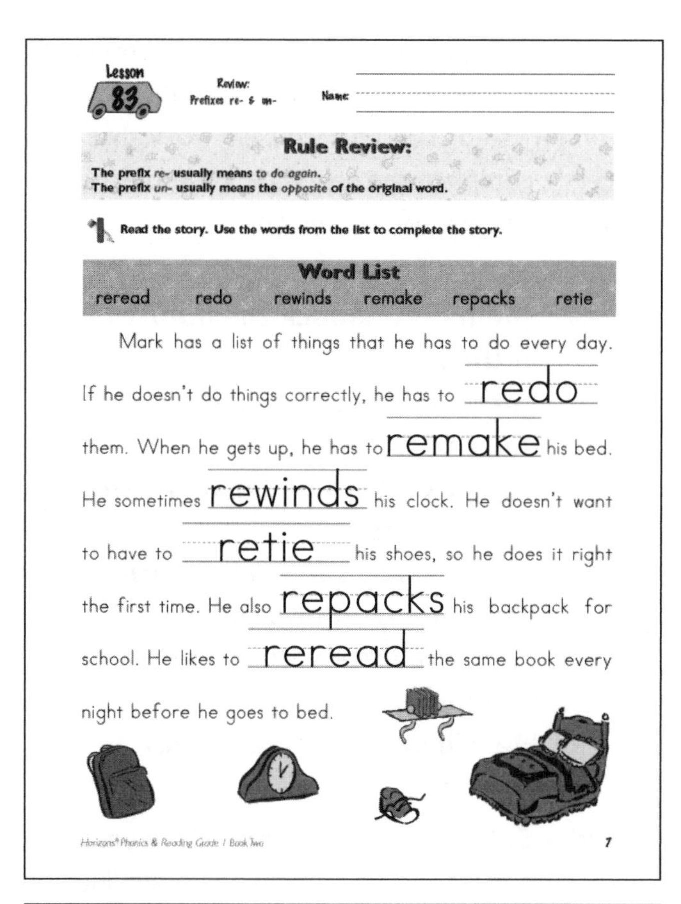

Lesson 83 Review: Prefixes re- & un- Name:

Rule Review:

The prefix re- usually means to do again.
The prefix un- usually means the opposite of the original word.

1. Read the story. Use the words from the list to complete the story.

Word List

reread redo rewinds remake repacks retie

Mark has a list of things that he has to do every day. If he doesn't do things correctly, he has to redo them. When he gets up, he has to remake his bed. He sometimes rewinds his clock. He doesn't want to have to retie his shoes, so he does it right the first time. He also repacks his backpack for school. He likes to reread the same book every night before he goes to bed.

Horizons® Phonics & Reading Grade 1 Book Two 7

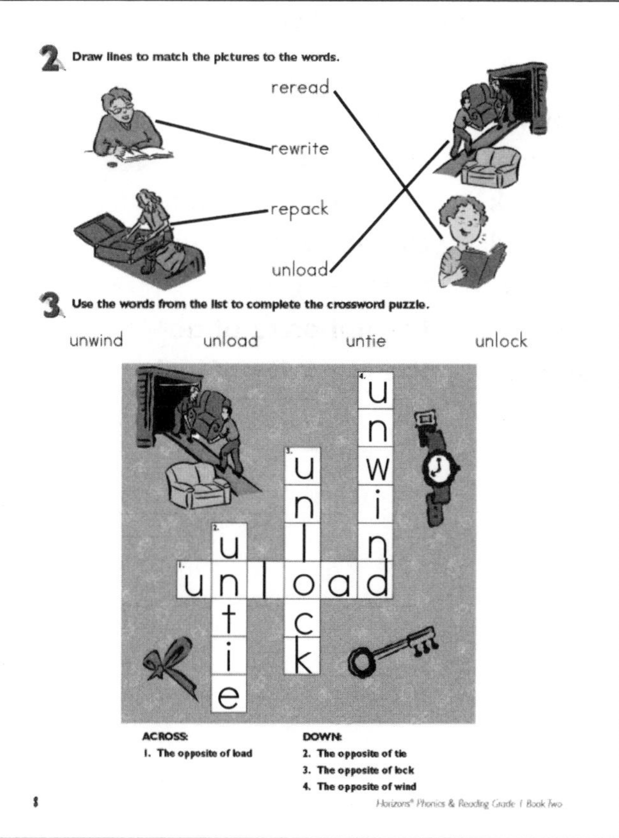

2. Draw lines to match the pictures to the words.

reread
rewrite
repack
unload

3. Use the words from the list to complete the crossword puzzle.

unwind unload untie unlock

ACROSS:
1. The opposite of load

DOWN:
2. The opposite of tie
3. The opposite of lock
4. The opposite of wind

8 Horizons® Phonics & Reading Grade 1 Book Two

Across: **1. unload**

Down: **2. untie**

3. unlock

4. unwind

Activity 4. Help the student read the sentences and the word choices. Instruct the student to add the prefix **re-** or **un-** to each base word that will correctly complete the sentence. Have the student write new word on the line.

Sentences:

1. **She had to unlock the door to get in the house.**
2. **I need to retie my shoes so that I don't trip.**
3. **I don't want to be unfair when I play a game.**
4. **I have to redo my homework because I didn't do my best.**
5. **Please rewrite your letter to Grandma.**
6. **He will unwrap his birthday presents.**

Activity 5. Have the student read the words and the meanings aloud. The student will draw lines to match the words with their meanings.

reread:	**to read again**
rewrite:	**to write again**
repack:	**to pack again**
unload:	**the opposite of load**
unwind:	**the opposite of wind**
reload:	**to load again**
untie:	**the opposite of tie**
unlock	**the opposite of lock**

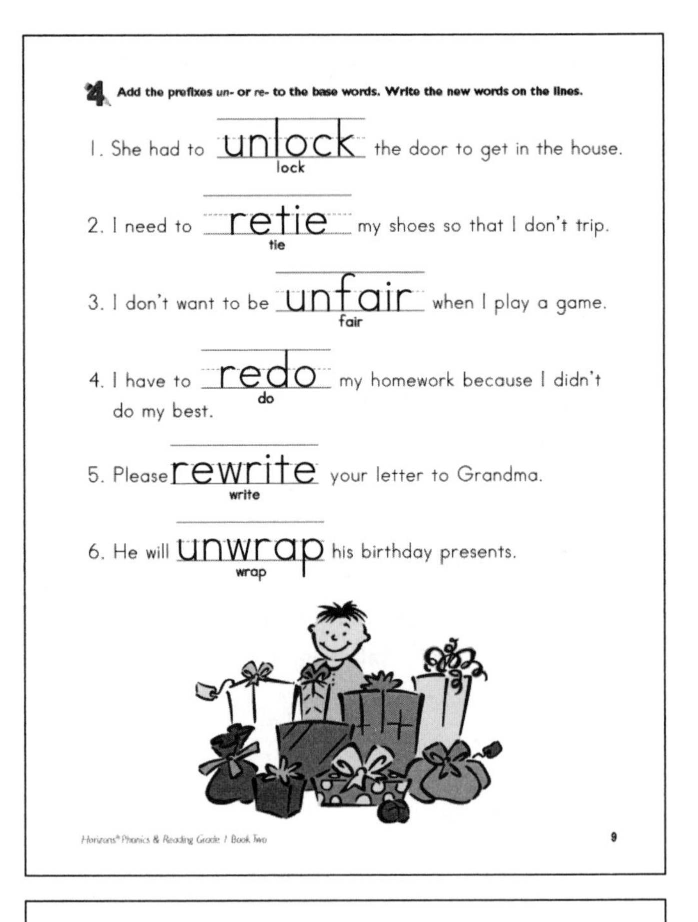

4 Add the prefixes *un-* or *re-* to the base words. Write the new words on the lines.

1. She had to unlock (lock) the door to get in the house.
2. I need to retie (tie) my shoes so that I don't trip.
3. I don't want to be unfair (fair) when I play a game.
4. I have to redo (do) my homework because I didn't do my best.
5. Please rewrite (write) your letter to Grandma.
6. He will unwrap (wrap) his birthday presents.

Horizons® Phonics & Reading Grade 1 Book Two 9

5 Draw a line to match the word with its meaning.

reread	to load again
rewrite	the opposite of wind
repack	to pack again
unload	the opposite of load
unwind	to write again
reload	the opposite of lock
untie	to read again
unlock	the opposite of tie

10 *Horizons® Phonics & Reading Grade 1 Book Two*

Lesson 84 - Prefix dis-

Overview:

- Add prefix **dis-** to base words
- Match words with meanings
- Sentence completion

Materials and Supplies:

- Teacher's Guide & Student Workbook
- White board or chalkboard
- Word cards (as necessary)
- Story: *The Disorderly Room*

Teaching Tips:

Review the rule. Have the student write examples of the rule on the chalkboard or white board. Assist the student as needed in identifying the pictures or reading the words in the lesson.

Activity 1. Have the student read the words aloud. The student will write new words by adding the prefix **dis-** to the beginning of each base word.

Words: **disobey**
disagree
disorder
disgrace
discolor
distrust
dislike
disappear

Activity 2. Have the student read the words and the meanings aloud. The student will draw lines to match the words with their meanings.

distrust:	**to not trust**
disorder:	**not in order**
dislike:	**to not like**
disagree:	**to not agree**
disconnect:	**opposite of connect**
disobey:	**to not obey**

Activity 3. Help the student read the sentences. Instruct the student to select a word from Activity 2 that will correctly complete each sentence and write the word on the line.

Sentences:

1. **It is not good to disobey your parents.**
2. **I dislike rainy days.**
3. **The room was in disorder, and needed to be cleaned up.**
4. **It is all right to disagree with someone, as long as you are polite.**

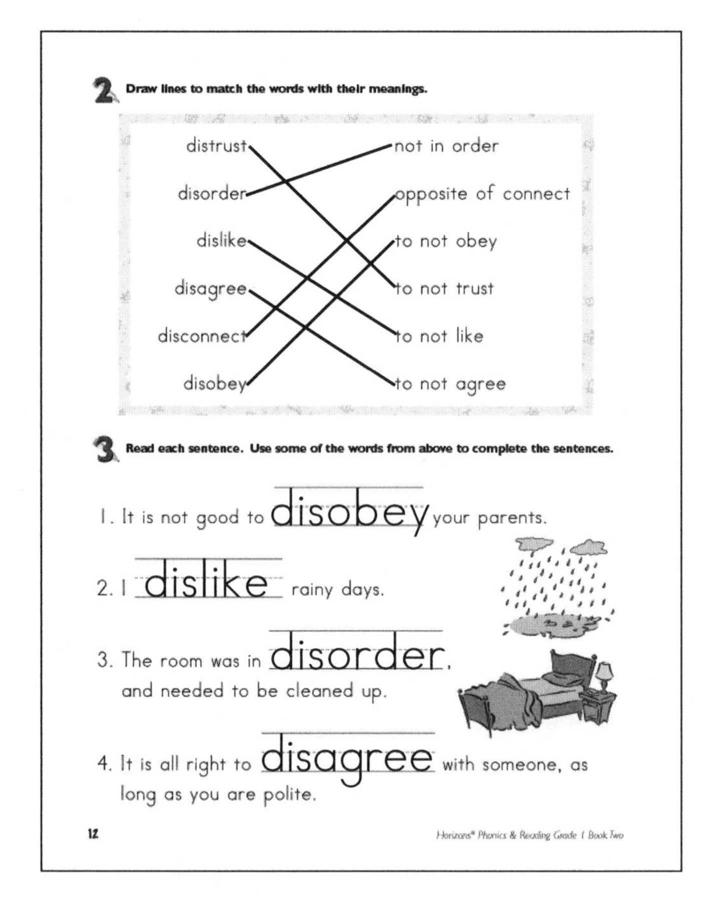

Lesson 85 - Review: Prefixes re-, un-, & dis-

Overview:

- Add prefixes to base words
- Match words with their opposites
- Sentence completion

Materials and Supplies:

- Teacher's Guide & Student Workbook
- White board or chalkboard
- Word cards (as necessary)
- Story: *The Disagreeing Girls*

Teaching Tips:

Review the rules. Have the student write examples of the rule on the chalkboard or white board. Assist the student as needed in identifying the pictures or reading the words in the lesson.

Activity 1. Have the student read the words aloud. The student will write new words by adding the correct prefix (**re-**, **un-**, or **dis-**) to the beginning of each base word. Remind the student that one of the words (appear) has two prefixes.

Words: **disagree, disobey, distrust, unlock, repay, disappear/reappear**

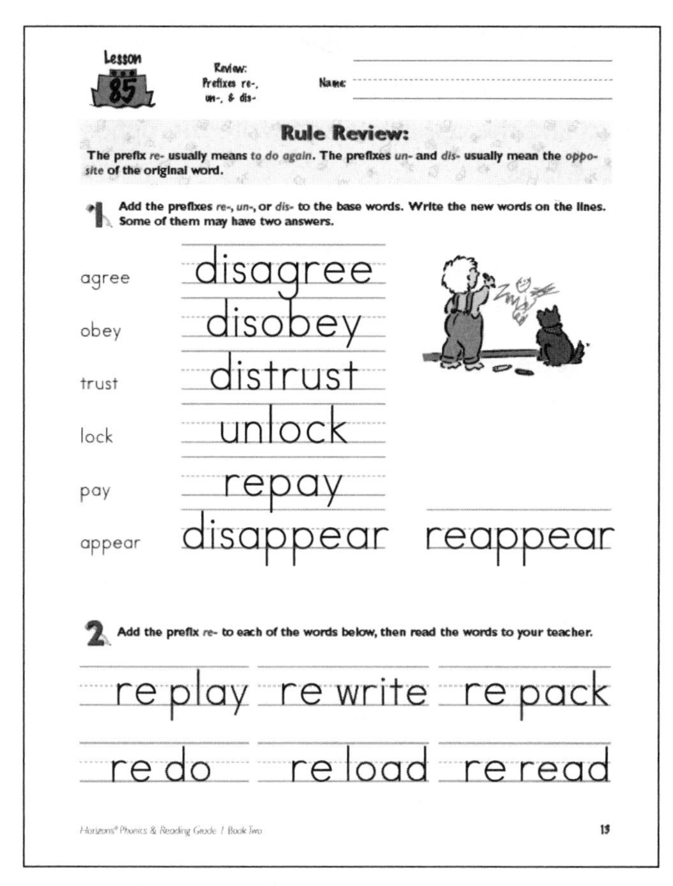

Lesson 85 Review: Prefixes re-, un-, & dis- Name:

Rule Review:

The prefix *re-* **usually means** *to do again*. **The prefixes** *un-* **and** *dis-* **usually mean the opposite of the original word.**

1. **Add the prefixes** *re-*, *un-*, **or** *dis-* **to the base words. Write the new words on the lines. Some of them may have two answers.**

agree disagree
obey disobey
trust distrust
lock unlock
pay repay
appear disappear reappear

2. **Add the prefix** *re-* **to each of the words below, then read the words to your teacher.**

re play re write re pack
re do re load re read

Horizons® Phonics & Reading Grade 1 Book Two 15

Activity 2. Have the student read the words aloud. The student will write new words by adding the prefix **re-** to the beginning of each base word. Have the student read the new words aloud.

Words: **replay, rewrite, repack redo, reload, reread**

Activity 3. Have the student read each word aloud. The student will use the words from the list to find the opposites and write the opposites on the lines.

Words: **disappear** **undo**
disobey **unhappy**
disagree

Activity 4. Help the student read the words in the list and the sentences. Instruct the student to select the word that will correctly complete each sentence and write the word on the line.

Sentences:

1. **When you get a gift, you unwrap it.**
2. **When things go away, they disappear.**
3. **When you disagree with someone, be polite.**
4. **Never skate on unsafe ice.**

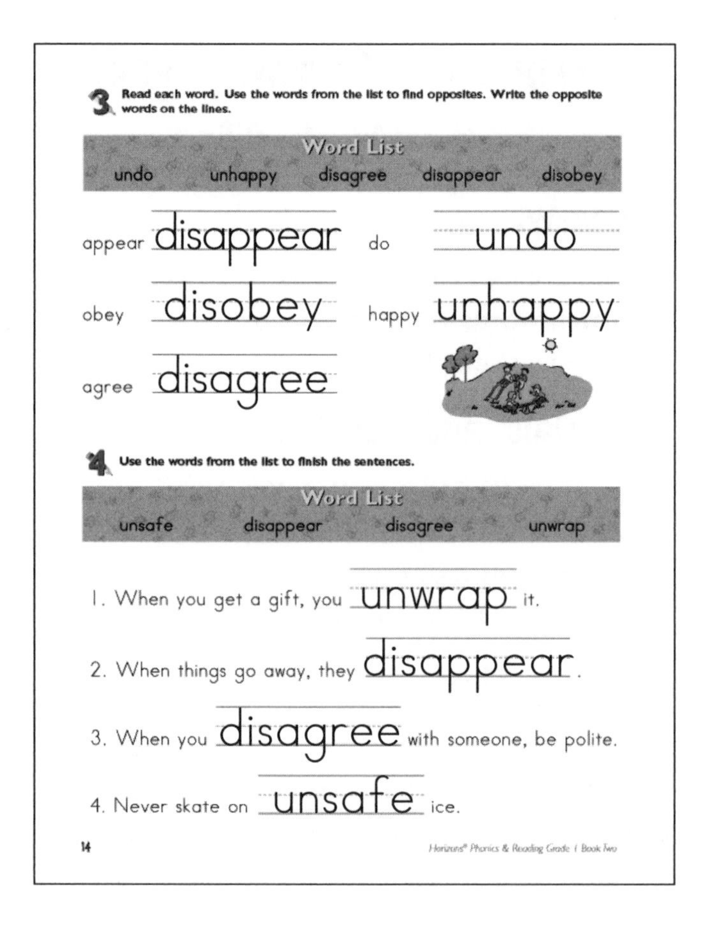

3 **Read each word. Use the words from the list to find opposites. Write the opposite words on the lines.**

Word List

undo unhappy disagree disappear disobey

appear disappear do undo

obey disobey happy unhappy

agree disagree

4 **Use the words from the list to finish the sentences.**

Word List

unsafe disappear disagree unwrap

1. When you get a gift, you unwrap it.
2. When things go away, they disappear.
3. When you disagree with someone, be polite.
4. Never skate on unsafe ice.

14 Horizons® Phonics & Reading Grade 1 Book Two

Lesson 86 - Checkup: Beginning Consonant Blends with r

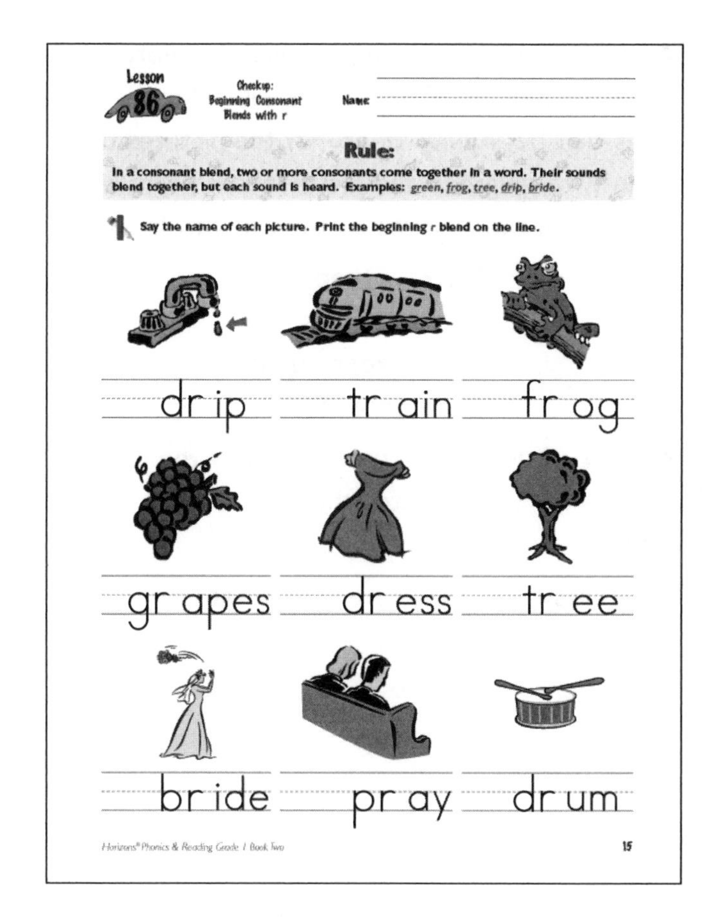
Lesson 86

Checkup: Beginning Consonant Blends with r

Name:

Rule:

In a consonant blend, two or more consonants come together in a word. Their sounds blend together, but each sound is heard. Examples: green, frog, tree, drip, bride.

1. Say the name of each picture. Print the beginning r blend on the line.

dr ip tr ain fr og

gr apes dr ess tr ee

br ide pr ay dr um

Horizons® Phonics & Reading Grade 1 Book Two 15

Overview:

- Add consonant blends with **r** to words
- Color pictures with same **r** blend
- Word/picture match

Materials and Supplies:

- Teacher's Guide & Student Workbook
- White board or chalkboard
- Word cards (as necessary)
- Story: *The Bride on the Train*

Teaching Tips:

Review the rule. This "Checkup" reviews the consonant blends with **r** that were studied in Lessons 18, 19, 23, and 37. Have the student write examples of the rule on the chalkboard or white board. Assist the student as needed in identifying the pictures or reading the words in the lesson.

Activity 1. Help student identify the pictures and print the correct beginning blend underneath each picture.

Pictures: **drip, train, frog**
grapes, dress, tree
bride, pray, drum

Activity 2. Have the student read the words and name the pictures. The student will color the pictures that begin with **tr** brown, the pictures that begin with **gr** green, the pictures that begin with **dr** red, and the pictures that begin with **fr** blue.

Pictures: Brown – **tree**
Green – **grass**
Red – **dress, drum**
Blue – **frog, fruit**

Activity 3. Have the student identify the pictures and draw a line to match the pictures with the words.

Pictures:	**brick**	**press**
	drive	**fruit**
	train	

2. Read each word and look at the pictures. Color the pictures with *tr* blends brown. Color the pictures with *gr* blends green. Color the pictures with *dr* blends red. Color the pictures with *fr* blends blue.

blue frog
brown tree
red dress
green grass
blue fruit
red drum

3. Draw lines to match the pictures with the words.

fruit
drive
train
press
brick

16

Horizons® Phonics & Reading Grade 1 Book Two

Lesson 87 - Checkup: Beginning Consonant Blends with l

Overview:

- Match words to ones with similar blend
- Picture/word match
- Word completion
- Color pictures that begin with same **l** blend

Materials and Supplies:

- Teacher's Guide & Student Workbook
- White board or chalkboard
- Word cards (as necessary)
- Story: *Sledding*

Teaching Tips:

Review the rule. This "Checkup" reviews the consonant blends with **l** that were studied in Lessons 18, 19, 21, 24, 29, 33, and 39. Have the student write examples of the rule on the chalkboard or white board. Assist the student as needed in identifying the pictures or reading the words in the lesson.

Activity 1. Have the student read the words aloud. The student will find the words with the same **l** blend and write the matching words on the lines.

Words:		
	clean	**glass**
	block	**play**
	fly	**slide**

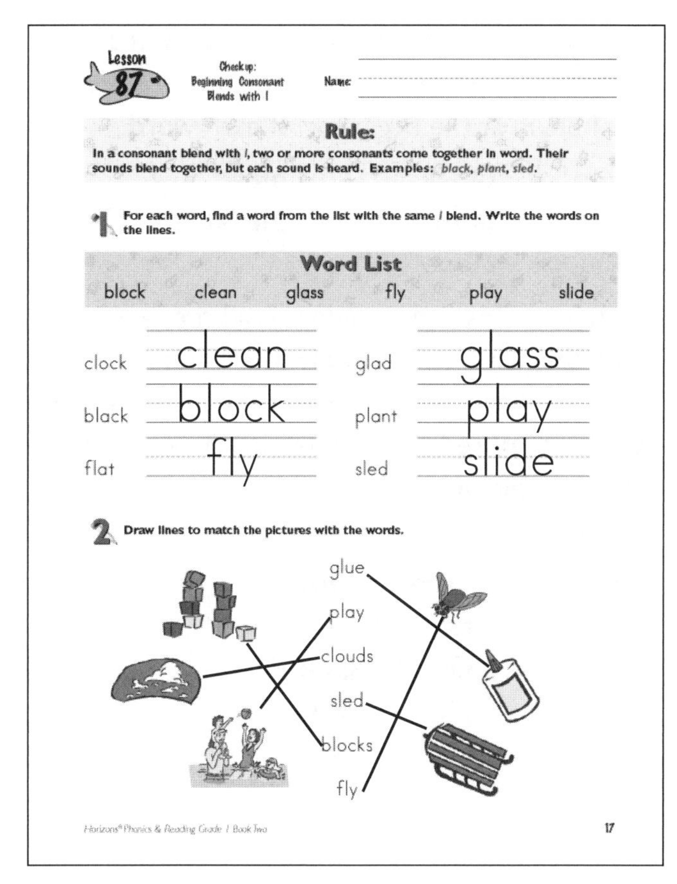

Lesson 87 Checkup: Beginning Consonant Blends with l

Name:

Rule:
In a consonant blend with *l*, two or more consonants come together in word. Their sounds blend together, but each sound is heard. Examples: *black, plant, sled.*

1 For each word, find a word from the list with the same *l* blend. Write the words on the lines.

Word List
block clean glass fly play slide

clock	clean	glad	glass
black	block	plant	play
flat	fly	sled	slide

2 Draw lines to match the pictures with the words.

glue
play
clouds
sled
blocks
fly

Horizons® Phonics & Reading Grade 1 Book Two 17

Activity 2. Have the student name the pictures and read the words aloud. The student will draw lines to match the pictures with the words.

Pictures:		
	blocks	**fly**
	clouds	**glue**
	play	**sled**

Activity 3. Have the student read all of the words in the list. The student will print the correct **l** blend at the beginning of each word.

Words:	**blocks**	**blow**
	blue	**please**
	close	

Activity 4. Have the student read the words and name the pictures. The student will color the pictures that begin with **bl** brown, the pictures that begin with **pl** red, the pictures that begin with **gl** green, the pictures that begin with **fl** blue, and the pictures that begin with **sl** orange.

Pictures:	Brown – **blocks**
	Red – **plane**
	Green – **glue**
	Blue – **flag, flowers**
	Orange – **sled**

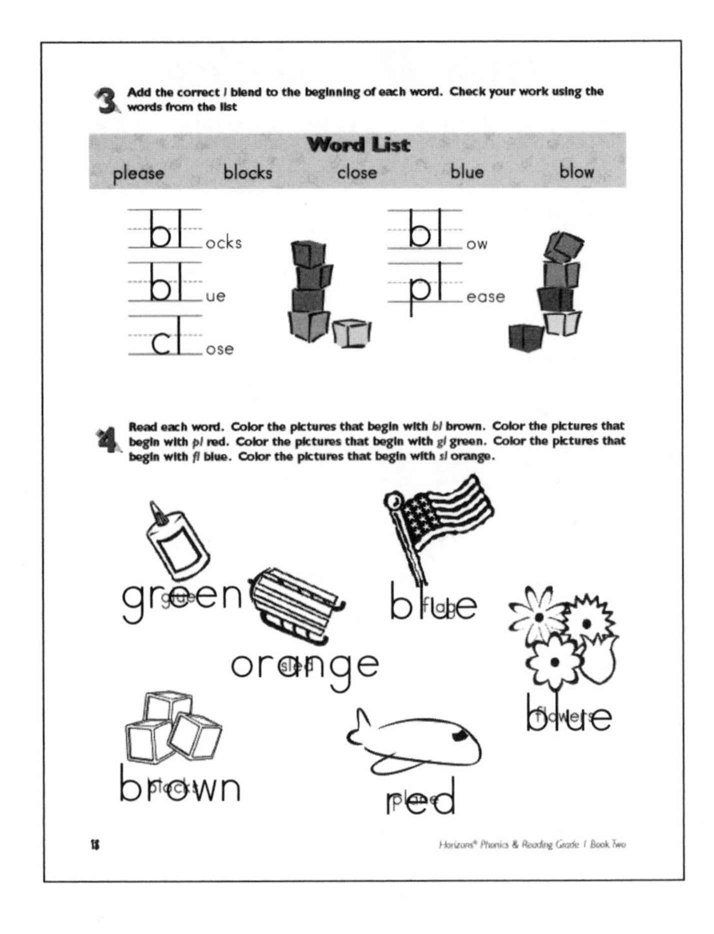

3 Add the correct *l* blend to the beginning of each word. Check your work using the words from the list

Word List

please blocks close blue blow

bl ocks

bl ue

cl ose

bl ow

pl ease

4 Read each word. Color the pictures that begin with *bl* brown. Color the pictures that begin with *pl* red. Color the pictures that begin with *gl* green. Color the pictures that begin with *fl* blue. Color the pictures that begin with *sl* orange.

glue green

sled orange

flag blue

flowers blue

blocks brown

plane red

15 Horizons® Phonics & Reading Grade 1 Book Two

Lesson 88 - Checkup: Ending Consonant Blends

Overview:

- Sentence completion
- Picture/word match
- Auditory recognition of ending consonant blends
- Add ending consonant blends to words

Materials and Supplies:

- Teacher's Guide & Student Workbook
- White board or chalkboard
- Word cards (as necessary)
- Story: *The Parade*

Teaching Tips:

Review ending consonant blends **nk**, **nt**, **mp**, **lp**, **lk**, **lt**, **lf**, **ft**, **st**, **sp**, **sk**, and **nk**. Have the student write examples of the rule on the chalkboard or white board. Assist the student as needed in identifying the pictures or reading the words in the lesson.

Activity 1. Help the student read the sentences and the word choices. Instruct the student to underline the word that will correctly complete each sentence and write the word on the line.

Sentences:

1. **I will study hard for my math test.**
2. **I drank half a glass of milk.**
3. **A camel has a big hump on his back.**
4. **I will ask my teacher for help.**
5. **I write with my left hand.**

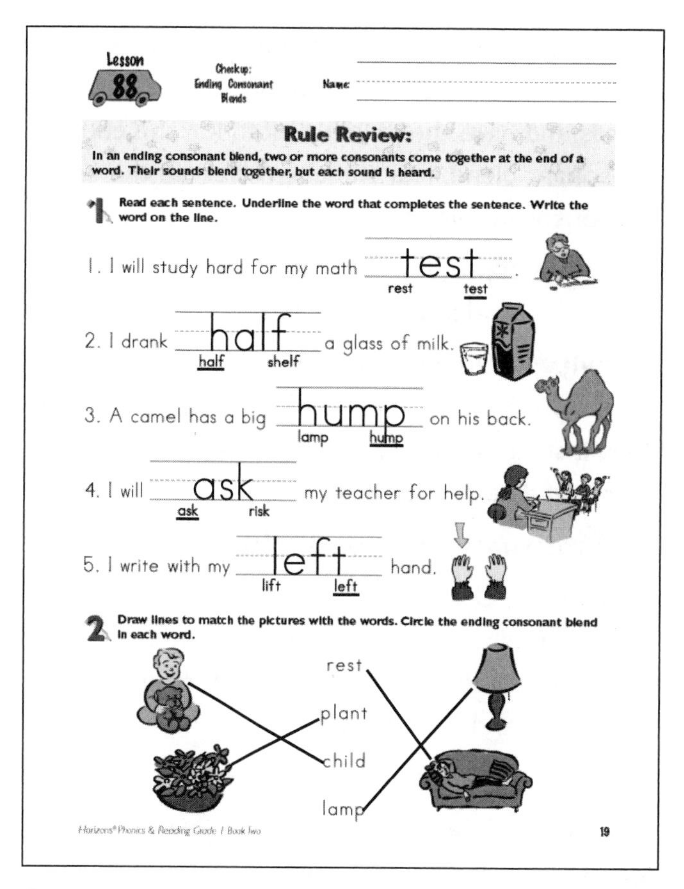

Lesson 88

Checkup: Ending Consonant Blends

Name:

Rule Review:

In an ending consonant blend, two or more consonants come together at the end of a word. Their sounds blend together, but each sound is heard.

1 Read each sentence. Underline the word that completes the sentence. Write the word on the line.

1. I will study hard for my math test. (rest, test)
2. I drank half a glass of milk. (half, shelf)
3. A camel has a big hump on his back. (lamp, hump)
4. I will ask my teacher for help. (ask, risk)
5. I write with my left hand. (lift, left)

2 Draw lines to match the pictures with the words. Circle the ending consonant blend in each word.

rest

plant

child

lamp

Horizons® Phonics & Reading Grade 1 Book Two 19

Activity 2. Have the student identify the pictures and draw a line to match the pictures with the words.

Pictures:	**child**	**lamp**
	plant	**rest**

Activity 3. Discuss each of the pictures so that the student can correctly identify them. Read the words and have the student listen for the ending consonant blend. The student will circle the ending consonant blend he hears.

Pictures: **hand, lamp, help, tent**
malt, milk, shelf, melt

Activity 4. Discuss the consonant blend rule for **sk** and have the student think of additional examples. Instruct the student to add **sk** to each of the words and read them aloud.

Words: **mask, tusk, desk, risk**

Activity 5. Discuss the consonant blend rule for **nk** and have the student think of additional examples. Instruct the student to add **nk** to each of the words and read them aloud.

Words: **think, wink, blank, stink**

Activity 6. Discuss the consonant blend rule for **sp** and have the student think of additional examples. Instruct the student to add **sp** to each of the words and read them aloud.

Words: **clasp, wisp, wasp, lisp**

Activity 7. Discuss the consonant blend rule for **ld** and have the student think of additional examples. Instruct the student to add **ld** to each of the words and read them aloud.

Words: **child, mold, mild, cold**

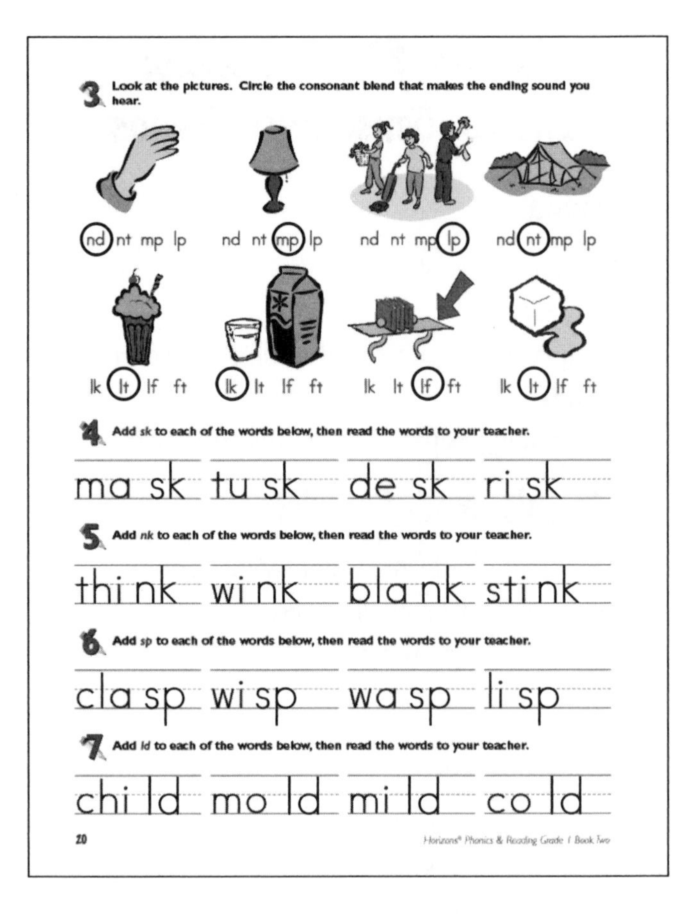

3 Look at the pictures. Circle the consonant blend that makes the ending sound you hear.

nd nt mp lp | nd nt mp lp | nd nt mp lp | nd nt mp lp

lk lt lf ft | lk lt lf ft | lk lt lf ft | lk lt lf ft

4 Add *sk* to each of the words below, then read the words to your teacher.

mask tusk desk risk

5 Add *nk* to each of the words below, then read the words to your teacher.

think wink blank stink

6 Add *sp* to each of the words below, then read the words to your teacher.

clasp wisp wasp lisp

7 Add *ld* to each of the words below, then read the words to your teacher.

child mold mild cold

20 Horizons Phonics & Reading Grade 1 Book Two

Lesson 89 - Writing Lesson: Personal Narrative

Overview:

- Write a narrative about a fun personal experience

Materials and Supplies:

- Teacher's Guide & Student Workbook
- White board or chalkboard
- Word cards (as necessary)
- Story: *Tammy's Vacation*

Teaching Tips:

The student will be writing a personal experience narrative. Define the word "narrative" for the student. The student will write about a fun experience that he or she had with family and /or friends. The teacher or writing partner should help the student think of ideas, narrow it down to one idea about which to write. The student should be sure to tell what he or she did, where and when he or she did it, and why it was fun. Help the student with spelling and punctuation as necessary. The student will write the rough draft on paper and the final copy in the student workbook.

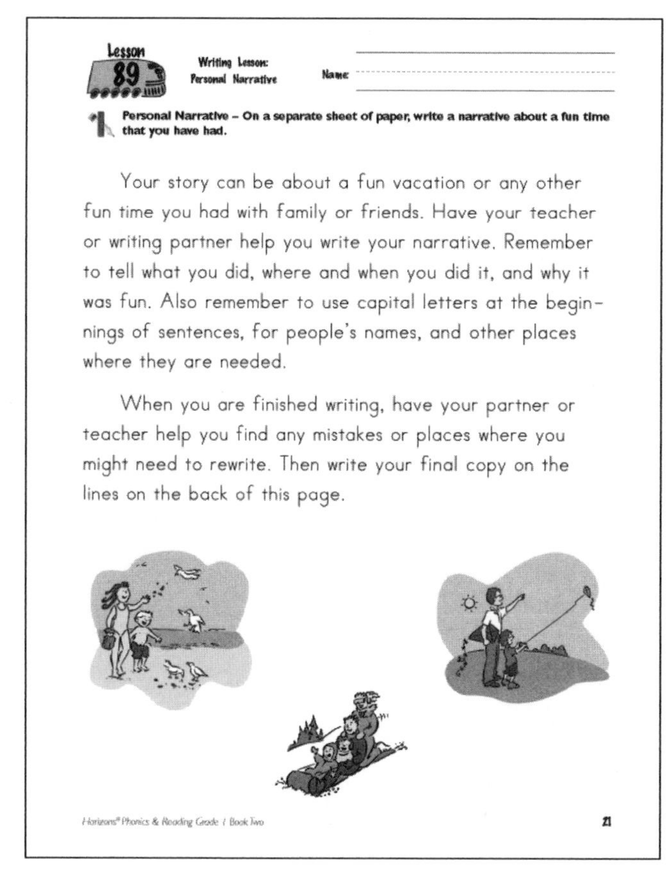

Lesson 89 Writing Lesson: Personal Narrative Name:

1. **Personal Narrative – On a separate sheet of paper, write a narrative about a fun time that you have had.**

Your story can be about a fun vacation or any other fun time you had with family or friends. Have your teacher or writing partner help you write your narrative. Remember to tell what you did, where and when you did it, and why it was fun. Also remember to use capital letters at the beginnings of sentences, for people's names, and other places where they are needed.

When you are finished writing, have your partner or teacher help you find any mistakes or places where you might need to rewrite. Then write your final copy on the lines on the back of this page.

Horizons® Phonics & Reading Grade 1 Book Two 21

Activity 1. The student will write about a fun experience that he or she had with family and/or friends.

12 Horizons® Phonics & Reading Grade 1 Book Two

Lesson 90 - Checkup: Beginning Consonant Blends with s

Overview:

- Word/picture match
- Word completion
- Sentence completion
- Auditory recognition of **s** blends

Materials and Supplies:

- Teacher's Guide & Student Workbook
- White board or chalkboard
- Word cards (as necessary)
- Story: *The Snake Slithered*

Teaching Tips:

Review the rule. Have the student write examples of the rule on the chalkboard or white board. Assist the student as needed in identifying the pictures or reading the words in the lesson.

Activity 1. Have the student identify the pictures and draw a line to match the pictures with the words.

Pictures:	**stamp**	**sky**
	spoon	**snail**
	swing	**street**

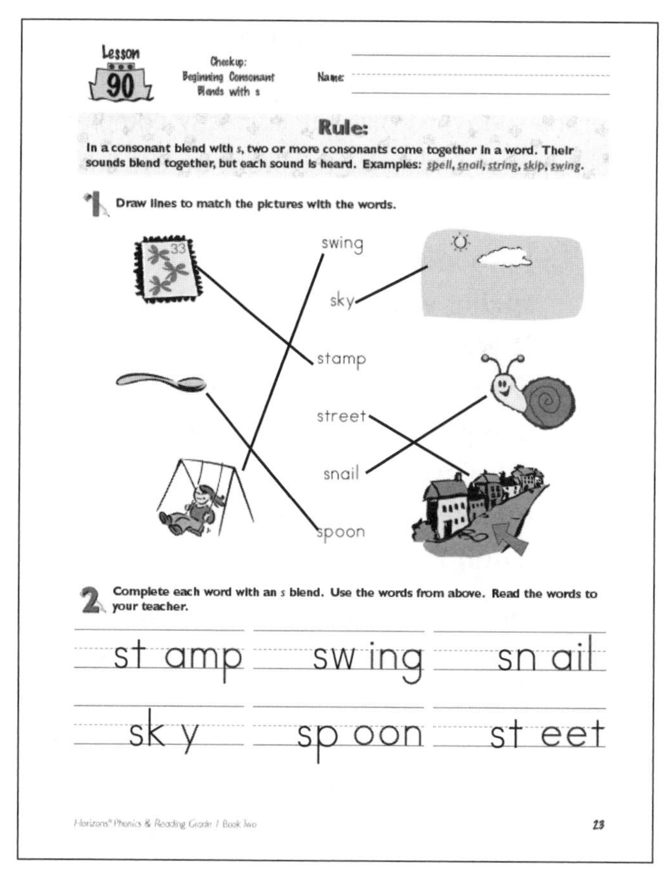
Lesson 90

Checkup: Beginning Consonant Blends with s

Name:

Rule:

In a consonant blend with s, two or more consonants come together in a word. Their sounds blend together, but each sound is heard. Examples: *spell, snail, string, skip, swing.*

1. Draw lines to match the pictures with the words.

swing
sky
stamp
street
snail
spoon

2. Complete each word with an s blend. Use the words from above. Read the words to your teacher.

st amp sw ing sn ail
sk y sp oon st eet

Horizons® Phonics & Reading Grade 1 Book Two 23

Activity 2. Discuss the rule for consonant blends with **s** and have the student think of additional examples. Instruct the student refer to Activity 1 and add the correct **s** blend to the words. Have the student read the words aloud.

Words: **stamp, swing, snail**
sky, spoon, street

Activity 3. Help the student read the sentences and the word choices. Instruct the student to underline the word that will correctly complete each sentence and write the word on the line.

Sentences:

1. **John went on a camping trip last spring with his mom and dad.**
2. **It was still cold.**
3. **Everyone wore sweaters.**
4. **They spent three days in the forest.**
5. **John saw a snake.**
6. **He screamed when he saw it.**
7. **Then it slithered away.**

Activity 4. Discuss each of the pictures so that the student can correctly identify them. Read the words and have the student listen for the beginning consonant blend. The student will circle the beginning consonant blend he hears.

Pictures: **strawberry, spoon, snail, swing**

3 **Read each sentence. Underline the word that completes the sentence. Write the word on the line.**

1. John went on a camping trip last spring with his mom and dad.
   spring spot
2. It was still cold.
   still stop
3. Everyone wore sweaters.
   stamp sweaters
4. They spent three days in the forest.
   spent sport
5. John saw a snake.
   spray snake
6. He screamed when he saw it.
   swept screamed
7. Then it slithered away.
   stood slithered

4 **Look at the pictures below. Circle the correct s blend for each word.**

sp sn str sk — sw sp sn str — sk sw sp sn — str sk sw sp

14

Horizons® Phonics & Reading Grade 1 Book Two

Test 9

Lessons 81-90

Instructions:

Review the prefixes **re-**, **un-**, and **dis-** and their meanings. Have the student do some examples of adding prefixes to different base words to make new words, such as **happy**, **please**, **lock**, **play**, and **safe**. Read through the test with the student. Help the student with any words that he/she is still unsure of. The teacher should be available to answer any questions that the student may have during the test.

Activity 1. Make sure the student understands the directions and can read the base words.

Words:			
	reread	**relock**	**unlock**
	unhappy	**reappear**	**disappear**
	disobey	**redo**	**undo**
	rewrite	**reorder**	**disorder**
	unsafe		
	displeased		

Activity 2. Make sure the student correctly identifies the pictures.

Pictures: **dress, presents, clock, glasses**
skirt, strawberry, brick, fruit

What do you know? Test 9 Lessons 81–90 Name:

1. Add the prefix *re-*, *un-*, or *dis-* to the base words. Some of the words may use two prefixes.

re read	re lock	un lock
un happy	re appear	dis appear
dis obey	re do	un do
re write	re order	dis order
un safe		
dis pleased		

2. Look at each picture. Circle the correct consonant blend.

br (dr) fr pr tr   br dr fr (pr) tr   (cl) fl gl bl pl   cl fl (gl) bl pl

(sk) sn sp str sw   sk sn sp (str) sw   (br) bl dr pr pl   cr cl (fr) fl gr

Horizons® Phonics & Reading Grade 1 Book Two   25

Activity 3. Make sure the student can read the sentences and the base words.

Sentences:

1. **Shawn is unhappy about losing his toy.**
2. **It is unsafe to ride your bike at night without a light.**
3. **Dad needed to rewrite his letter.**
4. **Unlock the door with the key.**
5. **The magician made the rabbit disappear.**
6. **She has to redo her homework.**

Activity 4. Make sure the student understands the instructions and can read the words and phrases to be matched.

Matching: **to heat again / reheat**
to wind again / rewind
opposite of pack / unpack
to play again / replay

3 Read each sentence. Add the correct prefix to the base word and write the new word on the line.

1. Shawn is unhappy (happy) about losing his toy.
2. It is unsafe (safe) to ride your bike at night without a light.
3. Dad needed to rewrite (write) his letter.
4. Unlock (lock) the door with the key.
5. The magician made the rabbit disappear (appear).
6. She has to redo (do) her homework.

4 Draw lines to match the words with the definitions.

to heat again	replay
to wind again	unpack
opposite of pack	rewind
to play again	reheat

26 Horizons® Phonics & Reading Grade 1 Book Two

Lesson 91 - Y as a Vowel

Overview:

- Word/picture match
- Categorize words from story
- Sentence completion
- Write words to match pictures
- Unscramble words

Materials and Supplies:

- Teacher's Guide & Student Workbook
- White board or chalkboard
- Phonics rule flashcards in **Teacher Resources**
- Word cards (as necessary)
- Story: *The Happy Baby*

Teaching Tips:

Review the rule. Have the student write examples of the rule on the chalkboard or white board. Assist the student as needed in identifying the pictures or reading the words in the lesson.

Activity 1. Have the student identify the pictures and draw a line to match the pictures with the words.

Pictures:		
	cry	**fly**
	bunny	**puppy**
	penny	**baby**
	happy	

Activity 2. Have the student read the story aloud. The student will underline all of the words in the story that end in **y** and write the words in the correct categories. (NOTE: do not let the student become confused about **everything**. It does not end in **y**.)

Y = long **e**: **Molly, baby, Tommy, happy, silly, finally**

Y = long **i**: **cry, try, fly**

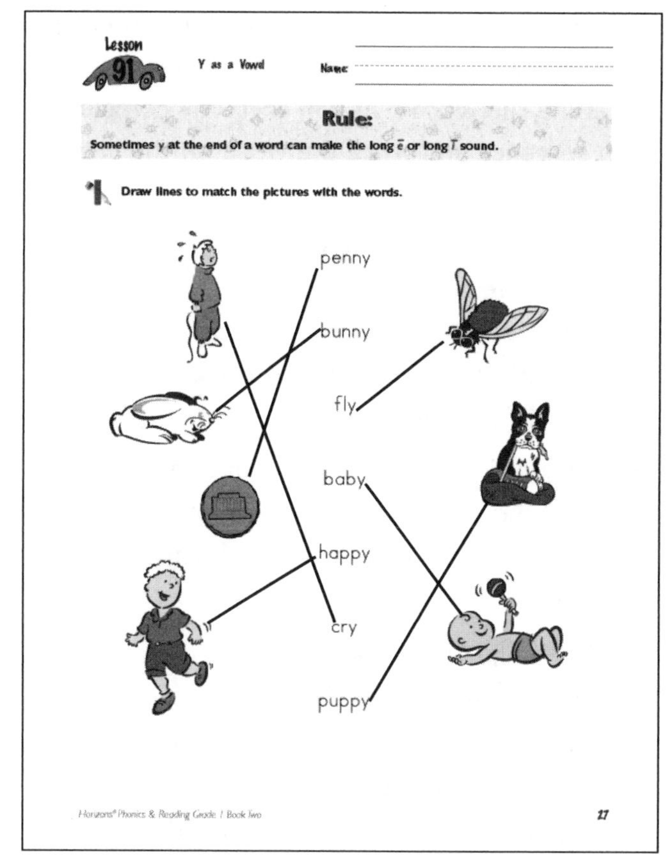
Lesson 91 Y as a Vowel Name:

Rule:
Sometimes y at the end of a word can make the long ē or long ī sound.

1 Draw lines to match the pictures with the words.

penny
bunny
fly
baby
happy
cry
puppy

Horizons® Phonics & Reading Grade 1 Book Two 27

2 Read the story. Underline all of the words that end in y. Put the words into the correct categories.

Molly was taking care of baby Tommy. She heard him cry in his crib. He was not happy. She had to try everything to calm him down. She read him a silly book about dogs that fly. Finally, he was better.

Y = long ē	Y = long ī
Molly	cry
baby	try
Tommy	fly
happy	
silly	
finally	

28 Horizons® Phonics & Reading Grade 1 Book Two

Activity 3. Help the student read the sentences and the word choices. Instruct the student to underline the word that will correctly complete each sentence and write the word on the line.

Sentences:

1. **The sky was cloudy.**
2. **The day was rainy.**
3. **We stayed inside to stay dry.**
4. **Mom wanted us to try to have fun.**
5. **I felt sleepy.**

Activity 4. Have the student name the pictures and read the words from the list aloud. The student will use the words from the list to name the pictures.

Pictures: **fly, cherry, bunny**
sky, fry, celery

Activity 5. Have the student read the riddles aloud. The student will unscramble the words at the ends of the sentences to answer the riddles.

Words: **bunny, sunny, sorry, why, muddy**

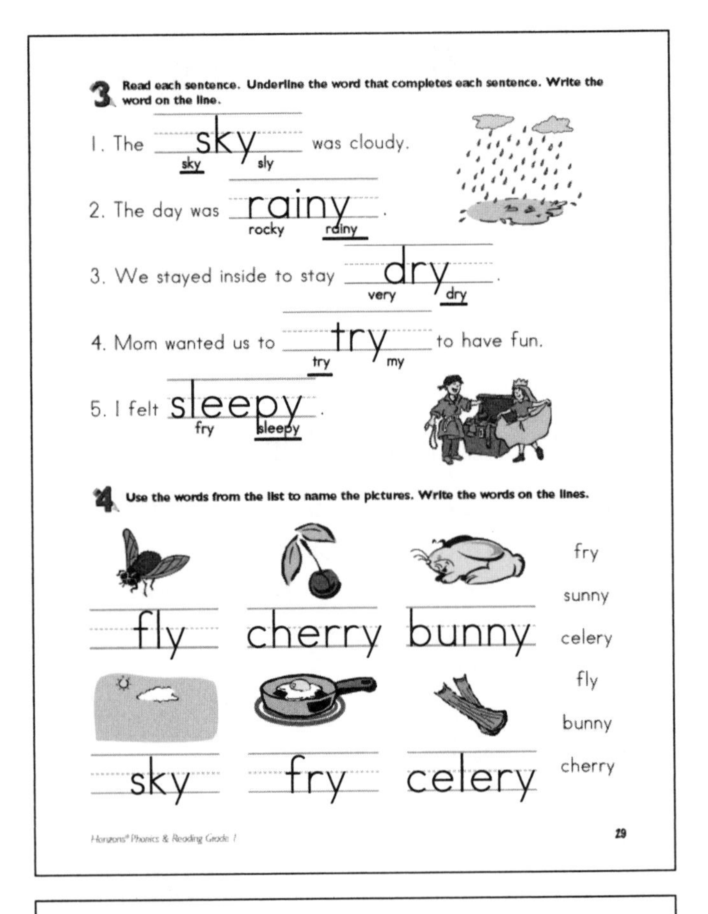

3 **Read each sentence. Underline the word that completes each sentence. Write the word on the line.**

1. The sky was cloudy. (sky / sly)
2. The day was rainy. (rocky / rainy)
3. We stayed inside to stay dry. (very / dry)
4. Mom wanted us to try to have fun. (try / my)
5. I felt sleepy. (fry / sleepy)

4 **Use the words from the list to name the pictures. Write the words on the lines.**

fly cherry bunny
sky fry celery

fry
sunny
celery
fly
bunny
cherry

Horizons® Phonics & Reading Grade 1 29

5 **Read each riddle. Unscramble the word that answers each riddle.**

1. This animal is furry and hops. bunny (nnyub)
2. If there are no clouds in the sky, it is this kind of day. sunny (ynuns)
3. If you did something that you wish you hadn't done, you might be this. sorry (oyrrs)
4. When you ask a question, you might use this word. why (hyw)
5. After it rains, dirt often gets this way. muddy (ddyum)

30 Horizons® Phonics & Reading Grade 1 Book Two

Lesson 92 - Checkup: Consonant Digraph th

Overview:

- Circle pictures that start with **th**
- Word completion
- Write words that name pictures
- Sentence completion

Materials and Supplies:

- Teacher's Guide & Student Workbook
- White board or chalkboard
- Word cards (as necessary)
- Story: *John's Thirteenth Birthday*

Teaching Tips:

Review the rule. Have the student write examples of the rule on the chalkboard or white board. Assist the student as needed in identifying the pictures or reading the words in the lesson.

Activity 1. Have the student name the pictures. The student will circle the pictures whose names begin with **th**.

Pictures: **thumb, tack, three**
thirteen, thimble, cheese

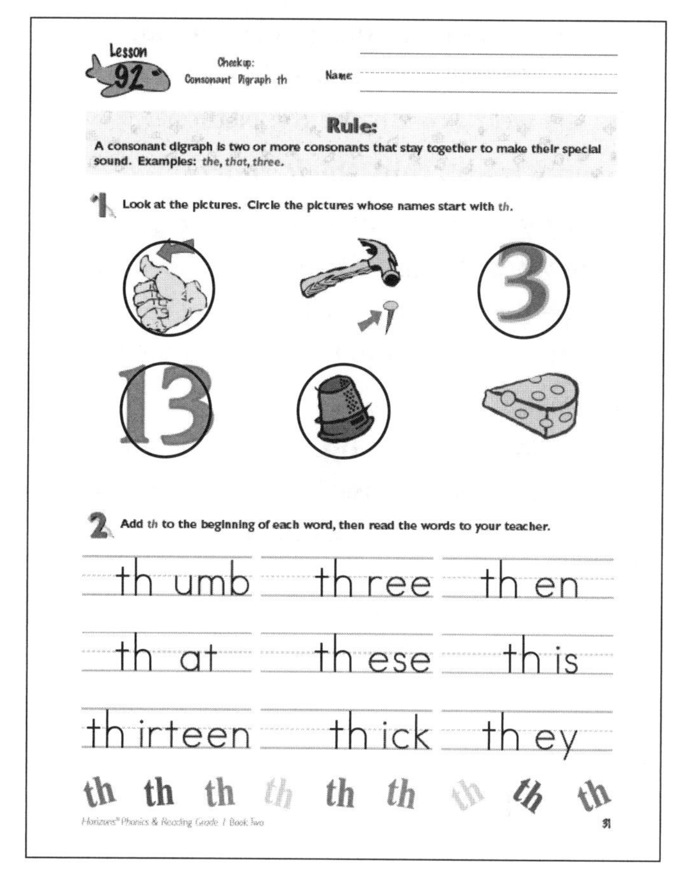
Lesson 92 Checkup: Consonant Digraph th Name:

Rule:
A consonant digraph is two or more consonants that stay together to make their special sound. Examples: *the, that, three.*

1. Look at the pictures. Circle the pictures whose names start with *th*.

2. Add *th* to the beginning of each word, then read the words to your teacher.

th umb	th ree	th en
th at	th ese	th is
th irteen	th ick	th ey

Horizons® Phonics & Reading Grade 1 Book Two 91

Activity 2. Discuss the consonant digraph rule for **th** and have the student think of additional examples. Have the student guess what each word in the activity might be. Instruct the student to add **th** to each of the words and read them aloud.

Words: **thumb, three, then**
that, these, this
thirteen, thick, they

Activity 3. Have the student read the words in the list and name the pictures. The student will write the words that name the pictures.

Pictures: **teeth, thin, thick, thorn**

Activity 4. Help the student read the sentences and the word choices. Instruct the student to underline the word that will correctly complete each sentence and write the word on the line.

Sentences:

1. **In the morning, we brush our teeth.**
2. **Mike's brother is three years old.**
3. **They are our friends.**
4. **This is my house.**

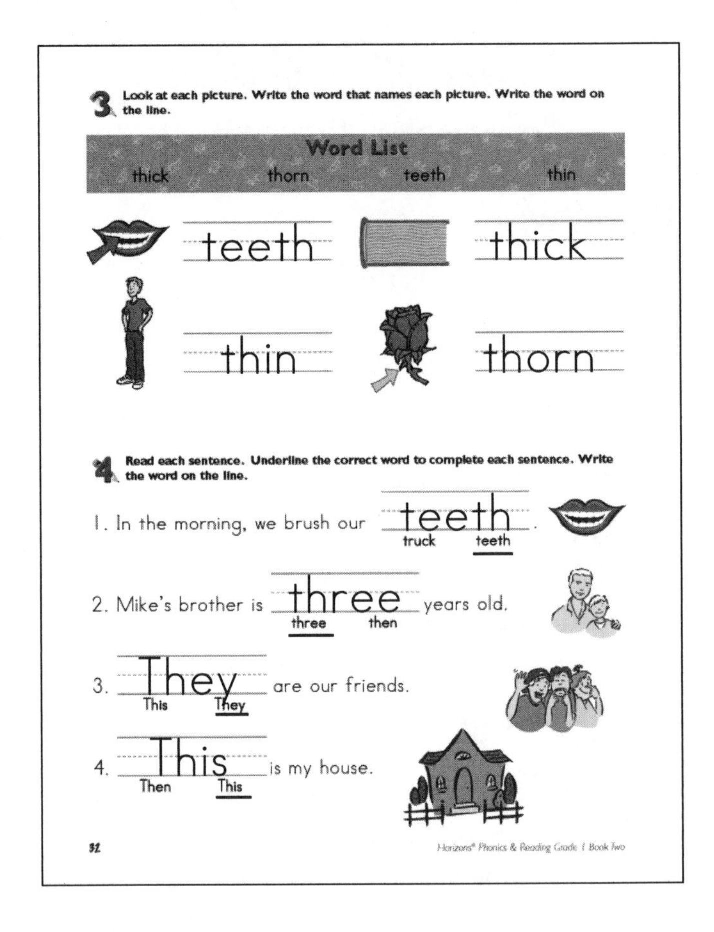

3 Look at each picture. Write the word that names each picture. Write the word on the line.

Word List

thick thorn teeth thin

teeth thick

thin thorn

4 Read each sentence. Underline the correct word to complete each sentence. Write the word on the line.

1. In the morning, we brush our teeth.
truck teeth
2. Mike's brother is three years old.
three then
3. They are our friends.
This They
4. This is my house.
Then This

Horizons® Phonics & Reading Grade 1 Book Two

Lesson 93 - Checkup: Consonant Digraph tch

Overview:

- Circle pictures that contain tch
- Word completion
- Sentence completion
- Unscramble words

Materials and Supplies:

- Teacher's Guide & Student Workbook
- White board or chalkboard
- Word cards (as necessary)
- Story: *A Batch of Cookies*

Teaching Tips:

Review the rule. Have the student write examples of the rule on the chalkboard or white board. Assist the student as needed in identifying the pictures or reading the words in the lesson.

Activity 1. Have the student name the pictures. The student will circle the pictures whose names contain **tch**.

Pictures: **watch, kitchen, catch**
pitcher, fetch, fence

Lesson 93 Checkup: Consonant Digraph tch Name:

Rule:
A consonant digraph is two consonants that stay together to make their special sound. Consonant digraph *tch* makes the sound you hear in *kitchen*, *watch*, and *stitch*.

1. Look at the pictures. Circle the pictures whose names contain *tch*.

2. Add *tch* to each of the words below, then read the words to your teacher.

watch kitchen catch pitcher
fetch match switch stitch

Horizons® Phonics & Reading Grade 1 Book Two 93

Activity 2. Discuss the consonant blend rule for **tch** and have the student think of additional examples. Instruct the student to add **tch** to each of the words and read them aloud.

Words: **watch, kitchen, catch, pitcher**
fetch, match, switch, stitch

Activity 3. Help the student read the words in the list and the sentences. Instruct the student to select the word that will correctly complete each sentence and write the word on the line.

Sentences:

1. **I use a watch to tell time.**
2. **We eat our meals in the kitchen.**
3. **I like to catch the ball when it is thrown to me.**
4. **Most of my socks match.**
5. **Mom made a batch of cookies.**

Activity 4. Review the words in the list with the student. Have the student unscramble the words, write the correct word on each line, and read the words aloud when they are unscrambled.

Words: **kitchen, stitch, watch**
match, itch, switch

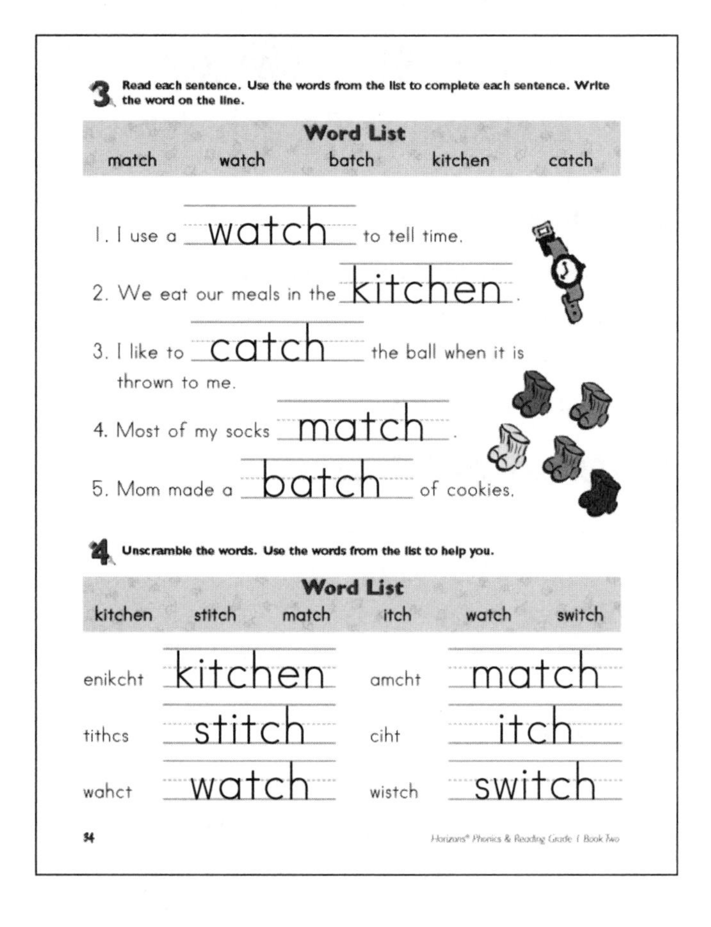

3 Read each sentence. Use the words from the list to complete each sentence. Write the word on the line.

Word List
match watch batch kitchen catch

1. I use a watch to tell time.
2. We eat our meals in the kitchen.
3. I like to catch the ball when it is thrown to me.
4. Most of my socks match.
5. Mom made a batch of cookies.

4 Unscramble the words. Use the words from the list to help you.

Word List
kitchen stitch match itch watch switch

enikcht	kitchen	amcht	match
tithcs	stitch	ciht	itch
wahct	watch	wistch	switch

54

Horizons® Phonics & Reading Grade 1 Book Two

Lesson 94 - Review: Consonant Digraphs th & tch

Overview:

- Circle pictures that contain **th** or **tch**
- Crossword puzzle
- Word/picture match
- Sentence writing

Materials and Supplies:

- Teacher's Guide & Student Workbook
- White board or chalkboard
- Word cards (as necessary)
- Story: *The Pitcher in the Kitchen*

Teaching Tips:

Review the rule. Have the student write examples of the rule on the chalkboard or white board. Assist the student as needed in identifying the pictures or reading the words in the lesson.

Activity 1. Have the student name the pictures. The student will circle the pictures whose names contain **th** or **tch**.

Pictures: **tent, teeth, kitchen**
pitcher, thumb, thimble

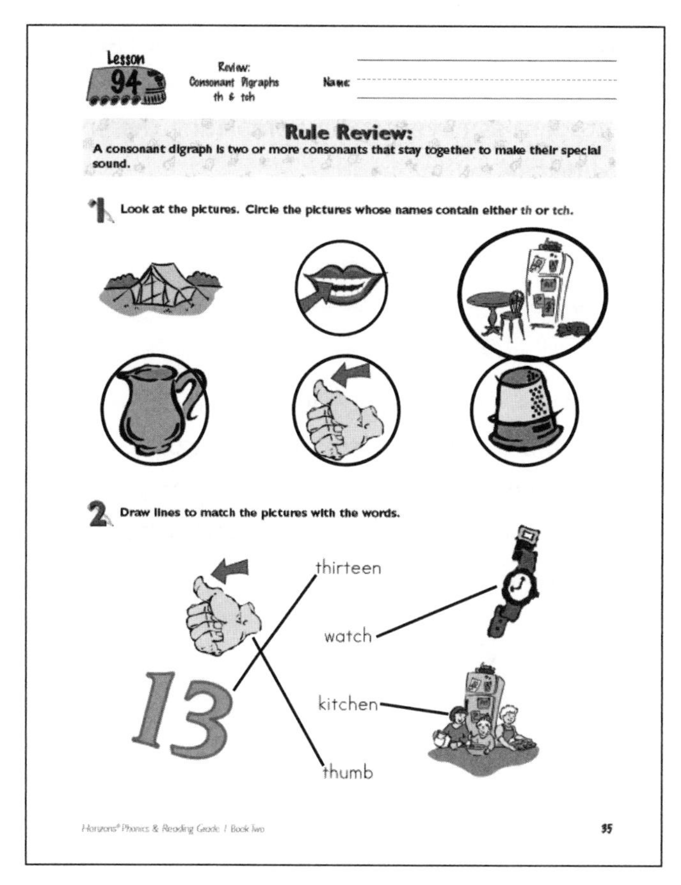

Lesson 94 Review: Consonant Digraphs th & tch Name:

Rule Review:
A consonant digraph is two or more consonants that stay together to make their special sound.

1 Look at the pictures. Circle the pictures whose names contain either *th* or *tch*.

2 Draw lines to match the pictures with the words.

thirteen
watch
kitchen
thumb

Horizons Phonics & Reading Grade 1 Book Two 95

Activity 2. Have the student identify the pictures and draw a line to match the pictures with the words.

Pictures:	**thumb**	**watch**
	thirteen	**kitchen**

Activity 3. Review the words in the list. Help the student read the crossword puzzle clues. Assist the student as necessary in completing the crossword puzzle.

Across: **1. This**

3. kitchen

Down: **2. think**

4. nothing

Activity 4. The student will write three sentences and use at least six of the words from the lesson. Help the student with writing and spelling as necessary. Emphasize correct capitalization and punctuation.

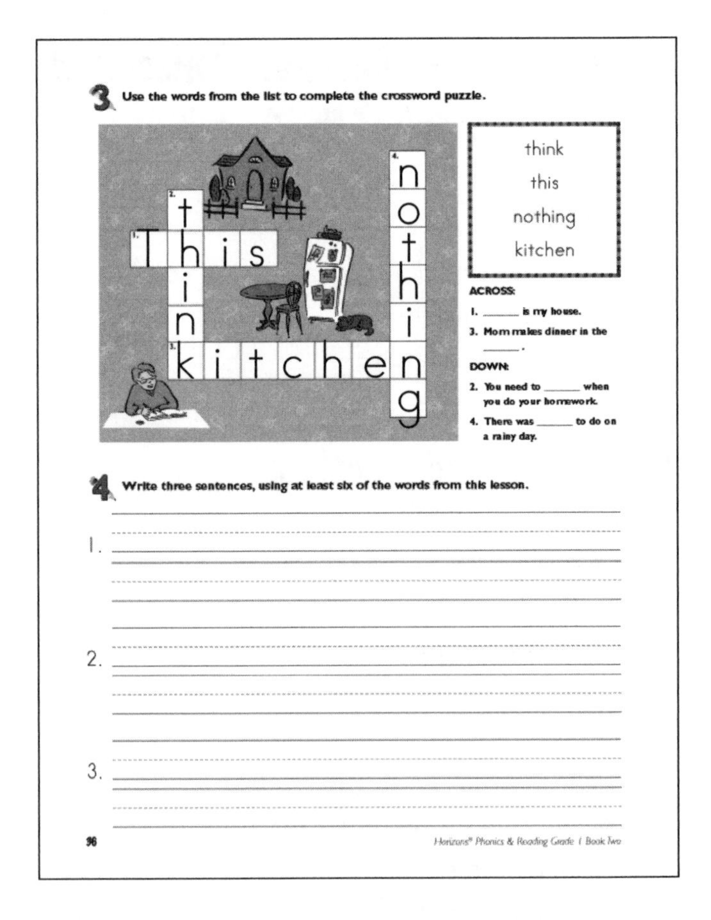

3 Use the words from the list to complete the crossword puzzle.
think
this
nothing
kitchen
ACROSS:
1. _____ is my house.
3. Mom makes dinner in the _____.
DOWN:
2. You need to _____ when you do your homework.
4. There was _____ to do on a rainy day.
This
think
kitchen
nothing
4 Write three sentences, using at least six of the words from this lesson.
1.
2.
3.
96
Horizons® Phonics & Reading Grade 1 Book Two

Lesson 95 - Review: Consonant Digraph sh

Overview:

- Circle pictures that contain **sh**
- Word completion
- Auditory recognition of **sh** at the beginning or end of a word
- Word/picture match
- Sentence completion

Materials and Supplies:

- Teacher's Guide & Student Workbook
- White board or chalkboard
- Word cards (as necessary)
- Story: *Shiny shells*

Teaching Tips:

Review the rule. Have the student write examples of the rule on the chalkboard or white board. Assist the student as needed in identifying the pictures or reading the words in the lesson.

Activity 1. Have the student name the pictures. The student will circle the pictures whose names begin with **sh**.

Pictures: **shoe, ship, shed, seven**
duck, shirt, shell, whale

Activity 2. Discuss the rule for **sh** and have the student think of additional examples. Instruct the student to add **sh** to each of the words and read them aloud.

Words: **shoe, shine, brush, fish**
ashes, shop, ship, shut

Lesson 95
Review:
Consonant Digraph sh
Name:

Rule:
A consonant digraph is two or more consonants that stay together to make their special sound. Examples: *shoe, show, shirt.*

1. Look at the pictures. Circle the pictures whose names begin with *sh*.

2. Add *sh* to each of the words below, then read the words to your teacher.

sh oe sh ine bru sh fi sh
a sh es sh op sh ip sh ut

3. Look at the pictures below. Circle the *sh* to show whether the *sh* sound is at the beginning or at the end of the word.

sh (sh) (sh) sh (sh) sh (sh) sh

Horizons® Phonics & Reading Grade 1 Book Two 37

Activity 3. Help the student identify the pictures. Have them listen as you say the names of the pictures, circle the **sh** that shows whether the word begins or ends in **sh**.

Pictures: **fish, shed, shell, shirt**

Activity 4. Have the student read the words in the list and name the pictures. The student will write the words that name the pictures.

Pictures: **brush, shell, shoe**
fish, dish, shin

Activity 5. Have the student read the words in the list (Activity 4) and the sentences. Instruct the student to select the word that will correctly complete each sentence and write the word on the line.

Sentences:

1. **Henry has three kinds of fish in his tank.**
2. **I found a shell on the beach.**
3. **I have a scrape on my shin.**
4. **Hank ate his food off a dish.**
5. **She uses a brush for her hair.**

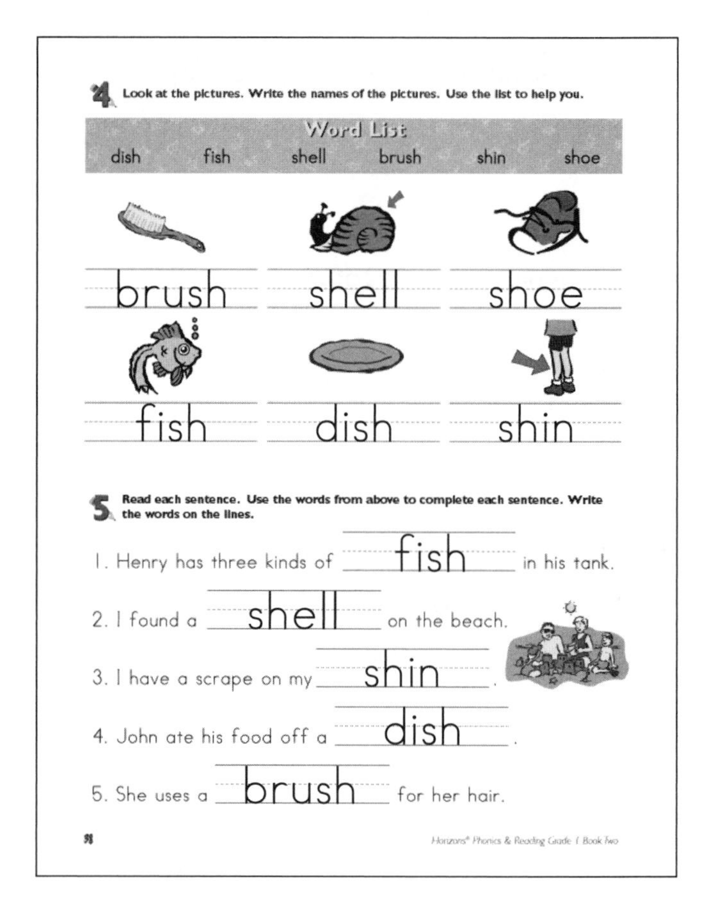

4 Look at the pictures. Write the names of the pictures. Use the list to help you.

Word List

dish fish shell brush shin shoe

brush shell shoe

fish dish shin

5 Read each sentence. Use the words from above to complete each sentence. Write the words on the lines.

1. Henry has three kinds of fish in his tank.
2. I found a shell on the beach.
3. I have a scrape on my shin.
4. John ate his food off a dish.
5. She uses a brush for her hair.

Horizons® Phonics & Reading Grade 1 Book Two

Lesson 96 - Checkup: Consonant Digraph ch

Overview:

- Circle pictures that start with **ch**
- Word/picture match
- Word completion
- Sentence writing

Materials and Supplies:

- Teacher's Guide & Student Workbook
- White board or chalkboard
- Word cards (as necessary)
- Story: *A Chip Sandwich*

Teaching Tips:

Review the rule. Have the student write examples of the rule on the chalkboard or white board. Assist the student as needed in identifying the pictures or reading the words in the lesson.

Activity 1. Have the student name the pictures. The student will circle the pictures whose names contain **ch**.

Pictures: **chair, sandwich, shoe, peach**
chimney, fish, cheese, dish

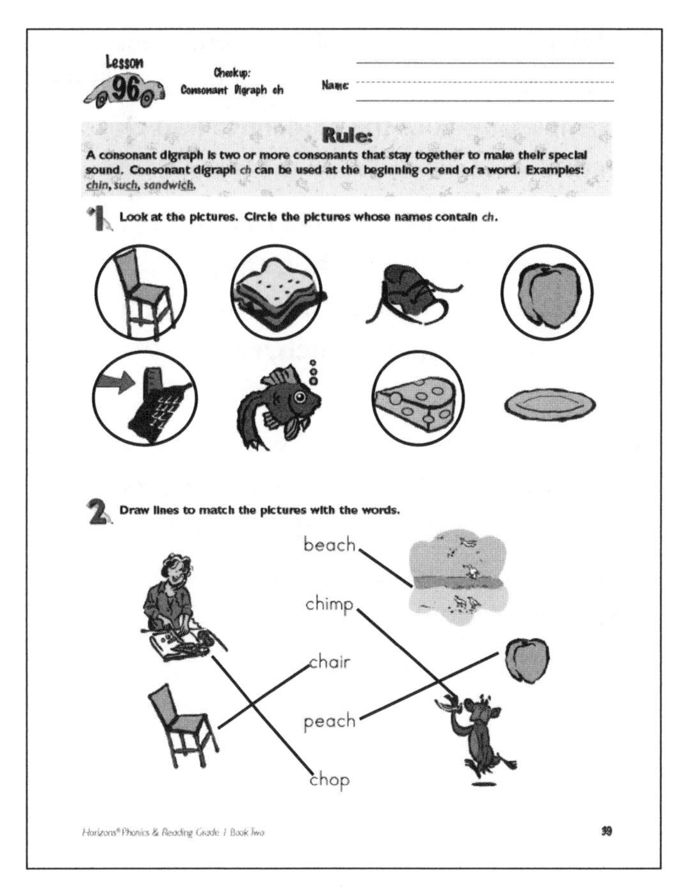
Lesson 96 Checkup: Consonant Digraph ch Name:

Rule:
A consonant digraph is two or more consonants that stay together to make their special sound. Consonant digraph *ch* can be used at the beginning or end of a word. Examples: chin, such, sandwich.

1. Look at the pictures. Circle the pictures whose names contain *ch*.

2. Draw lines to match the pictures with the words.

beach
chimp
chair
peach
chop

Horizons® Phonics & Reading Grade 1 Book Two 59

Activity 2. Have the student identify the pictures and draw a line to match the pictures with the words.

Pictures:	chop	beach
	chair	peach
		chimp

Activity 3. Discuss the rule for consonant digraph **ch** and have the student think of additional examples. Instruct the student to add **ch** to each of the words and read them aloud.

Words: **chair, chin, peach, much**
chest, churn, chill, chop
punch, crunch, branch, chunk
pinch, such, which, rich
chums, cheese, chips, chat

Activity 4. The student will write three sentences and use at least six of the words from the lesson. Help the student with writing and spelling as necessary. Emphasize correct capitalization and punctuation.

3 Add *ch* to each of the words below, then read the words to your teacher.

chair chin peach much
chest churn chill chop
punch crunch branch chunk
pinch such which rich
chums cheese chips chat

4 Write three sentences using at least six of the words from this lesson.

1.

2.

3.

40 Horizons® Phonics & Reading Grade 1 Book Two

Lesson 97 - Review: Consonant Digraphs sh & ch

Overview:

- Categorize words
- Word/picture match
- Sentence completion
- Crossword puzzle

Materials and Supplies:

- Teacher's Guide & Student Workbook
- White board or chalkboard
- Word cards (as necessary)
- Story: *The Cherry Tree*

Teaching Tips:

Review the rule. Have the student write examples of the rule on the chalkboard or white board. Assist the student as needed in identifying the pictures or reading the words in the lesson.

Activity 1. Assist the student in reading the story as needed. Have the student underline all the **ch** or **sh** words and categorize them correctly.

sh words:	**She**	**ch** words:	**each**
	show		**much**
	shoes		

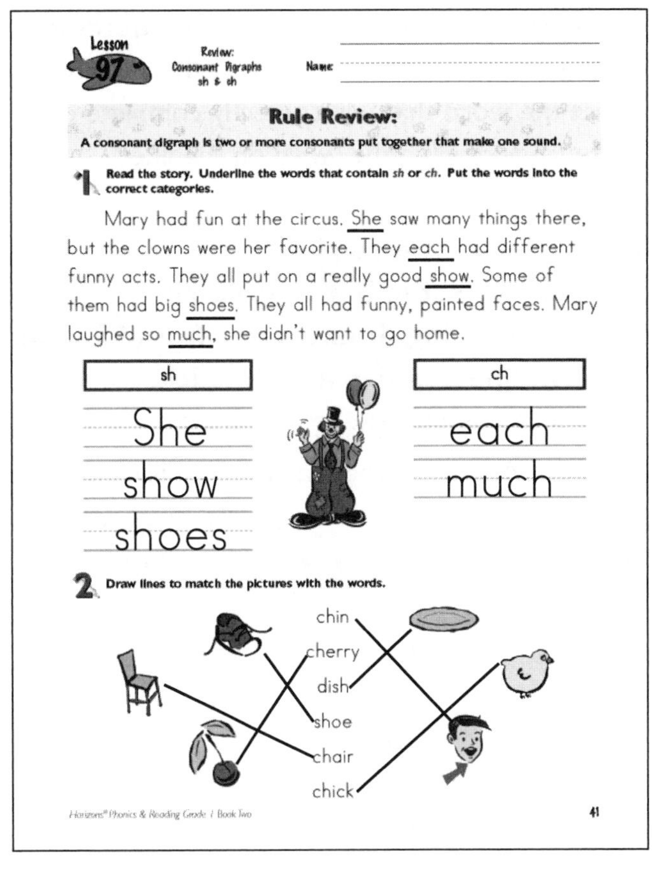
Lesson 97 Review: Consonant Digraphs sh & ch Name:

Rule Review:

A consonant digraph is two or more consonants put together that make one sound.

1 **Read the story. Underline the words that contain *sh* or *ch*. Put the words into the correct categories.**

Mary had fun at the circus. She saw many things there, but the clowns were her favorite. They each had different funny acts. They all put on a really good show. Some of them had big shoes. They all had funny, painted faces. Mary laughed so much, she didn't want to go home.

sh	ch
She	each
show	much
shoes	

2 **Draw lines to match the pictures with the words.**

chin
cherry
dish
shoe
chair
chick

Horizons® Phonics & Reading Grade 1 Book Two 41

Activity 2. Have the student identify the pictures and draw a line to match the pictures with the words.

Pictures:	**shoe**	**dish**
	chair	**chick**
	cherry	**chin**

Activity 3. Help the student read the words in the list and the sentences. Instruct the student to select the word that will correctly complete each sentence and write the word on the line.

Sentences:

1. **I like cherry pie.**
2. **She sat in her favorite chair.**
3. **The dog drinks water from his dish.**
4. **The hen had a baby chick.**
5. **I have a hole in my shoe.**

Activity 4. Review the words in the list. Help the student read the crossword puzzle clues. Assist the student as necessary with the crossword puzzle.

Across: **1. chair**
3. sandwich
4. shirt

Down: **2. cheese**
5. hush

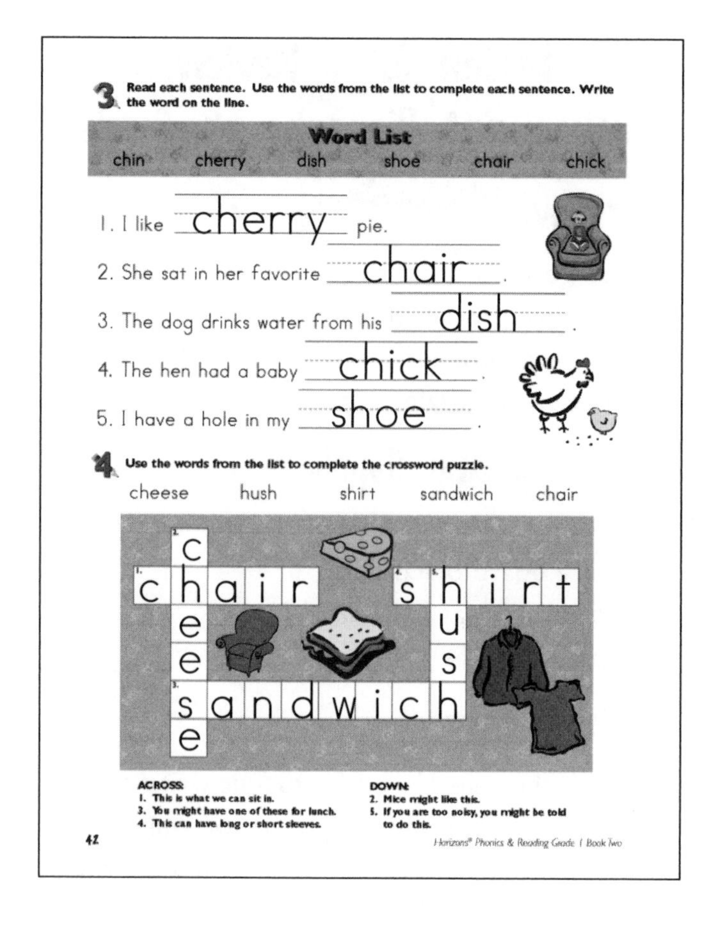

3 Read each sentence. Use the words from the list to complete each sentence. Write the word on the line.

Word List
chin cherry dish shoe chair chick

1. I like cherry pie.
2. She sat in her favorite chair.
3. The dog drinks water from his dish.
4. The hen had a baby chick.
5. I have a hole in my shoe.

4 Use the words from the list to complete the crossword puzzle.

cheese hush shirt sandwich chair

ACROSS:
1. This is what we can sit in.
3. You might have one of these for lunch.
4. This can have long or short sleeves.

DOWN:
2. Mice might like this.
5. If you are too noisy, you might be told to do this.

42 Horizons® Phonics & Reading Grade 1 Book Two

Lesson 98 - Writing Lesson: Report

Overview:

- Write a report about an animal

Materials and Supplies:

- Teacher's Guide & Student Workbook
- White board or chalkboard
- Word cards (as necessary)
- Story: *Zach's Report*

Teaching Tips:

The student will be writing a report on an animal. Go over the directions for the report with the student. The student will need some reference material to use to get information for the report. Help with this as necessary. The teacher or writing partner should help the student choose an animal and help find five facts about the animal. The student will write the facts down and arrange the facts in order for the report. This report does not have to be very detailed, considering the age of the student. Five sentences are sufficient, but more can be written if the teacher so desires.

The student should write a rough draft on a piece of paper. The teacher or writing partner should help with the editing process. The student should write the final copy in the student workbook.

Lesson 98 Writing Lesson: Report Name:

1 Writing a Report – Write a report about an animal.

You are going to write a report about an animal. A report tells the reader information about something. Only facts, or things that can be proven to be true, are written in a report. Have your teacher or writing partner help you find information about an animal on which you want to do your report. Pick out at least five facts about the animal. Your teacher or partner can help you write them down. Then decide what order to put them in.

Write your first copy on a piece of paper. Have your teacher or partner help you check for any mistakes, then write your final copy in your book.

Horizons® Phonics & Reading Grade 1 Book Two 49

Activity 1. Write a report about an animal.

My Report About ____________

Lesson 99 - Checkup: Compound Words

Overview:

- Write two words that make up the compound word
- Match words with meanings
- Word search

Materials and Supplies:

- Teacher's Guide & Student Workbook
- White board or chalkboard
- Word cards (as necessary)
- Story: *The Sandbox in the Backyard*

Teaching Tips:

Review the rule. Have the student write compound words on the chalkboard or white board. Assist the student as needed in identifying the pictures or reading the words in the lesson.

Activity 1. Review the rule for compound words. Help the student read the words in the activity. Review the pictures with the student. The student will write the two words that make up each compound word.

Words:		
	back	**yard**
	mail	**box**
	pea	**nut**
	pan	**cake**
	cup	**cake**
	rain	**coat**
	pop	**corn**
	sand	**box**
	back	**pack**
	sail	**boat**

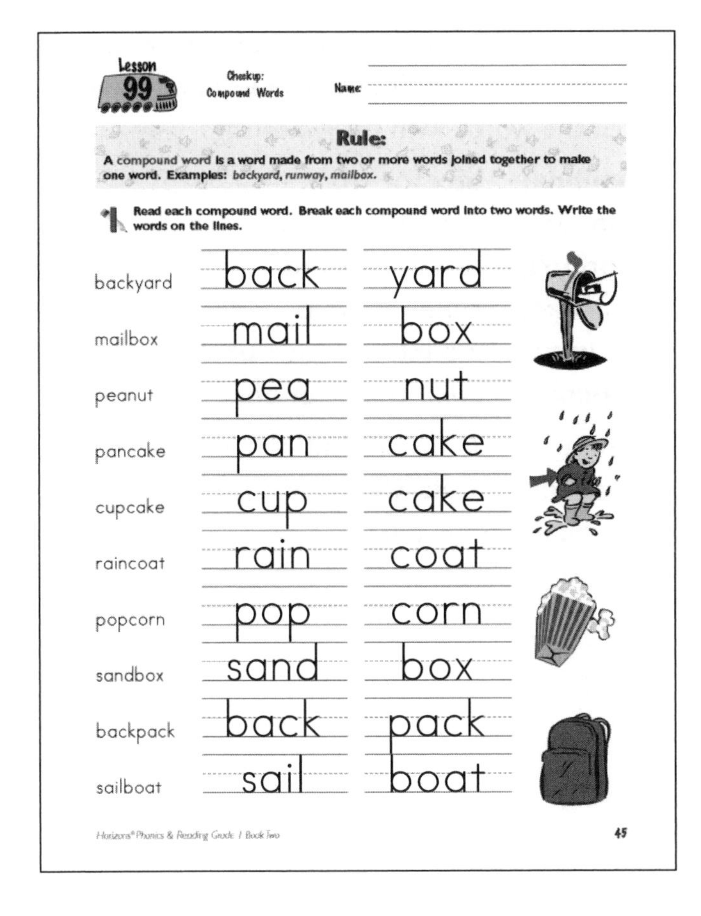

Lesson 99 Checkup: Compound Words Name:

Rule:
A compound word is a word made from two or more words joined together to make one word. Examples: *backyard, runway, mailbox.*

1 Read each compound word. Break each compound word into two words. Write the words on the lines.

backyard	back	yard
mailbox	mail	box
peanut	pea	nut
pancake	pan	cake
cupcake	cup	cake
raincoat	rain	coat
popcorn	pop	corn
sandbox	sand	box
backpack	back	pack
sailboat	sail	boat

Horizons® Phonics & Reading Grade 1 Book Two 45

Activity 2. Have the student read the words and the meanings aloud. The student will draw lines to match the words with their meanings.

mailbox:	**box for mail**
raincoat:	**a coat for rain**
sandbox:	**box with sand**
cupcake:	**cake in a cup**
backpack:	**a pack for your back**
popcorn:	**corn that can pop**

Activity 3. Help the student read the words in the list. The student will find and circle the words from the list in the puzzle.

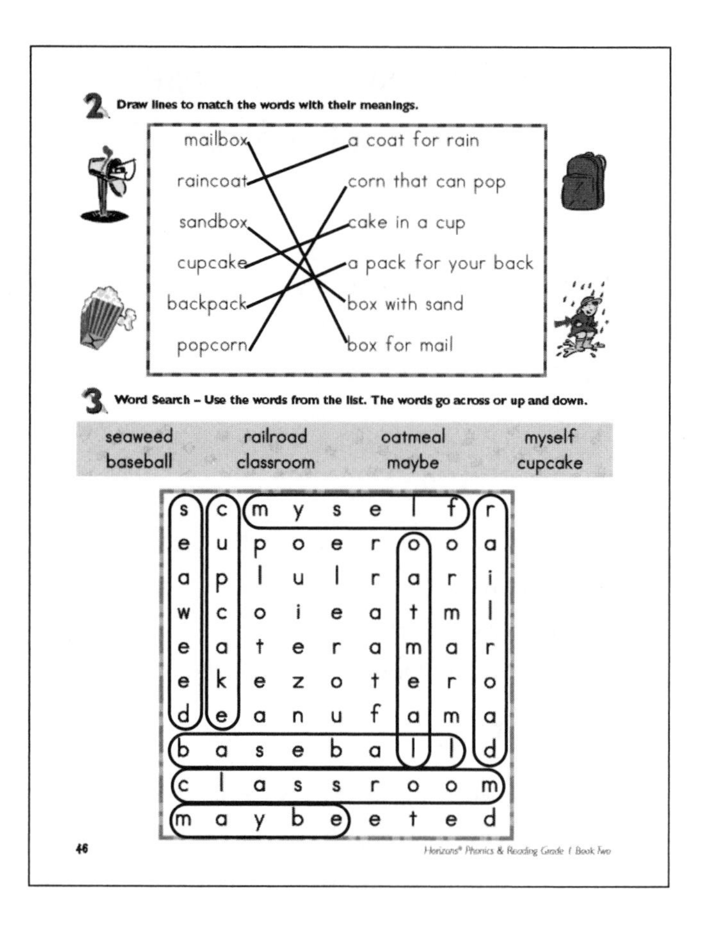

2. Draw lines to match the words with their meanings.

mailbox	a coat for rain
raincoat	corn that can pop
sandbox	cake in a cup
cupcake	a pack for your back
backpack	box with sand
popcorn	box for mail

3. Word Search – Use the words from the list. The words go across or up and down.

seaweed	railroad	oatmeal	myself
baseball	classroom	maybe	cupcake

s	c	m	y	s	e	l	f	r
e	u	p	o	e	r	o	o	a
a	p	l	u	l	r	a	r	i
w	c	o	i	e	a	t	m	l
e	a	t	e	r	a	m	a	r
e	k	e	z	o	t	e	r	o
d	e	a	n	u	f	a	m	a
b	a	s	e	b	a	l	l	d
c	l	a	s	s	r	o	o	m
m	a	y	b	e	e	t	e	d

46 Horizons® Phonics & Reading Grade 1 Book Two

Lesson 100 - Checkup: Prefixes & Suffixes

Overview:

- Divide words into prefix, base word, suffix
- Sentence completion
- Riddles

Materials and Supplies:

- Teacher's Guide & Student Workbook
- White board or chalkboard
- Word cards (as necessary)
- Story: *Kip, A Playful Puppy*

Teaching Tips:

Review the rule. Have the student write examples of the rule on the chalkboard or white board. Assist the student as needed in identifying the pictures or reading the words in the lesson.

Activity 1. Have the student read the words aloud. The student will divide the words into prefix, base word and suffix. Not all of the words will have a prefix and a suffix.

un	**like**	
re	**read**	**ing**
jump	**ing**	
try	**ing**	
un	**wind**	**ing**
re	**do**	**ing**

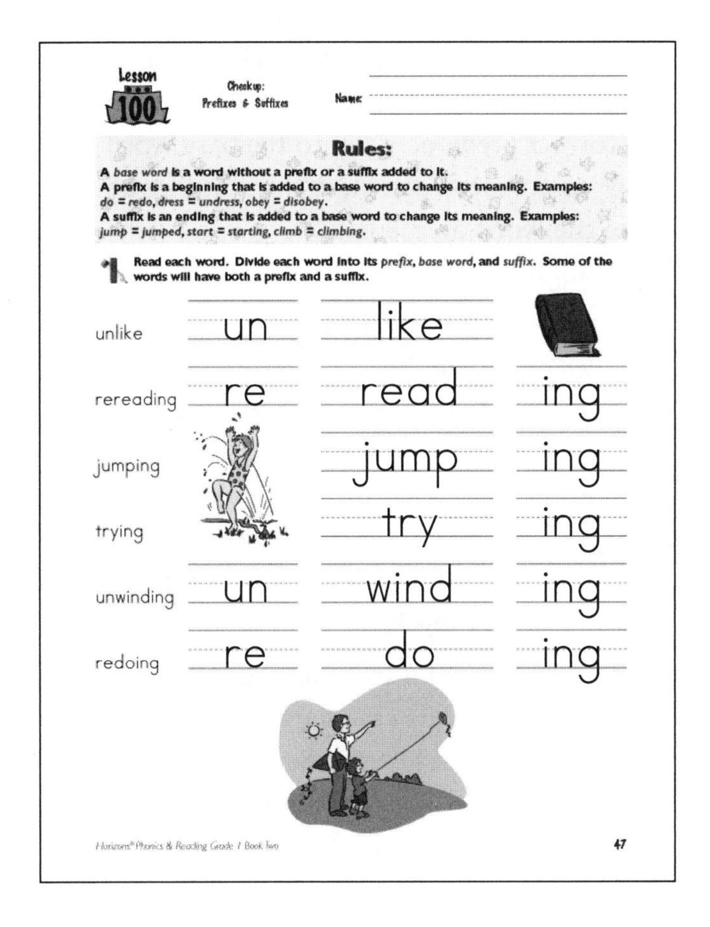

Lesson 100 Checkup: Prefixes & Suffixes Name:

Rules:

A *base word* is a word without a prefix or a suffix added to it.
A prefix is a beginning that is added to a base word to change its meaning. Examples: *do = redo, dress = undress, obey = disobey.*
A suffix is an ending that is added to a base word to change its meaning. Examples: *jump = jumped, start = starting, climb = climbing.*

1. Read each word. Divide each word into its *prefix*, *base word*, and *suffix*. Some of the words will have both a prefix and a suffix.

unlike	un	like	
rereading	re	read	ing
jumping		jump	ing
trying		try	ing
unwinding	un	wind	ing
redoing	re	do	ing

Horizons® Phonics & Reading Grade 1 Book Two 47

Activity 2. Help the student read the sentences and the base word. Instruct the student to add the correct prefix or suffix to the base word in order to correctly complete the sentence and write the word on the line.

Sentences:

1. **Nancy is going to redo her homework.**
2. **Our house is unlike any other house on our street.**
3. **My sister is jumping rope.**
4. **I am trying to do my best.**
5. **This book was so good that I am rereading it.**

Activity 3. Have the student read the words in the list and assist the student as necessary in reading the riddles. Instruct the student to write the correct answer to each riddle on the line.

Words: **1. careful**
2. playful
3. useless
4. sleepless

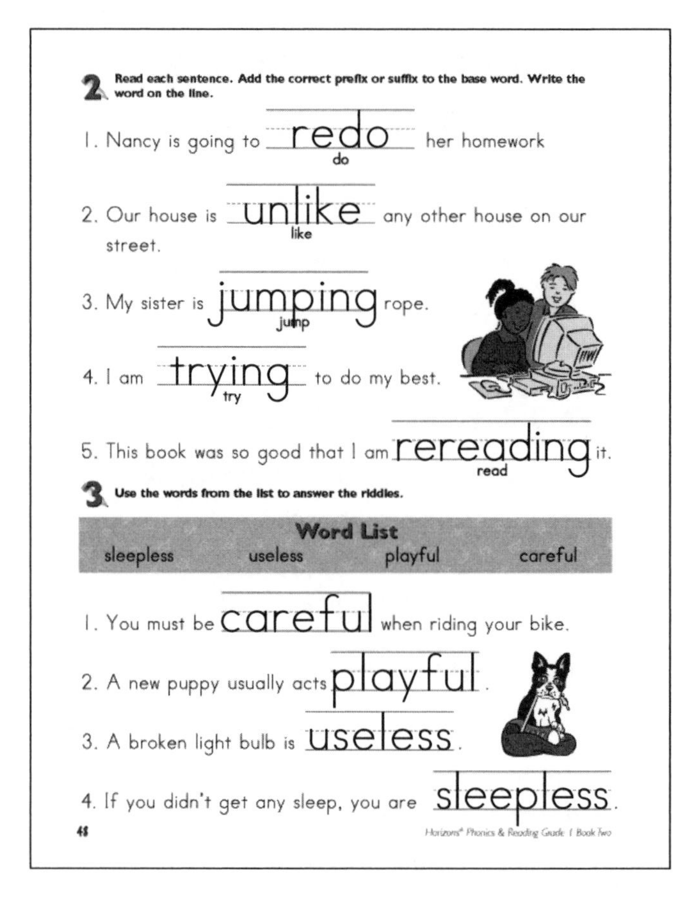

2 Read each sentence. Add the correct prefix or suffix to the base word. Write the word on the line.

1. Nancy is going to redo (do) her homework.
2. Our house is unlike (like) any other house on our street.
3. My sister is jumping (jump) rope.
4. I am trying (try) to do my best.
5. This book was so good that I am rereading (read) it.

3 Use the words from the list to answer the riddles.

Word List			
sleepless	useless	playful	careful

1. You must be careful when riding your bike.
2. A new puppy usually acts playful.
3. A broken light bulb is useless.
4. If you didn't get any sleep, you are sleepless.

48 Horizons Phonics & Reading Grade 1 Book Two

Test 10
Lessons 91-100

Instructions:

Review the long **i** and long **e** sounds of the letter **y**. Review the definition of a compound word. Have the student give some examples of compound words. Have the student break the compound words into their separate words. Review dividing words into prefix, base word, and suffix. Have the student do some examples of these. Read through the test with the student. Help the student with any words that he/she may still be unsure of. The teacher should be available to answer any questions that the student may have during the test.

Activity 1. Review the words in the list with the student.

Words:	**Y = long ī**	**Y = long ē**
	fly	**city**
	by	**every**
	why	**safely**
	my	**money**

Activity 2. Review the words and the instructions with the student.

Words:	**play**	**ground**
	mail	**box**
	day	**light**
	night	**gown**
	pea	**nut**

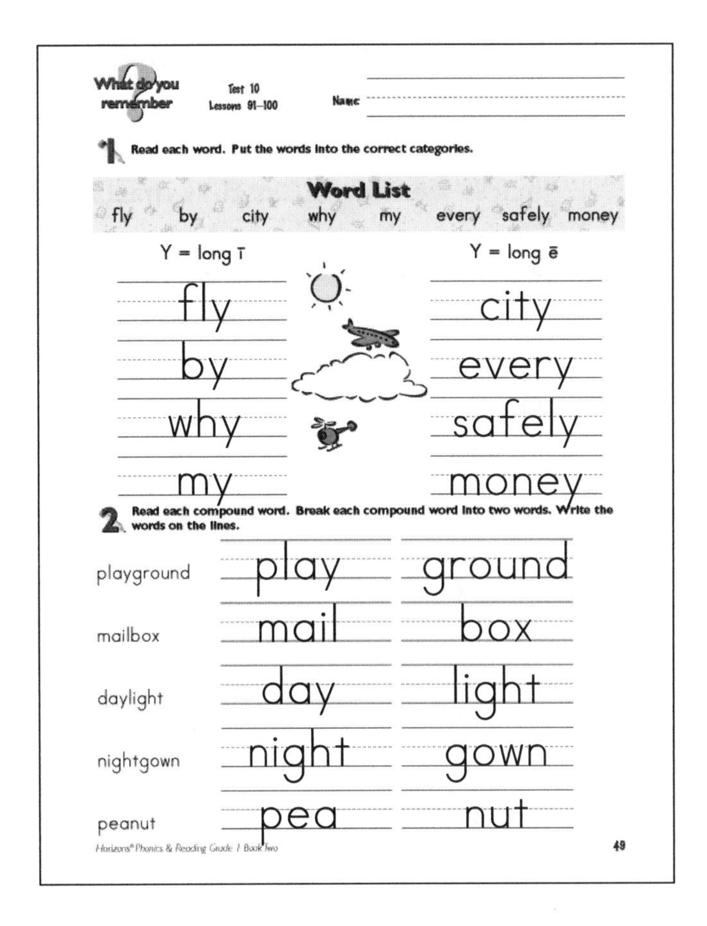
What do you remember

Test 10
Lessons 91–100

Name:

1. Read each word. Put the words into the correct categories.

Word List
fly by city why my every safely money

Y = long ī	Y = long ē
fly	city
by	every
why	safely
my	money

2. Read each compound word. Break each compound word into two words. Write the words on the lines.

playground	play	ground
mailbox	mail	box
daylight	day	light
nightgown	night	gown
peanut	pea	nut

Horizons® Phonics & Reading Grade 1 Book Two 49

Activity 3. Make sure the student can read the words in the list and the sentences.

Sentences:

1. **Jack is wearing socks that match.**
2. **Please don't touch the hot stove.**
3. **Mary needs a new pair of shoes.**
4. **That is my favorite chair to sit in.**
5. **It is a shame that our team didn't win the game.**

Activity 4. Review the instructions and the words with the student.

Words:			
	re	**play**	**ing**
	un	**do**	**ing**
	un	**safe**	**ly**
	dis	**obey**	**ing**
	un	**kind**	**ly**

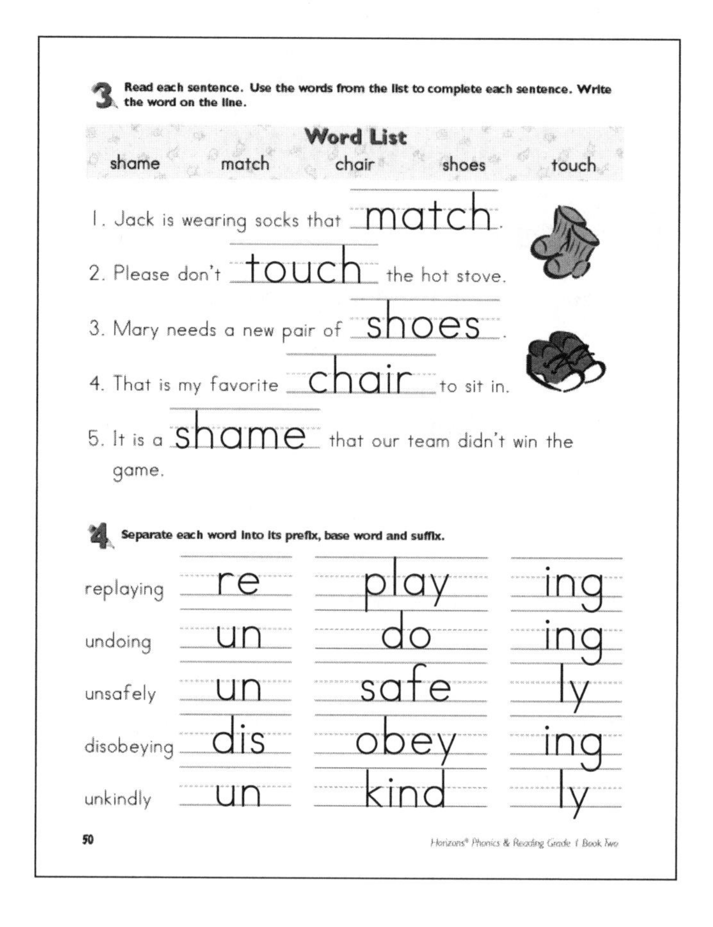

3 Read each sentence. Use the words from the list to complete each sentence. Write the word on the line.

Word List

shame match chair shoes touch

1. Jack is wearing socks that match.
2. Please don't touch the hot stove.
3. Mary needs a new pair of shoes.
4. That is my favorite chair to sit in.
5. It is a shame that our team didn't win the game.

4 Separate each word into its prefix, base word and suffix.

replaying	re	play	ing
undoing	un	do	ing
unsafely	un	safe	ly
disobeying	dis	obey	ing
unkindly	un	kind	ly

50 Horizons® Phonics & Reading Grade 1 Book Two

Lesson 101 - Syllables: Words with Prefixes

Overview:

- Divide words into syllables
- Choose words with prefixes
- Word/picture match
- Sentence completion

Materials and Supplies:

- Teacher's Guide & Student Workbook
- White board or chalkboard
- Word cards (as necessary)
- Story: *The Smiths Repaint the House*

Teaching Tips:

Review the rule. Have the student write examples of prefixes and suffixes on the chalkboard or white board. Instruct the student to add a word to the prefixes and suffixes they have written and read them aloud. Assist the student as needed in identifying the pictures or reading the words in the lesson.

Activity 1. Have the student read the words aloud. The student will divide the words into syllables, using a hyphen to divide the words.

un-safe	**re-new**
re-tell	**re-write**
un-paid	**dis-like**
un-kind	**un-wise**

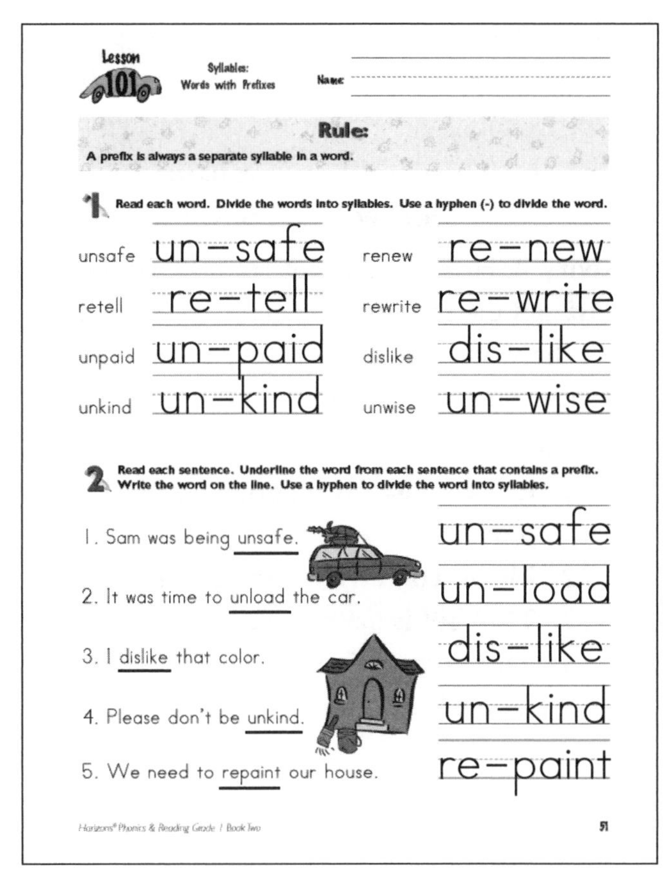

Lesson 101 Syllables: Words with Prefixes Name:

Rule:
A prefix is always a separate syllable in a word.

1 Read each word. Divide the words into syllables. Use a hyphen (-) to divide the word.

unsafe	un-safe	renew	re-new
retell	re-tell	rewrite	re-write
unpaid	un-paid	dislike	dis-like
unkind	un-kind	unwise	un-wise

2 Read each sentence. Underline the word from each sentence that contains a prefix. Write the word on the line. Use a hyphen to divide the word into syllables.

1. Sam was being unsafe. un-safe
2. It was time to unload the car. un-load
3. I dislike that color. dis-like
4. Please don't be unkind. un-kind
5. We need to repaint our house. re-paint

Horizons® Phonics & Reading Grade 1 Book Two 51

Activity 2. Assist the student as necessary in reading the sentences. Instruct the student to underline the word in each sentence that contains a prefix. The student will write the word on the line and divide the syllables with a hyphen.

Words: **1. un-safe**
2. un-load
3. dis-like
4. un-kind
5. re-paint

Activity 3. Have the student identify the pictures and draw a line to match the pictures with the words.

Pictures: **rebuild** **repaint**
replay **unwind**

Activity 4. Help the student read the words in the list and the sentences. Instruct the student to select the word that will correctly complete each sentence and write the word on the line.

Sentences:

1. **It is unwise to disobey your parents.**
2. **I have to rewrite my letter.**
3. **This bill is still unpaid.**
4. **The dog untied my shoe.**
5. **Don't be unkind to your friends.**

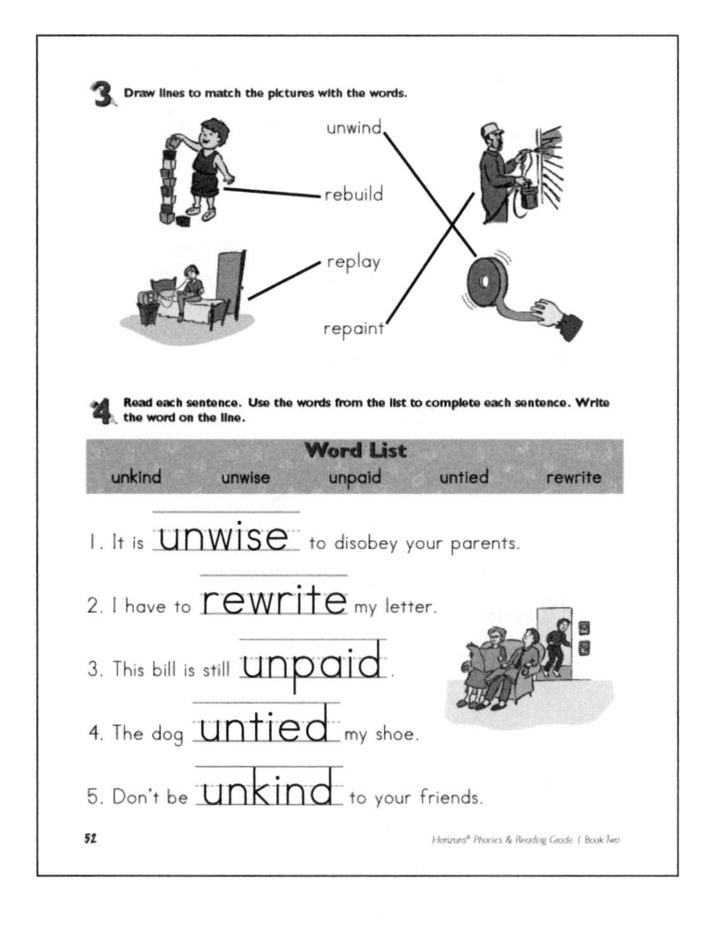

Lesson 102 - Syllables: Words with Suffixes

Overview:

- Divide words into syllables
- Word/picture match
- Sentence completion

Materials and Supplies:

- Teacher's Guide & Student Workbook
- White board or chalkboard
- Word cards (as necessary)
- Story: *Recess Time*

Teaching Tips:

Review the rule. Have the student write examples of the rule on the chalkboard or white board. Assist the student as needed in identifying the pictures or reading the words in the lesson.

Activity 1. Have the student read the words aloud. The student will divide the words into syllables, using a hyphen to divide the words.

cold-er	**build-ing**
spoon-ful	**play-ing**
care-ful	**care-less**
harm-less	**read-ing**
soft-ly	**soft-ness**

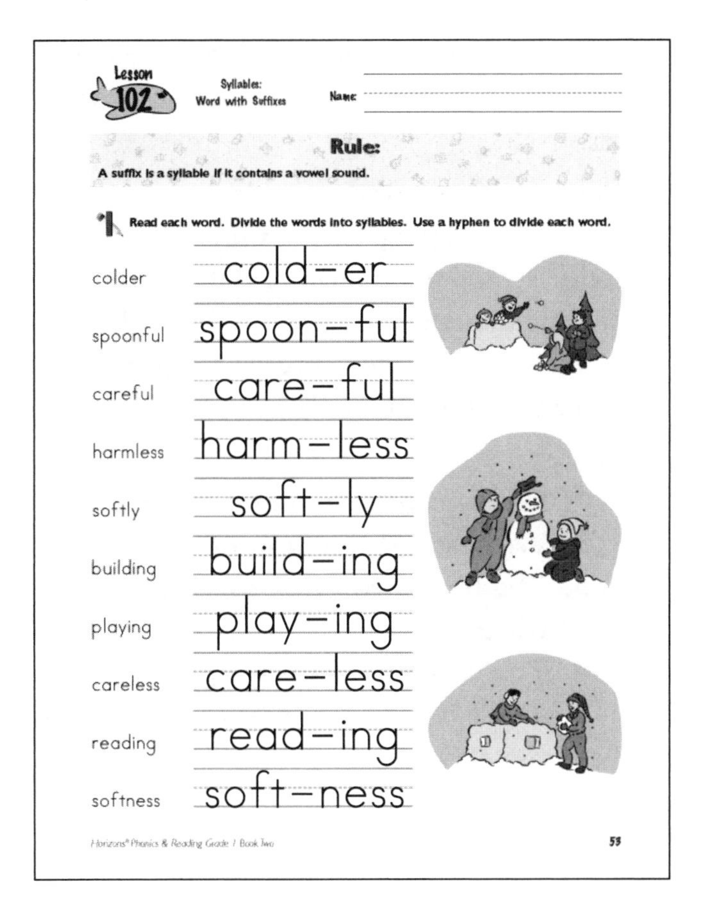

Lesson 102 Syllables: Word with Suffixes Name:

Rule:

A suffix is a syllable if it contains a vowel sound.

1 Read each word. Divide the words into syllables. Use a hyphen to divide each word.

colder	cold-er
spoonful	spoon-ful
careful	care-ful
harmless	harm-less
softly	soft-ly
building	build-ing
playing	play-ing
careless	care-less
reading	read-ing
softness	soft-ness

Horizons® Phonics & Reading Grade 1 Book Two 53

Activity 2. Have the student identify the pictures and draw a line to match the pictures with the words.

Pictures: **planted** **playing**
flying **spoonful**

Activity 3. Help the student read the words in the list and the sentences. Instruct the student to select the word that will correctly complete each sentence and write the word on the line.

Sentences:

1. **Nancy took a spoonful of medicine.**
2. **We planted the flowers.**
3. **The birds are flying south for the winter.**
4. **The children are playing at recess.**
5. **Don't be careless when you play on the slide.**

2. Draw lines to match the words with the pictures.

spoonful
planted
playing
flying

3. Read each sentence. Use the words from above to complete each sentence. Write the word on the line.

Word List
spoonful planted careless playing flying

1. Nancy took a spoonful of medicine.
2. We planted the flowers.
3. The birds are flying south for the winter.
4. The children are playing at recess.
5. Don't be careless when you play on the slide.

54 Horizons® Phonics & Reading Grade 1 Book Two

Lesson 103 - Syllables: Compound Words

Overview:

- Divide words into syllables
- Crossword puzzle

Materials and Supplies:

- Teacher's Guide & Student Workbook
- White board or chalkboard
- Word cards (as necessary)
- Story: *Rainbow Birthday*

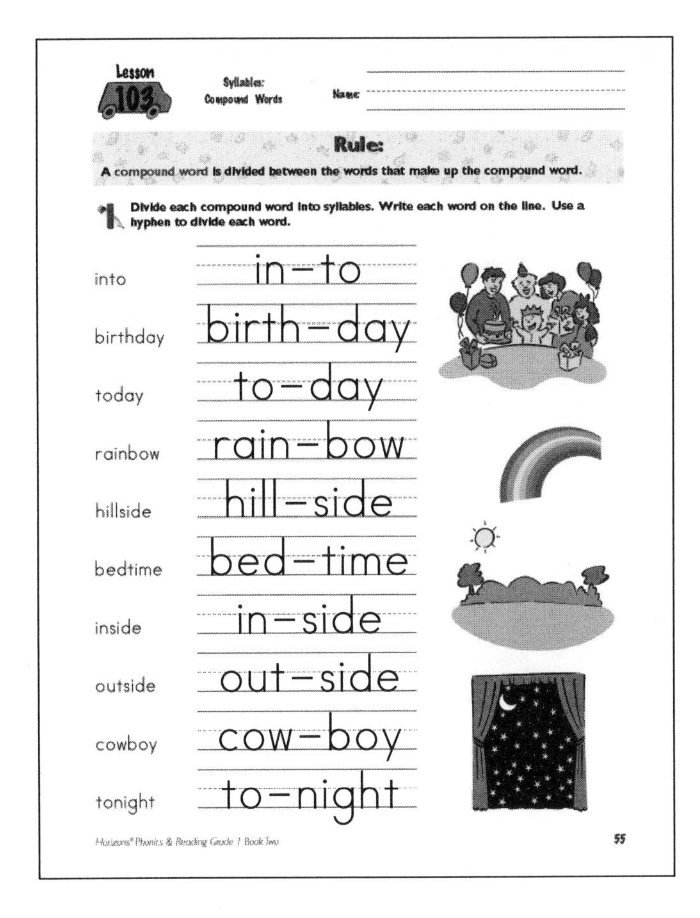

Lesson 103 Syllables: Compound Words Name

Rule:
A compound word is divided between the words that make up the compound word.

1. Divide each compound word into syllables. Write each word on the line. Use a hyphen to divide each word.

into	in-to
birthday	birth-day
today	to-day
rainbow	rain-bow
hillside	hill-side
bedtime	bed-time
inside	in-side
outside	out-side
cowboy	cow-boy
tonight	to-night

Horizons® Phonics & Reading Grade 1 Book Two 55

Teaching Tips:

Review the rule. Have the student write examples of the rule on the chalkboard or white board and divide the compound words into separate words using a hyphen. Assist the student as needed in identifying the pictures or reading the words in the lesson.

Activity 1. Have the student read the words aloud. The student will divide the words into syllables, using a hyphen to divide the words.

in-to	**bed-time**
birth-day	**in-side**
to-day	**out-side**
rain-bow	**cow-boy**
hill-side	**to-night**

Activity 2. Review the words in the list. Help the student read the crossword puzzle clues. Assist the student as necessary with the crossword puzzle.

Across: **1. tiptoe**
3. dustpan
5. bedtime

Down: **2. today**
4. pancakes

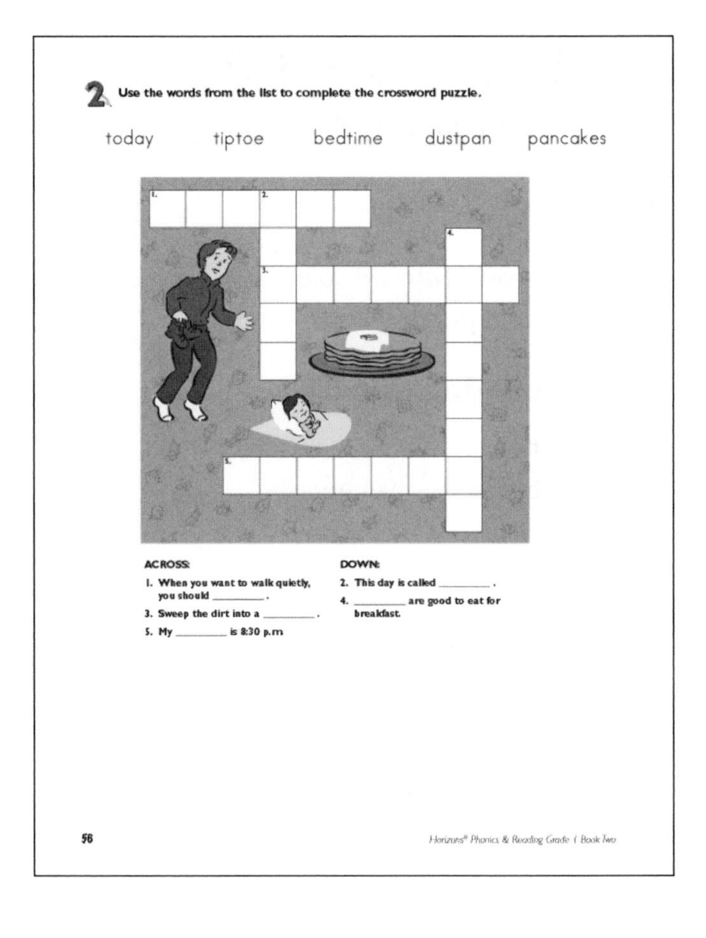

2 Use the words from the list to complete the crossword puzzle.

today tiptoe bedtime dustpan pancakes

ACROSS:

1. When you want to walk quietly, you should ________ .
3. Sweep the dirt into a ________ .
5. My ________ is 8:30 p.m

DOWN:

2. This day is called ________ .
4. ________ are good to eat for breakfast.

56 Horizons® Phonics & Reading Grade 1 Book Two

Lesson 104 - Review: Prefixes, Suffixes, Compound Words, Syllables

Overview:

- Divide words into syllables
- Sentence completion

Materials and Supplies:

- Teacher's Guide & Student Workbook
- White board or chalkboard
- Word cards (as necessary)
- Story: *The Medicine*

Teaching Tips:

Review the rule. Have the student write examples of the rule on the chalkboard or white board and practice word division using hyphens between the syllables. Assist the student as needed in identifying the pictures or reading the words in the lesson.

Activity 1. Have the student read the words aloud. The student will divide the words into syllables, using a hyphen to divide the words.

re-paint	**bed-time**
un-kind	**cow-boy**
build-ing	**dis-like**
in-side	**spoon-ful**
some-one	**un-load**

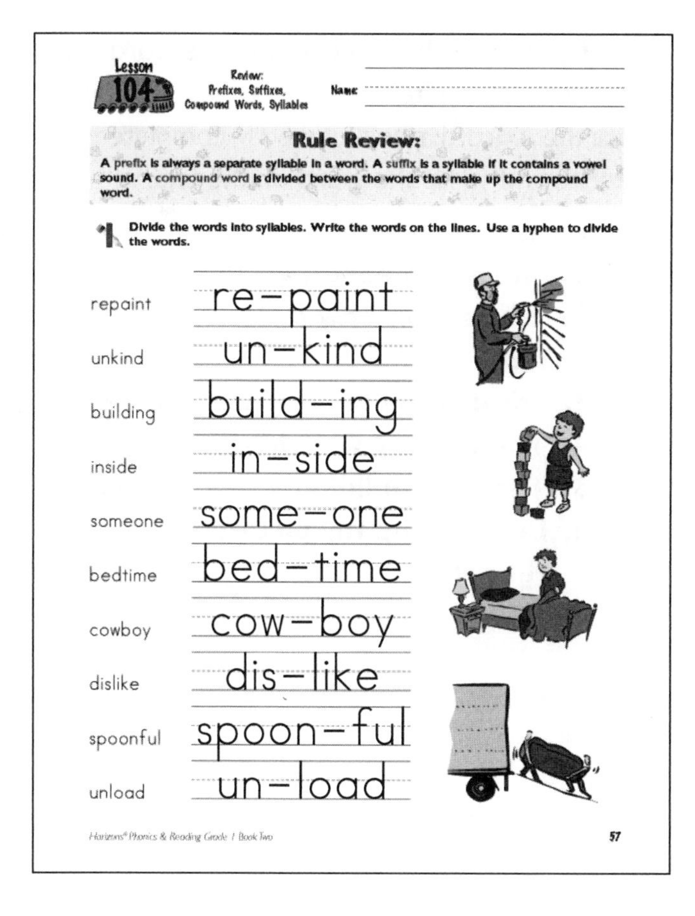

Lesson 104 Review: Prefixes, Suffixes, Compound Words, Syllables Name:

Rule Review:

A prefix is always a separate syllable in a word. A suffix is a syllable if it contains a vowel sound. A compound word is divided between the words that make up the compound word.

1. Divide the words into syllables. Write the words on the lines. Use a hyphen to divide the words.

repaint	re-paint
unkind	un-kind
building	build-ing
inside	in-side
someone	some-one
bedtime	bed-time
cowboy	cow-boy
dislike	dis-like
spoonful	spoon-ful
unload	un-load

Horizons® Phonics & Reading Grade 1 Book Two 57

Activity 2. Help the student read the words in the list and the sentences. Instruct the student to select the word that will correctly complete each sentence and write the word on the line.

Sentences:

1. **She is someone I know.**
2. **We have to stay inside when it is raining.**
3. **I dislike the taste of that medicine.**
4. **The cowboy was riding a horse.**
5. **They are building a new house.**
6. **I messed up my picture, so I will redo it.**

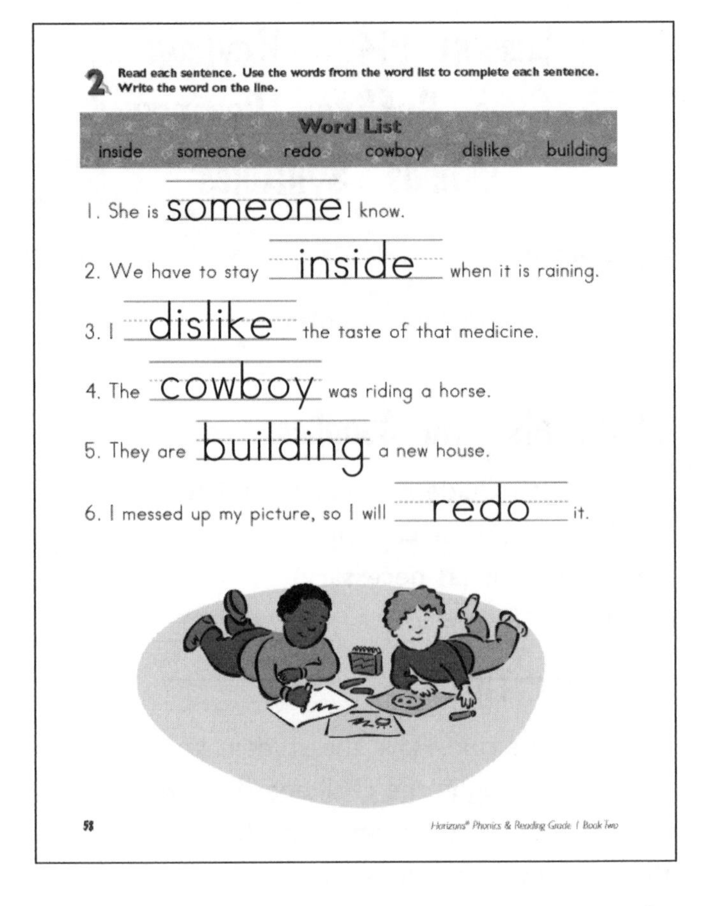

2 **Read each sentence. Use the words from the word list to complete each sentence. Write the word on the line.**

Word List

inside someone redo cowboy dislike building

1. She is someone I know.
2. We have to stay inside when it is raining.
3. I dislike the taste of that medicine.
4. The cowboy was riding a horse.
5. They are building a new house.
6. I messed up my picture, so I will redo it.

58 *Horizons® Phonics & Reading Grade 1 Book Two*

Lesson 105 - Writing Lesson: Thank You Note

Overview:

- Write a thank you note to a friend or relative

Materials and Supplies:

- Teacher's Guide & Student Workbook
- White board or chalkboard
- Word cards (as necessary)
- Story: *The Thank You Note*

Teaching Tips:

Go over the directions for the thank-you note with the student. The teacher or writing partner should help the student think of a person to write to and help the student get started on the note. Help with spelling and punctuation as necessary. Have the student write the rough draft on a piece of paper. The final copy will be written in the student workbook. It might be fun for the student to write a note to actually send to someone.

Activity 1. Write a thank you note. The final draft will be written in the student's workbook. NOTE: The back of the page is blank so that it may be removed from the book and mailed or given to the recipient, if desired.

Lesson 105 Writing Lesson: Thank You Note Name:

You write a thank you note to someone after they have given you a gift or have done something especially nice for you. Thank you notes are similar to friendly letters. They have a date, greeting, body, closing and signature.

In a thank you note, you thank the person for what he or she has given to you or has done for you. Here is an example of a thank you note:

September 13, 20__

Dear Grandma,

Thank you for the pretty dress. I don't have anything else like it. I can wear it to school and to church. I can also wear it to birthday parties and out to dinner.

Thanks again. It was nice of you to remember me on my birthday.

Love,

Nancy

Horizons® Phonics & Reading Grade 1 Book Two 59

1 Write a thank you note.

Think of a gift you have gotten or a nice thing that was done for you. Write a thank you note to the person who got you the gift or did the nice thing. Be sure that you name the gift or the deed and tell why it was special to you. Have your teacher or your writing partner help you write your note. Then have that person help you fix any mistakes. Write your note on a piece of paper. Then write your final copy in your book. You may mail your note if you wish.

60 Horizons® Phonics & Reading Grade 1 Book Two

Horizons® Phonics & Reading Grade 1 Book Two 61

62 Horizons® Phonics & Reading Grade 1 Book Two

Lesson 106 - Synonyms

Overview:

- Match words with their synonyms
- Sentence completion
- Sentence writing
- Crossword puzzle

Materials and Supplies:

- Teacher's Guide & Student Workbook
- White board or chalkboard
- Word cards (as necessary)
- Phonics rule flashcards in **Teacher Resources**
- Story: *The Deer in the Woods*

Teaching Tips:

Go over the definitions with the student. Write examples of synonyms on the chalkboard or white board. Assist the student as needed in identifying the pictures or reading the words in the lesson. Make word cards as needed. (**Optional**: Have a "synonym drill" where you call out a word and the student gives you a synonym as quickly as possible.)

Activity 1. Have the student read both sets of words aloud. The student will write the correct synonym for each word.

Synonyms:		
	glad	**discovers**
	silent	**present**
	forest	**drop**
	pretty	**piece**
	sad	**fast**

Activity 2. Help the student read the sentences and the word choices. Instruct the student to underline the word that will correctly complete each sentence and write the word on the line.

Sentences:

1. **Many kinds of animals live here in the forest.**
2. **You might get a present for your birthday.**
3. **You may feel sad when something bad happens.**

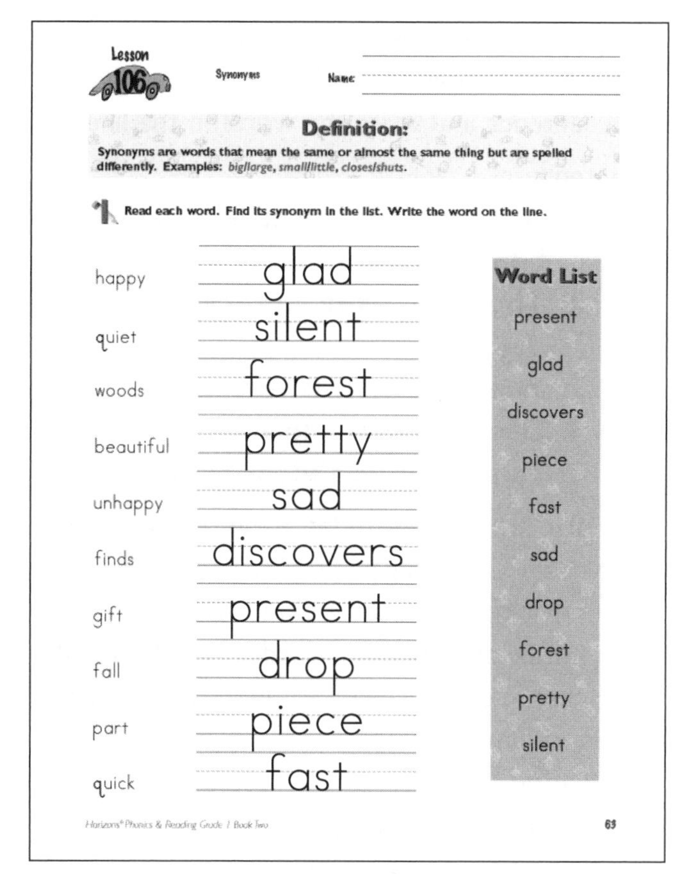

Lesson 106 Synonyms Name:

Definition:
Synonyms are words that mean the same or almost the same thing but are spelled differently. Examples: *big/large, small/little, closes/shuts.*

1 Read each word. Find its synonym in the list. Write the word on the line.

happy	glad
quiet	silent
woods	forest
beautiful	pretty
unhappy	sad
finds	discovers
gift	present
fall	drop
part	piece
quick	fast

Word List: present, glad, discovers, piece, fast, sad, drop, forest, pretty, silent

Horizons® Phonics & Reading Grade 1 Book Two 63

2 Read each sentence. Underline the word that completes each sentence. Write the word on the line.

1. Many kinds of animals live here in the forest. (forest / farther)
2. You might get a present for your birthday. (piece / present)
3. You may feel pretty when something bad happens. (sad / pretty)
4. It is fun to ride your bike fast. (fast / sound)
5. You might feel glad when something good happens. (tall / glad)

3 Read each sentence. Underline the word that completes each sentence. Write the word on the line.

1. Gail was sick, so she had to stay home. (take / stay)
2. The ship was sailing across the ocean. (ship / same)
3. The building was very tall. (took / tall)
4. Deer live in the forest. (forest / farther)
5. At night it was silent outside. (sound / silent)

64 Horizons® Phonics & Reading Grade 1 Book Two

4. **It is fun to ride your bike fast.**
5. **You might feel glad when something good happens.**

Activity 3. Help the student read the sentences

and the word choices. Instruct the student to underline the word that will correctly complete each sentence and write the word on the line.

Sentences:

1. **Gail was sick, so she had to stay home.**
2. **The ship was sailing across the ocean.**
3. **The building was very tall.**
4. **Deer live in the forest.**
5. **At night it was silent outside.**

Activity 4. Have the student read the words in the word list, assisting as needed and discussing word meanings. The student will write four sentences using at least eight words from the word list. Help the student with writing and spelling as necessary. Emphasize correct capitalization and punctuation.

Activity 5. Review the words in the list. Help the student read the crossword puzzle clues. Assist the student as necessary with the crossword puzzle.

Across: **1. sound**
5. silent
6. present

Down: **2. discover**
3. forest
4. fast
6. pretty

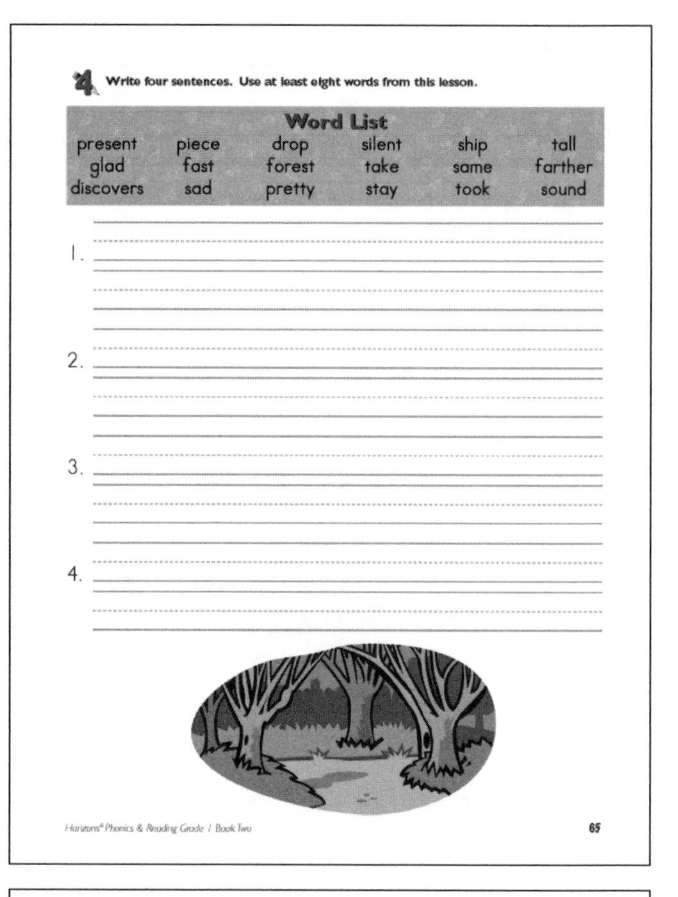

4 Write four sentences. Use at least eight words from this lesson.

Word List					
present	piece	drop	silent	ship	tall
glad	fast	forest	take	same	farther
discovers	sad	pretty	stay	took	sound

1.

2.

3.

4.

Horizons® Phonics & Reading Grade 1 Book Two 65

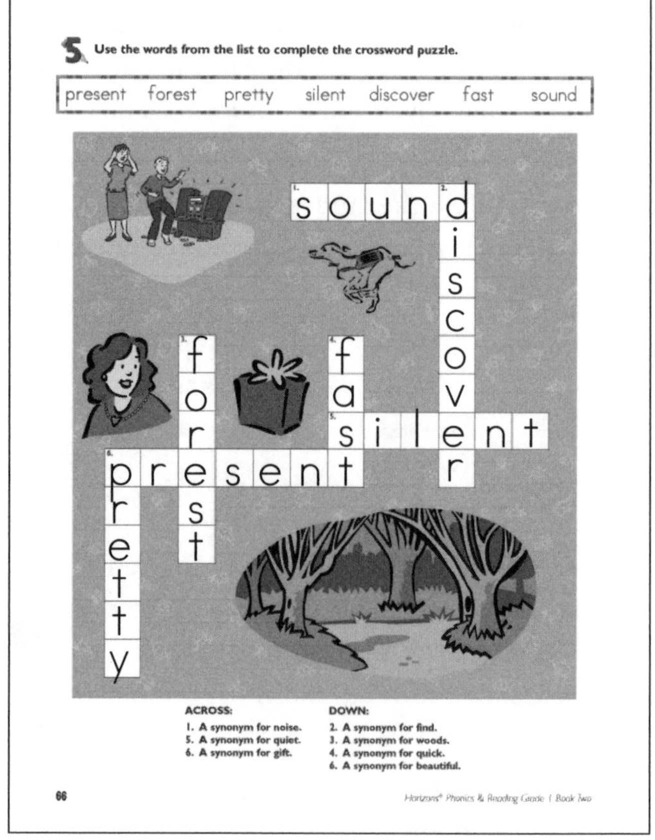

5 Use the words from the list to complete the crossword puzzle.

present forest pretty silent discover fast sound

ACROSS:
1. A synonym for noise.
5. A synonym for quiet.
6. A synonym for gift.

DOWN:
2. A synonym for find.
3. A synonym for woods.
4. A synonym for quick.
6. A synonym for beautiful.

66 Horizons® Phonics & Reading Grade 1 Book Two

Lesson 107 - Antonyms

Overview:

- Match words with their antonyms
- Word/picture match
- Riddles
- Sentence writing

Materials and Supplies:

- Teacher's Guide & Student Workbook
- White board or chalkboard
- Word cards (as necessary)
- Phonics rule flashcards in **Teacher Resources**
- Story: *The Opposite Twins*

Teaching Tips:

Go over the definitions with the student. Write examples of antonyms on the chalkboard or white board. Make word cards as necessary. (**Optional**: Have an "antonym drill" where you call out a word and the student gives you the correct antonym as quickly as possible.)

Activity 1. Have the student read the words aloud. The student will draw lines to match the words with their antonyms.

Antonyms: **noisy/quiet**
asleep/wake
young/old
hard/soft
under/over
thin/fat
loose/tight
weak/strong
dark/light
few/many

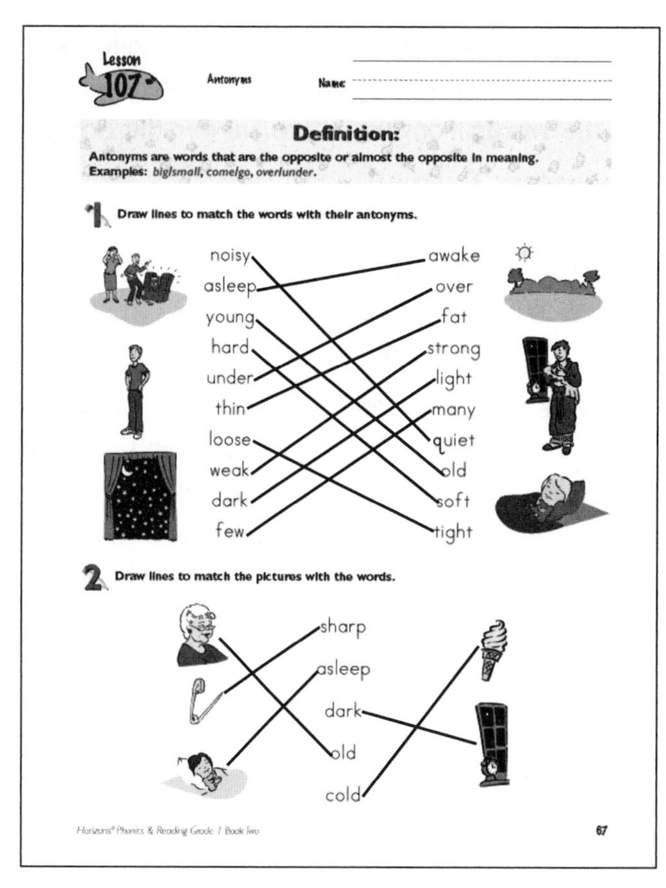
Lesson 107 Antonyms Name:

Definition:
Antonyms are words that are the opposite or almost the opposite in meaning.
Examples: *big/small, come/go, over/under.*

1 Draw lines to match the words with their antonyms.

noisy	awake
asleep	over
young	fat
hard	strong
under	light
thin	many
loose	quiet
weak	old
dark	soft
few	tight

2 Draw lines to match the pictures with the words.

sharp
asleep
dark
old
cold

Horizons® Phonics & Reading Grade 1 / Book Two 67

Activity 2. Have the student identify the pictures and draw a line to match the pictures with the words.

Pictures: **old** **cold**
sharp **dark**
asleep

Activity 3. Have the student read the riddles and the words from the list aloud. The student will use the words from the list to answer the riddles.

Answers: **1. small**
2. fast
3. soft
4. under
5. cold

Activity 4. The student will write four sentences and use at least eight of the words from the word list. Help the student with writing and spelling as necessary. Emphasize correct capitalization and punctuation.

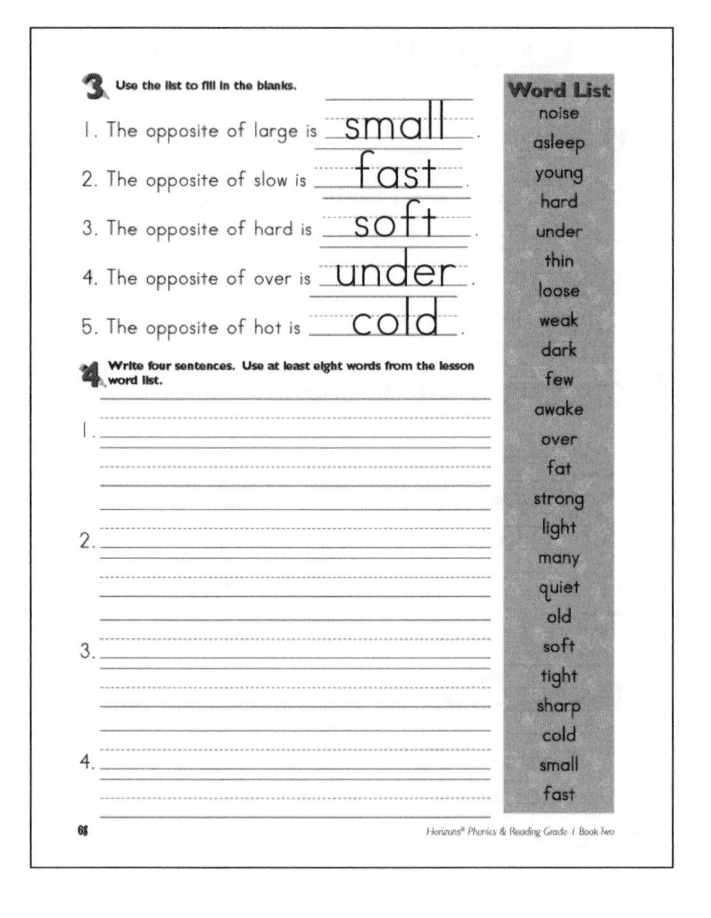

3 Use the list to fill in the blanks.

1. The opposite of large is small.
2. The opposite of slow is fast.
3. The opposite of hard is soft.
4. The opposite of over is under.
5. The opposite of hot is cold.

4 Write four sentences. Use at least eight words from the lesson word list.

1.
2.
3.
4.

Word List
noise
asleep
young
hard
under
thin
loose
weak
dark
few
awake
over
fat
strong
light
many
quiet
old
soft
tight
sharp
cold
small
fast

Horizons® Phonics & Reading Grade 1 Book Two

Lesson 108 - Homonyms

Overview:

- Match words to their homonyms
- Crossword puzzle
- Sentence writing

Materials and Supplies:

- Teacher's Guide & Student Workbook
- White board or chalkboard
- Word cards (as necessary)
- Phonics rule flashcards in **Teacher Resources**
- Story: *I Sent a Cent*

Teaching Tips:

Go over the definition with the student. Write examples of homonyms on the chalkboard or white board. Make word cards as necessary.

Activity 1. Have the student read the words aloud. The student will draw lines to match the homonyms.

Antonyms: **sent/cent**
blew/blue
made/maid
road/rode
wait/weight
bee/be
knot/not
ate/eight
fair/fare
won/one
right/write
sail/sale
eye/I

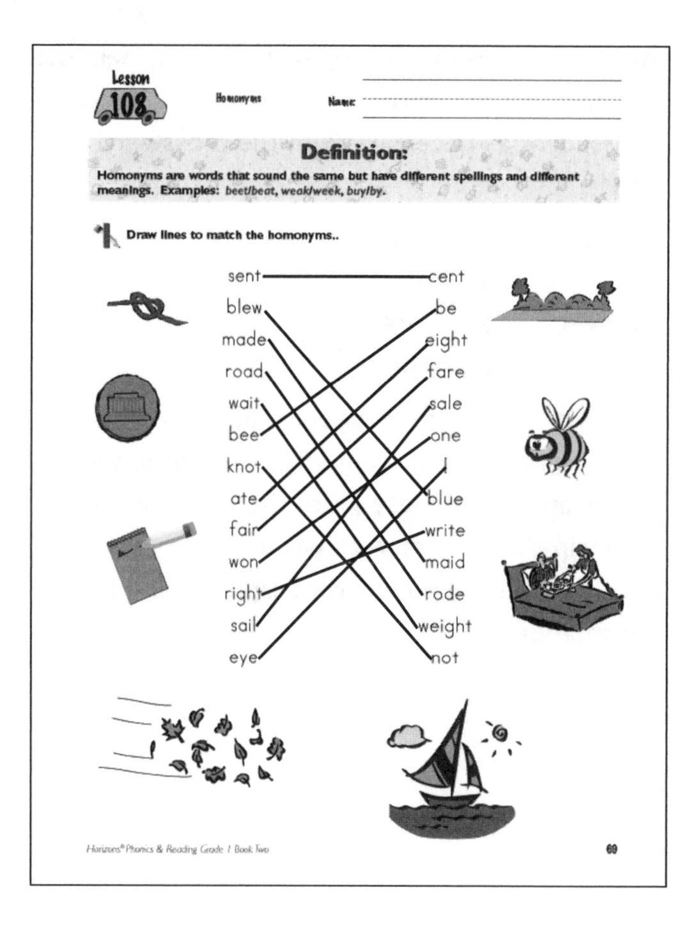
Lesson 108 Homonyms Name:

Definition:
Homonyms are words that sound the same but have different spellings and different meanings. Examples: *beet/beat, weak/week, buy/by.*

1 Draw lines to match the homonyms..

sent	cent
blew	be
made	eight
road	fare
wait	sale
bee	one
knot	I
ate	blue
fair	write
won	maid
right	rode
sail	weight
eye	not

Horizons® Phonics & Reading Grade 1 Book Two 69

Activity 2. Review the words in the list. Help the student read the crossword puzzle clues. Assist the student as necessary with the crossword puzzle.

Across:	**1. wrap**
	4. not
Down:	**2. write**
	3. pane

Activity 3. Have the student read the words in the list aloud. The student will write three sentences and use at least six of the words from the list. Help the student with writing and spelling as necessary. Emphasize correct capitalization and punctuation.

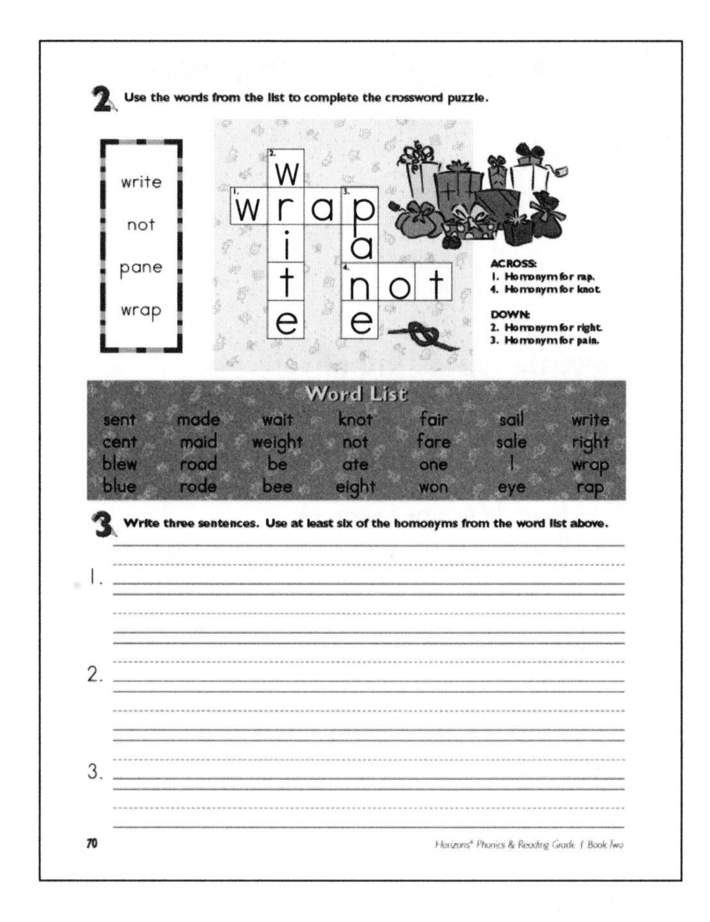

2 Use the words from the list to complete the crossword puzzle.

write
not
pane
wrap

ACROSS:
1. Homonym for rap.
4. Homonym for knot.

DOWN:
2. Homonym for right.
3. Homonym for pain.

Word List

sent	made	wait	knot	fair	sail	write
cent	maid	weight	not	fare	sale	right
blew	road	be	ate	one	I	wrap
blue	rode	bee	eight	won	eye	rap

3 Write three sentences. Use at least six of the homonyms from the word list above.

1.

2.

3.

70 Horizons® Phonics & Reading Grade 1 Book Two

Lesson 109 - Review: Synonyms, Antonyms, Homonyms

Overview:

- Sentence completion
- Short story reading comprehension
- Picture/word match

Materials and Supplies:

- Teacher's Guide & Student Workbook
- White board or chalkboard
- Word cards (as necessary)
- Story: *The Beet that Beat All of the Others*

Teaching Tips:

Review the definitions with the student. Have the student write examples of synonyms, antonyms, and homonyms on the chalkboard or white board. Review any word cards as necessary. (**Optional**: Write several pairs of antonyms, synonyms, and homonyms on the board. Point to each set of words and have the student correctly identify them as either antonyms, synonyms, or homonyms.)

Activity 1. Help the student read the sentences and the word choices. Instruct the student to underline the antonym or homonym that will correctly complete each sentence and write the word on the line.

Sentences:

1. I like to swim.
2. The boat sails on the water.
3. I can't go right now.
4. My friend knows a lot about sailboats.
5. We drove over the bridge.
6. We were happy when we got to go to the zoo.

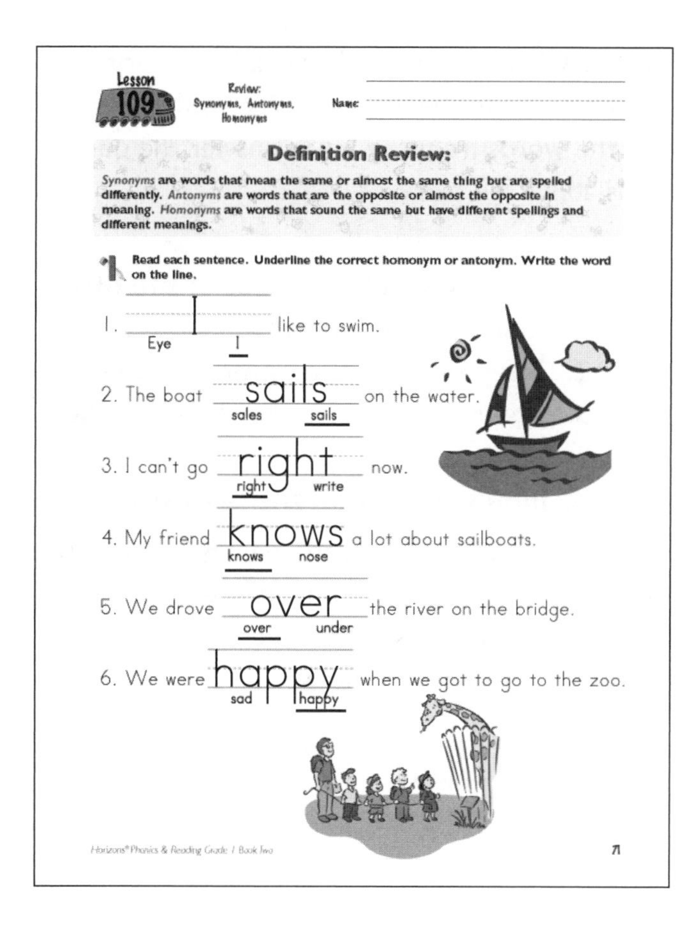

Lesson 109 Review: Synonyms, Antonyms, Homonyms Name:

Definition Review:

Synonyms are words that mean the same or almost the same thing but are spelled differently. *Antonyms* are words that are the opposite or almost the opposite in meaning. *Homonyms* are words that sound the same but have different spellings and different meanings.

1. Read each sentence. Underline the correct homonym or antonym. Write the word on the line.

1. I like to swim. (Eye / I)
2. The boat sails on the water. (sales / sails)
3. I can't go right now. (right / write)
4. My friend knows a lot about sailboats. (knows / nose)
5. We drove over the river on the bridge. (over / under)
6. We were happy when we got to go to the zoo. (sad / happy)

Horizons® Phonics & Reading Grade 1 Book Two 71

Activity 2. Have the student read the story and the words from the list aloud. The student will use the words from the list to answer the questions about the story.

Sentences:

1. **John's team beat most of the other teams in the league.**
2. **They rode to the game in a bus.**
3. **They wore their new shirts to the game.**
4. **John's team won the big game.**

Activity 3. Have the student identify the pictures and draw a line to match the pictures with the words. (**Optional**: Ask the student to spell the homonyms for each of the words – not, beat, wring, see, ate.)

Pictures:	**knot**	**sea**
	beet	**eight**
	ring	

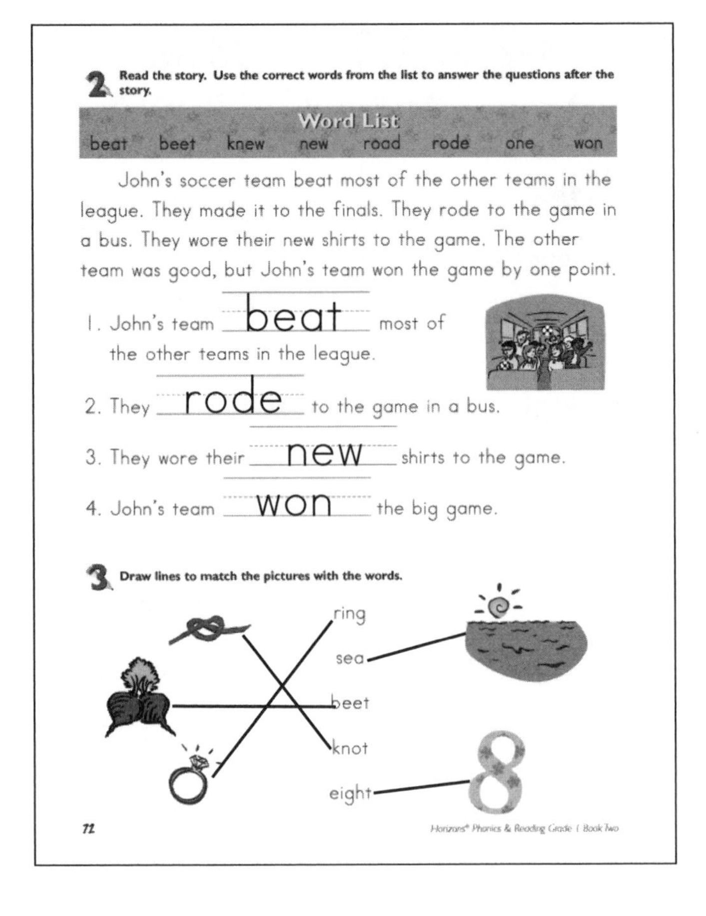

2 Read the story. Use the correct words from the list to answer the questions after the story.

Word List

beat beet knew new road rode one won

John's soccer team beat most of the other teams in the league. They made it to the finals. They rode to the game in a bus. They wore their new shirts to the game. The other team was good, but John's team won the game by one point.

1. John's team beat most of the other teams in the league.
2. They rode to the game in a bus.
3. They wore their new shirts to the game.
4. John's team won the big game.

3 Draw lines to match the pictures with the words.

ring
sea
beet
knot
eight

72 Horizons® Phonics & Reading Grade 1 Book Two

Lesson 110 - Writing Lesson: Personal Experience Narrative

Overview:

- Write a narrative about something special that you do

Materials and Supplies:

- Teacher's Guide & Student Workbook
- White board or chalkboard
- Word cards (as necessary)
- Story: *Dan's Music*

Teaching Tips:

Go over the directions with the student. The teacher or writing partner should help the student think of a topic for writing. This subject can be difficult for first-grade students, so much encouragement may be needed. The student should be encouraged to think of several ideas choose the one that he or she can write the most about. The student should write the rough draft on a piece of paper and the final copy in the student workbook.

Lesson 110 Writing Lesson: Personal Experience Narrative Name:

1. Write a personal experience narrative.

In this lesson you will be writing another personal experience narrative in which you tell about something that you have done or something that really happened to you.

You will be writing about something you do that is special. Do you take music or dance lessons? Do you take care of a pet or help around the house in some way? Those are some ideas. Maybe you can think of something else that you do that is special.

Have your teacher or writing partner help you write your ideas down. Choose one and begin writing. Your teacher or partner can help you with the writing. When you are finished, check for any mistakes. Write your final copy on the following page. Draw a picture below to go with your narrative.

Horizons® Phonics & Reading Grade 1 Book Two 73

Activity 1. Write a personal experience narrative.

74 Horizons® Phonics & Reading Grade 1 Book Two

Test 11

Lessons 101-110

Instructions:

Review dividing words into prefix, base word and suffix. Do some examples of these. Review the definition of a synonym. Have the student give synonyms for words that the teacher presents. Review the definition of an antonym. Have the student give antonyms for words that the teacher presents. Read through the test with the student. Help the student with any words that he/she is still unsure of. The teacher should be available to answer any questions that the student may have during the test.

Activity 1. Review the instructions and the words with the student. Instruct the student to use a hyphen or dash (–) to divide each word into syllables.

Words:		
	re–run	**re–do**
	un–like	**dis–like**
	jump–ing	**pea–nut**
	mail–box	
	re–tell–ing	
	play–ground	

Activity 2. Make sure the students understand the instructions and can read the words.

Words:		
	large	
	gift	
	close	
	quick	**little**

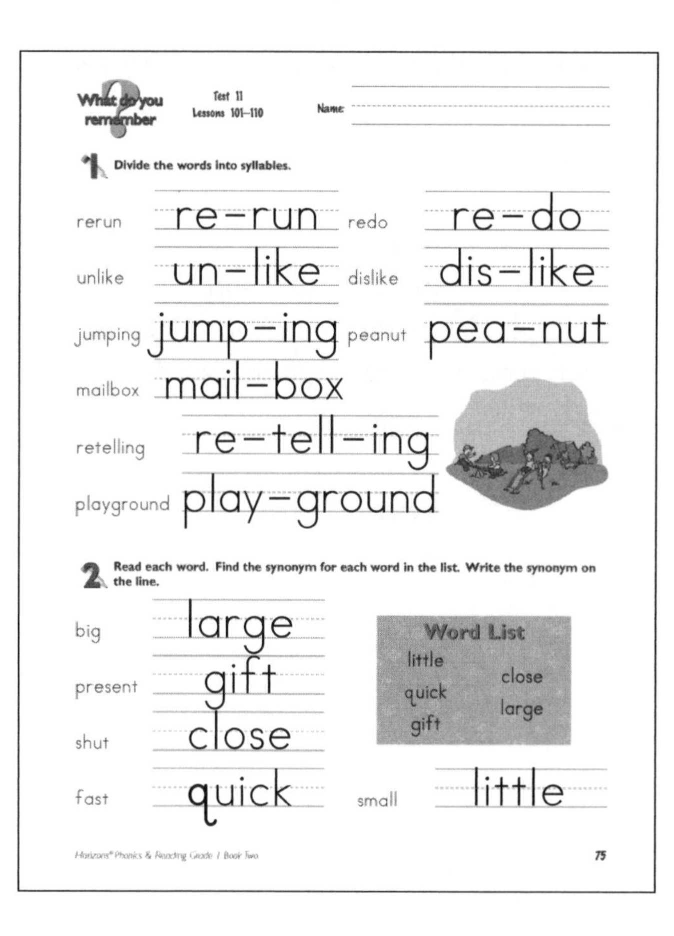
What do you remember

Test 11
Lessons 101–110

Name:

1 Divide the words into syllables.

rerun re–run redo re–do
unlike un–like dislike dis–like
jumping jump–ing peanut pea–nut
mailbox mail–box
retelling re–tell–ing
playground play–ground

2 Read each word. Find the synonym for each word in the list. Write the synonym on the line.

big large
present gift
shut close
fast quick
small little

Word List
little
quick
gift
close
large

Horizons® Phonics & Reading Grade 1 Book Two 75

Activity 3. Make sure the students understand the instructions and can read the words.

Words: **slow**
tight
young
under **soft**

Activity 4. Make sure the students understand the instructions and can read the words.

Words: **eight**
by
beat
week **fair**

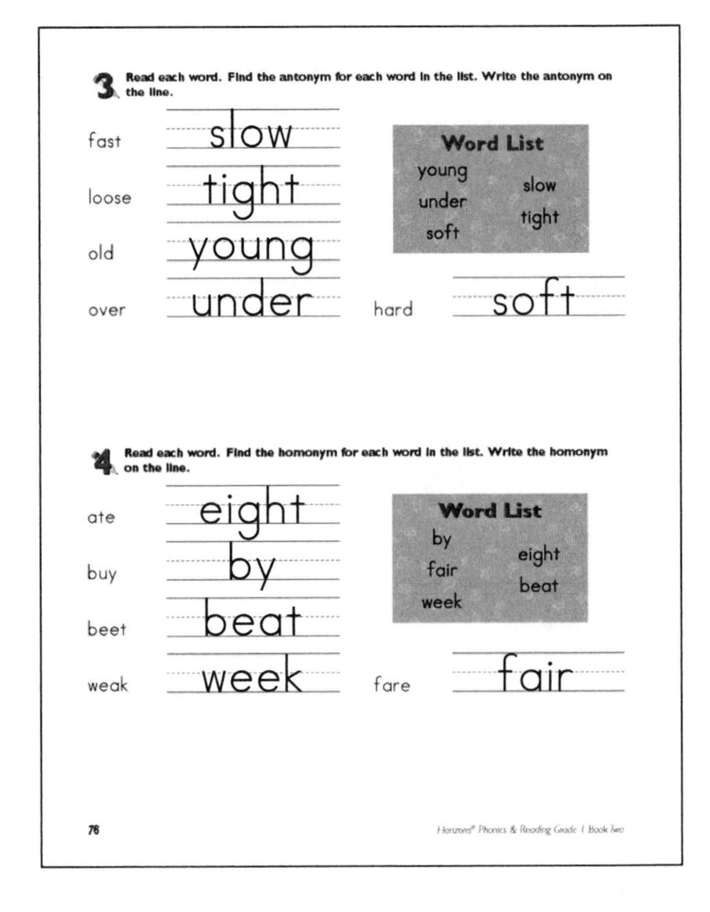

3 Read each word. Find the antonym for each word in the list. Write the antonym on the line.
fast slow
loose tight
old young
over under
hard soft
Word List
young
under
soft
slow
tight
4 Read each word. Find the homonym for each word in the list. Write the homonym on the line.
ate eight
buy by
beet beat
weak week
fare fair
Word List
by
fair
week
eight
beat
78

Lesson 111 - Alphabetical Order to First Letter

Overview:

- Write words in alphabetical order
- Sentence writing
- Crossword puzzle

Materials and Supplies:

- Teacher's Guide & Student Workbook
- White board or chalkboard
- Word cards (as necessary)
- Story: *The Fox and the Antelope*

Teaching Tips:

Go over the rule. Write some practice lists on the chalkboard or white board. Help the student number the words in alphabetical order by asking "Which word is first?" Ask the student why that word is first (because it starts with the letter that is closest to the beginning of the alphabet). Proceed in this manner through all the words in the list until the student has correctly alphabetized them all. Make word cards as necessary.

Activity 1. Have the student read the words aloud. The student will write the words in alphabetical order to the first letter.

Words: **antelope**
cat
dog
eagle
fox
goat

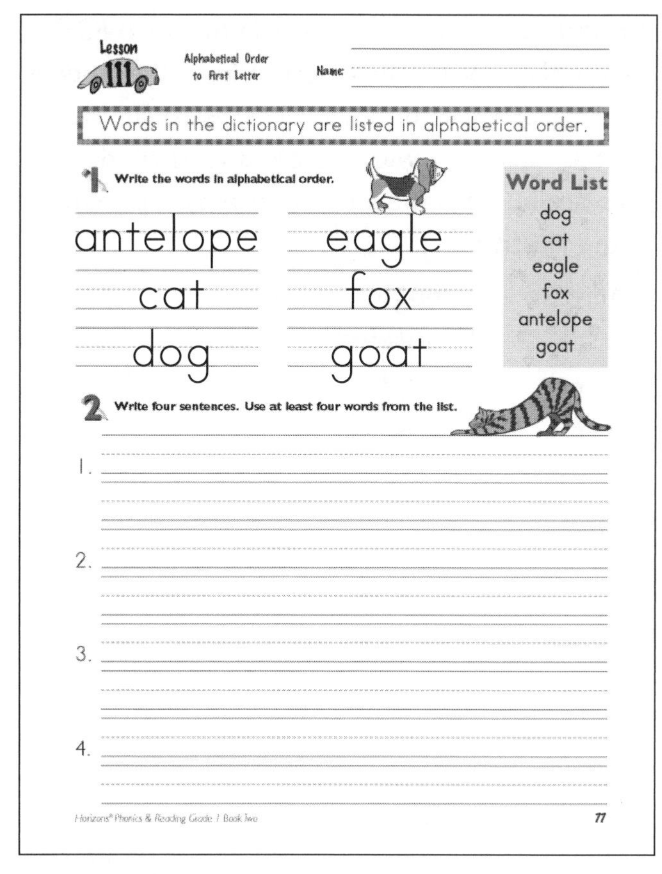

Lesson 111 Alphabetical Order to First Letter

Name:

Words in the dictionary are listed in alphabetical order.

1 Write the words in alphabetical order.

antelope	eagle
cat	fox
dog	goat

Word List: dog, cat, eagle, fox, antelope, goat

2 Write four sentences. Use at least four words from the list.

1.

2.

3.

4.

Horizons® Phonics & Reading Grade 1 Book Two 77

Activity 2. The student will write four sentences and use at least four of the words from the word list. Help the student with writing and spelling as necessary. Emphasize correct capitalization and punctuation.

Activity 3. Review the words in the list (NOTE: two of the words are not used). Help the student read the crossword puzzle clues. Assist the student as necessary with the crossword puzzle. (**Optional**: Have the student identify the animals in the illustration.)

Across:	**1. eagle**
	3. antelope
Down:	**2. goat**
	4. fox

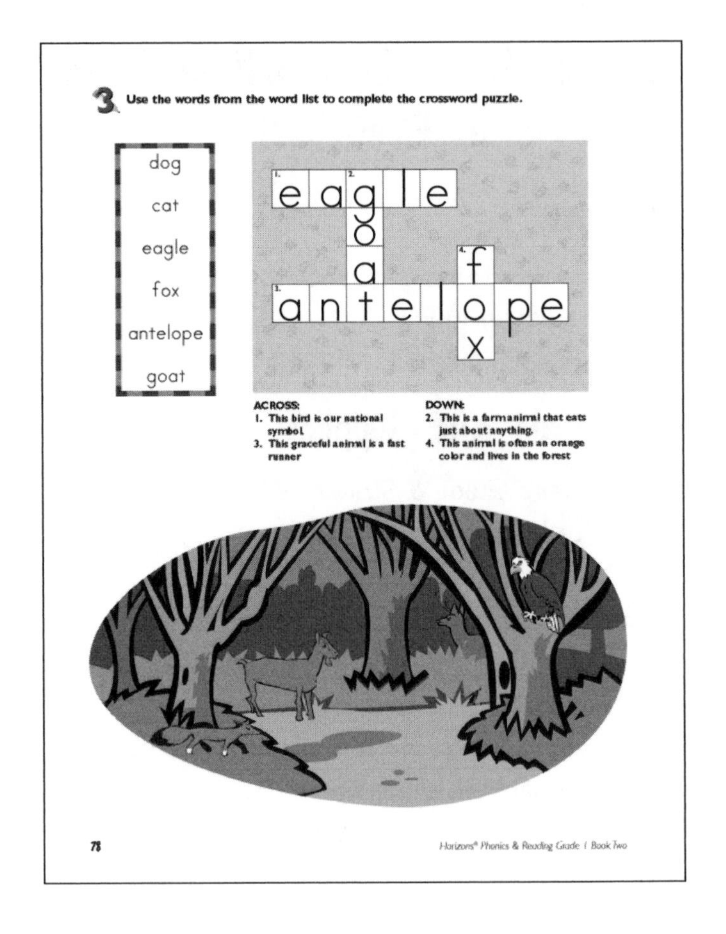

3 Use the words from the word list to complete the crossword puzzle.

dog
cat
eagle
fox
antelope
goat

ACROSS:
1. This bird is our national symbol.
3. This graceful animal is a fast runner

DOWN:
2. This is a farm animal that eats just about anything.
4. This animal is often an orange color and lives in the forest

78 Horizons® Phonics & Reading Grade 1 Book Two

Lesson 112 - Alphabetical Order to Second Letter

Overview:

- Write words in alphabetical order
- Word search
- Sentence writing

Materials and Supplies:

- Teacher's Guide & Student Workbook
- White board or chalkboard
- Word cards (as necessary)
- Story: *Bob's Bike*

Teaching Tips:

Go over the rule. Write some word pairs on the chalkboard or white board. These can be words that begin with the same letter such as **bike** and **bat**. Ask the student, "Which word is first?" Ask why that word is first (because its second letter is closer to the beginning of the alphabet). Do this with several pairs of words. Make word cards as necessary.

Activity 1. Have the student read the words in the list aloud. Instruct the student to alphabetize the list, using the second letter of each word.

Words: **bat**
bet
bike
blue
boat
bob
button

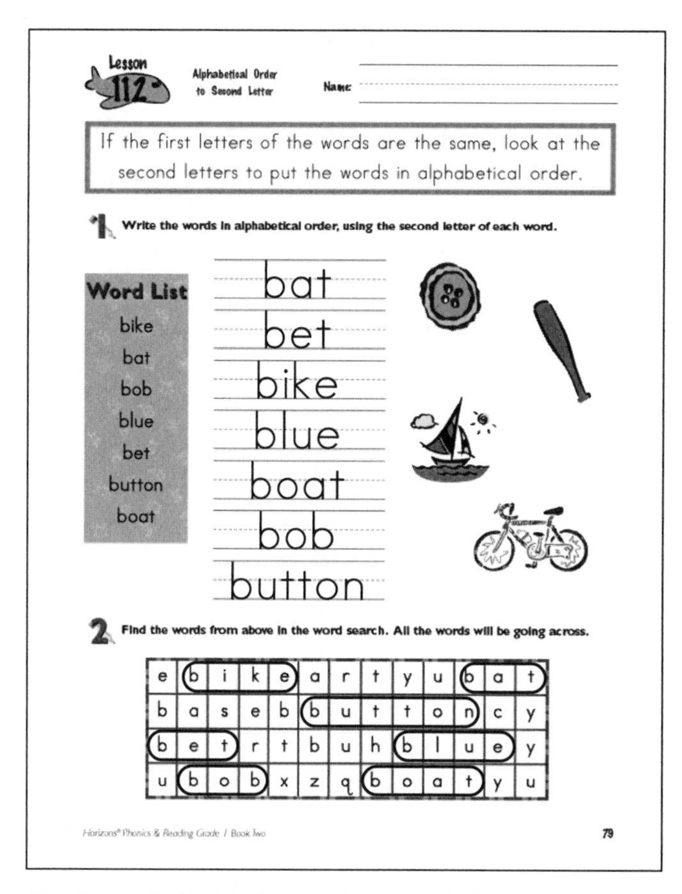

Lesson 112 Alphabetical Order to Second Letter Name:

If the first letters of the words are the same, look at the second letters to put the words in alphabetical order.

1. Write the words in alphabetical order, using the second letter of each word.

Word List: bike, bat, bob, blue, bet, button, boat

bat
bet
bike
blue
boat
bob
button

2. Find the words from above in the word search. All the words will be going across.

e	b	i	k	e	a	r	t	y	u	b	a	t
b	a	s	e	b	b	u	t	t	o	n	c	y
b	e	t	r	t	b	u	h	b	l	u	e	y
u	b	o	b	x	z	q	b	o	a	t	y	u

Horizons® Phonics & Reading Grade 1 Book Two 79

Activity 2. Help the student read the words in the list. The student will find and circle the words from the list in the puzzle. All the words are going across.

Activity 3. The student will write four sentences and use at least four of the words from the lesson. Help the student with writing and spelling as necessary. Emphasize correct capitalization and punctuation.

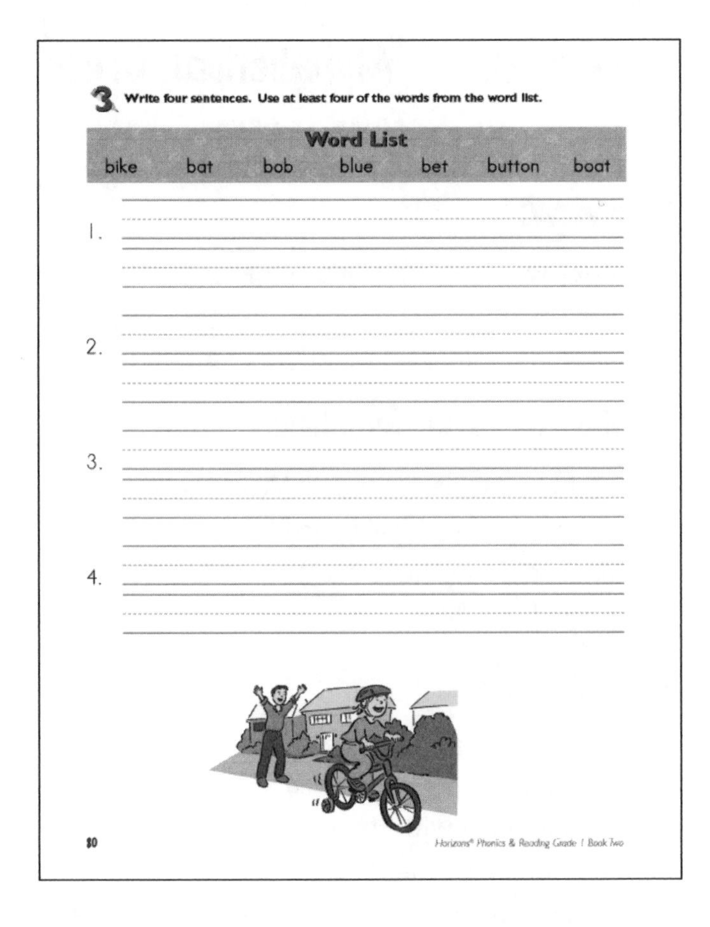

3 Write four sentences. Use at least four of the words from the word list.

Word List						
bike	bat	bob	blue	bet	button	boat

1. ______________________________

2. ______________________________

3. ______________________________

4. ______________________________

80 Horizons® Phonics & Reading Grade 1 Book Two

Lesson 113 - Review: Alphabetical Order to First & Second Letter

Overview:

- Alphabetize words to first and second letters
- Sentence completion
- Story completion

Materials and Supplies:

- Teacher's Guide & Student Workbook
- White board or chalkboard
- Word cards (as necessary)
- Story: *The Dog Who Dug*

Teaching Tips:

Review the rules for alphabetizing words to the first and second letter. Do some drills on the board, if desired. Assist the student as needed in identifying the pictures or reading the words in the lesson.

Activity 1. Have the student read the words in the list. Ask the student why the words all begin with capital letters (because they are proper names). Instruct the student to write the words in the correct order on the lines.

Words: **Ann**
Bob
Cathy
Don
Eve
Fran

Lesson 113 Review: Alphabetical Order to First & Second Letter Name:

1. Write the words in alphabetical order to the first letter.

Word List: Cathy, Don, Eve, Bob, Ann, Fran

Ann
Bob
Cathy
Don
Eve
Fran

2. Write the words in alphabetical order to the second letter.

damp
desk
dig
door
drive
duck

Word List: desk, drive, dig, door, duck, damp

Horizons® Phonics & Reading Grade 1 Book Two 81

Activity 2. Have the student read the words in the list. Instruct the student to write the words in the correct order on the lines, using the second letter to arrange them in alphabetical order.

Words: **damp**
desk
dig
door
drive
duck

Activity 3. Help the student read the words in the list and the sentences. Instruct the student to select the word that will correctly complete each sentence and write the word on the line.

Sentences:

1. **The dog likes to dig holes.**
2. **She sits at her desk in the classroom.**
3. **We fed the ducks some bread.**
4. **The ground was still damp after the rain.**
5. **Please close the door when you leave.**

Activity 4. Have the student read the story aloud. The student will use the words from Activity 3 to complete the story.

Story:

We have a pet dog who likes to dig holes in our yard. It is very easy for him to do when the ground is damp after a rain. He goes out the door and starts in. Dad says that he will drive the dog in the car and take him to dog training class. Maybe that will stop him!

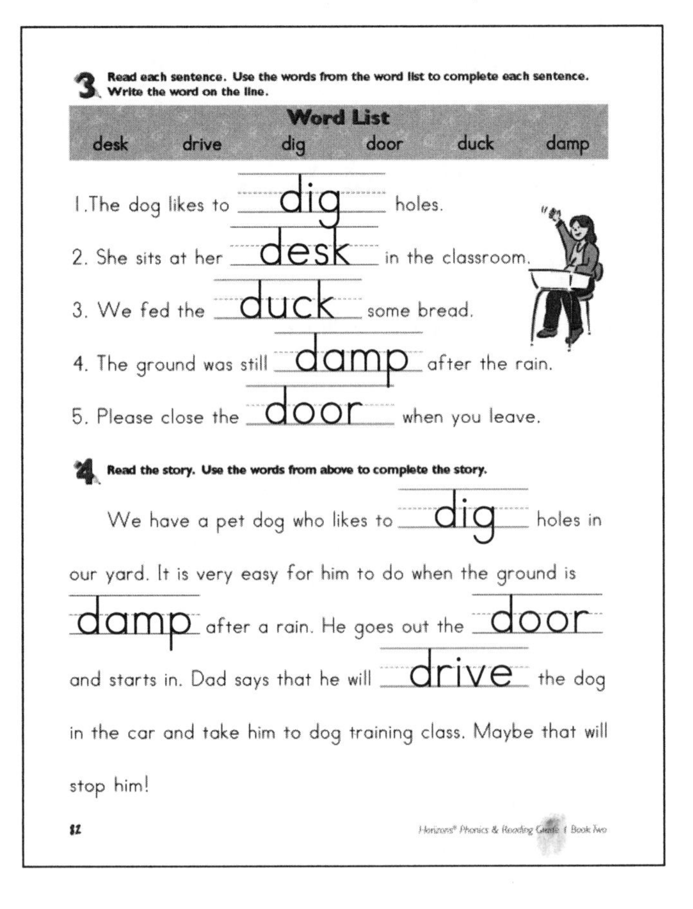

3 Read each sentence. Use the words from the word list to complete each sentence. Write the word on the line.

Word List					
desk	drive	dig	door	duck	damp

1. The dog likes to dig holes.
2. She sits at her desk in the classroom.
3. We fed the duck some bread.
4. The ground was still damp after the rain.
5. Please close the door when you leave.

4 Read the story. Use the words from above to complete the story.

We have a pet dog who likes to dig holes in our yard. It is very easy for him to do when the ground is damp after a rain. He goes out the door and starts in. Dad says that he will drive the dog in the car and take him to dog training class. Maybe that will stop him!

Lesson 114 - Checkup: Synonyms, Antonyms, Homonyms

Overview:

- Write synonyms for words
- Write antonyms for words
- Write homonyms for words

Materials and Supplies:

- Teacher's Guide & Student Workbook
- White board or chalkboard
- Word cards (as necessary)
- Story: *Synonyms, Antonyms, Homonyms*

Teaching Tips:

Review the definitions of synonyms, antonyms, and homonyms with the student. Have the student write examples on the chalkboard or white board. Assist the student as needed in reading the words in the lesson.

Activity 1. Have the student read the words aloud. The student will write the synonym for each word.

Words: **happy**
silent
forest
sad
large
beautiful

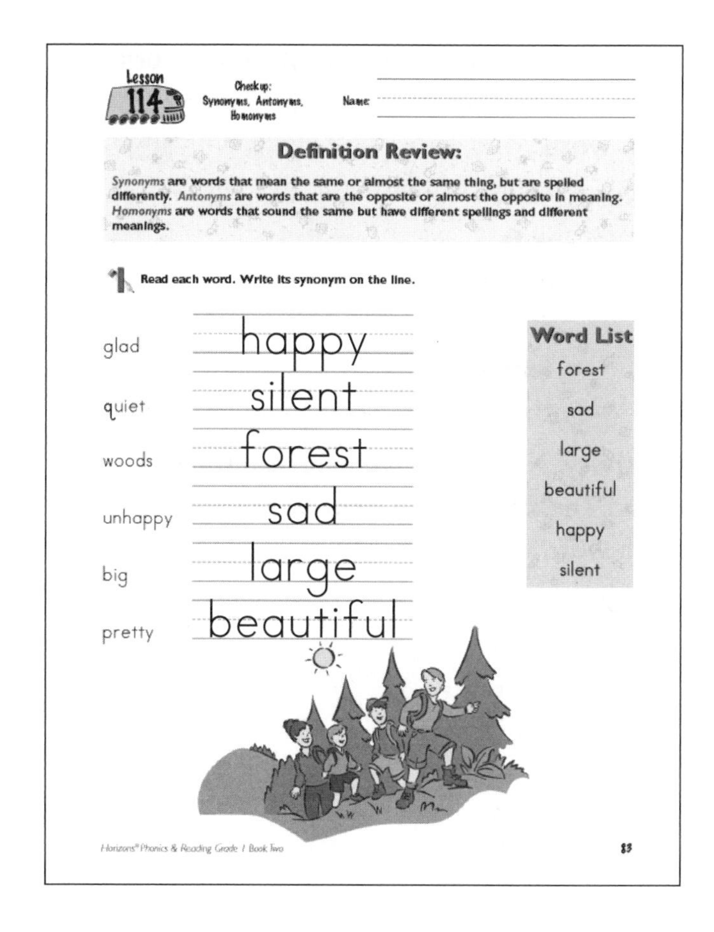

Lesson 114 Checkup: Synonyms, Antonyms, Homonyms

Name:

Definition Review:

Synonyms are words that mean the same or almost the same thing, but are spelled differently. *Antonyms* are words that are the opposite or almost the opposite in meaning. *Homonyms* are words that sound the same but have different spellings and different meanings.

1. Read each word. Write its synonym on the line.

glad happy
quiet silent
woods forest
unhappy sad
big large
pretty beautiful

Word List
forest
sad
large
beautiful
happy
silent

Horizons® Phonics & Reading Grade 1 Book Two

Activity 2. Have the student read the words aloud. The student will write the antonym for each word.

Words: **slow**
soft
empty
small
warm
thin

Activity 3. Have the student read the words aloud. The student will write the homonym for each word.

Words: **our**
won
weak
maid
blew
by

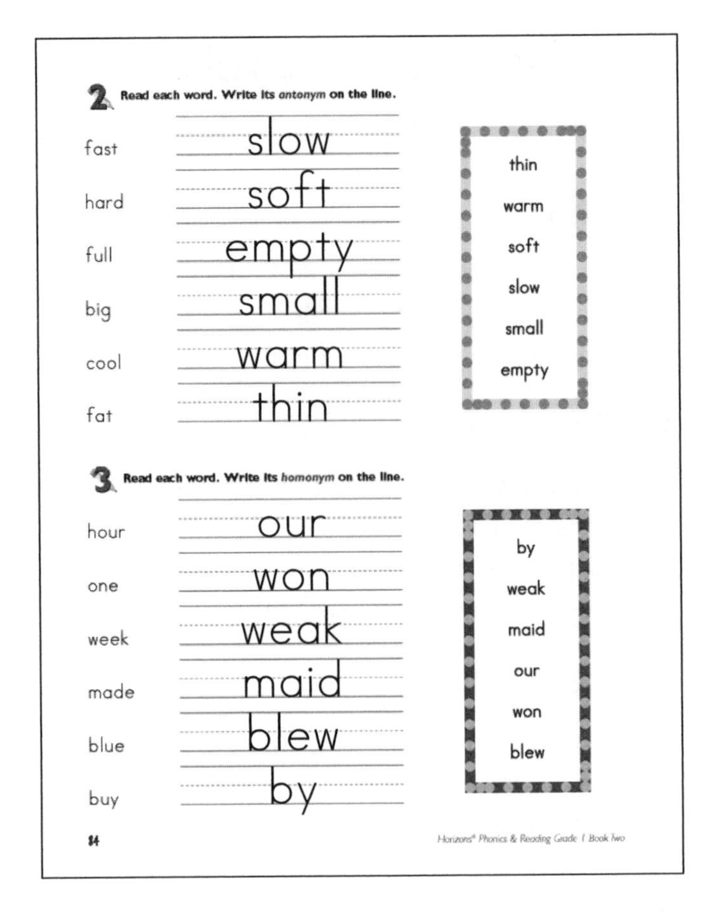

2 Read each word. Write its antonym on the line.
fast slow
hard soft
full empty
big small
cool warm
fat thin
thin
warm
soft
slow
small
empty
3 Read each word. Write its homonym on the line.
hour our
one won
week weak
made maid
blue blew
buy by
by
weak
maid
our
won
blew
14
Horizons Phonics & Reading Grade 1 Book Two

Lesson 115 - Checkup: Hard & Soft c

Overview:

- Picture/word match
- Word categorization
- Sentence completion

Materials and Supplies:

- Teacher's Guide & Student Workbook
- White board or chalkboard
- Word cards (as necessary)
- Story: *Climbing the Fence*

Teaching Tips:

Review the rule. Have the student write examples of the rule on the chalkboard or white board. Assist the student as needed in identifying the pictures or reading the words in the lesson.

Activity 1. Have the student identify the pictures and draw a line to match the pictures with the words.

Pictures: **cap**, **ice**, **pencil**, **mice**, **clock**

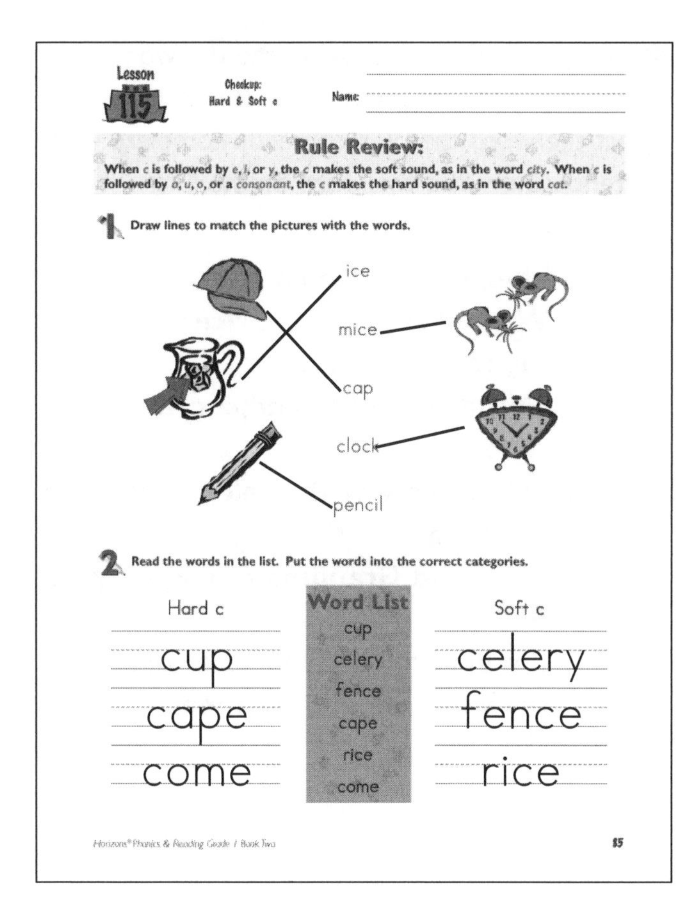
Lesson 115

Checkup:
Hard & Soft c

Name:

Rule Review:
When *c* is followed by *e*, *i*, or *y*, the *c* makes the soft sound, as in the word *city*. When *c* is followed by *a*, *u*, *o*, or a *consonant*, the *c* makes the hard sound, as in the word *cat*.

1. Draw lines to match the pictures with the words.

ice
mice
cap
clock
pencil

2. Read the words in the list. Put the words into the correct categories.

Hard c	Word List	Soft c
cup	cup	celery
cape	celery	fence
come	fence	rice
	cape	
	rice	
	come	

Horizons® Phonics & Reading Grade 1 Book Two

85

Activity 2. Have the student read the words from the list aloud. The student will write the words in the correct categories.

Hard **c**: **cup, cape, come**
Soft **c**: **celery, fence, rice**

Activity 3. Help the student read the words in the list and the sentences. Instruct the student to select the word that will correctly complete each sentence and write the word on the line.

Sentences:

1. **I helped my dad paint the fence.**
2. **We had chicken and rice for supper last night.**
3. **Grandma and Grandpa came to supper.**
4. **I liked the way the celery crunched when I ate it.**
5. **Mom and Grandma drank a cup of tea.**
6. **I'm glad my baby brother did not cry while we ate our meal.**

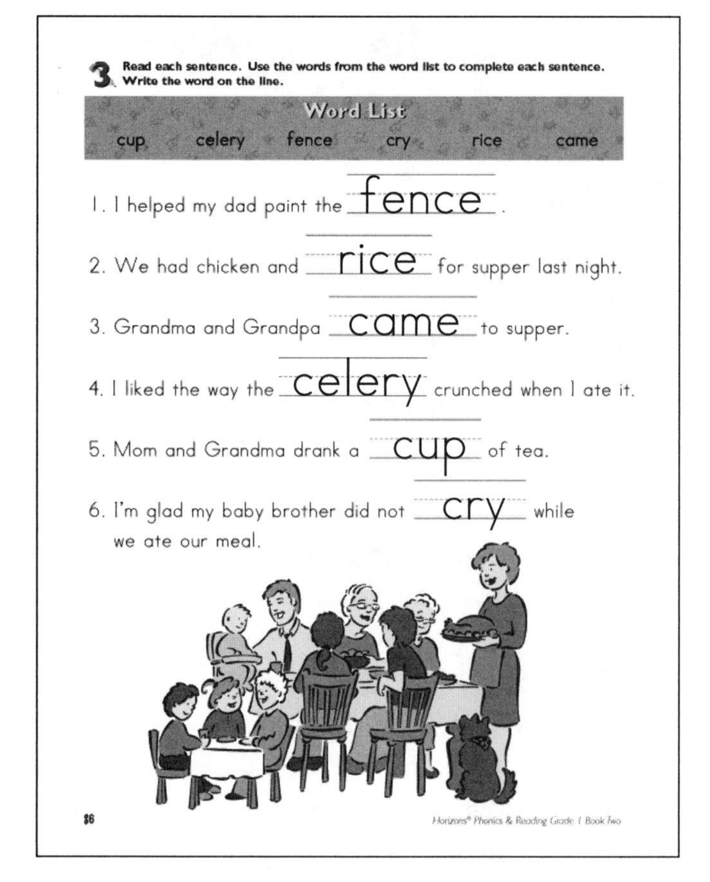

3 **Read each sentence. Use the words from the word list to complete each sentence. Write the word on the line.**

Word List

cup celery fence cry rice came

1. I helped my dad paint the fence.
2. We had chicken and rice for supper last night.
3. Grandma and Grandpa came to supper.
4. I liked the way the celery crunched when I ate it.
5. Mom and Grandma drank a cup of tea.
6. I'm glad my baby brother did not cry while we ate our meal.

86 Horizons® Phonics & Reading Grade 1 Book Two

Lesson 116 - Checkup: Hard & Soft g

Overview:

- Word/picture match
- Categorize words

Materials and Supplies:

- Teacher's Guide & Student Workbook
- White board or chalkboard
- Word cards (as necessary)
- Story: *The Giant Giraffe*

Teaching Tips:

Review the rule. Have the student write examples of the rule on the chalkboard or white board. Assist the student as needed in identifying the pictures or reading the words in the lesson.

Activity 1. Have the student identify the pictures and draw a line to match the pictures with the words.

Pictures:	**page**	**giant**
	gum	**goat**
	giraffe	

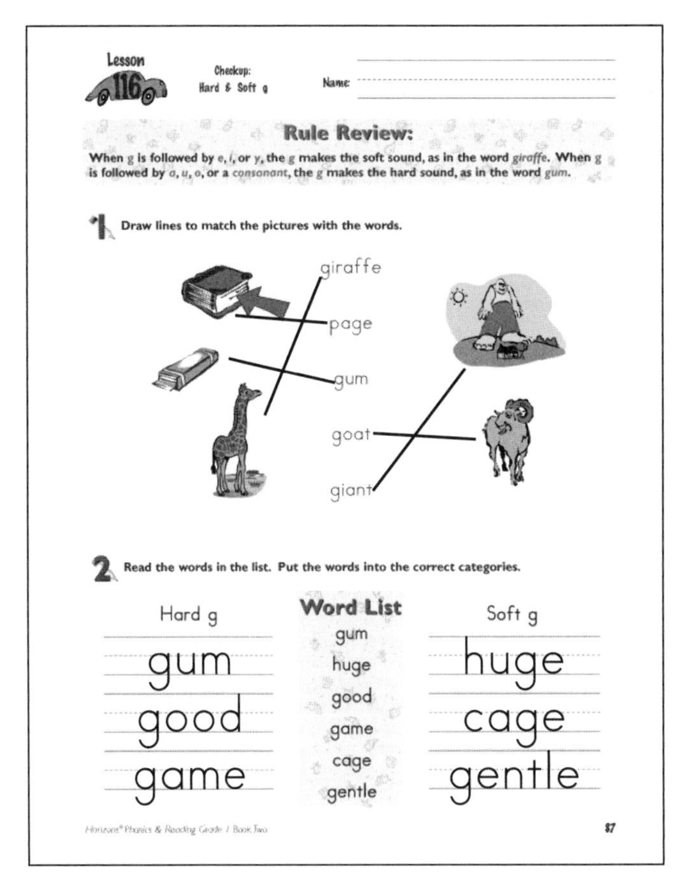
Lesson 116

Checkup: Hard & Soft g

Name:

Rule Review:

When g is followed by *e*, *i*, or *y*, the g makes the soft sound, as in the word *giraffe*. When g is followed by *a*, *u*, *o*, or a *consonant*, the g makes the hard sound, as in the word *gum*.

1. Draw lines to match the pictures with the words.

giraffe
page
gum
goat
giant

2. Read the words in the list. Put the words into the correct categories.

Hard g	Word List	Soft g
gum	gum	huge
good	huge	cage
game	good	gentle
	game	
	cage	
	gentle	

Horizons® Phonics & Reading Grade 1 Book Two

87

Activity 2. Have the student read the words in the list aloud. The student will write the words in the correct categories.

Hard g: **good, game, get**
Soft g: **age, huge, cage**

Activity 3. Have the student read the words in the list aloud. The student will write the words in the correct categories.

Soft g:	**gerbil, giraffe gem**
Hard g:	**go, got, grow**
Soft c:	**cent, cell, certain**
Hard c:	**cake, count, cross**

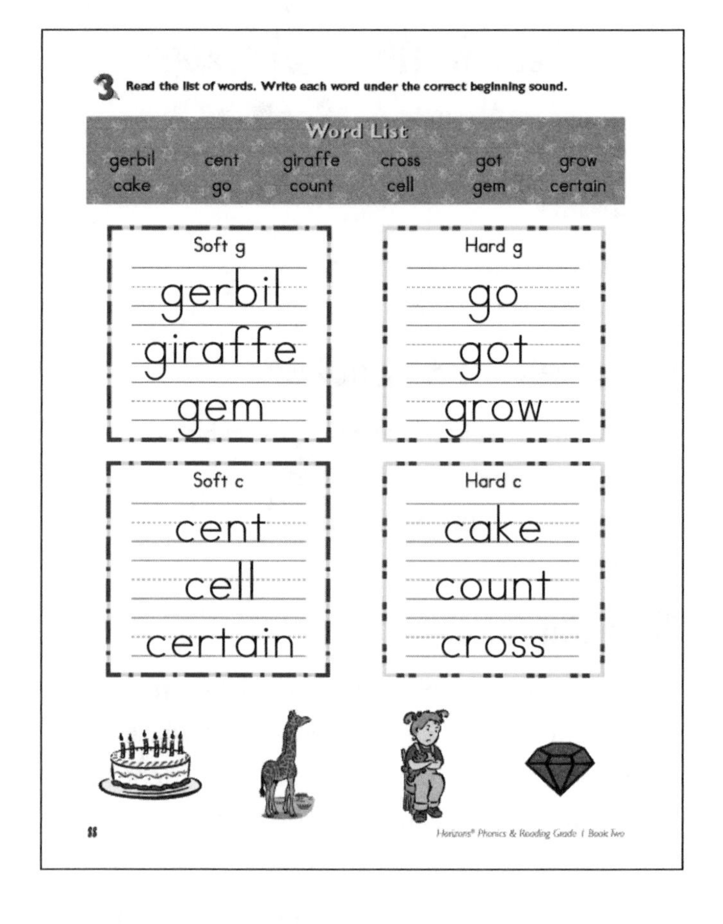

3. Read the list of words. Write each word under the correct beginning sound.

Word List

gerbil	cent	giraffe	cross	got	grow
cake	go	count	cell	gem	certain

Soft g	Hard g
gerbil	go
giraffe	got
gem	grow

Soft c	Hard c
cent	cake
cell	count
certain	cross

Horizons® Phonics & Reading Grade 1 Book Two

Lesson 117 - Words with qu

Overview:

- Picture/word match
- Sentence completion
- Sentence writing
- Story completion

Materials and Supplies:

- Teacher's Guide & Student Workbook
- White board or chalkboard
- Word cards (as necessary)
- Phonics rule flashcards in **Teacher Resources**
- Story: *A Quilt for the Queen*

Teaching Tips:

Review the rule. Have the student write examples of the rule on the chalkboard or white board. Assist the student as needed in identifying the pictures or reading the words in the lesson.

Activity 1. Have the student identify the pictures and draw a line to match the pictures with the words.

Pictures: **quarter** **queen**
quilt **question mark**

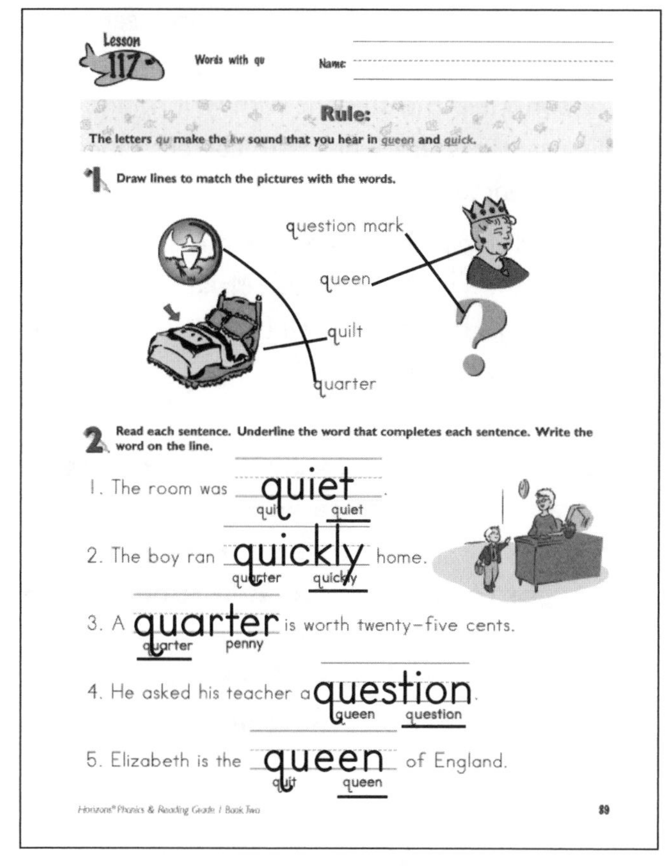

Activity 2. Help the student read the sentences and the word choices. Instruct the student to underline the word that will correctly complete each sentence and write the word on the line.

Sentences:

1. **The room was quiet.**
2. **The boy ran quickly home.**
3. **A quarter is worth twenty-five cents.**
4. **He asked his teacher a question.**
5. **Elizabeth is the queen of England.**

Activity 3. The student will write three sentences and use at least four of the **qu** words from the lesson. Help the student with writing and spelling as necessary. Emphasize correct capitalization and punctuation.

Activity 4. Help the student read the unfinished story and the words in the list. Make word cards as necessary. The student will use the words from the list to complete the story.

Story:

Tom heard the ice cream truck coming. He ran to meet it. He knew that he needed three quarters to get a treat. When Tom got to the truck he quit running. The woman in the truck had quite a lot of different things to choose from. Tom bought his treat and ran home quickly.

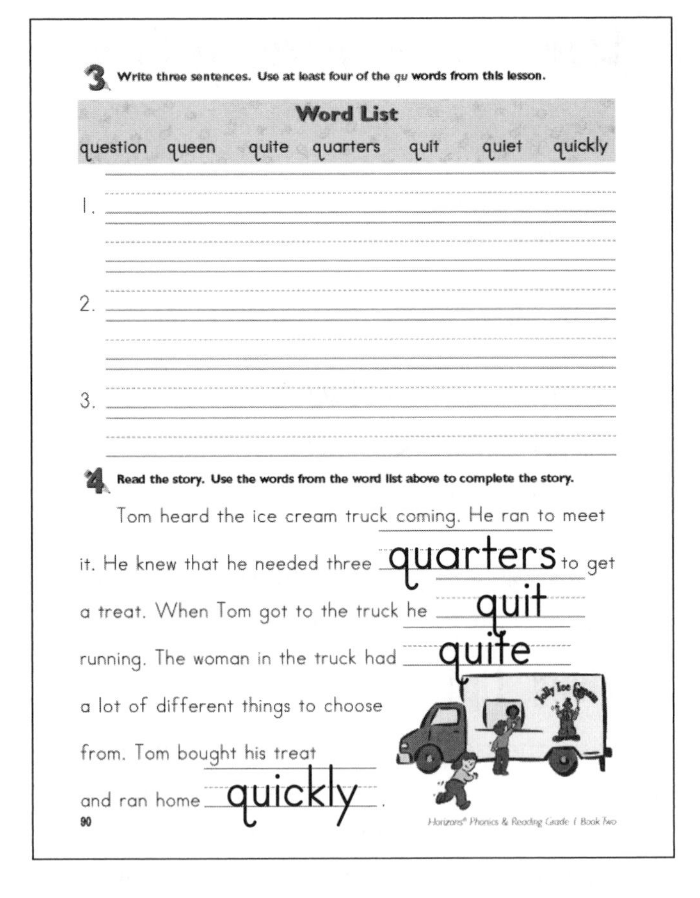

3 Write three sentences. Use at least four of the *qu* words from this lesson.

Word List

question queen quite quarters quit quiet quickly

1.

2.

3.

4 Read the story. Use the words from the word list above to complete the story.

Tom heard the ice cream truck coming. He ran to meet it. He knew that he needed three quarters to get a treat. When Tom got to the truck he quit running. The woman in the truck had quite a lot of different things to choose from. Tom bought his treat and ran home quickly.

90 Horizons® Phonics & Reading Grade 1 Book Two

Lesson 118 - Checkup: Consonant Digraphs ph & gh

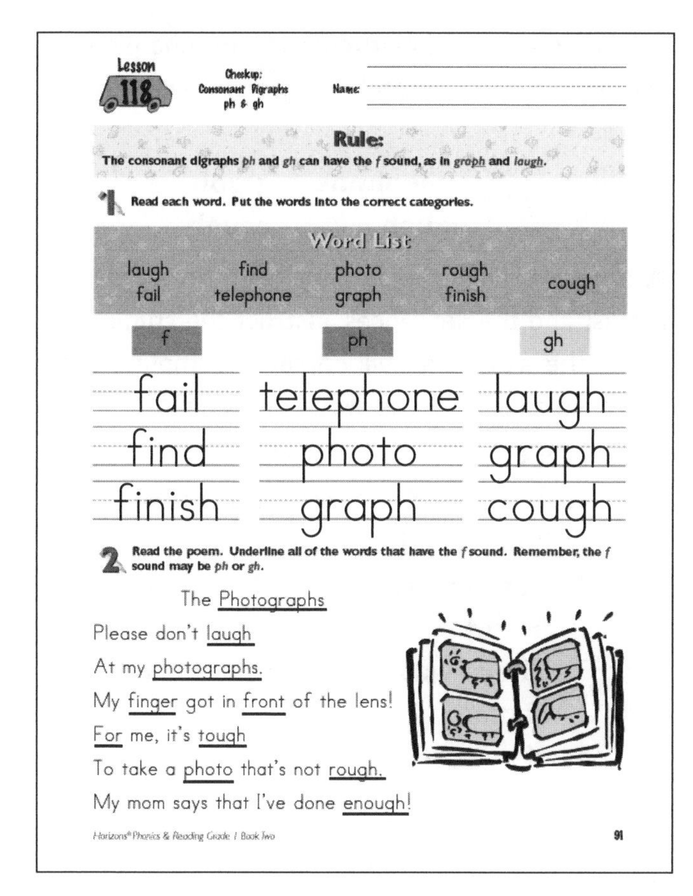
Lesson 118

Checkup: Consonant Digraphs ph & gh

Name:

Rule:
The consonant digraphs *ph* and *gh* can have the *f* sound, as in *graph* and *laugh*.

1. Read each word. Put the words into the correct categories.

Word List

laugh fail find telephone photo graph rough finish cough

f	ph	gh
fail	telephone	laugh
find	photo	graph
finish	graph	cough

2. Read the poem. Underline all of the words that have the *f* sound. Remember, the *f* sound may be *ph* or *gh*.

The Photographs

Please don't laugh
At my photographs.
My finger got in front of the lens!
For me, it's tough
To take a photo that's not rough.
My mom says that I've done enough!

Horizons® Phonics & Reading Grade 1 Book Two 91

Overview:

- Categorize words
- Read a poem and underline **f**-sound words
- Picture/word match
- Sentence completion

Materials and Supplies:

- Teacher's Guide & Student Workbook
- White board or chalkboard
- Word cards (as necessary)
- Story: *A Photo of Phillip*

Teaching Tips:

Review the rule. Have the student write examples of the rule on the chalkboard or white board. Assist the student as needed in identifying the pictures or reading the words in the lesson.

Activity 1. Have the student read the words in the list. The student will write the words in the correct categories.

f: **fail, find, finish**
ph: **telephone, photo, graph**
gh: **laugh, rough, cough**

Activity 2. Have the student read the poem aloud. The student will underline all of the words that have the sound of **f**.

The Photographs

Please don't laugh
At my photographs.
My finger got in front of the lens!
For me, it's tough
To take a photo that's not rough.
My mom says that I've done enough!

Activity 3. Have the student identify the pictures and draw a line to match the pictures with the words.

Pictures: **telephone** **graph**
laugh **cough**

Activity 4. Help the student read the words in the list and the sentences. Instruct the student to select the word that will correctly complete each sentence and write the word on the line.

Sentences:

1. **The wood felt rough because it hadn't been sanded.**
2. **I use the telephone to call my friend.**
3. **There was enough milk for my cereal.**
4. **My sister's son is my nephew.**

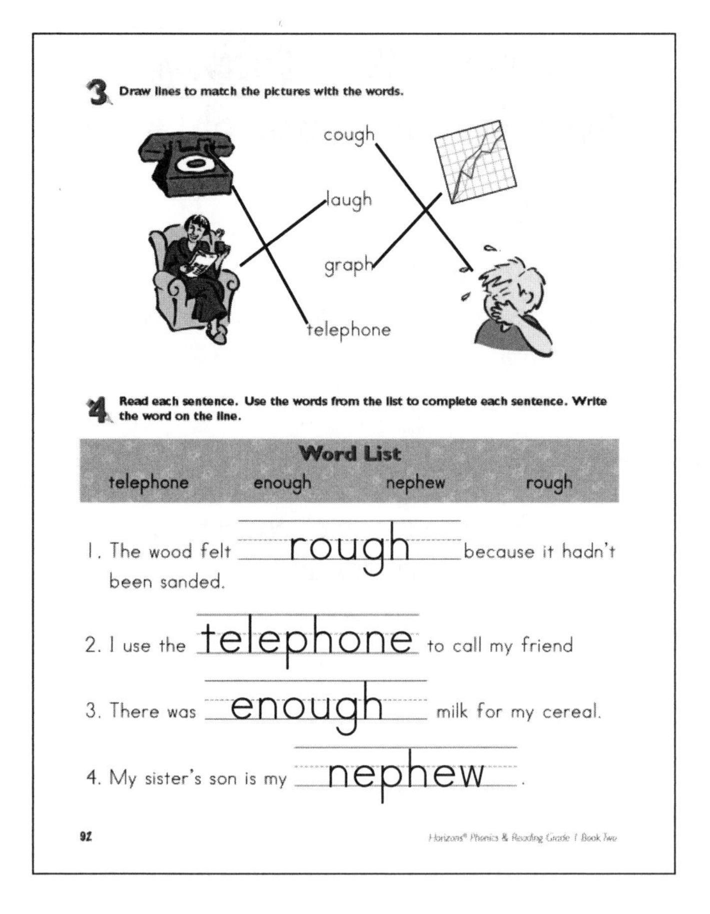
3 Draw lines to match the pictures with the words.
cough
laugh
graph
telephone
4 Read each sentence. Use the words from the list to complete each sentence. Write the word on the line.
Word List
telephone
enough
nephew
rough
1. The wood felt rough because it hadn't been sanded.
2. I use the telephone to call my friend
3. There was enough milk for my cereal.
4. My sister's son is my nephew.
92

Lesson 119 - Words with the s Sound

Overview:

- Categorize words
- Sentence completion
- Word match
- Crossword puzzle
- Add **s** to words and identify correct **s** sound
- Sentence writing

Materials and Supplies:

- Teacher's Guide & Student Workbook
- White board or chalkboard
- Word cards (as necessary)
- Phonics rule flashcards in **Teacher Resources**
- Story: *Raising the Flags*

Teaching Tips:

Review the rule. Have the student write examples of the rule on the chalkboard or white board. Assist the student as needed in identifying the pictures or reading the words in the lesson.

Activity 1. Have the student read the words aloud. Discuss word meanings if needed. The student will write the words into the correct categories.

s as in same: **Sam, stay, stem**
s as in rise: **raise, noise, close**
s as in sure: **surely, assure, reassure**

Activity 2. Help the student read the sentences. Instruct the student to select the word from the list in Activity 1 that will correctly complete each sentence and write the word on the line. NOTE: Not all of the words will be used.

Sentences:

1. **Please close the door when you go.**
2. **We stay inside when it rains.**
3. **The stem of a rose sometimes has thorns.**
4. **Every morning we raise the flag.**

Activity 3. Have the student read the words aloud. The student will match the words that have the same sound of **s**.

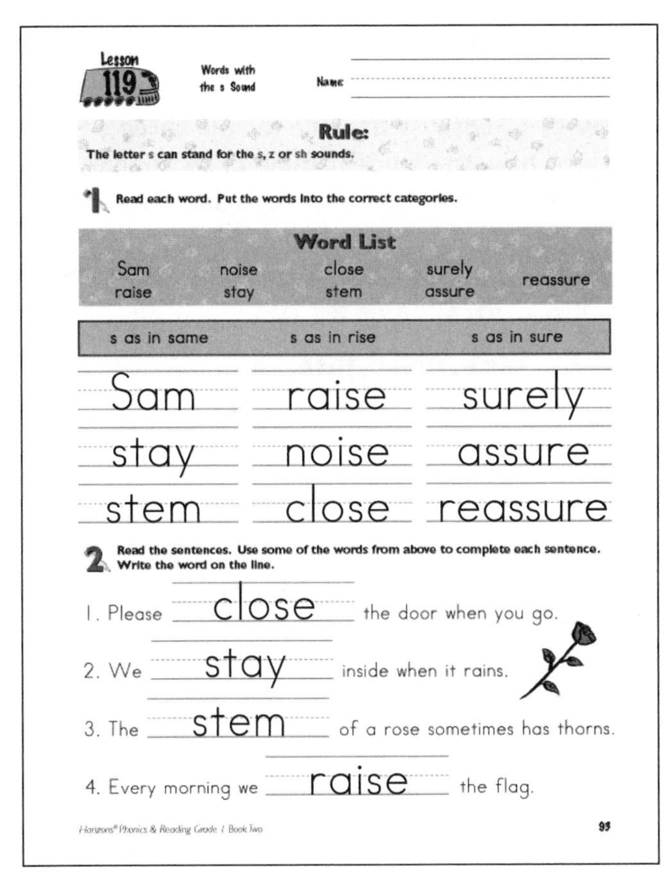
Lesson 119
Words with the s Sound
Name:

Rule:
The letter s can stand for the s, z or sh sounds.

1. Read each word. Put the words into the correct categories.

Word List
Sam, noise, close, surely, reassure, raise, stay, stem, assure

s as in same	s as in rise	s as in sure
Sam	raise	surely
stay	noise	assure
stem	close	reassure

2. Read the sentences. Use some of the words from above to complete each sentence. Write the word on the line.

1. Please close the door when you go.
2. We stay inside when it rains.
3. The stem of a rose sometimes has thorns.
4. Every morning we raise the flag.

Horizons® Phonics & Reading Grade 1 Book Two 93

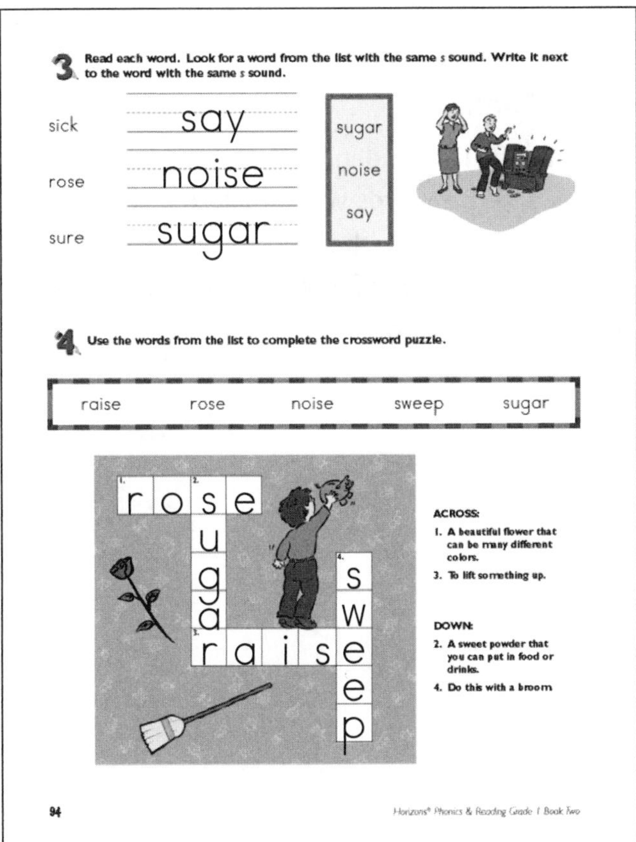
3. Read each word. Look for a word from the list with the same s sound. Write it next to the word with the same s sound.

sugar noise say

sick say
rose noise
sure sugar

4. Use the words from the list to complete the crossword puzzle.

raise rose noise sweep sugar

ACROSS
1. A beautiful flower that can be many different colors.
3. To lift something up.

DOWN
2. A sweet powder that you can put in food or drinks.
4. Do this with a broom.

94 Horizons® Phonics & Reading Grade 1 Book Two

Activity 4. Review the words in the list. Help the student read the crossword puzzle clues. Assist the student as necessary with the crossword puzzle.

Across: **1. rose** **3. raise**
Down: **2. sugar** **4. sweep**

Activity 5. Discuss the rule for the three sounds of **s**, and have the student think of additional examples. Instruct the student to add **s** to each of the words and read them aloud. Have the student circle the sound of **s** they hear in the words they have just read.

Words: **raise, noise, fuse, rise**
please, tease, nose, rose

Sound of s: **z**

Activity 6. Instruct the student to add **s** to each of the words and read them aloud. Have the student circle the sound of **s** they hear in the words they have just read.

Words: **seam, same, sign, sick**

Sound of s: **s**

Activity 7. Instruct the student to add **s** to each of the words and read them aloud. Have the student circle the sound of **s** they hear in the words they have just read.

Words: **sure, sugar, assure**

Sound of s: **sh**

Activity 8. The student will write three sentences and use words with a different **s** sound in each sentence. Help the student with writing and spelling as necessary. Emphasize correct capitalization and punctuation.

5. Add *s* to each of these words, then read the words to your teacher.

raise noise fuse rise

please tease nose rose

Circle the sound the *s* makes in the words above: s (z) sh

6. Add *s* to each of these words, then read the words to your teacher.

seam same sign sick

Circle the sound the *s* makes in the words above: (s) z sh

7. Add *s* to each of these words, then read the words to your teacher.

sure sugar a s sure

Circle the sound the *s* makes in the words above: s z (sh)

Horizons® Phonics & Reading Grade 1 Book Two 95

8. Write three sentences using words with a different *s* sound in each sentence.

1.

2.

3.

96 Horizons® Phonics & Reading Grade 1 Book Two

Lesson 120 - Review: Words with the Sounds of f & s

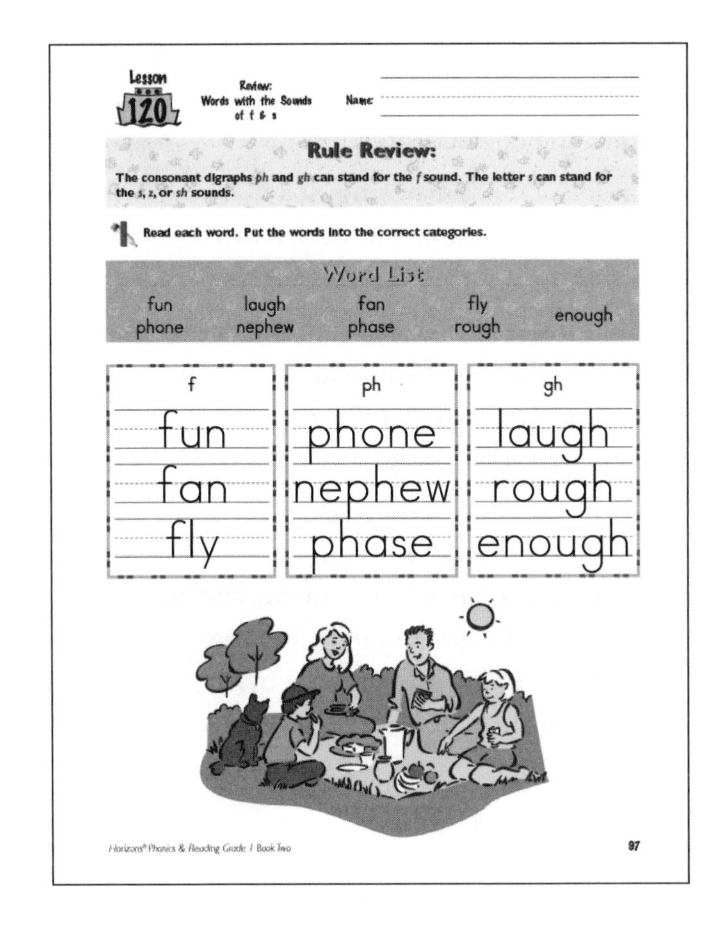
Lesson 120 Review: Words with the Sounds of f & s Name:

Rule Review:

The consonant digraphs *ph* and *gh* can stand for the *f* sound. The letter *s* can stand for the *s*, *z*, or *sh* sounds.

1. Read each word. Put the words into the correct categories.

Word List

fun phone laugh nephew fan phase fly rough enough

f	ph	gh
fun	phone	laugh
fan	nephew	rough
fly	phase	enough

Horizons® Phonics & Reading Grade 1 Book Two 97

Overview:

- Categorize words
- Sentence completion

Materials and Supplies:

- Teacher's Guide & Student Workbook
- White board or chalkboard
- Word cards (as necessary)
- Story: *Cousin Sue*

Teaching Tips:

Review the rules. Have the student write examples of the rule on the chalkboard or white board. Assist the student as needed in identifying the pictures or reading the words in the lesson.

Activity 1. Have the student read the words aloud. The student will write the words from the list into the correct categories.

f: **fun, fan, fly**
ph: **phone, nephew, phase**
gh: **laugh, rough, enough**

Activity 2. Have the student read the words aloud. The student will write the words from the list into the correct categories.

s as in sun: **Sam, sing, stay**
s as in sure: **sugar, surely, assure**
s as in rise: **please, noise, raise**

Activity 3. Help the student read the sentences and the word choices. Instruct the student to underline the word that will correctly complete each sentence and write the word on the line.

Sentences:

1. **Jason is my cousin**
2. **I am sure that I know the answer.**
3. **Dad puts sugar in his tea.**
4. **The day surely flew by!**
5. **It is my job to raise the flag every day.**

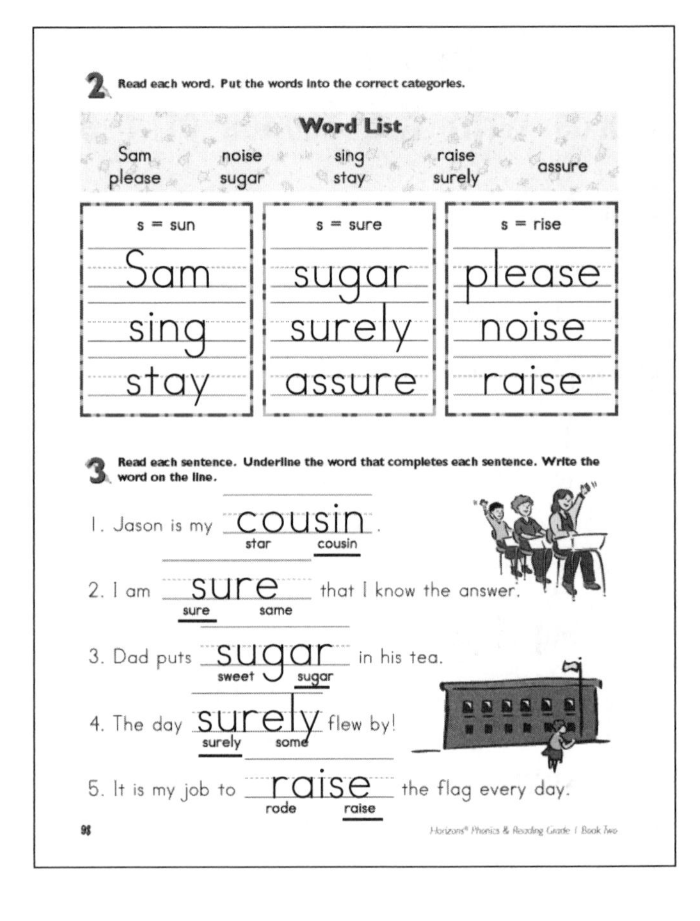

2. Read each word. Put the words into the correct categories.

Word List

Sam, please, noise, sugar, sing, stay, raise, surely, assure

s = sun	s = sure	s = rise
Sam	sugar	please
sing	surely	noise
stay	assure	raise

3. Read each sentence. Underline the word that completes each sentence. Write the word on the line.

1. Jason is my cousin. (star, cousin)
2. I am sure that I know the answer. (sure, same)
3. Dad puts sugar in his tea. (sweet, sugar)
4. The day surely flew by! (surely, some)
5. It is my job to raise the flag every day. (rode, raise)

Horizons® Phonics & Reading Grade 1 Book Two

Test 12

Lessons 111-120

Instructions:

Review putting words in alphabetical order to the first letter and to the second letter. Give the student a list of each type of alphabetizing to put in order. Have the student name the pictures in the test. Read through the test with the student. Help the student with any words that he/she is still unsure of. The teacher should be available to answer any questions that the student may have during the test.

Activity 1. Review the instructions and the words with the student.

Words:		
	Ann	**Eve**
	Brad	**Janet**
	Carol	**Luke**
	Dan	**Mark**

Activity 2. Review the instructions and the words with the student.

Words:		
	cake	**climb**
	cent	**come**
	city	**cream**

Activity 3. Review the instructions and the words with the student.

Words:	sh sound	s sound	z sound
	sure	**seal**	**noise**
	sugar	**sum**	**rose**

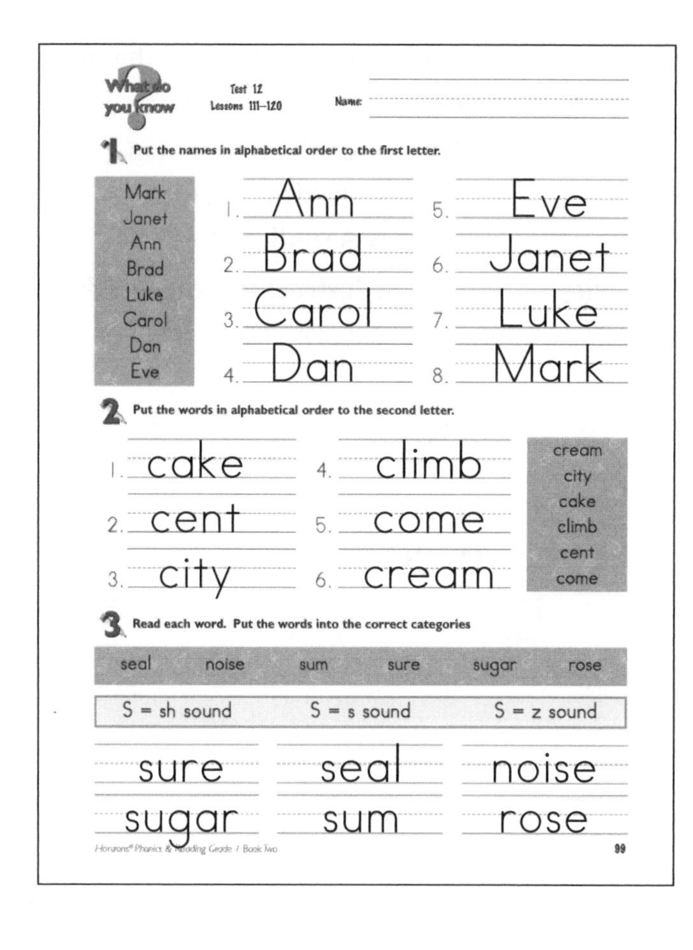

What do you know

Test 12
Lessons 111–120

Name:

1. Put the names in alphabetical order to the first letter.

Mark
Janet
Ann
Brad
Luke
Carol
Dan
Eve

1. Ann
2. Brad
3. Carol
4. Dan
5. Eve
6. Janet
7. Luke
8. Mark

2. Put the words in alphabetical order to the second letter.

cream
city
cake
climb
cent
come

1. cake
2. cent
3. city
4. climb
5. come
6. cream

3. Read each word. Put the words into the correct categories

seal noise sum sure sugar rose

S = sh sound	S = s sound	S = z sound
sure	seal	noise
sugar	sum	rose

Horizons® Phonics & Reading Grade / Book Two 99

Activity 3. Review the instructions and the pictures with the student.

Pictures: **The queen has a crown.**
She is making cookies.
This is a quill pen.

Activity 4. Review the instructions, the words in the list, and the sentences with the student.

Words: **cough**
rough
enough
phone
laugh

4. Circle the sentence that tells what it is in the picture.

The queen has a crown.
The king has a red hat.

She is making cookies.
She is making a quilt.

This is a quill pen.
You must be quick.

5. Use the words from the list to answer the riddles.

phone rough laugh cough enough

1. This is what you might do if you have a cold. cough
2. This is the way that wood feels before you sand it. rough
3. When you are full, you have had ________ . enough
4. You use this when you want to call someone. phone
5. When something is funny, you do this. laugh

100

Lesson 121 - Writing Lesson: Imaginative Story

Overview:

- Write an imaginative story

Materials and Supplies:

- Teacher's Guide & Student Workbook
- White board or chalkboard
- Word cards (as necessary)
- Story: *The Dog Who Could Fly*

Teaching Tips:

Go over the directions with the student. The student will write an imaginative story about an imaginary animal. The teacher or writing partner should help the student with ideas as necessary. The teacher or writing partner should also help the student get started on the story and assist as needed throughout the assignment. The student may need help with spelling and punctuation. The student should do the rough draft on a piece of paper and write the final copy in the student workbook. (**Optional**: Have the student draw a picture of the imaginary animal about which he is writing.)

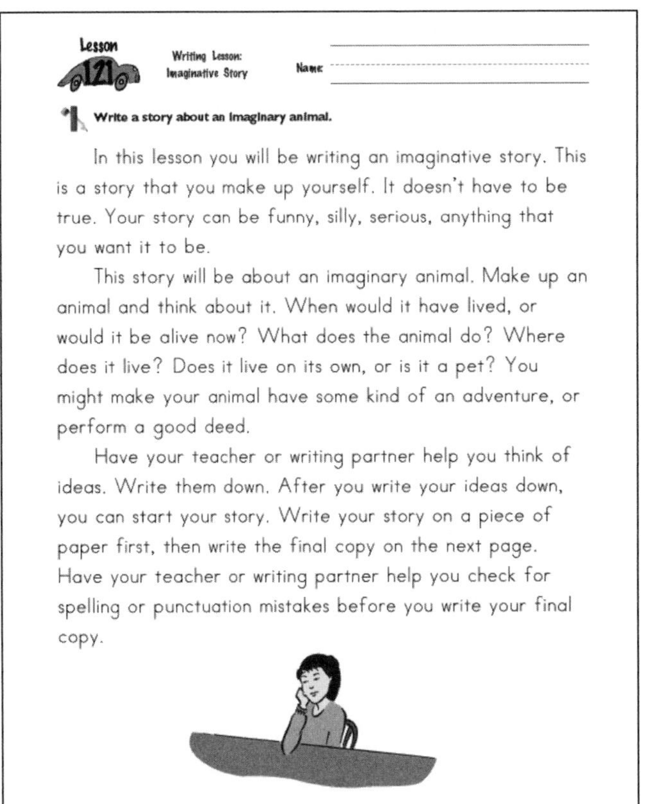

Lesson 121 Writing Lesson: Imaginative Story Name:

1. **Write a story about an imaginary animal.**

In this lesson you will be writing an imaginative story. This is a story that you make up yourself. It doesn't have to be true. Your story can be funny, silly, serious, anything that you want it to be.

This story will be about an imaginary animal. Make up an animal and think about it. When would it have lived, or would it be alive now? What does the animal do? Where does it live? Does it live on its own, or is it a pet? You might make your animal have some kind of an adventure, or perform a good deed.

Have your teacher or writing partner help you think of ideas. Write them down. After you write your ideas down, you can start your story. Write your story on a piece of paper first, then write the final copy on the next page. Have your teacher or writing partner help you check for spelling or punctuation mistakes before you write your final copy.

Horizons® Phonics & Reading Grade 1 Book Two 101

Activity 1. Write a story about an imaginary animal.

102

Horizons® Phonics & Reading Grade 1 Book Two

Lesson 122 - Checkup: Y as a Vowel

Overview:

- Picture/word match
- Sentence writing
- Sentence completion
- Crossword puzzle

Materials and Supplies:

- Teacher's Guide & Student Workbook
- White board or chalkboard
- Word cards (as necessary)
- Story: *A Crying Baby*

Teaching Tips:

Review the rule. Have the student write examples of the rule on the chalkboard or white board. Assist the student as needed in identifying the pictures or reading the words in the lesson.

Activity 1. Have the student identify the pictures and draw a line to match the pictures with the words.

Pictures:	**fly**	**cry**
	penny	**city**
	baby	**puppy**

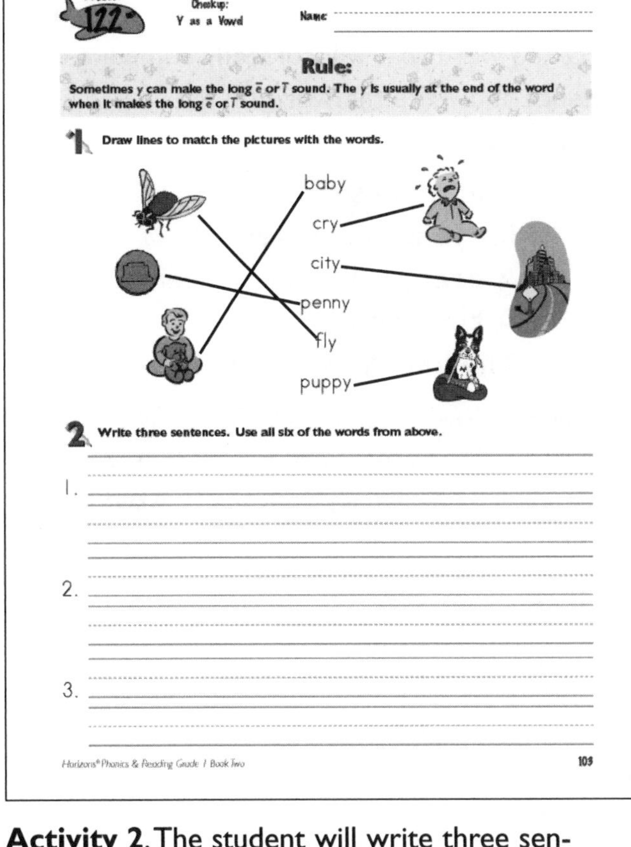
Lesson 122

Checkup: Y as a Vowel

Name:

Rule:
Sometimes y can make the long ē or ī sound. The y is usually at the end of the word when it makes the long ē or ī sound.

1 Draw lines to match the pictures with the words.

baby
cry
city
penny
fly
puppy

2 Write three sentences. Use all six of the words from above.

1.

2.

3.

Horizons® Phonics & Reading Grade 1 Book Two 103

Activity 2. The student will write three sentences using the six words from Activity 1. Help the student with writing and spelling as necessary. Emphasize correct capitalization and punctuation.

Activity 3. Help the student read the words in the list and the sentences. Instruct the student to select the word that will correctly complete each sentence and write the word on the line.

Sentences:

1. **We live in the city.**
2. **I have a baby sister.**
3. **A penny is worth one cent.**
4. **A bird can fly.**
5. **The loud noise made the baby cry.**

Activity 4. Review the words in the list. Help the student read the crossword puzzle clues. Assist the student as necessary with the crossword puzzle.

Across: **1. try**
2. funny

Down: **2. fly**
3. nearby

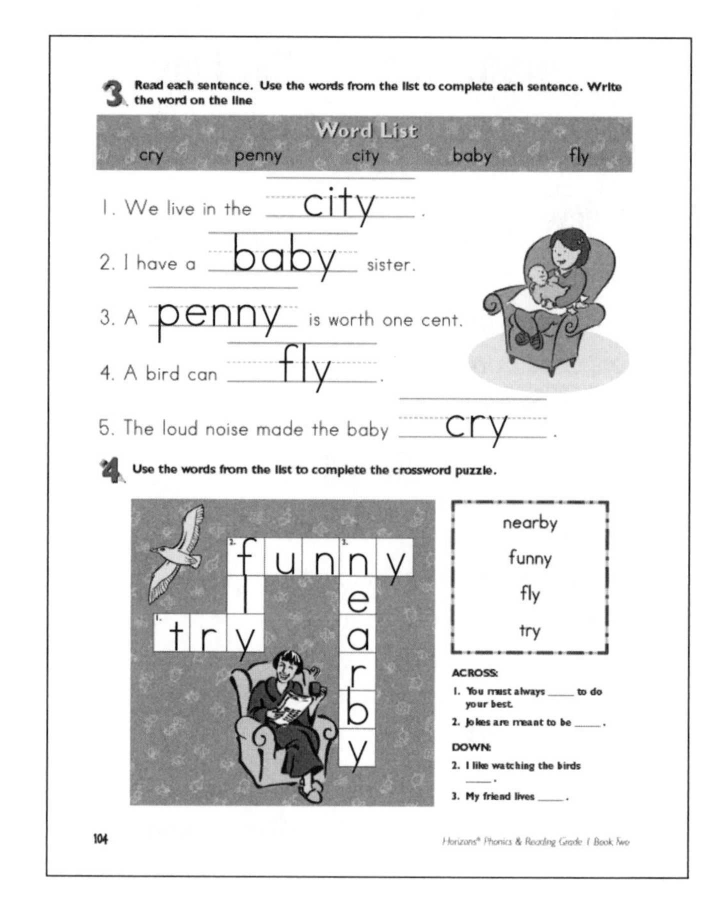

3 Read each sentence. Use the words from the list to complete each sentence. Write the word on the line

Word List

cry penny city baby fly

1. We live in the city.
2. I have a baby sister.
3. A penny is worth one cent.
4. A bird can fly.
5. The loud noise made the baby cry.

4 Use the words from the list to complete the crossword puzzle.

nearby
funny
fly
try

ACROSS:

1. You must always ____ to do your best.
2. Jokes are meant to be ____.

DOWN:

2. I like watching the birds ____.
3. My friend lives ____.

104 *Horizons® Phonics & Reading Grade 1 Book Two*

Lesson 123 - Checkup: Contractions with Will

Overview:

- Write contractions for phrases
- Write phrases for contractions
- Write missing letters in contractions
- Write sentences using contractions

Materials and Supplies:

- Teacher's Guide & Student Workbook
- White board or chalkboard
- Word cards (as necessary)
- Story: *He'll Go, She Won't*

Teaching Tips:

Review the definition. Have the student write examples of contractions on the chalkboard or white board. Assist the student as needed in reading the words in the lesson.

Activity 1. Have the student read the words aloud. The student will write the contraction for each group of two words.

Words:		
	they'll	**we'll**
	I'll	**you'll**
	she'll	**it'll**
	he'll	

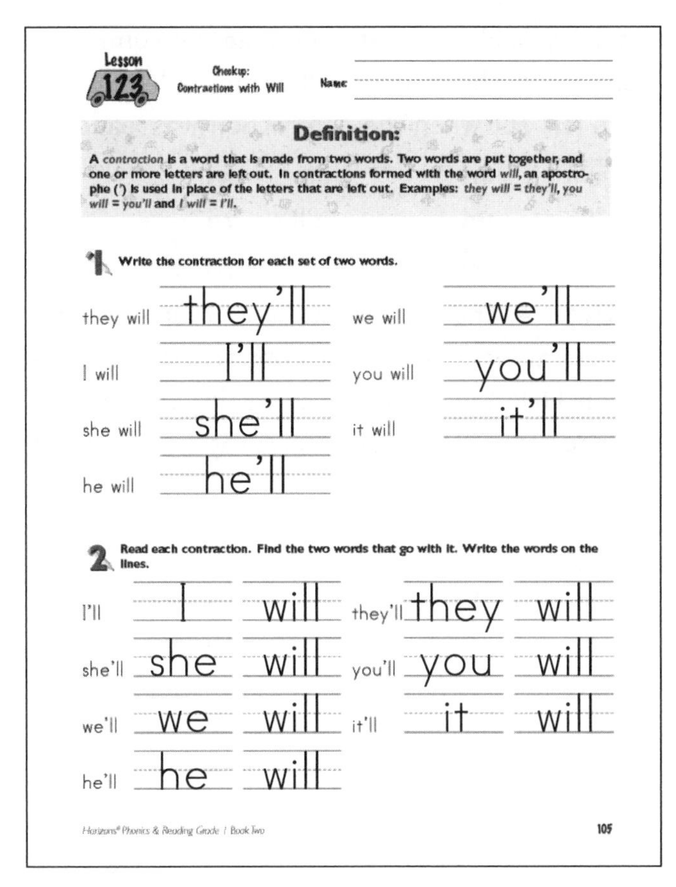
Lesson 123 Checkup: Contractions with Will Name:

Definition:

A *contraction* is a word that is made from two words. Two words are put together, and one or more letters are left out. In contractions formed with the word *will*, an apostrophe (') is used in place of the letters that are left out. Examples: *they will = they'll, you will = you'll* and *I will = I'll.*

1. Write the contraction for each set of two words.

they will they'll we will we'll
I will I'll you will you'll
she will she'll it will it'll
he will he'll

2. Read each contraction. Find the two words that go with it. Write the words on the lines.

I'll I will they'll they will
she'll she will you'll you will
we'll we will it'll it will
he'll he will

Horizons® Phonics & Reading Grade 1 Book Two 105

Activity 2. Have the student read the words aloud. The student will write the two words for each contraction on the lines.

Words:		
	I will	**they will**
	she will	**you will**
	we will	**it will**
	he will	

Activity 3. Have the student read the contractions aloud. The student will write the letters that were left out when the contraction was made.

you'll	**wi**	I'll	**wi**
he'll	**wi**	it'll	**wi**
she'll	**wi**		

Activity 4. The student will write four sentences and use at least four of the contractions from the lesson. Help the student with writing and spelling as necessary. Emphasize correct capitalization and punctuation.

3 **Read each contraction. Think about the letter or letters that were left out when the contraction was made. Write the missing letters on the line.**

you'll	wi	I'll	wi
he'll	wi	it'll	wi
she'll	wi		

4 **Write four sentences. Use at least four contractions from this lesson.**

1.

2.

3.

4.

106 *Horizons® Phonics & Reading Grade 1 Book Two*

Lesson 124 - Checkup: Contractions with Not

Overview:

- Write two words for each contraction
- Write missing letters
- Match contractions with two words for each
- Sentence writing

Materials and Supplies:

- Teacher's Guide & Student Workbook
- White board or chalkboard
- Word cards (as necessary)
- Story: *The Dance Lessons*

Teaching Tips:

Review the definition. Have the student write examples of the contractions on the chalkboard or white board. Assist the student as needed reading the words in the lesson.

Activity 1. Have the student read the words aloud. The student will write the contraction for each group of two words. NOTE: Explain that the contraction for **will not** seems to break the rule. It came from an old-fashioned English phrase (*woll not*) that we no longer use; however, the contraction that was derived from this phrase (*won't*) is still used.

don't	**do not**
won't	**will not**
can't	**cannot**
shouldn't	**should not**
didn't	**did not**
couldn't	**could not**
wouldn't	**would not**

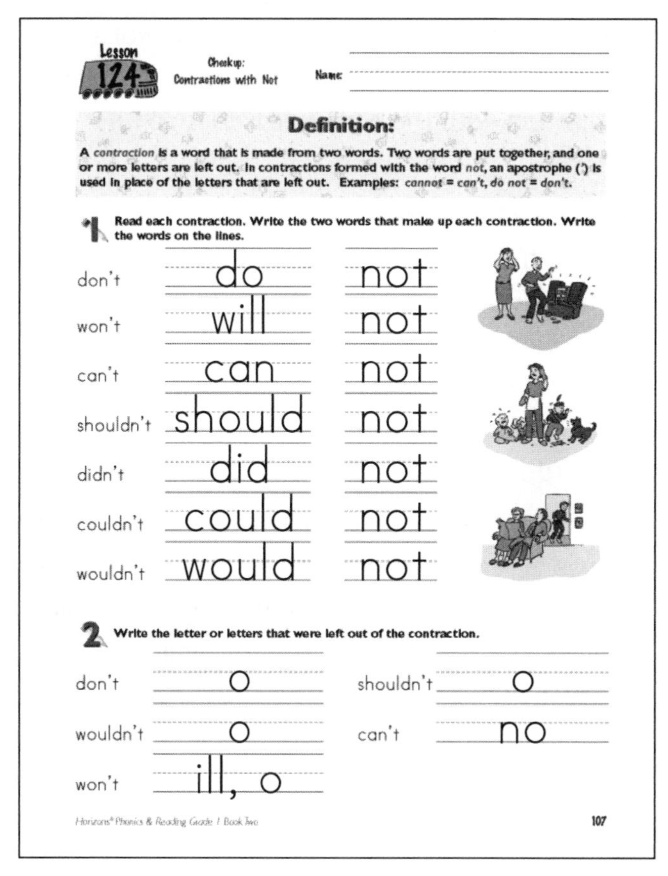

Lesson 124 Checkup: Contractions with Not Name:

Definition:

A *contraction* is a word that is made from two words. Two words are put together, and one or more letters are left out. In contractions formed with the word *not*, an apostrophe (') is used in place of the letters that are left out. Examples: *cannot* = *can't*, *do not* = *don't*.

1. Read each contraction. Write the two words that make up each contraction. Write the words on the lines.

don't	do	not
won't	will	not
can't	can	not
shouldn't	should	not
didn't	did	not
couldn't	could	not
wouldn't	would	not

2. Write the letter or letters that were left out of the contraction.

don't	o	shouldn't	o
wouldn't	o	can't	no
won't	ill, o		

Horizons® Phonics & Reading Grade 1 Book Two 107

Activity 2. Have the student read the words aloud. The student will write the letters that were taken out when the contraction was made.

don't	**o**	shouldn't	**o**
wouldn't	**o**	cannot	**no**
won't	**ill, o**		

Activity 3. Have the student read the words aloud. The student will draw lines to match each contraction with the two words that go with it.

wouldn't/**would not**
couldn't/**could not**
didn't/**did not**
can't/**cannot**
won't/**will not**
shouldn't/**should not**
don't/**do not**

Activity 4. The student will write four sentences and use at least four of the contractions from the lesson. Help the student with writing and spelling as necessary. Emphasize correct capitalization and punctuation.

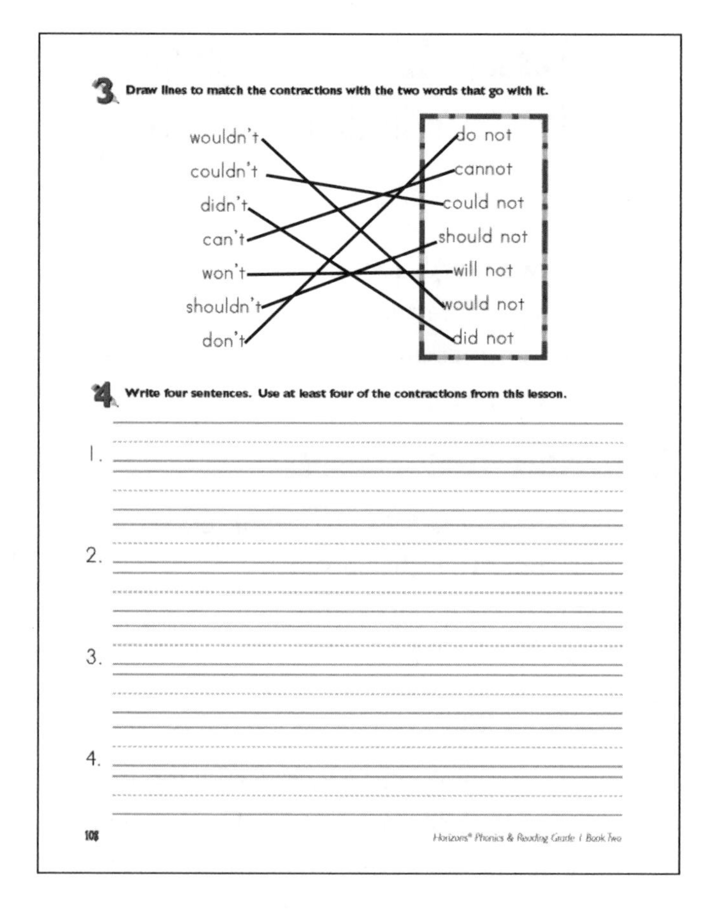

3 Draw lines to match the contractions with the two words that go with it.

wouldn't	do not
couldn't	cannot
didn't	could not
can't	should not
won't	will not
shouldn't	would not
don't	did not

4 Write four sentences. Use at least four of the contractions from this lesson.

1.

2.

3.

4.

108 Horizons® Phonics & Reading Grade 1 Book Two

Lesson 125 - Writing Lesson: Poem

Overview:

- Write a poem

Materials and Supplies:

- Teacher's Guide & Student Workbook
- White board or chalkboard
- Word cards (as necessary)
- Story: *Mark's Poem*

Teaching Tips:

The student will be writing a short poem. The poem should be about the student 's favorite food. The student should try to use some contractions in the poem. Go over the directions for the poem with the student. The teacher or writing partner should help the student with ideas and with the actual writing of the poem. The student may need to be reminded that poems do not have to rhyme. The student should write the rough draft on a piece of paper. The final copy should be written in the student workbook.

Lesson 125 Writing Lesson: Poem Name:

1. Write a short poem about your favorite food.

In this lesson you will write a short poem. Poems can rhyme, or not. You will write a poem about your favorite food. Think about this food and why it is your favorite. What do you like about it? Start with those ideas. Try to include in your poem some of the contractions that you have learned about. You might want to look at some poetry books before you start.

Your poem should be at least three lines long. Have your teacher or writing partner help you write your poem. He or she can help you with spelling and ideas. Write your first copy on a piece of paper. Write your final copy on the following page and draw a picture to go with your poem.

Horizons® Phonics & Reading Grade 1 Book Two 109

Activity 1. Have the student write a short poem about his or her favorite food. If desired, the student may also draw a picture to illustrate the completed poem.

110 Horizons® Phonics & Reading Grade 1 Book Two

Lesson 126 - Checkup: Contractions with Have

Overview:

- Write two words for each contraction
- Match contractions with the two words that go with them
- Write letters left out of contractions
- Sentence writing

Materials and Supplies:

- Teacher's Guide & Student Workbook
- White board or chalkboard
- Word cards (as necessary)
- Story: *Kay's Toys*

Teaching Tips:

Review the definition. Have the student write examples of contractions on the chalkboard or white board. Assist the student as needed in reading the words in the lesson.

Activity 1. Have the student read the words aloud. The student will write the contraction for each group of two words.

I've	**I have**
we've	**we have**
they've	**they have**
you've	**you have**

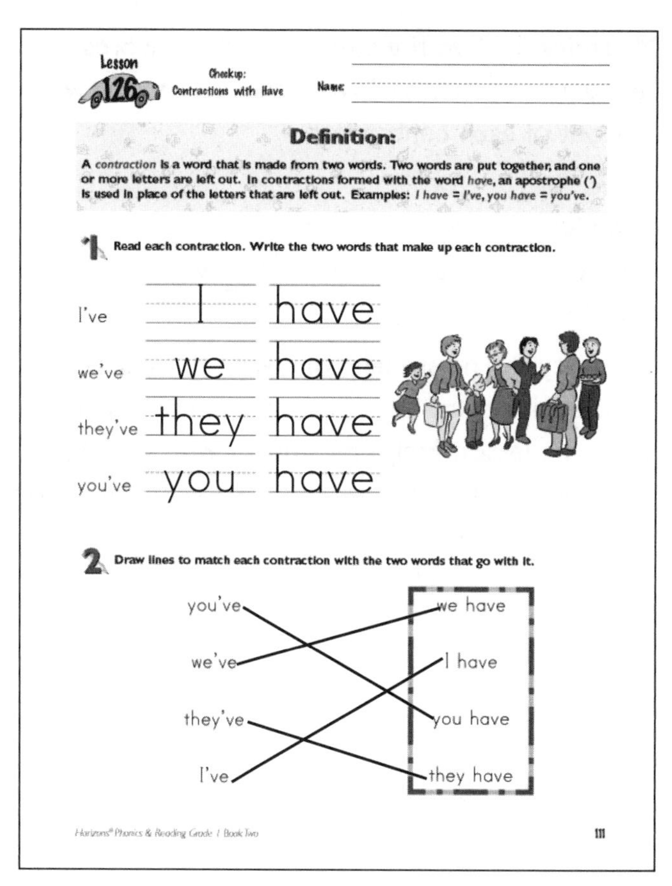

Lesson 126 Checkup: Contractions with Have Name:

Definition:

A *contraction* is a word that is made from two words. Two words are put together, and one or more letters are left out. In contractions formed with the word *have*, an apostrophe (') is used in place of the letters that are left out. Examples: *I have* = *I've*, *you have* = *you've*.

1. Read each contraction. Write the two words that make up each contraction.

I've I have
we've we have
they've they have
you've you have

2. Draw lines to match each contraction with the two words that go with it.

you've — we have
we've — I have
they've — you have
I've — they have

Horizons® Phonics & Reading Grade 1 Book Two 111

Activity 2. Have the student read the words aloud. The student will draw lines to match each contraction with the two words that go with it.

you've/**you have**
we've/**we have**
they've/**they have**
I've/**I have**

Activity 3. Have the student read the words aloud. The student will write the letters that were left out of each contraction.

I've	**ha**
you've	**ha**
they've	**ha**
we've	**ha**

Activity 4. The student will write three sentences and use at least three of the contractions from the lesson. Help the student with writing and spelling as necessary. Emphasize correct capitalization and punctuation.

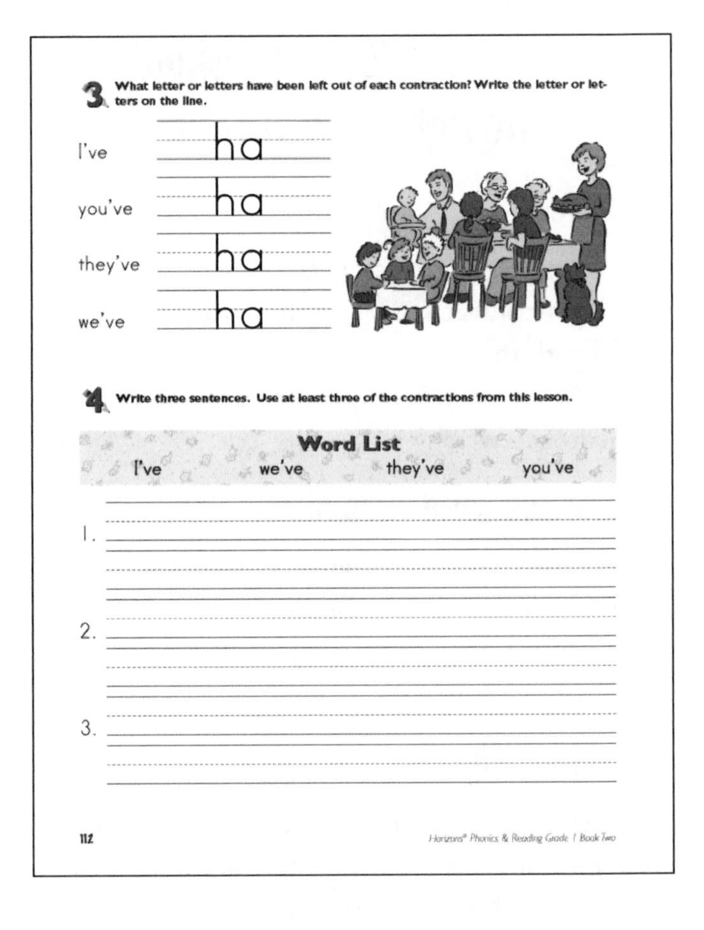

Lesson 127 - Checkup: Contractions with Is

Overview:

- Write two words for each contraction
- Match contractions with two words that go with them
- Write letters that are left out
- Sentence writing

Materials and Supplies:

- Teacher's Guide & Student Workbook
- White board or chalkboard
- Word cards (as necessary)
- Story: *Chet's Mud*

Teaching Tips:

Review the definition. Have the student write examples of contractions on the chalkboard or white board. Assist the student as needed in reading the words in the lesson.

Activity 1. Have the student read the words aloud. The student will write the two words that make up each contraction.

he's	**he is**
she's	**she is**
it's	**it is**

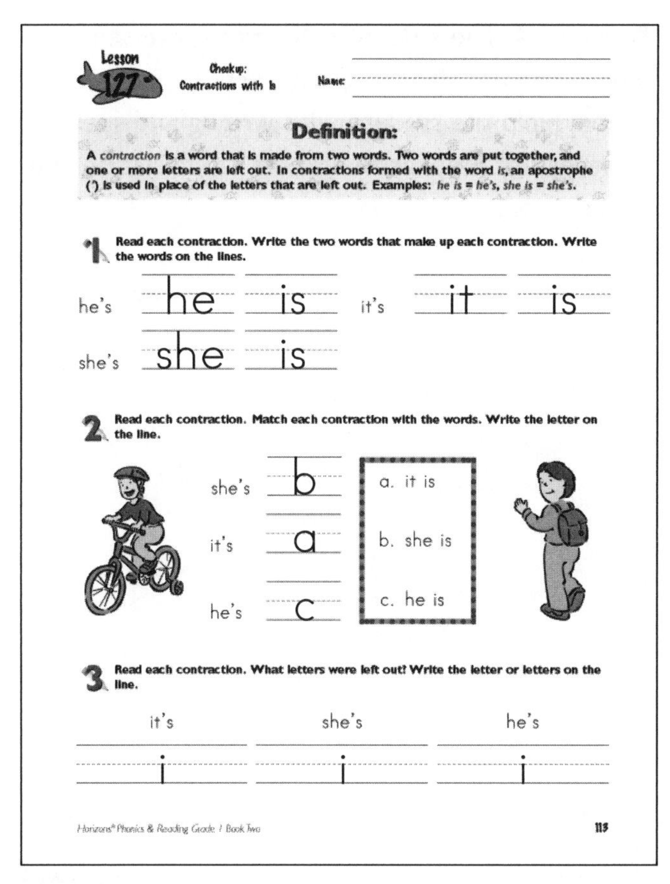
Lesson 127 Checkup: Contractions with Is Name:

Definition:

A *contraction* is a word that is made from two words. Two words are put together, and one or more letters are left out. In contractions formed with the word *is*, an apostrophe (') is used in place of the letters that are left out. Examples: *he is = he's, she is = she's.*

1. Read each contraction. Write the two words that make up each contraction. Write the words on the lines.

he's he is it's it is
she's she is

2. Read each contraction. Match each contraction with the words. Write the letter on the line.

she's b a. it is
it's a b. she is
he's c c. he is

3. Read each contraction. What letters were left out? Write the letter or letters on the line.

it's i she's i he's i

Horizons® Phonics & Reading Grade 1 Book Two 113

Activity 2. Have the student read the words aloud. The student will match each contraction with the two words that it is made from and write the letters on the lines.

1. **b**
2. **a**
3. **c**

Activity 3. Have the student read the contractions and on the line below write the letter that was left out of each contraction.

Omitted letter: **i i i**

Activity 4. The student will write three sentences and use the three contractions from the lesson. Help the student with writing and spelling as necessary. Emphasize correct capitalization and punctuation.

4. Write three sentences. Use one of the contractions from this lesson in each sentence.

Word List		
he's	she's	it's

1. ______________________________

2. ______________________________

3. ______________________________

114 Horizons® Phonics & Reading Grade 1 Book Two

Lesson 128 - Checkup: Contractions with Am & Us

Overview:

- Write two words for each contraction
- Picture/sentence match
- Write letters left out of each contraction
- Sentence writing

Materials and Supplies:

- Teacher's Guide & Student Workbook
- White board or chalkboard
- Word cards (as necessary)
- Story: *Let's Have Fun!*

Teaching Tips:

Review the definition. Have the student write examples of contractions on the chalkboard or white board. Assist the student as needed in identifying the pictures or reading the words in the lesson.

Activity 1. Have the student write the two words that make up each contraction.

I'm: **I am** let's: **let us**

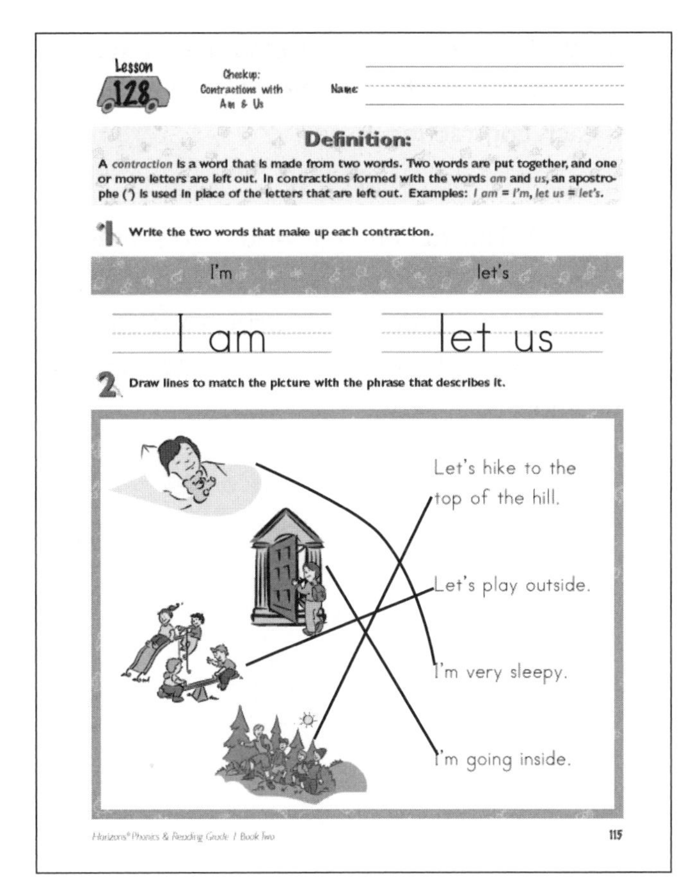

Lesson 128 Checkup: Contractions with Am & Us Name:

Definition:

A *contraction* is a word that is made from two words. Two words are put together, and one or more letters are left out. In contractions formed with the words *am* and *us*, an apostrophe (') is used in place of the letters that are left out. Examples: *I am = I'm, let us = let's.*

1. Write the two words that make up each contraction.

I'm	let's
I am	let us

2. Draw lines to match the picture with the phrase that describes it.

Let's hike to the top of the hill.
Let's play outside.
I'm very sleepy.
I'm going inside.

Horizons Phonics & Reading Grade 1 Book Two 115

Activity 2. Have the student identify the pictures and draw a line to match the pictures with the sentences.

Pictures: **I'm very sleepy.**
I'm going inside.
Let's play outside
Let's hike to the top of the hill.

Activity 3. Have the student read the contractions and write on the line the letter(s) omitted from each contraction.

I'm: **a** let's: **u**

Activity 4. The student will write two sentences, one for each of the contractions studied in the lesson. Help the student with writing and spelling as necessary. Emphasize correct capitalization and punctuation.

3 Read each contraction. What letters are left out? Write the letter or letters that were left out on the line.

I'm a let's u

4 Write a sentence for each contraction.

1.

2.

116 Horizons® Phonics & Reading Grade 1 Book Two

Lesson 129 - Checkup: Contractions with Are

Overview:

- Write two words for each contraction
- Match contractions with two words for each
- Write letters that were left out
- Sentence writing

Materials and Supplies:

- Teacher's Guide & Student Workbook
- White board or chalkboard
- Word cards (as necessary)
- Story: *We're Going on a Trip*

Teaching Tips:

Review the definition. Have the student write examples of the contractions on the chalkboard or white board. Assist the student as needed in reading the words in the lesson.

Activity 1. Have the student read the words aloud. The student will write the two words for each contraction.

they're	**they are**
we're	**we are**
you're	**you are**

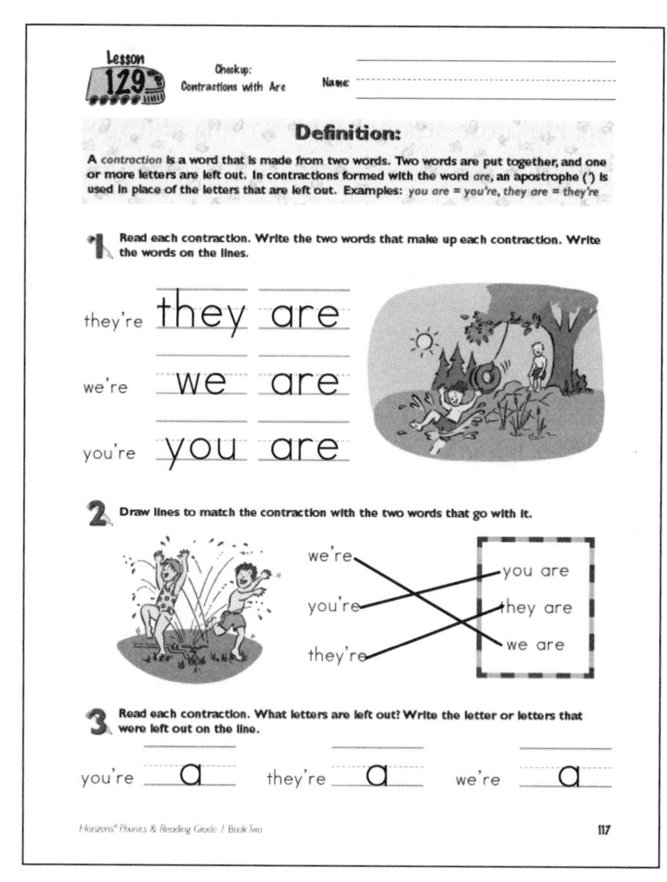
Lesson 129 Checkup: Contractions with Are Name:

Definition:

A *contraction* is a word that is made from two words. Two words are put together, and one or more letters are left out. In contractions formed with the word *are*, an apostrophe (') is used in place of the letters that are left out. Examples: *you are = you're, they are = they're*

1. Read each contraction. Write the two words that make up each contraction. Write the words on the lines.

they're they are
we're we are
you're you are

2. Draw lines to match the contraction with the two words that go with it.

we're — we are
you're — you are
they're — they are

3. Read each contraction. What letters are left out? Write the letter or letters that were left out on the line.

you're a they're a we're a

Horizons® Phonics & Reading Grade 1 Book Two 117

Activity 2. Have the student read the words aloud. The student will draw lines to match each contraction with the two words that go with it.

we're/**we are**
you're/**you are**
they're/**they are**

Activity 3. Have the student read the contractions and write on the line the letter(s) omitted from each contraction.

you're: **a** they're: **a** we're: **a**

Activity 4. The student will write three sentences and use the three contractions from the lesson. Help the student with writing and spelling as necessary. Emphasize correct capitalization and punctuation.

4 Write a sentence for each contraction.

you're	they're	we're

1. ____________________

2. ____________________

3. ____________________

118 Horizons® Phonics & Reading Grade 1 Book Two

Lesson 130 - Checkup: R-Controlled Vowel ar

Overview:

- Picture/word match
- Sentence completion
- Add r-controlled vowel **ar** to words

Materials and Supplies:

- Teacher's Guide & Student Workbook
- White board or chalkboard
- Word cards (as necessary)
- Story: *The Pickle Jar*

Teaching Tips:

Review the rule. Have the student write examples of the rule on the chalkboard or white board. Assist the student as needed in identifying the pictures or reading the words in the lesson.

Activity 1. Have the student identify the pictures and draw a line to match the pictures with the words.

Pictures:	**car**	**jar**
	farm	**star**
		bark

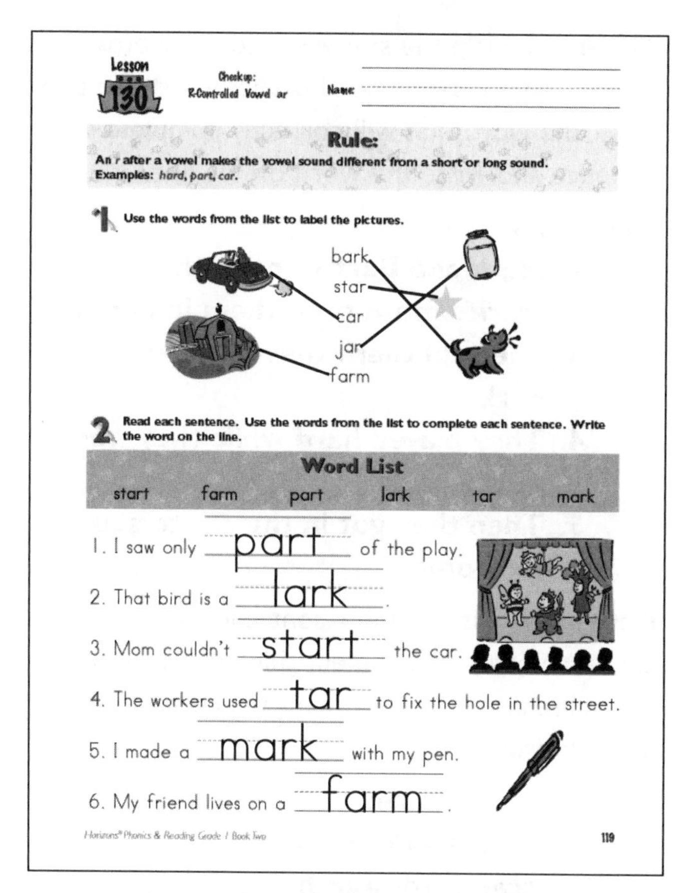

Lesson 130 Checkup: R-Controlled Vowel ar Name:

Rule:
An r after a vowel makes the vowel sound different from a short or long sound.
Examples: *hard, part, car.*

1 Use the words from the list to label the pictures.

bark
star
car
jar
farm

2 Read each sentence. Use the words from the list to complete each sentence. Write the word on the line.

Word List					
start	farm	part	lark	tar	mark

1. I saw only part of the play.
2. That bird is a lark.
3. Mom couldn't start the car.
4. The workers used tar to fix the hole in the street.
5. I made a mark with my pen.
6. My friend lives on a farm.

Horizons® Phonics & Reading Grade 1 Book Two 119

Activity 2. Help the student read the words in the list and the sentences. Instruct the student to select the word that will correctly complete each sentence and write the word on the line.

Sentences:

1. **I saw only part of the play.**
2. **That bird is a lark.**
3. **Mom couldn't start the car.**
4. **The workers used tar to fix the hole in the street.**
5. **I made a mark with my pen.**
6. **My friend lives on a farm.**

Activity 3. Help the student read the words in the list and the sentences. Instruct the student to select the word that will correctly complete each sentence and write the word on the line.

Sentences:

1. **Mark and Bart went to the park.**
2. **Mark's mom took them in her car.**
3. **She told them they could stay until dark.**
4. **They played hard while they were at the park.**
5. **Then they got in the car to start for home.**

Activity 4. Discuss the r-controlled vowel rule for **ar**, and have the student think of additional examples. Instruct the student to add **ar** to each of the words and read them aloud.

Words: **arch, charm, dart**
cart, shark, marsh
scar, yard, starch
smart, sharp, spark

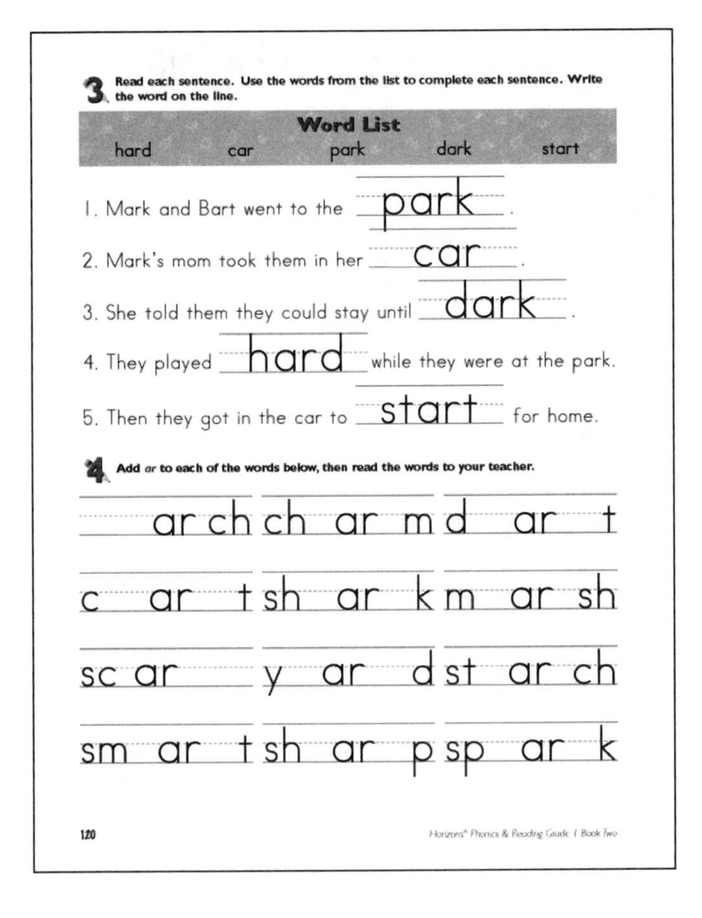

3 Read each sentence. Use the words from the list to complete each sentence. Write the word on the line.

Word List				
hard	car	park	dark	start

1. Mark and Bart went to the park.
2. Mark's mom took them in her car.
3. She told them they could stay until dark.
4. They played hard while they were at the park.
5. Then they got in the car to start for home.

4 Add *ar* to each of the words below, then read the words to your teacher.

ar ch	ch ar m	d ar t
c ar t	sh ar k	m ar sh
sc ar	y ar d	st ar ch
sm ar t	sh ar p	sp ar k

120 Horizons® Phonics & Reading Grade 1 Book Two

Test 13

Lessons 112-130

Instructions:

Review the definition of a contraction. Have the student do some examples of contractions with not, will, and have. Read through the test with the student. Help the student with any words that he/she is still unsure of. The teacher should be available to answer any questions that the student may have during the test.

Activity 1. Review the instructions, the words in the list, and the sentences with the student.

Sentences:

1. **Jack lives in the city.**
2. **The lights are pretty.**
3. **The bird flew by.**
4. **I don't know why that happened.**

Activity 2. Make sure the student can correctly identify the pictures and the words.

Pictures:	car	jar
	shark	bark
		park

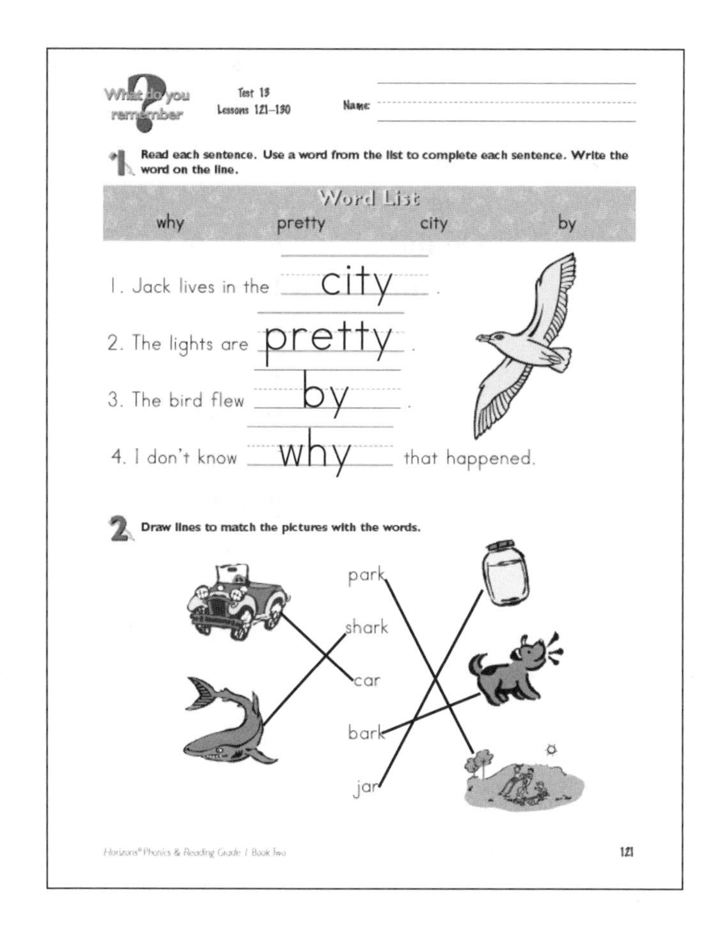
What do you remember

Test 13
Lessons 121–130

Name:

1. Read each sentence. Use a word from the list to complete each sentence. Write the word on the line.

Word List

why pretty city by

1. Jack lives in the city.
2. The lights are pretty.
3. The bird flew by.
4. I don't know why that happened.

2. Draw lines to match the pictures with the words.

park
shark
car
bark
jar

Horizons® Phonics & Reading Grade 1 Book Two

121

Activity 3. Review the instructions and the list of contractions with the student.

Words:

should not	
have not	
are not	**will not**
did not	**I will**
she will	**we will**
you have	**we have**
I have	**let us**
he is	**she is**
I am	**you are**
we are	**they are**

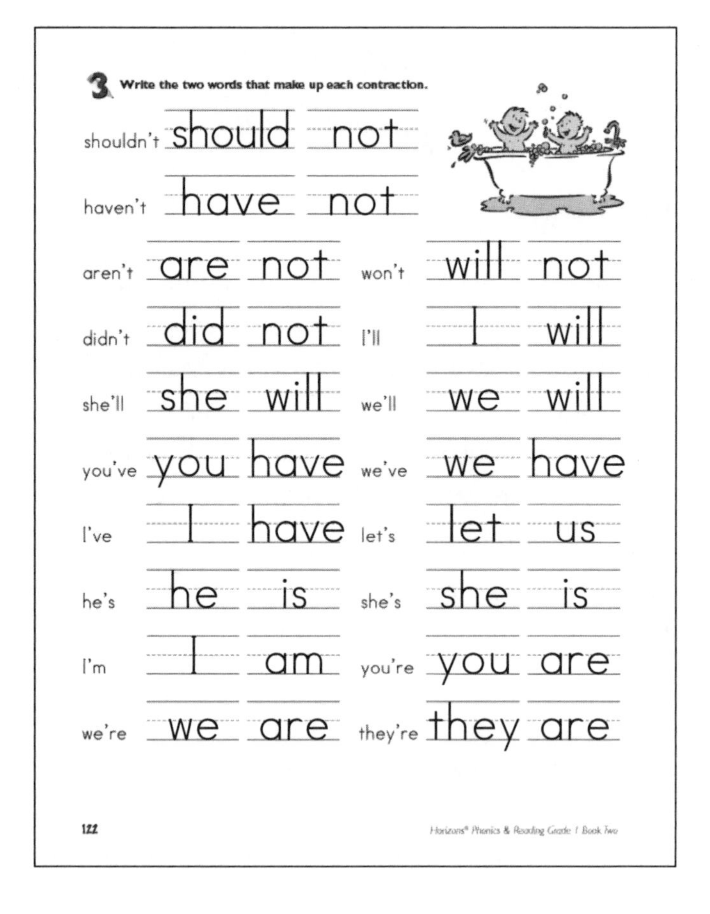
3 Write the two words that make up each contraction.

shouldn't	should	not			
haven't	have	not			
aren't	are	not	won't	will	not
didn't	did	not	I'll	I	will
she'll	she	will	we'll	we	will
you've	you	have	we've	we	have
I've	I	have	let's	let	us
he's	he	is	she's	she	is
I'm	I	am	you're	you	are
we're	we	are	they're	they	are

122 Horizons® Phonics & Reading Grade 1 Book Two

Lesson 131 - Checkup: R-Controlled Vowel or

Overview:

- Riddles
- Add r-controlled vowel **or** to words
- Crossword puzzle
- Auditory recognition of **or** sound
- Sentence completion

Materials and Supplies:

- Teacher's Guide & Student Workbook
- White board or chalkboard
- Word cards (as necessary)
- Story: *Popcorn with a Fork*

Teaching Tips:

Review the rule. Have the student write examples of the rule on the chalkboard or white board. Assist the student as needed in identifying the pictures or reading the words in the lesson.

Activity 1. Have the student read the riddles and the words from the list aloud. The student will use the words from the list to answer the riddles.

1. **popcorn**
2. **horn**
3. **storm**
4. **fork**
5. **thorn**

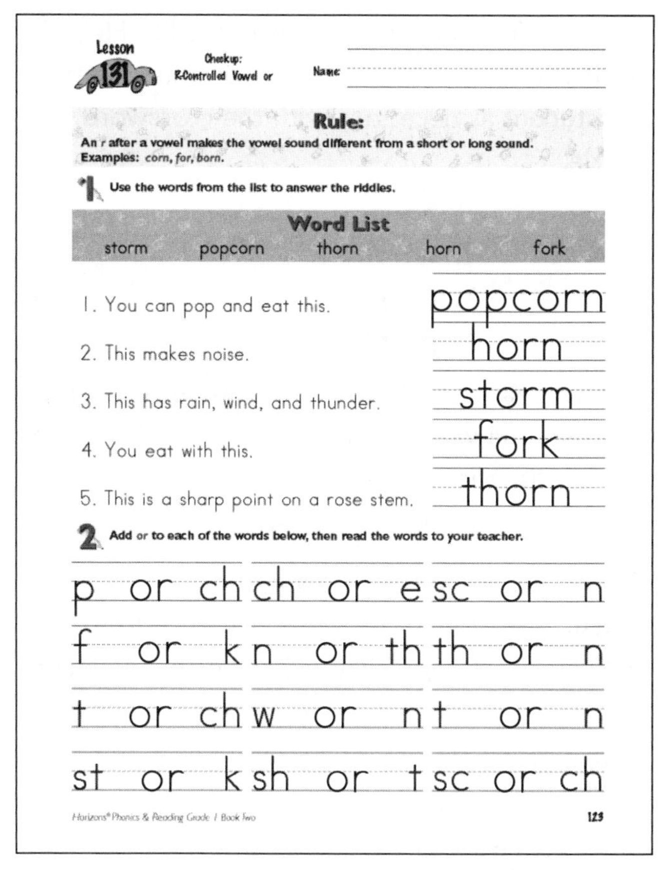

Lesson 131 Checkup: R-Controlled Vowel or Name:

Rule:
An *r* after a vowel makes the vowel sound different from a short or long sound.
Examples: *corn, for, born.*

1 Use the words from the list to answer the riddles.

Word List
storm popcorn thorn horn fork

1. You can pop and eat this. popcorn
2. This makes noise. horn
3. This has rain, wind, and thunder. storm
4. You eat with this. fork
5. This is a sharp point on a rose stem. thorn

2 Add or to each of the words below, then read the words to your teacher.

p or ch	ch or e	sc or n
f or k	n or th	th or n
t or ch	w or n	t or n
st or k	sh or t	sc or ch

Horizons® Phonics & Reading Grade 1 Book Two 123

Activity 2. Discuss the rule for r-controlled vowel **or** and have the student think of additional examples. Instruct the student to add **or** to each of the words and read them aloud.

Words: **porch, chore, scorn**
fork, north, thorn
torch, worn, torn
stork, short, scorch

Activity 3. Review the words in the list. Help the student read the crossword puzzle clues. Assist the student as necessary with the crossword puzzle.

Across: **1. born**
2. north

Down: **3. horn**
4. porch

Activity 4. Have the student name the pictures and read the words aloud. The student will circle the words that name the pictures.

Pictures: **cork, horn, thorn, shore, store**

Activity 5. Help the student read the sentences. Instruct the student to select the word from the choices in Activity 4 that will correctly complete each sentence and write the word on the line.

Sentences:

1. **We use a fork to eat our food.**
2. **The boy tore the paper.**
3. **We went down to the shore to look for crabs.**
4. **I want to have some more play time.**

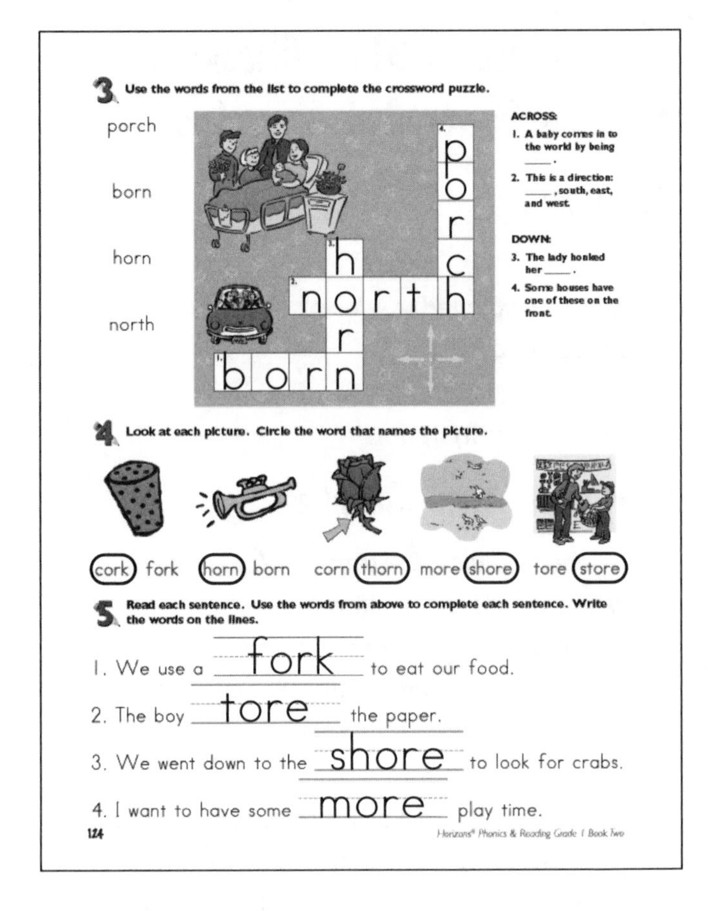

3 Use the words from the list to complete the crossword puzzle.

porch
born
horn
north

ACROSS:
1. A baby comes in to the world by being ____.
2. This is a direction: ____, south, east, and west.

DOWN:
3. The lady honked her ____.
4. Some houses have one of these on the front.

4 Look at each picture. Circle the word that names the picture.

cork fork horn born corn thorn more shore tore store

5 Read each sentence. Use the words from above to complete each sentence. Write the words on the lines.

1. We use a fork to eat our food.
2. The boy tore the paper.
3. We went down to the shore to look for crabs.
4. I want to have some more play time.

124 Horizons® Phonics & Reading Grade 1 Book Two

Lesson 132 - Review: R-Controlled Vowels ar & or

Overview:

- Categorize words
- Sentence completion
- Picture/word match
- Story completion

Materials and Supplies:

- Teacher's Guide & Student Workbook
- White board or chalkboard
- Word cards (as necessary)
- Story: *The Horse in the Barn*

Teaching Tips:

Review the rule. Have the student write examples of the rule on the chalkboard or white board. Assist the student as needed in identifying the pictures or reading the words in the lesson.

Activity 1. Have the student read the words aloud. The student will write the words in the correct categories.

ar: **barn, start, far**
or: **form, torn, forty**

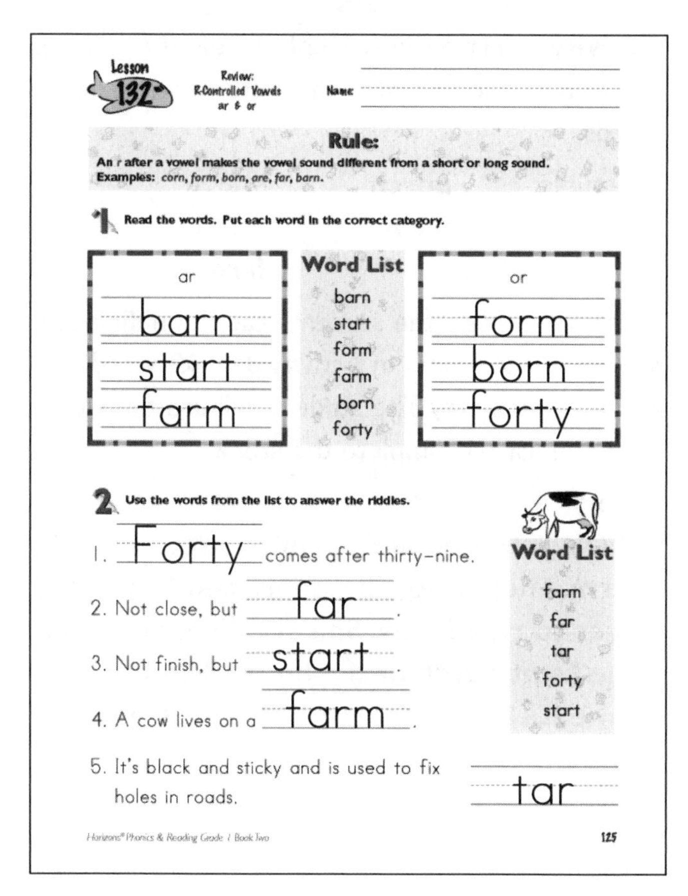

Lesson 132 Review: R-Controlled Vowels ar & or Name:

Rule:
An r after a vowel makes the vowel sound different from a short or long sound.
Examples: corn, form, born, are, far, barn.

1 Read the words. Put each word in the correct category.

ar	Word List	or
barn	barn	form
start	start	born
farm	form	forty
	farm	
	born	
	forty	

2 Use the words from the list to answer the riddles.

1. Forty comes after thirty-nine.
2. Not close, but far.
3. Not finish, but start.
4. A cow lives on a farm.
5. It's black and sticky and is used to fix holes in roads. tar

Word List: farm, far, tar, forty, start

Horizons® Phonics & Reading Grade 1 Book Two 125

Activity 2. Help the student read the words in the list and the riddles. Instruct the student to select the word that will correctly answer each riddle and write the word on the line.

Answers:

1. **Forty**
2. **far**
3. **start**
4. **farm**
5. **tar**

Activity 3. Have the student identify the pictures and draw a line to match the pictures with the words.

Pictures:	**porch**	**star**
	horn	**horse**
		farm

Activity 4. Help the student read the unfinished story and the words in Activity 3. Make word cards as necessary. The student will use the words from the list to complete the story.

Story:

Kay's grandma and grandpa lives on a farm. They have a horse named Betsy. Kay likes to ride Betsy. She also likes to sit on the front porch of the house. The last time Kay was there, she saw a falling star. She made a wish.

3 Draw lines to match the pictures with the words.

horn
porch
farm
star
horse

4 Read the story. Use the words from above to complete the story.

Kay's grandma and grandpa live on a farm. They have a horse named Betsy. Kay likes to ride Betsy. She also likes to sit on the front porch of the house. The last time Kay was there, she saw a falling star.

126

Horizons® Phonics & Reading Grade 1 Book Two

Lesson 133 - Checkup: R-Controlled Vowel er

Overview:

- Identify words with **er** sound
- Sentence completion
- Sentence writing
- Add r-controlled vowel **er** to words

Materials and Supplies:

- Teacher's Guide & Student Workbook
- White board or chalkboard
- Word cards (as necessary)
- Story: *The Office Clerk*

Teaching Tips:

Review the rule. Have the student write examples of the rule on the chalkboard or white board. Assist the student as needed in identifying the pictures or reading the words in the lesson.

Activity 1. Have the student name the pictures and read the words aloud. The student will circle the words that name the pictures.

Pictures: **fern, hammer, farmer, clerk**

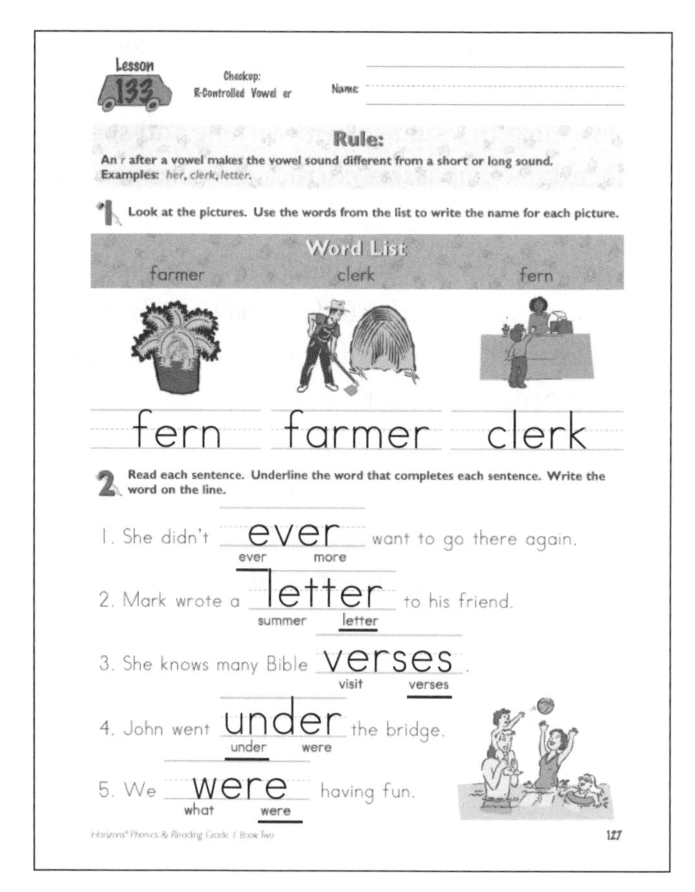

Lesson 133

Checkup: R-Controlled Vowel er

Name:

Rule:

An r after a vowel makes the vowel sound different from a short or long sound.
Examples: *her, clerk, letter.*

1. Look at the pictures. Use the words from the list to write the name for each picture.

Word List

farmer clerk fern

fern farmer clerk

2. Read each sentence. Underline the word that completes each sentence. Write the word on the line.

1. She didn't ever want to go there again. (ever / more)
2. Mark wrote a letter to his friend. (summer / letter)
3. She knows many Bible verses. (visit / verses)
4. John went under the bridge. (under / were)
5. We were having fun. (what / were)

Horizons Phonics & Reading Grade 1 Book Two 127

Activity 2. Help the student read the sentences and the word choices. Instruct the student to underline the word that will correctly complete each sentence and write the word on the line.

Sentences:

1. **She didn't ever want to go there again.**
2. **Mark wrote a letter to his friend.**
3. **She knows many Bible verses.**
4. **John went under the bridge.**
5. **We were having fun.**

Activity 3. The student will write three sentences and use at least three of the words from the list. Help the student with writing and spelling as necessary. Emphasize correct capitalization and punctuation.

Activity 4. Discuss the rule for r-controlled vowel **er**, and have the student think of additional examples. Instruct the student to add **er** to each of the words and read them aloud.

Words: **stern, better, never**
clerk, perch, term
herd, letter, fern
winter, summer, under

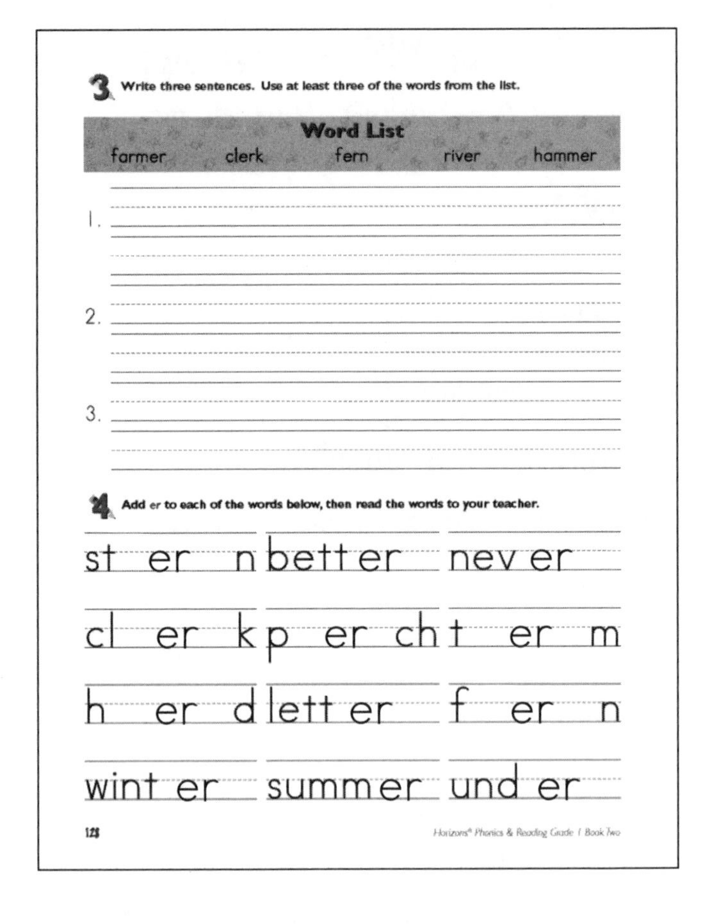
3. Write three sentences. Use at least three of the words from the list.

Word List
farmer clerk fern river hammer

1.

2.

3.

4. Add er to each of the words below, then read the words to your teacher.

st er n better never
cl er k p er ch t er m
h er d lett er f er n
wint er summer und er

123 Horizons® Phonics & Reading Grade 1 Book Two

Lesson 134 - Checkup: R-Controlled Vowel ir

Overview:

- Picture/word match
- Sentence completion
- Riddles
- Add r-controlled vowel **ir** to words

Materials and Supplies:

- Teacher's Guide & Student Workbook
- White board or chalkboard
- Word cards (as necessary)
- Story: *The Girl with the Dirty Face*

Teaching Tips:

Review the rule. Have the student write examples of the rule on the chalkboard or white board. Assist the student as needed in identifying the pictures or reading the words in the lesson.

Activity 1. Have the student identify the pictures and draw a line to match the pictures with the words.

Pictures:	**dirty**	**girl**
	shirt	**skirt**
		bird

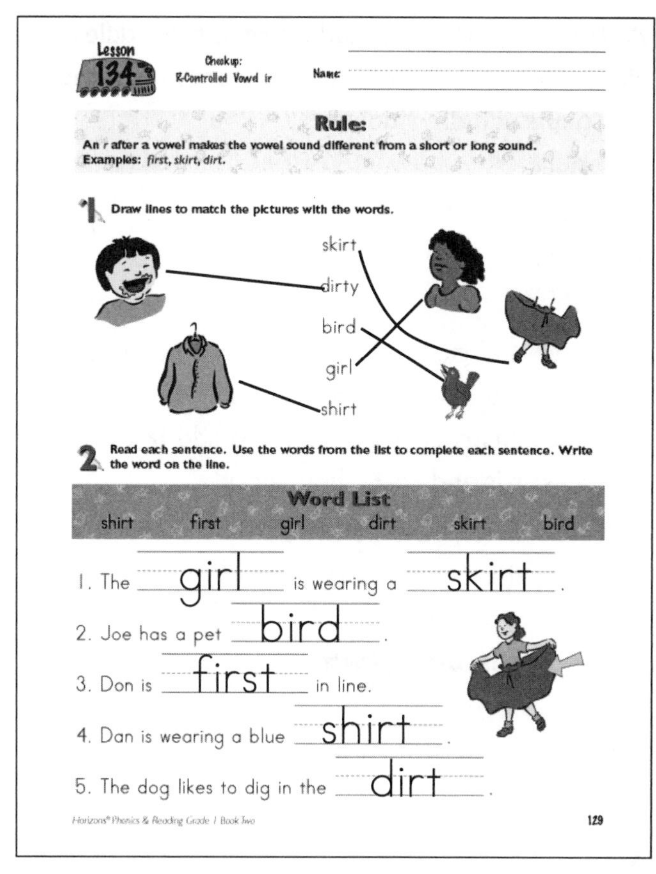

Lesson 134 Checkup: R-Controlled Vowel ir Name:

Rule:
An *r* after a vowel makes the vowel sound different from a short or long sound.
Examples: *first, skirt, dirt.*

1. **Draw lines to match the pictures with the words.**

skirt
dirty
bird
girl
shirt

2. **Read each sentence. Use the words from the list to complete each sentence. Write the word on the line.**

Word List
shirt first girl dirt skirt bird

1. The girl is wearing a skirt.
2. Joe has a pet bird.
3. Don is first in line.
4. Dan is wearing a blue shirt.
5. The dog likes to dig in the dirt.

Horizons® Phonics & Reading Grade 1 Book Two 129

Activity 2. Help the student read the words in the list and the sentences. Instruct the student to select the word that will correctly complete each sentence and write the word on the line.

Sentences:

1. **The girl is wearing a skirt.**
2. **Joe has a pet bird.**
3. **Don is first in line.**
4. **Dan is wearing a blue shirt.**
5. **The dog likes to dig in the dirt.**

Activity 3. Have the student read the riddles aloud. The student will use the words from the list to answer the riddles.

1. **first**
2. **girl**
3. **dirt**
4. **shirt**

Activity 4. Discuss the rule for r-controlled vowel **ir**, and have the student think of additional examples. Instruct the student to add **ir** to each of the words and read them aloud.

Words: **firm, swirl, thirst**
first, dirty, smirk
whirl, chirp, shirt
stir, birth, twirl

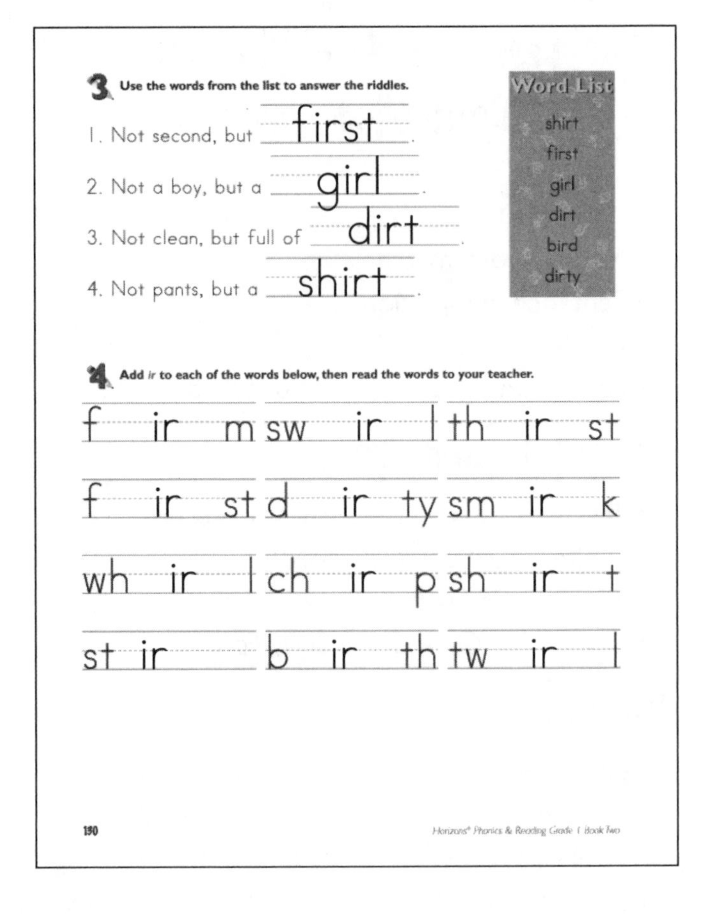

3. Use the words from the list to answer the riddles.
1. Not second, but first.
2. Not a boy, but a girl.
3. Not clean, but full of dirt.
4. Not pants, but a shirt.
Word List
shirt
first
girl
dirt
bird
dirty
4. Add ir to each of the words below, then read the words to your teacher.
f ir m sw ir l th ir st
f ir st d ir ty sm ir k
wh ir l ch ir p sh ir t
st ir b ir th tw ir l
190
Horizons® Phonics & Reading Grade 1 Book Two

Lesson 135 - Review: R-Controlled Vowels er & ir

Overview:

- Categorize words by r-controlled vowel sound
- Sentence completion
- Crossword puzzle
- Matching

Materials and Supplies:

- Teacher's Guide & Student Workbook
- White board or chalkboard
- Word cards (as necessary)
- Story: *The Boy Who Had to be First*

Teaching Tips:

Review the rules. Have the student write examples of the rules on the chalkboard or white board. Assist the student as needed in identifying the pictures or reading the words in the lesson.

Activity 1. Have the student read the words aloud. The student will write the words into the correct categories.

er: **her, clerk, ever**
ir: **third, first, dirt**

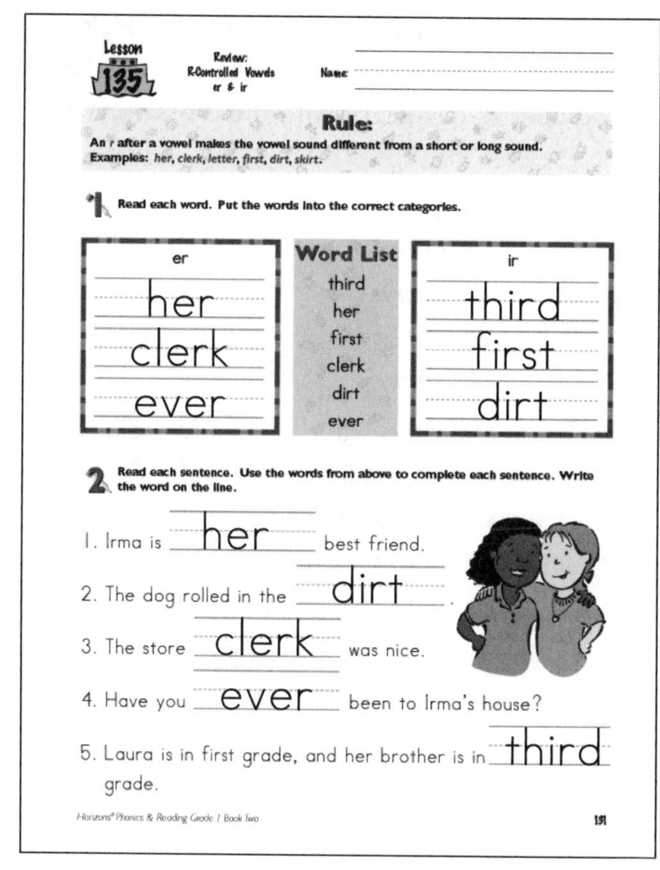
Lesson 135
Review: R-Controlled Vowels er & ir
Name:

Rule:
An *r* after a vowel makes the vowel sound different from a short or long sound.
Examples: *her, clerk, letter, first, dirt, skirt.*

1 Read each word. Put the words into the correct categories.

er	Word List	ir
her	third	third
clerk	her	first
ever	first	dirt
	clerk	
	dirt	
	ever	

2 Read each sentence. Use the words from above to complete each sentence. Write the word on the line.

1. Irma is her best friend.
2. The dog rolled in the dirt.
3. The store clerk was nice.
4. Have you ever been to Irma's house?
5. Laura is in first grade, and her brother is in third grade.

Horizons® Phonics & Reading Grade 1 Book Two 151

Activity 2. Help the student read the words in the sentences. Instruct the student to select the word from the list in Activity 1 that will correctly complete each sentence and write the word on the line.

Sentences:

1. **Irma is her best friend.**
2. **The dog rolled in the dirt.**
3. **The store clerk was nice.**
4. **Have you ever been to Irma's house?**
5. **Laura is in first grade, and her brother is in third grade.**

Activity 3. Review the words in the list. Help the student read the crossword puzzle clues. Assist the student as necessary with the crossword puzzle.

Across:	**3. bird**
	5. third
Down:	**1. skirt**
	2. river
	4. dirt

Activity 4. Have the student identify the pictures and find the corresponding word in the list. Instruct the student to write the letter for the word on the line beside the picture.

Pictures: **dirt (a)** **shirt (e)** **bird (d)** **girl (b)** **skirt (c)**

3. Use the words from the list to complete the crossword puzzle.

skirt third dirt river bird

ACROSS:
3. The ___ flew in the sky.
5. After second comes ___.

DOWN:
1. My mom got a new a ___.
2. The boat floated down the ___.
4. The farmer filled the hole with ___.

4. Look at each picture. Find the word that goes with it. Write the letter for the word on the line.

a. dirt
b. girl
c. skirt
d. bird
e. shirt

132 Horizons® Phonics & Reading Grade 1 Book Two

Lesson 136 - Checkup: R-Controlled Vowel ur

Overview:

- Picture/word match
- Sentence completion
- Story completion
- Add r-controlled vowel **ur** to words

Materials and Supplies:

- Teacher's Guide & Student Workbook
- White board or chalkboard
- Word cards (as necessary)
- Story: *The Nice Nurse*

Teaching Tips:

Review the rule. Have the student write examples of the rule on the chalkboard or white board. Assist the student as needed in identifying the pictures or reading the words in the lesson.

Activity 1. Have the student identify the pictures and draw a line to match the pictures with the words.

Pictures: **purse** **nurse** **turtle** **burn** **fur**

Lesson 136 Checkup: R-Controlled Vowel ur Name:

Rule:
An r after a vowel makes the vowel sound different from a short or long sound.
Examples: nurse, fur, burn.

1. Draw lines to match the pictures with the words.

turtle
burn
nurse
fur
purse

2. Read each sentence. Use the words from above to complete each sentence. Write the word on the line

1. The turtle went into its shell.
2. Jim got a burn when he touched the hot stove.
3. The nurse at the doctor's office takes care of us.
4. Mom carries a big brown purse to keep her things in.
5. Our dog has black fur to keep him warm.

Horizons® Phonics & Reading Grade 1 Book Two 133

Activity 2. Help the student read the sentences. Instruct the student to select the word from Activity 1 that will correctly complete each sentence and write the word on the line.

Sentences:

1. **The turtle went into its shell.**
2. **Jim got a burn when he touched the hot stove.**
3. **The nurse at the doctor's office takes care of us.**
4. **Mom carries a big brown purse to keep her things in.**
5. **Our dog has black fur to keep him warm.**

Activity 3. Help the student read the unfinished story and the words in the list. Make word cards as necessary. The student will use the words from the list to complete the story.

Story:

Carol is happy because her birthday is coming soon. Carol will turn seven. She will have a party and invite her friends and family. She plans to curl her hair so that she will look pretty. Even her pet turtle will be there!

Activity 4. Discuss the rule for r-controlled vowel **ur**, and have the student think of additional examples. Instruct the student to add **ur** to each of the words and read them aloud.

Words: **burst, curl, church**
hurt, plural, curb
turn, turtle, lurch
churn, spur, blur

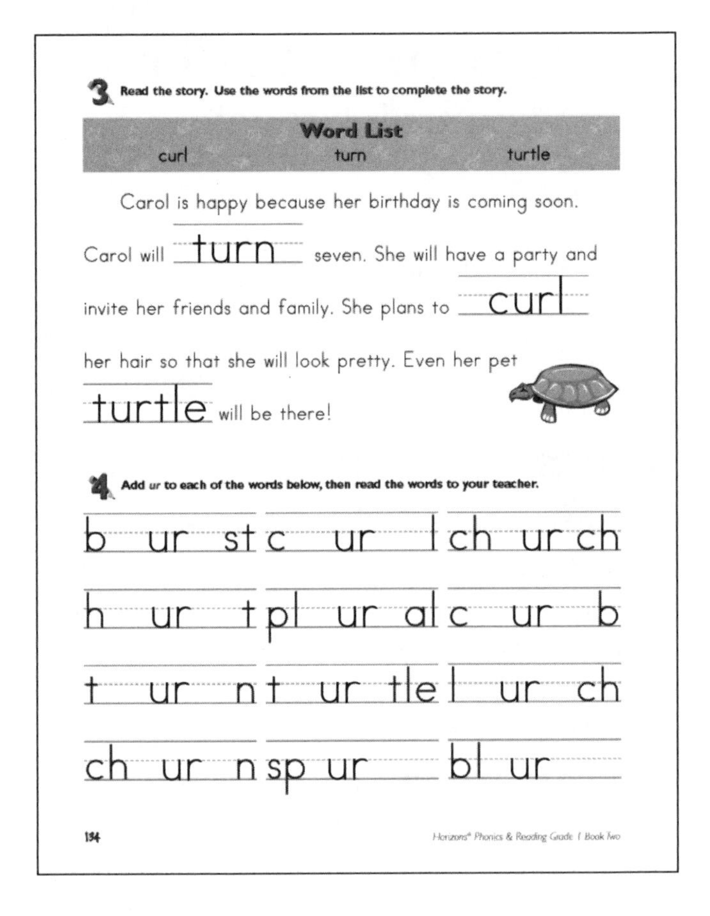

3 Read the story. Use the words from the list to complete the story.

Word List

curl turn turtle

Carol is happy because her birthday is coming soon. Carol will turn seven. She will have a party and invite her friends and family. She plans to curl her hair so that she will look pretty. Even her pet turtle will be there!

4 Add *ur* to each of the words below, then read the words to your teacher.

b ur st	c ur l	ch ur ch
h ur t	pl ur al	c ur b
t ur n	t ur tle	l ur ch
ch ur n	sp ur	bl ur

154 *Horizons® Phonics & Reading Grade 1 Book Two*

Lesson 137 - Writing Lesson: Journal Entry

Overview:

- Make a journal entry

Materials and Supplies:

- Teacher's Guide & Student Workbook
- White board or chalkboard
- Word cards (as necessary)
- Story: *Carol's Journal*

Teaching Tips:

Go over the directions for the journal entry with the student. Help the student think of ideas as needed. The teacher or writing partner should help the student with spelling and punctuation as necessary. The student will write the rough draft on a piece of paper and the final draft in the student workbook. (**Optional**: You may want to encourage the student to begin keeping a real journal at home to improve their spelling and writing skills.)

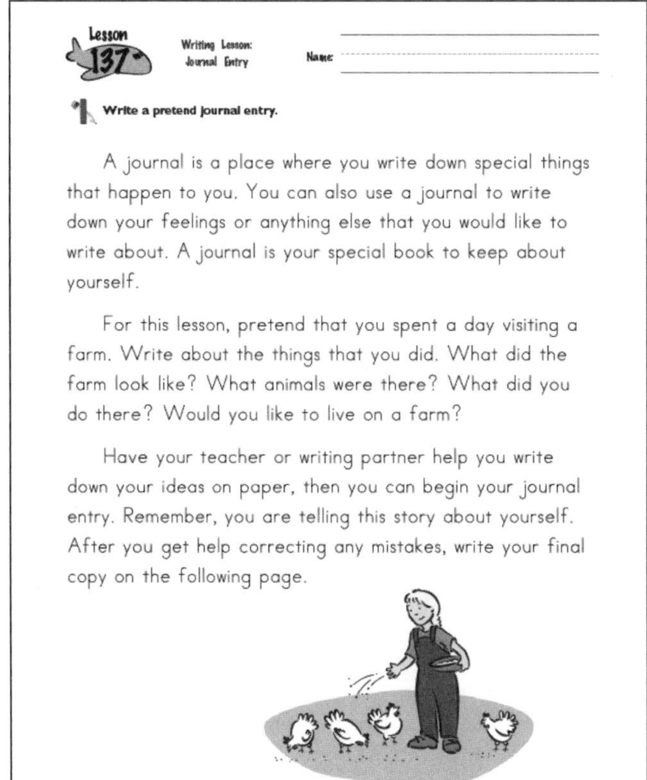
Lesson 137 Writing Lesson: Journal Entry Name:

1. Write a pretend journal entry.

A journal is a place where you write down special things that happen to you. You can also use a journal to write down your feelings or anything else that you would like to write about. A journal is your special book to keep about yourself.

For this lesson, pretend that you spent a day visiting a farm. Write about the things that you did. What did the farm look like? What animals were there? What did you do there? Would you like to live on a farm?

Have your teacher or writing partner help you write down your ideas on paper, then you can begin your journal entry. Remember, you are telling this story about yourself. After you get help correcting any mistakes, write your final copy on the following page.

Horizons® Phonics & Reading Grade 1 Book Two 195

Activity 1. Write a pretend journal entry.

196

Horizons® Phonics & Reading Grade 1 Book Two

Lesson 138 - Checkup: Prefix re-

Overview:

- Matching words with definitions
- Picture/word match
- Identifying base words
- Sentence writing

Materials and Supplies:

- Teacher's Guide & Student Workbook
- White board or chalkboard
- Word cards (as necessary)
- Story: *Repacking the Backpack*

Teaching Tips:

Review the rule. Have the student write examples of the rule on the chalkboard or white board. Assist the student as needed in identifying the pictures or reading the words in the lesson.

Activity 1. Have the student read the words aloud. The student will match the words with their meanings by writing the letter for each meaning on the lines.

reread	**d.**	**a.**	redo
retie	**g.**	**b.**	repack
rewrite	**e.**	**c.**	reload
rewind	**h.**	**f.**	remake

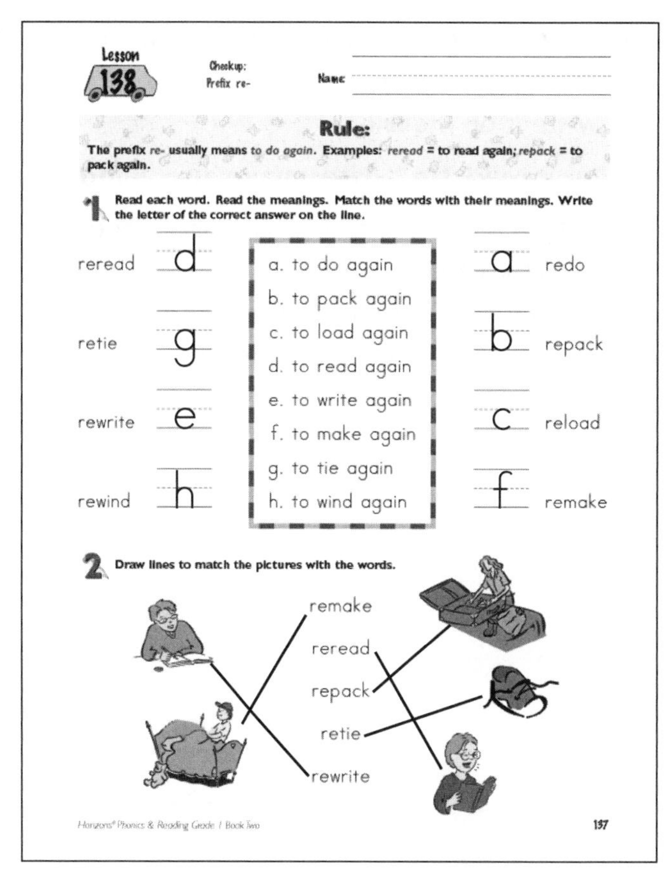

Lesson 138 Checkup: Prefix re- Name:

Rule:
The prefix re- usually means to do again. Examples: reread = to read again; repack = to pack again.

1. Read each word. Read the meanings. Match the words with their meanings. Write the letter of the correct answer on the line.

reread	d	a. to do again	a	redo
		b. to pack again		
retie	g	c. to load again	b	repack
		d. to read again		
		e. to write again		
rewrite	e	f. to make again	c	reload
		g. to tie again		
rewind	h	h. to wind again	f	remake

2. Draw lines to match the pictures with the words.

remake
reread
repack
retie
rewrite

137

Activity 2. Have the student identify the pictures and draw a line to match the pictures with the words.

Pictures:		
	rewrite	**repack**
	remake	**retie**
		reread

Activity 3. Have the student read the words aloud. Tell the student to identify the base word and write it on the line.

Words: **read, tie, write, make, use, wind**

Activity 4. The student will write four sentences and use at least eight of the words from the lesson. Help the student with writing and spelling as necessary. Emphasize correct capitalization and punctuation.

3 Read each word. Write the base word for each one.

reread	read	remake	make
retie	tie	reuse	use
rewrite	write	rewind	wind

4 Write four sentences. Use at least eight of the words from the word list.

Word List

reread, retie, rewrite, rewind, redo, repack, reload, remake, reuse

1. ______

2. ______

3. ______

4. ______

198 Horizons® Phonics & Reading Grade 1 Book Two

Lesson 139 - Checkup: Prefix un-

Overview:

- Picture/word match
- Sentence completion
- Identify the base word
- Sentence writing

Materials and Supplies:

- Teacher's Guide & Student Workbook
- White board or chalkboard
- Word cards (as necessary)
- Story: *The Unhappy Boy*

Teaching Tips:

Review the rule. Have the student write examples of the rule on the chalkboard or white board. Assist the student as needed in identifying the pictures or reading the words in the lesson.

Activity 1. Have the student identify the pictures and draw a line to match the pictures with the words.

Pictures: **unload** **unbutton** **unhappy** **unwrap**

Lesson 139 Checkup: Prefix un- Name:

Rule:
The prefix *un-* usually means the *opposite* of the original word. Examples: *unbutton, unlock.*

1. Look at each picture. Use the words from the list to write the word that goes with each picture.

unhappy
unbutton
unload
unwrap

unload unbutton
unhappy unwrap

2. Read each sentence. Use the words from above to complete each sentence.

1. The boy was unhappy about losing his toy.
2. She can unbutton her coat by herself.
3. On your birthday, you unwrap your gifts.
4. The men will unload the moving van.

Horizons® Phonics & Reading Grade 1 Book Two 199

Activity 2. Help the student read the sentences. Instruct the student to select the word from Activity 1 that will correctly complete each sentence and write the word on the line.

Sentences:

1. **The boy was unhappy about losing his toy.**
2. **She can unbutton her coat by herself.**
3. **On your birthday, you unwrap your gifts.**
4. **The men will unload the moving van.**

Activity 3. Have the student read the words aloud. Tell the student to identify the base word and write it on the line.

Words: **load, buckle, do, tie, happy, safe**

Activity 4. The student will write four sentences and use at least six of the words from the list. Help the student with writing and spelling as necessary. Emphasize correct capitalization and punctuation.

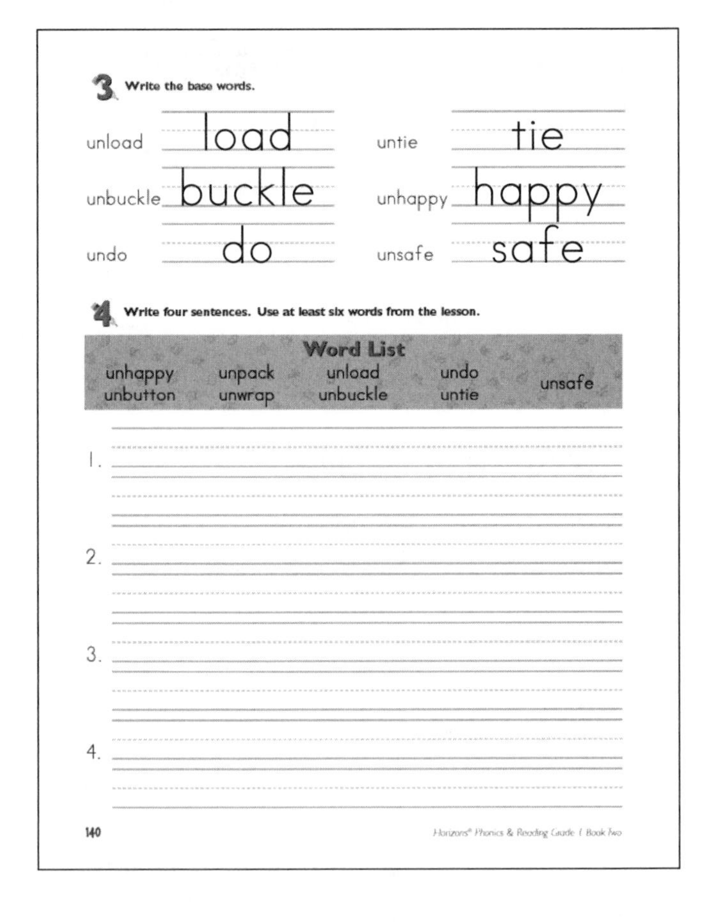

Lesson 140 - Checkup: Prefix dis-

Overview:

- Write base words
- Match words with meanings
- Sentence writing

Materials and Supplies:

- Teacher's Guide & Student Workbook
- White board or chalkboard
- Word cards (as necessary)
- Story: *Kyle Dislikes His Food*

Teaching Tips:

Review the rule. Have the student write examples of the rule on the chalkboard or white board. Assist the student as needed in identifying the pictures or reading the words in the lesson.

Activity 1. Have the student read the words aloud. The student will write the base words.

Base words: **agree** **grace**
order **cover**
obey **please**
like **trust**

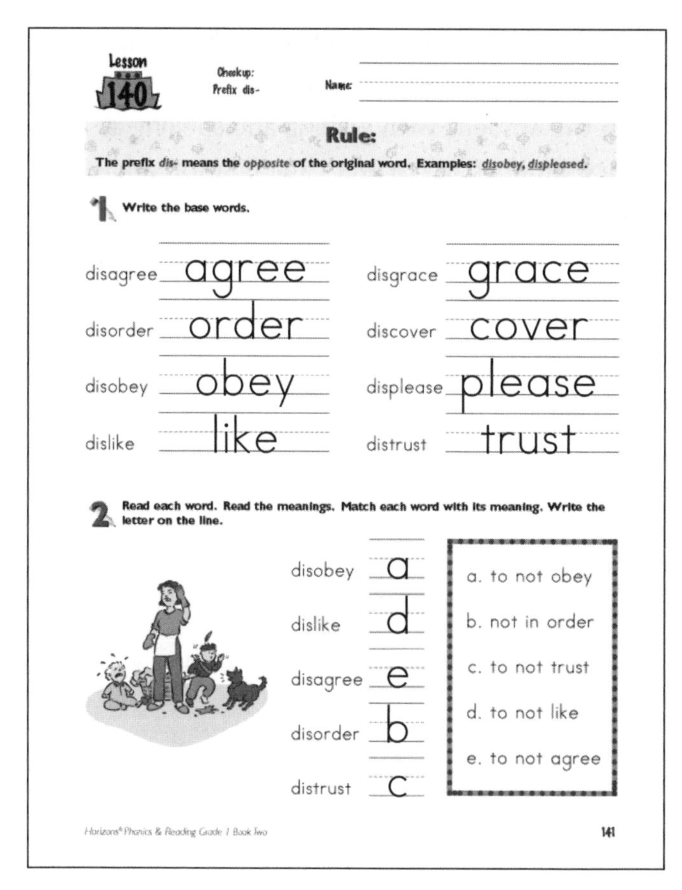

Lesson 140 Checkup: Prefix dis- Name:

Rule:
The prefix dis- means the opposite of the original word. Examples: disobey, displeased.

1 Write the base words.

disagree agree — disgrace grace
disorder order — discover cover
disobey obey — displease please
dislike like — distrust trust

2 Read each word. Read the meanings. Match each word with its meaning. Write the letter on the line.

disobey a
dislike d
disagree e
disorder b
distrust c

a. to not obey
b. not in order
c. to not trust
d. to not like
e. to not agree

Horizons® Phonics & Reading Grade 1 Book Two 141

Activity 2. Have the student read the words aloud. The student will match each word with its meaning by writing the letter for the meaning on the line next to the word.

disobey	**a**
dislike	**d**
disagree	**e**
disorder	**b**
distrust	**c**

Activity 3. The student will write five sentences and use at least five of the words from the list. Help the student with writing and spelling as necessary. Emphasize correct capitalization and punctuation.

3 Write five sentences. Use at least *five* words from this lesson.

Word List			
disagree	disobey	discover	displease
disorder	disgrace	dislike	distrust

1.

2.

3.

4.

5.

142 Horizons® Phonics & Reading Grade 1 Book Two

Test 14

Lessons 131-140

Instructions:

Review the rule on r-controlled vowels. Have the student give examples of words in which the r controls the sound of the vowel next to it (**turn**, **shirt**, **her**, **born**, **flower**). Review the prefixes **re-**, **un-**, and **dis-**. Have the student give the meanings of these prefixes. Read through the test with the student. Help the student with any words that he/she is still unsure of. The teacher should be available to answer any questions that the student may have during the test.

Activity 1. Review the words in the list and the sentences with the student.

Sentences:

1. **Grandma's house is far away from our house.**
2. **John is third in line.**
3. **Her name is Joan.**
4. **Were you at school today?**
5. **Jack is wearing a blue shirt.**
6. **The car made a wrong turn.**
7. **Mark got a bad burn when he touched the hot stove.**
8. **John baby brother was just born today.**
9. **A rose is a pretty flower.**

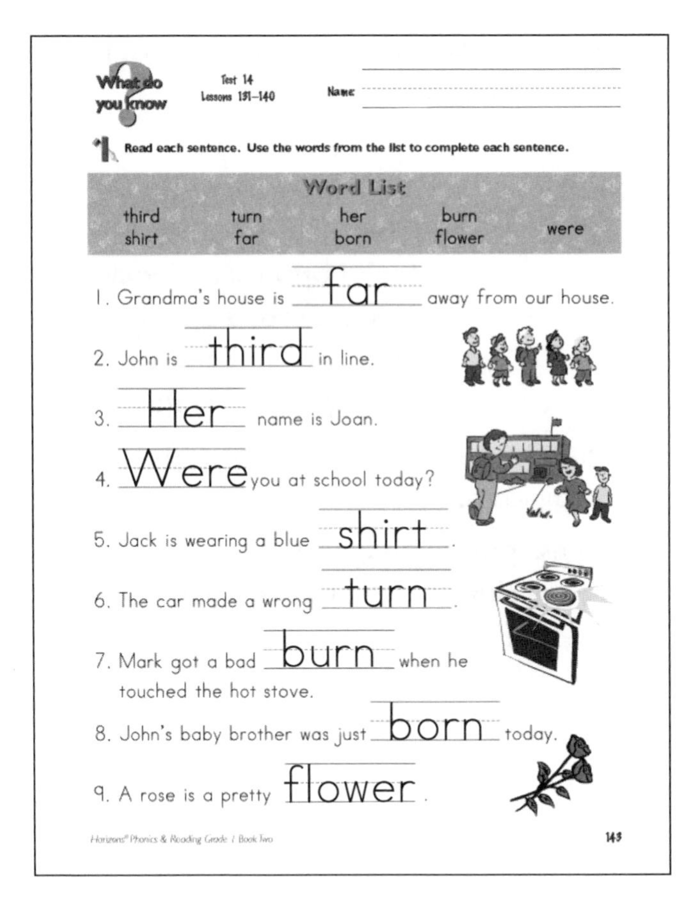

What do you know

Test 14
Lessons 131–140

Name:

1 Read each sentence. Use the words from the list to complete each sentence.

Word List				
third	turn	her	burn	were
shirt	far	born	flower	

1. Grandma's house is far away from our house.
2. John is third in line.
3. Her name is Joan.
4. Were you at school today?
5. Jack is wearing a blue shirt.
6. The car made a wrong turn.
7. Mark got a bad burn when he touched the hot stove.
8. John's baby brother was just born today.
9. A rose is a pretty flower.

Horizons® Phonics & Reading Grade 1 Book Two 145

Activity 2. Make sure the student can read the words and phrases to be matched.

Words: **redo / to do again**
untie / opposite of tie
disobey / to not obey
unlock / opposite of lock
reread / to read again
distrust / to not trust
undo / opposite of do

Activity 3. Make sure the student correctly identifies the pictures.

Pictures: **porch, dirt, park, fern**
skirt, turtle, horse, shirt

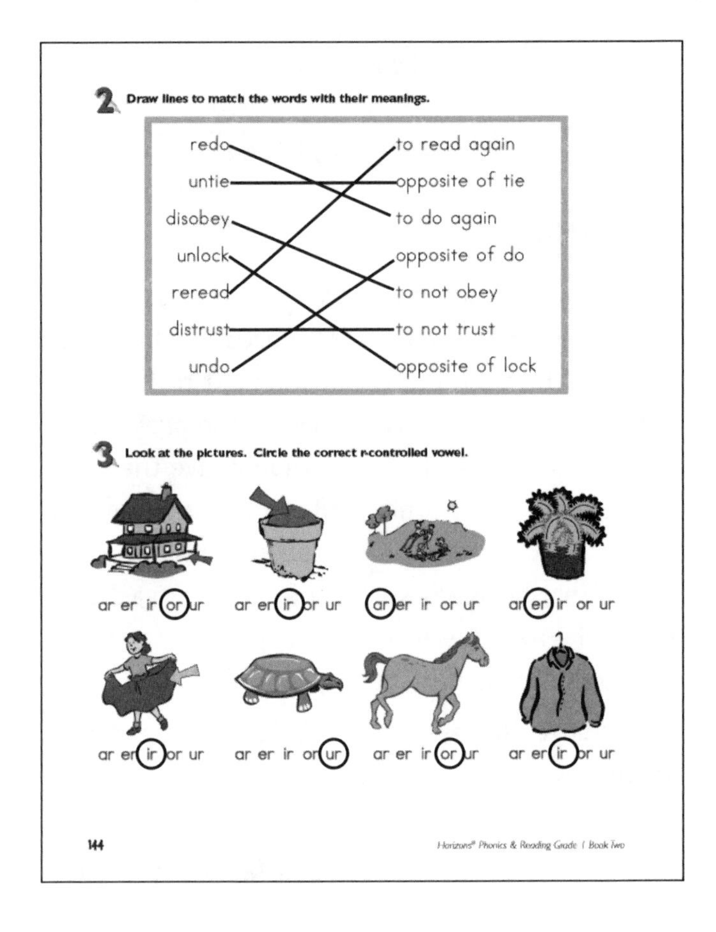

2. Draw lines to match the words with their meanings.

redo	to read again
untie	opposite of tie
disobey	to do again
unlock	opposite of do
reread	to not obey
distrust	to not trust
undo	opposite of lock

3. Look at the pictures. Circle the correct r-controlled vowel.

ar er ir or ur ar er ir or ur ar er ir or ur ar er ir or ur

ar er ir or ur ar er ir or ur ar er ir or ur ar er ir or ur

144 Horizons® Phonics & Reading Grade 1 Book Two

Lesson 141 - Checkup: Capitalization & Punctuation

Overview:

- Copy and punctuate sentences
- Read paragraph and recognize punctuation marks
- Copy and punctuate paragraph

Materials and Supplies:

- Teacher's Guide & Student Workbook
- White board or chalkboard
- Word cards (as necessary)
- Story: *Why Play a Xylophone?*

Teaching Tips:

Review punctuation rules from Lesson 11 in Student Book One. Write the three types of sentences on the board, omitting punctuation, and ask what type of sentence each one is (statement, question, exclamation). Ask the student what the correct ending punctuation is for each type of sentence. This lesson will also discuss quotation marks. Write several sentences and show how to correctly punctuate with quotation marks. Have the student punctuate some of the examples. Assist the student as needed in identifying the pictures or reading the words in the lesson.

Activity 1. Have the student read the first sentence aloud. Discuss what type of sentence it is: exclamation, statement, or question. Instruct the student to copy the sentence on the line below, adding the correct punctuation and capitalization. Do the same with the second sentence.

Sentences:
Are Jim and Jan ready yet?
Mrs. Davis is my mom's best friend.

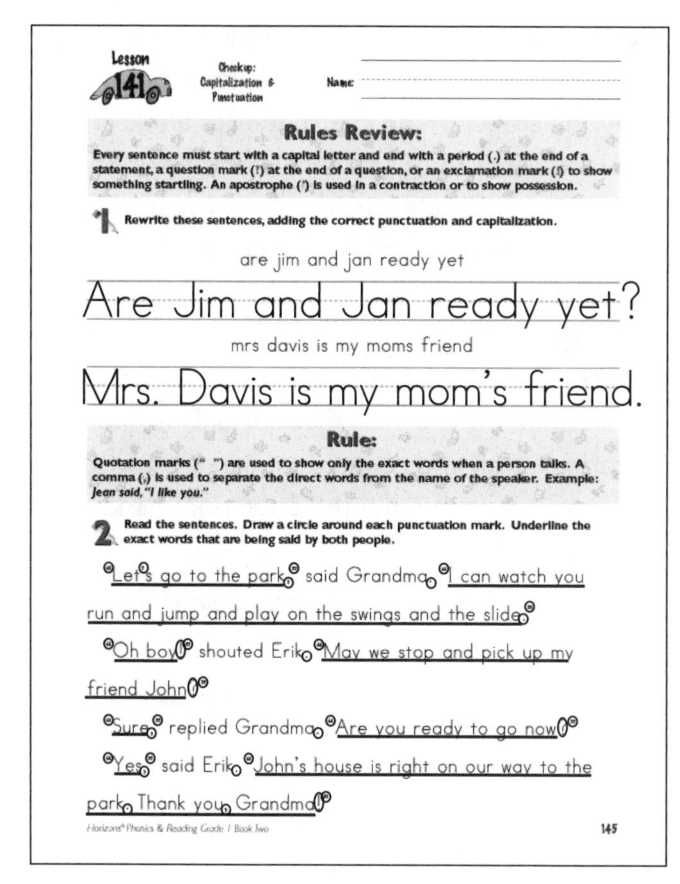

Lesson 141 Checkup: Capitalization & Punctuation Name:

Rules Review:
Every sentence must start with a capital letter and end with a period (.) at the end of a statement, a question mark (?) at the end of a question, or an exclamation mark (!) to show something startling. An apostrophe (') is used in a contraction or to show possession.

1 **Rewrite these sentences, adding the correct punctuation and capitalization.**

are jim and jan ready yet

Are Jim and Jan ready yet?

mrs davis is my moms friend

Mrs. Davis is my mom's friend.

Rule:
Quotation marks (" ") are used to show only the exact words when a person talks. A comma (,) is used to separate the direct words from the name of the speaker. Example: ***Jean said, "I like you."***

2 **Read the sentences. Draw a circle around each punctuation mark. Underline the exact words that are being said by both people.**

"Let's go to the park," said Grandma. "I can watch you run and jump and play on the swings and the slide."

"Oh boy!" shouted Erik. "May we stop and pick up my friend John?"

"Sure," replied Grandma. "Are you ready to go now?"

"Yes," said Erik. "John's house is right on our way to the park. Thank you, Grandma!"

Horizons® Phonics & Reading Grade 1 Book Two 145

Activity 2. Have the student read the paragraph aloud, assisting as needed. Review the rule about quotation marks and instruct the student to circle all punctuation marks, including commas, periods, quote marks, etc. Have the student underline the exact words that are being said. Remind the student that these words are found between the quotation marks.

"<u>Let's go to the park</u>," said Grandma. "<u>I can watch you run and jump and play on the swings and the slide</u>."

"<u>Oh boy</u>!" shouted Erik. "<u>May we stop and pick up my friend John</u>?"

"<u>Sure</u>," replied Grandma. "<u>Are you ready to go now</u>?"

"<u>Yes</u>," said Erik. "<u>John's house is right on our way to the park. Thank you, Grandma</u>!"

Activity 3. The sentences in this activity are correctly capitalized but completely unpunctuated. Have the student read the sentences aloud and discuss what type of sentence each one is. Review the punctuation rules for the three types of sentences, and have the student copy and correctly punctuate the sentences on the lines provided. The student may refer to the sentences in Activity 2 as needed for examples of how to punctuate within quotations. Stress that not only is quoted material set off with quotation marks, but also with punctuation within the quotation marks.

Sentences:

"How would you like to go sledding?" asked Dad.

"That would be great!" we yelled.

"Climb in the car," said Dad.

We found a great hill for sledding. It was steep and long.

"May we please do this again next week?" we asked Dad.

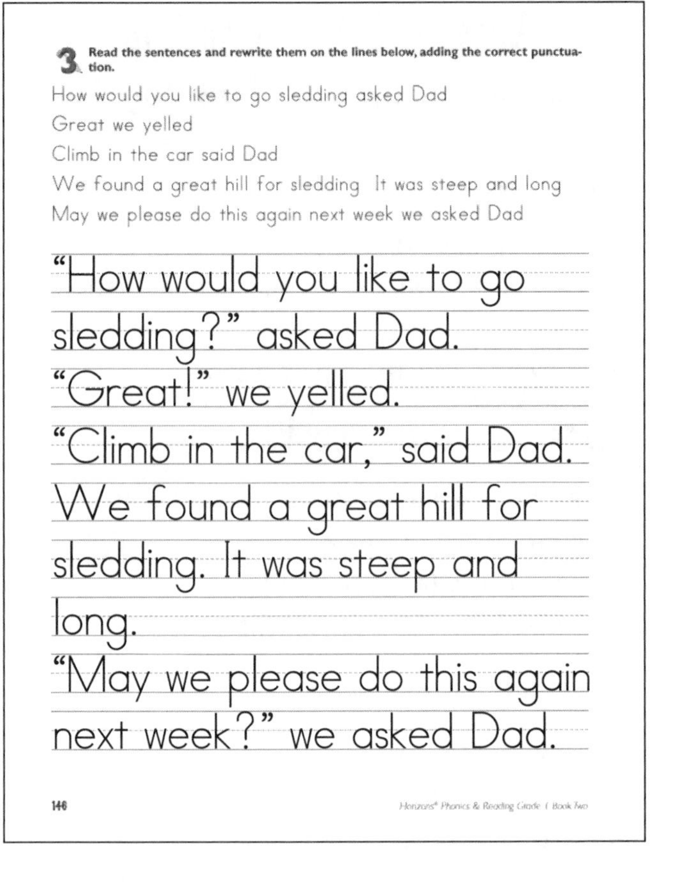

3 Read the sentences and rewrite them on the lines below, adding the correct punctuation.

How would you like to go sledding asked Dad
Great we yelled
Climb in the car said Dad
We found a great hill for sledding It was steep and long
May we please do this again next week we asked Dad

"How would you like to go sledding?" asked Dad.
"Great!" we yelled.
"Climb in the car," said Dad.
We found a great hill for sledding. It was steep and long.
"May we please do this again next week?" we asked Dad.

146 Horizons® Phonics & Reading Grade 1 Book Two

Lesson 142 - Checkup: Words with x

Overview:

- Picture/word match
- Sentence completion
- Story completion
- Adding **x** to words

Materials and Supplies:

- Teacher's Guide & Student Workbook
- White board or chalkboard
- Word cards (as necessary)
- Story: *The Man Who Fixed Cars*

Teaching Tips:

Review the rule. Discuss the fact that very few words in the English language begin with the letter **x**. If desired, have the student look in the dictionary to see how many words start with **x**. Have the student write examples of the rule on the chalkboard or white board. Assist the student as needed in identifying the pictures or reading the words in the lesson.

Activity 1. Have the student identify the pictures and draw a line to match the pictures with the words.

Pictures:	**ox**	**box**
	ax	**fox**

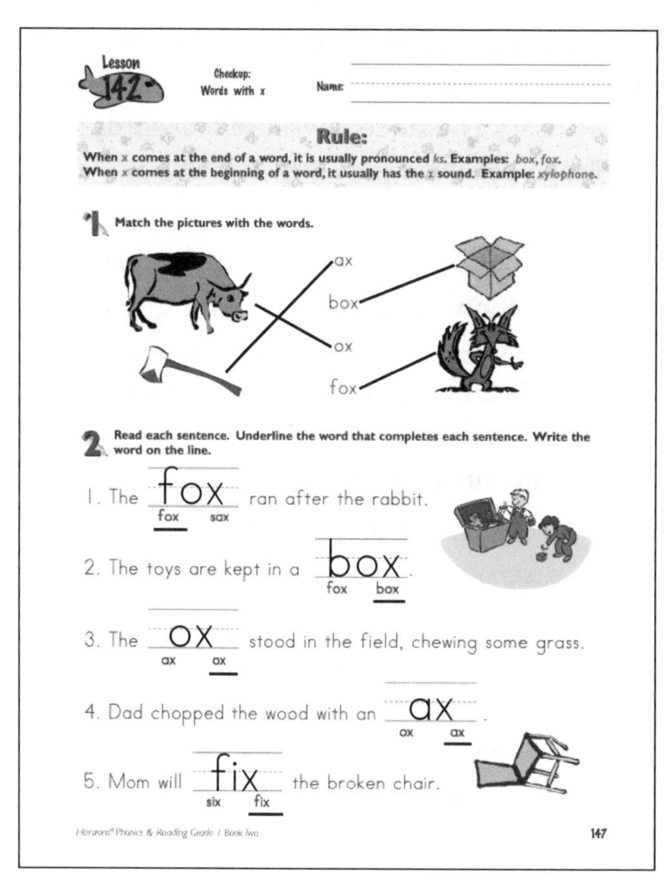

Lesson 142

Checkup: Words with x

Name:

Rule:

When x comes at the end of a word, it is usually pronounced ks. Examples: box, fox.
When x comes at the beginning of a word, it usually has the z sound. Example: xylophone.

1. Match the pictures with the words.

ax
box
ox
fox

2. Read each sentence. Underline the word that completes each sentence. Write the word on the line.

1. The fox ran after the rabbit. (fox, sax)
2. The toys are kept in a box. (fox, box)
3. The ox stood in the field, chewing some grass. (ax, ox)
4. Dad chopped the wood with an ax. (ox, ax)
5. Mom will fix the broken chair. (six, fix)

Horizons® Phonics & Reading Grade 1 Book Two

147

Activity 2. Help the student read the sentences and the word choices. Instruct the student to underline the word that will correctly complete each sentence and write the word on the line.

Sentences:

1. **The fox ran after the rabbit.**
2. **The toys are kept in a box.**
3. **The ox stood in the field, chewing some grass.**
4. **Dad chopped the wood with an ax.**
5. **Mom will fix the broken chair.**

Activity 3. Help the student read the unfinished story and the words in the list. Make word cards as necessary. The student will use the words from the list to complete the story.

Story:

Mary wanted to come home and just relax. When she got home, she saw that she needed to fix the broken vase. She also saw a box of things to put away. Things were a mess. It looked like a fox had run through her house.

Activity 4. Discuss the rule for the two sounds of the letter **x** and have the student think of additional examples. Instruct the student to add **x** to each of the words and read them aloud.

Words: **mix, fix, fox**
Max, tax, text
was, six, box
relax, xylophone

3 Read the story. Use the words from the list to complete the story.

Word List

fox relax fix box

Mary wanted to come home and just relax. When she got home, she saw that she needed to fix the broken vase. She also saw a box of things to put away. Things were a mess. It looked like a fox had run through her house.

4 Add *x* to each of the words below, then read the words to your teacher.

mix fix fox
Max tax text
wax six box
relax xylophone

148 Horizons® Phonics & Reading Grade 1 Book Two

Lesson 143 - Checkup: Alphabetical Order to the First Letter

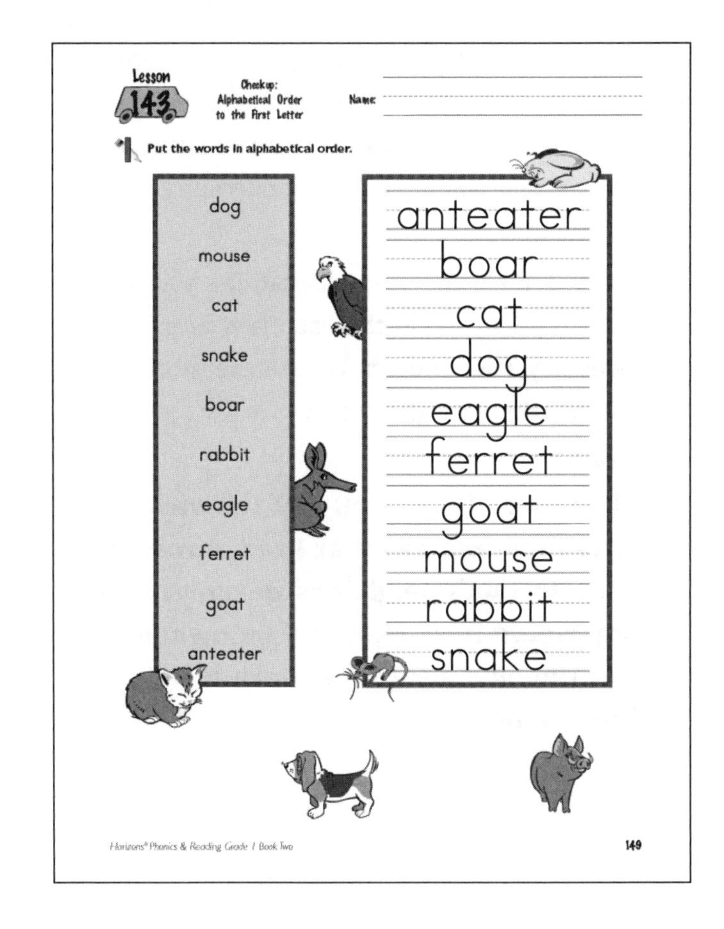
Lesson 143 — Checkup: Alphabetical Order to the First Letter — Name:

1. Put the words in alphabetical order.

dog	anteater
mouse	boar
cat	cat
snake	dog
boar	eagle
rabbit	ferret
eagle	goat
ferret	mouse
goat	rabbit
anteater	snake

Horizons® Phonics & Reading Grade 1 Book Two — 149

Overview:

- Alphabetize words to the first letter
- Sentence writing
- Story completion

Materials and Supplies:

- Teacher's Guide & Student Workbook
- White board or chalkboard
- Word cards (as necessary)
- Story: *The Alphabet*

Teaching Tips:

Write some practice lists on the chalkboard or white board. Help the student number the words in alphabetical order by asking "Which word is first?" Ask the student why that word is first (because it starts with the letter that is closest to the beginning of the alphabet). Proceed in this manner through all the words in the list until the student has correctly alphabetized them all.

Activity 1. Have the student read the words aloud. The student will write the words in alphabetical order to the first letter.

Words: **anteater**
boar
cat
dog
eagle
ferret
goat
mouse
rabbit
snake

Activity 2. The student will write three sentences and use at least three of the animal words from the list. Help the student with writing and spelling as necessary. Emphasize correct capitalization and punctuation.

Activity 3. Help the student read the unfinished story and the words in the list. Make word cards as necessary. The student will use the words from the list to complete the story.

Story:

Joshua's dog barked all day. He was barking at the black cat that lived across the street. Joshua's neighbors weren't happy. They would have liked it if he owned a quiet pet, like a slithery snake or a fluffy white rabbit with long ears.

2 Write three sentences using at least three of the animal words listed below.

Word List

dog	cat	boar	eagle	goat
mouse	snake	rabbit	ferret	anteater

1. ____________________

2. ____________________

3. ____________________

3 Read the story. Use the animal names from above to complete the story.

Joshua's dog barked all day. He was barking at the black cat that lived across the street. Joshua's neighbors weren't happy. They would have liked it if he owned a quiet pet, like a slithery snake or a fluffy white bunny with long ears.

150 Horizons® Phonics & Reading Grade 1 Book Two

Lesson 144 - Checkup: Alphabetical Order to the Second Letter

Overview:

- Alphabetize a list of names to the second letter
- Riddles
- Sentence writing

Materials and Supplies:

- Teacher's Guide & Student Workbook
- White board or chalkboard
- Word cards (as necessary)
- Story: *The Class in Alphabetical Order*

Teaching Tips:

Review the rules for alphabetizing words to the first and second letter. Do some drills on the board, if desired. Assist the student as needed in identifying the pictures or reading the words in the lesson.

Activity 1. Assist the student as needed in reading the list of names to be alphabetized. Have the student write the names in alphabetical order, using the second letter.

Words: **Sam, Scott, Seth, Sharon, Sidney, Stanley, Sue**

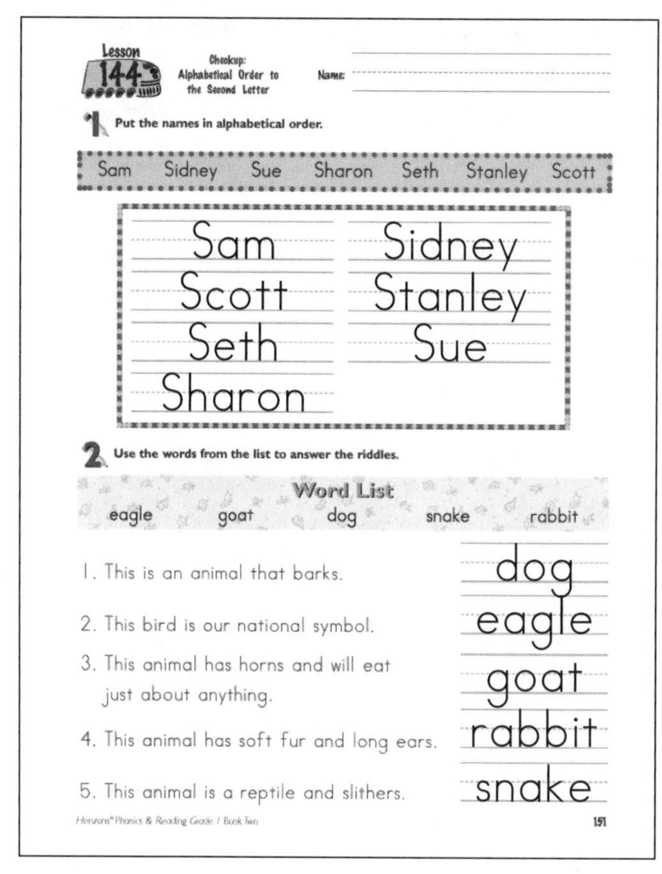

Activity 2. Help the student read the words in the word list and in the riddles. The student will select the correct answer from the word list for each riddle.

Words:
1. dog
2. eagle
3. goat
4. rabbit
5. snake

Activity 3. The student will write three sentences and use at least four of the names from the list. Help the student with writing and spelling as necessary. Emphasize correct capitalization and punctuation.

Activity 4. Have the student draw a picture about one of the sentences from Activity 3.

3 Write three sentences. Use four of the names from the word list.

Word List

Sam Sidney Sue Sharon Sean Stanley Scott

1.

2.

3.

4 Draw a picture about one of your sentences.

152 Horizons® Phonics & Reading Grade 1 Book Two

Lesson 145 - Review: Plural Words Ending in ss or s

Overview:

- Circle pictures that show more than one
- Write singular words as plurals
- Crossword puzzle

Materials and Supplies:

- Teacher's Guide & Student Workbook
- White board or chalkboard
- Word cards (as necessary)
- Story: *Martha's Dresses*

Teaching Tips:

Review the rule. Have the student write examples of the rule on the chalkboard or white board. Assist the student as needed in identifying the pictures or reading the words in the lesson.

Activity 1. Identify the pictures. Have the student choose which pictures represent more than one. Instruct the student to circle those pictures.

Pictures: **dresses, glass, crosses, glasses**

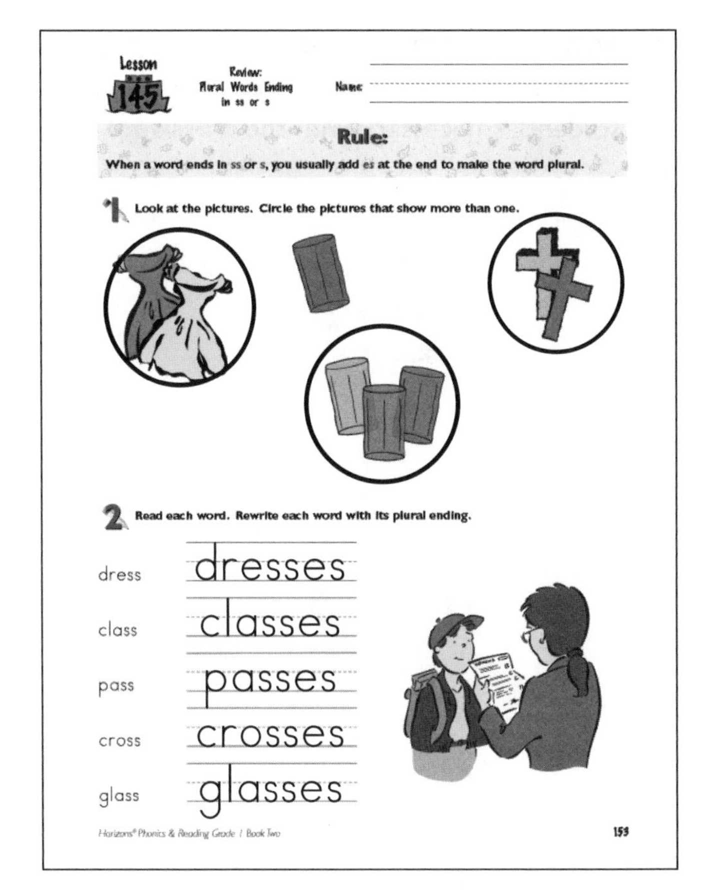

Lesson 145 — Review: Plural Words Ending in ss or s — Name:

Rule:
When a word ends in ss or s, you usually add es at the end to make the word plural.

1. Look at the pictures. Circle the pictures that show more than one.

2. Read each word. Rewrite each word with its plural ending.

dress — dresses
class — classes
pass — passes
cross — crosses
glass — glasses

Horizons® Phonics & Reading Grade 1 Book Two — 153

Activity 2. Have the student read the words aloud and rewrite each word on the line, adding its plural ending.

Words: **dresses, classes, passes, crosses, glasses**

Activity 3. Review the words in the list. Help the student read the crossword puzzle clues. Assist the student as necessary with the crossword puzzle.

Across: **1. classes**

3. glasses

Down: **2. dresses**

3. grasses

3 Use the words from the list to complete the crossword puzzle.

classes grasses passes glasses dresses

ACROSS:

1. I am taking three _____ this year.
3. Mom wears _____ so that she can see better.

DOWN:

2. Jan has two special _____ that she likes to wear.
3. We planted two kinds of _____ in our yard.

154 Horizons® Phonics & Reading Grade 1 Book Two

Lesson 146 - Review: Plural Words Ending in x

Overview:

- Write plural forms of words
- Sentence completion
- Riddles

Materials and Supplies:

- Teacher's Guide & Student Workbook
- White board or chalkboard
- Word cards (as necessary)
- Story: *Boxes of Books*

Teaching Tips:

Review the rule. Have the student write examples of the rule on the chalkboard or white board. Assist the student as needed in identifying the pictures or reading the words in the lesson.

Activity 1. Have the student read the words aloud. The student will write the plural form of each word.

Words: **foxes, boxes, axes, fixes, relaxes**

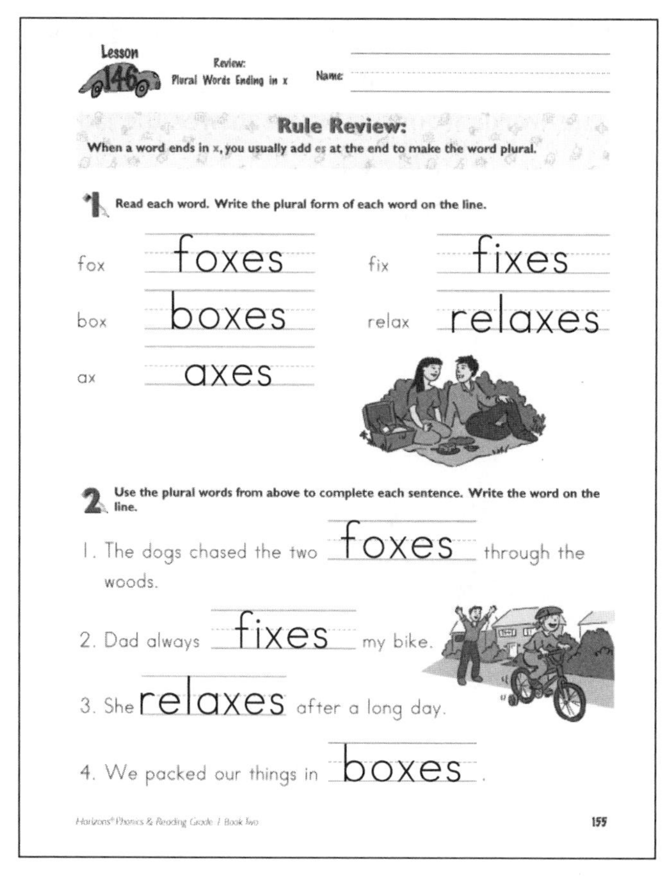

Lesson 146 Review: Plural Words Ending in x Name:

Rule Review:

When a word ends in x, you usually add es at the end to make the word plural.

1. Read each word. Write the plural form of each word on the line.

fox foxes fix fixes

box boxes relax relaxes

ax axes

2. Use the plural words from above to complete each sentence. Write the word on the line.

1. The dogs chased the two foxes through the woods.
2. Dad always fixes my bike.
3. She relaxes after a long day.
4. We packed our things in boxes.

Horizons Phonics & Reading Grade 1 Book Two 155

Activity 2. Help the student read the sentences. Instruct the student to select the word from Activity 1 that will correctly complete each sentence and write the word on the line.

Sentences:

1. **The dogs chased the two foxes through the woods.**
2. **Dad always fixes my bike.**
3. **She relaxes after a long day.**
4. **We packed our things in boxes.**

Activity 3. Have the student read the riddles and the words from the list aloud. The student will use the words from the list to answer the riddles.

Answers: **1. prefixes**
2. foxes
3. suffixes
4. axes
5. boxes

3 Use the words from the list to answer the riddles.

Word List
foxes axes prefixes boxes suffixes

1. These come at the beginning of words. prefixes
2. These wild animals live in the forest. foxes
3. These come at the end of words. suffixes
4. These are used to chop wood. axes
5. You pack things in these. boxes

156 Horizons® Phonics & Reading Grade 1 Book Two

Lesson 147 - Review: Plural Words Ending in sh

Overview:

- Write plural forms of words ending in **sh**
- Sentence completion
- Select pictures that show plurals
- Write base words

Materials and Supplies:

- Teacher's Guide & Student Workbook
- White board or chalkboard
- Word cards (as necessary)
- Story: *Rush Washes the Dishes*

Teaching Tips:

Review the rule. Have the student write examples of the rule on the chalkboard or white board. Assist the student as needed in identifying the pictures or reading the words in the lesson.

Activity 1. Have the student read the words aloud. The student will write the plural form of each word.

Words: **brushes, dishes, flashes, ashes**
wishes, crashes, dashes, gashes

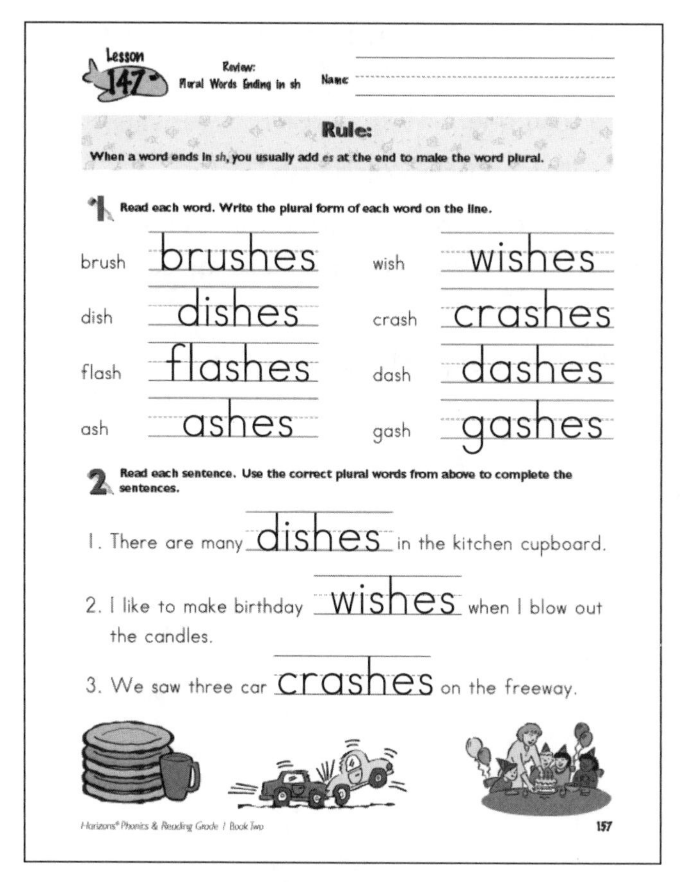

Lesson 147 Review: Plural Words Ending in sh Name

Rule:
When a word ends in *sh*, you usually add *es* at the end to make the word plural.

1 Read each word. Write the plural form of each word on the line.

brush	brushes	wish	wishes
dish	dishes	crash	crashes
flash	flashes	dash	dashes
ash	ashes	gash	gashes

2 Read each sentence. Use the correct plural words from above to complete the sentences.

1. There are many dishes in the kitchen cupboard.
2. I like to make birthday wishes when I blow out the candles.
3. We saw three car crashes on the freeway.

Horizons® Phonics & Reading Grade 1 Book Two 157

Activity 2. Help the student read the sentences. Instruct the student to select the word from Activity 1 that will correctly complete each sentence and write the word on the line.

Sentences:

1. **There are many dishes in the kitchen cupboard.**
2. **I like to make birthday wishes when I blow out the candles.**
3. **We saw three car crashes on the freeway.**

Activity 3. Review the pictures with the student, and instruct him to circle the pictures that show more than one.

Pictures: **brushes, dish, fish, dishes**

Activity 4. Have the student read the plural words aloud, write the base word for each on the line.

Words: **brush, dish, crash, wish**

Lesson 148 - Review: Plural Words Ending in ch

Overview:

- Write plural forms of words ending in **ch**
- Select pictures that show plurals
- Sentence completion
- Write base words

Materials and Supplies:

- Teacher's Guide & Student Workbook
- White board or chalkboard
- Word cards (as necessary)
- Story: *Fresh Peaches*

Teaching Tips:

Review the rule. Have the student write examples of the rule on the chalkboard or white board. Assist the student as needed in identifying the pictures or reading the words in the lesson.

Activity 1. Have the student read the words aloud. The student will write the plural form of each word.

Words: **peaches, watches, patches**
lunches, churches, coaches

Lesson 148 Review: Plural Words Ending in ch Name:

Rule Review:
When a word ends in ch, you usually add es at the end to make the word plural.

1 Read each word. Write the plural form of each word on the line.

peach	peaches	lunch	lunches
watch	watches	church	churches
patch	patches	coach	coaches

2 Look at each picture. Circle the pictures that show more than one.

Horizons Phonics & Reading Grade 1 Book Two 159

Activity 2. Review the pictures with the student, and instruct him to circle the pictures that show more than one.

Pictures: **peaches, church, patch**
watch, coach, lunches

Activity 3. Help the student read the words in the list and the sentences. Instruct the student to select the word that will correctly complete each sentence and write the word on the line.

Sentences:

1. **We bought fresh peaches at the store.**
2. **There are six different churches in our town.**
3. **Mom sewed patches on my jeans.**
4. **John has two different watches to wear on his wrist.**

Activity 4. Have the student read the plural words aloud, write the base word for each on the line.

Words: **coach, peach, bunch**
church, touch, lunch

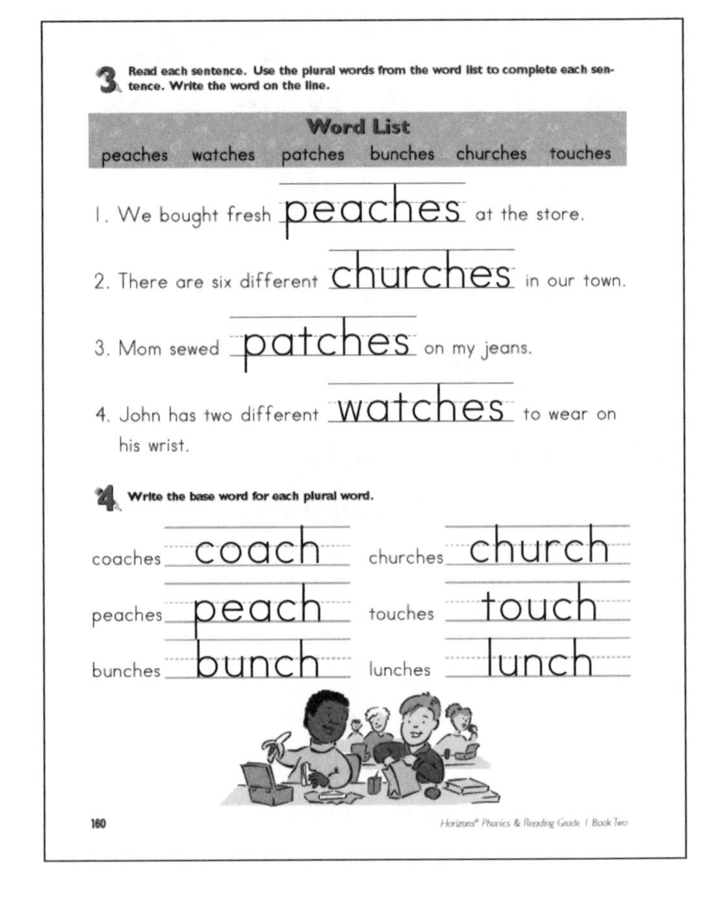

3 Read each sentence. Use the plural words from the word list to complete each sentence. Write the word on the line.

Word List
peaches watches patches bunches churches touches

1. We bought fresh peaches at the store.
2. There are six different churches in our town.
3. Mom sewed patches on my jeans.
4. John has two different watches to wear on his wrist.

4 Write the base word for each plural word.

coaches coach churches church
peaches peach touches touch
bunches bunch lunches lunch

160 Horizons Phonics & Reading Grade 1 Book Two

Lesson 149 - Review: Plural Words Ending in a Vowel plus y

Overview:

- Sentence completion
- Write plural words
- Sentence writing
- Story completion

Materials and Supplies:

- Teacher's Guide & Student Workbook
- White board or chalkboard
- Word cards (as necessary)
- Story: *The Monkeys*

Teaching Tips:

Review the rule. Have the student write examples of the rule on the chalkboard or white board. Assist the student as needed in identifying the pictures or reading the words in the lesson.

Activity 1. Help the student read the words in the list and the sentences. Instruct the student to select the word that will correctly complete each sentence and write the word on the line.

Sentences:

1. **Mary took two trays of food to the table.**
2. **Lynn plays with her friend after school.**
3. **The house has two chimneys.**
4. **They had two turkeys for Thanksgiving.**
5. **There are twelve boys in the class.**

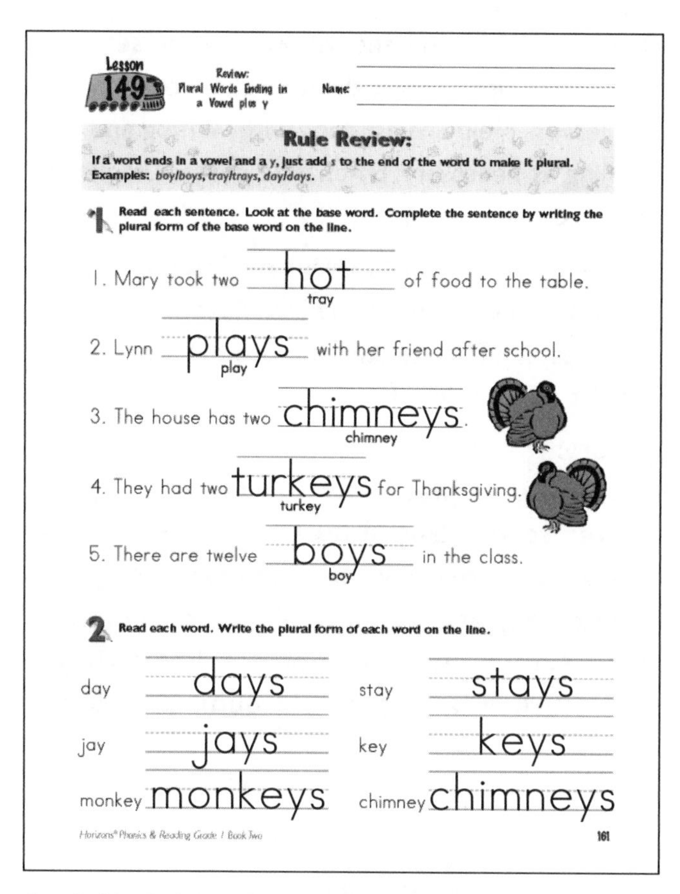
Lesson 149 Review: Plural Words Ending in a Vowel plus y Name:

Rule Review:
If a word ends in a vowel and a y, just add s to the end of the word to make it plural.
Examples: boy/boys, tray/trays, day/days.

1 Read each sentence. Look at the base word. Complete the sentence by writing the plural form of the base word on the line.

1. Mary took two hot of food to the table. (tray)
2. Lynn plays with her friend after school. (play)
3. The house has two chimneys. (chimney)
4. They had two turkeys for Thanksgiving. (turkey)
5. There are twelve boys in the class. (boy)

2 Read each word. Write the plural form of each word on the line.

day days — stay stays
jay jays — key keys
monkey monkeys — chimney chimneys

Horizons® Phonics & Reading Grade 1 Book Two 161

Activity 2. Have the student read the base words aloud, write the plural word for each on the line.

Words: **days, jays, monkeys**
stays, keys, chimneys

Activity 3. The student will write three sentences and use at least three of the words from the lesson. Help the student with writing and spelling as necessary. Emphasize correct capitalization and punctuation.

Activity 4. Help the student read the unfinished story and the words in the list. Make word cards as necessary. The student will use the words from the list to complete the story.

Story:

Jane always plays with her friend Lucy after school. She stays there until dinnertime on most days. Sometimes they pretend they are monkeys living in the jungle. Other times they pretend that they are turkeys and gobble around the house.

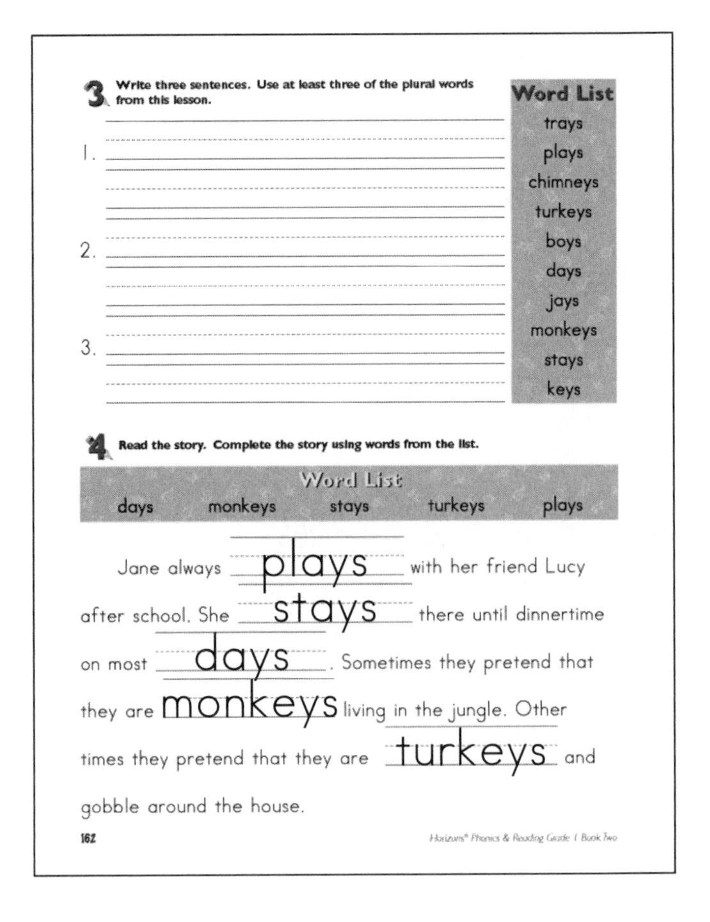

Lesson 150 - Irregular Plurals

Overview:

- Picture/word match
- Write plural words
- Sentence completion
- Crossword puzzle

Materials and Supplies:

- Teacher's Guide & Student Workbook
- White board or chalkboard
- Word cards (as necessary)
- Story: *The Children and the Geese*

Teaching Tips:

Review the rule. Have the student write examples of the rule on the chalkboard or white board. Assist the student as needed in identifying the pictures or reading the words in the lesson.

Activity 1. Have the student identify the pictures and draw a line to match the pictures with the words.

Pictures:	**children**	**mice**
	teeth	**geese**
	men	**feet**

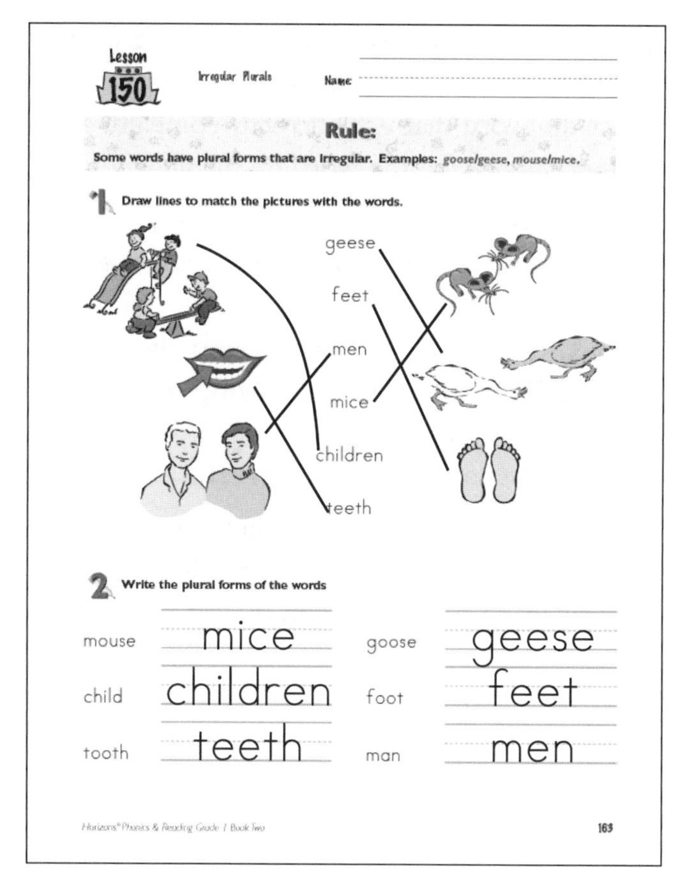
Lesson 150 Irregular Plurals Name:

Rule:
Some words have plural forms that are irregular. Examples: *goose/geese, mouse/mice.*

1. Draw lines to match the pictures with the words.

geese
feet
men
mice
children
teeth

2. Write the plural forms of the words

mouse	mice	goose	geese
child	children	foot	feet
tooth	teeth	man	men

Horizons Phonics & Reading Grade 1 Book Two 163

Activity 2. Have the student read the base words aloud and write the plural word for each on the line.

Words: **mice, children, teeth**
geese, feet, men

Activity 3. Help the student read the words in the list and the sentences. Instruct the student to select the word that will correctly complete each sentence and write the word on the line.

Sentences:

1. **There were three geese on the farm.**
2. **The mice got away from the cat.**
3. **The children are playing on the playground.**
4. **A shark has sharp teeth.**

Activity 4. Review the words in the list. Help the student read the crossword puzzle clues. Assist the student as necessary with the crossword puzzle.

Across: **1. men**
2. children

Down: **1. mice**
3. feet

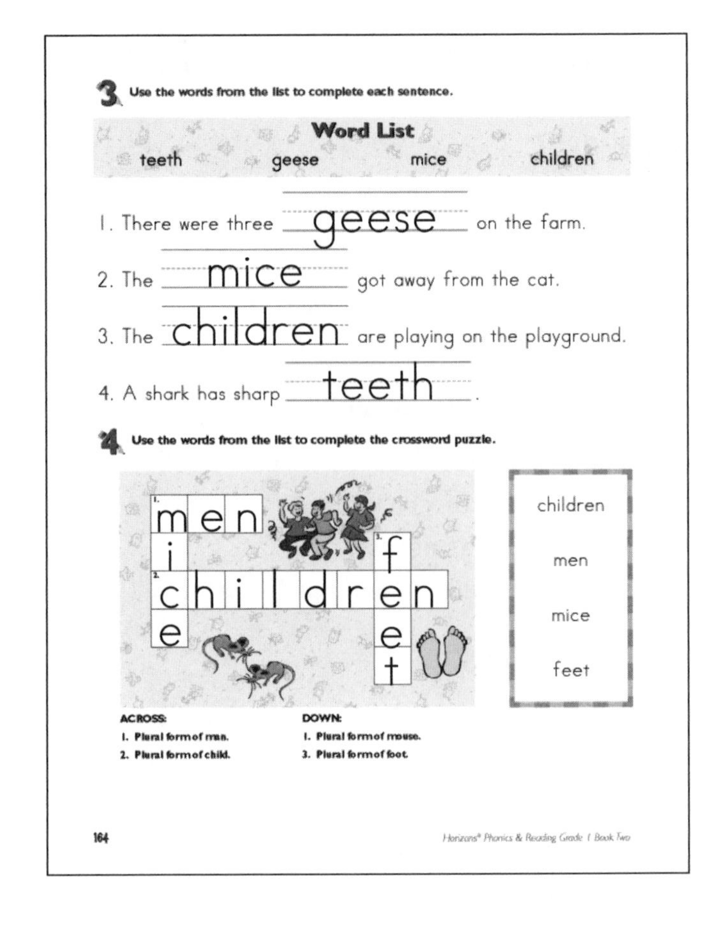
3 Use the words from the list to complete each sentence.

Word List
teeth geese mice children

1. There were three geese on the farm.
2. The mice got away from the cat.
3. The children are playing on the playground.
4. A shark has sharp teeth.

4 Use the words from the list to complete the crossword puzzle.

children
men
mice
feet

ACROSS:
1. Plural form of man.
2. Plural form of child.

DOWN:
1. Plural form of mouse.
3. Plural form of foot.

164 Horizons® Phonics & Reading Grade 1 Book Two

Test 15

Lessons 141-150

Instructions:

Review the sounds of **x** at the end of a word. Review putting words in alphabetical order to the first and second letter. Have the student alphabetize a list of words for both types. Review making words plural that end with **ss**, **ch**, **sh**, or **x**. Also review making words plural that end in a vowel and a **y**. Read through the test with the student. Help the student with any words that he/she is still unsure of. The teacher should be available to answer any questions that the student may have during the test.

Activity 1. Remind the student to use correct capitalization, punctuation, and spelling.

Answers will vary.

Activity 2. Review the instructions and the words in the list with the student.

Words: **blinds**
chair
desk
lamp
sofa
table

What do you know? Test 15 Lessons 141–150 Name:

1. Write a sentence to go with each picture. Include the word under the picture in the sentence.

1. fox

2. box

3. ax

2. Put the words in alphabetical order to the first letter.

desk	blinds
chair	chair
table	desk
blinds	lamp
sofa	sofa
lamp	table

Horizons® Phonics & Reading Grade 1 Book Two 165

Activity 3. Review the instructions and the words in the list with the student.

Words: **Barbara**
Beth
Bill
Bob
Brenda

Activity 4. Review the instructions and the words in the list with the student.

Words:

classes	**keys**
dresses	**grasses**
boxes	**crunches**
brushes	**mice**
bunches	**geese**
monkeys	**teeth**

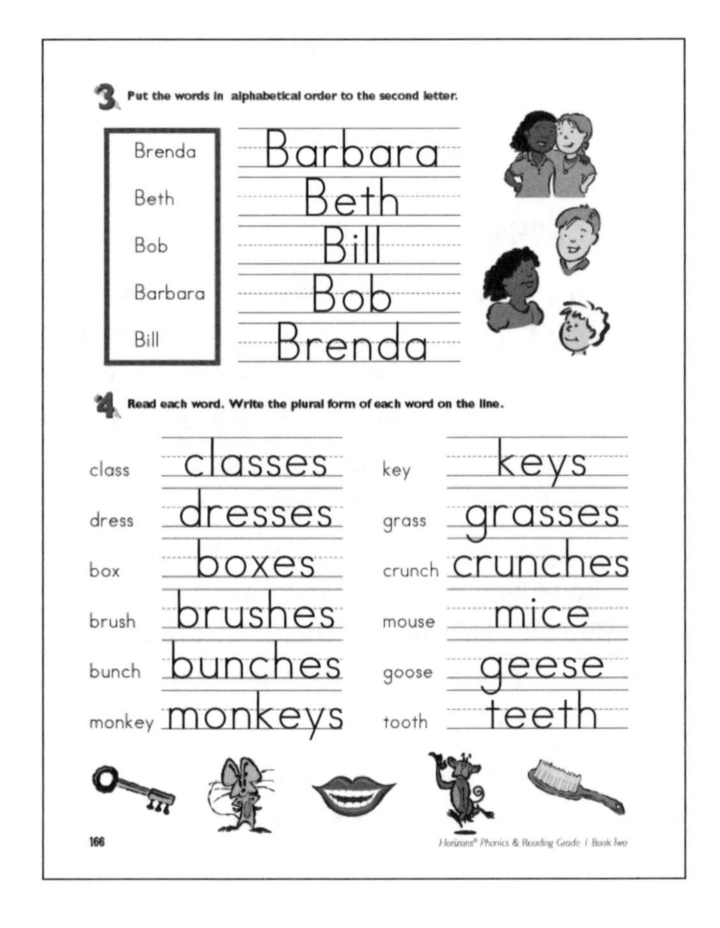

3 Put the words in alphabetical order to the second letter.

Brenda	Barbara
Beth	Beth
Bob	Bill
Barbara	Bob
Bill	Brenda

4 Read each word. Write the plural form of each word on the line.

class	classes	key	keys
dress	dresses	grass	grasses
box	boxes	crunch	crunches
brush	brushes	mouse	mice
bunch	bunches	goose	geese
monkey	monkeys	tooth	teeth

166 Horizons® Phonics & Reading Grade 1 Book Two

Lesson 151 - More Irregular Plurals

Overview:

- Picture/word match
- Sentence completion
- Story completion
- Sentence writing

Materials and Supplies:

- Teacher's Guide & Student Workbook
- White board or chalkboard
- Word cards (as necessary)
- Story: *Moose in Alaska*

Teaching Tips:

Review the rule. Have the student write examples of the rule on the chalkboard or white board. Assist the student as needed in identifying the pictures or reading the words in the lesson.

Activity 1. Have the student identify the pictures and draw a line to match the pictures with the words.

Pictures:	**sheep**	**deer**
	moose	**fish**
		elk

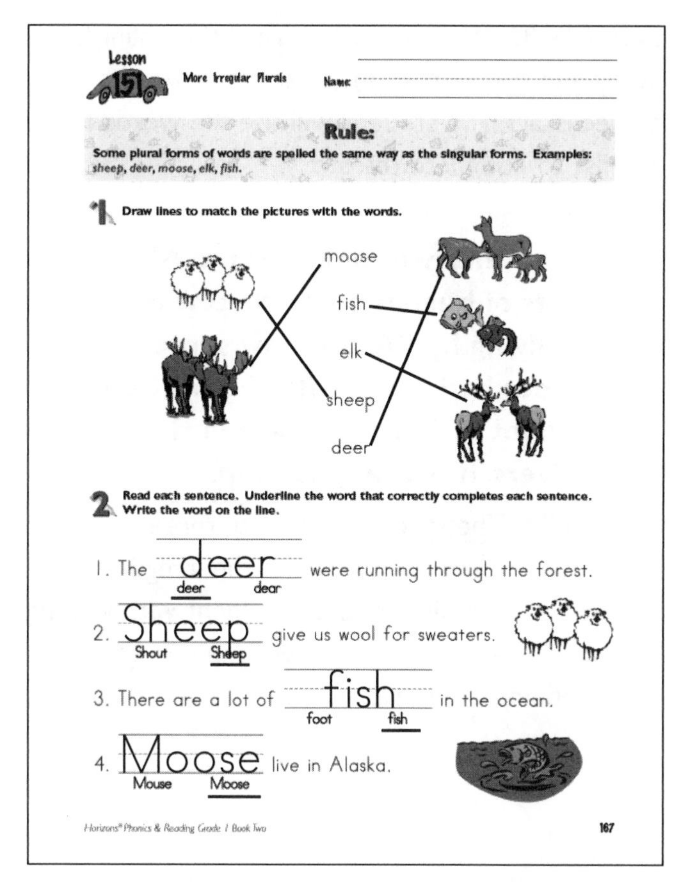

Lesson 151 More Irregular Plurals Name:

Rule:
Some plural forms of words are spelled the same way as the singular forms. Examples: *sheep, deer, moose, elk, fish.*

1 Draw lines to match the pictures with the words.

moose
fish
elk
sheep
deer

2 Read each sentence. Underline the word that correctly completes each sentence. Write the word on the line.

1. The deer were running through the forest. (deer / dear)
2. Sheep give us wool for sweaters. (Shout / Sheep)
3. There are a lot of fish in the ocean. (foot / fish)
4. Moose live in Alaska. (Mouse / Moose)

Horizons® Phonics & Reading Grade 1 Book Two 167

Activity 2. Help the student read the sentences and the word choices. Instruct the student to underline the word that will correctly complete each sentence and write the word on the line.

Sentences:

1. **The deer were running through the forest.**
2. **Sheep give us wool for sweaters.**
3. **There are a lot of fish in the ocean.**
4. **Moose live in Alaska.**

Activity 3. Help the student read the unfinished story and the words in the list. Make word cards as necessary. The student will use the words from the list to complete the story.

Story:

Last summer we took a trip to Alaska. We saw lots of huge moose. We saw many geese flying by. We also saw some deer. The does had fawns with them. There were a lot of fish swimming in the lakes and rivers. It was a great trip!

Activity 4. The student will write three sentences and use at least three of the irregular plurals in the word list. Help the student with writing and spelling as necessary. Emphasize correct capitalization and punctuation.

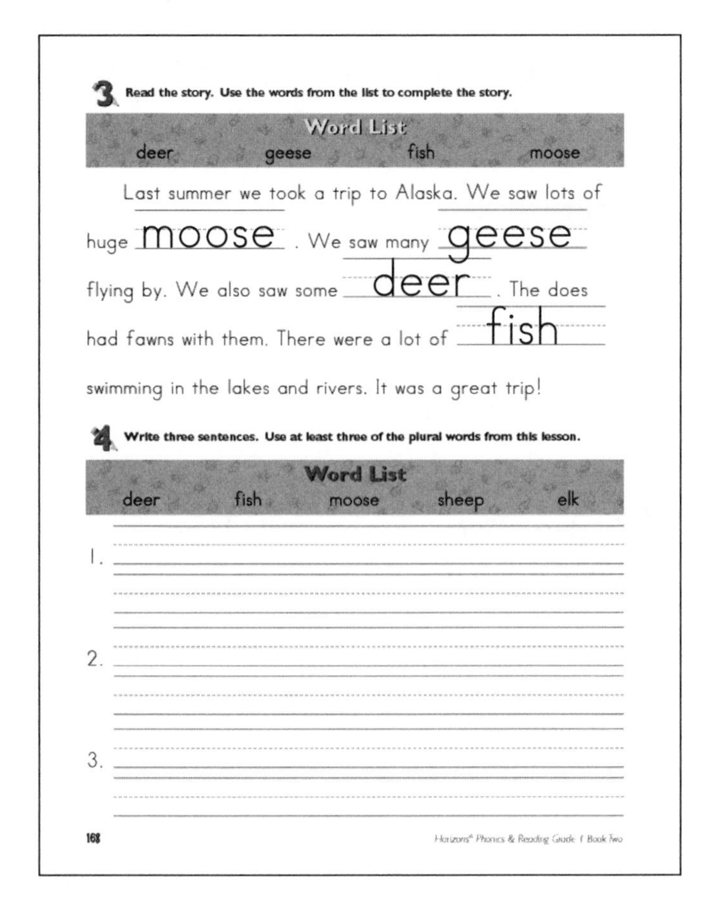

3 Read the story. Use the words from the list to complete the story.

Word List			
deer	geese	fish	moose

Last summer we took a trip to Alaska. We saw lots of huge moose. We saw many geese flying by. We also saw some deer. The does had fawns with them. There were a lot of fish swimming in the lakes and rivers. It was a great trip!

4 Write three sentences. Use at least three of the plural words from this lesson.

Word List				
deer	fish	moose	sheep	elk

1.

2.

3.

168 Horizons® Phonics & Reading Grade 1 Book Two

Lesson 152 - Possessives

Overview:

- Picture/phrase match
- Sentence completion
- Write possessive versions of base words
- Sentence writing

Materials and Supplies:

- Teacher's Guide & Student Workbook
- White board or chalkboard
- Word cards (as necessary)
- Story: *John's Ball*

Teaching Tips:

Review the rule. Have the student write examples of the rule on the chalkboard or white board. Assist the student as needed in identifying the pictures or reading the words in the lesson.

Activity 1. Have the student identify the pictures and draw a line to match the pictures with the phrases.

Pictures:	**the lady's bag**	**the baby's rattle**
	the man's robe	**the boy's cast**
		the girl's doll

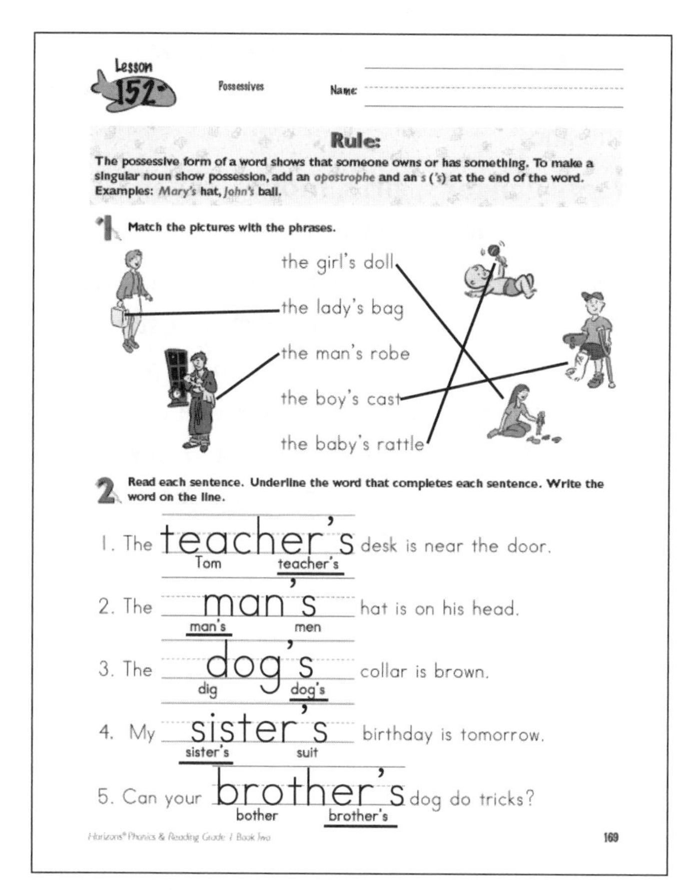
Lesson 152 Possessives Name:

Rule:
The possessive form of a word shows that someone owns or has something. To make a singular noun show possession, add an *apostrophe* and an s ('s) at the end of the word.
Examples: *Mary's* hat, *John's* ball.

1. Match the pictures with the phrases.

the girl's doll
the lady's bag
the man's robe
the boy's cast
the baby's rattle

2. Read each sentence. Underline the word that completes each sentence. Write the word on the line.

1. The teacher's desk is near the door. (Tom / teacher's)
2. The man's hat is on his head. (man's / men)
3. The dog's collar is brown. (dig / dog's)
4. My sister's birthday is tomorrow. (sister's / suit)
5. Can your brother's dog do tricks? (bother / brother's)

Horizons® Phonics & Reading Grade 1 Book Two 169

Activity 2. Help the student read the sentences and the word choices. Instruct the student to underline the word that will correctly complete each sentence and write the word on the line.

Sentences:

1. **The teacher's desk is near the door.**
2. **The man's hat is on his head.**
3. **The dog's collar is brown.**
4. **My sister's birthday is tomorrow.**
5. **Can your brother's dog do tricks?**

Activity 3. Have the student read the words aloud and write the possessive form of each word on the line.

Words: **dancer's, girl's, mom's, cat's friend's, doctor's**

Activity 4. Discuss places the student has visited. Ask which places he enjoyed the most. Have the student write four sentences about places he has been, using at least four possessive nouns, one for each sentence. Help the student with writing and spelling as necessary. Emphasize correct capitalization and punctuation.

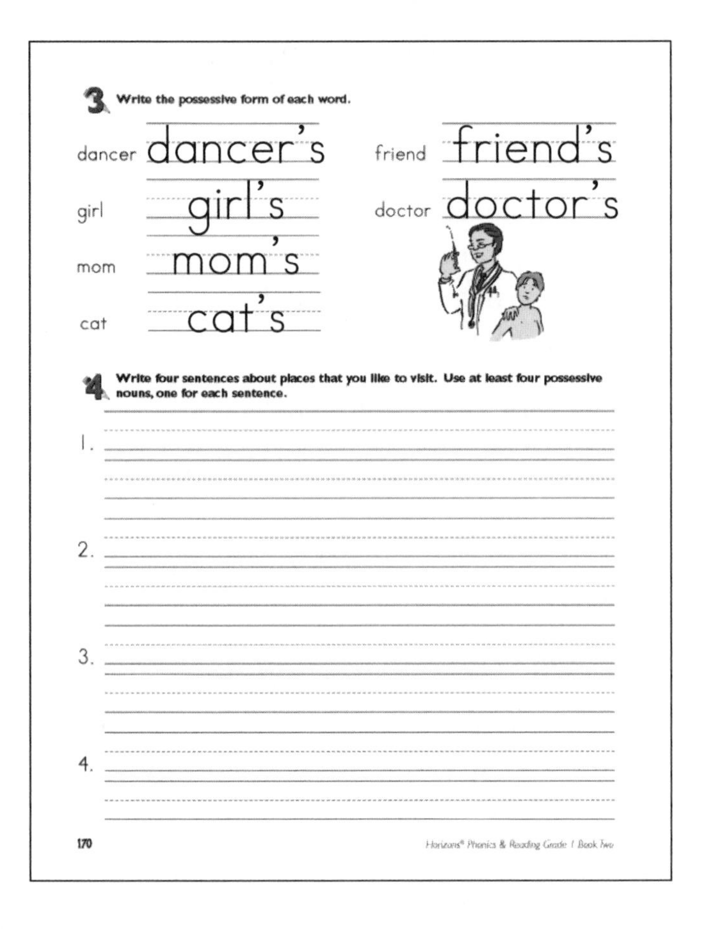

3 Write the possessive form of each word.

dancer	dancer's	friend	friend's
girl	girl's	doctor	doctor's
mom	mom's		
cat	cat's		

4 Write four sentences about places that you like to visit. Use at least four possessive nouns, one for each sentence.

1.

2.

3.

4.

170 Horizons® Phonics & Reading Grade 1 Book Two

Lesson 153 - Review: Possessives & Contractions

Overview:

- Sentence completion
- Read short story and answer comprehension questions
- Sentence writing

Materials and Supplies:

- Teacher's Guide & Student Workbook
- White board or chalkboard
- Word cards (as necessary)
- Story: *Josh's Hat*

Teaching Tips:

Review the rule. Discuss the difference between a contraction and a possessive form. Have the student write examples of the rule on the chalkboard or white board. Assist the student as needed in identifying the pictures or reading the words in the lesson.

Activity 1. Help the student read the sentences and the word choices. Instruct the student to underline the word that will correctly complete each sentence and write the word on the line.

Sentences:

1. **I'm going to the zoo.**
2. **I'll have a lot of fun there.**
3. **My friend's dad is taking us.**
4. **I can't wait to see the lion's new cubs.**
5. **I'm sure that I'll enjoy myself!**

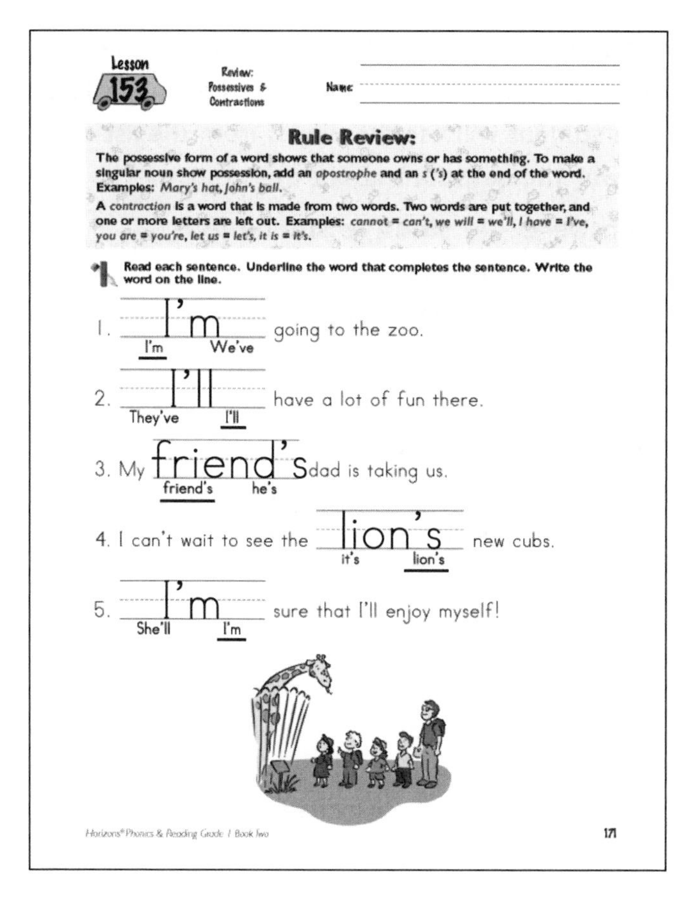

Lesson 153 Review: Possessives & Contractions Name:

Rule Review:

The possessive form of a word shows that someone owns or has something. To make a singular noun show possession, add an *apostrophe* and an *s* ('s) at the end of the word. Examples: *Mary's hat, John's ball.*

A *contraction* is a word that is made from two words. Two words are put together, and one or more letters are left out. Examples: *cannot = can't, we will = we'll, I have = I've, you are = you're, let us = let's, it is = it's.*

1 Read each sentence. Underline the word that completes the sentence. Write the word on the line.

1. I'm going to the zoo. (I'm / We've)
2. I'll have a lot of fun there. (They've / I'll)
3. My friend's dad is taking us. (friend's / he's)
4. I can't wait to see the lion's new cubs. (it's / lion's)
5. I'm sure that I'll enjoy myself! (She'll / I'm)

Horizons® Phonics & Reading Grade 1 Book Two 171

Activity 2. Have the student read aloud the story, the questions, and the words from the list. The student will use the words from the list to answer the questions about the story.

Answers: **1. sled (go sledding)**
2. John's
3. hats and mittens

Activity 3. The student will write two sentences, one containing a possessive noun and the other containing a contraction. Help the student with writing and spelling as necessary. Emphasize correct capitalization and punctuation.

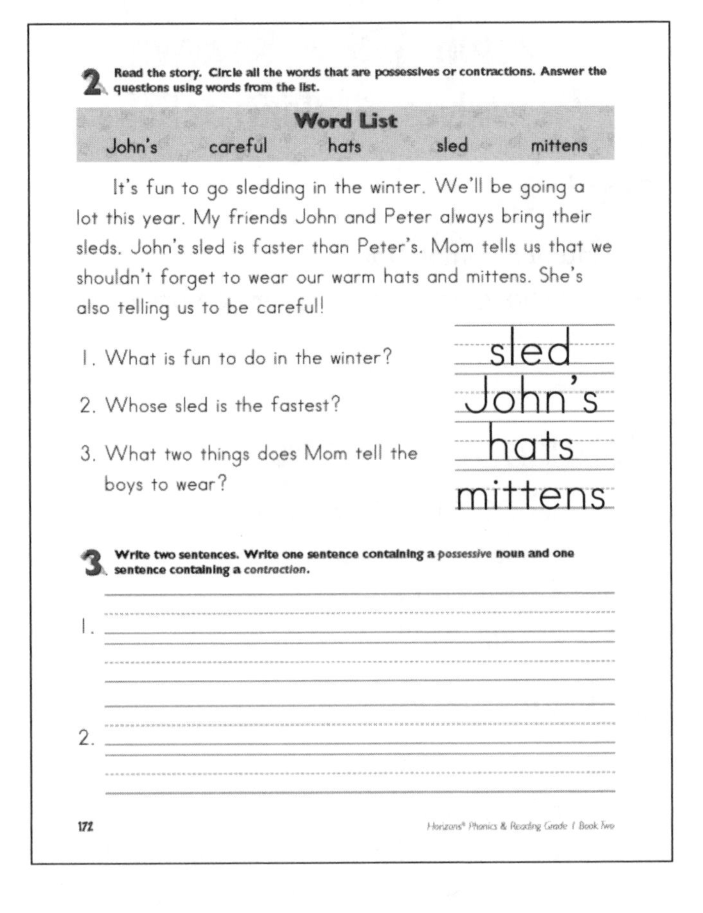

2 **Read the story. Circle all the words that are possessives or contractions. Answer the questions using words from the list.**

Word List

John's	careful	hats	sled	mittens

It's fun to go sledding in the winter. We'll be going a lot this year. My friends John and Peter always bring their sleds. John's sled is faster than Peter's. Mom tells us that we shouldn't forget to wear our warm hats and mittens. She's also telling us to be careful!

1. What is fun to do in the winter? sled
2. Whose sled is the fastest? John's
3. What two things does Mom tell the boys to wear? hats mittens

3 **Write two sentences. Write one sentence containing a** possessive noun **and one sentence containing a** *contraction*.

1.

2.

172 *Horizons® Phonics & Reading Grade 1 Book Two*

Lesson 154 - Checkup: Suffixes

Overview:

- Add suffixes **-ed**, **-er**, or **-ing** to base words
- Sentence completion
- Sentence writing

Materials and Supplies:

- Teacher's Guide & Student Workbook
- White board or chalkboard
- Word cards (as necessary)
- Story: *The Biggest Nap*

Teaching Tips:

Review the rule. Have the student write examples of the rule on the chalkboard or white board. Assist the student as needed in identifying the pictures or reading the words in the lesson.

Activity 1. Have the student read the base words aloud. Discuss possible suffix choices with the student. Instruct the student to add either **-ed**, **-er**, or **-ing** to each base word and write the new word on the line (alternate choices are listed in parentheses).

Words: **tagged** (or **tagging**)
hotter
madder
bigger
napped (or **napping**)
sadder
fitted (or **fitting**)
wrapped (or **wrapper**, **wrapping**)
setting

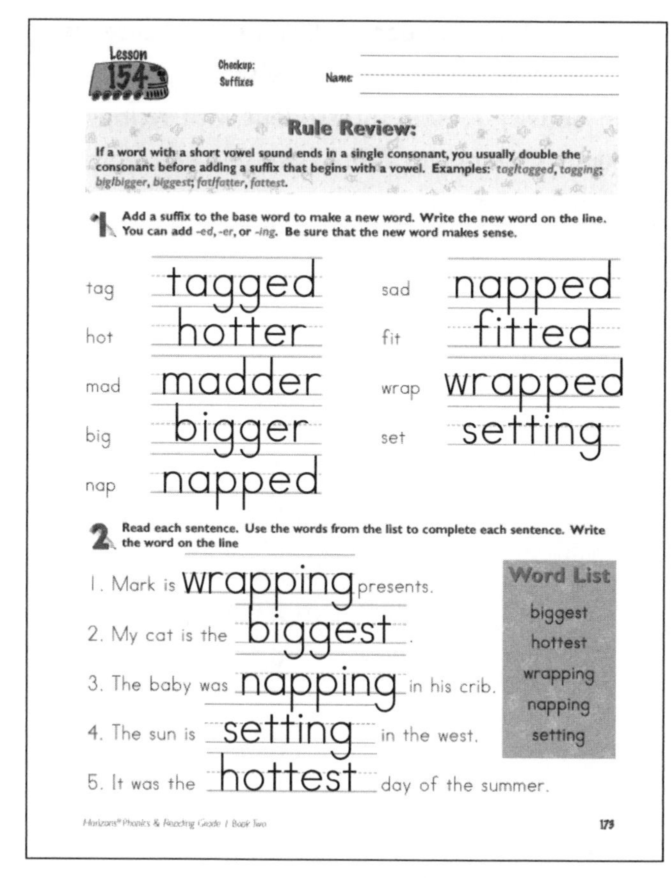
Lesson 154
Checkup: Suffixes
Name:

Rule Review:
If a word with a short vowel sound ends in a single consonant, you usually double the consonant before adding a suffix that begins with a vowel. Examples: *tag/tagged, tagging; big/bigger, biggest; fat/fatter, fattest.*

1. Add a suffix to the base word to make a new word. Write the new word on the line. You can add *-ed*, *-er*, or *-ing*. Be sure that the new word makes sense.

tag	tagged	sad	napped
hot	hotter	fit	fitted
mad	madder	wrap	wrapped
big	bigger	set	setting
nap	napped		

2. Read each sentence. Use the words from the list to complete each sentence. Write the word on the line

1. Mark is wrapping presents.
2. My cat is the biggest.
3. The baby was napping in his crib.
4. The sun is setting in the west.
5. It was the hottest day of the summer.

Word List: biggest, hottest, wrapping, napping, setting

Horizons® Phonics & Reading Grade 1 Book Two 179

Activity 2. Help the student read the words in the list and the sentences. Instruct the student to select the word that will correctly complete each sentence and write the word on the line.

Sentences:

1. **Mark is wrapping presents.**
2. **My cat is the biggest.**
3. **The baby was napping in his crib.**
4. **The sun is setting in the west.**
5. **It was the hottest day of summer.**

Activity 3. The student will write five sentences and use at least five of the new words they created in Activity 1. Help the student with writing and spelling as necessary. Emphasize correct capitalization and punctuation.

3 Write five sentences. Use at least five of the new words from Exercise 1.

1. ______________________________

2. ______________________________

3. ______________________________

4. ______________________________

5. ______________________________

174 Horizons® Phonics & Reading Grade 1 Book Two

Lesson 155 - Writing Lesson: Friendly Letter

Overview:

- Write a letter to a friend or relative

Materials and Supplies:

- Teacher's Guide & Student Workbook
- White board or chalkboard
- Word cards (as necessary)
- Story: *Ryan's Letter*

Teaching Tips:

The student will be writing another friendly letter. Go over the directions with the student. Review the five parts of a friendly letter. The teacher or writing partner should help with spelling and/or writing ideas as necessary. Have the student write the rough draft on a piece of paper and the final copy in the student workbook.

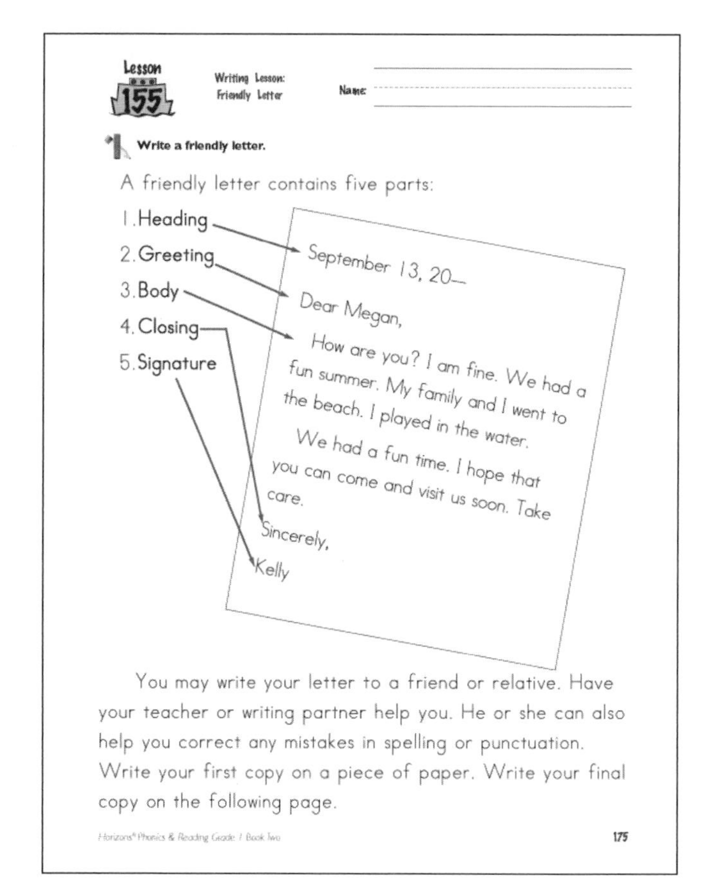

Lesson 155 Writing Lesson: Friendly Letter Name:

1 Write a friendly letter.

A friendly letter contains five parts:

1. Heading
2. Greeting
3. Body
4. Closing
5. Signature

September 13, 20__

Dear Megan,

How are you? I am fine. We had a fun summer. My family and I went to the beach. I played in the water.

We had a fun time. I hope that you can come and visit us soon. Take care.

Sincerely,

Kelly

You may write your letter to a friend or relative. Have your teacher or writing partner help you. He or she can also help you correct any mistakes in spelling or punctuation. Write your first copy on a piece of paper. Write your final copy on the following page.

Horizons® Phonics & Reading Grade 1 Book Two 175

Activity 1. Write a friendly letter.

176 Horizons® Phonics & Reading Grade 1 Book Two

Lesson 156 - Review: Suffixes with Words Ending in Silent e

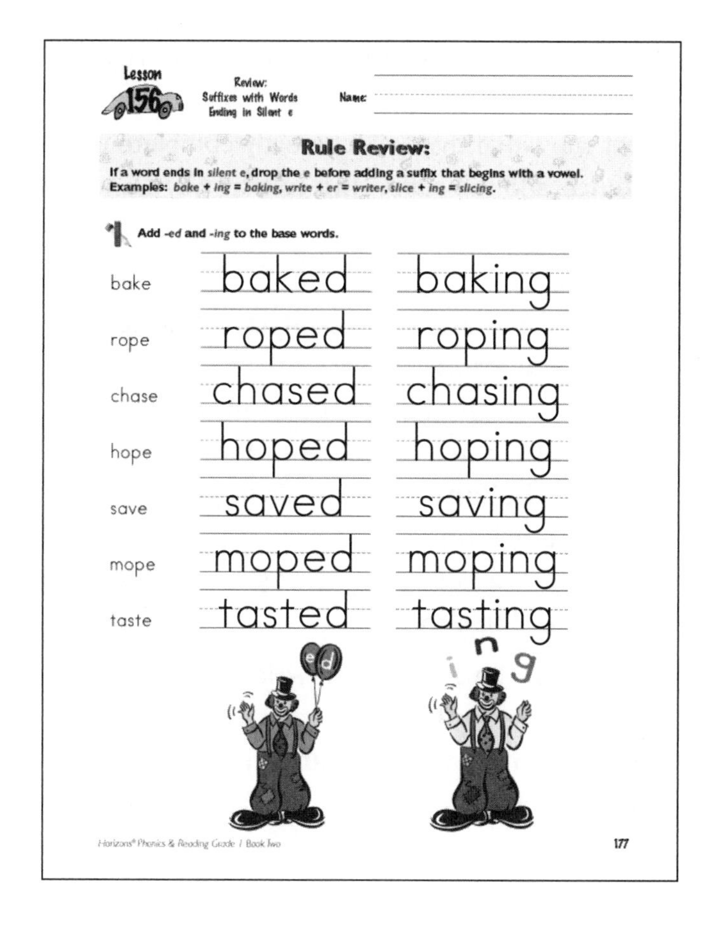

Lesson 156

Review:
Suffixes with Words
Ending in Silent e

Name:

Rule Review:

If a word ends in *silent e*, drop the *e* before adding a suffix that begins with a vowel.
Examples: *bake + ing = baking, write + er = writer, slice + ing = slicing.*

1 **Add *-ed* and *-ing* to the base words.**

bake	baked	baking
rope	roped	roping
chase	chased	chasing
hope	hoped	hoping
save	saved	saving
mope	moped	moping
taste	tasted	tasting

Overview:

- Add suffixes to base words
- Sentence completion
- Sentence writing

Materials and Supplies:

- Teacher's Guide & Student Workbook
- White board or chalkboard
- Word cards (as necessary)
- Story: *Saving Money*

Teaching Tips:

Review the rule. Have the student write examples of the rule on the chalkboard or white board. Assist the student as needed in identifying the pictures or reading the words in the lesson.

Activity 1. Have the student read the words aloud. The student will add **ed** and/or **ing** to the base words.

Words: **baked, baking**
roped, roping
chased, chasing
hoped, hoping
saved, saving
moped, moping
tasted, tasting

Activity 2. Help the student read the words in the list and the sentences. Instruct the student to select the word that will correctly complete each sentence, add the suffix **-ing** to that word, and write the word on the line.

Sentences:

1. **Cara and her family are taking a vacation.**
2. **Cara is saving her money so that she can buy some gifts there.**
3. **The family will be flying on an airplane.**
4. **Cara is hoping that she will have a great time.**

Activity 3. The student will write three sentences and use at least three of the words from the list. Help the student with writing and spelling as necessary. Emphasize correct capitalization and punctuation.

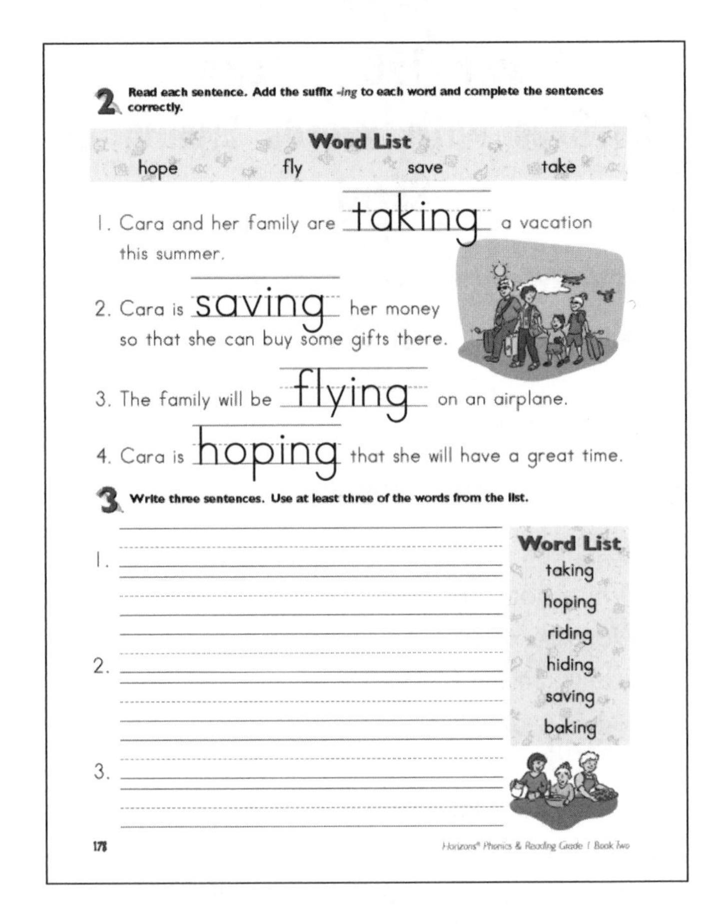

2 Read each sentence. Add the suffix *-ing* to each word and complete the sentences correctly.

Word List
hope fly save take

1. Cara and her family are taking a vacation this summer.
2. Cara is saving her money so that she can buy some gifts there.
3. The family will be flying on an airplane.
4. Cara is hoping that she will have a great time.

3 Write three sentences. Use at least three of the words from the list.

1.
2.
3.

Word List
taking
hoping
riding
hiding
saving
baking

178 Horizons® Phonics & Reading Grade 1 Book Two

Lesson 157 - Checkup: Synonyms

Overview:

- Match words to their synonyms
- Sentence completion
- Story completion
- Sentence writing

Materials and Supplies:

- Teacher's Guide & Student Workbook
- White board or chalkboard
- Word cards (as necessary)
- Story: *The Synonym Story*

Teaching Tips:

Review the rule. Have the student write examples of the rule on the chalkboard or white board. Assist the student as needed in identifying the pictures or reading the words in the lesson.

Activity 1. Have the student read the words aloud. The student will write the synonyms next to the words that they match.

Words: **junk/trash**
close/shut
sick/ill
quick/fast
large/big
small/little
glad/happy
damp/wet

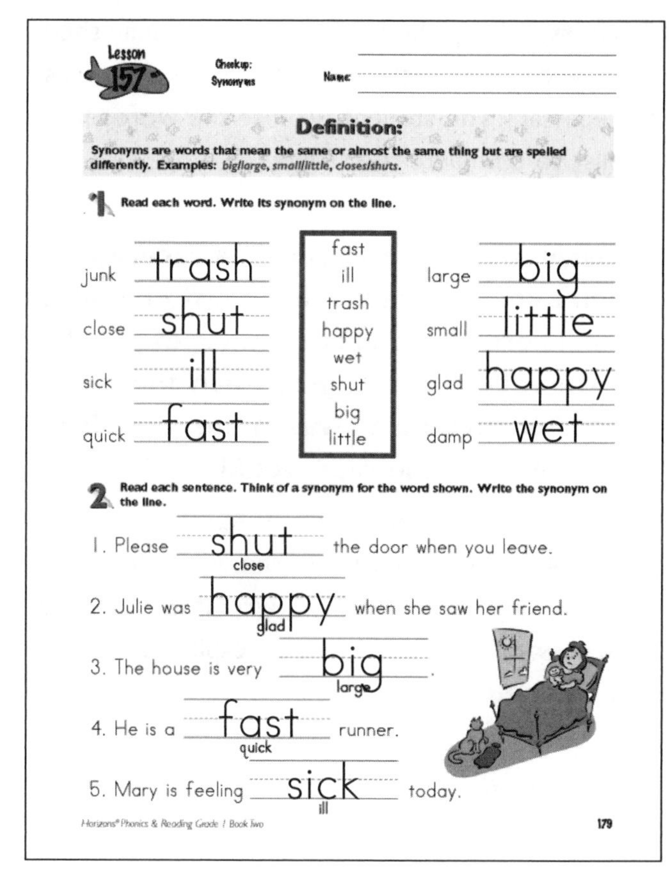

Lesson 157 Checkup: Synonyms Name:

Definition:
Synonyms are words that mean the same or almost the same thing but are spelled differently. Examples: *big/large, small/little, close/shuts.*

1 **Read each word. Write its synonym on the line.**

junk	trash	fast	large	big
close	shut	ill	small	little
sick	ill	trash	glad	happy
quick	fast	happy	damp	wet
		wet		
		shut		
		big		
		little		

2 **Read each sentence. Think of a synonym for the word shown. Write the synonym on the line.**

1. Please shut (close) the door when you leave.
2. Julie was happy (glad) when she saw her friend.
3. The house is very big (large).
4. He is a fast (quick) runner.
5. Mary is feeling sick (ill) today.

Horizons® Phonics & Reading Grade 1 Book Two 179

Activity 2. Help the student read the sentences and the word choices. Instruct the student to select a synonym for each word that will correctly complete each sentence and write the word on the line.

Sentences:

1. **Please shut the door when you leave.**
2. **Julie was happy when she saw her friend.**
3. **The house is very big.**
4. **He is a fast runner.**
5. **Mary is feeling sick today.**

Activity 3. Help the student read the unfinished story and the words in the list. Make word cards as necessary. The student will use the words from the list to complete the story.

Story:

Sharon was going to ride in a race. She didn't know if she would be fast enough to win. There was a large number of people in the race. She was glad when she saw that her friend Dan was in the race also. Sharon knew the race would be close.

Activity 4. The student will write three sentences and use at least six of the words from the lesson. Help the student with writing and spelling as necessary. Emphasize correct capitalization and punctuation.

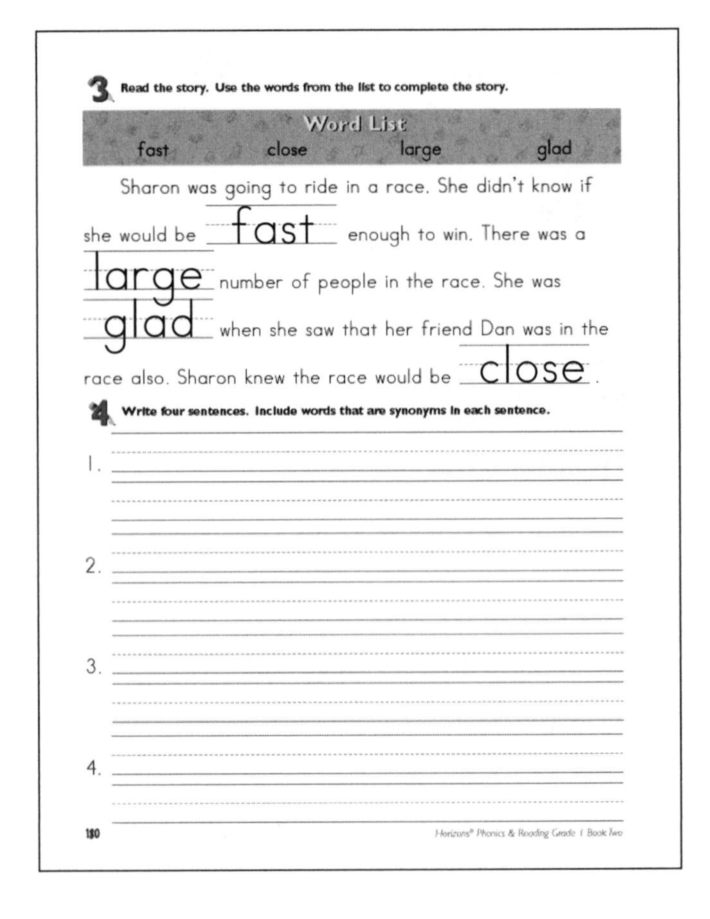

3 Read the story. Use the words from the list to complete the story.

Word List

fast close large glad

Sharon was going to ride in a race. She didn't know if she would be fast enough to win. There was a large number of people in the race. She was glad when she saw that her friend Dan was in the race also. Sharon knew the race would be close.

4 Write four sentences. Include words that are synonyms in each sentence.

1.

2.

3.

4.

180 Horizons® Phonics & Reading Grade 1 Book Two

Lesson 158 - Checkup: Antonyms

Overview:

- Match words to their antonyms
- Sentence completion
- Crossword puzzle
- Sentence writing

Materials and Supplies:

- Teacher's Guide & Student Workbook
- White board or chalkboard
- Word cards (as necessary)
- Story: *The Girl Who Frowned*

Teaching Tips:

Review the rule. Have the student write examples of the rule on the chalkboard or white board. Assist the student as needed in identifying the pictures or reading the words in the lesson.

Activity 1. Have the student read the words aloud. The student will write the antonyms next to the words that they match.

Words: **come/go**
over/under
big/small
full/empty
go/stop
awake/asleep
down/up
wet/dry

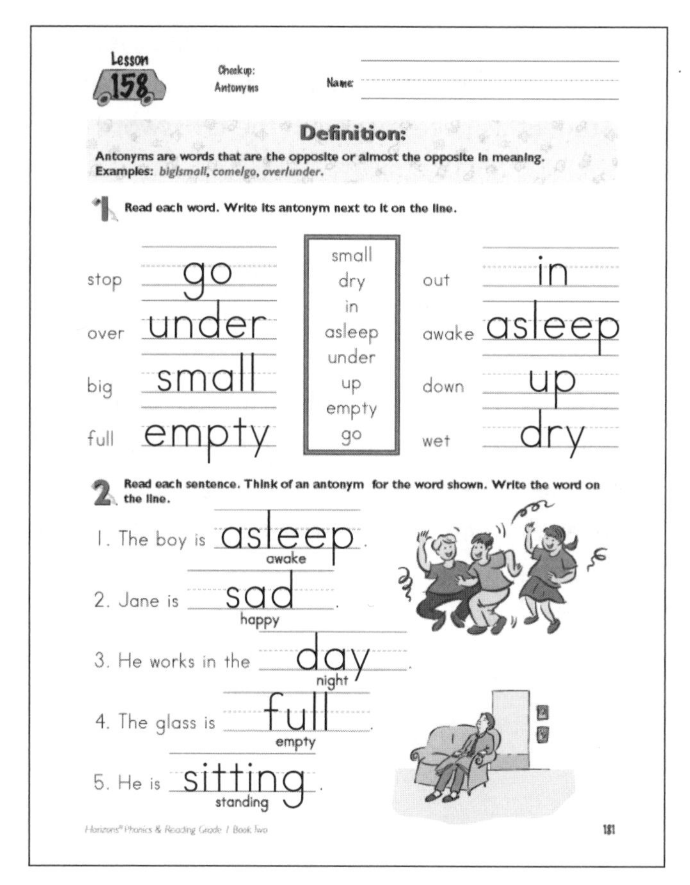

Lesson 158 Checkup: Antonyms Name:

Definition:
Antonyms are words that are the opposite or almost the opposite in meaning.
Examples: *big/small, come/go, over/under.*

1. Read each word. Write its antonym next to it on the line.

small, dry, in, asleep, under, up, empty, go

stop go
over under
big small
full empty
out in
awake asleep
down up
wet dry

2. Read each sentence. Think of an antonym for the word shown. Write the word on the line.

1. The boy is asleep. (awake)
2. Jane is sad. (happy)
3. He works in the day. (night)
4. The glass is full. (empty)
5. He is sitting. (standing)

Horizons® Phonics & Reading Grade 1 Book Two 181

Activity 2. Help the student read the sentences and the word choices. Instruct the student to write the correct antonym to complete each sentence and write the word on the line.

Sentences:

1. **The boy is asleep.**
2. **Jane is sad.**
3. **He works in the day.**
4. **The glass is full.**
5. **He is sitting.**

Activity 3. Review the words in the list. Help the student read the crossword puzzle clues. Assist the student as necessary with the crossword puzzle.

Across: **1. frown**
2. light
Down: **1. full**
3. tall

Activity 4. The student will write four sentences, using the antonym for each of the words in the boxes. Help the student with writing and spelling as necessary. Emphasize correct capitalization and punctuation.

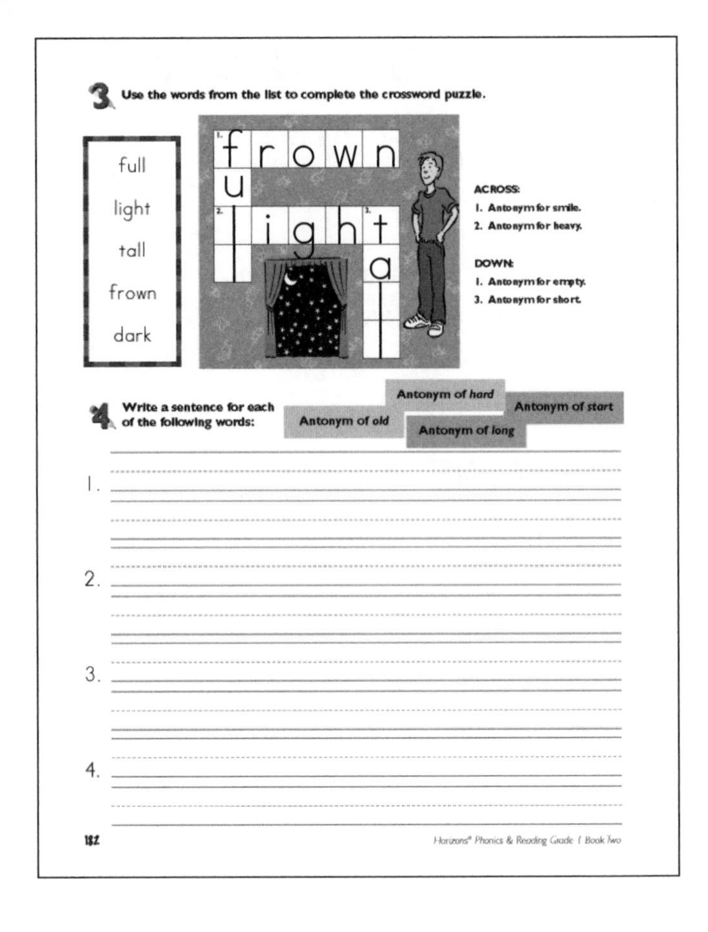

3 Use the words from the list to complete the crossword puzzle.
full
light
tall
frown
dark
frown
full
light
tall
ACROSS:
1. Antonym for smile.
2. Antonym for heavy.
DOWN:
1. Antonym for empty.
3. Antonym for short.
4 Write a sentence for each of the following words:
Antonym of hard
Antonym of start
Antonym of old
Antonym of long
1.
2.
3.
4.
182
Horizons Phonics & Reading Grade 1 Book Two

Lesson 159 - Checkup: Homonyms

Overview:

- Match words to homonyms
- Complete sentences by using correct homonym

Materials and Supplies:

- Teacher's Guide & Student Workbook
- White board or chalkboard
- Word cards (as necessary)
- Story: *Two at Sea*

Teaching Tips:

Review the rule. Have the student write examples of the rule on the chalkboard or white board. Assist the student as needed in identifying the pictures or reading the words in the lesson.

Activity 1. Have the student read the words aloud. The student will write the homonyms next to the words that they match.

Words: **weight/wait**
week/weak
sew/so
heel/heal
blew/blue
pane/pain
meat/meet
sea/see
to/two
son/sun

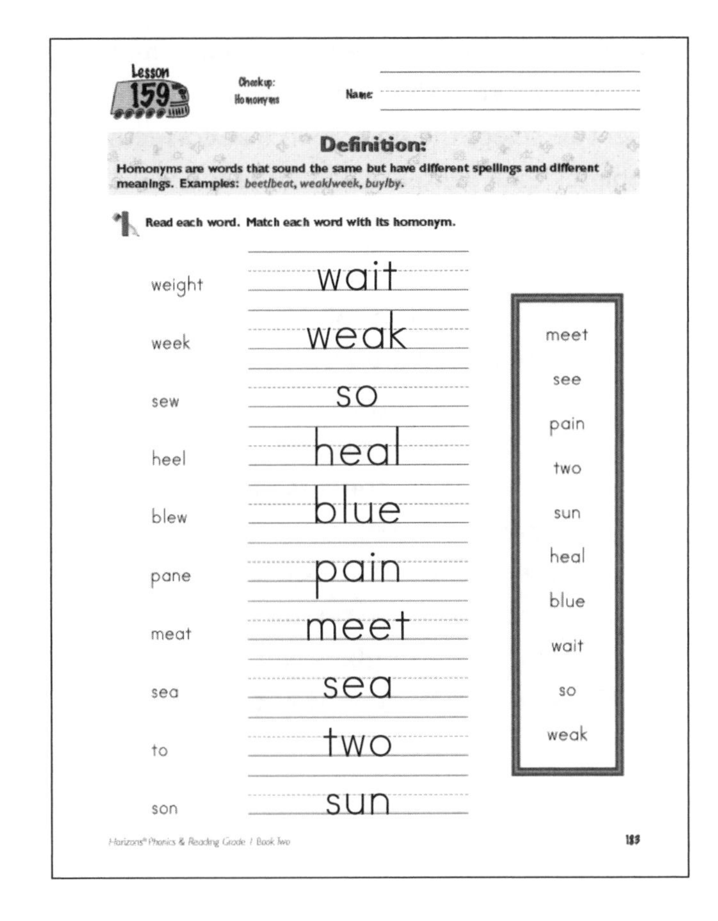

Lesson 159
Checkup: Homonyms
Name:

Definition:
Homonyms are words that sound the same but have different spellings and different meanings. Examples: *beet/beat, weak/week, buy/by.*

1 Read each word. Match each word with its homonym.

weight wait
week weak
sew so
heel heal
blew blue
pane pain
meat meet
sea sea
to two
son sun

meet
see
pain
two
sun
heal
blue
wait
so
weak

Horizons® Phonics & Reading Grade 1 Book Two 183

Activity 2. Help the student read the homonyms in the list and read the sentences. Instruct the student to select the homonym that correctly completes each sentence and write the word on the line.

Sentences:

1. **Dan can lift a lot of weight.**
2. **The ship sailed on the sea.**
3. **There are seven days in a week.**
4. **After one comes two.**
5. **My favorite color is blue.**
6. **Grandma likes to sew clothes.**
7. **Sarah likes to meet new people.**
8. **John had a blister on his heel.**
9. **The pane of glass is broken.**
10. **The sun is very hot today.**

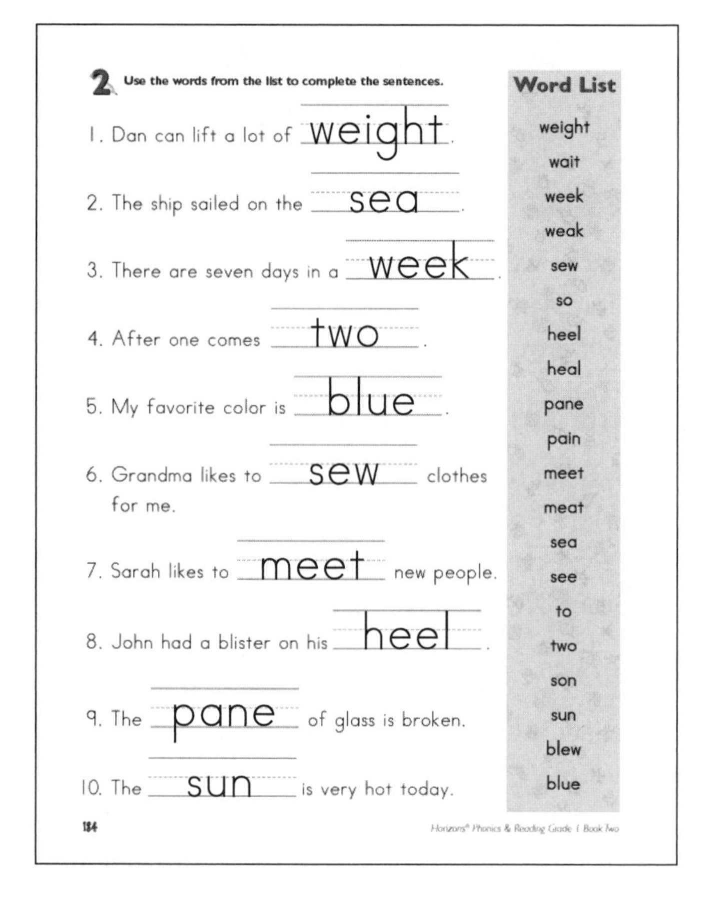
2 Use the words from the list to complete the sentences.
1. Dan can lift a lot of weight.
2. The ship sailed on the sea.
3. There are seven days in a week.
4. After one comes two.
5. My favorite color is blue.
6. Grandma likes to sew clothes for me.
7. Sarah likes to meet new people.
8. John had a blister on his heel.
9. The pane of glass is broken.
10. The sun is very hot today.
Word List
weight
wait
week
weak
sew
so
heel
heal
pane
pain
meet
meat
sea
see
to
two
son
sun
blew
blue

Lesson 160 - Writing Lesson: Poem

Overview:

- Write a poem using synonyms, antonyms and homonyms

Materials and Supplies:

- Teacher's Guide & Student Workbook
- White board or chalkboard
- Word cards (as necessary)
- Story: *Ron's Poem*

Teaching Tips:

The student will write a poem using synonyms, antonyms or homonyms. The poem should be about playing with a friend or relative. The teacher or writing partner should help with ideas and with spelling and punctuation as necessary. The student should write the rough draft on a piece of paper and the final draft in the student workbook.

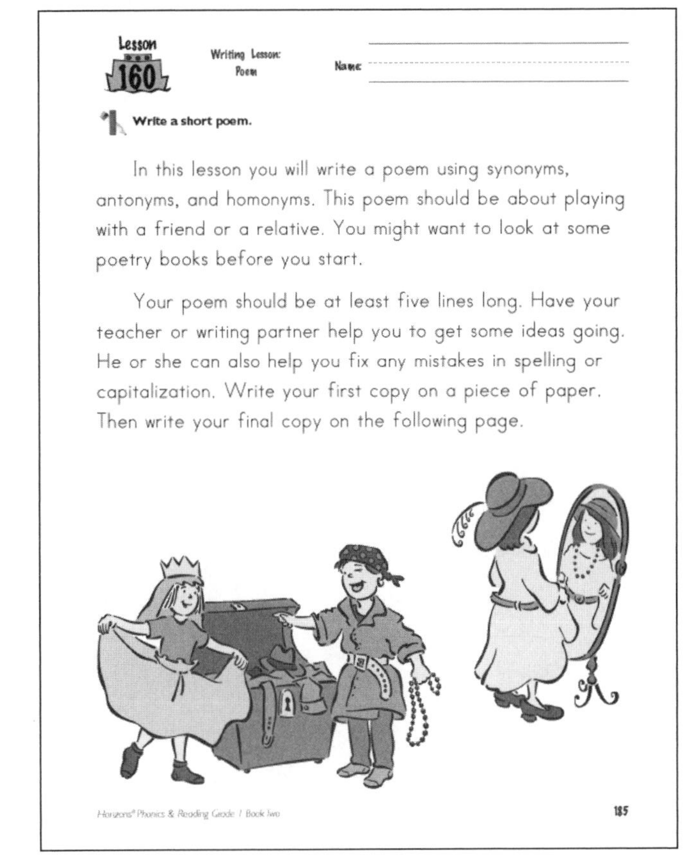

Lesson 160 Writing Lesson: Poem Name:

1. **Write a short poem.**

In this lesson you will write a poem using synonyms, antonyms, and homonyms. This poem should be about playing with a friend or a relative. You might want to look at some poetry books before you start.

Your poem should be at least five lines long. Have your teacher or writing partner help you to get some ideas going. He or she can also help you fix any mistakes in spelling or capitalization. Write your first copy on a piece of paper. Then write your final copy on the following page.

185

Activity 1. Write a short poem.

186 Horizons® Phonics & Reading Grade 1 Book Two

Test 16

Lessons 151-160

Instructions:

Review irregular plurals. Have the student give some examples of irregular plurals (**deer, sheep, fish, child, man, goose, tooth**). Review possessive forms of singular words (adding an apostrophe and **s**). Review adding **-ing** and **-er** to words in which the consonant must be doubled before adding the suffix. Have the student give examples (**sad, run, fit, dig**). Review adding **-ed, -ing, -er,** and **-est** to words ending in silent **e** (**smile, cute, nice**). Have the student give some examples. Review synonyms, antonyms, and homonyms. Have the student give examples of each type of word from words presented by the teacher. Read through the test with the student. Help the student with any words that he/she is still unsure of. The teacher should be available to answer any questions that the student may have during the test.

Activity 1. Review the instructions and the words with the student.

Words:	**sheep**	**feet**
	deer	**geese**
	children	**teeth**
	men	**mice**

Activity 2. Review the instructions and the base words with the student.

Words:	**boy's**	**girl's**
	man's	**John's**
	friend's	**teacher's**

Activity 3. Review the instructions and the base words with the student.

Words:	**running**	**runner**
	digging	**digger**
	planning	**planner**
	sadder	
	fitting	**fitter**

Activity 4. Review the instructions and the base words with the student.

Words:	**cuter**	**cutest**
	loved	**loving**
	coming	
	smiled	**smiling**
	nicer	**nicest**
	later	**latest**

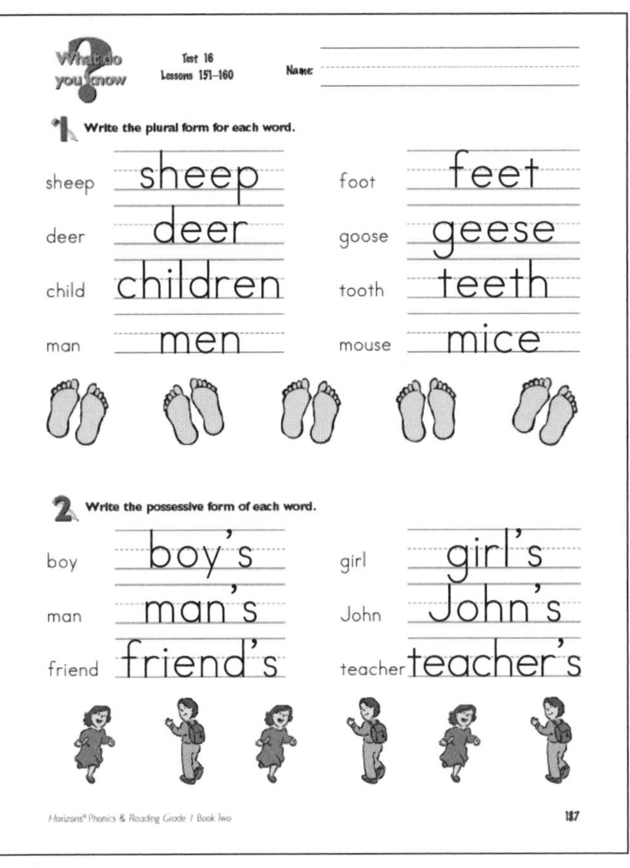
What do you know? Test 16 Lessons 151–160 Name:

1. Write the plural form for each word.

sheep	sheep	foot	feet
deer	deer	goose	geese
child	children	tooth	teeth
man	men	mouse	mice

2. Write the possessive form of each word.

boy	boy's	girl	girl's
man	man's	John	John's
friend	friend's	teacher	teacher's

Horizons® Phonics & Reading Grade 1 Book Two 187

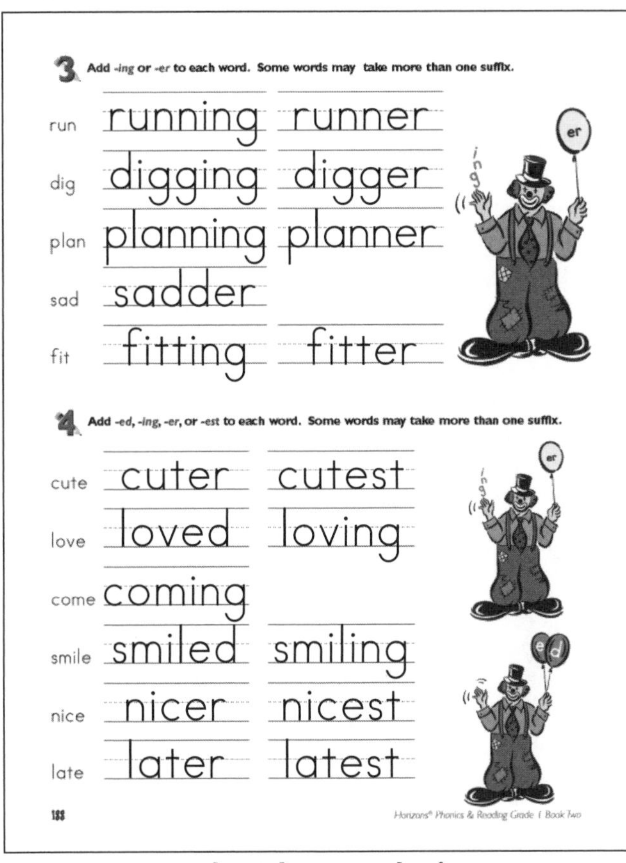
3. Add -ing or -er to each word. Some words may take more than one suffix.

run	running	runner
dig	digging	digger
plan	planning	planner
sad	sadder	
fit	fitting	fitter

4. Add -ed, -ing, -er, or -est to each word. Some words may take more than one suffix.

cute	cuter	cutest
love	loved	loving
come	coming	
smile	smiled	smiling
nice	nicer	nicest
late	later	latest

188 Horizons® Phonics & Reading Grade 1 Book Two

Activity 5. Review the instructions and the words with the student.

Words:	**big**	**happy**
	little	**tidy**
	fast	**wet**

Activity 6. Review the instructions and the words with the student.

Words:	**cold**	**empty**
	dry	**slow**
	strong	**down**

Activity 7. Review the instructions and the words with the student.

Words:	**mail**	**pain**
	to	**ate**
	know	**blue**

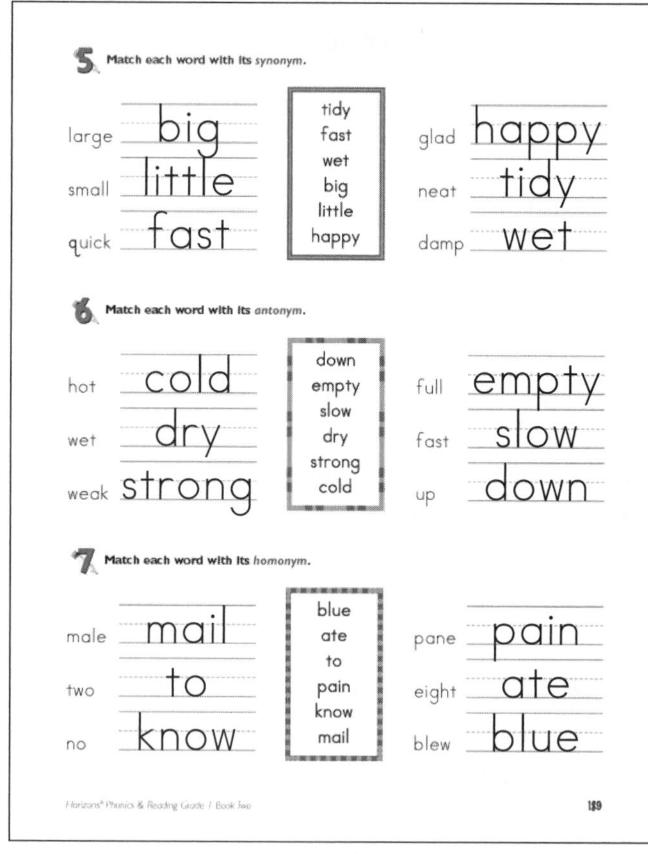
5. **Match each word with its** ***synonym.***

Word box: tidy, fast, wet, big, little, happy

large big
small little
quick fast
glad happy
neat tidy
damp wet

6. **Match each word with its** ***antonym.***

Word box: down, empty, slow, dry, strong, cold

hot cold
wet dry
weak strong
full empty
fast slow
up down

7. **Match each word with its** ***homonym.***

Word box: blue, ate, to, pain, know, mail

male mail
two to
no know
pane pain
eight ate
blew blue

Horizons® Phonics & Reading Grade 1 Book Two 189

190 Horizons® Phonics & Reading Grade 1 Book Two

Teacher Resources

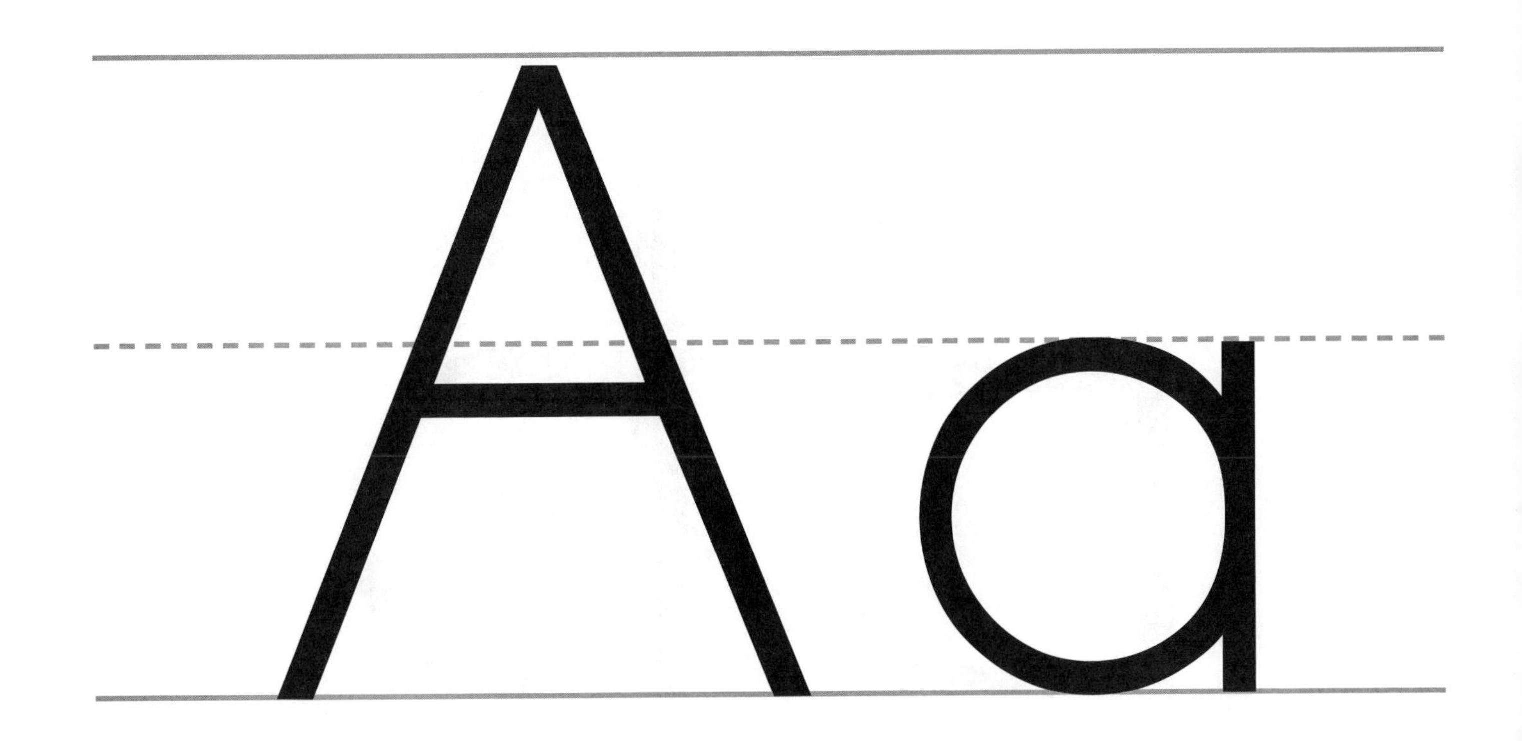

short ă

Bb

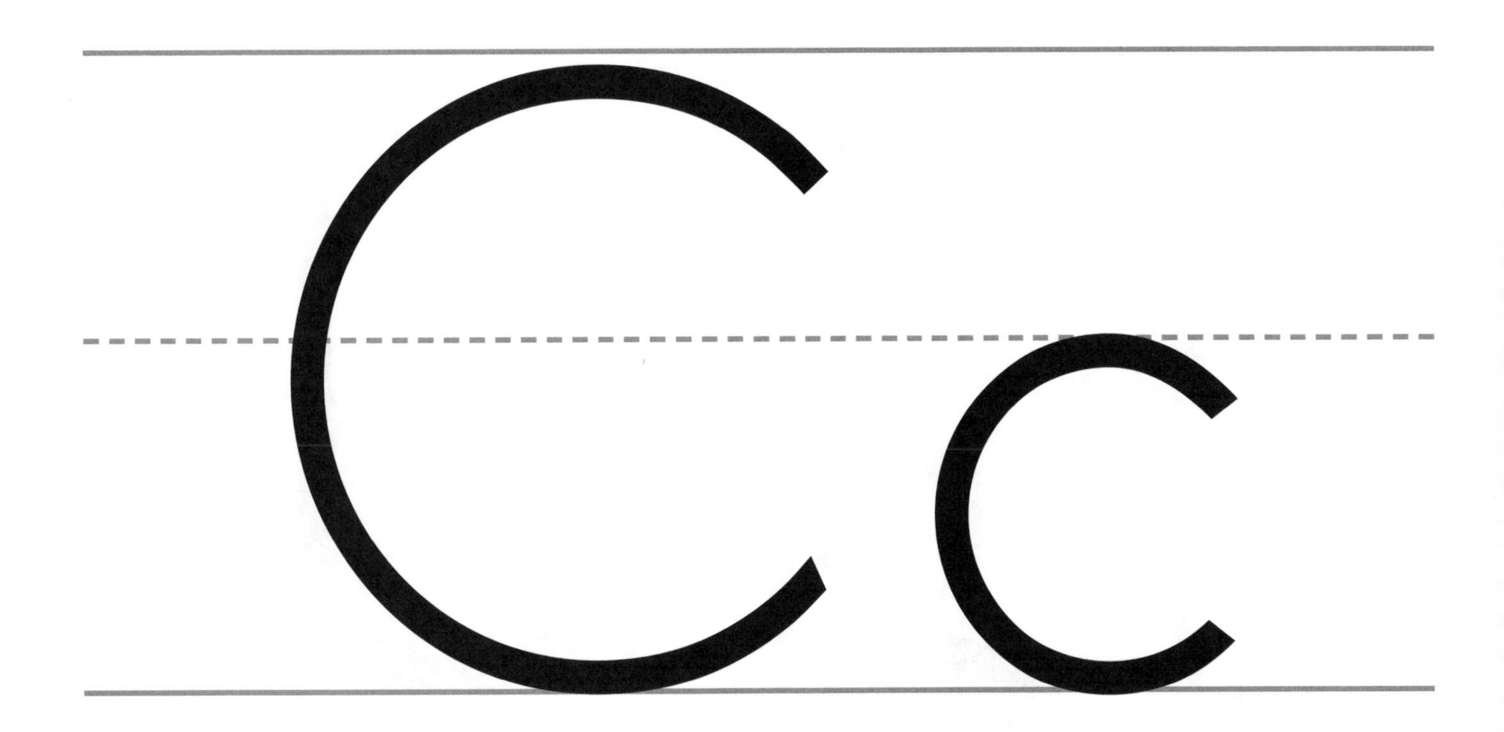
Cc

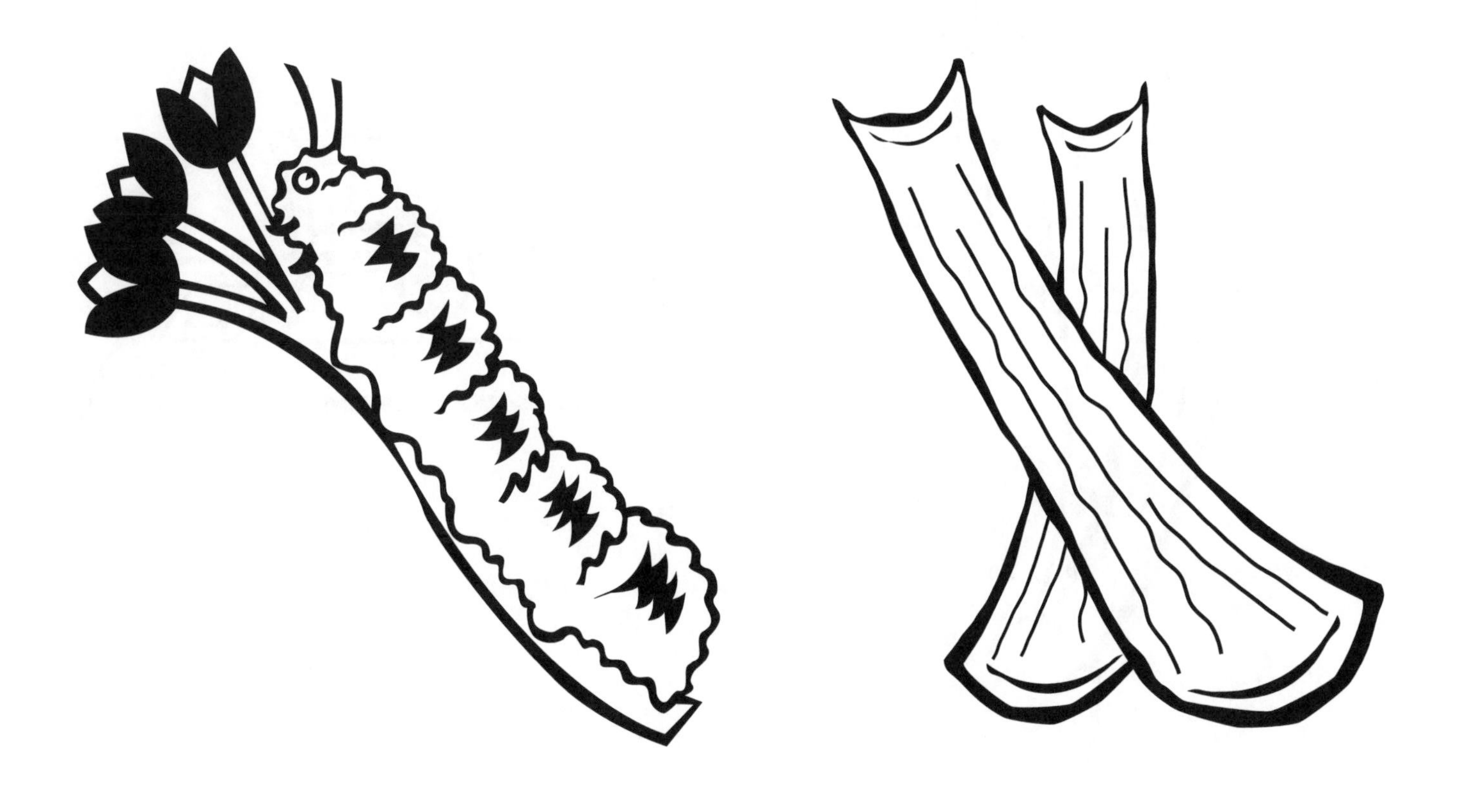

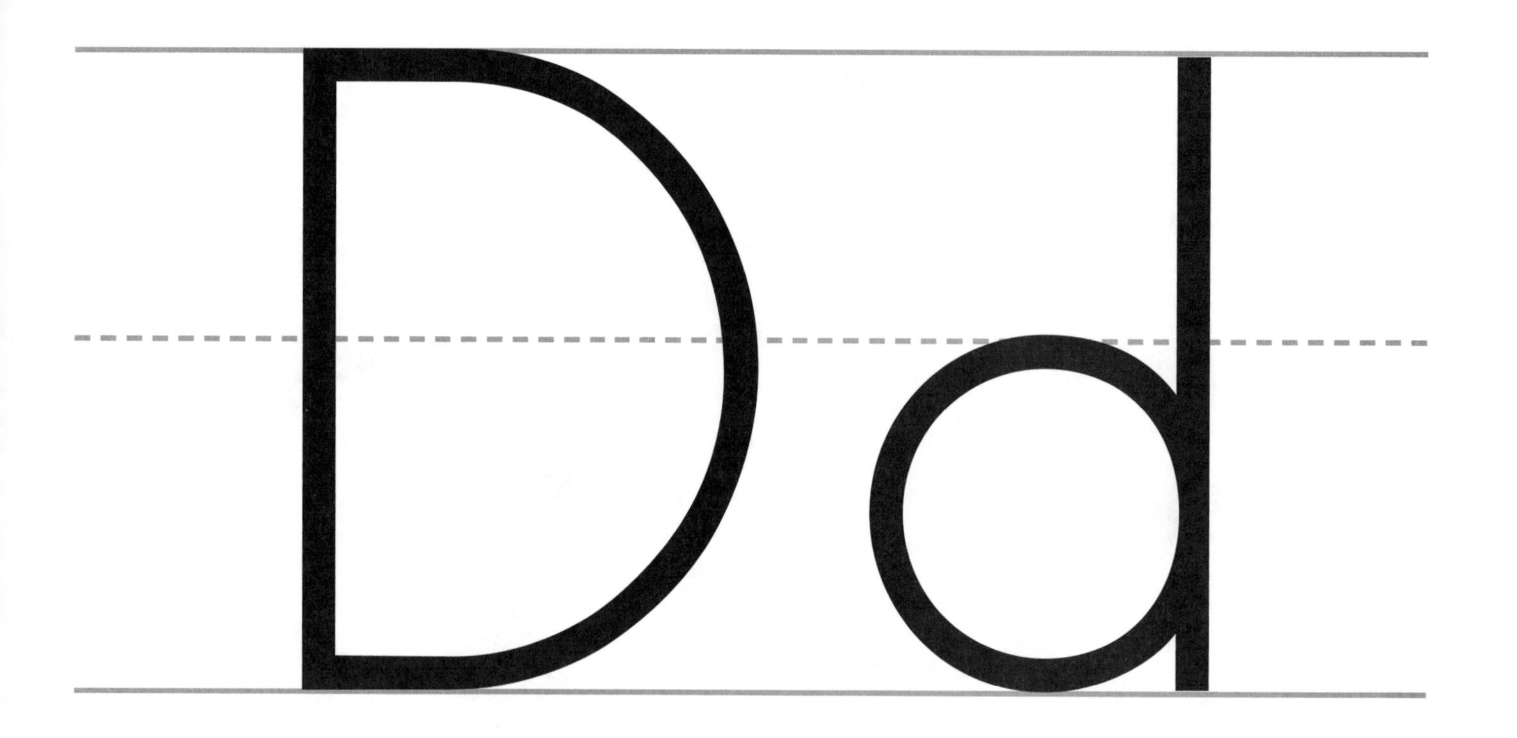

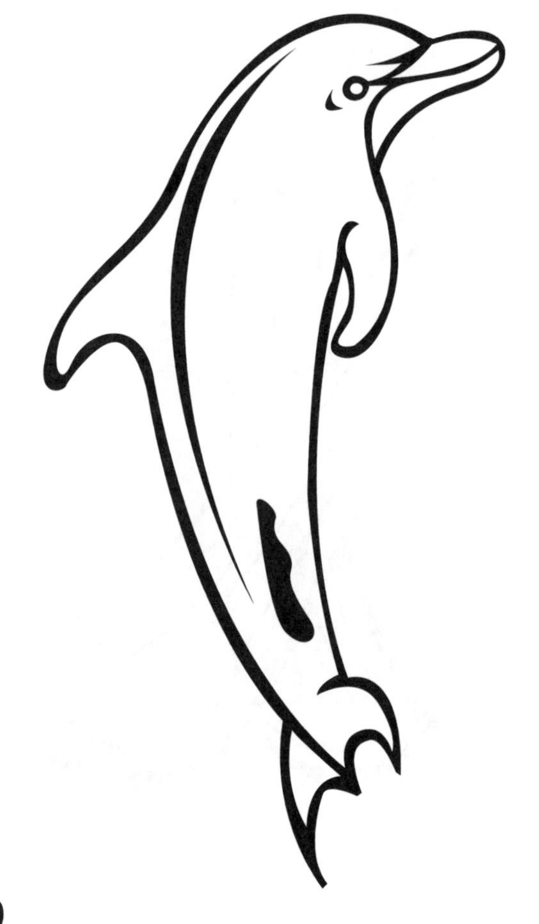

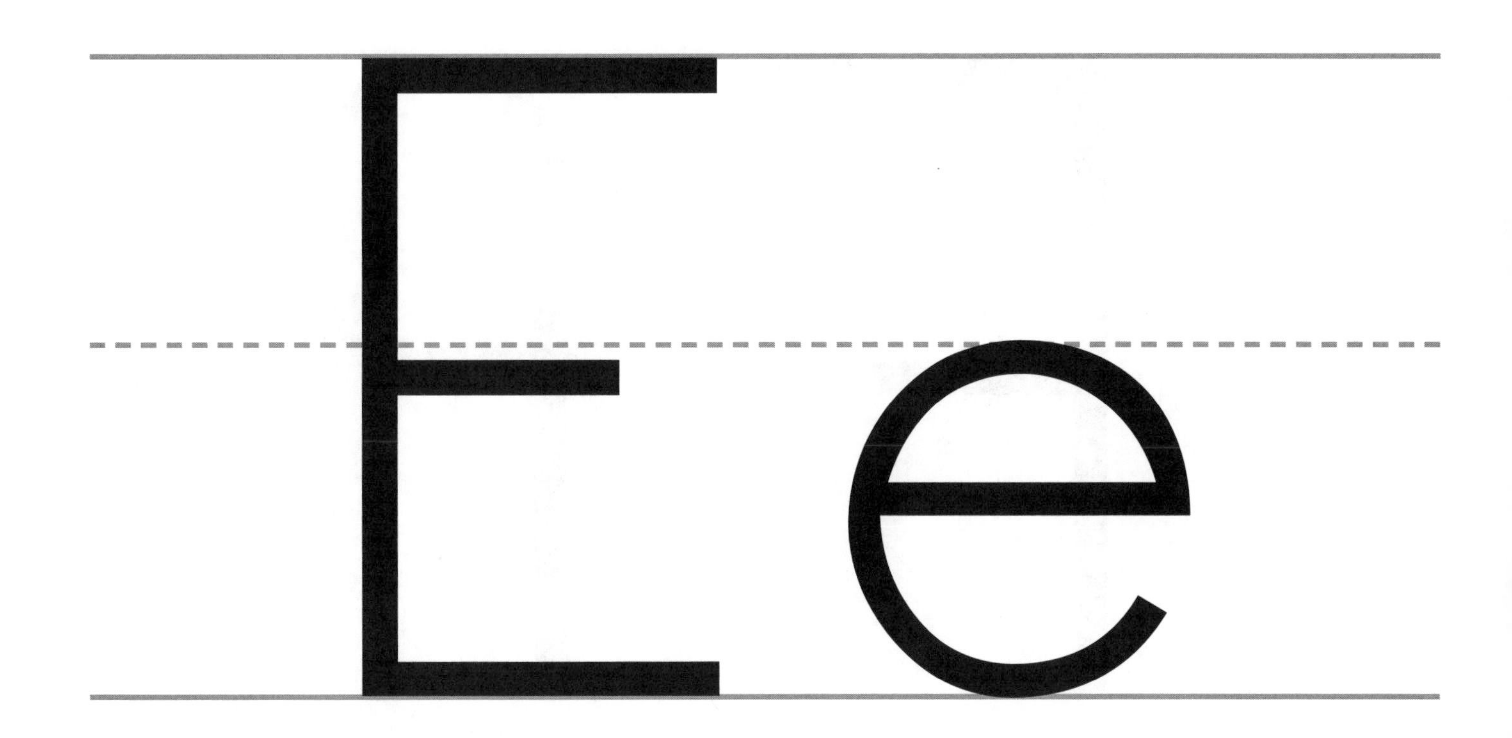

short ĕ

long ē

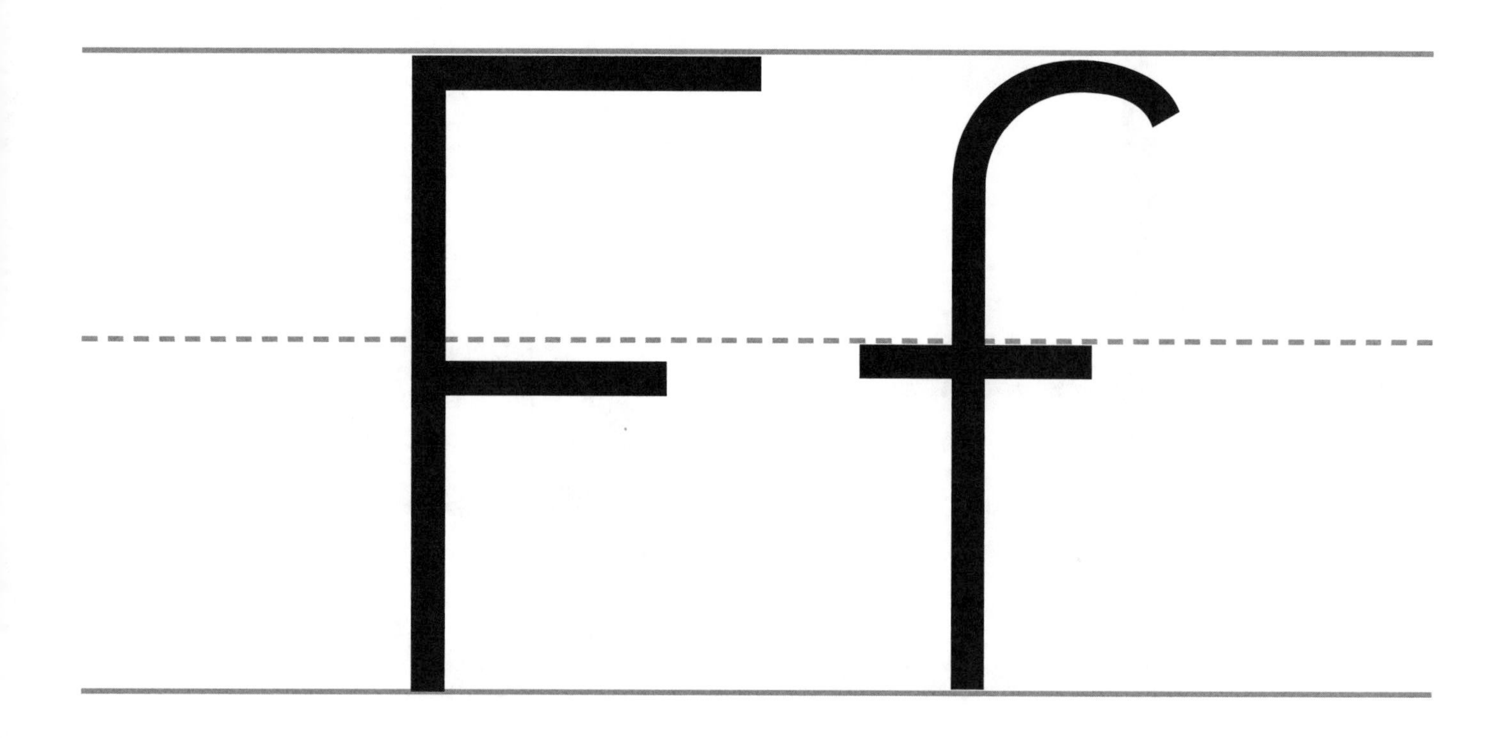
Ff

Gg

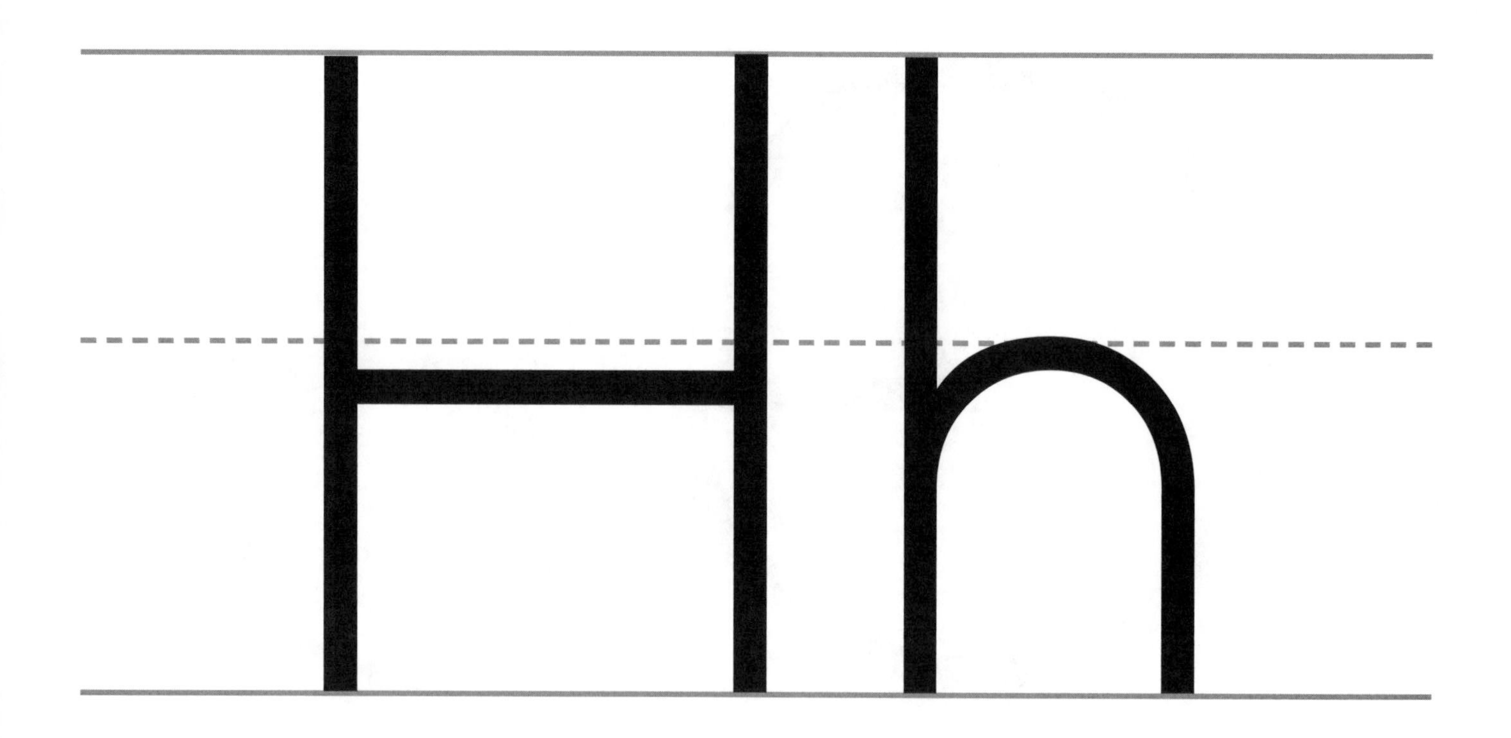
Hh

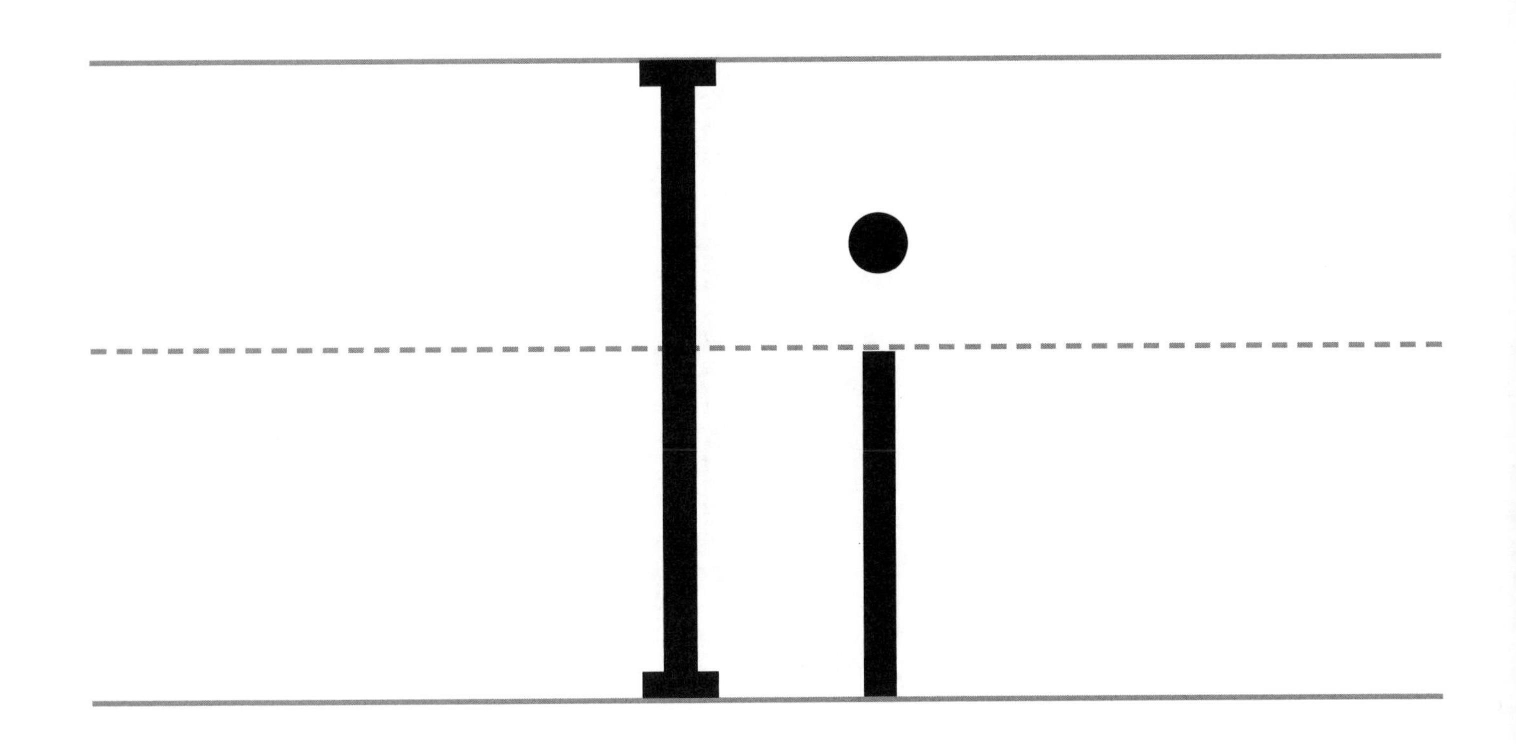

short ĭ

long ī

Jj

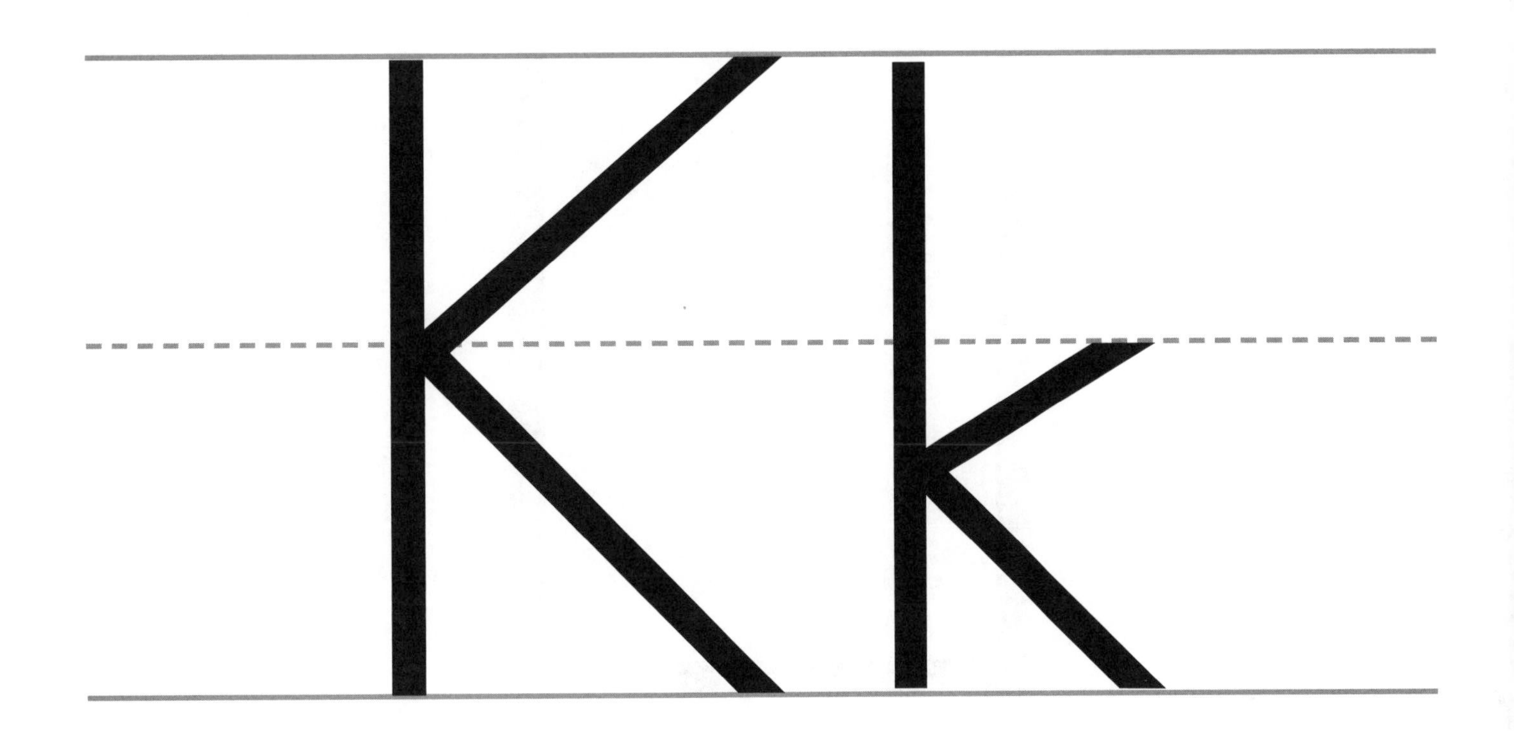

Kk

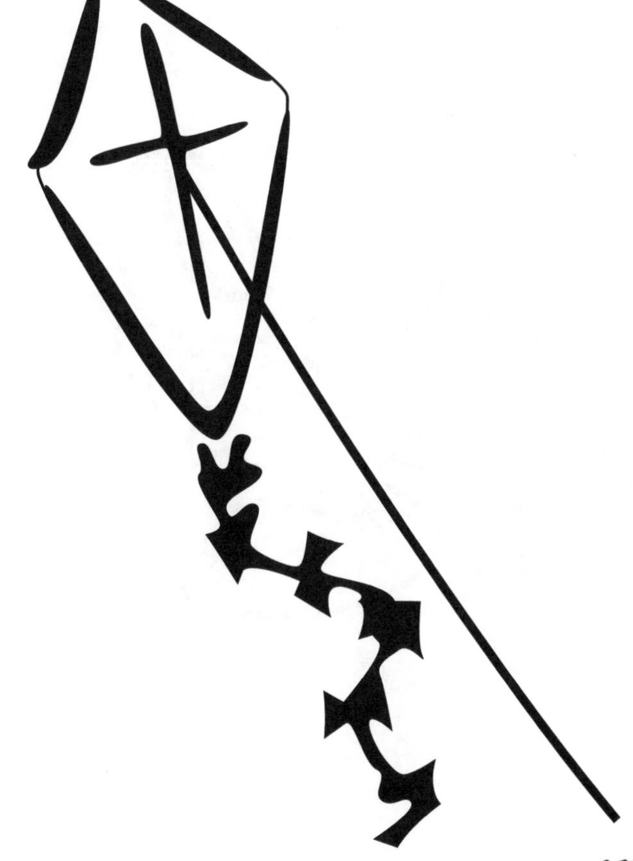

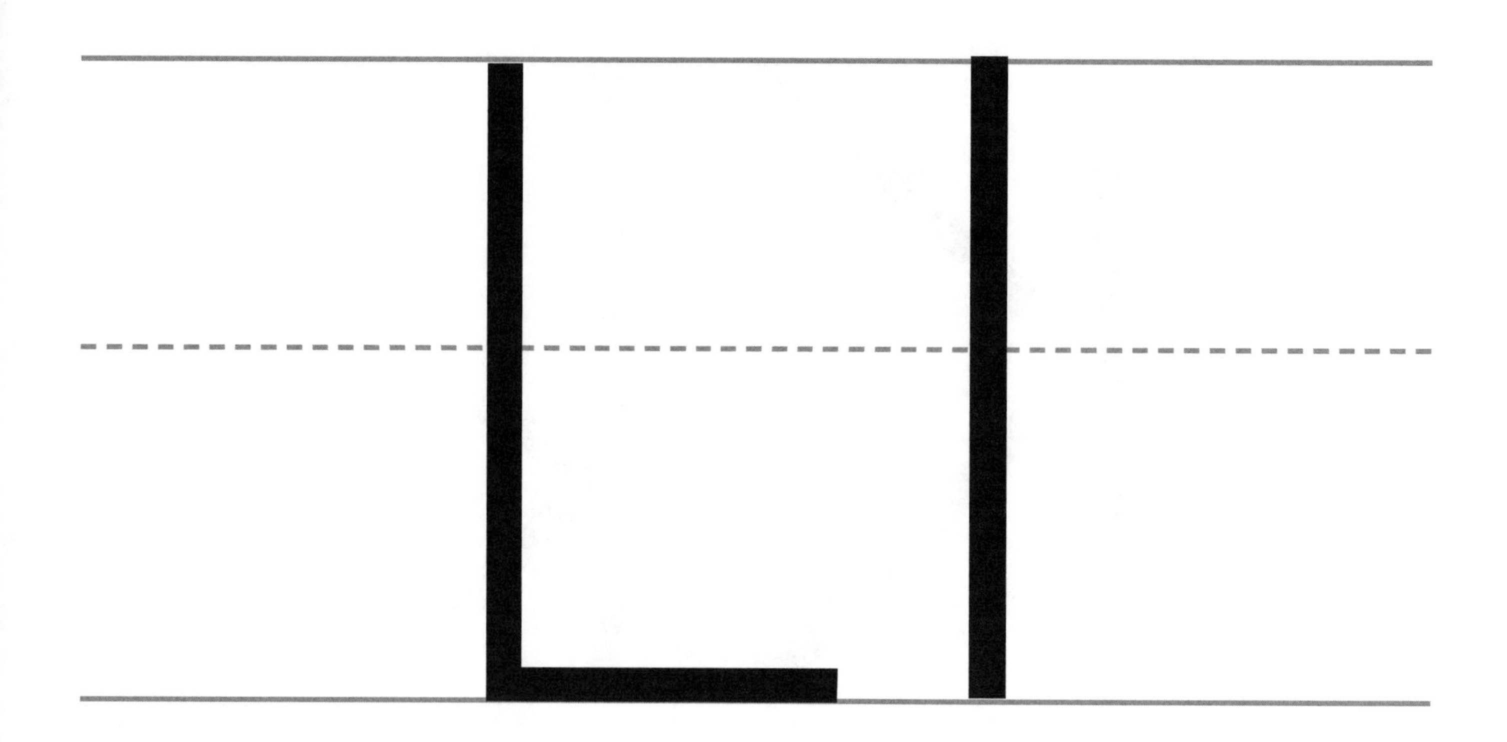
Ll

Mm

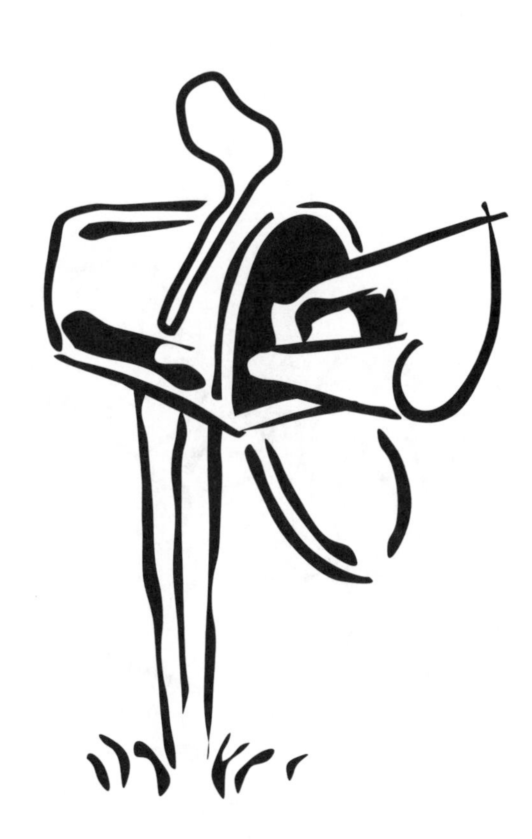

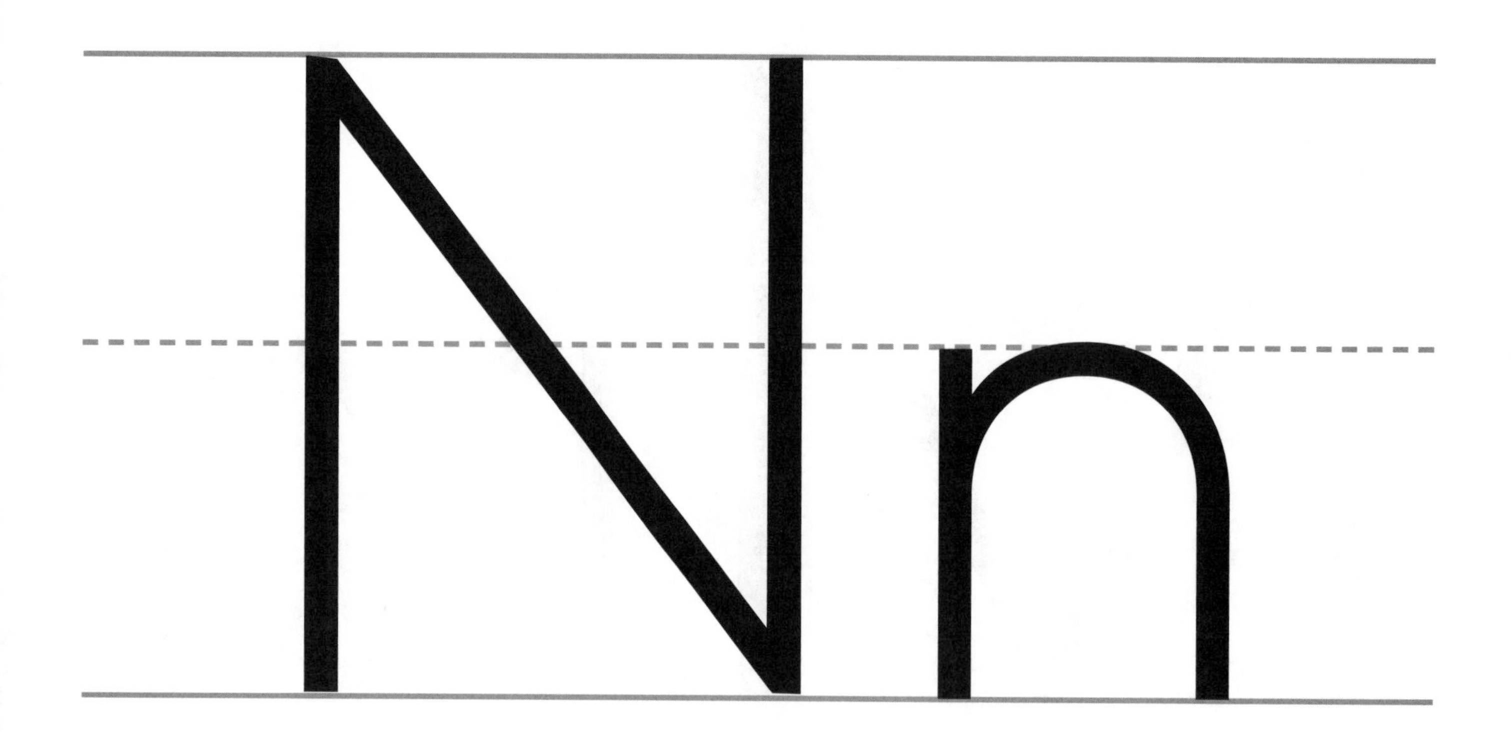
Nn

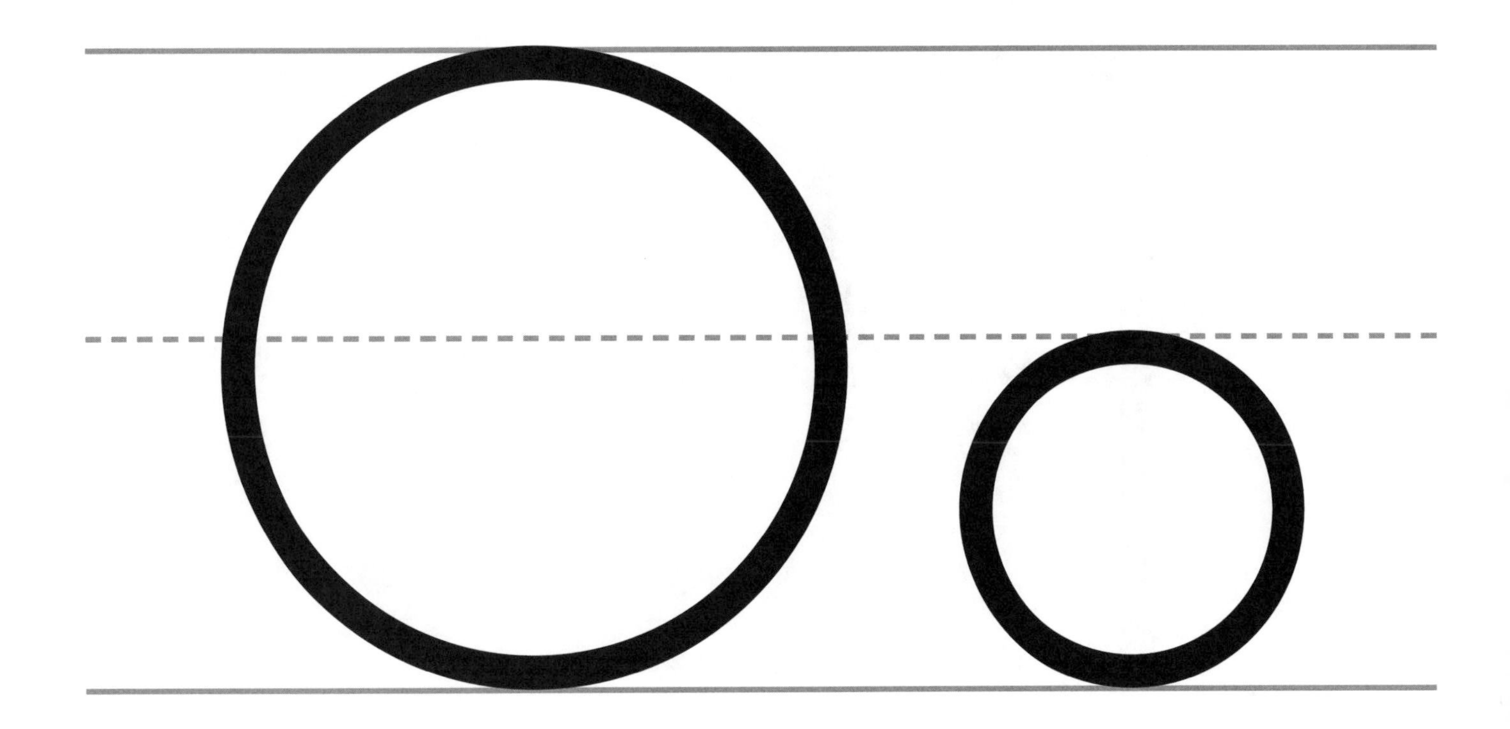

short ŏ

P p

Qq
25¢

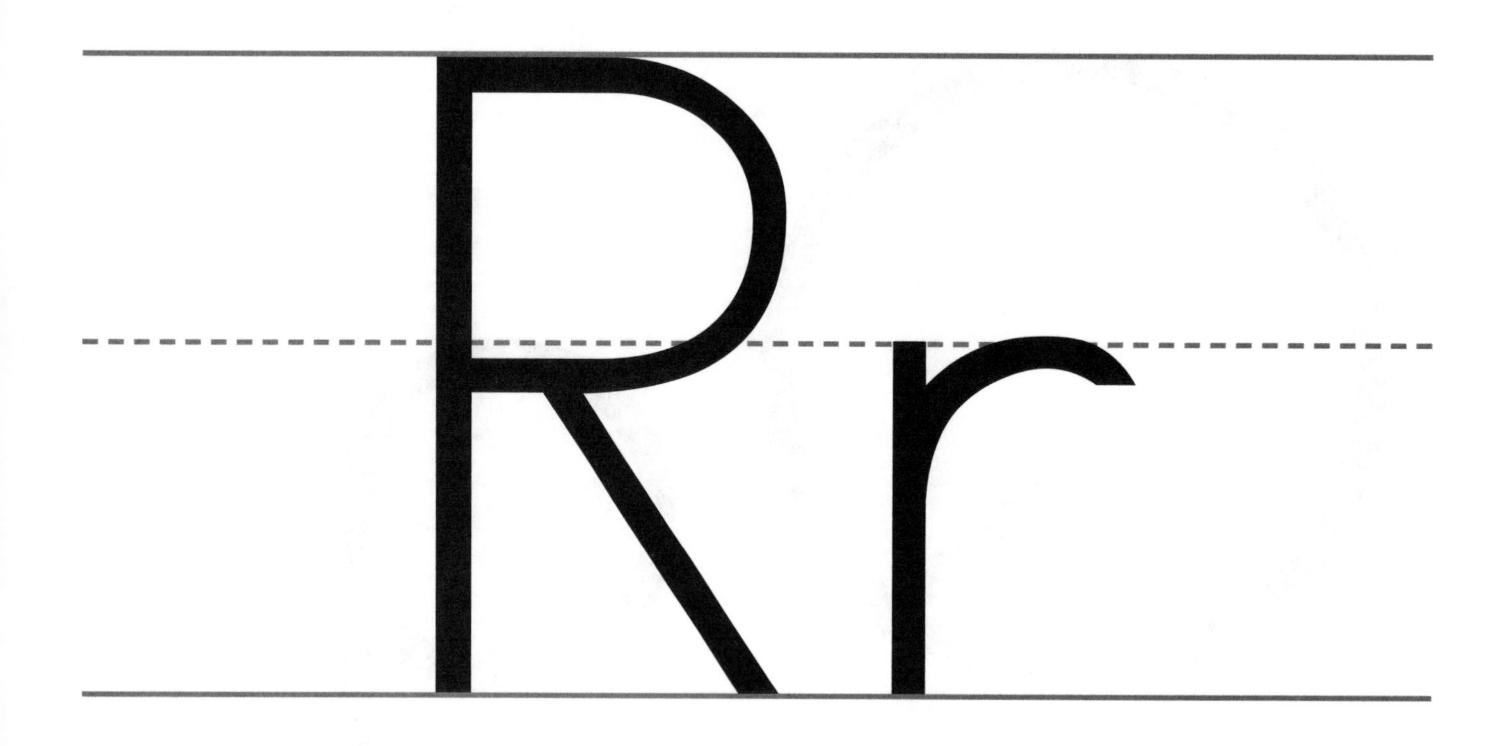
Rr

Ss

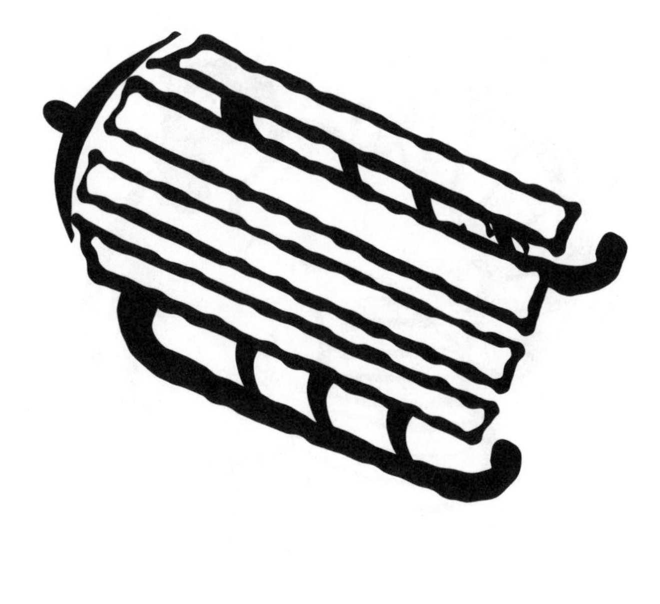

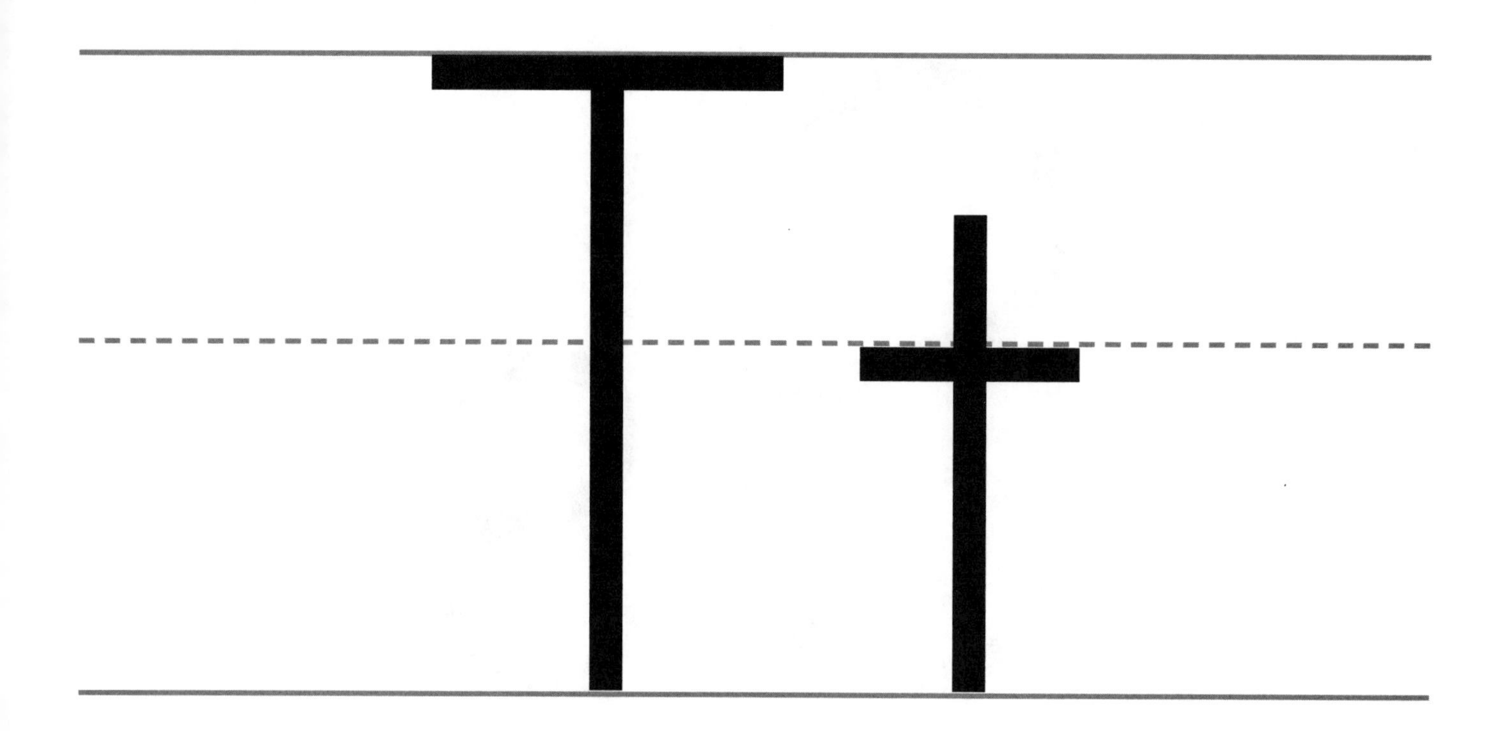

Tt

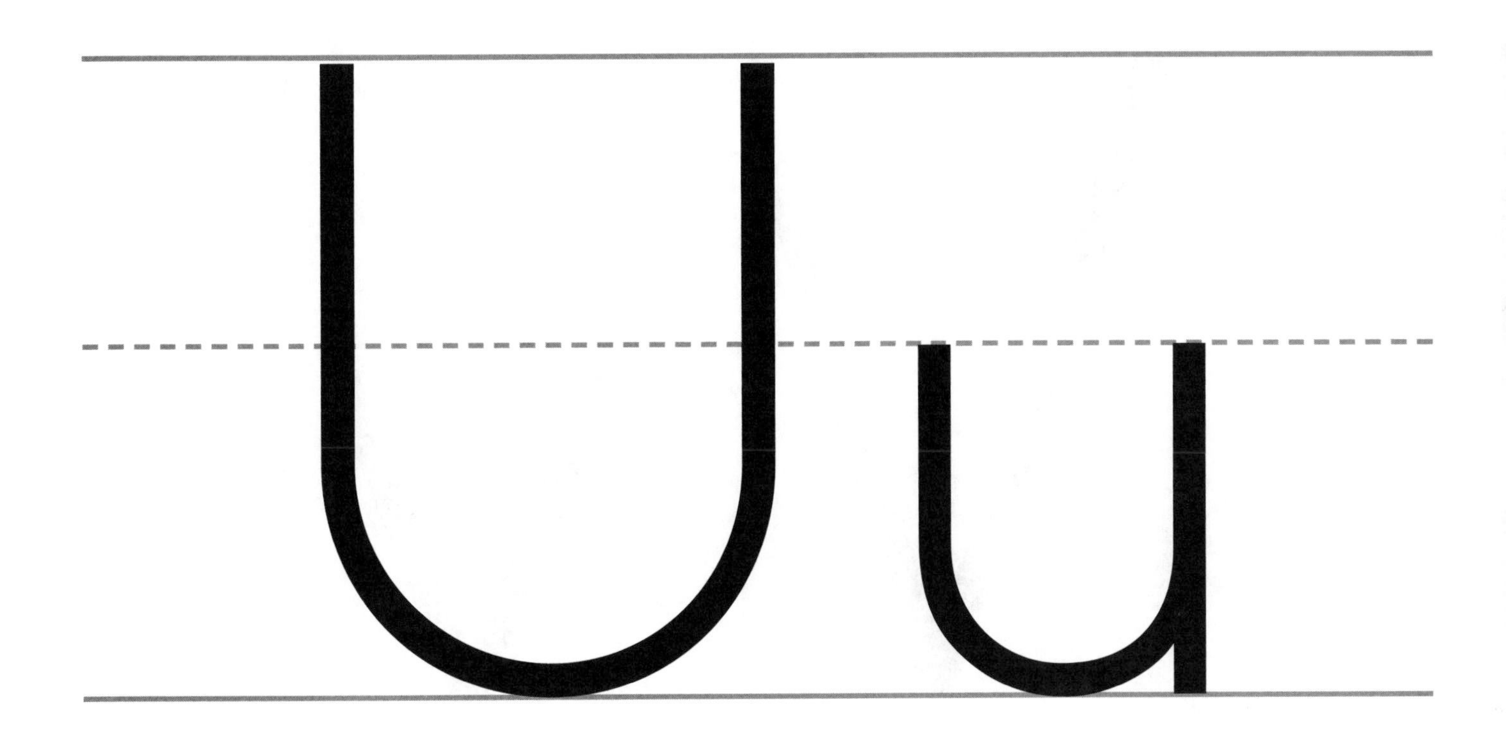

short ŭ

long ū

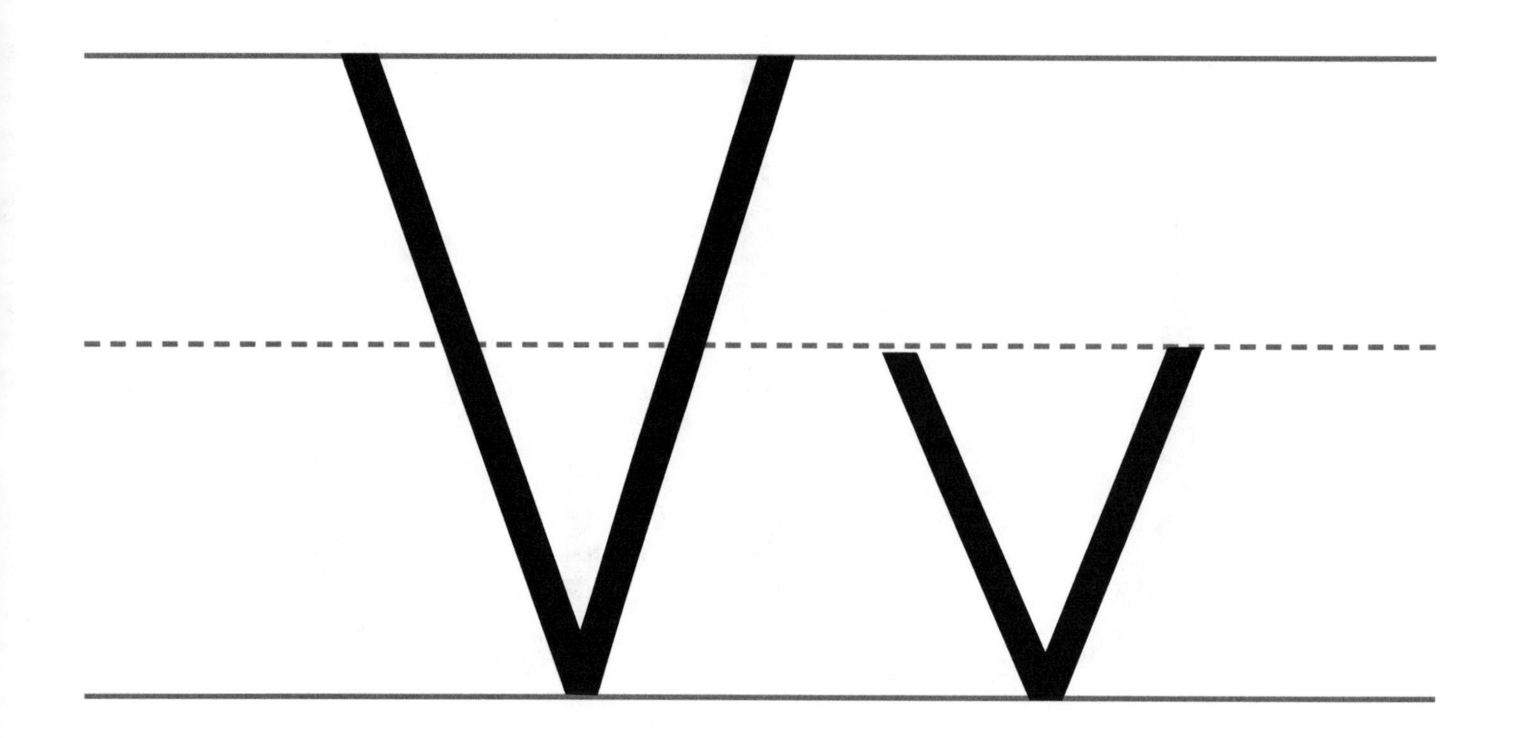
Vv

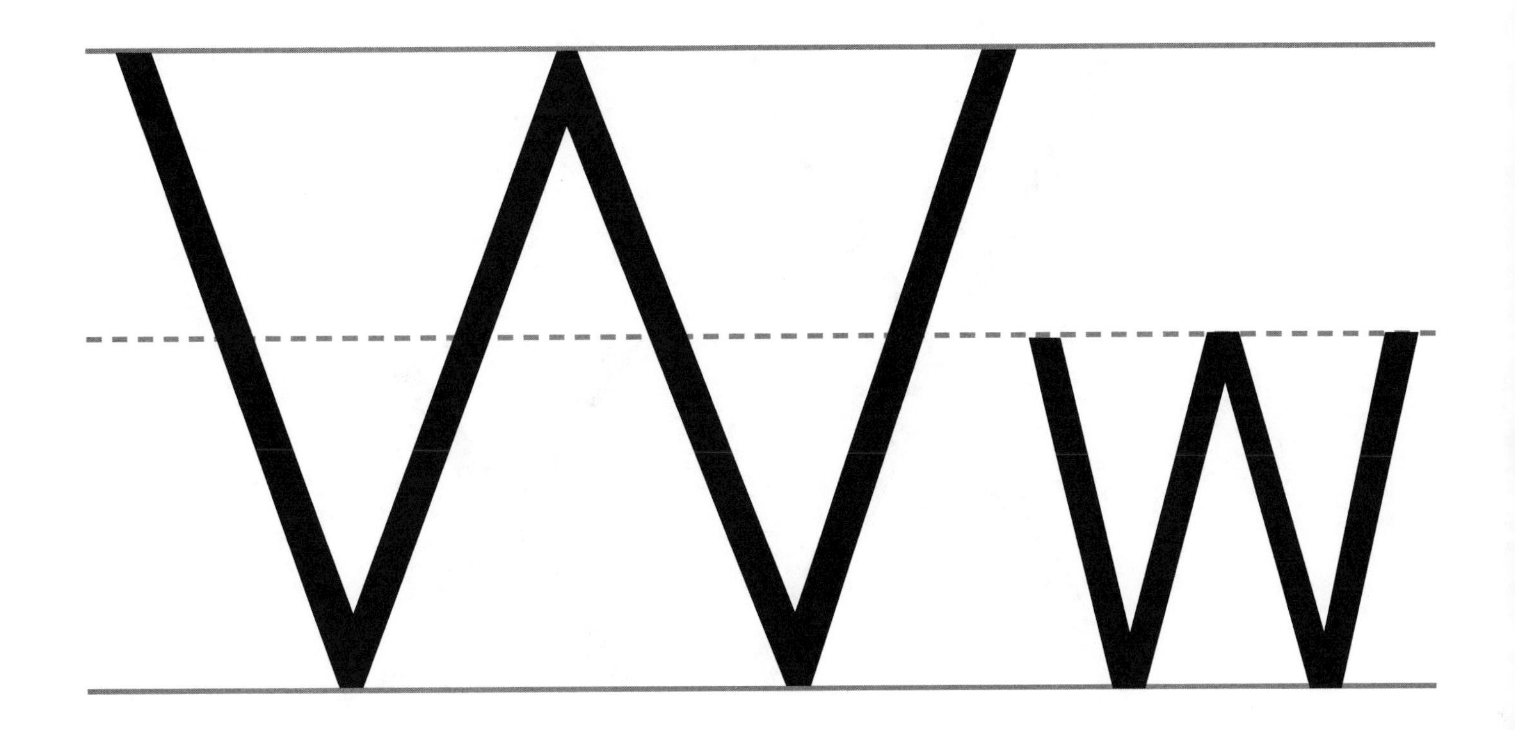

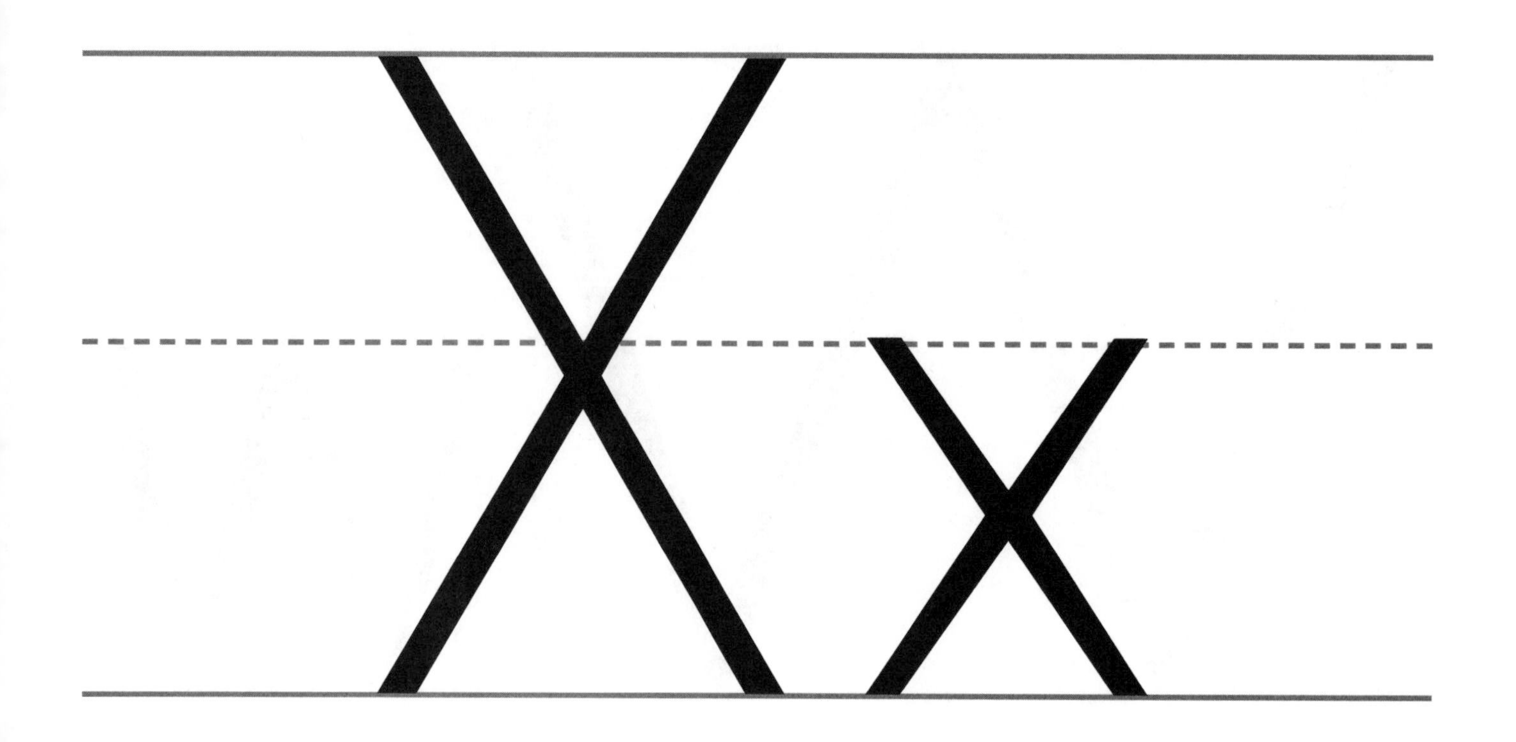

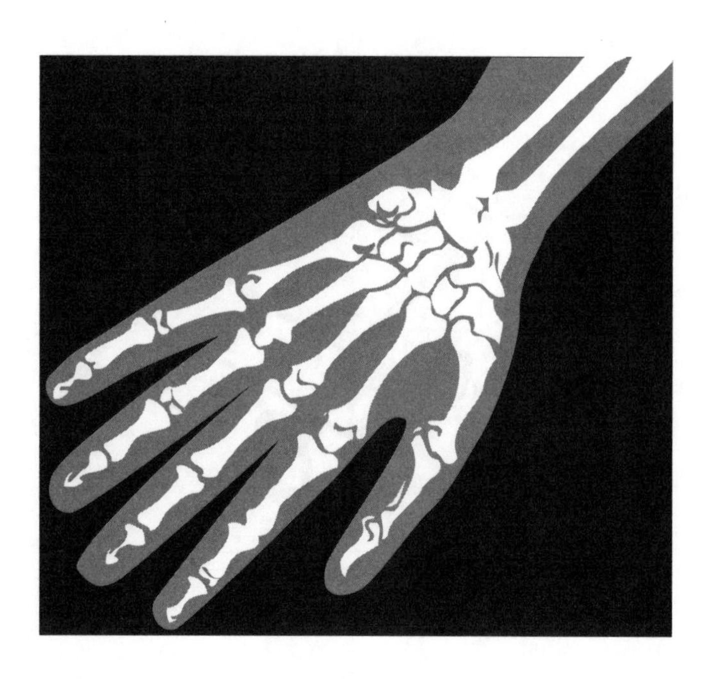

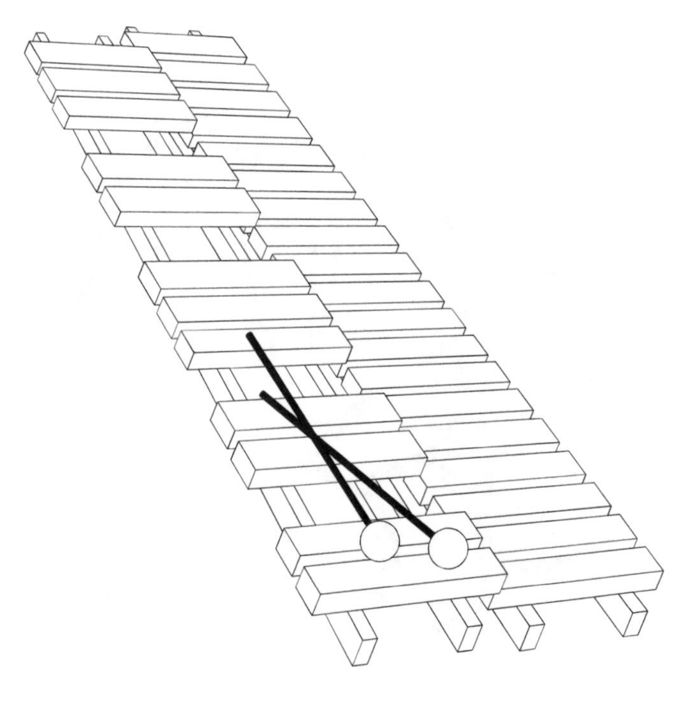

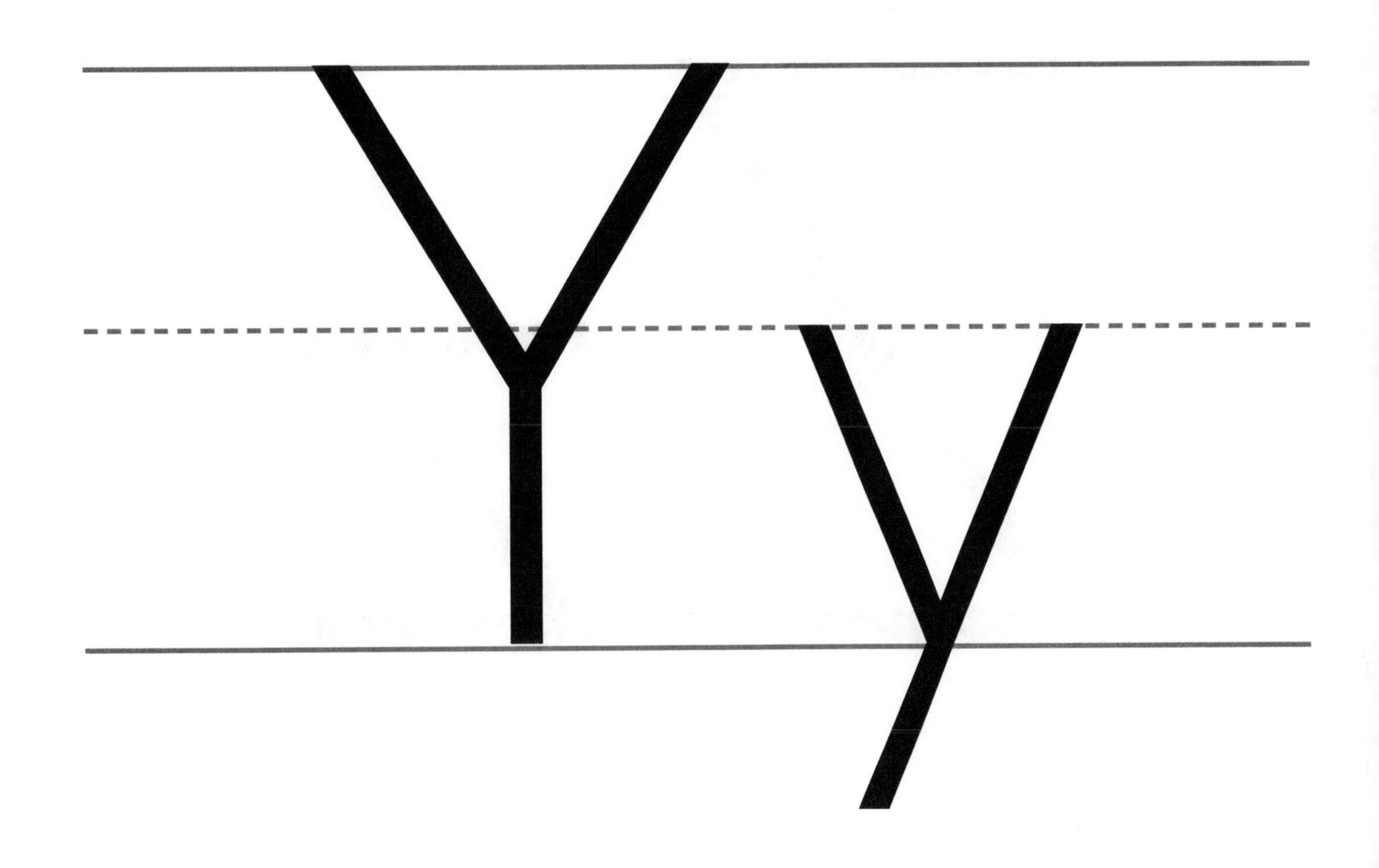
Yy

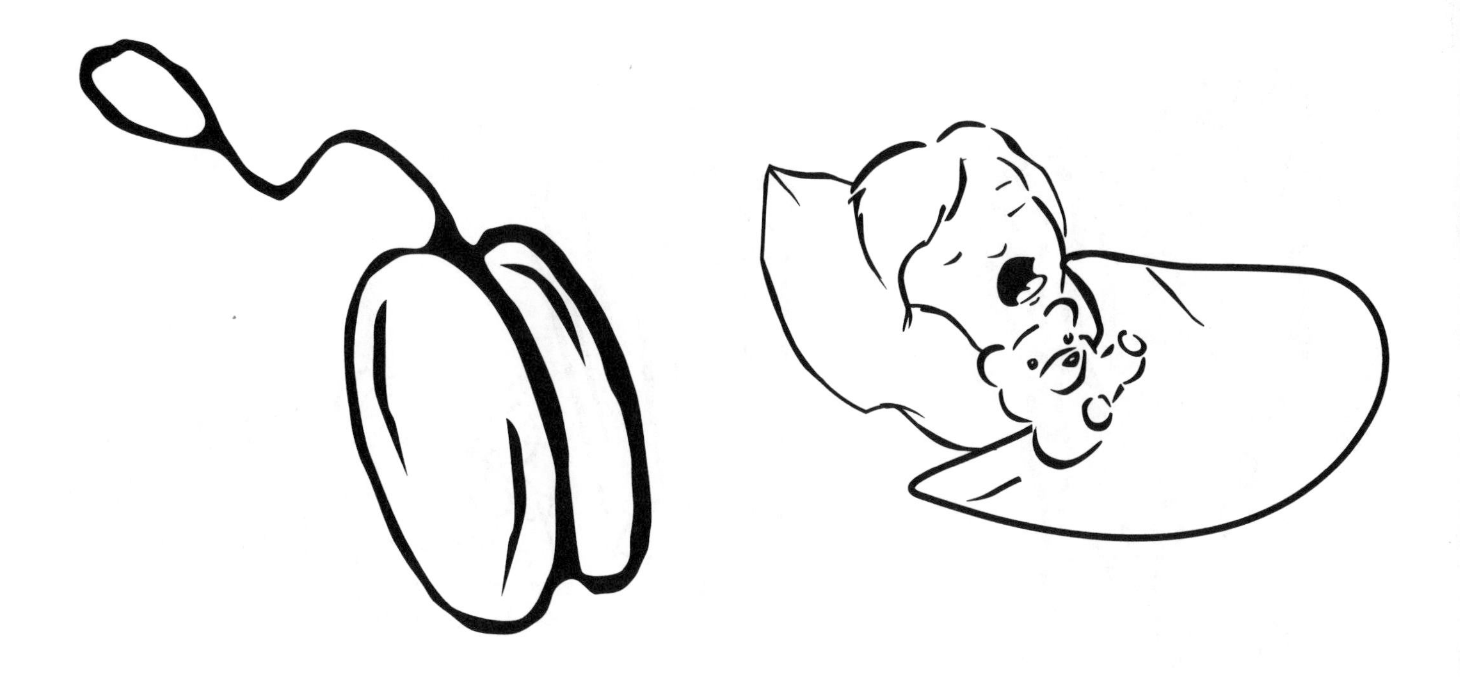

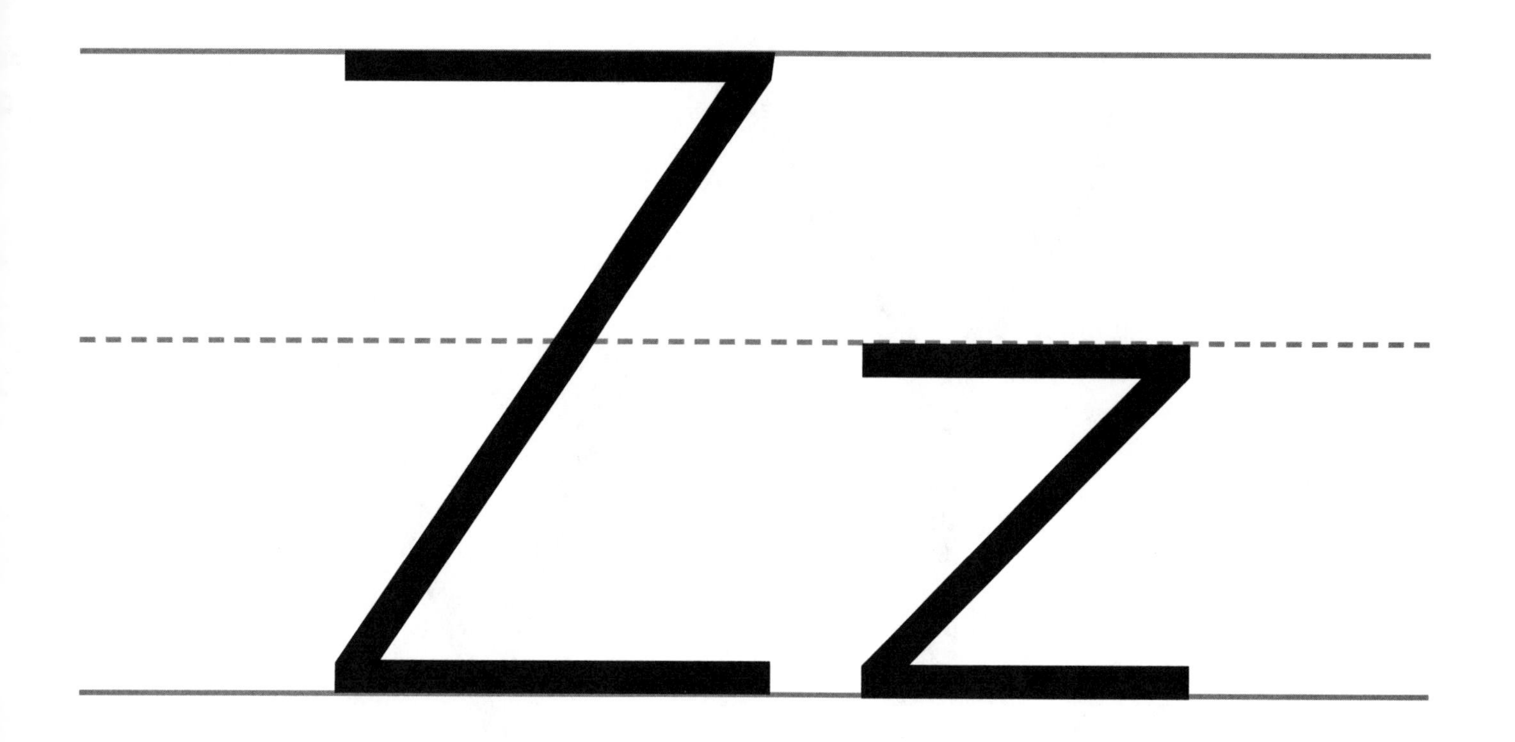
Zz

1. Long vowels say their names.

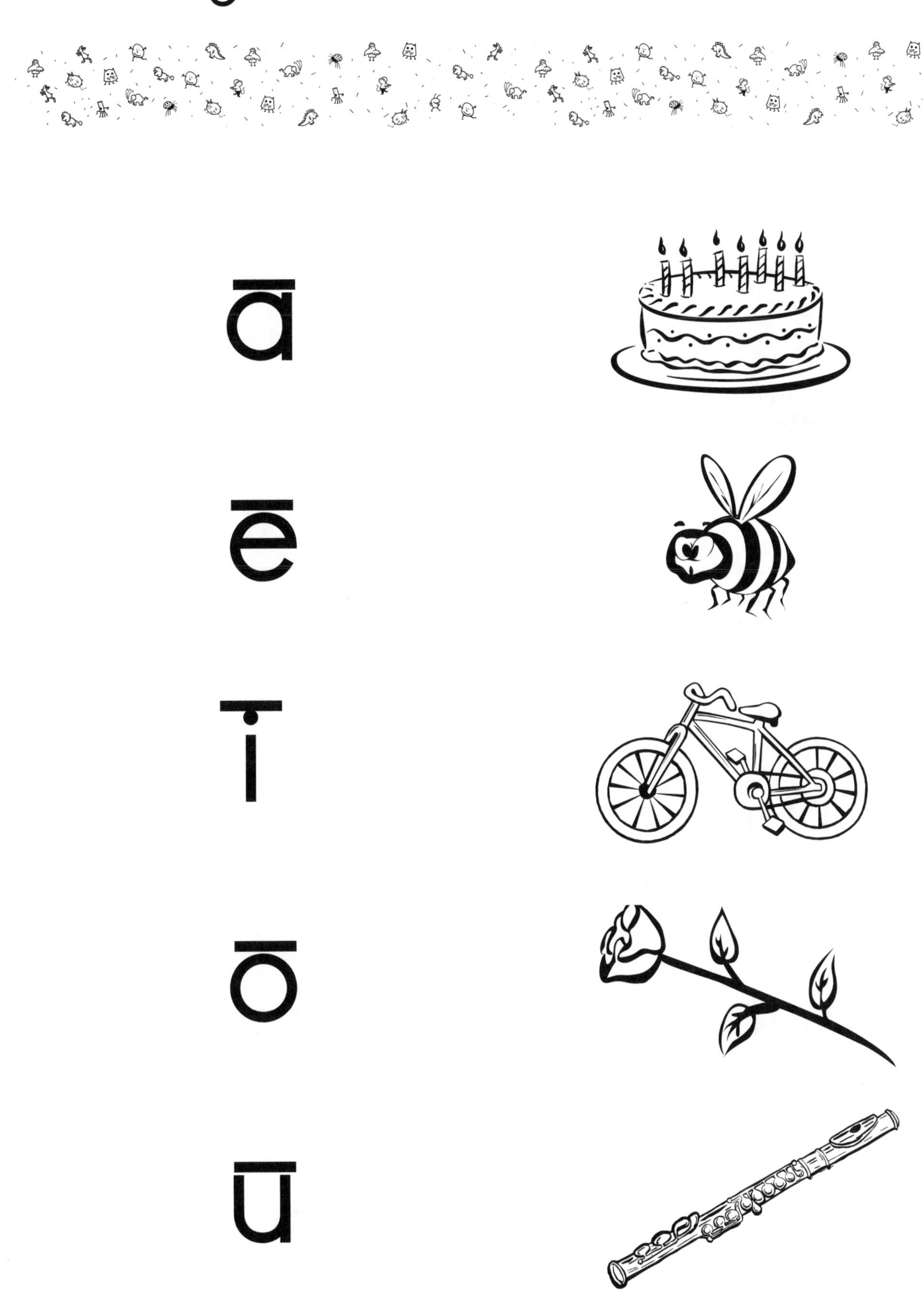

2. When a word has one vowel, the vowel usually has the short sound.

căt	răn
bĕd	pĕp
pĭn	dĭg
cŏt	hŏt
hŭt	gŭm

3. In words with a vowel, a conso- nant, and an e at the end, the first vowel sound is long and the e is silent.

mād~~e~~	tīr~~e~~
rāk~~e~~	flūt~~e~~
hōp~~e~~	tūb~~e~~
cōn~~e~~	dīm~~e~~
bīk~~e~~	hīd~~e~~

4. When c or g are followed by e, i, or y, they make the soft sound. When c or g are followed by a, u, o, or a consonant, they make the hard sound.

Soft c	ceiling, city, ice
Hard c	cake, cut, cane
Soft g	gem, giant, giraffe
Hard g	sugar, grape, glass

5. A consonant digraph is two or more consonants that stay together to make their special sound.

Beginning	Ending	
thin	path	bright
chop	much	sign
shop	dish	catch
phone	graph	comb
knife	doubt	phlegm
chorus	John	
gnaw	column	
whip	clock	
write	laugh	

6. A vowel pair is two vowels that come together to make one long vowel sound. The first vowel is long, and the second vowel is silent.

āi̸	rain, train, paint
āy̸	pray, hay, tray
ēe̸	peek, creek, teeth
ēa̸	dream, seal, read
īe̸	pie, tie, lie
ōa̸	goat, roam, soap
ōe̸	doe, hoe, toe

7. A sentence is a complete thought that tells who did what. Every sentence starts with a capital letter and ends with a period (.), a question mark (?), or an exclamation mark (!).

Statement (.):

I am in the first grade.

Question (?):

What grade are you in?

Exclamation (!):

Wow! We are in the same grade!

8. A capital letter is used at the beginning of every sentence. Names of people and places begin with a capital letter.

Does Jane like ice cream?

Jim and Jill will take a trip to Texas.

Will Ann and Bob go with them?

9. A compound word is made from two or more words joined together to make one word.

mail + box = mailbox

cup + cake = cupcake

dog + house = doghouse

rain + coat = raincoat

pop + corn = popcorn

10. When a word ends in ss, ch, sh, or x, you usually add es at the end to make the word plural.

dress + es = dresses

church + es = churches

dish + es = dishes

fox + es = foxes

11. When a word ends in a vowel plus y, you usually add s at the end to make the word plural.

turkey	+	s	=	turkeys
jay	+	s	=	jays
toy	+	s	=	toys
monkey	+	s	=	monkeys

12. When a word ends in f or fe, change the f to a v and add es to make the word plural.

wolf – f + v + es = wolves

leaf – f + v + es = leaves

wife – fe + v + es = wives

calf – f + v + es = calves

13. A suffix is an ending that is added to a base word. Many words do not have to have their spelling changed before a suffix is added.

Base Word	+	Suffix	=	New Word
rain	+	ed	=	rained
lift	+	ing	=	lifting
hope	+	ful	=	hopeful
safe	+	ly	=	safely
care	+	less	=	careless
kind	+	ness	=	kindness
open	+	s	=	opens
trick	+	y	=	tricky

14. The suffix -er is used to compare two things.
The suffix -est is used to compare more than two things.

Suffix -er:

Bill is taller than Ben and shorter than Dan.

Suffix -est:

Dan is the tallest of the three boys.

15. If a word with a short vowel ends in a single consonant, you usually double the consonant before adding a suffix that begins with a vowel.

tag + g + ed = tagged

hot + t + er = hotter

big + g + est = biggest

run + n + ing = running

16. If a word ends in silent e, drop the e before adding a suffix that begins in a vowel.

bake − e + ing = baking

shine − e + ing = shining

hide − e + ing = hiding

cute − e + est = cutest

smile − e + ed = smiled

17. When a word ends in a single or a double consonant, the spelling does not usually need to be changed when adding the suffixes -y, -en, or -able.

Base Word	+ Suffix	= New Word
speed	-y	speedy
sharp	-en	sharpen
break	-able	breakable

18. A consonant blend is two or more consonants that work together at the beginning or end of a word. Each consonant says its own sound.

Beginning				Ending	
bl	br	sc	str	ft	nd
cl	cr	scr	st	ld	ng
fl	dr	sk	sw	lf	nk
gl	fr	sm	tw	lm	nt
pl	gr	sn		lt	sk
sl	pr	sp		lk	sp
	tr	spr		lp	st
		spl		mp	xt

19. Vowel digraphs are two vowels put together in a word that make a long or short sound or have a special sound all their own.

aw, au	saw, auto, draw, Paul
ea	head, dread, sweater
ei	eight, weigh, sleigh
ew	few, threw, knew
oo	good, stood, book
oo	pool, school, tool

20. When x comes at the end of a word, it usually is pronounced ks. When it comes at the beginning of a word, it often makes the z sound.

Beginning "z" sound	Ending "ks" sound
xylophone	box
Xerox	fox
	suffix
	prefix

21. When a word ends in y after a consonant, change the y to i before adding –er or –est to the end.

busy – y + er = busier

early – y + est = earliest

happy – y + er = happier

sunny – y + er = sunnier

funny – y + est = funniest

22. A contraction is a word that is made from two words. Two words are put together, and one or more letters are left out. An apostrophe (') is used in place of those letters.

cannot	–	no	+	'	=	can't
let us	–	u	+	'	=	let's
it is	–	i	+	'	=	it's
I am	–	a	+	'	=	I'm
you have	–	ha	+	'	=	you've
we are	–	a	+	'	=	we're

23. In an r-cor
after the v
sound diffe
long sounc

24. A vowel diphth
that blend to
sound.

ow

ar farm, pu

er clerk, fern, swerve, perch

ir twirl, shirt, dirt, whirl

or born, storm, horse, corn

ur purse, church, purr, surf

ong is two vowels
ogether to make one

cow, town, brown, clown

ow snow, elbow, know, throw

ou mouth, south, house, round

oi boil, coin, soil, voice

oy toy, joy, boy, enjoy

25. Sometimes y at the end of a word can make the long ē or long ī sound.

Long ē sound	Long ī sound
baby	fly
happy	cry
puppy	try
penny	why

26. Synonyms are words that mean the same or almost the same thing but are spelled differently.
Antonyms are words that are the opposite or almost the opposite in meaning.
Homonyms are words that sound the same but have different spellings and different meanings.

Synonyms	Antonyms	Homonyms
happy/glad	hot/cold	sent/cent
gift/present	light/dark	won/one
unhappy/sad	loose/tight	fair/fare

27. The letters qu make the kw sound.

queen	quit
quilt	quite
quarter	quiet
question	quick

28. The letter s can stand for the s, z or sh sounds.

s sound	z sound	sh sound
seam	raise	sure
sign	noise	sugar
sock	please	assure
	rise	